The World Book of Math Power

THE
WORLD BOOK OF
MATH
POWER

Volume 1

Math Skills Builder

Published by
World Book Encyclopedia, Inc.
a Scott Fetzer company
Chicago

Staff

Editorial director

William H. Nault

Editorial

Executive editor
Robert O. Zeleny

Senior editor
Seva Johnson

Editors
Suzanne B. Aschoff
Cynthia Fostle
Mike Urban
Judith A. Witt

Administrative assistant
Janet T. Peterson

Editorial assistant
Valerie Steward

Writers
Bryan H. Bunch
Everett T. Draper

Art

Executive art director
William Hammond

Art director
Roberta Dimmer

Assistant art director
Joe Gound

Photography director
John S. Marshall

Photographs editor
Karen M. Koblik

Designer
Randi Brill

Illustrations
ANCO/Boston
Bill Anderson
Trudy Rogers

Copyright © 1983 by
World Book Encyclopedia, Inc., Merchandise
Mart Plaza, Chicago, Illinois 60654

Printed in the United States of America

ISBN 0-7166-3160-1
Library of Congress Catalog Card
No. 82-51271
a/hc

Product production

Executive director
Peter Mollman

Manufacturing
Joseph C. LaCount, director

Research and development
Henry Koval, manager

Pre-press services
J. J. Stack, director

Production control
Barbara Podczerwinski, manager

Editorial services

Director
Susan C. Kilburg

Research services
Mary Norton, head

Rights and permissions
Paul Rafferty

Advisers

Lola J. May, Ph.D.
Mathematics Consultant
Winnetka Public Schools
Winnetka, Illinois

Peter Pereira, M.A.
Assistant Professor
School of Education
DePaul University
Chicago

Contents

Volume 2 Everyday Math

Introduction

Math power is a term important for everyone. We use mathematics every day. Telling time from a clock or counting the change returned by the grocer requires math skills. So do a number of games and hobbies. Many people do not realize that managing a household or business successfully are directly related to their ability to use math properly. Math power can mean the difference between confidence and insecurity; vitality and boredom; goals and regrets.

What *Math Power* offers

Math Power was prepared with two goals in mind: first, to provide a close and thorough look at modern mathematics as a vital part of home, school, and work life; second, to provide a complete review of math coursework and show how best to take advantage of opportunities to study and use mathematics, in and out of school.

The two-volume set is divided into seven parts. Each part has a different focus. The first four parts comprise the *Math Skills Builder*.

Part I, "Relaxing with Math," is designed to help you feel at ease with math by showing how math is a natural part of the way you think. Your first math challenge also comes in this part. You are shown how to do "quick math," or mental arithmetic, to speed up the computation process and make your math more accurate.

Part II puts mathematics into perspective for students and parents alike. "School Math: Learning the Third *R*" talks about how children first start learning math as preschoolers and how the school mathematics curriculum builds on mathematics concepts the children bring with them to kindergarten or first grade. In this part, the history of mathematics education in the United States is also presented, giving some insights into what the future of mathematics instruction might be. How mathematics can influence career success is also covered in Part II.

"Tips and Tools for Math Students," Part III, is a handy, well-organized aid for students who wish to excel in mathematics. Studying, taking tests, controlling math anxiety—all are covered here. Special features in this part are sections on calculators and computers: tools that are becoming increasingly important in the study and performance of mathematics.

For those who wish a sound review, Part IV, the "Complete Math Review Program," provides dozens of math lessons and exercises that will recap the coursework in mathematics from kindergarten through grade 12. This part is not only useful to students but also to adults who have found that their math skills are inadequate to meet their needs.

Volume II, *Everyday Math,* puts your new math skills into practice. The volume opens with Part V, "Putting Math to Work." This part shows how math is used in the workshop and kitchen, on the road, and in personal and business affairs. Then Part VI, "Math Marvels," brings the extraordinary world of mathematical thought to you in the form of everyday entertainments. Have you ever thought of a jacket and vest as having entertainment potential? Would you like to make up words like *googolplex* or *maximillion*? Have you ever played Sprouts or Pentominoes? You will learn how to do so in Part VI.

Math Power ends with Part VII, the "Math Powerhouse." It is a fingertip source for all sorts of mathematical information. Math history opens the part, and next comes an overview of U.S. math competitions that encourage mathematical excellence through individual and team effort. Following are math symbols, formulas, and tables, as well as summaries of mathematical operations. A section on math reading gives you an excellent list of math books for independent work. Each book entry is *annotated,* or described, for you.

How to use *Math Power*

Presented in these volumes are many aids to understanding math. Using them properly might determine how much you will learn. Make sure, for example, to read all the introductory material, both to each part and to each section. You will feel far more comfortable if you know the direction your study is about to take. And make sure you have a mathematics notebook and pencil or pen handy at all times. Some lessons call for more equipment, including compass, protractor, and ruler.

Precisely follow all explanations and directions. With them are hundreds of diagrams and other illustrations. Study them well. When appropriate, copy them.

Unless your math is strong, don't jump from one part to another. Start at the beginning of volume 1 and go straight through. Stop, relax, and reread when concepts seem difficult; math learning can't be hurried.

If you need to review a concept but can't remember where it was, use the index at the end of volume 2. It is a final aid in the mathematical journey these books hold in store.

Part

I

Relaxing with Math

Many people, especially those who have "always had trouble with math," think that it is impossible to relax with mathematics. What they probably don't know is that math is a part of every life. People come by math understandings very early and very naturally. In other words, everyone relaxes with math quite often.

Math is much more than adding up long columns of figures and working algebra formulas. These exercises merely sharpen math skills that you already have, just as speaking and writing develop language skills. Mathematics includes so many different subjects that it is hard to define. One definition that fits most of the mathematics you learn in school is that mathematics is the study of quantities and relations through the use of numbers and symbols. Does that sound difficult? Then think of it this way. Whenever you rush to be on time, take two aspirins, or select the "biggest piece of fudge," you are using math. See how mathematically inclined you are?

You are about to explore your everyday world with mathematics as a lively companion instead of a silent partner, as it may have seemed until now. First, you will learn how math is not only part of you, but of animals about you, as well. Then, you will see how you can "touch" math. Finally, you will find out how you can speed up math operations—or skip them entirely—and still arrive at correct or usable solutions to mathematical problems, perhaps without even using pencil and paper. Sound impossible? Relax, you've got what it takes. You see, the math is already in your mind.■

(Preceding photo)
Math games are a favorite pastime for many families.

The Math in Your Mind

From an early age, all human beings use some mathematics, even in cultures that have no written language. Other animals also use mathematics. Crows have been known to keep track of up to thirty persons. Bees can measure angles and lengths. And almost all animals learn to recognize shapes and sizes. (Yes, shapes and sizes are a part of math.) Rabbits must learn, for example, the shape of a flying hawk so that they can take cover. They must also learn the shapes of edible leaves. For animals, mathematics means survival.

Humans are probably born with some very basic mathematical abilities. With no teaching whatsoever, almost anyone can tell the difference between one object and two objects, know that one object is much larger than another, and recognize the difference between a circle and a triangle. But higher levels of mathematics require training. You must learn special techniques to tell the difference between 137 sheep and 141 sheep, or between a liter of water in a pail and a quart of water in a carton. The purpose of mathematics education is to build on inborn abilities and gradually take them to higher levels.

Counting

How can you be sure that crows count? In farming areas, crows can be a nuisance because they eat young plants. Scarecrows sometimes help keep crows away, but often the only way to get rid of crows is to shoot them. Crows are smart, however. If they see a person with a shotgun, they won't invade the field until the person leaves. You see, crows recognize the shape of a shotgun. So to shoot crows, a farmer may build a hiding place in the field, called a *blind*. Even then the crows are hard to fool. If they see a farmer enter the blind, they won't attack the corn until the farmer leaves.

One farmer had an "easy" solution to this problem. Two people would enter the blind, but only one would come out. The person who was left would shoot the crows when they flew into the field. But when the plan was tried, the crows did not come into the field until the second person left the blind.

More help was needed. Three people went into the blind and two came out. The crows were not fooled. Four people going in and three coming out did not fool the crows either. At this point, everyone became very curious about how high the crows could count. So the farmer in charge asked more people to enter the blind. It was not until thirty people entered the blind and twenty-nine came out that the crows were fooled into the field. That is, the crows had finally "lost count."

What is counting? Adult human beings can usually count up to five objects without any special technique. A person can look at a stack of four or five books and tell how many there are without actually counting. If a stack contains six or seven books, however, the person must count in order to tell their exact number. Counting is done by matching each book in the stack with a number name. People learn different number names and rules for combining the names to form numbers in order from one upward. A person may count the books by saying, "One, two, three, four, five, six, seven." The person matches each number name with one of the books in the stack. If seven is matched with the last book in the stack, it tells how many books there are.

Crows, however, probably "count" by the mental technique that humans use for five or fewer objects. Since crows cannot use language, they have developed the ability to judge larger quantities by sight.

The number-name method was probably not the first way that humans used to count. Long ago, humans probably used sets of objects to match things they wanted to count. For example, a shepherd who wanted to make sure that all the sheep were safe for the night could match each sheep with a pebble and keep the pebbles in a bag. Each night, the shepherd could check to see if there was a sheep for each pebble and a pebble for each sheep. In that way, the sheep were counted, even though no number name was used. The matching process was more important than the use of number names.

Along trade routes in the Middle East, archeologists have found hollow clay balls filled with markers. The archeologists believe that ancient merchants used these balls to tell buyers how many items they had sent. For example, if seventeen bars of copper were shipped from Cyprus to Turkey, a ball containing seventeen markers would be shipped, too. When the shipment got to Turkey, the buyer could break open the ball, match the markers with the bars of copper, and know if the proper amount had arrived safely.

Eventually, the markers were shown as dents on the outside of the ball, so people could check the number along the way without breaking the ball open. The clay was baked hard after the dents were made so no new dents could be added or old dents removed. The dents became the first system of writing numbers, the *cuneiform* system. In fact, people developed ways to write numerals before they developed ways to write words. About five thousand years ago, Babylonians used numerals that looked like this

1	2	3	4	5	6	7	8	9	10

Measurement

The counting process results in a whole set of numbers—1, 2, 3, 4, 5, and so forth—that can go on indefinitely. These numbers are often called the *counting numbers* or the *natural numbers*. The counting numbers are the basis of all numbers, but they are not enough to solve all the mathematical problems that might arise.

Suppose, for example, that the merchant in Cyprus had more than enough copper to make 16 bars but not enough to make 17 bars. If the merchant wanted to ship all the copper, he would need a way to show that he was sending sixteen whole bars and one partial bar. How could he relate this information to the buyer? The answer is to use what today are called fractions.

Fractions are numbers but they are different from the counting numbers. If two partial bars make one whole bar, then each bar is a half, or $\frac{1}{2}$, of a whole bar. If three partial bars make one whole, then the size of each partial bar is a third, or $\frac{1}{3}$. In each case, a *measurement* takes place. The merchant is *measuring* the size of the partial bar in terms of the whole number 1. Fractions thus allow the merchant to measure the partial quantity against the whole quantity.

Things may become a bit more complicated for the merchant. Perhaps the amount of leftover copper he wishes to send will not "go evenly" into one bar. For example, it will take three partial copper bars to make up two (not one) whole bars. The easy solution is to use the fraction $\frac{2}{3}$.

A fraction is always a way of showing a relationship between two numbers—the number of parts and the number of wholes. If you had any difficulty following the example of the merchant, try this: You divide a candy bar and give your friend one-half. He has half of the whole bar. You just split the whole down the middle, in other words. Neither one of you is confused because fractions are a natural part of the way you think. You share via fractions.

One number in a fraction tells how many parts the whole was divided into. The other number tells how many parts are in the piece being measured. Here is a new way of thinking about the merchant's copper bars using fractions to split the bars mentally.

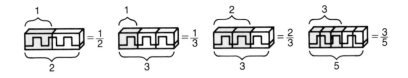

Can you split a candy bar into halves? thirds? fifths? Then you can use fractions correctly, and you understand the mathematical concept ratio. A *ratio* between two quantities is the number of times one contains the other. Since fractions show a ratio of two numbers, mathematicians call fractions the *rational numbers*. You don't need mathematicians to explain this concept to you. You've been using it for years.

Shape

Shape is an important concept in mathematics. Shape can be defined in terms of numbers. Can you think of a shape that has three sides? four sides? five sides? Did you think of these?

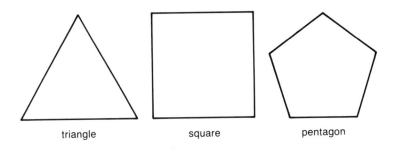

triangle   square   pentagon

All of these shapes are associated with numbers. A figure made with three straight lines has to be a triangle; it cannot be a square. Four straight lines of equal length can make a square, but never a pentagon. The five sides of the pentagon cannot be put into the shape of a triangle. Each figure has its own characteristics, which mathematicians call *properties*. The properties can be defined in terms of the numbers 3, 4, and 5. The properties vary from figure to figure.

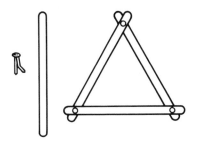

Take three sticks from a frozen dessert and fasten them at the ends. (Note that the sticks are of equal length.) You have just made a triangle. You can try pushing it into different forms, but it doesn't change. It is rigid. Now add a fourth stick. Push the sticks into different positions. Do you always have a square? No, sometimes you have what's called a *parallelogram*. What does this mean in terms of numbers? It means that if you have a shape made of three straight lines, you are going to have a triangle no matter how you try to move the sides around. If you have a shape made of four straight lines of equal length, you may have more than one type of four-sided figure. This difference in properties between the triangle and the four-sided figure is intricately interwoven with the numbers 3 and 4 that are associated with the figure.

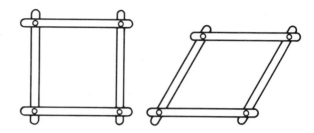

Measurement enters into shape as well. If all sides of a four-sided figure made from straight lines are the same length, as above, the shape has one set of properties. Otherwise, the shape has another set of properties. The same goes for triangles. Here are some more examples of three- and four-sided shapes.

Look at the third triangle more closely. It is a very important shape in mathematics. The sides of this triangle have the measurements 3 cm, 4 cm, and 5 cm. Any triangle whose sides have the measurements 3, 4, 5—no matter what the measurement *units* are—always makes an angle of the same size between the three-unit side and the four-unit side. This angle is the one called a *right angle*. This triangle is a *right triangle*.

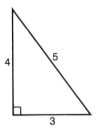

The right triangle can also have sides of different lengths, as shown here.

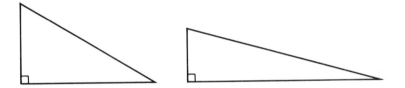

The properties of the right triangle have interested many mathematicians for thousands of years, Pythagoras among them. You will learn more about the right triangle and Pythagoras in the math review lessons at the end of this volume and in other discussions in this publication.

Patterns

Through the ages, people didn't have to go to school to see that number and measurement were closely related. They saw that there were patterns in counting and measuring physical objects. For example, ancient peoples recognized that everyone had two feet and two eyes, but only one nose.

Still, language shows that numbers have not always been used for measurement. Sometimes, *number words* are used. For example, a *pair* of shoes and *twin* engines both mean two objects, but no one ever says "a twin of shoes." In one North American Indian language, different number words are used for living things, for round things, for long things, and for days. The Fiji language uses one word for ten coconuts and another word for ten boats. These words developed without the basic pattern involved in "twoness," "tenness," "hundredness," or number in general.

Similarly, people began to see that the properties that triangles made from sticks shared with triangles made from gold rods also formed a pattern. The important idea was the triangular shape, not what the triangle was made from—just as twoness did not depend on whether the objects were shoes or engines. In fact, people began to think that a triangle, like a number, was a pattern.

This observation led to a major conclusion. Mathematics deals with both number and shape because both follow patterns. In other words, mathematics is the study of patterns, and the study of patterns is mathematics.

Logic and Proof

While some patterns of mathematics are fairly obvious, others are less so. Consider a pattern such as the following:

$$2 + 3 = 3 + 2 \qquad 9 + 5 = 5 + 9$$
$$27 + 58 = 58 + 27 \qquad 132 + 6 = 6 + 132$$

You can observe that this pattern holds true for a great many pairs of counting numbers. But no matter how many pairs of numbers you check, there will always be pairs that you have not checked. If you want to be sure that the pattern holds true for all pairs of counting numbers, you must go beyond simply seeing that the pattern is true for a great many pairs.

One way to convince yourself that the pattern is true for all pairs of counting numbers is to use *logic*. Logic is also called *reasoning*. In its simplest form, logic is the argument that because one set of conditions is true, a given result must follow. For example, if you know that

All men are mortal.
Socrates is a man.
Then you also know that
Socrates is mortal.

This example is a famous *syllogism,* a kind of logical scheme of formal argument. But the arguments of logic can be less formal than that. For example, suppose that an addition problem such as 9 + 5 is shown as two sets of dots, with nine dots on the left and five dots on the right.

• • • • • • • • •   • • • • •

You can also show the problem 5 + 9 with five dots on the left and nine dots on the right. If you turn this book upside down, you get the second problem. Obviously, turning the book upside down does not change the total number of dots, so you have reasoned that 9 + 5 = 5 + 9. The same reasoning would apply to twenty-seven dots, to fifty-eight dots, and, in fact, to any number of dots on the left and any number on the right. This line of thinking is a *proof* of the following: For counting numbers, called *n* and *m* here, it is always true that

$$n + m = m + n$$

no matter which two counting numbers *n* and *m* are.

Logic is not the same as mathematics, but it is the main tool for finding patterns. Logic by itself, however, does not go far enough. Since the time of the ancient Greeks, more than 2000 years ago, mathematicians have tried to set up perfect rules for logic and math, rules that everyone could agree on. Then it would be possible to say what really was a proof and what was not. For example, how do you know that turning the book upside down does not change the number of dots? Should turning the book upside down be accepted as a proof—a legitimate way to solve problems in math?

The Greeks believed that there were a few simple rules of logic and math that everyone could accept. They called the rules of logic *axioms* and the rules of math *postulates*. This idea turned out to be extremely useful. When applied to the study of shapes, for example, the Greek mathematician Euclid (305–285 B.C.) was able to show that about five axioms and five postulates were enough to prove everything that was known. (Later mathematicians improved on his system, but not on the basic idea.) This approach to mathematics is called an *axiomatic system*. As a result of Euclid's success, it became common to think of proof as something that happened only in axiomatic systems. But in reality, early mathematicians proved results in whatever ways they could. You will learn more about Euclid's system and other approaches to proof in Part IV, Section 10, "Formal Geometry."

Counting, measurement, shape, patterns, logic and proof—these are all parts of math that are basically easy to think about. Now get ready to reach out and actually touch math.

Section 2

Math You Can Touch

People usually think of mathematics as a mental process. But this is not exactly so. Math in many ways represents the physical part of your life. An example from the ancient Greeks will show you how this is true.

Although the Greeks had a system of writing numbers based on letters of the alphabet (similar to Roman numerals), the ordinary people found it too complicated to work with. But they needed to use math just as much as the mathematicians. So, instead of using the "bulky" letters, they computed with small stones, or counters, on a board. They were literally able to move their numbers around on the board.

The Greek mathematicians didn't find the letter system very efficient, either. But they went beyond using stones for counting and instead used pictures of stones drawn in the sand. It was a bit more convenient for them to work with a clean board covered with sand than with a board and a bag of stones. They showed their numbers as holes in the sand—dots, in other words. The Greeks had developed a method of picturing numbers as arrangements of dots. They merely had to touch the sand in a certain way and the numbers (dots) would appear. They could just as easily remove them.

Mathematical Models

The ordinary Greek people's stones and the mathematicians' pictures in sand are two examples of mathematical *models*. Stones on a board are a good model of counting numbers because they can be combined in the same way that counting numbers are. An example of a poor mathematical model would be to try to use drops of water on a board. The drops might run together, making this model an unreliable method of counting. But if you have three stones on a board and put four more on, you will always get seven stones.

Models are used by modern educators to help students learn math. The educators have several names for the models they use. One, the *concrete model,* is like the stone-and-board method. This model, like the ancient one, makes it possible to put objects into *one-to-one correspondence* with the objects to be counted. For example, stones are concrete models. If you want to represent three pairs of sandals, you can use three stones to do so. In modern schoolrooms, you may represent three apples with three blocks, instead.

Sometimes a single stone or other marker is used to represent two, ten, one hundred, or some other number. It is still a physical object that can be touched and manipulated, but it is less concrete than using exactly as many markers as the number of objects to be counted. A model that uses single objects to stand for collections of objects is called *semiconcrete.*

Concrete and semiconcrete models help people visualize numbers, but they are not always practical to use. Imagine a teacher taking home a class's homework made up of individual counting boards with loose stones for every problem from every student. In such a case, it would be easier to work with pictures of the counting boards and stones. The pictures would be considered *semiabstract models.*

The semiabstract model shows what physical operations are supposed to have taken place. For example, a lesson may show pictures of blue dots, each representing one object. Maybe the children were asked to circle the number of fingers the teacher held up. By circling the right number of dots, the children have "grouped" them. A lesson may also have different-colored dots. If the blue dots represent one object and the red dots represent two, and there are three windows in the classroom, the students can show how many windows there are by circling one blue and one red dot.

The next level of model is the *abstract* level. *Abstract models* represent numbers and operations on numbers with actual numerals and mathematical signs. For example, both the symbols $3 + 4 = 7$ and

$$\begin{array}{r} 3 \\ +4 \\ \hline 7 \end{array}$$

are abstract models for numbers.

There is yet another model, but it is one you cannot reach physically. This model is the idea of the numbers themselves:

no objects, no pictures, no numerals, just the thought of "one," "two," and other numbers. This model has no name.

Understanding the first four kinds of math models—concrete, semiconcrete, semiabstract, and abstract—is important to understanding the discussion that follows. If you don't have a clear understanding of these four models, review the previous discussion before reading on.

Concrete Counting Numbers

You already know one way that counters can be used for counting. That is, if you match a set of counters with another set of objects so that there is one counter for each object and one object for each counter, you know the number of objects you have.

Now suppose that you are counting people entering a store through a turnstile. As each person passes through the turnstile, you place a counter on a board. At the end of the day, the number of counters is the same as the number of people who passed through the turnstile. This matching process suggests an important model for the counting numbers. The empty board represents 0, which is not a counting number. (The counting numbers and 0 taken together are called the *whole numbers*). Put a counter on the board and you have the first counting number, 1. Add another and you have the second, which is $1 + 1$, or 2. Add another, and you have $2 + 1$, or 3. Each counting number is formed from the one before it in the same way. This provides a model of the counting numbers that does not depend on one-to-one correspondence. In fact, it is the *plus-one model* that is generally used to teach the counting numbers to small children, often combined with the idea of one-to-one correspondence.

The next level of dealing with the counting numbers includes the four familiar operations of addition, subtraction, multiplication, and division. Each operation combines two counting numbers to get a third. Each also has a model at the concrete level.

Keep in mind as you read that concrete models help you understand the nature of the mathematical computations you perform every day. Some of the examples may seem farfetched, but concentrate on them anyway. Get some counters, like pennies, and work through appropriate examples. The physical process will show an interrelationship of mathematical operations you may not know exists.

Addition

Suppose that you are counting people entering a store, but there is no turnstile. Instead of entering the store one at a time, people can enter in groups of any size. If you are using stones on a board to keep track of the number entering, you have to change your strategy. As each group (or individual person) enters, you quickly model the group with stones using one-to-one correspondence. When a group of three people enters, you grab three stones as a group and place them on the board. When a group of four people enters, you add four stones to the board in one handful. At this point, the number of stones on the board is the same as if seven people had entered one by one through a turnstile. This grouping can replace counting one at a time. Manipulating stones or other counters in this way is the basic concrete model of addition.

There is another way that addition can be modeled. Let's say that it's getting late in the day, and you already have 217 stones on the board. A large group of people comes in, and you do not have time to match them with a group of stones. So instead of matching the whole group and putting all the stones on the board at once, you take a random handful of stones from the pile and, one-by-one, put a stone on the board for each person in the group. You get the same result either way. This represents the *counting-on model* of addition. If you said the numbers aloud, you would say 218, 219, 220, 221, 222, 223, 224, 225. It is the same as putting stones on the board in one handful.

The counting-on model is an important tool in learning addition and in finding a number when you have forgotten how to add abstractly. It always works for counting numbers. If you have 6 and want to add 5, you can always think "7, 8, 9, 10, 11," counting the numbers you are thinking until you have five of them. Notice that it is necessary to start counting on with the number just after the number that is being added to.

The numbers that are combined in an addition problem are called *addends*, and the number that is obtained as a result is called the *sum*. It is not practical to use a concrete model every time you need to add. For the smaller counting numbers, through nine at least, you must memorize the sums of each possible pair of addends. These sums, which include all possible combinations from $0 + 0$ to $9 + 9$, are called the *basic addition facts*. There are one hundred of them. You'll find the addition facts and other mathematics facts soon to be mentioned in Part VII, the "Math Powerhouse." You may want to refer there before going on.

One hundred addition facts are a lot for children to remember at first. So they need strategies to learn all the facts and to recall the ones that they forget. One strategy is to return to the concrete model, using counters. Often the handiest counters are their fingers, which they can use either in one-to-one correspondence for sums less than ten, or in the counting-on strategy for larger sums. For efficient computation, however, youngsters must pass beyond the finger-counting stage and memorize all the basic addition facts.

Subtraction

Suppose that your job at the store includes making sure that all customers have left at the end of the day. You can also use a concrete model to determine this. As each group of people leaves the store, you simply remove from the board the number of counters that matches one-to-one with that group. If, at the end of the day, there are no counters on the board, you know that everyone who has entered has also left. In fact, at any time during the day, the number of counters on the board represents the number of persons in the store. Say that there are thirty-eight customers in the store and six of them leave in a group. You remove six counters from the board. There are thirty-two counters left, so you know that there are now thirty-two customers left in the store. This is the *take-away model* for subtraction.

Another model for subtraction is just as useful. It is similar to the counting-on model for addition. As the six customers leave the store, instead of removing six counters all at once, you can remove one counter at a time. This is the *counting-back model* for subtraction. Like the counting-on model of addition, it is a useful way to learn or to recall the answers to subtraction problems.

Here is another concrete model for subtraction. The store hopes to attract 500 customers to a big sale. Late in the day, not subtracting for people who have left the store, you have 437 counters on the board. How many more people need to come into the store to reach 500? This is the subtraction problem $500 - 437$, but the answer cannot be found by removing counters from the board. Instead, it is necessary to *add* counters. If you do not know the answer, you can add one counter at a time until you reach 500, keeping track of how many counters you have added. The number you added will be the answer to $500 - 437$. This is sometimes called the *missing-addend* or *difference model* of subtraction.

Like the addition facts, the *basic subtraction facts* must be memorized. One hundred facts are generally labeled basic. These include all the whole-number facts from $0 - 0 = 0$ to $18 - 9 = 9$. In subtraction, the number you are subtracting from is generally called the *minuend,* although sometimes—thinking of the missing-addend model—it is called the *sum.* The number you subtract is called the *subtrahend.* The answer is most often called the *difference*—thinking of the missing-addend model—or the *remainder*—thinking of the take-away model. The 100 basic subtraction facts are those for which both the subtrahend and the difference is 9 or less.

Multiplication

One concrete model for multiplication is simply *repeated addition.* For example, assume you want to count the people riding a roller coaster. Each car holds 8 passengers and there are 6 cars. One way to find the answer using counters is to add 8 counters to a board 6 times. This is the same as $8 + 8 + 8 + 8 + 8 + 8$, but it is also the same as 6×8.

In another concrete model, if you want to multiply 6×8, you can arrange your counters in a rectangle that has 6 rows with 8 counters in a row.

```
• • • • • • • •
• • • • • • • •
• • • • • • • •
• • • • • • • •
• • • • • • • •
• • • • • • • •
```

While this is essentially the same as repeated addition, this model, called the *array model,* is often easier to use. Furthermore, the array model can be used to make discoveries about multiplication that are hard to see using the repeated-addition model. For example, since a 6-by-8 array and an 8-by-6 array have the same number of counters, $6 \times 8 = 8 \times 6$.

A third physical model for multiplication is quite different from the other two in that its relation to addition is not at all obvious. Place 6 counters on one side of the board. Place 8 counters opposite those 6. Now connect each counter in one set to every other counter in the other set, using pieces of string as the connectors. You get 48 connectors, which is the same number as 6×8.

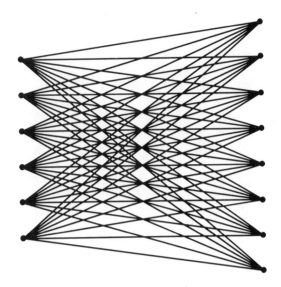

This model is the *Cartesian-product,* or *matching* model. The matching model is not very useful for learning the multiplication facts, but it is handy for understanding certain kinds of problem situations, such as "If Sarah has 3 blouses and 4 skirts that all match, how many different outfits can she put together?" The answer is 3 × 4, or 12, which is a direct result of the matching model.

Two numbers that are multiplied are sometimes called *factors.* The answer is always called the *product.* If you want to make a distinction between the two factors—based on the addition model for multiplication—the number of addends is called the *multiplier* and the addend that is repeated is called the *multiplicand.* A peculiarity of the way people write multiplication is that the order of the factors is changed when going from the horizontal form 6 × 8 = 48 to the vertical form

$$\begin{array}{r} 8 \\ \times 6 \\ \hline 48 \end{array}$$

In both the horizontal and vertical forms, 6 is the multiplier and 8 is the multiplicand.

Like the basic addition and subtraction facts, it is important to memorize the 100 *basic multiplication facts.* They are the facts for which both factors are 9 or less. In fact, it is even more important to memorize the multiplication facts because it is harder to use concrete models to get the products than it is for addition or subtraction.

Division

Just as one model for subtraction is a missing-addend model, suggesting the relationship between addition and subtraction, one model for division is the *missing-factor model,* which indicates the relationship between multiplication and division. The name for this kind of relationship is *inverse operation.* Subtraction and addition are inverse operations, and division and multiplication are inverse operations. Therefore, if you need to find 48 ÷ 6, you can use your memorized multiplication fact 6 × 8 = 48 to find the answer. This model can be made into a concrete model by using the array model for multiplication. If you have 48 stones that you want to divide into 6 groups, you can put the 48 stones into an array that has 6 stones on one side. The number of stones on the other dimension of the array is the missing factor.

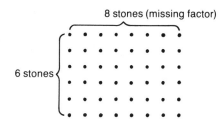

8 stones (missing factor)

6 stones

There is also a subtraction model for division. You can find the answer to 48 ÷ 6 by subtracting 6 from 48 until you have subtracted all the 6s you can. There will be 8 of them. Note that this is not identical to 6 × 8 = 48, which would be to subtract groups of 8 from 48.

Here's another method to find 48 ÷ 6. Make a picture of 48 dots. Then, circle 6 dots at a time until all dots are circled.

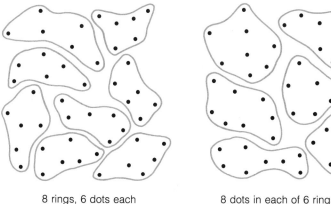

8 rings, 6 dots each
8 = missing factor

8 dots in each of 6 rings
8 = missing factor

Count the rings. Or use only 6 rings, so that the same number of dots is in each ring. Count the dots inside a ring.

How, you may well ask, can you circle the dots when you don't know how many dots to put into each circle? There is a physical model for doing this that you probably know. Suppose that you have 48 cents that you want to divide equally among 6 friends. You give the first friend a penny, then the next friend a penny, and so on until you reach the sixth friend. Then you start all over. You keep repeating the process until you run out of pennies. When you are finished, each of your 6 friends has 8 pennies: the missing factor. If you have ever used this technique, you were dividing via a model of the concrete counting numbers without knowing it.

For the problem here, to translate into circles and dots, you may begin by drawing six circles and placing 48 dots to the side. Then start moving the dots into the circles, crossing out a dot each time you move it. First you move one dot into each circle, then another dot into each, and so forth until all the dots have been moved. There will be eight dots per circle.

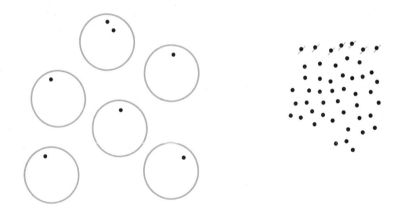

In division, the number you are dividing by is called the *divisor,* the number you are dividing into is called the *dividend,* and the answer is called the *quotient.* So in $48 \div 6 = 8$, 48 is the dividend, 6 is the divisor, and 8 is the quotient.

The answers to the division problems used thus far have "come out even." Answers that do not come out even are a problem with division that does not occur with the other whole-number operations. For example, if you divide 50 by 6, you end up with 2 counters left over. The number of leftover counters is called the *remainder.*

In the concrete models of division based on subtraction, the remainder emerges naturally. For example, if you subtract 6 from 50 over and over, you will end up with 2 left over. In the concrete models based on multiplication, however, the remainder requires a bit of extra work.

Every number has a relatively small number of factors. For example, 2 and 5 are factors of 10 because $2 \times 5 = 10$; 1 and 10 are also factors of 10. The factors of 48 are 1, 2, 3, 4, 6, 8, 12, 16, 24, and 48. If 48 is divided by any number other than one of its factors—5, for example—there will be a remainder. The missing-factor approach involves asking the question ''5 times what number is equal to 48?'' When you are restricted to the whole numbers, there is no answer. Therefore, the missing-factor model must be modified to become ''5 times what number *plus what number* is equal to 48?'' In that case the answer can be determined to be $(5 \times 9) + 3 = 48$. (The parentheses mean that you multiply 5×9 before you add the 3.)

By combining multiplication and addition, you can almost always find an answer to division problems involving whole numbers. No physical model works for division by zero, however, so division by zero is undefined. For example, if you have nine dots and try to circle zero of them and then count the circles, you will never have any circles to count. Or, if you start out with zero circles and move one dot at a time into the circles, you won't have any place to put your dots.

Because division by 0 is ruled out, there are only 90 *basic division facts*. They correspond to the situations in which the divisor is a counting number from one through nine and the quotient is a whole number from zero through nine. (Note that while a divisor cannot be 0, a dividend can. When the dividend is 0, the quotient is 0.) When there is a remainder, the problem is not counted as a basic fact.

Now that you have learned the many ways you can ''touch'' math, you should go back and review each model. If you haven't already done so, set up your own models of the different problems. Change the problems, too, using different numbers. If you take the time to practice with the models, you will have a firm foundation for the next section. It will explain how you can do math more quickly than you had ever thought possible.

Section 3

Quick Math: Mental Arithmetic

There is little doubt that everyone would like to perform mathematical operations as quickly and as accurately as possible. In this section, you will learn many techniques for achieving the ability to do "quick math." One caution, however, is that there are times when you are expected to "show your work" in arriving at a mathematical answer. This is true both in the classroom and outside. When the situation is appropriate, using quick math is rewarding; it is also fun. But never use quick math when your instructions do not permit you to do so.

Another very important caution in reading this section is not to become discouraged. The opening discussion isn't difficult to understand, given a few pauses to reflect on what has been said. You will learn several shortcut techniques more quickly than you thought you could. However, as the discussion continues, you will find that if you haven't mastered certain mathematical concepts and operations, you will have trouble grasping the techniques. The short reviews presented here may not give you enough help.

The best thing to do in this case is to go to Part IV, the "Complete Math Review Program," and review the operations being discussed. For example, to understand quick math for fractions, decimals, and percents, you must first completely understand what they are and how to convert from one to the other. You will find lessons with plenty of exercises on fractions, decimals, percents, and other math subjects in the review program.

Most important, don't hurry. Relax, read and reread, if necessary. Take your time and enjoy yourself. You are in for many surprises in learning how to make numbers work fast for you.

Memory and Memory Tricks

Some people have remarkable memories for numbers. Even if they are no brighter than other people, their ability to remember number combinations allows them to make calculations as fast as a machine. In fact, on certain problems, such "mathematical wizards" outperform calculating machines.

When the first atomic bomb was being designed at Los Alamos, New Mexico, during World War II, there were three physicists there who would frequently race one another to compute the effects of various experiments. One used a desk calculator, another used a slide rule, and the third worked in his head. John von Neumann, the one who worked in his head, won the race most of the time.

Some calculating wizards, such as von Neumann, are also mathematicians. Although not all mathematicians are calculating wizards, most good mathematicians have developed their memories to recall those numbers that are useful to them. Mathematician Alexander Craig Aitken may hold the record for this kind of memory because he was able to memorize a one-thousand-digit number that had no recognizable pattern.

Of course, mathematicians with good memories for numbers excel in branches of mathematics where quick and accurate mental figuring may suggest important patterns. And if you develop a memory for useful numbers, it can help you too.

Useful Numbers

One

One certainly is a useful number. If you add 1 to any counting number, you get the next counting number: $2 + 1 = 3$; $7 + 1 = 8$. If you subtract 1, you get the previous counting number: $10 - 1 = 9$; $5 - 1 = 4$. If you multiply by 1, you get a product that is equal to the multiplicand: $1 \times 3 = 3$; $1 \times 15 = 15$.

Similarly, if you divide by 1, the quotient is the same as the dividend: $6 \div 1 = 6$; $9 \div 1 = 9$. Finally, if you divide 1 by a counting number, the result is a fraction that is already in simplest form: $1 \div 2 = \frac{1}{2}$; $1 \div 8 = \frac{1}{8}$. All of this is extremely useful in many operations, and the rules are easily learned. In fact, the rules for adding 1 and subtracting 1 are among the earliest topics taught in grade 1 and are useful in developing the other basic addition facts using the counting-on model.

Two

The number 2 is very easy to use. No one knows why, but the ability to double numbers comes very easily to most people. As a result, doubling numbers is an important aid in learning addition and subtraction and in mental computation with multiplication and division. Perhaps the ability to double numbers is common because the basic multiplication facts of 2s are the first ones people learn.

But there is good reason to suspect that doubling ability is more basic. For one thing, children are good doublers for a couple of years before they learn the multiplication facts (although they may have learned the 2s in disguised form through counting by 2s). The most likely explanation is that children teach themselves to double at a very early age, possibly by arranging toys in pairs.

In any case, the chances are good that you can instantly add $6 + 6$ or $8 + 8$, but that you may have to think a second to add $6 + 7$ or $8 + 7$. (Try a few such doubles and near-doubles to see the difference.) Therefore, a good way to solve a problem quickly in your head is to think of a double that is near it. If you know $5 + 5$ is 10, then $4 + 5$ will be 1 less, or 9, and $5 + 6$ will be 1 more, or 11.

This pattern carries over to subtraction as well, although it usually takes a little more thought. If you want to subtract 9 from 17, it is quick to think of the next highest even number, which is 18. You probably remember $9 + 9 = 18$ and $18 - 9 = 9$ very easily. Since you added 1 to 17 to get 18, you need to subtract 1 from 9 to find the answer to $17 - 9$, which is 8.

In fact, people who are good at doing math in their heads are usually familiar with the doubles of at least all the counting numbers to 50—and sometimes far beyond. Confronted with a problem such as $37 + 39$, such people do not begin by thinking "$7 + 9 = 16$ and carry the 1. Rather, they think "$37 + 37 = 74$, and add 2 more." Or they think, "$39 - 1 = 38$; $37 + 1 = 38$; and $38 + 38 = 76$." While all three thought patterns if carried out correctly will produce the right result, 76, the doubling methods are more direct and lead to quicker results with fewer errors. Memorizing the doubles of numbers less than 50 is not hard to do and is well worth the effort. If you can memorize even more doubles, so much the better.

Of course, since doubles are also the products of counting numbers and 2, an added benefit of learning doubles is that you extend your knowledge of multiplication beyond the basic 100 facts. Similarly, since doubling is the inverse operation of halving, you also know how to instantly solve a wide range of division problems.

Because doubling is so easy, it can be used to solve problems that do not show a 2 at all. For example, it is easy to solve 13×4 by doubling twice. The first doubling is 26 and the second 52. As a result of the ease of doubling twice, 4 is also a useful number.

Going one step further, doubling three times can be used to solve multiplication problems that have 8 as a factor. For small counting numbers, doubling three times is often faster and more accurate than multiplying the long way. For example, to multiply 13 by 8, the additional doubling from 52 to 104 is easy even if you have not memorized doubles above 50.

In fact, doubling repeatedly makes it easy to use any number where 2 can be used as the only factor. Many people find this process so easy that they have memorized the first 10 such numbers. These numbers, which are called *powers* of 2, are often handy in other ways as well. For example, computers work in powers of 2, so there are computers that are based on 4, 8, 16, and 32. Computer memories are expressed in terms of 1024 times some other number, which is often 16, 128, 256, or 512. And displays on commonly used computer programs may involve 256 rows or 256 columns. All of the numbers in the last sentence are powers of 2. Here are the first 10 powers of 2. Note the small numerals written to the right and just above the main body of each 2. These numerals are called *exponents*. They indicate the power, or the number of times, 2 is multiplied by itself.

first power of 2 $\quad = 2^1 \ = 2$
second power of 2 $= 2^2 \ = 4$
third power of 2 $\quad = 2^3 \ = 8$
fourth power of 2 $= 2^4 \ = 16$
fifth power of 2 $\quad = 2^5 \ = 32$
sixth power of 2 $\quad = 2^6 \ = 64$
seventh power of 2 $= 2^7 \ = 128$
eighth power of 2 $= 2^8 \ = 256$
ninth power of 2 $\quad = 2^9 \ = 512$
tenth power of 2 $\quad = 2^{10} = 1{,}024$

Ten—the most useful number

For multiplication, ten is useful because any number times 10 is almost like the original number. The product is just the multiplicand with a 0 written after it. Thus, $10 \times 17 = 170$, $10 \times 932 = 9320$, and $10 \times 1,234,567,890 = 12,345,678,900$.

Furthermore, for division, the same rule works in reverse. If a number ends in 0, dividing it by 10 produces a quotient that is just like the dividend, but with the 0 taken off.

The way that 10 behaves in multiplication and division makes 5 a useful number too. The number 10 is the product of 5 and 2. Therefore, you can use the properties of both 10 and 2 to get answers in which 5 is a factor or divisor. For example, to solve 48×5 in your head, you can begin by multiplying 48 by 10 and getting 480. This is twice the desired answer because you multiplied by twice 5 instead of by 5. So you use doubles to find half of 480. Therefore, $5 \times 48 = 240$.

The same idea also works for division—but reversed, of course. If you need to divide 330 by 5, you can begin by dividing by 10. The answer, 33, will be half the size of the answer you get when you divide by 5, since 10 is twice 5. Therefore, the solution to $330 \div 5$ is 66.

The number 10 is also easy to add and subtract. Adding a number from 0 through 9 to 10 is almost automatic; for example, the word *eighteen* is easily perceived as $8 + 10$. *-Teen* means "ten." Similarly, learning to recognize two numbers whose sum is 10, such as 3 and 7 or 6 and 4, is very easy. This ease in working with 10 provides another important strategy for learning the basic addition and subtraction facts. For example, someone who has learned such facts as $8 + 2$ or $10 - 2$ can use these facts as a bridge to facts such as $8 + 5$ or $13 - 5$. The person can think "I know $5 = 2 + 3$, and I know $2 + 8 = 10$, so $8 + 5$ is the same as $8 + 2 + 3$; $8 + 5 = 13$."

Similarly, subtraction facts can often be related to 10. To find $13 - 5$, the same thought pattern is used in reverse: "I know $5 = 2 + 3$. And $13 - 3$ leaves me with 10, so the answer is $10 - 2$, or 8."

One advantage of learning strategies such as these is that the basic facts can be relearned quickly if temporarily forgotten, such as during a test. But taking a problem apart into simple pieces that can be done quickly, and then reassembling the pieces into the original problem is the essence of mental arithmetic. Mastering these strategies gives you an advantage no matter what the situation.

The number ten can be used as a touchstone in addition problems of any complexity. When adding columns of numbers, they can be grouped to form 10s as you go along. For example, if you need to add

$$
\begin{array}{r}
25 \\
37 \\
15 \\
53 \\
+46 \\
\hline
\end{array}
$$

the best way to begin is to look for the 10s. From the first and third numbers, you find $5 + 5$ and from the second and fourth numbers, you find $7 + 3$. The only unmatched number in the second column is 6. Therefore, the sum of the first column is $10 + 10 + 6$, or 26. This is much easier than thinking "$5 + 7 = 12; 12 + 5 = 17; 17 + 3 = 20;$ and $20 + 6 = 26$." Similarly, in the first column, you now have 2 (from the 26), 2, 3, 1, 5, and 4. You can begin either by noting that $2 + 3 + 5 = 10$ or that $1 + 4 + 5 = 10$. In the first case, the remaining sum is $2 + 1 + 4 = 7$, so the total in the first column is $10 + 7 = 17$ (tens, since you are working in the tens column). If you begin with $1 + 4 + 5$, the remaining numbers are 2, 2, and 3, which are also easily summed to 17 (tens). In either case, the answer will be easier to find than thinking "$2 + 2 = 4; 4 + 3 = 7; 7 + 1 = 8; 8 + 5 = 13;$ and $13 + 4 = 17$ (tens)." The sum of the addends in the problem is 176 (17 tens and 6 ones).

The powers of 10 are also easy to use, just as the powers of 2 are. What is more, you do not have to memorize the powers of 10, since each is found simply by writing 1 followed by the same number of zeros as the number of the power. For example,

the first power of 10 $\quad = 10^1 = 10$
the second power of 10 $= 10^2 = 100$
the third power of 10 $\quad = 10^3 = 1000$
the fourth power of 10 $\; = 10^4 = 10,000$
the fifth power of 10 $\quad = 10^5 = 100,000$
the sixth power of 10 $\quad = 10^6 = 1,000,000$

Multiplying or dividing by a power of 10 is quite similar to multiplying or dividing by 10. To multiply, you merely need to add on the appropriate number of zeros—which is the same number as the exponent of the power. For example, to find 1000×349, you write 349 followed by three zeros, so the answer is 349,000. If a number ends in several zeros, you can use the same method in reverse to divide. The quotient of 83,000,000 divided by 100 is just 83,000,000 with the last two zeros removed, or 830,000. The hardest part is keeping track of where to put the commas.

Other small numbers

So far you have looked at 1, 2, 4, 5, 8, and 10, all of which are easy to use in mental computation. Now look at some other small numbers that are useful in varying degrees.

On the surface, the number 0 seems to be nearly as easy to use as 1. After all, what could be easier than adding or subtracting 0, since any number plus or minus 0 is unchanged?

For addition, 0 really is quite easy, but many people have trouble with the other operations. In fact, the concept of 0 poses much difficulty. A symbol for 0 was not invented until long after people had become familiar with counting numbers and fractions.

It is generally believed that the first clear notions about 0 date from about A.D. 500, and that these ideas were worked out in India. In the Western Hemisphere, the Mayan mathematicians of Central America independently worked out the notion of 0. But 0 as a separate number—meaning something more than just "nothing"—was apparently unknown to the great Greek mathematicians, people who produced enduring works of mathematical beauty for over a thousand years, from the sixth century B.C. until the fifth century A.D.

For many people, it is not easy to solve a subtraction problem like

$$
\begin{array}{r}
500{,}000 \\
-\ \ 49{,}928 \\
\hline
\end{array}
$$

The difficulty arises from all the zeros in the top number. People become lost when they have to "carry over" numbers to complete the computation. (If you have trouble with this sort of computation, there is a quick solution. Subtract 50,000 from the top number and you get 450,000—a number easily arrived at mentally. Then, find 50,000 − 49,928. The answer is 72, which you can also arrive at mentally. Add this to 450,000 and you get 450,072. You have the correct answer. And you've done all the work in your head.)

Multiplication by 0 is not very hard in theory, either. Yet many students have problems with 0 in multiplication, especially if it appears as part of another number. In a problem such as 509 × 34, students are apt to forget that the 0 is there, which produces errors. (The correct answer here is 17,306.) Similarly, students have trouble recalling that 0 divided by any number is 0, but that it is impossible to divide any number by 0.

All in all, 0 is not so easy as it might appear at first glance. In mental computation, the main use of 0 is with powers of 10, which have already been discussed.

The number 3, on the other hand, is easier than it might seem at first glance. Because 3 is such a low number, addition problems with 3s can be solved by counting on, for example.

Multiplication by 3 can often be done in your head by first doubling, then adding the original number. For example, to multiply 37 by 3, you can think "2 × 37 is 74; and 74 + 37 is _____ ." Here it is good to remember how useful 10s can be. You should complete the mental computation by thinking "and 74 + 37 is (70 + 30) + (4 + 7), or 100 + 11 = 111."

This technique can be carried over to make 6 easier than it might otherwise be. Since 6 is the double of 3, you can first use the method for multiplying by 3 and then double the result. For example, to find 6 × 24 in your head, you can think "2 × 24 is 48, and 48 + 24 is 72, so 6 × 24 is the same as 2 × 72, or 144." Sometimes, it turns out to be easier to double first, and then use the method for 3. Had the problem been 6 × 25, for instance, most people would find it easier to think "2 × 25 is 50, 2 × 50 is 100, and 100 + 50 is 150." When you work in this order, it is important to remember that the number to be added at the end is not the original number, but the result of the first doubling. You need to make a mental note such as "(doubling) 2 × 25 = 50; (tripling) 2 × 50 = 100; 100 + 50 = 150." Otherwise, you may wind up with the wrong answer.

The method for 3 can be used twice to compute mentally with 9. For example, if you know that 3 × 15 is 45, to find 9 × 15 you may want to think "To triple 45, I double it to get 90 and add 45 to get 135." In that circumstance, tripling twice is an efficient method for multiplying by 9 in your head.

Another way of working with the number 9 is based on its closeness to 10. If you are adding 9 to a number, it is sometimes easier to add 10 and subtract 1. For example, you can find 37 + 9 by thinking "37 + 10 is 47, and 47 − 1 is 46." Especially when you have several 9s in a row, as in 3984 + 999, going to the nearby power of 10 is definitely easier than working the problem out the long way. Think: "3984 + 1000 is 4984, and 4984 − 1 is 4983." In fact, the same method can be used for numbers that are not quite so near a power of 10. If you are adding 3984 to 996, for example, you merely need to subtract 4 at the end, instead of subtracting 1.

One number has been overlooked in this survey of the whole numbers from 0 through ten—the number 7. The sad truth is that 7 is not very easy to work with. The best thing to do with problems involving 7 is to look for other numbers in the problem that are more useful and rely on them to get you through.

Does becoming familiar with useful numbers really help? Absolutely. The mathematical wizards mentioned at the beginning of this section always used them. For example, when eight-year-old Zerah Colburn was asked how he could multiply 21,734 by 543 so quickly, he replied that he began by noting that 543 is 181 × 3. Since it is easier to multiply a large number by 181 than by 3 (note the useful 1s and 8), he first multiplied 21,734 by 3 to get 65,202 and then multiplied 65,202 by 181 to get 11,801,562.

Clues from Division

Although many people have trouble with division, it provides a set of helpful clues to mental computation. As usual, some numbers are easier to work with than others. If you memorize the division clues, you will find easy ways both to compute in your head and to check computations you do with paper and pencil or a calculator.

First, here is some necessary vocabulary. A counting number *divides* a whole number if the resulting quotient is also a whole number—that is, if the remainder is 0. The property of dividing a number is called *divisibility*. Thus, you can talk about a *divisibility test* of a given whole number with respect to a given counting number. For example, the divisibility test for 3 tells whether a given whole number can be divided by 3 with a zero remainder. The number 9 passes the divisibility test for 3 because 9 ÷ 3 = 3. The number 10 does not pass the divisibility test for 3 because 10 ÷ 3 = 3R1. You should memorize the divisibility tests for the single-digit counting numbers because they have many uses in mental arithmetic and checking computations.

Every number is divisible by 1, and no number is divisible by 0. After that, the tests become progressively more complicated. The next easiest test is for 10. You probably know it already because it is an easy consequence of the rule for multiplying by 10. If a whole number ends in 0, the number is divisible by 10.

Other numbers follow the same pattern. To test for divisibility, you look at the last digit or digits of a number. You should be familiar with the rule for divisibility by 5, since it was referred to earlier. If a number ends in 0 or 5, it is divisible by 5. The first part of that rule, pertaining to 0, is a consequence of the rule for 10. If a number is divisible by 10, because $10 = 5 \times 2$, it also must be divisible by 5. The second part of the rule is also a result of the fact that $10 = 5 \times 2$, for it means that 5 is just halfway between 0 and 10. Since each multiple of 5 is 5 greater than the multiple preceding it, the end digits go from 0 to 0 (10 greater) in *exactly* two steps. Thus, every other multiple of 5 must end with 5.

A number that ends in 0 is also divisible by 2, since $10 = 5 \times 2$. Furthermore, for the same reasons that numbers ending in 5 must be divisible by 5, numbers ending in 2, 4, 6, or 8 must be divisible by 2. The fact that 2 divides 10 means that there is a cycle of numbers that repeat themselves each *decade*. (A decade in this sense consists of the numbers from one number that ends in 1 to the next number that ends in 0, just as a decade of years is defined.)

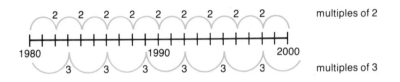

multiples of 2

multiples of 3

The principle involved here is a general one that can be used to explore divisibility in other ways. If one number divides another, the multiples of the divisor will repeat in a cycle that is exactly equal to the dividend. If the dividend is a power of 10, for instance, the cycle will be the same between each two powers of 10 and show in the last few digits of the number.

For example, the second power of 10 is 100 [$(5 \times 2) \times (5 \times 2)$]. The numbers that divide 100, then, are 2, 5, $2 \times 2 = 4$, $2 \times 5 = 10$, $5 \times 5 = 25$, and $5 \times 5 \times 2 = 50$. You already know divisibility tests for 2, 5, and 10. But the general rule suggests that the last two digits of any number can be used to determine whether that number is divisible by 4, 25, or 50. This discussion will demonstrate the rules for 4.

Clearly, if the last two digits of a number are divisible by 4, then the number must be divisible by 4. You know that this is true of the first one hundred whole numbers; that is, the numbers 0 through 99. Since the cycle repeats every one hundred numbers, the same will hold true from 100 through 199, from 200 through 299, and so forth. Suppose you want to know if 398,882 is divisible by 4. The last two digits are 82. It is easy to check that 82 is *not* divisible by 4; nor is 398,882. On the other hand, you can also see that 398,872 *is* divisible by 4, because $72 = 4 \times 18$. The rule will work no matter how large the number is.

The third power of 10 is 1000, which equals $10 \times 10 \times 10$ and can be factored into primes as $5 \times 2 \times 5 \times 2 \times 5 \times 2$. Since three factors of 2 are involved, one number that has a cycle of 1000 for divisibility is 8 because $8 = 2 \times 2 \times 2$. By the same line of reasoning that was used in the last paragraph, if the last three digits of a number are divisible by 8, the number must also be divisible by 8. As a result, you can reduce a problem such as determining whether 123,456,972 is divisible by 8 to the simpler problem of whether 972 is divisible by 8.

You can quickly rule out any number that does not end in 0, 2, 4, 6, or 8 as being divisible by 4 or 8. For a number to be divisible by 4 or 8, it must also be divisible by 2. (But the reverse does not hold; numbers divisible by 2 are not necessarily divisible by 4 or 8.) Thus, if a number is odd, you know immediately that it is not divisible by 4 or 8. Only if the number is even can you use the specific test for divisibility.

Mathematics is the study of patterns. If you see the way this pattern has been developed, you should also be able to see that the following statement is always true: For any number, if the last n digits are divisible by 2^n, the number is also divisible by 2^n. Notice how easy it can be in mathematics to go from a few specific examples to a far-ranging rule for all numbers.

Since 3 is not a factor of 10, its divisibility test is not based on the last digits of the dividend. Instead, if the sum of the digits of a number is divisible by 3, the number itself is divisible by 3. Thus, for example, 298,341 *is* divisible by 3 because $2 + 9 + 8 + 3 + 4 + 1 = 27$. But 392,521 is *not* divisible by 3 because $3 + 9 + 2 + 5 + 2 + 1 = 22$.

In practice, you do not have to add the numbers. Instead, you can look for sums of two or more digits that are divisible by 3 and "cast them out," working with only the ones that are left over. For example, the efficient way to determine whether 298,341 is divisible by 3 is to cast out the 9 and the 3, which are divisible by 3, leaving 2, 8, 4, and 1. You can cast out the 8 and 1, because they sum to 9, and also the 2 and 4, because they add to 6. Since all the digits were cast out, the number is divisible by 3. On the other hand, with the number 392,521, when you cast out the 3, 9, and $2 + 5 + 2 = 9$, you are left with 1. Since the 1 cannot be cast out, the number is not divisible by 3.

The same rule that works for 3 also works for 9, only this time the digits cast out must sum to 9. To find whether 293,837 is divisible by 9, cast out 9s. Because $2 + 7 = 9$, they can be cast out, as can be the digit 9. You are then left with 3, 8, and 3. You can cast out one more 9 by adding $3 + 8 = 11$ and subtracting 9. That leaves 2 and 3. Since $2 + 3 = 5$, there are no more 9s to cast out. Therefore, 293,837 is *not* divisible by 9. If a number is divisible by 9, the result when all the 9s have been cast out will be 0.

Now you have divisibility tests for 0, 1, 2, 3, 4, 5, 8, and 9. The only remaining single-digit numbers are 6 and 7.

The number 6 is easy to work with. Since $6 = 2 \times 3$, if a number is divisible by both 2 and 3, it must also be divisible by 6. Therefore, to determine whether 205,384 is divisible by 6, you note that it is even (and therefore divisible by 2) and proceed to cast out 3s. You are left with a remainder of 1, so 205,384 is *not* divisible by 6. Also, 205,383, which is divisible by 3, is not divisible by 6 because it is odd. But 205,386 is divisible by both 3 and 2, so it *is* divisible by 6.

A number of divisibility tests have been developed for 7, but all are very complicated. Here is one that is somewhat easier than the others. Given a number, remove its last digit and subtract twice that digit from the number you obtained by removing the digit. Repeat this until you get a single digit. If the last digit is 0 or 7, the original number is divisible by 7. Unless the single digit is either 0 or 7, the original number was not divisible by 7. Here is an example.

$$
\begin{array}{r}
493,826 \\
-\quad 12 \\
\hline
493\ 70 \\
-\quad\ \ 0 \\
\hline
493\ 7 \\
-\ 14 \\
\hline
479 \\
-\ 18 \\
\hline
29 \\
-\ 18 \\
\hline
-\ 16 \\
-\ 12 \\
\hline
-\ 13 \\
-\ 6 \\
\hline
-7
\end{array}
$$

The last digit you get may be positive or negative. But to apply the rule, you must end up with 0 or 7 (-7 does not count). The number in the example is *not* divisible by 7.

While this divisibility rule is interesting, you can see that it takes a lot of work. For most practical purposes, it is easier to divide the number by 7 to see if there is a remainder than it is to apply the rule. (Now for more practice in divisibility, *see* Pt. IV, Sec. 2, p. 233.)

Fractions, Decimals, and Percents

The discussion so far has been limited to whole numbers. But mental computations can also be done with fractions, decimals, and percents as long as you memorize certain relationships.

Unlike the basic addition, subtraction, multiplication, and division facts, the basic facts about fractions, decimals, and percents are not drilled over and over in school (although there is usually a lesson or two in which some of the most important ones are discussed). As a result, most people have a good command of the basic facts of whole numbers, but few have a good command of the basic facts of fractions, decimals, and percents. Because understanding the relationships among fractions, decimals, and percents can be extremely helpful, you should seriously try to learn them.

Fractions and whole numbers

Much of what you have learned about the small whole numbers is immediately useful with fractions. In multiplying a whole number by a fraction that has a *numerator* (top number) of 1, the result is the same as dividing the whole number by the *denominator* (bottom number) of the fraction. Thus, to find $\frac{1}{2}$ of 52, you can divide 52 by 2. The divisibility tests become helpful as a result. For example, to find $\frac{1}{51}$ of 192, you can begin by noting that both 51 (5 + 1 = 6) and 192 (1 + 9 + 2 = 12) are divisible by 3. Dividing each by 3 changes the problem to $\frac{1}{17}$ of 64. Since 17 and 64 have no common divisors, the only operation left is to divide 64 by 17, which gives 3 with a remainder of 13. In stating the answer to a fraction problem, however, you should use fractions instead of remainders. The fraction form is found by writing the remainder over the divisor, so the final form of the answer to $\frac{1}{51}$ of 192 is $3\frac{13}{17}$. Working this way, you can do most problems involving whole numbers and fractions in your head if the numbers involved are fairly small.

There are other methods you can memorize for specific fractions. One group of rules applies to $\frac{1}{2}$ and $\frac{1}{5}$. Sometimes it is easier to multiply a number by 5 than it is to find $\frac{1}{2}$ of it, for example. The product will then be 10 times the answer you really want, so you must divide by 10. For example, to find $\frac{1}{2}$ of 25, you might find it easier to think "5 × 25 = 125, and 125 ÷ 10 = 12$\frac{5}{10}$, or 12$\frac{1}{2}$." Similarly, to find $\frac{1}{5}$ of a number, you can multiply by 2 and divide the result by 10. Suppose that you want to find $\frac{1}{5}$ of 193. The answer is 2 × 193 = 386, and 386

÷ 10 = $38\frac{6}{10}$, or $38\frac{3}{5}$. While the same result can be obtained by dividing 193 by 5, in this case it is easier to multiply by 2 and divide by 10 than it is to divide by 5.

You can use the same ideas in reverse as well. To multiply by 5, you can take $\frac{1}{2}$ of a number and multiply by 10. This is a convenient way to find 5×58, for example. The result is 290. Also, to multiply by 2, you *could* take $\frac{1}{5}$ of the number and multiply by 10, but that method is usually less convenient than doubling.

Since 4 and 25 are related to 100, a similar set of relationships holds for $\frac{1}{4}$ and $\frac{1}{25}$. To find $\frac{1}{4}$ of a number, you can multiply by 25 and divide by 100. This can be convenient for a few numbers. For example, $\frac{1}{4}$ of 1000 is $1000 \times 25 = 25,000$, and $25,000 \div 100 = 250$. Similarly, to find $\frac{1}{25}$ of a number, multiply by 4 and divide by 100. Thus, $\frac{1}{25}$ of 87 is $87 \times 4 = 348$, and $348 \div 100 = 3\frac{48}{100}$, or $3\frac{12}{25}$.

Using fractions with decimals and percents

If you have learned the fraction-decimal-percent equivalents, you can often convert a difficult problem with decimals or percents into an easy problem with fractions.

Decimals are just another way to write a fraction whose denominator is a power of 10. For example, 0.3 is the decimal form of $\frac{3}{10}$. Each decimal place is the next power of 10, so 0.003 is 3 over the third power of 10, or $\frac{3}{1000}$. The basic way to convert a decimal to a fraction is to write a whole number over the appropriate power of 10 and simplify. For example, the decimal 0.25 is $\frac{25}{100}$, which simplifies to $\frac{1}{4}$. Similarly, the decimal 0.375 is $\frac{375}{1000}$, which simplifies to $\frac{3}{8}$.

Recall that the rule for dividing a whole number by 10 or by a power of 10 worked only if the whole number ended in 0 or a number of 0s. When working with decimals you can convert the rule to apply to any number. All you need to do is to move the decimal point as many places to the left as there are zeros in the power of 10. For example, $511 \div 100 = 5.11$.

It is often hard to change a fraction into a decimal in your head. So the best solution is to memorize the most common fractional forms of decimals. Some of the most useful are in the table on the next page. In that table, you may recognize that the relationships between 0.25 and $\frac{1}{4}$ and between 0.5 and $\frac{1}{2}$ form the basis of the shortcuts for using fractions with whole numbers. The same ideas can be used even more easily with decimal problems. For example, if you need to find 0.25×488, it is much easier to solve as $\frac{1}{4} \times 488 = 122$. The same applies to the other relationships. For example, to solve any multiplication or division problem using 0.875, you can first consider whether it would be easier to use $\frac{7}{8}$. In some cases, such as 1600×0.875, it is much easier to use $\frac{7}{8}$, because $1600 \div 8 = 200$, and $200 \times 7 = 1400$.

0.05	$= \dfrac{1}{20}$	0.375	$= \dfrac{3}{8}$	0.75	$= \dfrac{3}{4}$
0.1	$= \dfrac{1}{10}$	0.4	$= \dfrac{2}{5}$	0.8	$= \dfrac{4}{5}$
0.125	$= \dfrac{1}{8}$	0.5	$= \dfrac{1}{2}$	0.875	$= \dfrac{7}{8}$
0.2	$= \dfrac{1}{5}$	0.6	$= \dfrac{3}{5}$	0.9	$= \dfrac{9}{10}$
0.25	$= \dfrac{1}{4}$	0.625	$= \dfrac{5}{8}$		
0.3	$= \dfrac{3}{10}$	0.7	$= \dfrac{7}{10}$		

Sometimes you must be very alert to spot a situation in which a fraction equivalent will simplify the problem. For example, $140 \div 0.875$ can be solved using fraction equivalents, although the solution may not be immediately obvious. You must recall that division by a fraction is accomplished by inverting the divisor and multiplying. Thus, the fraction form of $140 \div 0.875$, which is $140 \div \frac{7}{8}$, is solved by finding $140 \times \frac{8}{7}$. Since 7 divides 140, you can complete the solution in your head: $140 \div 7 = 20$, and $20 \times 8 = 160$.

Percents are easily converted to decimals. Therefore, the same fraction equivalents you learned for decimals can be used with percents. To convert a percent to a decimal, divide the percent by 100. In practice, this means that you place the decimal point (which is not shown for whole-number percents) two places to the left, writing or dropping 0s as needed. For example, 20% is the same as 0.20, or 0.2; $37\frac{1}{2}$ is the same as 0.375 (note that $\frac{1}{2}$% is 0.005); and 115% is 1.15.

Decimals are not usually written with fractions, but as the example of $37\frac{1}{2}$% illustrates, percents often do include fractions. Therefore, you need to learn some of the percents in fraction form and their corresponding decimal forms. Furthermore, many percents that correspond to fractions have decimal forms with an infinite number of digits that repeat a particular pattern. For example, $33\frac{1}{3}$% is equivalent to the decimal 0.3333 . . . , where the pattern of 3s repeats forever. Here is a list of percents that use fractions and have easy fraction equivalents.

$$12\tfrac{1}{2}\% = \frac{1}{8} \qquad 33\tfrac{1}{3}\% = \frac{1}{3} \qquad 66\tfrac{2}{3}\% = \frac{2}{3}$$

$$14\tfrac{2}{7}\% = \frac{1}{7} \qquad 37\tfrac{1}{2}\% = \frac{3}{8} \qquad 83\tfrac{1}{3}\% = \frac{5}{6}$$

$$16\tfrac{2}{3}\% = \frac{1}{6} \qquad 62\tfrac{1}{2}\% = \frac{5}{8} \qquad 87\tfrac{1}{2}\% = \frac{7}{8}$$

It is often easier to use the fraction equivalent of a percent than the decimal equivalent. For example, to find 66⅔% of 99, it is much easier to multiply 99 by ⅔ than it is to use the decimal equivalent: 99 ÷ 3 = 33, and 33 × 2 = 66.

On the other hand, you may find it easier in some cases to convert from a fraction problem to a decimal or percent problem. Once you have the common equivalents memorized, you can choose the easiest form to use in a given situation. For example, to find ⅖ of 24, you can think "0.4 × 24 is twice 24, or 48, twice 48, or 96, divided by 10, or 9.6." Then, if the answer needs to be in fraction form, you think "0.6 is ⅗, so ⅖ of 24 is 9⅗." While the same result can be found by thinking "Twice 24 is 48, and 48 divided by 5 is 9 with a remainder of 3, so the answer is 9⅗," many people prefer not to divide in their heads.

The important skill is to be able to convert instantly from fractions to decimals or percents and vice versa. Once you have the equivalents firmly in your memory, you will have many opportunites to use them. In particular, you will find them useful in working with handheld calculators because most calculators use decimals, but not fractions. If you know the decimal equivalents for the commonly used fractions, you can more easily solve problems using a calculator.

Mnemonics

The number that Alexander Craig Aitken memorized to a thousand digits was pi (π), which is the ratio of the circumference of a circle to its diameter and which also crops up in many math situations, often quite unexpectedly. Pi is a mathematical *constant*—that is, a number that has a constant value. When written as a decimal, pi has no pattern that repeats, as does, for example, the decimal representation of ⅓. In fact, although pi is an infinite decimal like 0.33333 . . . , the calculation of the digits from various formulas is more trouble than it is worth. Therefore, people memorize as many of the digits of pi as they need. If you want, you can take pi to 3.1415926 and further. But, for most purposes, pi to hundredths, or 3.14, is sufficient. It is also often useful to know a close fractional approximation of pi. For most purposes, $3\frac{1}{7}$, or $\frac{22}{7}$, is sufficient.

People who want more accuracy, of course, need to know more decimal places. Modern computers have calculated pi to thousands, and even millions, of digits. But Aitken himself had no practical use for knowing a thousand digits of pi. He just memorized them to amuse himself.

One trick for memorizing digits in any situation is to use a *mnemonic*, or memory aid. A mnemonic is usually a sentence in which the order and number of letters in each word correspond to the order and value of the digits to be remembered. For example, to memorize 3.14 you could think "Now I know," or "See a word," or some similar phrase that has a three-letter word, then a one-letter word, and then a four-letter word. (Note that the decimal point is not taken into account.) For a more lengthy version of pi, someone coined the mnemonic, "May I have a large container of coffee?" This translates into 3.1415926, which is certainly precise enough for most purposes. The physicist Sir James Jeans went a little further, however, with "How I want a drink, alcoholic of course, after the heavy chapters involving quantum mechanics" (3.14159265358979—skip the punctuation).

Patterns as Shortcuts

There are many ways to convert a difficult problem into an easier one. Some involve patterns in arithmetic, while others call for patterns that can be found only by using algebra. In some cases, special methods of computing may be easier for mental calculation than the usual methods.

Although these methods are especially helpful for mental calculation, they can also be used when working with paper and pencil. It is a mistake to approach every problem in the same way. If you have many different weapons in your arsenal, you can choose the weapon that fits the situation. You can also use these methods to check answers that you've computed in other ways.

The fundamental rule of arithmetic

Almost every branch of mathematics has one rule that mathematicians have termed *fundamental*. For arithmetic, the fundamental, or basic, rule is that any counting number can be expressed as the product of *primes* in just one way. A prime is a counting number greater than 1 that has no factors other than 1 and itself. For example, 2 is prime because its only factors are 1 and 2. Based on this rule, 12 could only be expressed in primes as 2 × 2 × 3. Although 12 is also 4 × 3 and 2 × 6, 4 and 6 are not primes. The only *prime factorization* of 12 is 2 × 2 × 3. (The order of the factors is not considered important, so 2 × 3 × 2 and 3 × 2 × 2 are considered to be the same prime factorization.)

When two numbers are multiplied, the product is also the product of the two unique prime factorizations. Often, it is possible to rearrange the prime factors to find numbers that simplify the multiplication. For example, to find 12 × 35, you can begin by factoring each number, to obtain (2 × 2 × 3) × (5 × 7). This product can be rearranged as (2 × 5) × (2 × 3 × 7), or 10 × 42. Thus, the answer is 420. In general, to solve a multiplication problem this way, you begin by looking for pairs of 2 and 5, since each pair becomes a 10. For example, to multiply 425 by 44, factoring gives (5 × 5 × 17) × (2 × 2 × 11). There are two pairs of 2 and 5, so the answer is 100 times the product of 17 and 11. Since 11 × 17 is 187, the product of 425 and 44 is 18,700.

The fundamental rule of arithmetic is also useful in working division and fraction problems. You may recall that if a fraction contains the same factor in the numerator as it does in the denominator, that factor can be "cancelled." For example, $\frac{4}{6}$ contains a factor of 2 in both the numerator and denominator. If you write the fraction in prime-factored form, you can cancel the common 2s.

$$\frac{4}{6} = \frac{\cancel{2} \times 2}{\cancel{2} \times 3}$$

This means that $\frac{4}{6}$ and $\frac{2}{3}$ are the same number.

It is usually easiest to cancel common factors by using prime factorizations when the numbers are fairly large. For small numbers, you may recognize common factors without using primes. For example, to put $\frac{357}{924}$ in simplest form, you can begin by finding the prime factors of 357. Since 357 is a multiple of 3, mentally divide 357 by 3 to get 119. Since 119 is not a multiple of 2, 3, or 5, try 7: 7 × 17 = 119. Since 17 is prime, the factored form of 357 is 3 × 7 × 17.

Now work on 924. Since 924 is even, 2 is a prime factor. Divide by 2, to obtain 462, another even number. Divide by 2 again, obtaining 231, a multiple of 3. Divide by 3; the result is 77, which is easily recognizable as 7 × 11. Now you have all the prime factors, so 924 = 2 × 2 × 3 × 7 × 11. You can proceed to cancel.

$$\frac{357}{924} = \frac{3 \times 7 \times 17}{2 \times 2 \times 3 \times 7 \times 11}$$

so $\frac{357}{924}$ is equal to $\frac{17}{44}$.

To find the prime factors of any number, you need only check for factors up to the square root of the number. After that, you will find that the same factors repeat in reverse order. For example, after 7, the next factor of 119 is 17, so you get 17 × 7—the same as 7 × 17. If you have memorized the squares of the counting numbers through 15, you can easily recognize that 119 is just a little less than 121, or 11 squared. Thus, 11 is too big to bother checking. The next prime less than 11 is 7, so 7 is the largest prime that needs to be checked.

If you can recognize the factors easily, the same method can be used for mentally computing division problems or for turning a difficult division problem into an easier one to solve with paper and pencil. Fractions can be viewed as just another way of writing division. Thus, a problem such as 969 ÷ 105 can be quickly seen to have a common factor of 3 that can be eliminated, reducing the problem to 323 ÷ 35. Since 7 and 5, the factors of 35, are not factors of 323, that is the best you can do; but it does simplify the problem somewhat: 323 ÷ 35 = 9.23.

The distributive law

Another principle that helps you break a problem down into simpler parts is the *distributive law*. For counting numbers, the distributive law can be illustrated by dot diagrams. Consider 6 × 5, for example:

The vertical line separates the diagram into two parts. The part on the left is the dot array for 6 × 2, while the part on the right is the dot array for 6 × 3. This diagram proves that 6 × 5 = (6 × 2) + (6 × 3).

Now suppose that you move the vertical line to another place in the diagram.

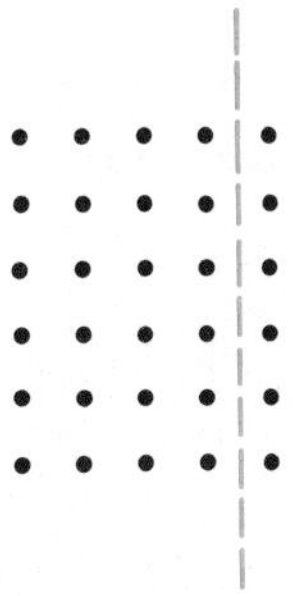

In this position, the diagram proves that 6 × 5 is equal to (6 × 4) + (6 × 1).

Such diagrams can be used for any product of counting numbers. In each case, the vertical line would separate the original factor into two parts whose sum is the original factor. In fact, if *a, b,* and *c* are any numbers (not just counting numbers), it is true that

$$a \times (b + c) = (a \times b) + (a \times c)$$

This is the general statement of the distributive law.

The distributive law is useful because it enables you to separate a multiplication problem into two problems. Furthermore, you can always choose at least one of the numbers so that it will be easy to work with. In fact, the most common use for the distributive law occurs when the factor to be separated is close to a power or multiple of the easiest of all numbers, 10.

For example, both 11 and 12 are close to 10. Therefore, one way to multiply 17 × 11 is to use the distributive law to change the problem to (17 × 10) + (17 × 1), or 170 + 17 = 187. Similarly, in multiplying by 12, you can change 12 × 341 to (10 × 341) + (2 × 341). The result is 3410 plus twice 341, or 3410 + 682 = 4092.

Notice that the rule suggests a mechanical way of multiplying by 11. You can always multiply by 11 by writing the original number twice, with the second version under the first, but moved 1 place to the left. Then you add as in the regular multiplication procedure. So to multiply 4937 by 11, merely write

```
  4937
  4937
 54307
```

The same procedure can be used for numbers that are near multiples of 10. For example, to multiply 21×84, you can think "20 times 84 is 1680, and $1680 + 84$ is 1764."

The distributive law also applies to subtraction. That is, for any numbers a, b, and c it is true that

$$a \times (b - c) = (a \times b) - (a \times c)$$

This version of the distributive law makes 9 a very useful number. Since $9 = 10 - 1$, you can solve multiplication problems involving 9 using the distributive law. To find 78×9, think "10×78 is 780, and $780 - 78$ is 702."

Also, you can use the subtraction version of the distributive law with factors that are near to multiples of 10 or powers of 10. So to solve 56×998, you would change the problem to $(56 \times 1000) - (56 \times 2) = 56,000 - 112 = 55,888$.

A pattern from algebra

In algebra, certain relationships become apparent that are not obvious in arithmetic. One of these is called the *difference of two squares*. It is based on the relationship that is always true for any two numbers a and b that

$$(a \times b) \times (a - b) = a^2 - b^2$$

For example, $(5 + 3) \times (5 - 3) = (5 \times 5) - (3 \times 3)$. You can check this for yourself: $8 \times 2 = 16$ and $25 - 9 = 16$.

The difference of two squares is useful when both factors in a problem are the same distance from a number whose square you know. Therefore, it is a good idea to memorize the squares of the smaller numbers. From learning the basic multiplication facts, you already know the squares of the numbers from 0 to 9, and you also know that $10 \times 10 = 100$. But it is helpful to know the squares through 15 (or even through 25) as well. For your convenience, here are the squares from 11 through 15:

$$11 \times 11 = 121$$
$$12 \times 12 = 144$$
$$13 \times 13 = 169$$
$$14 \times 14 = 196$$
$$15 \times 15 = 225$$

It is also helpful to remember that the square of 25 is 625.

Here is how the difference of two squares can help you to find 23×17. First notice that each factor is just 3 units away from 20. Therefore, think "$(20 + 3) \times (20 - 3)$ is 20 squared minus 3 squared, or 2 squared times 10 squared minus 9, or $400 - 9 = 391$." The differences that are close to a multiple of 10, such as 20 in this case, are the easiest to recognize. However, you can also use this method to multiply 17×13 if you remember the square of 15. In that case, you can think "this problem is $(15 + 2) \times (15 - 2)$, or $225 - 4 = 221$." First, of course, you have to notice that the difference of two squares can be used. Then you need to remember the appropriate squares.

If one factor is 5 more than a multiple of 10 and the other factor is 5 less than a multiple of 10, a particularly easy pattern emerges. Consider, for example, 35×45, which is the square of 40 minus the square of 5. In any problem of this kind, the first square will end with two 0s, so subtracting 25 from it will result in 75. Furthermore, the subtraction will reduce the square of the multiple of 10 by 100. Experiment to see that the following rule always works: To multiply two two-digit numbers, one of which is 5 more than a multiple of 10 and the other of which is 5 less than the same multiple of 10, first write 75. Then square the larger of the digits in the tens place of the two original factors, subtract 1 from the square, and write the difference in front of the 75. The four-digit number that results is the correct answer. In the case of 35×45, after writing 75, you would square 4 to get 16, subtract 1 to get 15, and, writing the 15 in front of the 75, come up with the answer 1575.

Estimating

There is an old saying that "Close only counts in horseshoes," which refers to the scoring system of the game of tossing horseshoes at a post. If one of the horseshoes that you toss lands within a certain distance of the post, you receive points, although not so many as when the shoe touches or circles the post. Similarly, in mathematics, you can receive "points" for being close, although perhaps not so many as you would receive for the exact answer. In fact, for many purposes, close is good enough in mathematics—an estimate will do.

For example, a bright young student announced to her teacher that the last Ice Age ended 11,005 years ago. When asked for an explanation, the student reported that her textbook said that the Ice Age ended 11,000 years ago, but that the copyright indicated that the book was five years old.

In this case, close is not merely good enough. It is really *better* than the student's more exact estimate. The textbook statement is intended to express a not-very-certain date. It implies that the Ice Age ended 11,000 years ago *plus or minus* 500 years. That is, the textbook statement was expressed "to the nearest thousand." Had the textbook been over 500 years old, the student would have been right to correct the date, but not to 11,505. Rather, the corrected date should be 12,000 years ago.

This example illustrates an important point. Mathematical statements must be reasonable. This especially applies to the solutions of word problems. And there are a number of short-cuts to determining whether an answer is reasonable.

Reasonable answers

In solving any math problem, the first question you should ask about an answer is "Does this answer make sense? Is it reasonable or 'way out of the ballpark'?" For practical problems, such a test merely means comparing the answers to reality. In using algebra to solve some geometry problems, for example, you often end up with two answers. If the problem is about the dimensions of a rectangle, and one of the answers is 0 or less than 0, that answer must be discarded as unreasonable. (Such an answer may be acceptable in another context, but it cannot describe a rectangle.)

Some tests for reasonableness do not depend on physical reality. They are purely mathematical. People who are good at math apply such tests almost without thinking. This is a habit that you should develop. Automatically checking the reasonableness of your answers is one of the best ways to avoid making "dumb" mistakes.

The first test to apply in checking your work is to look at the relationship between the size of the proposed answer and the size of the numbers in the problem. The following relationships hold true for the four basic operations with counting numbers:

Addition: The answer will be larger than the largest number in the problem.
Subtraction: The answer will be smaller than the largest number in the problem.
Multiplication: The answer will be larger than the largest number in the problem.
Division: The answer will be smaller than the largest number in the problem.

In a problem of only counting numbers, if you obtain an answer that does not meet these four rules, your answer cannot possibly be right. Furthermore, you can use the rules in reverse to help you solve problems. For example, suppose that you are given this word problem: "Jack is 5 years older than his sister. Jack is 23. How old is his sister?" A good first step is to think "The largest number in the problem is 23. Clearly, the answer must be smaller than 23, so the solution cannot be found by addition or multiplication." This reduces your choices to subtraction and division, from which it is easy to choose subtraction as the correct method.

Some people may think that following such a procedure for problems involving counting numbers isn't necessary because these problems are so simple. But when a problem involves fractions, decimals, or percents, the story is quite different. People often make mistakes in working with these that could be avoided if the people first determined what a reasonable answer would be.

The situation is complicated by the fact that the rules for multiplying and dividing that apply here are different from those for counting numbers. Since many people learn the rules for counting numbers early in life, they make mistakes because they unconsciously apply a counting-number rule to a fraction, decimal, or percent situation.

For example, consider the problem "How many quarters are there in 8 dollars?" One temptation is to multiply $\frac{1}{4}$ times 8, producing the product 2. If you think about the four basic rules beforehand, however, you will realize that the answer must be greater than 8. Then you would know that $4 \times 8 = 32$ is the more likely solution. Similarly, some people might be misled by the word *divided* in the problem "24 apples are divided so that each person gets $\frac{1}{4}$ of the apples. How many does each person get?" They may think that $24 \div \frac{1}{4}$ should be the answer. Since $24 \div \frac{1}{4}$ is 96, however, it is unreasonable. The answer must be smaller than 24, the largest number in the problem, so the correct solution is $24 \div 4 = 6$ apples.

You should become familiar with the rules for numbers that are not counting numbers. The rules for counting numbers continue to apply for all numbers *larger* than 1. For numbers *between* 0 and 1, however, the rules for both multiplication and division are different. The rules for addition and subtraction, however, remain the same. Here is a summary of all the rules:

Addition: Answers are larger than the largest number for all numbers greater than 0.
Subtraction: Answers are less than the largest number for all numbers greater than 0.

Multiplication: Answers are larger than the largest number for all numbers greater than 1. Answers are less than the largest number for all numbers between 0 and 1. *Division:* Answers are less than the largest number for all divisors greater than 1. Answers are larger than the largest number for all divisors between 0 and 1.

Notice that in division, it matters whether the numbers are dividends or divisors. While 24 ÷ ¼ is greater than 24, ¼ ÷ 24 is less than 24.

Getting closer

Merely knowing whether an answer should be larger or smaller than the largest number in a problem does not get you very close to the actual answer, of course. In many situations, you want an answer that is much more precise than that. For example, you may want to use an estimate to check a problem that you have already solved. There are various ways to make estimates that are good enough for such purposes.

Probably the most common way of estimating relies on rounding numbers. Numbers can be rounded according to three different rules, however. The most common rule is the one that is generally taught in arithmetic. If you want to round to a particular place, look at the digit just to the right of that place. If it is less than 5, change all the digits following the place to which you are rounding to 0s. But if the digit to the right is 5 or greater, increase the digit in the place you are rounding to by 1 and change succeeding digits to 0. Following this rule

543,056 rounds to hundreds as 543,100
124,497 rounds to thousands as 124,000
1,923,846 rounds to millions as 2,000,000

The second method of rounding is used by stores in dealing with money. Any part of a cent rounds up to the next higher cent. This rule, which is important in dealing with purchasing problems, also has a place in estimating, as you will see. Refer to it as the *commercial method*. Using the commercial method

$1.3333 rounds to $1.34
$10.575 rounds to $10.58
$6.999 rounds to $7.00

The third method of rounding is sometimes called *statistical rounding*. It depends on whether the place to which you are rounding is odd or even. When the digit to the right of the place to which you are rounding is not a 5, the statistical method is just like the method taught in arithmetic. If the digit to the right is 5, however, you round up (that is, increase the place to which you are rounding by 1) if the place is odd; if the place is even, you round down (that is, do not change the digit in the place to which you are rounding). This technique is based on the laws of probability. Using statistical rounding

> 64,643 rounded to tens is 64,640
> 289,662 rounded to hundreds is 289,700
> 796,551 rounded to hundreds is 796,600
> 796,551 rounded to thousands is 796,000

In adding long columns of numbers or in long operations of any kind, you get a better estimate using statistical rounding. In short problems, it is not essential.

Ideally, to get the best estimate possible, you should round as little as possible. But some people feel that this rule is too general. As a result, more and more textbooks provide more specific rules about how to use rounding for estimating. These rules should be taken only as general guidelines. For solving the math problems you run into in everyday life, the rules are not very helpful. Nevertheless, they give you a place to start improving your estimation skills.

Rounding with addition and subtraction

The smallest number that is longer than one digit should be rounded to its first digit. All other numbers should be rounded to the same place.

2394	rounds to	2400
598		600
9508		9500
+ 4		+ 0
		12500

The actual answer is 12,504, so the estimate is close enough for many purposes. If you had rounded to thousands instead of hundreds, the estimate would have been 13000. If you had rounded to tens instead of hundreds, the estimate would have been 12,500, the same estimate.

Similarly, for subtraction

83748	rounds to	83700
− 451		− 500
		83200

The actual answer is 83,297. While the estimate is close enough for checking a calculator computation, it would be closer if you ignored the rule and rounded to the nearest 50, making the problem 83750 − 450, which gives 83300. Good estimators will take the second way, but people just learning to estimate may be better off following the rule.

Rounding with multiplication and division

The rounding methods that work fairly well for addition and subtraction do not work for multiplication and division because they produce problems that are almost as hard to do mentally as the original problems. Therefore, another rule is used: Round each number to its first place. For example,

$$
\begin{array}{r}
5937 \\
\times\ \ 64 \\
\end{array}
\qquad \text{rounds to} \qquad
\begin{array}{r}
6000 \\
\times\ \ \ 60 \\
\hline
360000 \\
\end{array}
$$

The actual answer is 379,968, so this estimate should be close enough. Multiplication estimates are seldom as precise as addition and subtraction estimates.

In division, the same rule works.

$$
48\overline{)392864} \qquad \text{rounds to} \qquad 50\overline{)400000}^{\,8000}
$$

The actual answer is 8184 R 32.

If you are in a hurry, a fourth kind of rounding can be used for any of the four operations. It is similar to the method used for multiplication and division, but one step easier. Instead of rounding to a particular place, you drop all places beyond the first and work with the leading digit only. Here's how the previous examples would work out using the *leading-digits* method of rounding:

$$
\begin{array}{r}
2394 \\
598 \\
9508 \\
+\ \ \ \ 4 \\
\end{array}
\qquad \text{becomes} \qquad
\begin{array}{r}
2000 \\
500 \\
9000 \\
+\ \ \ \ 4 \\
\hline
11504 \\
\end{array}
$$

$$
\begin{array}{r}
83748 \\
-\ \ 451 \\
\end{array}
\qquad \text{becomes} \qquad
\begin{array}{r}
80000 \\
-\ \ \ 400 \\
\hline
79600 \\
\end{array}
$$

$$
\begin{array}{r}
5937 \\
\times\ \ 64 \\
\end{array}
\qquad \text{becomes} \qquad
\begin{array}{r}
5000 \\
\times\ \ \ 60 \\
\hline
300000 \\
\end{array}
$$

$$
48\overline{)392,864} \qquad \text{becomes} \qquad 40\overline{)300000}^{\,7500}
$$

Compare these estimates with the previous estimates and the actual answers:

Addition: Previous estimate, 12,500; actual answer, 12,504
Subtraction: Previous estimate, 83,200; actual answer, 83, 297
Multiplication: Previous estimate, 360,000; actual answer, 379, 968
Division: Previous estimate, 8000; actual answer, 8184 R 32

As you can see, the standard rounding method tends to give more precise estimates than the leading-digits method. Since you are "throwing away" part of each number, leading-digits will always give you an answer that is too low for both addition and multiplication. Still, the leading-digits method is good enough if you need only a rough estimate.

All of these, and other, methods of estimating should be part of everyone's math skills. In many cases, an accurate answer is not essential. People who have studied the use of mathematics in everyday life have found that estimates are often as useful as exact computations. And in some cases, estimates are even more useful.

Use your intuition—Guess!

So far, this discussion has presented some methods of mental computation that give exact answers by unusual means, plus some ways to estimate approximate answers. But there is yet another important mental operation that can be used in problem solving—guessing. Many people overlook this useful mathematical tool or consider it less than honest.

These people are missing out on one of the most helpful approaches to math. Guessing can be especially helpful when you encounter a problem that you don't know how to solve. On a test, for example, where there is no penalty for wrong answers, a carefully considered guess may be all you need to gain added points.

Many famous mathematical problems began as guesses. For example, no one knows for sure who first guessed that all prime numbers can be expressed as $2^n - 2$, but the guess drew interest for hundreds of years before it was finally shown to be wrong. That was a guess that didn't work, but it kept some mathematicians very busy. On the other hand, in 1850, a seventeen-year-old student named Francis Guthrie guessed that every map of any kind needed only four colors to color it in a way so that no two countries with a common boundary shared the same color. His guess was communicated to his brother, who was studying mathematics at the University College in London. His brother told his mathematics professor, who passed the guess on to other mathematicians. By 1878, the guess was in print, but no one could prove or disprove it. Finally, just a few years ago, mathematicians using the powerful electronic computer managed to prove that Guthrie's guess had indeed been correct. (For further discussion of prime numbers and Guthrie's four-color problem, *see* Pt. VI, Sec. 2 and 4.)

Particularly in everyday situations, identifying a problem is often the hardest part in solving it. You may begin thinking that you need to solve one problem and find out that you really need to solve a different problem altogether. In such cases, knowing how to look for patterns and make good guesses are important problem-solving skills. You can develop them by practicing on all the problems that come your way. Having good guessing skills can save you much time in the long run.

Guessing has another use. In many kinds of problems, one guess can be corrected into a better guess. This method is called *iteration*. It is the best way to find the square root of a number. For example, you can use iteration to find the square root of 300. Since the square of 15 is 225, you might logically guess that the square root of 300 is about 18. You would then divide 300 by your guess. The quotient is $16\frac{2}{3}$, which tells you that 18 was too large. Now *average* your original guess of 18 and the quotient of $16\frac{2}{3}$ to get $17\frac{1}{3}$ ($18 + 16\frac{2}{3} = 34\frac{2}{3}$, and $34\frac{2}{3} \div 2 = 17\frac{1}{3}$). Consider $17\frac{1}{3}$ as a new, improved guess and repeat the procedure. The result this time is $17\frac{4}{13}$, which is very close to $17\frac{1}{3}$. The actual square root of 300 to six decimal places is 17.320508, while $17\frac{1}{3}$ to six decimal places is 17.333333 and $17\frac{4}{13}$ to six decimal places is 17.307692. If you need a more accurate answer than 17.3, you merely use $17\frac{4}{13}$ as a new divisor and repeat the process.

There are whole classes of problems that the method of iteration applies to. Suppose that you need to know what number twice itself plus 3 equals 11. While that problem is easily solved by algebra, you can also use iteration. You can start with any guess—for example, 10. Twice 10 plus 3 is 23, so 10 is the wrong answer. But you can assume that 10 is to the right answer what 23 is to 11 (this is not actually so, but it is a way of getting on the right track). Since 23 is about twice 11, you can improve your guess by assuming that 10 is about twice the number you really want. So change your guess to 5. Twice 5 plus 3 is 13, so 5 is still too high, but it is getting closer. Since 13 is too high, try $\frac{11}{13}$ of 5, or $4\frac{3}{13}$. Twice $4\frac{3}{13}$ plus 3 is $11\frac{6}{13}$, so you are getting quite close. The correct answer, if you have not already guessed, is 4.

All the tools discussed in this section work together in problem solving. You need quick math to compute, estimate, and guess mentally for problems or parts of problems in order to solve them quickly and accurately. And, as you have seen, quick math also provides a means to check your results that goes beyond simply redoing them the same way and taking the risk that you will make the same mistake twice.

Chances are that, by the end of this first part of *Math Power,* you feel you have been given some real challenges in understanding math. As you learned earlier, math is a natural part of you. Your math understanding progresses with each new concept mastered, and sometimes each new concept requires a real effort.

Your schools are responsible for presenting math to you in progressive stages based on what you have already learned and on what, at any given stage of your development, you are able to study successfully. In the next part, you will read about the care with which your schools plan your mathematics curriculum based on your childhood experiences as well as your plans for the future.

Part

II

School Math: Learning the Third *R*

Part II of *Math Power* is especially useful for students, though parents will also greatly benefit from it. Here you will learn about preschool math learning and about math programs in the schools. You will also look at how mastering math at school can make adult success in personal and business matters much easier to achieve.

Often, parents don't realize how much they can help their children acquire mathematics understandings before entering school. Friends also shape a child's earliest math experiences. The discussion to follow shows the mathematics that children can do and how family and friends can go about helping them do it well.

Schools plan their mathematics programs around experiences students are likely to have had, and the types of math the children can reasonably be expected to do as they mature. The school math program, from nursery school through 12th grade, is charted for you here. Knowing it will help you understand the pattern that instruction is likely to follow, plus the reasons why educators have adopted that pattern.

Finally, you will look at trends in mathematics education—some abandoned and some in force. And this part will end by showing you specifically how mathematics is an everyday part of the business and professional worlds. This insight is important, since no one can do without mathematics and still be in top form for day-to-day living.■

(Preceding photo)
*Math learning ranges
from assembling blocks
to solving complex
equations.*

Math for Youngsters

Nearly everyone starts learning mathematics before going to school. When television first became popular in the 1950s, some people joked that children were coming to kindergarten already able to count at least as high as the numbers on the channel selector. But the joke turned serious when people realized that very young children really were learning to count from TV, especially if they watched educational shows such as today's "Sesame Street." The tots also learned colors, shapes, and directions—subjects that usually form a large part of the kindergarten mathematics program.

Modern children in advanced societies are especially fortunate in how they can learn mathematics. Not only do these children have TV and other electronic devices as learning aids, but they also still have important sources other children have used for centuries—school, friends, and family, and all the mathematical experiences that go with them. In the discussion that follows, you will learn more about how these sources help young children.

Beginning Math Learning

Have you ever thought of your childhood games as math experiences? How about hide and seek? This is a childhood game that involves counting. Even prekindergarten children who cannot count by themselves are often exposed to this and other games that involve the sequence, or order, of counting numbers. When the children hear common expressions such as, "One, two, three, go!" they notice that one always comes first, three last, and two in between. That's math.

Parents know that counting is an important skill, so they often make an effort to teach it to their little children. For example, they may read children picture books that call for counting objects from one through ten. From these and many similar experiences, children develop an idea of counting before they have any formal math instruction.

Of course, children who reach school able to recite the first ten or twelve counting numbers do not necessarily know what the numbers mean. So, one of the first goals of a kindergarten mathematics program is to present numbers and counting in ways that show how words, meanings, and the symbols that represent them are related. The symbols, such as the numerals 1 through 10, are especially important because many children can count correctly before they are able to get any meaning from the symbols.

At first, brand-new students are taught to keep track of numbers by matching real objects that have been placed in two different groups, called sets. There will be exactly one object in the first set for each object in the second set. Because of this exactness, the learning process is called *one-to-one matching,* or *one-to-one correspondence.* The children, of course, are not expected to learn these terms. Kindergartners follow a path from sets of real objects to pictures of objects and then to the numerals themselves through a series of guided activities.

As the children learn to match real objects, they are given some sets that have equal numbers to match and other sets that do not have equal numbers. In this way, they learn the difference between the two situations. Next, the real objects are replaced by pictures of objects. Now the children learn to draw lines between pictures of two sets. Usually, this is a very early workbook activity in kindergarten or grade 1.

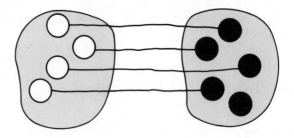

Finally, the children are introduced to the numerals one at a time. They progress once again from real objects to pictures to numerals, first finding actual sets that have the number of members specified by 1, 2, and so forth, then circling the appropriate pictures of sets that match the numerals. At the same time, they may learn to write the words for the numbers. The children learn about zero after they have had some experience with other numbers.

These activities are generally followed by or combined with work on comparing numbers and on placing numbers in order. Children need to learn to do fill-in-the-blank exercises such as 3, __?__, 5; 7, 8, __?__; and __?__, 5, 6.

Children learn two ways to compare numbers. When they first do exercises in one-to-one correspondence, they encounter two situations in which one-to-one correspondence fails— when the second set of numbers has more members than the first and when the second set has fewer members. Thus, even before they learn the order of the numbers, children can understand that some numbers are larger than others and that some numbers are smaller. Later, when they know the order of numbers, children can equate "comes before" with "less than" and "comes after" with "greater than."

One problem that arises at this early stage is that some children can progress at a pace faster than the rest of their classmates. As a result, they may grow bored and lazy. When doing exercises that they consider too easy, they may take shortcuts or fail to follow directions. Although no one has proved that such "jumping the gun" actually interferes with children's later progress in arithmetic, it is possible that their failure to see the purpose of early mathematical activities may give them negative attitudes. Otherwise bright students may then keep "anti-math" attitudes through school and into adult life. Some studies suggest that the best thing to do with such children is to let them explore other topics or the same topics in different ways, returning them to the basics at a later time.

Another important early skill is writing numerals. This skill is essential because it enables children to communicate on paper with their teachers and with others in later life.

Although understanding the meaning of numbers is the main goal of beginning mathematics education, it is not the only goal. There are numerous subgoals. In kindergarten or grade 1, the first subgoal may be to teach such basic concepts as *top, left,* and *before*. These ideas have many important uses both inside and outside the classroom. For example, a teacher will lose much time explaining if children do not understand a simple direction such as "Look at the picture at the top of the page."

Another early goal is to teach children to understand patterns. Because mathematics is the study of patterns, the teaching of pattern recognition has become a part of the standard curriculum in kindergarten through grade 3. At first, children are presented with simple patterns to complete.

Then they move on to more complex patterns of the same kind.

These exercises are sometimes called *attribute studies* because such attributes (or characteristics) as being colored or not and being square or not are the focus of attention in addition to the attribute of pattern. Students may use blocks and pictures to do these exercises.

At the same time, students may begin some simple work with geometry. One goal of beginning geometry is to teach children to recognize the most simple shapes—the square, the circle, the triangle, and the rectangle. Teaching such basic terms simplifies classroom explanations and lays the foundation for future work with geometry. Also, some shapes are used when fractions are introduced.

Children respond better to three-dimensional shapes than they do to two-dimensional pictures in books. This probably occurs because, aside from printed materials and television, the shapes around them actually are three-dimensional. Therefore, most educators believe that early experiences with geometry should include such solid shapes as the cube, sphere, cone, cylinder, and pyramid. (*See* Pt. IV, sections on geometry, for examples of these solids.) In fact, the solid figures are often taught first, and the two-dimensional shapes are explained in terms of the solids. A square, for example, is one *face* of a cube. This "analytic" approach to geometry is usually not tried in kindergarten, but it may be started as early as grade 1.

Another geometric concept that is nearly always taught early is *symmetry,* specifically what mathematicians call *line symmetry*. The reason for including symmetry at this level is that it is useful in design. Also, it is not difficult for young children to recognize the difference between symmetrical objects, such as the capital letters *A* and *B*, and an asymmetrical object, such as the letter *F*.

It is clear that for *A* and *B,* the dotted line separates two parts that are identical. One part is the reflection of the other. No such line can be drawn for *F*.

Another goal of early elementary education is to teach children about measurement. This involves many skills and concepts. Often the first notion taught is that a measurement is a number of standard units. It is easiest to explain this idea by measuring straight lines. Many teachers like to use units that students standardize themselves. For example, the class may measure the length of a line in paper clips. This form of measurement is convenient because it uses an object that students can hold in their hands. A child can actually lay several clips along the object to be measured, then count the number of clips to determine the measurement.

Measuring this way calls for several subskills. One is laying the paper clips in the proper way to obtain the measurement—they must be parallel to the length being measured. Another is rounding to the nearest number of clips. This involves judgment about whether the object is closer to, say, five paper clips long or six paper clips long. For beginners, most teachers and textbooks structure situations so that lengths are very nearly whole numbers of paper clips. As children gain experience, they are given lengths that are close to halfway between two clips, but they are asked to report the measurements as whole numbers, not as fractions.

Soon the teacher introduces conventional standardized units, such as centimeters or inches. Most schools now teach the metric system and the customary (sometimes called the English) system side by side. Almost all elementary science textbooks and most social studies textbooks use the metric system, so students must learn it. Although the customary system is currently used more than the metric system in the United States, the schools teach metrics on the assumption that the metric system will eventually be universally adopted. But they also teach the customary system because people have been slow to accept the metric system.

After working with length for some time, teachers move on to other measures—usually capacity, weight, and temperature. *Capacity*—liquid measures such as the liter or quart—is usually taught before *volume*—space measures such as the cubic centimeter or cubic inch—because capacity can be taught as a system separate from measurement of length. Area is also taught before volume because the idea of volume is a logical extension of area.

For students to progress beyond measuring objects to the nearest whole unit, they must develop a firm understanding of fractions. Actually, one way to explain fractions is in terms of measurement. (For more information about this approach, *see* Pt. IV, Sec. 3, "Fractional Numbers.") Two other approaches to fractions are generally used earlier, however: fractions of a whole and fractions of a set. Both illustrations below indicate $\frac{1}{2}$ by coloring one-half and leaving one-half uncolored. But the illustration on the left shows $\frac{1}{2}$ as a fraction of a whole, while the illustration on the right shows $\frac{1}{2}$ as a fraction of a set.

Experience suggests that children need much practice with fractions of a whole before going on to fractions of a set. Fractions of measurement are similar to fractions of a whole. But students must remember the whole is the unit of measurement.

Typically, children first learn the *unit fractions;* that is, the fractions with 1 as a numerator. (In the unit fraction $\frac{1}{2}$, 1 is the *numerator* and 2 is the *denominator*.) Most educators believe that fraction work should be largely restricted to commonly used fractions with small denominators, such as halves, thirds, fourths, fifths, sixths, eighths, tenths, and sometimes twelfths. Sevenths and ninths, although they have small denominators, are rarely used in practical problems at the elementary level. These fractions and fractions with higher denominators are usually left until later.

An important skill that is practiced almost from the beginning with young children is problem solving. It seems to be the hardest math skill for children to master, so teachers start working on it early. Because most kindergartners and first graders are not yet strong readers, their teachers usually give them math problems orally. As students gain reading ability, they are given *word problems* (also called *verbal problems*) in textbooks.

The National Assessment of Educational Progress has found that many students who have good basic mathematical skills are often unable to apply these skills to word problems. As a result, for several years, educators have given special effort to developing youngsters' problem-solving abilities.

Math from the Child's Viewpoint

When working with beginning math students, teachers try to see things from the child's point of view. Teachers know that many basic ideas of mathematics can (and must) be taught without textbooks or written exercises. Beginning learners either cannot read and write, or are just learning those skills. Textbooks and written lessons are therefore out of the question, although it is possible to use materials that require children to show answers by coloring or by drawing lines or circles. The teacher's most important concern is to make math a part of daily life in the classroom so that children absorb it as practical information.

A number of teaching techniques are employed. Many kindergartens have a snack time that is used as much for math teaching as for nourishment. One child counts the number of children in the room that day. Another child counts the number of cookies. They then pass the cookies out, one cookie to a child. In the process, everyone practices counting and one-to-one correspondence. (Everyone becomes involved because the other children carefully watch in the hope of catching the assigned counters in a mistake!) Putting on boots and buttoning coats can be made into counting and matching activities. Shapes in drawings can also be discussed.

Along with using common situations as they arise, teachers may plan games and other activities to promote learning. Such activities have many different goals, including teaching pre-reading and social skills as well as mathematical concepts. Perhaps the most familiar game that has a mathematical element is musical chairs, but many other games call for counting too. Children may learn about *top* or *bottom* by placing a toy on top of a desk or at the bottom of a pile. They may use blocks to learn about geometric shapes. In addition, many children's games that the teacher may not plan, such as jacks and jump rope, also require counting.

Cuisenaire rods

Children move from unstructured play to structured mathematics one step at a time. By the time they start working with pictures in a workbook, they have had many experiences to pave the way. Many schools use sets of carefully designed blocks called *Cuisenaire rods* to help students move from concrete objects to abstract ideas.

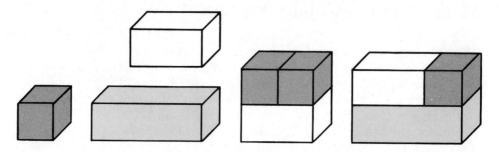

Cuisenaire rods are colored blocks in various lengths. The smallest rods are one-centimeter cubes. The rest are one centimeter thick by one centimeter wide but vary in length—from two centimeters up. Since each length is a different color, the teacher can tell students to do such things as find a rod that is the same length as two green rods put together—meaning find the sum of the numbers symbolized by the green and white rods.

After sufficient practice, students can equate the rods with numbers and relate them to addition, subtraction, multiplication, and division. The rods can also be used to teach about measurement and fractions.

Shorts, longs, and flats

While Cuisenaire rods are mainly meant to teach basic facts, they can also be used to illustrate ideas in geometry (for example, area) and more complex computations. In these, rods ten centimeters long are used with one-centimeter cubes. And sometimes squares ten centimeters by ten centimeters are added to the cubes and rectangles. Children can then use these pieces to learn how to add, subtract, multiply, and divide whole numbers beyond the basic facts. The pieces look like the illustration that follows.

You can make similar pieces for home use out of cardboard or flat sticks. Small square counters represent ones, rectangular counters tens, and large square counters hundreds. The blocks pictured represent the number 127.

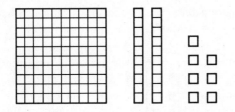

Students first memorize the basic addition facts. Then they learn methods—called *algorithms*—for computations beyond the basic facts. Some of these methods used to be called "carrying," "saving," and "borrowing." Now, the same methods are called "regrouping," "renaming," and "exchanging." With the physical counters, 10 of the small squares, called *shorts,* can be exchanged for 1 of the rectangles, called a *long.* Or the exchange can go the other way, exchanging 1 long for 10 shorts. Similarly, 10 longs can be exchanged for 1 large square, called a *flat,* or vice versa. This pattern of exchanging enables anyone who has memorized the basic facts to add or subtract all whole numbers. For example, to add 127 and 388, begin by representing each number with shorts, longs, and flats.

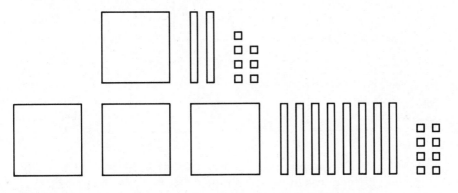

Working from the right, combine the ones, getting 15 shorts. Then exchange 10 shorts for 1 long.

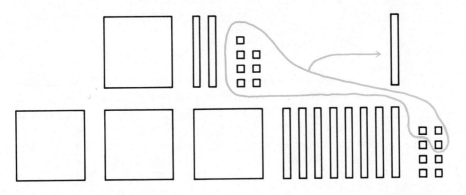

Now you have 4 flats, 11 longs, and 5 shorts. Since you have more than 10 longs, exchange them for 1 flat.

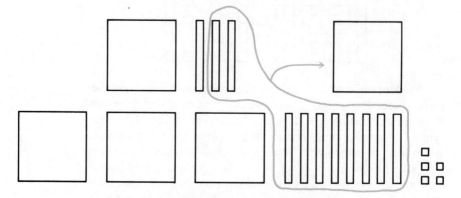

If you had been working with the actual blocks instead of pictures, you would be left with the following:

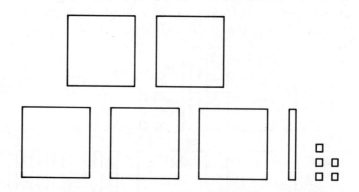

This represents the number 515. After students have learned to add using regrouping with shorts, longs, and flats, they transfer the process to pictures and then to written figures:

```
 11
127
388
515
```

Subtraction can be done similarly, but the exchange process goes from left to right. To subtract 276 from 324, for example, you begin by laying out the flats, longs, and shorts that represent 324. Working from the ones to the hundreds, you find that you cannot take away 6 shorts because there are only 4 shorts. So you exchange 1 long for 10 shorts.

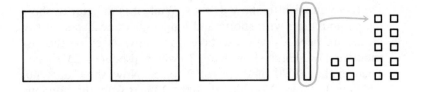

Then you can subtract by removing 6 shorts. This is shown in the picture by crossing out 6 shorts. If you were working with physical counters, you would actually remove them from your work area.

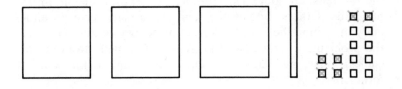

Now you move on to the longs, or tens. You need to subtract 7 longs, but only 1 is showing. Therefore, you exchange 1 flat for 10 longs. Then you are able to complete the subtraction of 7 longs. To finish the problem, subtract 2 flats from the remaining flats. Here is an illustration of the whole problem.

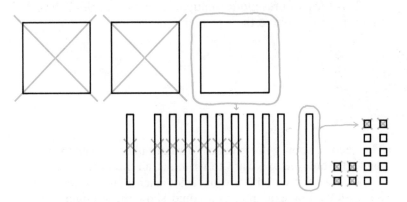

This diagrams a process that is often shown as

$$
\begin{array}{ccc}
2 & 11 & 14 \\
3 & 2 & 4 \\
2 & 7 & 6 \\
\hline
 & 4 & 8
\end{array}
$$

Multiplication and division can be shown similarly, but not so easily. You might enjoy experimenting with how to show them. It may help to make your own set of shorts, longs, and flats, although you can work with drawings.

Say you wish to show 8 × 43. While it is difficult to show the computation with shorts and longs—just because so many pieces are needed—you can take it in steps, based on the distributive law. First show 8 × 3, which produces 24 shorts. Then exchange 20 of them for 2 longs. Now show 8 × 40, which is 32 longs. You already have 2 longs from the previous operation, so the result is 34 longs and 4 shorts, or 344. Use of shorts and longs not only implies the correct way of multiplying (add the 2, meaning 2 tens, *after* multiplying 4 by 8), but also shows "carrying" into the hundreds place.

Many teachers insist that students make an exchange when the 34 tens are obtained, turning 30 of the tens in for 3 hundreds. Others, finding that children usually have no difficulty in writing the 3 in the correct place, ignore this aspect of the problem. In any case, the transition is made from actual shorts, longs, and flats, to pictures of them, to the written form:

$$
\begin{array}{r}
2 \\
43 \\
\times\ 8 \\
\hline
344
\end{array}
$$

This form of presenting multiplication by a single-digit multiplier is preferable to the alternative of writing

$$
\begin{array}{r}
43 \\
\times\ 8 \\
\hline
24 \\
32 \\
\hline
344
\end{array}
$$

The second form will be used with multipliers larger than one digit. It would be awkward to write out all the partial products if the second method were used for each digit, although not impossible. For example, you could show the product 123 × 45 as

$$
\begin{array}{r}
123 \\
\times\ 45 \\
\hline
15 \\
10 \\
5 \\
12 \\
8 \\
4 \\
\hline
5535
\end{array}
$$

But the conventional algorithm in which each single-digit multiplier is used with the multiplicand as a whole, perhaps with "helping numbers" written small to indicate exchanging, takes less space, involves less writing, and is easier to use.

Helping Out at Home

Children who have a supportive home environment learn better than those who encounter mathematics only in the classroom. Math should be an important part of every young child's daily routine. Knowing how schools go about teaching mathematics helps parents to reinforce school math experiences at home. While many classroom activities cannot and need not be duplicated at home, others can be used in modified form. Also, parents and children can do some mathematical activities on a one-to-one basis that would be difficult for a teacher to carry out with a class of 20 or 30 pupils.

Some techniques that can be used at home are used daily by teachers. They include counting aloud while helping a young child button a coat and planning mathematically oriented chores as part of a child's regular activity. Setting the table, for example, involves counting, or at least one-to-one matching. Games and toys that involve the use of numbers or shapes, such as jacks or building sets, can be added to the toy box. Long car trips can be opportunities for spotting particular numbers on license plates, such as finding the largest or smallest license number or finding 0 through 9 consecutively. Similarly, road signs can be scanned for geometric shapes. Reading counting books with children is also a worthwhile activity, although perhaps not so meaningful as games or chores that use mathematics.

Older children should be included too. For the most part, they are glad to show off their superior knowledge by helping a younger brother or sister. If older children know that the reason for certain activities is to develop mathematical awareness, they can help make those activities a larger part of a younger child's environment.

To be effective, most home math activities need to be planned as part of the regular routine. But parents should also take advantage of opportunities that occur in the course of shopping and other common activities. During a visit to the zoo, children can count the animals. Or, if there are twelve candies to be shared among three children, the children can be shown how to count them out, one item for each child, round and round, until all candies have been distributed. In such situations, parents should use the language of mathematics: "You divided the twelve candies among the three of you. Now each of you has four candies."

Young children ask many questions that bring up opportunities to use math. A question as simple as "How old is Grandpa?" can be productive if the answer is made into more than an off-hand "62." A parent can make a game or puzzle out of the answer, with its complexity geared to the child's level of mathematical knowledge. At its simplest, the answer could be something like "6 tens and 2 ones. What number is that?" or "There is a 2 and a 6 in his age. Do you think he is 26 or 62?" When children have begun to learn addition or subtraction, answers such as "3 years older than grandma, and she's 59" or "In 8 years he will be 70" become appropriate.

If youngsters don't ask questions with numerical content, parents can take the initiative. Good occasions frequently occur during family dinners. Adults' standard topics of dinner conversation are usually not very interesting to younger children. But parents can include their youngsters in the conversation by addressing problems to them. Doing number puzzles may seem an odd dinner-time activity to some people, but it is an effective way to encourage mathematical thinking and include younger children in the conversation.

This approach is most successful with children who have had at least two or three years of school because the problems can be made challenging enough to pique their interest. These can be practical problems or puzzles taken from daily life. For example, a third or fourth grader might be asked a question based on how long it takes to get to school. "If it takes you about ten minutes to get to school on the bus every day, how much time do you spend on the bus each week? How many hours and minutes is that?" A puzzle can be made up about anything. "How many different routes could we take to drive from here to the shopping center?" The most important thing to remember when posing math questions is to keep them easy enough for the child to solve but hard enough to be interesting. As much as possible, the question topics should grow out of the conversation.

Parents who encourage their children's mathematical abilities to grow in nonschool settings may be rewarded when report cards come. And very importantly, youngsters who develop a mathematical outlook in daily dealings with the world learn to appreciate the purpose of studying mathematics in school.

The School Math Program

Often older children question the importance of learning mathematics. Now that handheld calculators and home computers are commonly available, questions about the relevance of learning math have become louder. Nevertheless, educators continue to make math the second most time-consuming subject in elementary school (after reading). The reasons for teaching math are many, and the goals of general education require that math be a major part of the curriculum.

The goals of math eduation change slowly from grade to grade. Most children require all the time from nursery school through the end of grade 6 just to learn the meaning of whole numbers, fractions, and decimals and how to perform operations with them. (Of course, a number of other mathematical ideas are also taught along the way.) Although actual computations can often be done with a calculator, answers are of no use without an understanding of basic math processes.

In grades 7 and 8, earlier work is consolidated and preparation for algebra and geometry begins. A student who has successfully completed math through grade 8 should be able to deal with most mathematical situations that occur in running a home or holding a nontechnical job. An eighth-grade graduate is not prepared for many possible jobs and hobbies, however. For example, a lathe operator needs to know trigonometry, a field of mathematics that relates angles to lengths. Businesspeople who are involved in setting prices find that elementary algebra is helpful. Geometry is more than useful in planning many sewing projects. Scientists of all kinds, including biologists and social scientists, need calculus to solve problems and do research.

As a result, high-school math courses are largely designed to provide the basics that are needed in such situations and to prepare students for college. Some colleges require all students to take mathematics, but many have math requirements only for students of science, engineering, and advanced planning for business. Required courses are chosen by the instructors in those fields. They know what math their students will need to succeed in their course work and in the working world.

Mathematics learning is sequential—one idea builds on another. While it is possible to learn a lot about nineteenth-century American literature without knowing much about earlier literature, it is not possible to do calculus without the ability to add, subtract, multiply, and divide whole numbers, fractions, and decimals. Consequently mathematics is taught in nearly the same sequence in almost every school in the United States.

A Tour of U.S. Mathematics Education

Due to the near uniformity of the mathematics curriculum in the United States through the end of high school, it is possible to give a broad outline of the topics children study at each grade level. Such a list can be helpful in planning home math activities and in checking the progress of an individual child.

Some schools may vary the schedule by a year or two, but seldom by more than that. Private schools and specialized schools are more likely to speed up or slow down the curriculum than are ordinary public schools. In many states, the topics covered and the years in which they are taught are set by a state education agency, which adds to the uniformity. Frequently, large cities also set an exact curriculum for mathematics.

The information presented here can be used as a general guide. But it should not be used to assess an individual math program because variations are bound to occur from school to school and from teacher to teacher.

There are many math terms and concepts used in this section. Some terms are defined and some concepts are discussed in length, or references are given to other discussions in these volumes that will explain the topic being explored. To benefit fully from this section, you should make sure that you firmly understand all terms and concepts under discussion. Unless you are quite familiar with math, to do so you may have to review all or portions of Part IV, the "Complete Math Review Program." Also remember that the reference material in Part

VII and the index (both in volume 2) are excellent guides to all the information in this publication.

Nursery school

Mathematics learning among young children has already been discussed generally in Section 1 of this part, "Math for Youngsters." In nursery school, as you would expect, the children gain informal practice with counting and shapes. They also learn the meaning of words such as *top, in,* and *left.* Nursery schools put much emphasis on games and activities that use simple counting. Reading and writing numerals are almost never taught.

Not all children go to nursery schools. All of the topics covered at that level are taught again in kindergarten and grade 1. The schools cannot assume that all children will have had the same early math experiences.

Kindergarten

Today, nearly all children in the United States go to kindergarten. The beginning part of kindergarten focuses on informal experiences similar to those used in nursery school. Later in the year, more formal experiences start. Sometimes books or kits are used to organize mathematics learning, but many kindergarten teachers believe that it is too early to ask children to work with books or even with specific mathematics materials. The use of books in kindergarten seems to be on the increase, however.

A formal kindergarten math program usually starts at least six weeks into the year and often as late as the beginning of the second term. It generally includes counting; ordering and comparing numbers; preparation for addition and subtraction; comparing size; preparation for telling time; the concept of a penny; recognizing squares, triangles, and circles; such concepts as top, bottom, front, back, in, on, between, left, and right (which are needed to explain lessons); classifying objects; and recognizing patterns. Most time is spent on counting and learning to understand numbers through one-to-one matching and comparing and ordering numbers.

Every grade has a major goal for mathematics achievement, although it is not always formally defined. While it is useful to know the many different topics that are taught in each grade, the lists become so long that they are impossible to memorize. An alternative is to remember each grade's major goal. This goal will appear in dark type in this book. Thus, for kindergarten, the major goal is **counting.** Because the major goals often overlap from year to year, grades 1 through 8 will be discussed in pairs.

Grades 1 and 2

The main emphasis in grade 1 is on teaching **addition and subtraction of whole numbers,** but many other topics must be introduced as well. Counting generally stops at ten in kindergarten. In grade 1, counting is extended to ninety-nine or one hundred.

Children also learn to count by twos, fives, and tens, and perhaps by threes and twenty-fives. Counting by twos, threes, and fives prepares children for multiplication. Counting by tens is important for multiplication and for developing understanding of place value. Counting by fives, tens, and twenty-fives is important in learning to deal with money because children need to learn the value of nickels, dimes, and quarters. Related activities, such as putting numbers in order and comparing two numbers, which were introduced in kindergarten for the numbers zero through ten, are also extended to ninety-nine or one hundred.

The addition facts are given much attention during the first term of grade 1. In some courses, each fact is developed around the concept of like sums. For example, a given lesson will be based on sums of five. Such a lesson would focus on the following six basic facts:

$$0 + 5 = 5 \qquad 5 + 0 = 5$$
$$1 + 4 = 5 \qquad 4 + 1 = 5$$
$$2 + 3 = 5 \qquad 3 + 2 = 5$$

When facts are grouped this way, each sum includes more facts until sums of ten, for which there are nine basic facts.

After ten, the number of basic facts diminishes with each higher sum. For sums of eleven, for example, there are only eight basic facts—$11 + 0 = 11$, $0 + 11 = 11$, $1 + 10 = 11$, and $10 + 1 = 11$ are excluded because they are not basic facts. As the school year progresses and the children become more comfortable with addition, lessons begin to group two or more sums together so that the total number of facts to be learned stays about the same.

Most schools would like to teach all addition facts—that is, the facts through sums of eighteen—in grade 1, but sometimes there is not enough time. Schools that do not reach sums of eighteen often stop at sums of twelve, leaving the rest of the facts for grade 2.

Not all schools use this method of grouping the addition facts. In some programs, facts are grouped by operations that can be used to find the sums: counting on one, counting on two, doubling, making a ten, and so forth. For example, a lesson based on counting on one might include such facts as:

$$1 + 1 = 2 \qquad 2 + 1 = 3$$
$$3 + 1 = 4 \qquad 4 + 1 = 5$$
$$5 + 1 = 6 \qquad 6 + 1 = 7$$
$$7 + 1 = 8 \qquad 8 + 1 = 9$$
$$9 + 1 = 10$$

While a lesson based on doubling might include such facts as:

$$2 + 2 = 4 \qquad 3 + 3 = 6$$
$$4 + 4 = 8 \qquad 5 + 5 = 10$$
$$6 + 6 = 12 \qquad 7 + 7 = 14$$
$$8 + 8 = 16 \qquad 9 + 9 = 18$$

Once children have learned one fact, such as that $4 + 1 = 5$, they learn to use the commutative property of addition to find the reverse, that $1 + 4 = 5$, and so on through the sums. With this method, at the same time that children are learning the facts, they are also learning ways to find the facts.

Besides the basic facts, addition with three addends is taught for the first time at this level. Some programs also introduce addition beyond the basic facts that does not include renaming (carrying or exchanging).

Many years ago, it was customary to teach all addition facts before starting on subtraction. Because subtraction is closely related to addition, however, shortly after World War II, many schools began to teach subtraction along with addition. In some cases, subtraction facts with a given number were presented in the same lesson as the corresponding addition facts. More commonly, lessons alternated between addition and subtraction.

Although the logic of this approach was excellent, teachers did not like to switch back and forth. Futhermore, some evidence showed that when addition and subtraction were taught together, children did not learn either so well as when the two operations were taught separately. Consequently, the recent trend has been to return to the old way, or to a modification of it. For example, addition and subtraction may be alternated, so that after the "easy" addition facts (those with a sum of ten or less) are taught, the corresponding subtraction facts are studied. Then the class will return to addition to learn the "harder" facts.

Research suggests that the order of learning mathematics greatly influences its difficulty. So schools and textbook publishers work hard to find just the right approach to make learning easy and ensure that ideas and skills are thoroughly incorporated into children's thinking patterns.

Whether introduced at the same time as addition or not, subtraction facts are generally taught through sums of eighteen in grade 1, although some teachers believe in stopping at sums of 12. If a program includes addition of two-digit numbers without renaming, then it will also probably teach subtraction of two-digit numbers without renaming. In any case, it is assumed that subtraction will not be learned so well as addition in grade 1, so it continues to be a major focus in grade 2.

While the focus in grade 1 is on addition and subtraction of whole numbers, other topics are at least touched on. The first fractions are introduced, typically one-half, one-third, and one-fourth, or perhaps all the halves, thirds, and fourths less than one (that is, one-half, one-third, two-thirds, one-fourth, two-fourths, and three-fourths). Although most students do not read well enough to do word problems on their own, they are taught problem-solving skills in other ways. They also learn their first standard units of measurement, typically centimeters, inches, liters, and quarts.

Telling time is a major topic in first grade, although the situation has become considerably confused by the widespread acceptance of digital clocks and wristwatches. Formerly, teachers spent a great deal of time explaining the complexities of the "big hand, little hand" system. First-grade classes were equipped with special clocks without works that could be used to demonstrate hours and minutes, and many books were written to help students learn to tell time. Now, even though digital clocks are so popular, most teachers continue to try to teach the conventional dial system of telling time. But students may have their own digital watches and reject the whole notion as unnecessary. As a result, teachers find themselves explaining two competing systems at once. This situation may not be resolved for years.

Two other topics regularly introduced in grade 1 are geometry and graphing. In geometry, the shapes from kindergarten are reviewed and three-dimensional shapes—cube, sphere, cone, and cylinder—are introduced. An introduction to symmetry is usually included. Students also learn to read or make bar graphs and pictographs.

Place value is introduced through the tens place in grade 1. In grade 2, the topic is drilled and drilled and then extended to the hundreds place and, perhaps, the thousands place. Students must master place-value concepts in order to learn the standard algorithms for addition, subtraction, multiplication, and division with whole numbers. Thus, even though **place value** is not a new topic, its mastery becomes the main goal of grade 2.

Another basic goal, almost equally important, is to finish any undone work on subtraction facts. Even if children have been exposed to all one hundred subtraction facts in grade 1, they often fail to learn them as well as they learn the basic addition facts. If the addition facts through eighteen were not finished in grade 1, they also become a major topic in grade 2. All schools have the goals of teaching place value and all the basic addition and subtraction facts by the end of grade 2.

Addition and subtraction with renaming are taught for the first time at this level, but not for mastery. Usually operations with renaming are limited to the tens and ones (that is, two-digit problems). But many teachers find that it makes sense to also include addition problems in which two-digit addends lead to three-digit sums (80 + 20 = 100) and subtraction problems in which the number subtracted from has three digits (100 − 80 = 20).

Fractions are reintroduced at this level, but with little extension. Word problems can be presented for the first time in grade 2 with the hope that students will be able to read them. Of course, the problems must be kept very simple. A typical word problem for this level is

> Jack has 5 apples.
> Jill has 3 apples.
> How many apples do they have in all?

The subject of measurement is extended, with the meter, foot, yard, kilogram, pound, and pint being introduced. Telling time is practiced once again. All money units through the dollar are presented, using dollar signs ($50), decimal points, ($.50), and cents signs (50¢). There are small advances in geometry (rectangle and pyramid, for example) and a review of previously learned graphing concepts.

Sometimes a little multiplication work is introduced in grade 2. Although it is possible to teach the multiplication facts through 5 times 5 or so, there is little chance that they will be learned by any but the best students. Many teachers believe that the time is better spent on helping students master the addition and subtraction facts and the fundamental ideas of place value.

Grades 3 and 4

In grade 3, the principal goal is to teach the **multiplication facts.** Basic division facts are also taught, but they definitely take second place to multiplication. Although many old and new topics are covered in grade 3 mathematics, many teachers believe that from early in the school year until the very end, *daily* drill on multiplication is essential.

The amount of attention paid to multiplication facts in grade 3 has varied over the years, but the subject has always held center stage. Many years ago, it was common to teach not only the basic facts but also the facts of tens, elevens, and twelves. At the end of grade 3, a child was expected to know $12 \times 12 = 144$ as firmly as $2 \times 2 = 4$. This was thought to be too hard for some students, so adjustments were made. After much trial and error, it was decided that the best place to stop was at $9 \times 9 = 81$—that is, after teaching all the basic facts. And that is where the curriculum stands today.

Of course, there is still much variation in *how* the basic multiplication facts are taught. For the most part, the differences of opinion revolve around the sequence in which the facts should be taught. About the only agreement is that the ones and zeros should not be taught first. (The multiplication facts are named by the multiplicand, so the twos are 0×2, 1×2, 2×2, 3×2, and so forth.) Also, nearly everybody begins with the twos because students have had several years of practice in counting by twos.

After the twos, various sequences may be followed, each with its own pros and cons. The most plodding sequence is to proceed in order from the threes through the nines, stopping along the way (perhaps after the fives) to catch up on the ones and zeros.

A more common approach is to build on students' practice in counting by fives, so multiplication facts of five are taught after the twos. Ones and zeros can then be treated before returning to the main sequence with threes, fours, sixes, sevens, eights, and nines. Or, ones and zeros may be held off until after the fours.

Finally, a few teachers do the nines before the sixes, sevens, and eights because they believe that the pattern of products in the nines is easier to learn than the other products. Each nines product has two digits that sum to nine [18($1 + 8 = 9$), 27 ($2 + 7 = 9$), 36 ($3 + 6 = 9$)], for example). Furthermore, the first digit is always one less than the multiplier, so students can easily learn that $8 \times 9 = 72$ because 7 is 1 less than 8 and $9 - 7 = 2$.

The commutative property of multiplication says that the product of two factors is the same no matter what order the factors are multiplied in. Since the facts are always taught with multipliers through nine, the number of new facts to learn steadily decreases for each new multiplicand once children know how to use the commutative property. If the nines are taught last, at that point, students need to learn only one new fact: $9 \times 9 = 81$. All the other facts of nine can be arrived at using the commutative property. That is, if $9 \times 2 = 18$, then $2 \times 9 = 18$ also.

The division facts are closely related to the multiplication facts. And the same problem occurs in sequencing the multiplication and division facts in grade 3 that occurred in sequencing the addition and subtraction facts in grade 1. Logic suggests that the corresponding multiplication and division facts should be taught together, but experience suggests that it is better to teach them separately. As a result, most schools make the same kind of compromise in teaching multiplication and division that they do for addition and subtraction. After teaching some easy multiplication facts, they teach the corresponding division facts. Then the more difficult multiplication facts are followed by the corresponding division facts.

While place value is normally extended to thousands or ten thousands in grade 3, the basic conceptual work has usually been done earlier. Place value is of particular importance in grade 3 because the time has come to give serious attention to addition, subtraction, and multiplication with renaming. Teaching the algorithms for renaming is as important in grade 3 as teaching multiplication and division. Little effort, however, is made to teach renaming with division, which is really a different skill.

In addition to place value, rounding numbers is introduced in grade 3 and reviewed every year thereafter. Measurement is extended to include measures of weight, and new units for length and capacity may be introduced. Geometry and measurement are combined with the introduction of perimeter and area, although area problems are usually confined to rectangles. All measurement and geometry ideas from the earlier grades are, of course, reviewed.

Fraction concepts are also reviewed and extended. Sometimes decimals (to tenths only) are introduced, but students are not usually expected to do computations with fractions or decimals.

Problem-solving skills are greatly expanded in grade 3. Techniques for solving problems, such as drawing diagrams, begin to be introduced at this level.

The main goal in grade 4 is to teach **addition and subtraction of fractions.** To add and subtract fractions, students must understand the concept of *equivalent fractions,* such as $\frac{1}{2} = \frac{2}{4}$ $= \frac{3}{6} = \frac{4}{8} = \frac{5}{10}$. Most fourth graders learn to form equivalent fractions by multiplying the numerator (top number) and denominator (bottom number) in a fraction by the same number. For example, to show that $\frac{1}{2}$ is equivalent to $\frac{5}{10}$, they learn to think, "1×5 is the new numerator, and 2×5 is the new denominator."

Fourth graders are also taught to *simplify fractions,* or to *put a fraction in simplest form.* To simplify a fraction, its numerator and denominator must be divided by the same number. So to simplify $\frac{2}{10}$ to $\frac{1}{5}$, a student would think, "$2 \div 2$ is the new numerator, and $10 \div 2$ is the new denominator."

Addition and subtraction of fractions is taught in two steps. First students add and subtract fractions that have the same denominator, called *like fractions* ($\frac{1}{5} + \frac{1}{5} = \frac{2}{5}$). Then the children use renaming to convert *unlike fractions* (those with different denominators) to like fractions before adding or subtracting ($\frac{1}{2} - \frac{1}{4} = \frac{2}{4} - \frac{1}{4} = \frac{1}{4}$).

Multiplication of fractions is not taught in depth until grade 5, but it may be touched on in grade 4, possibly in a disguised form. A problem such as "Find $\frac{1}{4}$ of 8" is really a multiplication problem, but it can be solved by dividing 8 by 4. Such problems using "of" are often presented to prepare students for multiplication of fractions.

Computations with decimals are also introduced in grade 4, although they are limited to addition and subtraction. The methods for adding and subtracting decimals are simple extensions of the methods used for whole numbers, so they are more easily taught than addition and subtraction with fractions. At this level, decimals are usually limited to tenths and hundredths, but thousandths may be introduced in some cases.

Fourth graders also get their first taste of *long division.* This algorithm for dividing any whole number by a counting number is easily the most difficult mathematical operation taught in elementary school. The basics of long division are carefully taught in grade 4, but students are not expected to master the whole process until it is presented even more thoroughly in grade 5. Consequently, the long-division teaching sequence is explained in more detail in the section on the curriculum for grade 5.

Addition, subtraction, and multiplication of whole numbers are repeated with larger numbers. This pattern continues in every grade from now on, so it will not be mentioned again. You can safely assume that all previously taught topics are reviewed and extended in succeeding grades.

A new topic, estimation, is often presented at this level, although some preparatory work may have been done in grade 3. Students cannot estimate very well until they have had some practice with rounding numbers, so grade 4 (a year after the children have learned to round) is a good time to start teaching estimating techniques. Measurement is extended to include units for volume and temperature.

The geometry sequence differs more from school to school than do other parts of the mathematics curriculum. In some schools, geometry beyond area and volume is barely taught at all. In other schools, geometry is given much attention. The volume of a rectangular prism (or box) is often introduced in grade 4. Students may also learn to identify lines, line segments (parts of lines that are bounded on each end), rays (parts of lines that are bounded on one end only), and angles, including right angles. Some mathematics programs introduce the idea of *congruence*. Two figures are congruent if they are the same size and the same shape.

An important advance in problem solving is often made in grade 4 when students move from one-step problems to two-step problems. A one-step problem can be solved with a single operation. An example of a one-step problem is "John is 3 years older than his sister. His sister is 12. How old is John?" The solution can be found by adding 3 to 12, which is one operation.

A two-step problem requires two operations. A typical two-step problem would be "John is 3 years older than his sister. In 5 years his sister will be 12. How old is John?" Many two-step problems can be solved in more than one way. For example, in this case, you can subtract 5 from 12 to get 7 and then add 7 and 3 to get 10. Or you can add 12 and 3 to get 15 and then subtract 5 from 15 to get 10. Both solutions call for two operations. In everyday life, many problems involve more than two steps, but the biggest adjustment in learning to solve such problems is the transition from a single step to two steps.

Grades 5 and 6

The major goal in grade 5 is to perfect students' skills in **long division.** There are so many different methods of teaching long division that it is impossible to explain them all here. Long division is so difficult to teach and to learn that every known technique for simplifying it has been tried at one time or another. In addition, most methods of presenting long division involve a long sequence of carefully planned steps, so to explain any one method in detail can be very time consuming.

The most commonly used algorithm for long division looks like this:

```
      341  R  6
23)7849
   69
   ‾‾
    94
    92
    ‾‾
     29
     23
     ‾‾
      6
```

All methods of teaching long division currently used in schools aim at this algorithm as a final product, but they take different routes to get there.

The traditional approach is to learn how to estimate the first number in the answer (or *quotient*), which is 3. The most common way is to round 23 (called the *divisor*) to 20 and to note that 20 "goes into" 78 (the first two figures of the *dividend*) about 3 times. The phrase "goes into" is in quotation marks to call attention to the common nickname for this approach—the *guzinta* algorithm.

When the first trial quotient figure has been obtained, the student multiplies the divisor by the trial quotient figure, writes the product at the left of the region below the dividend as if 78 were the only part of the dividend to consider, and subtracts from 78. The logic of this step may or may not be explained to the child. In fact, the trial quotient figure does not represent just 3—it represents 3 hundreds. Therefore, the product is not just 69; it is 69 hundreds, or 6900. The procedure of writing the number to be subtracted at the left omits the last two zeros. In some approaches to division, the zeros are written at first, and then dropped later.

Subtracting 69 from 78 gives 9. The student is taught to "bring down" the 4 from 7849; that is, to write the next digit in the dividend after the numeral for the difference just obtained. Then, a new estimate based on 94 ÷ 20 is made. The correct estimate is 4, so 4 becomes the next trial divisor. Of course, the 4 really represents 40, since it is in the tens place.

The student multiplies 23 × 4 to obtain 92. From this point on, the product is written below the number obtained in the last step. Again, the student subtracts, 94 − 92 = 2, and "brings down" the next (and last) digit from the dividend. The whole process is then repeated with the 29 thus obtained. This time the partial quotient figure is 1, and after subtraction, there are no more digits in the dividend to bring down. The 6 that is left is the *remainder* and is labeled as such next to the quotient.

Many approaches to long division use other formats to prepare students for the final algorithm. Some of these formats are fairly easy to recognize for someone who has learned the final algorithm. For example, one such transitional format is

$$
\begin{array}{r}
341 \quad \text{R} \quad 6 \\
\underline{} \\
1 \\
40 \\
300 \\
23\overline{)7849} \\
\underline{6900} \\
949 \\
\underline{920} \\
29 \\
\underline{23} \\
6
\end{array}
$$

Much besides long division is accomplished in grade 5. For one thing, fractions are extended to include *mixed numerals* (also called by other names such as *mixed forms* and *mixed numbers*). Mixed numerals are numerals used to indicate the sum of a whole number and a fraction, such as $2\frac{1}{2}$ and $3\frac{7}{8}$, which mean the same as $2 + \frac{1}{2}$ and $3 + \frac{7}{8}$. Most math programs also include multiplication of fractions at this level, and some even begin preliminary work with division of fractions.

Work with decimals continues in grade 5. Addition and subtraction are reviewed, multiplication of decimals is introduced, and, usually, division of a decimal by a whole number is given light treatment. Rounding of decimals is also taught.

In measurement, volume is extended, new units are introduced, and all preceding work is reviewed. The amount of geometry taught continues to vary from school to school. A typical new topic in grade 5 would be finding the area of a triangle. If parallel and perpendicular lines have not yet been taught, they may be brought in here. There is also likely to be much review of the geometry taught in previous years. Many teachers choose to focus on computation and skip geometry, especially in the lower grades. Therefore, teachers at middle and higher grade levels cannot safely assume that all students have already learned particular geometry concepts and must give extensive "review."

Sometimes students in grade 5 will have a first look at ratio, proportion, and percent. But these related topics are usually postponed until grade 6 or 7, when more time can be spent on them.

By tradition, **decimals** have always been emphasized in grade 6. But many schools have recently started to teach decimals more extensively in the lower grades, especially in grade

5. Today's earlier emphasis on decimals stems from classroom use of the metric system, which is based on decimals, and the popularity of handheld calculators, which use decimals instead of fractions. As a result, in schools where decimals are studied earlier, the curriculum for grade 6 may emphasize percent. In fact, so many different topics are covered for the first time, or at least covered *thoroughly* for the first time, that it is much harder to point out a main goal for grade 6 than it is for the earlier grades. This discussion assumes the traditional view that decimals will receive major emphasis, but accepts that many other topics will also be taught.

By grade 6, most students have done all operations with decimals except division. If students have thoroughly learned division of whole numbers in grade 5—which is not usually the case—then division by a decimal can be taught simply and mechanically, based on "moving the decimal point." If students have not yet mastered long division, or if the teacher prefers a less mechanical approach, the teaching of division by a decimal may require more explanation.

In addition to work on decimals, exponents are often introduced in grade 6. The number system is extended to include negative numbers, and division of fractions is taught.

In geometry, sixth graders are often introduced to the properties of circles, including circumference and area. Measurement of angles may also be presented. These topics all lead to the development of circle graphs. Ratio and percent, the other requirements for reading and making circle graphs, are covered too. These topics may have been introduced in grade 5, and they will get thorough treatment in grade 7. But they are not ignored in grade 6.

By the time students finish grade 6, they have been introduced to virtually all the basic concepts of elementary-school mathematics. In addition to the main topics mentioned so far, they are likely to have encountered probability, statistics (mean, median, and mode), simple algebraic equations, graphing of all kinds, scale drawing, and perhaps elementary computer programming. They will also have had much practice in solving word problems.

Grades 7 and 8

The traditional focus in grade 7 has been on **ratio, proportion, and percent.** In recent years, more and more time has been devoted to these related topics in earlier grades. Nonetheless, the goal of understanding percent is usually not reached until grade 7—and sometimes not until grade 8.

The problems that involve percent have been divided into three categories, or "cases." Case 1 problems call for finding a percent of a number—for example, "Find 20% of 50." Case 2 problems call for finding what percent one number is of another—for example, "10 is what percent of 50?" Case 3 problems call for finding the original number when a percentage of it is given; for example, "10 is 20% of what number?"

Much time in grade 7 is spent on review of math concepts taught in earlier grades. Some mathematics teachers joke that grade 7 reviews the first six grades and grade 8 reviews grade 7. This is less true today than it once was, but there is still a tendency to use the last two grades of elementary school to make sure that students have learned the basics before they go on to high school.

One result of this extensive review and reteaching in grades 7 and 8 is that better students can easily learn all the new topics of both grades in a single year. Therefore, at this level, some students may be given an algebra course that most students take in grade 9.

New topics in grade 7 frequently include scientific notation, computer literacy (if not begun earlier), new measures such as the calorie and the kilowatt-hour, many new concepts of geometry, and further operations with negative numbers, generally involving multiplication and division with negative numbers. The geometry topics, as always, vary more from school to school than do other topics of elementary mathematics. Plane figures may include the trapezoid, the parallelogram, and the rhombus. More formulas are given for the volume and surface area of solid figures. Frequently grade 7 is where students first learn that the sum of the angles in a triangle is 180°.

Another common emphasis at this grade level is mental computation. By grade 7, students should be familiar with the standard pencil-and-paper algorithms for whole numbers, so they are ready to learn mental techniques. Estimation is also stressed in grade 7 for much the same reasons.

In grade 8, the main focus is **preparation for high school.** Thus, much emphasis is given to pre-algebra and descriptive geometry. The approach to algebra and geometry in grade 8 differs from the approach in most high-school courses. But math teachers believe that the experiences of grade 8 help students prepare for their first two math courses in high school.

Topics covered in some depth in grade 8 and taught again in grade 9 are signed numbers (that is, both positive and negative numbers), first-degree equations in one variable (equations such as $2x + 3 = 15$), exponents, and properties of numbers.

Descriptive geometry does not require formal proofs. Instead, it emphasizes the names and properties of figures. Descriptive geometry forms a large part of the grade 8 curriculum. New topics are likely to include construction of geometric figures, such as bisecting a line and making a specified triangle; similar figures; the Pythagorean theorem; more work on volume and surface area of solids; and classification of angles, triangles, and lines. Similar figures and the Pythagorean theorem are frequently presented as individual units of instruction. Two geometric figures are similar if they have the same shape but not (generally) the same size. Similar figures include both enlargements and reductions and are a good application of the work on ratio and proportion. The Pythagorean theorem describes a relationship between the squares of the sides of right triangles. Therefore, using it requires work with square roots. As a result, finding square roots becomes another topic of grade 8.

In the effort to preview high school, most grade 8 math courses also present a small amount of trigonometry based on the properties of right triangles. At this level, trigonometry is used to find distances or angles by *indirect measurement*—although it has many other applications in higher mathematics. Typical trigonometry problems ask students to find the height of a tree or building or the distance across a river or canyon. Since such lengths cannot be measured directly using a measuring stick or tape, the object being measured is made into one side of a right triangle for which another side can be measured directly. Students are taught to use angles, ratios, and tables to determine the unknown measurement. Or they may solve such problems using a handheld calculator that has keys to calculate specific trigonometric ratios.

Teaching probability in grade 8 may serve one of two possible purposes. In some cases, it prepares students for the probability course they'll take in high school. In other cases, it is the only chance that students will have to work with probability. While probability is often offered as a one-term course in larger high schools and sometimes forms a unit in either second-year algebra or precalculus, it may be omitted. Inclusion of a unit on probability in grade 8 provides one additional chance for children to become familiar with this important topic.

If computer literacy has been part of grade 7, it is likely to be included and extended in grade 8. Statistics may also be extended to include more advanced topics (range, frequency distribution, and average deviation, for example). Applications of percent, as noted before, may include percents greater than 100% or less than 1%. But for the most part, the work with percent is similar to that in grade 7, with harder problems. The remainder of grade 8 is spent as necessary reviewing and reteaching the computational development of the previous years of elementary school.

Grade 9

Once students enter high school, they have greater freedom in their choice of mathematics courses. In fact, many students choose to take only one year of high-school math. Therefore, this survey can include only some of the possibilities that exist in the last four grades.

Most students in grade 9 will take math—either **algebra 1** or **general mathematics.** Nationally, about equal numbers of students are in each course. A small group of students take algebra 1 in grade 8. These students move directly into geometry and stay a grade level ahead for the rest of their math education. For those students, subtract one grade from the discussions that follow.

Algebra 1 is usually taken by the better mathematics students. The primary goal of most teachers of algebra 1 is to reach the study of *quadratic equations* by the end of the year. A quadratic equation is an equation in one variable for which at least one term involves the square of the variable. A typical quadratic equation is $2x^2 + 3x - 5 = 0$. Equations that do not contain a squared variable can be solved using addition, subtraction, multiplication, and division. But quadratic equations must be solved by finding square roots or by *factoring*.

The factoring method relies on the fact that if the product of two numbers is 0, then one or both of the numbers must be 0. For example, the quadratic equation $2x^2 + 3x - 5 = 0$ can be factored into the form $(2x + 5)(x - 1) = 0$. Therefore, either $2x + 5 = 0$ and/or $x - 1 = 0$ must be true. Each of the possible solution equations can be solved by the easier methods of addition, subtraction, multiplication, or division.

Much of the work in algebra 1 is aimed at developing the skills that students need to solve quadratic equations. These skills are using positive and negative numbers, solving equations in one variable that do not have a square, using radicals (roots, such as the square root), factoring, and operating with algebraic expressions, including algebraic fractions.

Three main topics in algebra 1 are not part of the sequence leading to quadratic equations. Students must learn to graph equations. They need some practice in solving two equations at the same time, which was formerly called solving simultaneous equations but is now known as solving *systems of equations*. And students learn to handle inequalities such as $2x + 5 > 3$ (which is read "two ex plus five is greater than three") as well as equations. Some courses include trigonometry, partly on the assumption that this topic may have been skipped in grade 8. Other courses may introduce the general idea of *function*. A function is a rule that connects two quantities in such a way that if a value is assigned to one quantity, the other quantity is defined uniquely. This simple idea has turned out to be one of the most useful in mathematics. Most of the real applications of function are too difficult for algebra 1, however.

Most schools agree on what to teach in algebra 1. But just the opposite is true of general mathematics. Courses that are called general mathematics range all the way from remedial computation to pre-algebra study that is almost as difficult as algebra 1. Courses that explore interesting aspects of higher mathematics may also be included in the general-mathematics category and given such names as "mathematics for the liberal arts student." Large high schools may offer several different general-math courses.

Probably the most common course in general mathematics repeats the work of grades 7 and 8 for students who need review. Other fairly common courses teach consumer or business math. Such courses (which may also be given at higher grade levels) focus on applications of mathematics to consumer or business situations, such as finding the interest on a loan or keeping track of the expense of running an automobile. A pre-algebra course may take an entire school year to cover the first term of algebra 1. Students are placed in pre-algebra courses in preparation for further math courses. But students in more computational courses are often viewed as getting their last chance at learning math before leaving school.

Grade 10

The majority of high schools in the United States teach **geometry** in grade 10, although a significant minority teach algebra 2. This discussion assumes that geometry is offered in grade 10 and that algebra 2 is given in grade 11, since that is the more common pattern.

A few decades ago, plane geometry was taught in grade 10 and solid geometry was taught a few grades later, usually in grade 12. For many years, however, concepts of solid geometry have been included in the grade 10 course, and a separate solid geometry course is seldom offered in high school.

For many years, geometry courses were based on Euclid's *The Elements*, a 2000-year-old textbook. In the nineteenth century, however, mathematicians began to find flaws in some of Euclid's methods. They developed new approaches to geometry that were adapted into American textbooks around 1960 and have since come to dominate geometry teaching. Therefore, people who learned geometry before 1960 often find the modern courses quite unfamiliar.

Today's geometry still emphasizes proof from a set of *axioms* (also called *postulates*), as did Euclid's geometry. But the axioms are different from the ones Euclid used. So are some of the definitions. What remain the same, however, are the *theorems,* the results that have been proved (or must be proved by the student). For example, a theorem such as "The line segment joining the midpoints of two sides of a triangle is still parallel to the third side and half its length" remains true. Only the method of arriving at this result has changed.

In the most widespread approach, after the first few chapters, textbooks begin to look a lot like Euclidean geometry. This occurs because most changes in axioms or definitions concern ideas that are so elementary that Euclid forgot to specify them. Thus, they apply largely to the beginning of the course.

Some geometry courses take a different approach throughout, however. Of these, the most popular—although it forms only a small fraction of the geometry taught in the United States—is the *transformational approach.* Again, the theorems are largely the same, but the method of proving them relies on an "algebra of transformations" rather than on deductive proof from the axioms. A transformation is an operation on a figure that moves in some well-described way or changes its size or shape. For example, the transformation *rotation* rotates the figure about a point by some specific angle. The transformation *reflection* reflects the figure in a line as if the line were a mirror. The transformed figure is the mirror image of the original figure. Rules for combining transformations form a sort of algebra. Even less common than transformational geometry are approaches that use *coordinate geometry* (graphs) or *vector geometry* (vectors can be thought of as a kind of transformation).

Geometry is an essential course for anyone who plans to go further in mathematics or science. One reason is that it is the main course in which mathematical proof is discussed, especially in the more traditional approaches. Also, the theorems that are proved frequently have many applications.

Grade 11

As noted earlier, the most common course in grade 11 is **algebra 2,** frequently **algebra 2 with trigonometry.** It is a much more varied course than algebra 1, as many different topics can be taught at this level. Few schools can cover all the topics, so most choose the ones they prefer and omit the rest. Among the possibilities are coordinate geometry, relations and functions, conic sections, sequences and series, limits, trigonometric functions, probability theory, logic, vectors, complex numbers, and set theory. Since many of these topics are little related, it is possible to treat them separately.

In addition, the primary task in grade 11 is to review and extend algebra 1. In algebra 2, all topics from algebra 1 are retaught to some extent. Furthermore, many of the topics from algebra 1 can be dealt with in more complicated situations. For example, the systems of equations taught in algebra 1 usually involve only two equations, neither of which is quadratic. In algebra 2, it is common to teach the solution of systems of three equations (or more) and the solution of systems involving one or more quadratic equations. Similarly, the exponents used in algebra 1 may be limited to whole numbers, while algebra 2 investigates the meaning of fractional exponents. Reviewing and extending the topics from algebra 1 usually take more than half the course in algebra 2, leaving only a small amount of time for other topics.

Larger high schools sometimes solve this problem by offering some topics as separate courses for students who wish to take more than one math course at a time. These elective courses can also be substituted for algebra 2 in most instances. Probably the most frequently offered elective is probability theory. Also, the elective courses can be taken in either grade 11 or grade 12, which allows still more flexibility.

Grade 12

The most common course in grade 12 consists largely of topics that were not covered in algebra 2. It is most often called **precalculus mathematics.** Coordinate geometry (also called *analytic geometry*), sequences and series, logic, and limits are emphasized. Transformations and vectors are usually taught as well. Knowledge of algebra 1 is assumed, so that the entire year of grade 12 can be spent on ideas that may have been crowded into the second semester of algebra 2 or postponed.

Accelerated students take precalculus mathematics in grade 11. So they commonly take calculus in grade 12. Although some materials have been prepared especially for high-school students, most courses use a regular college textbook. Students who complete the course and pass an advanced-placement test can usually get college credit for calculus.

Fewer and fewer students take math in each succeeding grade of high school. Only about half of all high-school students take algebra 1. Only about half the students who take algebra 1 continue as far as algebra 2. In most schools, fewer than 10 percent of seniors (and sometimes none) take calculus.

The Goals of Math Education

As the description of the mathematics curriculum from nursery school through high school indicates, schools make an extensive effort to ensure that all citizens are mathematically literate. At every level there are two concerns. One is to develop the skills that the child will need in dealing with everyday life. Thus, telling time, recognizing shapes, using money, counting, and the fundamental operations with numbers play a large part in the early grades. At the same time, the sequential nature of mathematics requires that another goal be met—preparing for future study.

For example, division of fractions is almost never used in daily life, but it is still taught. An important reason not to drop division of fractions from the curriculum is that students who go on to algebra need this skill. Similarly, most geometry is rarely used by anyone who is not an engineer, scientist, or mathematician (and perhaps not even by some people in those professions). The method of geometry, however, is important for later work in mathematics that may be required for other fields of study. It is also an important part of a well-rounded education because geometry dominated scientific thought and the visual arts for centuries.

For students who have taken only algebra 1 or general mathematics, most colleges offer a course that includes both algebra 1 and algebra 2. Most students who have gone as far as algebra 2 will be prepared for most freshman college courses in mathematics. But the best preparation for college courses in mathematics, science, engineering, and economics is the full four-year high-school mathematics curriculum.

In fact, preparation for college is the primary purpose of the four-year high-school programs. From time to time, college educators issue reports on the preparation needed for college. Their reports are taken seriously by high schools and are influential in determining the high-school curriculum.

Concepts versus techniques

Youngsters who are familiar with the subject matter that precedes and follows their current level can be better math students. For one thing, there is a psychological factor at work. If they know that they are going to need a particular concept or technique in the next year, they are more likely to learn it.

Mathematics is a mixture of concepts and techniques. Knowledge of a concept does no good without knowledge of the techniques for applying the concept. Similarly, it is hard to learn techniques and know when to use them without understanding the concepts behind the techniques. Students do best when they study a mixture of both. This is especially true in problem solving.

Techniques cannot be mastered without rote memorization. Because automatic recall is so important, repetitive drills are commonly used in teaching mathematics. Teachers know that drills can be boring, so they try to alternate them with more interesting math activities whenever possible. But the basic nature of drills cannot be changed—they present the same kinds of problems over and over. As a result, some people lose interest, assuming that drill is all there is to math. If they understood that drill is needed only until responses become automatic, they might be more appreciative of these lessons.

The logic of the math sequence

Youngsters who lose patience with the methods required to learn math might enjoy and learn from a famous story about Euclid. The ruler of Egypt at the time Euclid lived was Ptolemy I. Around 300 B.C., Ptolemy decided to establish a school that would attract the leading scholars of the time. The school came to be called the Museum. One scholar brought to the Museum was Euclid, the author of the basic geometry textbook, *The Elements*. Apparently Ptolemy had tried to learn geometry by studying *The Elements,* but found the step-by-step development from axioms and postulates too slow and boring. So he called Euclid to him and asked if there was a quicker way to learn geometry. Euclid allegedly answered, "There is no royal road to geometry."

The same remark applies to all mathematics. There is simply no easy way to learn it, although some ways are easier than others. Everyone must begin at the beginning and proceed step by step. For example, the following statement is taken from a grade 4 textbook: "To find $328 - 174$ you must rename a hundred." That comment would certainly be meaningless to a student in grade 1. A student near the end of grade 2 might be able to guess what it means. But by the end of grade 3, most students would know exactly what the remark means.

Because math must be learned in sequence, it must be taught in sequence. Problems can arise for students who miss part of the sequence. If they do not make up the missed work, their progress may be stalled.

For example, long division cannot be taught much earlier than grade 4. Before students can do long division, they need to know the division facts and how to multiply and subtract. They also need to be able to round if they use the algorithm that is most popular today. Addition and subtraction are started in grade 1, but it takes until some time in grade 2 before most students really know how to subtract. As a result, there is no time to teach multiplication and division facts before grade 3. Learning multiplication and division takes at least a year. So by the time students know enough to begin to learn long division, they are in grade 4.

Students who have trouble learning long division may have failed to learn one of the necessary basic skills. If so, they may need *remediation* or *reteaching*. Remediation usually takes the form of more drill. A response that ought to have become automatic has failed to do so. Reteaching involves work on a concept instead of work on a technique.

Of course, not all difficulties with math come from losing a step in the sequence. In long division, for example, new skills must be learned that have little to do with earlier work. For one thing, the order of operations (estimate the trial quotient figure, multiply, subtract, repeat as needed) is unique to long division. A youngster who fails to learn that order of operations fails to learn long division.

Whatever the problem in mastering mathematics, teachers, parents, and students together must decide where the failure to understand stems from. For those fortunate students who appreciate the importance of solving a learning problem when it occurs, rather than waiting until a complex network of misunderstandings sets in, steady progress in the math curriculum is a reality.

Math: Yesterday, Today, and Tomorrow

Approaches to mathematics education, like the approaches to all other areas of education, change to reflect new thinking and the needs of society. This section will trace the development of mathematics education in the last several decades. The discussion will include an overview of what will be called "old math," a mixture of approaches to teaching math that lasted through the 1950s, and new math, which for a while significantly changed the approach to mathematics education. Finally, you will take a look at the way math is taught today and the advantages a sound understanding of math gives to anyone entering or working in today's job market.

"Old Math"

It is helpful to look at the overall changes in math education since World War II before tackling the question of what the new math was, why it is no longer taught, and what has replaced it. Although the practice of reciting the basic facts in unison had probably died out in most places in America by World War II, math teaching just after the war was still largely based on rote learning, with no understanding required. A popular textbook of the time, for example, presented long division as a series of steps to be memorized. It gave no explanation of the meaning of the steps.

Even though people who used that textbook learned to divide, many educators felt that rote memorization was a bad teaching technique. They formed a group known as the *school of meaningful mathematics*. Shortly after World War II, they introduced explanations of why operations worked into the math curriculum. These methods produced students who could do math, but they weren't noticeably better than students who had learned by rote.

In the 1950s, other learning theories came into play. One was *discovery learning*. According to this theory, students, who by now were learning the meaning of what they were doing, would learn better if they discovered the meaning for themselves. In fact, with a little help, many students can build from one group of ideas to the next. But, of course, it takes time for students to discover the meaning of what they are doing. Partly because of this, the amount of math taught in each grade was reduced.

Another innovation also occurred in the 1950s. It is known that a series of short, spaced practice sessions produces longer-lasting improvement than does a single, long practice session. Based on this notion, educators reorganized the sequence in which math was taught so that an idea recurred several times, each time with increased complexity. They called this reorganization *spiral learning*. Teachers disliked this approach, and students seemed to learn less when it was used.

New Math

In October 1957, the launching of the Russian satellite *Sputnik I* shocked Americans into looking closely at their educational process. Problems were observed in the teaching of mathematics, science, and foreign language. So the government invested huge amounts of money to correct the situation.

Much of this money went to mathematicians (as opposed to math educators), who were brought in to reeducate teachers and develop new curricula. The mathematicians immediately focused on meaningful education, discovery learning, and spiral learning. They believed that the meaningful movement had not gone far enough. The real meaning of mathematics, said the mathematicians, is not found in operations with numbers. Operations with numbers are the logical consequence of operations with sets.

You learned in previous sections that sets are used today in mathematics education. But they are not used in a formal, abstract way. These mathematicians, declaring that sets should be used to get at the true meaning of mathematics, introduced abstract sets for doing formal operations.

When abstract sets appeared in elementary school, everyone was optimistic. Textbooks were produced. Teachers were reeducated. Parents were reeducated. But the mathematicians said children would not need to be reeducated. When teachers had trouble with some of the ideas, they were told, "Your students will understand this before you do. They do not have to unlearn old ideas." Perhaps this was true. But over a ten-year period, students' math performance dropped more rapidly than ever.

There was, predictably, a rebellion against the new math and other innovations in teaching. It was called the *back-to-basics movement*. In some extreme cases, back to basics led schools to discard every new idea since World War II. But in mathematics, most people were content to return to the beginning of the meaningful mathematics era. Only a few schools went back to rote learning.

Abstract sets disappeared from textbooks and classrooms as quickly as they had emerged fifteen years earlier. Time spent on other new-math topics was reduced, but not eliminated. The properties of numbers, after all, had been taught (without naming them) in the meaningful math era. It was all right to teach properties as long as their names were not too prominent. It was all right to correct outright errors in instruction too. Before the meaningful math period, for example, it was frequently taught that zero was not a number. No one wanted to return to that notion.

Today's Math

Since the disappearance of new math, several other minirevolutions have swept the curriculum. One revolved around the metric system. Since the middle of the nineteenth century the U.S. Congress has accepted the metric system as one official way to make measurements . But the metric system has never gained wide acceptance in this country. When both England and Canada officially went metric, the United States was left the only major country in the world that used a different measurement system. Congress then passed some bills that were taken to mean that the United States would follow in the footsteps of England and Canada.

Preparing students for metrics suddenly became an important concern of math teachers. When the schools realized that they were going metric but the public was not, they downplayed the whole idea. By that time, most teachers had learned quite a lot about the metric system. They now teach metric and customary measurement side by side.

Another recent revolution was caused by handheld calculators. No one knew what to do about them when they first appeared. The National Association for the Advancement of Colored People (NAACP) in Maryland tried to have them banned from the schools. Prominent educators suggested that the curriculum be revised to get the most out of calculators. Some students concluded that they no longer needed to learn mathematics. Most parents sided with the Maryland NAACP.

But more and more teachers found out that there was no way to keep children from using calculators at home even if the machines could be kept out of the schools, and that helping children learn to use calculators was also a way to teach useful mathematical ideas. Some teachers even found ways to make mathematical games that used calculators. Several years into this situation, it appears that the calculators are a useful tool in the mathematics class but that they will not revolutionize mathematics education so drastically as many thought at first. (*See* Pt. III, Sec. 4, "Calculators," for a thorough discussion of calculator use in the classroom.)

Next there was the problem-solving movement. Tests, especially the tests administered by the National Assessment of Educational Progress, revealed that American children were not able to solve word problems—something that most teachers already knew. For most people, mathematics is useful only if it helps in solving the problems of daily life. The public reacted strongly when the national test results were released.

Studies suggested that part of the difficulty in solving word problems came from lack of attention to problem-solving practice in most elementary and high schools. Word problems were hard for teachers to explain and for children to solve.

As a result of the problem-solving movement, both practice and methods soon became top priorities in mathematics education. Problem solving continues as a major concern today, but it may have lost some status to the newest development—the computer.

Computers began to arrive in schools a few years after the problem-solving movement had reached its height. As had been the case with handheld calculators, educators were at first uncertain about the role of computers. But the computer now appears to have gained a more secure position in education than did many changes that came before. Whether the computer will revolutionize the *mathematics* curriculum is in much greater doubt. Although the computer is often called a "number cruncher," many of its principal uses in schools will probably have little to do with computing. (*See* Pt. III, Sec. 5, "The Computer," for further discussion of computers in education.)

Math and the Job Market

Mathematics is included in the curriculum for all students from nursery school through at least grade 9. Yet many students complain that they do not see the purpose that so much math will have in their lives. In fact, the needs for math in everyday life are both real and varied. Math, like reading and writing, is recognized as one of the most basic subjects just because it is so necessary. This section discusses some of the different needs a good math education can serve, especially in terms of your career.

For students who want to go to college—and that number increases every year—one of the most practical reasons for studying math is that the colleges simply will not admit students who have no math background. While most colleges require only a year of high-school math, the more selective colleges prefer applicants with two or three years of math on the record.

Nearly all colleges furthermore use either the Scholastic Aptitude Test (SAT) or the American College Testing Assessment (ACT) to predict applicants' success in college. Both tests are nearly half mathematics. And both report math scores separately. Students who take four years of high-school math are likely to be better prepared for these tests than students who drop math at the end of grade 9. While it may be possible to find colleges that admit students with weak math backgrounds, the choices are severely limited and more selective schools are generally not among them.

Many students need to take math courses to prepare for their chosen careers. What students want to do with their working lives to a great extent determines the amount of math they need to know. Most students who want to be mathematicians, physicists, or engineers realize that their success depends on their knowledge of advanced math.

For example, engineers regularly use calculus in solving problems. Most people who use calculus admit that it took them several years of working with calculus concepts before they felt natural and comfortable. Therefore, a youngster who wants to be an engineer should plan a math program that reaches calculus as soon as possible, preferably by the senior year in high school.

Scientists of all kinds now use more math than ever before. One biology book, for example, Edward O. Wilson's *Sociobiology: The New Synthesis,* has seventy-three uses of mathematics in its first one hundred pages (and math use increases throughout the book). Included are statistics, differential equations, partial differential equations, and matrix algebra. This book was aimed largely at the general reader, so the math level is considerably lower than it would be in a technical article written for other biologists.

People might think that scientists who study the environment could get by with little math, but that is also far from true. The most influential theories about how the environment functions are full of higher mathematics. Someone who has enough mathematical knowledge to read the *American Mathematical Monthly,* the journal of the Mathematical Association of America, might easily be lost in a typical issue of the *Journal of Limnology,* which is devoted to the biology and environment of freshwater lakes and rivers. The problem would not be technical language about lakes and rivers. It would be the highly specialized mathematics that limnologists have developed to explore their subject. And chemists and other scientists probably use more math than biologists.

Many people associate computers with mathematics. Surprisingly, advanced math is not needed for many computer-programming jobs. Nevertheless, math training is helpful in many aspects of work with computers, and most people who have better jobs in the computer field know and use math. Of course, the people who design computers are engineers, whose work requires a strong mathematics background.

In the social sciences, mathematics has become much more important in recent years. Anthropologists and archaeologists, especially, have found that mathematics helps to unravel the relationships among various peoples. The same is true for sociologists. Even historians have begun to use more math in their work. All these groups have discovered that math can be useful for both description and prediction. Statistics has been particularly helpful.

Economics is highly mathematical. The basic ideas of many economic theories are expressed as differential equations, which are based on calculus. Analysis of economic trends is done with matrix algebra, which allows the study of many relationships all at once.

Actuaries are another group of high-mathematics users. They work for insurance companies, calculating the probabilities of illness, death, accidents, and other occurrences that affect insurance rates and payouts.

Not all people who regularly use mathematics in their work use advanced concepts, however. Some stick largely to adding, subtracting, multiplying, and dividing whole numbers, fractions, decimals, and percents. Accountants fit this description. Most accountants are concerned with determining how much money a company has, how much it is spending, how much it is likely to earn, and how much it could save by handling money more effectively. For even a medium-sized business, an enormous amount of mathematics is involved, although higher mathematics is not usually required.

Similar to accountants, although with considerably less responsibility, are bookkeepers. In larger companies, bookkeepers gather numbers for the accountants to process. In smaller companies, however, bookkeepers may have many of the same responsibilities as accountants. Again, these people use math every working day.

Of course, there are people who do not use math in their jobs every day. Many workers use math only occasionally. But some math is required for almost every kind of job.

Anyone who has to set prices needs to know mathematics, although an old joke seems to contradict this. Two former grade-school classmates met for the first time in twenty years. One had always been a terrible math student, while the other had always been outstanding. The poor math student was dressed in a custom-tailored suit and had arrived in a chauffeur-driven limousine. "How did you do it?" the former good student asked. "You were terrible in school, especially in math."

"Since I got out of school I learned how to make math work for me," replied the weak student. "I run my business on math, in fact. I buy shirts from the factory for $1 each and sell them to retailers for $5. And that little 5 percent profit has brought me all the wealth I would ever want."

In everyday business, of course, things do not work quite that simply. Pricing goods and services is a complex task that requires more math knowledge than how to compute a simple markup. The pricing examples in most textbooks are much simplified compared to the decisions made in even small businesses. Businesspeople who are good at math have a definite advantage over those who are not.

Almost every business and profession requires mathematics. A doctor prescribing medication may have to adjust the prescribed dosage in ratio to the patient's weight. Pharmacists and nurses may have to understand strengths and dosages of medicine, as well. Technicians of all kinds must use math to set up equipment properly. For example, an X-ray technician needs to determine the proper strength of the X rays for a particular body size or part of the body.

A farm is a small business with the same mathematical needs of any other business. Today many farmers are turning to computers to help ease the load of math they need to perform to stay in business. Interest rates, fertilizer rates, growth rates, loss rates, and, of course, prices must be carefully managed to make sure the farmer doesn't go bankrupt.

You just can't get away from math, whether you're building homes, designing toys, or doing income taxes for a living. Real-estate agents, bankers, appliance sellers, even gardeners estimating seed and fertilizer—all need to know how to compute not only with whole numbers but also with fractions, decimals, and percents.

It is difficult to picture how a person could work in modern society with no knowledge of math at all. At the most elementary level, workers must be able to get to work on time, read numbers, and handle their earnings. Students who believe that they will be able to get through their careers without using mathematics should ask any adult to find out how mistaken they are. And the students should ask soon, before the opportunity to learn math slips away.

Part

III

Tips and Tools
for Math
Students

Mathematics is not an easy subject to learn. Everyone has trouble with mathematics sometimes—even good mathematicians. But some people seem to have trouble with mathematics *all* of the time. You need not be one of those people.

There are some keys to success in mathematics, whether at school or elsewhere. Some of the most useful ones are discussed in this part. Though the suggestions may not make you into a great mathematician, they will at least help you learn mathematics well enough to get through school and life confidently. (And, at most, who knows what you can do with this help?) The suggestions include proper habits that you can develop, plus instructions for operating useful equipment that is being adapted more and more to teach and perform math.

First, you will learn how to study mathematics for classwork. Math is the type of subject that needs to be learned steadily, a little more each day. And it must be read properly. You will learn how to read math here, too.

Next you will learn how to take math tests. While studying is essential to good test performance, other factors can make good scores better. The full picture is presented, with special attention given to "math anxiety"—a nervousness about doing math that makes many people test and, generally, handle math less well than they might. Math anxiety can be overcome—this part explains how.

The discussion ends with an overview of a recent trend in mathematics education: the use of the calculator and the computer for classroom and home study. Chances are that you are already familiar with both of these tools, but here you will also learn about the history and the future these electronic tools have in mathematics education.■

(Preceding photo)
Precision is one key to success in math studies.

Studying for Math Class

You can save time preparing for math class and improve your performance if you develop good learning habits and use them both at school and at home. This section talks about the basic skills you need to learn math, helps you to find out how you learn best, and suggests ways that you can improve your math-learning and problem-solving skills.

Reading Math

Knowing how to read mathematics correctly will greatly improve math performance. Most people's problems do not stem from the *inability* to read mathematics but from the *failure* to read mathematics. Tutors find that almost all students who have trouble with math either fail to read instructions or fail to understand the instructions they have read.

This problem may be traced to very early school experience. Mathematics books for kindergarten and first grade often contain no instructions because the pupils cannot read well enough. Instead, the teacher gives all instructions. As the children progress through school, they continue to rely on the teacher to provide all the mathematics instruction they need. They persist in this habit long after they have learned to read and instructions have become part of their classroom materials. At some point, relying on only what the teacher has said inevitably fails. The teacher talks about one kind of problem but assigns another. Or the teacher is absent, and a substitute presents the lesson. By this time, students have begun to make serious errors on homework and tests. Instead of reading direction lines, they guess at what is expected. As a result, they make many unnecessary mistakes.

Examine your own habits. Where do you start reading a mathematics lesson? At the beginning of the explanation? At the beginning of the directions for the exercises? Or at the first assigned exercise? Unless you get in the habit of reading the whole lesson—and especially all directions—you will have trouble with mathematics.

There are also more subtle cases of failure to read mathematics. Many people regularly skip important parts of a mathematics test. For example, the text says:

> With only that scanty evidence to go on, Euclid was able to find a pattern. He showed that if a number is a prime and also of the form
>
> $$(2 \times 2 \times 2 \times 2 \times 2 \times \ldots \times 2) - 1$$
>
> where the number of times 2 is used is n, then the product of that prime and $2 \times 2 \times 2 \times \ldots \times 2$, where the number of times 2 is used is $n - 1$, will always be a perfect number.

But for some readers, the mathematical expressions just disappear. They read:

> With only that scanty evidence to go on, Euclid was able to find a pattern. He showed that

MATHEMATICS

This tendency to skip reading the mathematics usually increases as the mathematical expressions grow more complicated. For readers who fail to stop and decipher the mathematics, the text makes little or no sense. They learn that Euclid discovered something about prime numbers but they don't know what it was. (For an explanation and examples of Euclid's pattern for perfect numbers, *see* Pt. VI, Sec. 2, "Pythagorean Discoveries.")

People who read nonmathematical texts quickly and easily are particularly likely to misread mathematics in this way. Perhaps that explains why many people who are very good in literature classes are not very good in mathematics. The same reading technique that works so well for them in reading a novel or short story defeats their efforts to understand mathematics. It is impossible to learn much by skimming a mathematics book.

Diagrams are also more important in mathematics than they are in most other subjects. But in everyday reading, many people read the text and skip the illustrations. In mathematics, these people may miss significant information.

If you can read other subjects, you can develop correct reading habits in mathematics. First, you must read the entire text, including all mathematical expressions and all diagrams. If you find a word that you do not recognize, look up its definition. Nearly all mathematics books define the special terms they use. If there is a list of definitions in the back of the book, try it first. If there is no list, use the index to find where the word was first defined and reread that section. Read slowly. If you fail to understand something, don't skip over it—go back and try again.

Writing Math

Almost as troublesome as the failure to read mathematics properly is the failure to write mathematics properly. Many students get wrong answers because they do not write mathematics well.

The easiest mistake to correct is miscopying. To avoid this common error, get in the habit of checking your written work against the original problem both before and after you compute. Mistakes stemming from miscopying are extremely frustrating. Missing an item on a test due to miscopying is more painful, somehow, than not knowing how to do the problem at all.

Failure to set up a problem correctly is another common, but less obvious, source of error. If you get in the habit of labeling everything you do, you will make many fewer mistakes. Labeling is particularly important for word problems. Consider a problem such as

> Leslie had 35 tickets to sell for the school play. If 7 families each bought an equal number of tickets, how many tickets did each family buy?

A good way to approach such a problem is to copy the key parts:

> Leslie had 35 tickets.
> 7 families bought equal numbers of tickets.
> $35 \div 7 = 5$

It also helps to label the answer:

> Each family bought 5 tickets.

Many students think that writing all these words is wasted effort. But if they learn to write out problems this way, they will find that the time they spend in writing the words will save them time when they try to solve the problem. Furthermore, they will be much more likely to notice nonsensical answers such as "Each family bought 42 tickets" or "Each family bought 2345 tickets."

Another difficulty that may seem minor but often causes many errors is bad penmanship. Sometimes students make mistakes because they can't read their own handwriting. But more often, teachers must mark answers wrong because they cannot read them. Here are some poorly written numerals.

Here are some clearly written numerals. They are easy to write this way and remain distinct even when they are made in a hurry. Unless your handwriting is especially neat and precise, you should learn to write these numerals like this.

$$0123456789$$

Good Math Habits

The key to success with mathematics is the development of good habits. The best student in a mathematics class may not necessarily have the best mathematical insight. Rather, the best student probably has the best study habits. What are some good study habits?

Take notes

Many students do not start taking notes in class until they reach high school or college. But note taking is an excellent habit to develop as early as possible. Notes bridge the gap between your work in class and your work at home. They help you to study for tests. And they help you learn in several ways at once: you *hear* what the teacher says, you *see* what is written on the chalkboard, you *think* about how to summarize the information, you *write* the pertinent facts, and you *read* your notes later on. As a result, you *remember* the mathematics.

There are certain hard-and-fast rules in taking notes. Always keep your mathematics notes in a separate notebook or in a separate section of your notebook. Always write the date and the name of the class on each page. If possible, use a separate page for each class session. Always write down words that are defined in class along with their definitions. Always write down all assignments.

It is important that your notes reflect both your methods of learning and the teacher's methods of teaching. Some people underline important words; others draw diagrams. Your notes must be meaningful to you, both when you take them and when you look at them later.

Read the textbook

As noted earlier, failure to read explanations and directions is a common problem. Even if you think you understand what your teacher said in class, you should read your textbook to make sure that you didn't miss anything. And even if you are not assigned to read the text, you should get in the habit of using it to review what your teacher said.

Sometimes a teacher's explanation differs from the explanation in the textbook. This can actually be very helpful because you can then see two ways of approaching the same problem. If one technique doesn't work for you, you can try the other. In the process, both techniques may become clearer.

Set up work correctly

Most teachers will tell you how they want you to present problems on your paper. Follow their format and try to see the logic behind it. Proper presentation is especially important in higher mathematics, such as algebra, geometry, trigonometry, and calculus. By the same token, lining up the digits in a simple addition problem or a division problem with decimals is a good way to make sure that your work is not only neat, but accurate. In fact, if you tend to let your digits sprawl across the page, you can improve your handwriting by using squared paper. Younger children can use paper with centimeter-by-centimeter squares, while older children get better results—and better grades—working with quarter-inch-square graph paper. Once you get in the habit of lining up your digits on squared paper, you will find it easier to line them up even when no squared paper is available.

By setting up your paper correctly, you can help both yourself and your teacher. When all the students in the class follow the same format, the teacher can grade their papers more easily. A teacher is likely to be more impressed with the work of a student whose papers are neat and easy to grade than with one whose papers are messy.

Use drawings

You already know that you should carefully read the diagrams in your text. But you also should include, where appropriate, careful drawings in your notes and homework. As you think through a problem, it often helps to copy any accompanying diagrams. When there is no diagram, you may gain understanding by making your own drawing. Put the drawing in your homework. Often a teacher will give you credit for a correct diagram that shows your understanding of the problem—even if you make an error in calculation.

Use references

Your first references should be your notes and your textbook, but you should definitely check other sources if you are having difficulties. Your teacher or librarian may be able to suggest some books (like this one) that explain how to do mathematics. Encyclopedias can also help. Do not feel bound to rely only on your memory, your notes, and your textbook.

Ask for help

When you have trouble solving a problem or understanding a lesson, do not hesitate to ask your teacher for assistance. A teacher's job is to help students. In elementary school, teachers are usually available all day and for some time after school as well. In high school and college, most teachers have special times set aside to help students outside of class. Teachers are the best source for help because they know the subject matter and probably understand why you are having trouble.

While your teacher is the best source of aid, your parents and other adults can often help too. When you ask adults for help, tell them what you have been studying, show them your textbook and assignment, and try to explain what you don't understand. Then be patient while they try to familiarize themselves with the subject and your difficulties.

Above all, do not be ashamed to ask for help. No one expects you to learn everything on your own. You will learn more about how others can help you with math at the end of this section when you read "Learning Math from Others."

Learning Styles

People learn mathematics in different ways. For example, most mathematicians are either *geometers* or *algebraists*. This classification refers not to the field of mathematics that is their specialty but to the way they think. Geometers tend to tackle problems geometrically. They use diagrams and mental pictures to gain insight into how a problem should be solved. Other people might see the same problem algebraically. Algebraists manipulate abstract ideas and symbols easily but do not necessarily have good geometric intuition. (Of course, a few lucky people can use both approaches to a problem with equal ease.)

Recent research has shown that differences between the right and left halves of the brain may account for the division into geometric intuition and algebraic intuition. The left half of the brain approaches problems algebraically, while the right half sees patterns and pictures. Of course, people use both sides of the brain, but they tend to depend more on one side or the other.

This situation suggests two approaches to learning mathematics. First, make sure to follow your basic tendency. If you feel more comfortable drawing pictures, by all means draw them. If pictures don't help you, use your ability to manipulate abstract symbols.

Second, it is better to exercise both geometric and algebraic approaches. For example, your teacher may be a geometric thinker, while you are an algebraic thinker. This is a good opportunity for you to develop your geometric intuition. But you should also make sure to translate the material into your natural way of thinking. It is always better to have more than one method available when you are solving a difficult problem.

Geometric intuition and algebraic intuition are the two most basic styles of learning mathematics. But educators have also discovered that students favor different senses as modes, or ways, of learning. Thus, some students learn better from *seeing* information, others learn better from *hearing,* and still others learn better from *physical participation*. And each mode is developed to different degrees in different individuals. Better teachers try to determine their students' learning modes and teach accordingly.

If you know your own learning modes, you can use them to your advantage. When you are studying, you can apply your favored mode or modes to learn better.

Here is one way that you can discover your best learning modes with the help of a friend or parent. Your partner should write down four strings of random digits, such as 1938562934. You will then try to memorize each string. A good goal is to recall ten digits, but there should be more digits in each string than you can actually memorize.

Now use a different mode to learn each string. Concentrate on one mode at a time, and repeat it until you think you have learned the digits.

1. Look at the digits written on the piece of paper. (visual)
2. Listen to the digits as your partner reads them aloud. (aural)
3. Copy the digits on a piece of paper. (mainly physical)
4. Say the digits aloud. (mainly oral)

Keep track of how long it takes you to learn a string using each mode. The modes can also be combined in various ways. For example, you can write the digits as your partner reads them aloud.

Continue these exercises until you see a clear pattern emerge that indicates your best learning modes. Once you know what those modes are, use them in class and when studying at home. (Do not repeat aloud in class if it will disturb the teacher and other students.)

But the difference in learning styles goes beyond the modes of learning. The Learning Styles Network—a teachers' organization whose goal is to improve education by adapting teaching techniques to individual learning styles—has classified eighteen different learning factors into four categories.

1. Environmental: Sound, light, temperature, design
2. Emotional: Motivation, persistence, responsibility, structure
3. Sociological: Peers, self, pair, team, adult, varied
4. Physical: Perceptual (corresponds to the learning modes), intake, time, mobility

Under *environment,* questions asked are how do sound, light, temperature and room design affect the learner? With regard to *emotions,* what makes the learner want to work, keep at the task, and assume an obligation to learn the lesson at hand? How well can he plan his own learning; how much must it be planned for him?

The *sociological factors* relate to a learner's favored ways of learning from and with others. For example, some people learn best from peers, some when working by themselves, and others prefer learning in varied situations. Finally, the *physical* category covers: the learner's perceptions (which correspond to the learning modes); preferences for food and drink—or the lack of it—during study; efficiency in studying at particular times of the day (some people are "morning people" and others are "night people"); and ability to sit still for long periods of time versus the need to interrupt study in order to move around and stretch one's legs.

You probably know how these stimuli affect your learning. Thus, whenever possible, you should make use of this knowledge to help yourself to learn more effectively.

Learning Disabilities

Sometimes you will hear teachers speak of a condition called *dyslexia.* The word *dyslexia* means "inability to read." It is used to describe apparently intelligent and unhandicapped children who have difficulty learning to read.

Children with dyslexia often reverse words, reading *was* for *saw;* reverse letters, reading *bog* for *dog;* invert letters, reading *pill* for *bill;* or have other difficulties. With special tutoring most children can overcome these problems.

Today, most teachers no longer use the word dyslexia. They prefer to call children who cannot read "learning disabled." One reason that the phrase "learning disabled" has become popular is that many children who have difficulty learning to read also have difficulty learning mathematics. In fact, some children who are good readers have the same problems in learning mathematics as other children have in learning to read. Mathematics educators have coined the term *dyscalcia* to describe this set of problems in learning mathematics.

Dyscalcia's cause is still uncertain, but the disability can be corrected with proper educational techniques. Although estimates vary considerably, the number of children with dyscalcia is certainly under 20 percent of the school population. More and more schools are developing special programs to handle dyscalcia.

Some students have the same difficulty learning to read numbers that they have learning to read letters and words. Sometimes they make the same kinds of reversals with numbers that they do with words. Other children may confuse addition and subtraction signs. When such problems occur, usually in the early grades of elementary school, special help from the teacher or a tutor may be needed. If the school has a special program for students with dyscalcia, they will join the program. If not, other help will be set up.

Far more common than children with dyscalcia are those children who have not learned the special techniques, already mentioned, that are required to read mathematics. For example, children who make mathematics errors in class and in their homework can often make correct calculations on the playground and in other social situations. Such children are not learning disabled. They are actually capable of doing mathematics, but they don't understand the printed mathematics they encounter in the classroom.

Solving Math Problems

A simple five-step system can help you organize your approach to solving mathematics problems:

1. Reading
2. Planning
3. Estimating
4. Computing
5. Looking Back

Each step is important but three—reading, planning, and doing—are crucial. The way that you carry out all five steps greatly affects their usefulness.

Reading

Obviously, if a problem is presented in written form, you must read it to solve it. But reading a problem is not enough. You must understand the situation it presents. Several factors affect your understanding.

Vocabulary

To solve a problem, you must understand all the key words. Use a dictionary or the glossary at the end of your textbook to look up all words that are new to you.

Clues

Most word problems contain important clues to their solution. For example, a problem that contains the phrase "in all" can usually be solved by addition. Some common clues and the solutions they suggest are:

Addition	Subtraction	Multiplication or Division
in all	how much more	how many in (time period)
altogether	how many more	each
both	how much less	how many times
	how many fewer	
	how much left	
	beyond	

Clues can be misleading. Don't forget always to interpret them on a problem-by-problem basis.

Sketches

A problem can often be represented as a sketch, or rough drawing. Such a sketch can help clarify the solution to the problem.

Last and first sentences

Most problems in textbooks end with a question or set of instructions. Others present a question or instructions at the beginning. Since it is least common for a question or instructions to be in the middle of a problem, always look for such important information at the beginning or end first.

Acting out

If you have difficulty understanding a problem, you can sometimes act it out, either mentally or physically, as you reread it. If you picture yourself going through the steps of a problem (or actually go through the steps, perhaps with a friend), the whole situation often becomes clearer.

Planning

Although planning is an essential step in solving word problems, many students skip it. They do not realize that good planning can save time in the long run. Careful reading, as just described, is the first part of any plan, so the two steps overlap somewhat. Looking for clues, making sketches, and acting out a problem can all contribute to a plan, as can the following.

Labels

Begin by labeling the units of measure the problem calls for. If you know that the answer will be a number of boys, a number of meters, or some other specific measure, you have part of the problem solved already.

Working backward

Sometimes it is possible to develop a plan by starting with the answer and working backward to the conditions of the problem. For example, consider a problem such as

Jack saved $50 by buying a suit at a 22% discount. How much did he pay for the suit?

Make a guess at the answer. A new suit might cost $200. Since 22% of $200 is $44, the original price of the suit must be more than $200. But the question does not ask for the original price of the suit; it asks how much Jack actually paid.

Suppose he spent $200. Would the original price of the suit be 122% of $200? Check: 122% of $200 is $244, and 22% of $244 is $53.68. Therefore, $200 is not right, although it is fairly close.

At this point, you should begin to see a pattern. There is a number, call it N, for which $0.22 \times N = 50$. And the answer to the problem is going to be $N - \$50$. You need to solve $0.22 \times N = 50$ as the first step in the problem. You can do so by dividing 50 by 0.22, which shows that N is 227.2727. Rounding this result to allow conversion to dollars and cents, you find that the original price of the suit was $227.27. Since Jack saved $50 off the original price, he spent $177.27.

Using different numbers

Sometimes it is hard to think through a problem because the numbers are either very large or very small. Fractions and decimals can also make a problem harder to think about. You can develop a plan for solving the problem by using small whole numbers instead of the numbers given in the problem. For example, suppose the problem is:

> 21,265 persons each ate 0.3 foot of the world's largest hero sandwich. How long was the sandwich?

You can plan by thinking: "Suppose 5 people each ate 2 feet of a giant hero sandwich. How would I find the answer?" Using those numbers, it is easy to see that you would multiply 5×2, so the plan for the original problem would be to multiply $21,265 \times 0.3$. The answer is 6379.5.

Estimating

Like the reading and planning stages of problem solving, the planning and estimating stages should overlap. A good estimate should help you with your plan. There are many useful ways to estimate.

Practical estimates

Most problems in textbooks are planned to have reasonable answers. In the problem about Jack's new suit, for example, it would be unlikely that the suit would cost less than $50 or more than $1000, simply because most suits do not have such extremely low or high prices. People who write problems usually try to include reasonable information, although errors may occur and textbooks may become outdated. In math problems from everyday life, the answers are even more likely to make sense; therefore, an estimate based on your practical experience is often useful.

Size of answer

You can often tell if an answer will be larger or smaller than the largest or smallest number in the problem. For example, if your plan suggests that a problem should be solved by addition, you would expect the answer to be larger than the largest number in the problem. While this is a very rough estimate, it is usually easy to do and can keep you from making mistakes. Often the size of an answer can be determined from a practical estimate as well. If you know that a number of objects is to be divided among a number of people, you can estimate that the number each person gets will definitely be smaller than the total number of objects. You do not have to think about the mathematical operation here; the estimate of size can come from the physical operation of dividing the objects.

Rounding

Of course, the traditional way to estimate is to use rounded numbers. In most cases, this is the easiest and best way to get an estimate. (For more information about estimating, *see* Pt. I, Sec. 3, "Quick Math.")

Computing

If you have read the problem carefully, planned well, and made a good estimate, actually doing the problem becomes a simple matter of performing the arithmetic correctly. For more difficult problems, you may wish to use a calculator. And for very difficult problems, you may find a computer helpful.

Looking back

When you have finished your arithmetic, write a full sentence that states the answer to the problem, making sure that the answer is correctly labeled. Such a statement can often help you spot a mistake. Of course, you should also check your final answer against your estimate. You can also use several other methods to make sure that your answer is correct. If you have time on a test or if you are solving a problem of some consequence, it is a good idea to check your answer as many ways as you can.

Using the answer in the problem

With appropriate rewording, this method can be used as a check for almost any problem. For example, suppose the problem is

> Mary has some little lambs. If she has 5 more little lambs than little goats, and she has 3 little goats, how many little lambs does she have?

After you have solved the problem and gotten an answer of 8, you can plug that number back into the problem. Think:

> Mary has 8 little lambs. She has 5 more little lambs than little goats, and she has 3 little goats.

It is easy to see that you have solved the problem correctly. Often you can spot mistakes quickly by running though this mental exercise.

Using endings and divisibility rules

In most instances, you should be able to tell if an answer will be odd or even, if it should end in a 0 or a 5, and if it will be a whole number or not. A quick check of this kind is often worthwhile. (For more about endings and divisibility rules, *see* Pt. I, Sec. 3, "Quick Math" and Pt. IV, Sec. 2, p. 233.)

Working the problem another way

When the answer to a problem is particularly important, see if the problem can be solved in more than one way. Many problems can. For example, if a problem has two or more steps, the order of the steps may not matter. In such cases, you can solve the problem again by changing the order of the steps. Often a problem that is solved the first time through division by a whole number can be solved a second time through multiplication by a fraction. (For example, half of 4 can be found through $4 \div 2$ or $4 \times \frac{1}{2}$. The answer in either case is 2.) If the second answer agrees with the first, your answer is more likely to be right (although sometimes you will make the same mistake twice, even though you did the problem differently).

Checking the answer key

Textbooks for the upper school grades often include answers for all or some of their problems. Unless your teacher has told you not to look at such answers, you should feel free to use them. They were put there to help you. In many cases, *how* you do a problem is more important than getting the correct answer. In such cases, having the answer in the back of the book can be a great help. Although the answer does not tell you how to solve the problem, it often provides clues about what you are doing wrong when your answer does not agree. Your paper should show the process you used to arrive at your answer, so you cannot simply copy the answer from the answer key.

Learning Math from Others

Most people learn nearly all their mathematics from other people rather than from books. Even books such as this one are meant to supplement the mathematics you learn from your teachers and parents, not to replace those sources. Learning mathematics from other people means that you can carry on discussions and get immediate answers to your questions. The helpers can correct you if you make mistakes. They can give you hints. Also, learning mathematics from other people can be fun.

You already know that with a helper you can learn to use your best learning modes at school and at home. But there is more than that to learning mathematics from other people. You need to know how and when to ask questions, what kind of help to expect, how you can help yourself, and where to get more help if you need it.

It is also useful to think about how you could help other people to learn mathematics. Helping others to learn mathematics is a wonderful way to learn it yourself. Many teachers, in fact, admit that they learn more from teaching a subject than they ever did from studying it in school.

Asking questions

When you have not understood an explanation the first time, it is always reasonable to ask your teacher questions. Don't be afraid to ask the question in the first place. But asking good questions is not an easy task. To get the best results, you need to know when to ask a question, what to ask, and how to ask it.

It may seem correct that you should ask a question as soon as you realize that you do not understand something. But, in fact, that is not always the best time to ask. For example, you may become confused in the middle of an explanation. But if you wait a minute, your question will probably be answered. If you interrupt, you may complicate the issue by asking about details that will be discussed later. And you are likely to break the train of thought of other students and of the teacher. In most instances, you would do best to write the question in your notes and delay asking it until you are sure the explanation is complete. If, however, you fail to understand the meaning of a key word (or if you simply did not hear a word), it is probably a good idea to interrupt with a quick question, for it is difficult to follow an explanation if you lack an important term.

Once your teacher has finished an explanation, don't wait too long to ask your question. For example, if you do not ask until the next day, both you and your teacher may have trouble remembering the context in which the problem arose.

Questions should be neither too picky nor too general. For example, a question such as, "Why does the person in this problem want to buy a car?" is picky and unimportant. It has nothing to do with mathematics and problem solving. On the other hand, a question such as, "How do you do this kind of problem?" is too general for the teacher to answer well. As a rule, you should direct your questions to the specific point that the teacher is trying to make. For example, during an explanation of the long-division process, you should not ask for an explanation of how to rename in subtraction. (Although, if you have really forgotten how to rename in subtraction, you should ask at some other time—perhaps after class or while other students are doing written work.)

The way you ask a question influences the quality of the answer. Politeness is important. Start by describing your difficulty. Then ask your question. A good form to follow is: "I did not understand _____. Why did you _____?" If you still do not understand, ask a follow-up question. Do not be discouraged if you fail to understand the first answer to your question. Be willing to ask a follow-up question when one is needed.

Getting answers

There are times, of course, when no amount of preplanning ensures that you will be able to use the answer you receive. One story people in the math profession like to tell is about the famous mathematician Norbert Weiner.

When Norbert Weiner was teaching, his absent-mindedness sometimes got in the way. One day he was presenting a difficult problem to his class. After stating the problem, he turned his back to the class, stared at the chalkboard for five minutes, and wrote down a number, which he said was the answer. One brave student raised his hand and said, "Professor Weiner, I didn't quite follow your explanation. Could you please go through it again?" Weiner replied, "I'll do something even better. I'll do it another way." He turned to the chalkboard, stared at it for another five minutes, and once again wrote down the same number.

You may expect more help than that student supposedly received. But when a teacher, a parent, or another student is helping you, don't expect that person to do your work for you. If someone else solves a problem for you, it is unlikely that you will learn to solve similar problems in the future. A good teacher will give you hints or ask you questions that will guide you toward solving the problem on your own. Often a teacher will answer your question with another question. For example, if you say, "I can't solve problem number 7. How do you solve it?" Your teacher might answer, "Do you think that the answer will be larger than 34 or smaller than 34?'' or "Is this a one-step problem or a two-step problem?''

This technique helps you to think about the problem in a new way. It also shows you the kinds of questions you should ask yourself when you get confused.

A teacher may also give you some hints when you ask for help. Such hints may take the form of a question ("Did you try multiplying?") or a statement of fact ("You have to find two triangles that are similar"). Sometimes your teacher may tell you to read a passage in your textbook.

Of course, if you find that hints do not help you to solve a problem on your own, you may need to ask for a step-by-step presentation. After a demonstration of one such problem, your teacher will probably watch you carefully while you solve another problem or two without help. Such step-by-step explanations are most useful for basic math processes, such as renaming in multiplication. They are usually less useful for word problems, which tend to be more varied in their solutions.

Helping others

When you help a student, either someone in your class or someone younger, you should follow the methods just discussed. Do not do the problem for the other person unless it is the kind of problem that needs a step-by-step explanation and it is clear that the person has no idea of how to solve the problem. Instead, think of a hint or question that will start the person thinking. If you are doing a word problem, make sure that the other person understands what is required. For example, have the person explain the problem to you and make a rough estimate. If the estimate is reasonable, ask how the person made the estimate. Suggest the use of the problem-solving techniques discussed previously—drawing pictures, using simpler numbers, and the like. You may even let the person work through to a wrong answer. Then provide the correct answer and discuss why the two answers differ.

This method of helping takes much thought. But it is the best way to help the other person learn. And in the process, you too will become a better problem solver.

When help doesn't work

Sometimes you will remain confused after you've been helped. If your helper is someone who can solve the problem, then perhaps you have not asked the right questions. Most teachers will explain things another way if you tell them that you still do not understand. And if the second way doesn't work, they will try a third way. It is your job to make sure that your teacher knows that you still don't understand. Otherwise, the teacher will move on to another topic or question.

Once in a while, of course, you will encounter a person who does not give clear explanations. No matter what the person says, you cannot understand. In such a case, another student who does understand the explanation may be able to help you. Above all, don't give up.

Unfortunately, getting help from other students has some possible pitfalls. Fellow students may not necessarily be good teachers. They are much more likely to tell you step-by-step how to find an answer, even when that is not the most helpful response. Worst of all, other students may not know how to do the problem either. If they show you the wrong method, you may become even more confused. Therefore, make sure that fellow students really know how to solve a problem before you accept their suggestions without question.

In some cases, you can learn a lot by working with someone who is just as confused as you are. If you work together, using such resources as your textbook or class notes, you may be able to solve a problem that neither of you could do alone. Such cooperation can lead to valuable learning, and it is quite different from accepting the advice of someone who is misinformed.

Using all the study tips you've learned about in this section will bring about an improvement in your understanding of math and, with it, a change in your attitude toward math studies. And solid math study habits will also mean that you'll find your job much easier on those special days when you face a math test.

Section 2

Taking Math Tests

Throughout your school career, you will probably encounter two basic kinds of tests—*teacher-made tests* and *standardized tests*. Most of the tests you take are teacher-made tests. They range from pop quizzes on last night's homework to final exams on everything you have learned in an entire term. Most teacher-made tests are designed to be used in only one class or school.

Teachers are usually free to choose what they want to put on a teacher-made test. They decide what kinds of questions to ask, what information to ask for, and how long the test will last. After the test is given, they correct the students' answers and assign grades.

Standardized tests, by contrast, are usually written by professional testing companies and are intended for use by teachers and students across the country. A standardized test is designed to provide a standard, or uniform, measure of performance. Thus, every student who takes a standardized test is expected to follow the same directions, rules, and conditions. When you take a standardized test, your scores can be compared to the scores of other test takers nationwide.

Standardized tests may be used to measure achievement, learning ability, readiness to progress to higher levels of learning, personality, occupational preferences, and many other factors that interest educators.

Some people always get high scores on tests, no matter the type, while others always get low scores. It may seem that the people who always score high on tests have a special talent or a secret method of studying. But the way to get good scores is no secret.

People who do not do well on tests can greatly improve their scores by following a program of preparation and test taking that is mostly common sense. Poor test takers carry bad habits into the test room. They fail to make special preparations for tests, and they do not think carefully about how tests are constructed. Replacing these bad habits is not hard to do. If you want to improve your scores on mathematics tests, here are some steps that you can take. These steps apply to both teacher-made tests and standardized tests. Some specific advice about college-entrance tests follows the general discussion.

Seven Steps to Better Test Scores

The steps to follow in preparing for and taking a mathematics test range from using ideas that generally reflect the way you should be studying and doing your homework to specific ideas that apply to test taking only. They include:

1. How to study
2. How to start a test
3. How to time yourself
4. How to sequence a test
5. How to guess answers
6. How to check answers
7. How to outguess the test maker

The seven steps are presented roughly in their order of importance. You may be surprised at the emphasis on guessing. But students who guess intelligently will generally get better scores than those students who make wild guesses or don't guess at all.

Nearly everyone has to do a little guessing on long tests. There may not be time to finish a test if you work out every problem in detail. And some tests will cover topics that you do not know. For example, in large high schools, the same test may be given to all the algebra classes, but your class may not have studied one of the topics. Your not having studied all the topics is even more likely when you take standardized tests, such as college-entrance exams. So intelligent guessing may be an excellent aid.

How to study

Naturally, the earlier suggestions about how to study for class also apply to studying for tests. Take notes in class. Use your best modes of learning. Read the textbook carefully, including all the mathematical sentences, long mathematical expressions, and diagrams. And use other references if they are appropriate.

But studying for a test is a specific kind of studying as well. Nearly everyone studies differently for a test than for everyday classwork.

The worst way to study is to *cram*, or try to learn everything the night before the test. While there is nothing wrong with studying the night before, cramming is a concentrated way of studying that usually does not work very well. Research has shown that people who try to learn a lot in one concentrated session do not usually remember the information for very long.

Everyone uses two different forms of memory—long-term and short-term. When you need to remember a telephone number from the time you look it up until the time you dial, you put the number into your short-term memory. A few minutes later—if the line was busy, for example—you will have to look the number up all over again. Short-term memory is just temporary storage.

If you dial the same telephone number every day, however, it will become part of your long-term memory. You may remember it for many years. Then, if you stop using the number, it will gradually fade from your long-term memory.

Cramming puts information into your short-term memory, so you may forget it by the time you take the test. In addition, cramming is hard work, and it goes on far too long. The last thing you want to do before a test is to tire yourself out. Instead of cramming, you should set aside some time for relaxation the night before a test, and you should get a good night's sleep.

Finally, cramming puts you in the wrong mood for test taking. Cramming builds anxiety. You want to approach a test with confidence, not with the worry and tension that cramming causes. If you wait until the last minute to study, you may feel overwhelmed by having to learn a great deal in a very short time. Especially if you cram late into the night, you will feel the tension increase.

Instead of cramming, you should prepare for a test from the beginning of a course, or from the time a test is announced. In fact, four to six weeks of special preparation in addition to regular study is the best way to get ready for a major test. With extra study two or three times a week, you can be sure to get the main ideas into your long-term memory.

Use some study time to improve your notes. Recopying is an important learning tool that many people find extremely useful. Reorganizing your notes also helps you to group related information.

Notes taken in class are usually sketchy because the teacher keeps moving on to new topics. Recopying them, and adding information from your textbook and memory, help in several ways.

Your new set of notes becomes a useful study guide. If you can get people to quiz you on important facts, they can use the notes more easily if they are neat and well organized. If you arrange your notes so that all important topics are on a few sheets, you can use them for the last-minute review that you should plan instead of cramming.

To get a good score on a mathematics test, you usually need three different kinds of information. You need to know: (1) specific math vocabulary, (2) certain general rules, and (3) how to solve problems and do calculations.

You can often study both vocabulary and general rules with a friend or parent. After you think you have learned all the terms and rules, have your friend or parent quiz you and mark the ones that you miss the first time. Give these words, phrases, and rules special attention. Then ask someone to quiz you on the whole list again.

On most tests, solving problems and doing calculations are the most important. They make up the bulk of most mathematics tests, and they are the hardest to study. For a teacher's test, the best way to study is to do all your homework. If you miss a problem, you should redo it so that you have a correct model to study. If you keep all your mathematics homework in one place, you can use it to review. Look especially closely at the problems you missed, do them again without looking at the corrected version, and be sure that you do not make the same mistake again.

For standardized mathematics tests, good classroom study habits and testing skills are important. But you cannot know the specifics of the test beforehand. Study groups and review books are available, however, to show you the types of subjects and test items on some standardized tests. Still, there's no substitute for good classroom performance.

The night before any major test, make a quick check of your notes and do one last quiz on the vocabulary items and rules that have given you special trouble. Then do something to relax, such as watching a television show or movie, and go to bed early.

How to start a test

Before you start a test, make sure that you have the necessary pencils or pens and paper. If the test will be timed, or if you know that you have only one class period to finish the test, wear a watch, if possible. The test room may not have a clock that you can easily see. If you are taking an open-book test, remember to bring your book. And if calculators are permitted, check that you have your calculator with you and that it works. When you are sure that you have everything you need, relax.

One good way to relax is to arrive at the testing room several minutes before the test is supposed to start. Then do something that has nothing to do with the test, such as reading a magazine or talking with a friend. You will then be as relaxed as possible when you start taking the test.

When the test is about to begin, pay careful attention to any information the test giver provides about how to take the test. Make sure you know the total time allowed, the scoring methods, and any special instructions about how to mark your paper or test booklet. Also, check again to see if you can use such helps as a book or calculator. For many mathematics tests, there are special instructions about how to do scratch work. Should it be done on a separate sheet or in the margins of the test booklet? Should it be handed in along with the test? Make certain that you know the answers to all these questions before you begin the test.

When you are told that you can start to work, read through the whole test quickly before trying to put any answers on paper. As you look through the test, watch for two kinds of items—those that you think you can do easily and those that may be difficult. Note where they are. Also pay particular attention to all instructions. If they are not clear, question the test giver right away.

At this point, how you should proceed depends on how long the test is. If the test is long, you are still not ready to answer questions. But on a short test or quiz, you can begin to write the answers.

On a short test, or as you do each section on a longer test, begin by reading each instruction twice. Even if you know the material well, you can lose many points if you fail to follow the instructions.

How to time yourself

Most tests are timed in one way or another. Testing time is often limited by the need to go to another class or to another test. A common problem of poor test takers is that they fail to answer all the questions within the time limit. When the test is over, they leave many questions unanswered, including some that they could have answered if they had had more time. For a test that is longer than ten minutes or so, you should plan your time before you begin to answer the questions.

Most longer math tests have several different sections with different kinds of problems. And often the point value per problem varies from section to section. You need to take account of this in planning your time. For example, if a test contains twenty true-false items, ten computational items, and five word problems, the test maker may have assigned 1 point to each true-false item, 3 points to each computational item, and 10 points to each word problem. If you start with the true-false items and do not get to the last three word problems, there is no way that you can score above 70%. To avoid that possibility, you should plan your time carefully. Thus, if this were an hour's test, you would assign twelve minutes to the true-false items, eighteen minutes to computational items, and thirty minutes to the word problems. Then, using a special format, write the time limits you assign to each section on your scratch paper. Put down the actual time that you should finish each section. In this case, if the test starts at 9:30 and you do the sections in order, you should write:

True-false: 9:42
Computation: 10:00
Word problems: 10:30

Obviously, if you finish one section early, you can use the extra time on the next section. Similarly, if you fall a little behind on a section, you can borrow a minute or two from the next section to finish what you are doing.

The time limits you give to each section should be treated more as general guidelines than as rigid rules. Also, if you finish all the true-false items that you know in ten minutes, don't waste the remaining two minutes thinking about the items that you don't know how to answer. Guess the answers and move on quickly.

How to sequence a test

It is usually not a good idea to start with the first test item and work in sequence to the end. Test scores are based on the total number of correct answers. If all answers are worth the same number of points, first do all the items that you know you can solve quickly. When you begin by reading through the whole test, you can notice which items look easy and which look hard. Then, you can go back and answer the easy questions first. The more answers you can give that you know are correct, the more points you will score.

When some items are worth more points than others, you may want to tackle the items that count more first. It is not usually necessary to do all the sections of a test in order unless the test is given one part at a time. In the example of the one-hour test with three sections discussed earlier, you might want to reverse the order of the sections to maximize your score:

Word problems: 10:00
Computation: 10:18
True-false: 10:30

It is not always a good idea to do the problems with high point values first, however. If you don't know how to solve those problems, you may get bogged down and lose valuable time. In addition, despite the possible scoring advantages of doing the hard items first, many people feel better if they warm up on the easy items. No matter what order you give the sections, within each section, you should first answer all items that you can do quickly. As you work, keep track of the time limits that you've given each section.

How to guess answers

A test maker does not usually expect everyone who takes a test to get a perfect score. In fact, for some kinds of tests, that result would be undesirable. But most teachers would like to think that all their students have learned all the required material. Therefore, a test on which everyone gets a perfect score should be a goal for all teachers, as long as the test reflects the information that the students should know.

Not all tests are based on material that has been studied in class, however. In contrast with a teacher-made test for a specific subject, a test for college admissions is supposed to be "discriminating." That is, some people should get higher scores than others. In fact, very difficult items are included on such tests on the assumption that only the very best students will solve them correctly. Thus, students should develop a good strategy for guessing answers that they do not know how to find in other ways. You should never guess an answer if you know how to work a problem. But guessing is a useful way to improve your score when you do not know what else to do.

On most tests, students are not punished for wrong guesses. But on some tests, wrong guesses are deducted from the total score for correct answers. Be sure you know which kind of test you are taking. Finally, some tests deduct a number of points that is supposed to balance the effect of guessing, whether a test taker guesses or not. This is a controversial practice that will be discussed in more detail in the part of this section that deals with standardized tests.

When wrong guesses are not counted against your final score, you should guess as often as possible once you have worked all the items you can. If wrong guesses are deducted from correct answers, you should guess only if you are quite sure that your response is correct.

All guesses should be as informed as possible. (See pp. 53–61 for some techniques.) Consider the odds of making a correct guess. On a true-false item, you have a fifty-fifty chance of guessing right. On a multiple-choice item, your chance is $1/n$, where n is the number of choices. Thus, if there are four choices, you have one chance in four of guessing the correct answer. The hardest guesses are for questions that allow a free choice—that is, questions for which you must compute and supply the answer on your own, with no choices shown. Your odds on these test items depend entirely on how much you know.

Actually, the odds for all informed guesses depend on your accumulated knowledge. Often on a multiple-choice test, for example, you can easily see that one or more of the possible choices cannot be correct. (You don't know the right answer, but you know one of the wrong ones.) The right answer must be among the choices that remain. This increases the odds that you will guess correctly. Even on a true-false item, you may lean toward one answer or the other, and your guess is usually based on a hunch derived from former learning.

Some free-choice items are easier than others. For example, consider the question:

What is the name of the rule that says the order of addends does not make a difference in the sum?

This is really a kind of multiple-choice item. Someone who has studied the material could probably narrow the name of the rule down to three choices—the associative law of addition, the commutative law of addition, or the distributive law of addition. (Although there is really no distributive law of addition mentioned in textbooks, a person making a guess might come up with such a choice.) The odds are one chance in three that one of the answers will be right, so it would probably be worth the effort to make a guess.

When you cannot even guess how a problem should be done, quickly proceed to the next item. Then, if you have some time left over at the end of the test period, return to each unanswered question and put your unconsious mind to work. Sometimes you cannot recall a piece of information because you are trying too hard. But if you stop worrying and think about something else, the fact may suddenly pop into your mind. This occurs because the unconscious still works on the problem while the conscious mind thinks of other things. But the unconscious must first be prepared by deep thought about the problem.

The mathematician Jules Henri Poincaré (1854–1912) described in detail how his unconscious mind helped him. He had spent months trying to solve a particular problem without success. Finally, he turned to other matters. Then, as he was getting on a bus, thinking of something else entirely, the answer to the difficult problem just popped into his head—and he knew immediately that it was right.

How to check answers

You may think it's better to spend your time checking the answers you do know instead of guessing the answers you don't know. But on a timed test, it is best not to make elaborate checks of answers as you go along. While checking can eliminate annoying errors, the time it takes to do a careful check is better spent on completing more items.

Simple checks, however, are extremely useful. Simple checks include making estimates as you work, looking at patterns of odd and even numbers, and watching for unreasonable answers of any kind. You should make such checks automatically at the time you do a problem. But skip even simple checks if they take up too much time.

If you complete a test early, using more elaborate checks can often improve your score. Subtraction can be checked with addition. Division can be checked with multiplication. A long column of addition can be checked by adding in reverse order. Multiplication can often be checked using divisibility rules. Decimals and percents can be checked with fractions, or vice versa. (See index for where these operations are discussed at length.)

Check as many problems as you can. Do not leave a test early just because you've put down an answer for each question. Use any extra time to review your work once more.

How to outguess the test maker

In the days before missiles and nuclear weapons, it used to be said that wars were conducted largely between the cannon makers and the armor-plate makers. As soon as the cannon makers produced a cannon that could pass through an inch of armor, the armor-plate makers would produce armor an inch-and-a-half thick. Then the cannon makers would develop a cannon that could cut through two inches of armor. The rivals would continue that way indefinitely.

The same might be said of test makers and test takers. When test makers find a new way to prevent test takers from guessing correct answers, the test takers catch on to the new approach and base their guesses on it. All this is to say that guessing is at best a risky business. The following discussion will show you why.

People who write true-false tests usually make the number of true items approximately equal to the number of false items. Therefore, after you have completed as many items as you can without guessing, you can count the number you found true and the number you found false. If the test has been constructed with equal numbers of true and false items, you can adjust your guesses accordingly.

Of course, test makers may counter this practice with a test that presents many more true items than false ones, or vice versa. You may suspect this from the balance between true and false among the items you know how to answer. In that case, you can figure the *ratio* of answers in the finished test to be about the same as the ratio in the part that you have already done. That is, if you have three times more true statements than false ones among the items that you know how to answer, you can keep the same proportion of true to false among the items that you guess at.

But by the time you have finished all this figuring, you may be cannon fodder indeed. You've used up some of your time, and if you weren't that well prepared for the test to begin with, basing your guesses on your correct (?) answers isn't all that desirable.

The choice is yours, but the solution is probably to get out of the line of fire by preparing for the test in the first place. You have a better chance at making successful guesses the fewer guesses you have to make. If you have to make only one or two, you don't have to bother with figuring.

Test makers must often use certain important clues, or trigger words, in their questions. You need to watch for these and know how they might affect your answer. Some common trigger words are:

always
often
may
never
none
some
rarely

Be suspicious when a test item says that something *always* happens or *never* happens. Using the words *always* and *never* is an easy way for a test maker to produce a believable, but incorrect, choice. On the other hand, a test maker who wants to turn an unlikely choice into a true statement may use a word such as *sometimes* or *rarely*. And a test maker may try to outwit test takers by using a trigger word in the opposite way from the expected one. You should pay particular attention to trigger words when you are taking a test. But don't be tricked into thinking that they always mean the same thing. Read carefully.

One big problem test makers have in writing multiple-choice tests is that the correct choice tends to be the longest choice. Test takers have noticed this, of course, and have learned to pick the longest answer when they had to guess. So test makers countered by making sure that the longest choice was not always correct. As a result, it is now most common for the second-longest choice to be correct. If test takers begin to notice that this is the case, test makers may have to change their tactics again. Meanwhile, remember your solution. And never fail to keep in mind that, all strategies aside, the battle is really won when you know the material on the test, not when you outwit the test makers.

Kinds of Test Items

So far, most of this advice has applied to mathematics tests in general. Now you will look closely at the most common kinds of test items you will encounter in mathematics. For the most part, you will run into the same items in homework too. So while these suggestions apply to test items, you don't need to wait until test time to put most of them into practice.

Some tests contain only one kind of item, while other tests mix different kinds of items throughout. When a test contains different kinds of questions, you may have to switch strategies for each one.

Multiple-choice items

A typical multiple-choice question consists of two parts. The first part is called the *stem*. The stem is either a paragraph, a sentence, or a part of a sentence. The stem is followed by two or more *choices*. One of these choices either answers a question asked in the stem, results from following directions given in the stem, or completes an incomplete sentence in the stem. This is the *correct choice*. The remaining choices are called *distractors* because they are intended to distract your attention from the correct choice.

Here are some typical multiple-choice items:

1. Four children divided a pizza so that each got an equal amount. How much did each child get?
   a. $\frac{4}{1}$ b. $\frac{1}{4}$ c. 0.4

2. Round 13,593 to the nearest thousand.
   a. 13,000   b. 13,500   c. 14,000   d. 13,600

3. 30 quarts = ___?___ liters.
   a. 28.5   b. 2.85   c. 3.17   d. 31.71

4. If the scale on a map is 1 cm = 150 km, and the measured map distance is 3.2 cm, the actual distance on the ground is
   a. $46\frac{5}{6}$ km
   b. 480,000 km
   c. 480,000 cm
   d. 480 km
   e. none of the above

In item 1., the stem is a short paragraph of two sentences. In 2., the stem is a command, not a question. In 3., the stem is a fill-in-the blank statement, and in 4., the stem is an incomplete sentence. Typically, test makers number the stems and assign letters to the choices. Directions for indicating the correct choice vary. If a test consists of all multiple-choice items, a common direction is, "Circle the letter of the correct answer." On standardized tests, or other tests that are machine scored, there is usually a row of dashed or dotted lines that are labeled with the same letters as the choices. The instructions say to fill in the space corresponding to the correct answer.

Answer formats

Fill in the lettered circle.

a b c d e

Fill in the lettered space between two broken lines.

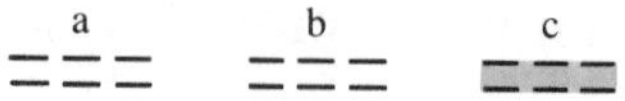

a   b   c

Fill in the numbered rectangle.

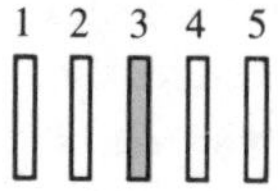

1 2 3 4 5

Fill in the numbered oval.

1 2 3 4 5

Circle the correct answer.

Yes   No

Fill in the circle under a symbol.

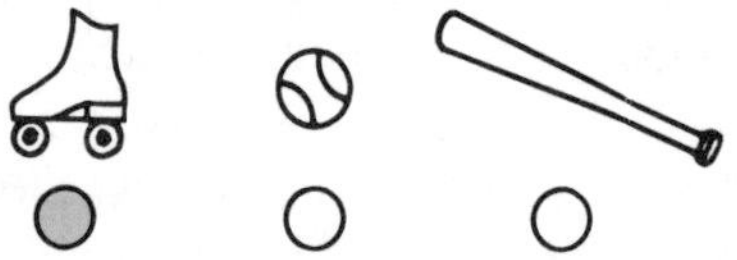

Circle the number corresponding to the best statement. Enter the number in the box at the bottom.

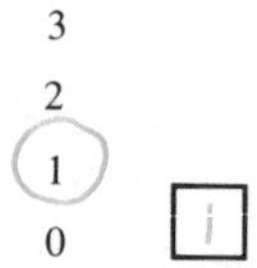

3
2
1
0

When doing multiple-choice questions, be sure to follow the instructions for how to indicate a correct answer. Your teacher may give you credit for correct answers that are wrongly recorded if, say, you underlined the right choice instead of circling it. But when a test is graded by machine, you will lose points if you do not follow the directions exactly.

Most commonly, four or five choices are given. Often the fifth choice is "none of the above," "not given," "all of the above," or "don't know." Any of these may be correct. For the most part, test makers use the fifth choice as a distractor, but you cannot count on it. You should always consider that it may be the correct answer.

When possible, people who write mathematics tests like to use common errors as distractors. For example, in item 3. of the previous multiple-choice samples, students may make two possible kinds of mistakes. First, they may confuse the fact that 1 quart equals 0.95 liters with the fact that 1 liter = 1.057 quarts. Second, when they multiply, they may misplace their decimal points. Of course, sometimes using common errors as distractors backfires by making it obvious, to better students at least, that one of two answers must be correct.

True-false items

A true-false item is simply a multiple-choice item for which there are two choices—true and false. Because test takers have a fifty-fifty chance of getting the correct choice, most test makers do not use true-false items so much as they use other kinds of questions. Nevertheless, true-false items make a good quick quiz because students can usually answer them fast without long computation. Of course, it is possible to have

True or false?
The product of 289 and 394 is 110,976.

But the purpose of such a format is questionable. A clearer and more desirable format would be:

Compute the following. $\begin{array}{r} 394 \\ \times 289 \\ \hline \end{array}$

The product must be computed in either case, and the answer is 113,866.

True-false items are better for checking understanding of concepts than they are for testing computational skills. For example, if you have been studying how to tell whether an answer to a computation should be even or odd, you might get a true-false quiz with items like the following:

Some of the computations below are true and some are false. You can tell which are false by using odds and evens. For each statement, write T for true or F for false.
1. $2945 + 6187 = 9132$
2. $289 \times 394 = 110,967$
3. $5902 - 3856 = 2045$
4. $47 \times 953 = 44,791$

Since you are expected to know such rules as odd + odd = even and odd × even = even, you should be able to mark each item true or false without doing any computation. If you stop to do the computations, you will probably not have enough time to complete all the items. The answers are: 1. T; 2. F (113,866); 3. F (2046); 4. T.

Matching items

Another common test item is the matching exercise. Words, phrases, or numbers in one list must be matched with the appropriate words, phrases, or numbers in another list. Sometimes both lists have the same number of entries, but often one list is longer than the other. In such cases, if the matching is supposed to be one-to-one, some terms will be left over. In other cases, several terms from one list can be matched with a single term from the other list.

Lists of equal length with one-to-one matches are the easiest, while lists of unequal length with multiple matches are the hardest. For example, if each list contains the same number of terms and the matching is one-to-one, the last match is automatic if you knew all the previous matches. If the two lists are different lengths and the matching is one-to-one, then the number of possibilities for each remaining match decreases by one every time you make a match. But if the matching is not one-to-one, terms that have already been matched offer no clues about terms that remain unmatched.

Noticing whether one-to-one matching is possible is to your advantage. This is usually spelled out in the directions, as shown in this example.

Match each number in the first list with one number in the second list by writing the letter of the correct answer in the blank provided.

1. 0.4 _____   a. 0.04
2. $\frac{2}{3}$ _____   b. $\frac{4}{10}$
3. 9.2 _____   c. 9.20
                     d. $\frac{4}{6}$
                     e. $\frac{4}{5}$

Here the directions specify that only the letter of the correct answer needs to be written. Sometimes answers will have to be written out in full.

You may also be asked to draw lines that connect each pair of matching terms. In such cases, people often lose points because they draw sloppy lines. Therefore, if you have a straight edge, such as a ruler or the edge of a piece of paper, use it.

Free-response items

On most classroom mathematics tests, free-response questions asking for computation are especially common. Unlike other kinds of test items, free-response questions do not give you a choice of answers. For teachers such tests are easier to prepare but harder to grade. They are easier to prepare because the teacher does not need to spend time on such problems as inventing good distractors or working out matching lists. They are harder to grade because the answers may appear in different forms on each student's paper. Free-response computation items do not usually appear on standardized tests because they cannot be scored by machine.

Three Standardized Tests

Students take a variety of standardized tests during their years in school. In fact, so many standardized tests exist, and they vary so greatly in goals and content, that we cannot possibly mention them all here. Instead, we will focus on the math portions of three of the most commonly taken standardized tests.

For many students, the most worrisome standardized tests are the college-entrance examinations. High-school grades and scores on the Scholastic Aptitude Test (SAT) and/or the American College Testing Program (ACT) often play a strong role in whether students are accepted into college, and which colleges they may go to. Few employers care about where a job applicant went to grade school or high school. But many are interested in where a potential employee attended college. Therefore, people who want to go to very selective colleges may actually agonize over the scores they receive on the SAT and ACT.

For adults who have not graduated from high school, another test is extremely important—the General Educational Development Test (GED), or high-school-equivalency examination. Many colleges and business and trade schools recognize a passing score on the GED as a valid standard for admission. Some government employers, at both the state and federal levels, require either a high-school diploma or a passing score on the GED, as do many private employers.

If you are interested in the SAT, ACT, or GED at this time, you should read the next discussion carefully.

The SAT and the ACT

Some colleges require applicants to take the SAT. Others require the ACT. The SAT is an aptitude test designed to measure reading comprehension, vocabulary, and mathematics, while the ACT is an achievement test designed to assess English usage, mathematics usage, social studies reading, and natural sciences reading.

The mathematics sections of these tests require an understanding of algebra and geometry. The full range of first-year algebra concepts and the easier parts of geometry appear in the questions, as well as some math concepts you should have acquired on the junior-high level. If you are planning to take the SAT or the ACT, it is much to your advantage to keep up with your mathematics studies each year and to take first-year algebra and geometry. Otherwise, you have placed yourself at a great disadvantage.

Courses beyond first-year algebra and geometry are also helpful. Although few questions relate directly to the higher-level courses, those that do help to identify the brightest students. Also, mathematics skills gradually fade if they are not practiced. Taking a full mathematics curriculum in high school is one of the best ways to prepare for college-entrance exams (and college mathematics courses).

For many students, additional preparation through coaching or other review programs is also helpful. Some studies have shown that this type of preparation can raise scores only by about 10 points. For example, the maximum score on the SAT is 800, and a good score is around 500. Whether you have a score of 500 or 510 isn't going to make much of a difference. The extra effort of additional preparation would not be very worthwhile.

But other studies do not agree. The organizations that offer intensive preparation for these tests say they are able to raise scores by 50 to 70 points on the average—and that is a significant amount. One company that sells computer software for use in improving SAT scores has studies showing that use of their materials will raise scores by as much as 100 points.

There is agreement that students who haven't studied math for several years can improve their scores through math review. And test makers provide test takers with a list of important mathematics concepts to study.

Both the SAT and ACT are *norm-referenced tests*. They enable you to compare your scores with those received by other people who took the test. A *norm* is an average. It is determined before the test is put into use by giving the test to a carefully selected experimental group of students and analyzing the results.

Scores on the ACT and SAT are presented in two ways. Test takers receive a point score and a *percentile score*. A percentile score of 75 means that the individual scored better than

75 percent of the students in the norm group. It also means
that 25 percent of the students in the norm group scored better.
From year to year, the relationship between the numerical
scores and the percentile scores varies. But on the SAT, a difference of 100 points in the numerical score would usually
translate into a difference of about 10 points in the percentile
score.

Students about to take the college-entrance exams should
begin to prepare about six weeks before the test date. Special
publications, intensive courses, and computer programs are
available, but most cost money. Some high schools may offer
free seminars, and the testing services themselves provide free
materials that can be helpful, including the math concepts already mentioned and sample tests or test items. These materials are sent to the high-school guidance counselors across the
country for distribution to interested test takers. Students may
also write for them.

Most students should begin by taking one of these sample
tests. If you take a sample test and are very disappointed by
your score, you might want to consider spending some money
on special help. If you are reasonably satisfied with your score
on the sample, you can probably rely on the free materials for
adequate preparation. It would be a mistake, however, not to
prepare at all. Some of the questions, especially in the math
section of the SAT, are very different from other test questions
you have seen, and they may confuse you.

Two kinds of mathematics questions appear on the SAT.
The first is a simple multiple-choice question, which takes a
form similar to the following:

17. If $7x = 3y$ and $y \neq 0$, then $\dfrac{x}{y} =$

(A) $\frac{7}{3}$
(B) 1
(C) $\frac{3}{7}$
(D) 21
(E) $\frac{1}{21}$

You indicate answers on a separate score sheet by dark-
ening an oval containing a letter (in this case, C).

About one-third of the test items in the mathematics sections of the SAT are presented in a two-column format. The
columns are labeled *Column A* and *Column B*. Each column
indicates a quantity. Often, an expression or diagram between
the columns suggests how the quantities are related. Your job
is to tell if one quantity is greater than the other, if they are
equal, or if it is impossible to tell their relationship from the

information given. The four possible answers are designated with letters:

A the quantity in column A is greater
B the quantity in column B is greater
C the quantities are equal
D you can't tell how they are related

The SAT also offers certain guidelines. It notes, for example, that if the same symbol appears in both columns, it always means the same thing and that all the lower-case letters are variables that represent real numbers.

An important thing to remember for this two-column question format is that, unlike other mathematics questions on the SAT, only four choices are possible. Choice E, which is shown on the answer sheet only, is never a possible answer. If you must guess an answer, make sure that you do not guess E.

A typical item from this part of the SAT looks like this:

Column A	Column B
$x > y$	
$x - y$	$y - x$

For this item, you must think, "If x is greater than y, then $x - y$ is positive and $y - x$ is negative; therefore the correct choice is A. On the other hand, if the mathematical sentence between the columns were $x \geq y$ (that is, x is greater than or equal to y), the correct choice would be D, since you would not know if the expressions $x - y$ and $y - x$ each represent 0 or different positive and negative numbers.

Items in this format are not necessarily more difficult than regular multiple-choice items, but they take some getting used to. You should practice these problems in the sample materials provided by the SAT test makers, even if you do no other studying for the test.

The SAT and the ACT are administered in timed sections. You can't set up a timing schedule for the entire test because you cannot proceed to the next section until you receive permission. It is important to read quickly through each section before you start work on it. Be sure to read the instructions twice because they tend to be somewhat complex.

The distractors on these tests can be very appealing. Therefore, be careful that you are not led astray by some of the incorrect choices.

You will probably not have enough time to answer every question of every section, let alone carefully check your answers. So you should make quick, informal checks as you work. Try to do the easiest items first in order to score the most points in the least amount of time.

The people who write the SAT try to eliminate the role of guessing. They do so by subtracting $\frac{1}{4}$ point for each incorrect answer to a multiple-choice question and $\frac{1}{3}$ point for each incorrect answer to a two-column question. (A correct choice scores 1 point.) If you guess at random, you should, on the average, neither gain nor lose points with this system because there is one correct choice and four incorrect choices for each multiple-choice question and one correct choice and three incorrect choices for each item in the two-column format.

No one should have to make a random guess, however, because it is almost always possible to make an informed guess. Nonetheless, when you know nothing about any of the choices, a random guess should not hurt your score very much. People who run intensive preparation courses for the SAT recommend that you guess anytime that you do not know an answer—but first you should make sure that you cannot find the correct choice.

The initial score you obtain (1 point for each correct choice minus a fraction of a point for each incorrect choice) is your *raw score*. The publishers of the SAT then convert your raw score into a number between 200 and 800. Their method of doing so does not necessarily mean that a score of 200 indicates a raw score of 0. Nor does a score of 800 mean that all items were answered correctly. The scores of 200 to 800 are then converted into percentiles, as discussed earlier.

The ACT differs from the SAT in some ways. The formats of the multiple-choice questions and answer sheets are different, for example. And there are no two-column math items. Also, not all ACT questions are multiple-choice. Nothing is deducted from the total point score for an incorrect answer. In general, however, the same methods you would use to prepare for the SAT can also be used for the ACT.

The GED

The General Educational Development Test (GED) for high-school equivalency is a multiple-choice test. Its five sections cover five different areas of the high-school curriculum. You must receive passing scores on all five sections to pass the test. Rules for passing scores have varied from time to time, but the current requirement for mathematics in most states is that you must get 40 of the 50 items correct to pass. (Your state's department of education sets GED standards.) The content of the GED is similar to the SAT. The GED places somewhat more emphasis on arithmetic, but knowledge of both algebra and simple geometry is expected. There are slight differences in the format of the multiple-choice items. For example, choices are assigned numbers instead of letters, and the fifth choice in the mathematics test is almost always "none of these." No points are deducted for incorrect answers.

A peculiarity of the GED is that you can receive passing scores for all five sections and still receive a failing total score. The passing total score in most states is 225, which is 5 points greater than the sum of the passing scores for the individual parts. Therefore, to pass the entire test, you must score at least 41 in each of the sections, or at least 40 in some sections and a total of at least 5 more points in others.

The same kind of review that helps for the SAT and ACT is also useful for the GED. Special courses and publications that apply specifically to the GED are available. When using special GED study materials, check the copyright dates because the test has changed several times in the past.

Now that you know more about the kinds of math tests you will take, you may do better on them. You should also be able to relax more and keep a positive outlook. Fear of math and negative feelings toward the subject are a real problem for many students, as you will find out in the next section.

Beating Math Jitters
(And Other Woes)

Every year a test called the National Assessment of Educational Progress is given to a selected group of students ages nine, thirteen, and seventeen across the United States. The test results are analyzed in many ways. Every five years, the National Assessment deals with mathematics.

The first National Assessment, in 1973, found that seventeen-year-old students disliked mathematics more than any other school subject. Perhaps their dislike stemmed from the fact that they thought math was the most difficult topic in the school curriculum. But mathematics and English tied when the seventeen-year-olds voted on the most important subject. In the second National Assessment of Mathematics, the percentage of seventeen-year-olds who disliked mathematics and who thought it was important did not change, but the percentage who thought it was difficult was considerably lower.

Math Jitters

Given these findings, it is not surprising that many Americans, both young and old, suffer from *math jitters*. People with math jitters shy away from anything that involves mathematics, usually on the grounds that they cannot understand math, or they don't like math, or math is too hard.

Research has shown that math jitters are not related to intelligence. Even many highly successful and intelligent people try to avoid tasks that require mathematics.

As society becomes more complex, however, it becomes more and more difficult to avoid mathematics. For one thing, colleges that stopped requiring math courses are now starting to require them again. They recognize that the ability to think mathematically is a necessity. If you have math jitters, the sooner you overcome them, the better off you'll be.

People who have math jitters fall into two main categories: those who think they cannot do mathematics and those who think there is some reason why they should not do mathematics. Neither group has many valid arguments on their side of the question. Almost everyone, and certainly everyone of normal intelligence, can learn to do mathematics—although it is true that some people need less help than others.

Can women master math?

Women seem to have math jitters more often than men do. This shows up in a number of ways. For example, although the second National Assessment showed that nine-year-old girls were ahead of nine-year-old boys in mathematics knowledge and skills, seventeen-year-old girls were behind boys in every area tested. This may occur because more girls than boys drop mathematics after geometry. But that is not the whole story because, among boys and girls who have taken the same courses, boys still do better than girls.

No one knows for sure why women tend to have trouble with mathematics. Theoretical explanations range from the pressures society puts on women to be wives and mothers to the biological differences between men and women. Fifty or a hundred years ago, many people actually believed that women were not so bright and capable as men, but that idea has been disproved frequently. Here are some of the more current ideas on the subject.

Studies have shown that teachers' attitudes have a strong influence on their students' achievement. In one study, teachers were asked to teach matched classes—that is, classes that were as similar in ability as the researcher could make them. But the teachers were told that the students in one class had below-average ability while those in the other class had above-average ability. At the end of the experiment, the class that had been falsely labeled superior actually performed better on the tests that were administered. This response to a teacher's attitude is called the *Pygmalion effect*.

Some people believe that women's lack of achievement in mathematics is caused by the Pygmalion effect. They think that society conditions teachers to expect lower math performances from girls and higher math performance from boys. As a result, as girls progress through school, they reflect their teachers' expectations and do not achieve so highly as boys. Some studies confirm this theory and some studies refute it, so the matter remains undecided.

Other researchers have looked for biological differences. For example, more men than women tend to be left handed, which suggests that more men are right-brained learners. In right-brained people, spatial intuition is better developed than language ability. Spatial intuition is an important aspect of mathematical ability. Therefore, to some degree at least, men may have more spatial intuition—and more basic math ability—than women. In fact, tests of spatial intuition administered to large numbers of men and women tend to show this difference does exist. Perhaps right-brainedness accounts for male dominance in mathematics. Test evidence also shows that women tend to be better with the left-brained skills in language.

Both algebraic thinkers and geometric thinkers can be good mathematicians. Algebraic thinkers tend to think of math in abstract terms while geometric thinkers tend to approach math through diagrams. (For more about these two ways of thinking, *see* Pt. III, Sec. 1 under "Learning Styles.") The theory that claims men dominate the mathematical professions due to biological differences also states that geometric intuition is more fundamental to mathematics. It is not clear, however, that geometric intuition is really more fundamental than algebraic intuition.

Many educators are trying to remedy the differences between men's and women's mathematics achievement, often with success. Some women have reached the first rank of mathematicians, so we know that women can excel. Emmy Noether (1882–1935) made major contributions in both mathematics and physics. Although she may be best known for a remarkable proof that has become the basis for much of modern physics, her work in mathematics also strongly influenced the way that modern algebra is perceived. She also made great contributions to number theory, the purest and least applied branch of mathematics. Since more and more women have entered the mathematics profession in the past twenty-five years (although still not so many as men), there are probably more Emmy Noethers already working. As time passes, these women will gain recognition.

Math and the minorities

Minority learners also appear to suffer math jitters more than the rest of the population does. The National Assessment found that at all three ages tested, blacks and Hispanics scored lower than the nation as a whole. Furthermore, the ratio of girls to boys in high-school math classes does not begin to drop until second-year algebra. But the number of blacks taking first-year algebra is almost 20 percentage points below the national average.

Despite these problems, the percentage of blacks who dislike mathematics is only slightly greater than the national average at ages nine and seventeen, and equals the national average at age thirteen. Even more encouraging, many more blacks than the national average would like to take more math. Thus, it appears that the problem with minority students is not so much that they fear or dislike mathematics, but that they are not given adequate opportunities to study math. As opportunities increased between the first (1973) and second (1978) National Assessments of Mathematics, scores for blacks and Hispanics did improve. But much more progress is still possible.

The city of Minneapolis has demonstrated what schools can do to improve mathematics opportunities for both women and minorities. In 1976 the school system began a major effort to interest more female and minority students in mathematics and to improve their scores and opportunities. At the beginning of the program, three times more boys than girls were taking calculus in high school. And no blacks were taking calculus, even though 12 percent of the high-school population was black.

Efforts were made to eliminate teaching materials that portrayed mathematics as an activity restricted for the most part to white men and boys. Teachers were trained to improve their attitudes. Successful women scientists and engineers visited the schools to discuss what mathematics had meant to them and to their careers. Black students in junior high were encouraged to take algebra in high school instead of general mathematics, and special help was offered to prepare them for success in algebra. By 1981, the percentage of girls taking calculus had gone up from 25 percent to 43 percent, and the percentage of blacks had risen from 0 percent to 4 percent. The improvement in the number of female and black students taking four years of high-school mathematics is certainly a sign that the program helped these students overcome some traditional obstacles to continued math study.

Objections to Math

"Math is too hard."

Of course, math jitters aren't confined to women and minorities. Many white males reach a point in mathematics at which they declare, "Mathematics is too hard for me. I don't have a mathematical mind." Of course, not everyone has the same amount of mathematical ability. But working on mathematics will improve anyone's skill.

Compare mathematics with other skills that you know—music or drawing, for instance. Some people are clearly better than others, often from a very early age. Yet anyone who is willing to invest the time and effort can learn to play an instrument. And anyone can make an accurate drawing by learning and following certain rules.

The difference is that being unable to play the piano or draw will probably not have a major effect on your ability to hold a job or manage your finances. But if you never learn mathematics, you will have problems in most jobs and will need help handling your money.

There is no secret to learning mathematics. In fact, it is easier for a mathematically untalented person to learn mathematics than it is for a nonmusical person to learn to play an instrument. In mathematics, you do not need to learn a complicated sequence of muscle movements in addition to specific intellectual skills.

The history of mathematics education in the United States clearly shows that more and more mathematics can be taught to more and more students. At one time, mathematics education for most students stopped with arithmetic, and beginning algebra was taught only in colleges attended by the elite. By the end of World War II, the high-school mathematics curriculum included intermediate algebra, but the topics were spread over two years. Most of the topics now in precalculus were taught only in college. Today, calculus is gaining more and more attention during the last year of secondary school.

People's ability to understand mathematics has been present, but school systems did not develop it. Over the long period of increasing mathematics opportunities, the number of youngsters who complete high school has increased immensely. As a result, vast numbers of students who, had they been born a century earlier, would know no mathematics beyond arithmetic, now know at least the basics of higher math.

Mathematics is not necessarily more difficult than other subjects, but it does differ in various ways. For example, math answers are, for the most part, either right or wrong. Mathematics homework and tests can usually be graded with complete objectivity, unlike essays in English or history. As a result, you cannot usually write fuzzy responses to math questions when you don't really know the answers.

You will do better in any school subject if you work at it regularly, but this is especially true for math. It is almost impossible to learn math if you study only off and on. In some cases, math jitters are simply caused by laziness.

"Math isn't necessary."

Sometimes even students who have always done well in math suddenly stop taking math courses and refuse to have anything further to do with the subject. Although they have no reason to believe that they cannot do mathematics, they decide for one reason or another that they do not want to do math.

Some of these people argue that math knowledge is not a cultural necessity. In social situations, people don't expect you to be able to discuss the latest mathematical theory the way you might discuss sports or politics. And, these critics say, unless you are going to use math in your work, anything beyond arithmetic is a waste of effort when there are so many more important and practical things to learn about life.

Such people are mistaken. Science is rapidly and dramatically changing our world. People who hope to survive and prosper must understand these changes. But to understand most of what is happening in science today requires a good mathematics background. Many people, most notably the scientist-novelist C. P. Snow, have argued that scientific knowledge must become a part of every person's culture. Science can be a meaningful part of culture only if mathematics is too.

"It's too late."

Some people feel that they have passed the point where they can learn mathematics. They know that mathematics learning is sequential. So they assume that if they fail at some stage of learning math, they can never catch up. Sometimes these people would like to learn more mathematics, but they think it is impossible.

There are a number of mistakes in this line of reasoning. While it is true that mathematics learning is sequential, more than one sequence is involved. For example, although you need to be able to multiply and subtract to do long division, you do not need to know geometry to do algebra. Thus, if you have had difficulty with one part of mathematics, you are not necessarily blocked from studying another part.

Furthermore, the various branches of mathematics call for different skills and appeal to different interests. Often someone who thinks algebra is boring will find geometry fascinating.

Finally, even if you have missed some important basics of mathematics, you can always backtrack. Information that you found difficult to learn the first time may seem easier the second time. In fact, some mathematical ideas take a long time to understand. Most students, for example, do not become really comfortable with the concepts of elementary algebra until they study them a second time in intermediate algebra.

"Math is boring."

Yet another reason some people offer for not learning math is that math is boring. But perhaps such people just don't know enough about math. In fact, many of the brightest people in the world have had a passionate interest in mathematics.

Blaise Pascal (1623–1662) was a brilliant mathematician. When he was thirty-one, however, he gave up mathematics to devote his time to religion. One day, after four years of ignoring mathematics, Pascal had an excruciating toothache. No matter what he did, he couldn't get his mind off his tooth. Finally, he thought of mathematics. He began working on a problem and got so involved that he forgot about his pain. Clearly, Pascal was using math to get his mind off his troubles. How many boring subjects can do that?

Every year a number of popular books about the most interesting aspects of mathematics are published. You will find a list of good math books in Part VII, and some of these fascinating topics are presented in Part VI of this book. They include math games, puzzles, and paradoxes; a look at strange and interesting numbers; and mathematical relationships that are tricky and intricate—and surprising. Try some of these and see what fun math can be. Once you start really enjoying math, you will have licked math jitters for good.

Calculators: When and How to Use Them

Blaise Pascal built the first workable mechanical calculator in 1642, although it could only add and subtract. A few years later, Gottfried Wilhelm Leibniz (1646–1716) developed a mechanical calculator that could multiply and divide. For several hundred years, businesses and offices used mechanical calculators based on Leibniz's invention.

Then, during World War II, scientists at Bell Laboratories developed a new technology that led to the transistor. Transistor technology, in turn, led to the development of tiny devices called silicon chips. These chips are now commonly used to operate watches, radios, automobiles, and calculators.

The Calculator Revolution

This new technology had a dramatic effect on calculating machines. Within a few years, calculators changed from mechanical machines that were almost as big as typewriters to devices the size of credit cards (and even smaller). At the same time, their cost fell from hundreds of dollars to less than ten dollars for the least expensive models. Carrying a calculator at all times became as easy—and almost as cheap—as carrying a handkerchief.

The new calculators have progressed a long way from Pascal's mechanical adder and subtracter. An inexpensive calculator can usually only add, subtract, multiply, and divide (and maybe find percentages). But slightly more expensive calculators can also take square roots; find factorials, powers, and nth roots; get values of trigonometric functions; call forth both common and natural logarithms; and perform many other scientific, business, and statistical calculations. Another step up in price buys calculators with even more features, including calculators that can be programmed to perform the same string of operations over and over.

A calculator's price tends to reflect the amount of its computing ability. The more need you have for complicated calculations, the more worthwhile it is to purchase an expensive calculator that can perform complex operations.

Calculators cannot solve problems for you, but they can certainly ease the sometimes tedious work of calculation. Adding a long column of numbers, for example, is faster and easier to do on a calculator than on a sheet of paper.

Of course, calculators are not foolproof. You can still get a wrong answer if you press the wrong keys or set up a problem incorrectly. In addition, calculators themselves may make mistakes on certain kinds of computations. On one popular calculator, for example, the result of $2^3 - 8$ is 2×10^{-10}, or 0.0000000002, instead of the correct answer 0. Most such mistakes occur because of the way that a particular calculator rounds. They are usually not harmful, although in a programmable calculator used for long computations, the mistakes can add up and cause serious confusion. Fortunately, newer calculators are programmed so that fewer such mistakes occur.

Calculators have become so helpful and easy to use that you see them everywhere. Many people take calculators to the supermarket, using them to keep track of how much they are spending, to figure out which of two similar products is a better bargain, or to determine the nutritional value of certain foods. Accountants take along handheld calculators when they call on clients. Scientists and engineers carry programmable calculators on field trips. They can then get instant results to long calculations without having to copy the data and wait until they return to the laboratory to compute the results. And, of course, students use calculators to do their homework.

Before the handheld calculator revolution, most homes did not have access to a calculator. But today, nearly every household has at least one. If you have a calculator, use it as you read this section. If you perform the suggested keystrokes, you will find out more about your own calculator and about calculators in general.

How Calculators Work

Every calculator has two visible parts—a *keyboard* and a *display*. The keyboard consists of about fifteen to thirty keys that are used to enter information into the calculator. Ten of the keys are *digit keys* for 0, 1, 2, 3, 4, 5, 6, 7, 8, and 9. Another key or a switch may be used to turn the calculator on and off. When the calculator is turned on, pressing one of the digit keys will cause the digit to appear on the display. If you press another digit key, it will appear following the first digit. On most calculators, once the display is filled (often in eight digits, but perhaps in as many as twelve or fifteen digits on scientific calculators), further pressing of the digit keys will produce no change. You have entered as many digits as the calculator will accommodate.

Each calculator has specific arithmetical functions built into the silicon chips in its interior. These are represented by *operation keys* such as ⊞, ⊟, ⊠, and ⊡. When the proper commands are given in the proper order, the chips will make the calculations and display the correct answer on the screen. It is therefore important for a user to know the sequence of keystrokes to use to tell a given calculator to perform a desired calculation.

The steps that must be taken to perform a calculation vary from calculator to calculator. Therefore, you should always follow the instruction manual on how to operate the calculator you are using.

Calculator logic

There are three basic kinds of calculator logic: *arithmetic, algebraic,* and *reverse Polish.* Algebraic logic can work two different ways, which will be explained below. Arithmetic is pronounced with the accent on *met,* since the word is an adjective.

You can tell which kind of logic your calculator uses by the presence or absence of certain keys. If a calculator uses arithmetic logic, it has both plus and equals on one key and both minus and equals on another. These will be shown here as $\boxed{+=}$ and $\boxed{-=}$.

If a calculator uses either form of algebraic logic, there will be a separate equals key, $\boxed{=}$, and no keys will be marked $\boxed{+=}$ and $\boxed{-=}$. If a calculator uses reverse Polish logic, there will be no equals key of either kind. Check your calculator to see which type of logic it uses.

Arithmetic logic

Arithmetic logic comes from the form of logic that was used in mechanical calculators for business. After inserting a number, the operator would indicate whether it was a credit ($+$) or a debit ($-$). Therefore, to add 17 and 34 on such a calculator, the operator would press 17$\boxed{+=}$ 34$\boxed{+=}$. To subtract 21 from 83, the operator would press 83$\boxed{+=}$ 21$\boxed{-=}$, although the same result could be obtained by pressing 21$\boxed{-=}$ 83 $\boxed{+=}$. This is a handy system to use in most business situations, but it is awkward for other uses.

Some arithmetic-logic calculators also have a separate equals key for multiplication and division, $\boxed{=}$, while others use the $\boxed{+=}$ key for those operations. Either method is likely to cause confusion. In the first case, you have to remember which equals key to use for which operation. In the second case, you have to remember when to press $\boxed{+=}$ and when not to. For example, if a problem requires both multiplication and addition, two different situations can occur. In one case, you add first and then multiply the sum by the third number, for example $(5 + 3) \times 2$. In the other case, you multiply first and then add the third number to the product, as in $(5 \times 3) + 2$. To find $(5 + 3) \times 2$, you enter both numbers to be added with the $\boxed{+=}$ key, then indicate multiplication with the $\boxed{\times}$ key, then enter the 2 with the $\boxed{+=}$ key:

$$5 \boxed{+=} 3 \boxed{+=} \boxed{\times} 2 \boxed{+=}$$

On the other hand, to multiply first, you do not need to use the ⬚+=⬚ key to enter the first digit, since it can be entered with the ⬚×⬚ key. Therefore, the usual way to perform (5 × 3) + 2 would be

5 ⬚×⬚ 3 ⬚+=⬚ 2 ⬚+=⬚

although you get the same answer by pressing

5 ⬚+=⬚ ⬚×⬚ 3 ⬚+=⬚ 2 ⬚+=⬚

Mathematics teachers discourage their students from using calculators with arithmetic logic. The sequence of operations is too different from standard mathematics and few arithmetic-logic calculators are characteristically equipped only with addition, subtraction, multiplication, and division functions.

Algebraic logic

In the more basic of the two forms of algebraic logic, the operator has to take care of the order of operations, while in the *algebraic operating system,* the calculator is programmed to multiply and divide automatically before adding and subtracting. If you have a calculator with just one equals key (that is, no ⬚+=⬚), it will have one of these logic systems built into it. The way to tell which you have is to see what solution you get to pressing 5 ⬚+⬚ 3 ⬚×⬚ 2 ⬚=⬚ , or some similar expression. With simple algebraic logic the result will be 16, but with an algebraic operating system the result will be 11.

Simple algebraic logic is the most common form found in handheld calculators, especially in lower-priced models. Most people find simple algebraic logic natural to use because it roughly corresponds to the way that paper-and-pencil calculations are made. For more extensive calculator use, the algebraic operating system has some advantages in ease of entry. With both kinds of algebraic-logic calculators, as with all calculators, you must very carefully think through complex computations to make sure that your calculator performs the operation you have in mind.

Algebraic calculators of both kinds sometimes have keys for parentheses, which allows you to indicate the order of operations when you are not sure which order the calculator would follow. This discussion will center on simple algebraic logic, which is more commonly used, with a few remarks at the end about the algebraic operating system.

In algebraic logic (without parentheses), the numbers are usually entered by pressing operation keys. The result is immediately displayed, so that if you press 5 ⊞ 3 ⊞ , the display will show 8. You do not have to press ⊟ . To avoid error, however, it is a good idea to get in the habit of always pressing ⊟ rather than the final operational sign when you complete a computation. For example, if you use operation signs to enter each number and then press ⊟ , you may get a wrong answer: 5 ⊞ 3 ⊞⊟ may result in displays of 8, 11, 16, or no answer, depending on your calculator. On the other hand, if you forget to press ⊟ , pressing only 5 ⊞ 3, the answer will not be displayed at all; you will still see a 3. The correct procedure is to use 5 ⊞ 3 ⊟ . But when you are performing a long series of calculations, it is nice to be able to check at each stage that the right numbers have been pressed without having to press the ⊟ .

As you are going through a calculation that involves different operations, say (3 × 8) ÷ 6, the number you see on the display when you press the second operation key will be the result of the first operation; that is, after you press 3⊠8⊞, the display will show 24. The operation key at this point acts merely to enter the number, keeping in memory that the next number entered will be a divisor.

A calculator with an algebraic operating system will not always display the same intermediate computations that a calculator with simple algebraic logic will. For example, to compute 5 + 3 × 4 on a calculator with simple algebraic logic, either you must use parentheses:

5 [+] [( ] [3] [×] [4] [ )] [=]

Or, if parentheses are not available on your calculator, you must reverse the problem:

3 [×] [4] [+] [5] [=]

In the first case (with parentheses), the display will show the following sequence as you press each key: 5 5 5 3 3 4 12 17. You see the result of 3 × 4 as an interim step. In the second case, the displays will be 3 3 4 12 5 17, so you also see the 12 along the way. To get the answer using the algebraic operating system, however, you can simply press

5 [+] [3] [×] [4] [=]

But the display will show only 5 5 3 3 4 17, concealing the interim results.

Reverse Polish logic

Perhaps a more accurately descriptive name for reverse Polish logic would be parentheses-free logic. But this form of logic gets its name from its developer.

In the 1920s, the Polish mathematician Jan Lukasiewicz developed a parentheses-free system for writing statements in symbolic logic. The key to Lukasiewicz's system was to start by listing connections between statements. (In logic you work with statements instead of numbers). The connections are listed first, and then the statements themselves are listed. When the list is ordered correctly, parentheses are not needed. This greatly simplified the usual systems of reading and writing logic in use at that time.

Using the Lukasiewicz notation for logic is rather like saying "Loves John Mary" to mean "John loves Mary." This system is usually called *Polish notation* because Lukasiewicz and a number of other logicians in Poland developed and used it, and because people had trouble pronouncing *Lukasiewicz*.

Because keeping track of parentheses is also a problem with calculators, the system was modified for calculator use. On calculators, you first enter numbers and then indicate which operations to perform. This is the reverse of the way that Polish notation works. Hence, a calculator that functions in this way is said to use reverse Polish logic, or reverse Polish notation.

For reverse-Polish-logic calculators, to add 2 + 3, you enter 2, then 3, then ⊞ . To enter the 3, you have to press a special enter key, ENT , so that the calculator will know that 2 and 3 are two separate numbers, not 23. Therefore, the whole operation would be shown as

For a more complicated problem, the order of operations at the end tells the calculator what to do. For example, 5 × (3 + 4) would be shown as

The last operation key you press indicates the main operation, the one that dominates the numerical expression. If you use parentheses, and are calculating with paper and pencil or in your head, first you must add 3 and 4, then multiply that sum by 5. The reverse-Polish calculator does the same thing in the same order, but the operation seems odd because it is not usu-

ally written down in that way. Similarly, to calculate 5 + (3 ×
4), you would press

5 [ENT] 3 [ENT] 4 [×] [+]

Of course, the main operation does not always occur first.
To indicate that the main operation does not occur first, you
press an operation key between two numbers. Thus, some operations may be indicated before all numbers have been entered. For example, to calculate (5 + 3) × 4, you would press

5 [ENT] 3 [+] 4 [×]

Note the main operation is still the last information entered.
    While reverse Polish logic seems strange at first, it is amaz-
ingly easy to get used to. In fact, mathematics educators believe that in the long run, reverse-Polish-logic calculators are
the best for teaching purposes. For one thing, such calculators
are extremely flexible and efficient. But also, more than other
systems, they force students to think about the meaning of
mathematics operations. As a result, students make fewer errors in complex calculations.

Calculator memories

Despite the advantages of reverse Polish notation, the simple
form of algebraic notation is the most common. Therefore, to
avoid confusion and showing every calculation three times, algebraic notation will be used in this discussion. If your calculator uses arithmetic or reverse Polish logic, consult your
user's manual to see how to make the appropriate adjustments.
    Generalizing about how all calculators work is impossible
because most calculators have a *memory* feature, and the
memory feature works slightly differently in different kinds of
calculators. Since the memory is a great help in making calculations, some sample operations with memory on two different
kinds of algebraic-logic calculators appear here. Your calculator is probably like one of these, although it may vary slightly.
    The basic idea of all calculator memories is the same.
When you are performing a long series of calculations, you
may want to have the results of some intermediate calculations
available in addition to the final result. Suppose, for example,
that you are determining the cost of a repair job. You need the
cost of the parts, the cost of the labor, the total of these two,
the sales tax, and the final total for the entire job. By using the

memory keys you can obtain all of the subtotals as well as the total cost. If you do not use memory, some of the subtotals will not appear separately on the display.

Most calculators have at least a key that clears the memory, a key that recalls the memory (which may be combined with the clear key), a key for adding a number into memory, and a key for subtracting a number from memory. These last two keys are usually designated as M+ and M-. Some calculators have other features, such as a key that enters a number directly into memory and replaces anything that was there before. The labels on such keys may vary. In addition to M+ and M-, this discussion will use CM for the key that clears the memory and RM for the key that recalls the memory.

Assume that you are an auto mechanic calculating the cost of repairing a car. You have installed parts that cost the customer $50, $15, and $34.95, you worked 3 hours at your standard rate $24 an hour, and the sales tax in your locality is 6%. To calculate this on one kind of calculator, you would begin by pressing

$$50 \boxed{+} 15 \boxed{+} 34.95 \boxed{M+}$$

The display would read 99.95, the cost of the parts. Then you would press

$$24 \boxed{\times} 3 \boxed{M+}$$

And the display would read 72, the cost of the labor. Next you would enter

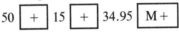

And the display would read 10.317, the sales tax (not rounded). Finally you would press

$$\boxed{RM}$$

And the display would read 182.267, the total cost. In the third step, when you pushed RM for the first time, the cost before sales tax (171.95) would appear.

On another calculator, the basic process would be the same, but variations might include having to push the equals key, =, before anything but the last number entered would go into memory. If that is the case, you would get the same results as above by pressing

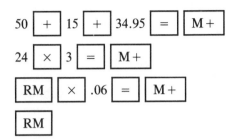

You should always be careful to clear the memory before starting any memory calculation.

In addition to the memory keys, all calculators have a form of pseudomemory called the *constant operation*. This means that when two numbers are entered into the calculator, one of them stays in the memory as a constant. If you continually press the equals key, the number in the display will be operated upon by the constant number and the last operation entered. Thus, on some calculators, if you enter

5 ☐×☐ 3 ☐=☐ ☐=☐ ☐=☐ ☐=☐

You will get subsequent displays of 15, 75, 375, and 1875.

Sometimes such a key is called an *accumulator key*. Use of an accumulator key is very helpful when you need to make a series of calculations in which you add, subtract, multiply, or divide the same number over and over. (Calculators that use algebraic logic will not hold minuends or dividends constant. Other calculators may vary in this regard. The instructions that come with your calculator should tell which numbers can be held constant, but if they don't, you can find out with a little experimentation.)

The constant operation is also extremely useful in computing powers on calculators that do not have a special key for that purpose. For example, to find the tenth power of 2, you merely need enter 2 ☐×☐ and press the equals key ten times.

If you want to hold an addend as a constant, some calculators will keep the second number entered in their pseudomemory. Thus to find 23 + 5, 23 + 8, and 23 + 13, you would enter

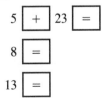

The display will show 28 when you press ☐ the first time, 31 when you press ☐ the second time, and 36 when you press ☐ the last time.

For subtraction, the subtrahend is held constant, so the same procedure would be followed. But in multiplication, it is the first factor that is held constant in the pseudomemory. Thus, to multiply 23 × 5, 23 × 8, and 23 × 13, you would enter

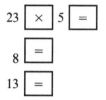

And the display would show the products 115, 184, and 299.

With division, the divisor is held constant, so division follows the same pattern as addition and subtraction. It is only in multiplication that the first number entered is retained.

Programmable calculators

More advanced calculators can be programmed to perform long, complex computations. For example, they are especially handy for computing the results of formulas and graphing. As a result, scientists, engineers, and accountants find programmable calculators extremely useful.

Because programmable calculators are intended to handle complicated algebraic and arithmetic expressions, most use either the algebraic operating system or reverse Polish logic. They also have numerous special mathematical functions (which may also be found on the more advanced nonprogrammable calculators), including the trigonometric functions, conversions from one coordinate system or system of measure to another, powers and roots, logarithms, and factorials. This discussion deals only with the programmable function of such calculators, however, not their full range of capabilities.

The key to programming a calculator is memory. A nonprogrammable calculator may have one memory location and a pseudomemory. The memory location holds only a single number, while the pseudomemory holds a single number and an operation. In contrast, a typical programmable calculator has forty-eight memory locations. The locations can hold a number, an operation, or a programming instruction. Furthermore, it is possible to partition these memory locations into several different memories—although the partitioned memories cannot hold so many numbers, operations, or programming instructions as the memory does before it is separated.

With a partitioned memory, you can load a number into one memory location and call it up when needed while other numbers or parts of the program are in other locations. Also, you can load a small program, called a *subroutine,* into one of the parts of memory and the main program into another part. Then the subroutine can be called from the main program several times. In effect, this increases the number of steps the program can do from forty-eight to perhaps an infinite number. Although there are still only forty-eight different steps, each is used over and over again.

Programs involving many steps that are repetitions of earlier steps are built around *loops.* Loops usually involve the decision-making instructions built into the calculator. For example, there are keys for such decisions as "Is x equal to some number?" or "Is x greater than some number?" If the answer is no, the calculator proceeds to the next step in the program. If the answer is yes, the calculator can be told to do something other than proceed to the next step.

In a loop, if the answer is no, the next step tells the calculator to return to an earlier step and start again. This is the loop. (There is actually more flexibility than this. The calculator could also be told to proceed to the next step if the answer is yes and to enter the loop if the answer is no.) Other loops can be constructed by telling the calculator to repeat the operation for the next larger number or the next even number or the next multiple of some number, then return to an earlier part of the program and do it again.

Now to the actual programming: first you tell the calculator that you are going to write a program, not make a calculation. There is a key that puts it into the program (or learn) mode. Before you can write a program, you must have a clear idea of what the program is going to do. For example, if you want the program to calculate the values you could use in drawing a graph of an equation, you need to tell the calculator what the equation is and store that information in one part of the memory. Then you need to tell the calculator to show you the value you put into the equation, followed by the value of the equation. Next you would tell the calculator to add some number to the value being put into the equation, loop back, and do it again. Often a flow chart is used to indicate the steps.

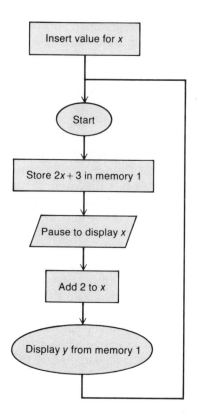

The flow chart describes a program that will calculate the coordinates, *(x,y),* of the equation $y = 2x + 3$ for every other integral value of x that is higher than the one you select to start with. (It may be easier to use every other value so that the points on the graph are not so close. If you wanted every integral value, you would add 1, not 2, to x each time.) To put this program into the calculator, you need to follow the same sequence as the flow chart.

1. Turn the calculator on and partition the memory into two parts.
2. Enter the learning mode and clear any previous programs.
3. Enter the expression $2x + 3 = y$ by letting x be the number in memory 0—the two partitions of the memory in this case are called 0 and 1—and then telling it to calculate 2 times the value in memory 0 and add 3.
4. Store the value from the previous step in memory 1.
5. Call up the value from memory 0 and display it. This is the x coordinate.
6. Add 2 to the value in memory 0.

7. Call up the value from memory 1 and display it. This is the y coordinate.
8. Tell the calculator to go back to the beginning of the program and run it again. (This involves pressing only one key because programs are frequently rerun.)
9. Exit the learning mode.

Of course, this is a lot of work for a simple equation such as $2x + 3 = y$, but it is not much more work to calculate a long equation involving several powers of x. (You have to change only step 3.)

To run the program, you start by storing some value of x in memory 0. Each time you push the run key, the program will display first the x coordinate, then the y coordinate for a value on the graph, moving the x coordinates up in intervals of 2. If you wanted to graph the equation from -10 to 10, you would begin by storing -10 in memory 0. Then, as you repeatedly pressed the run key, you would see this displayed.

RUN	-10
	-17
RUN	-8
	-13
RUN	-6
	-9
RUN	-4
	-5
RUN	-2
	-1
RUN	0
	3
RUN	2
	7
RUN	4
	11
RUN	6
	15
RUN	8
	19
RUN	10
	23

A programmable calculator may not be necessary for everyone. But it is an enormous timesaver for people who make extensive calculations.

Calculators in the Classroom

Although some mathematics teachers and many parents initially believed that calculators did not belong in the classroom, experience has proven otherwise. Calculators have not only turned out to be useful in teaching problem solving without the distraction of making computations by hand, but they have also proved helpful in teaching basic operations.

Young children like calculators. They enjoy pressing the keys and seeing the results on the display. This enjoyment can be used to good advantage. Schools often have a set of inexpensive calculators for use in teaching basic operations. School-owned calculators serve an important purpose. When young children are first learning to use a calculator, all must have the same model. Otherwise, the teacher's instructions would become too varied, time consuming, and confusing.

The accumulator key is often used to teach addition, subtraction, multiplication, division, and exponents. For example, first graders may be taught the counting-on strategy by accumulating ones. To add 3 to 8, they would be told to press 8, press $+$, press 1, and press $=$ three times. A similar approach may be used to teach the counting-back strategy for subtraction. To subtract 2 from 9, press 9, press $-$, press 1, and press $=$ two times. Counting by twos, fives, or some other number can be easily done with the accumulator key. To count by fives, press 5, press $+$, and press $=$ repeatedly. Since counting by a particular number is a good start toward multiplication, the accumulator key can be used to introduce that skill too. Older children can use the same idea for exponents, but instead of pressing $+$, they press $\times$.

Older children may also use calculators to learn properties of decimals. For example, multiplying a number by 0.2, 0.20, 0.200, and so forth produces the same answer on the calculator, making it clear that these different decimals are forms of the same number. Similarly, since the calculator places the decimal point correctly in multiplication and division, students can try to predict where the decimal point will be for specific problems, then put the calculator to work to find out if they were right. In that way, the children soon discover the rules for themselves.

By treating these operations as experiments or games, teachers can often encourage students to discover for themselves certain facts about numbers. At the same time, the youngsters get a strong introduction to how calculators work.

For example, children can use calculators to play games against one another. The teacher can choose a large number (depending on the age of the students) and have the children take turns adding specific numbers until they reach the designated number. The first child to reach the chosen number wins. (This includes an element of strategy too.) For example, very young children can race to 10 using only the numbers 0, 1, 2, and 3 as addends. Taking turns on the same calculator, each child gets to enter one of the allowable addends and ⊞. The first one to hit exactly 10 wins.

As children get older, the designated total numbers and addends can be increased. As the race goes on, the children learn the addition facts and think about their own and their opponents' strategies. Children who are learning factoring can play the same game with multiplication. The race might be to 36 with numbers less than 6. Any child who enters a number that is not a factor of 36 will be out. The one who reaches 36 first will win. By changing numbers, such games can be played over and over with continued enjoyment and considerable new learning.

Specific calculator skills can also be taught from the middle grades of elementary school on through college. For example, teachers can show their students how to minimize the number of keystrokes they use to solve a problem. This is an important skill because the fewer times you press a key, the fewer chances there are to make an error.

For example, in solving two-step problems that involve multiplication and addition, each of several terms must often be both added and multiplied by a constant number. Consider a problem in which several people earn the same hourly wage but put in different numbers of hours. There are two approaches to finding the total salary on the calculator. You can multiply each number of hours by the wage per hour, then add the products. Or you can add the number of hours, then multiply the sum by the wage per hour. The second method takes fewer keystrokes, even if the calculator has a memory that can be used to accumulate the products. If the calculator does not have a memory, the second method is even more desirable. Such instruction not only improves students' calculator skills, but also teaches an important property of mathematics, the distributive property.

Students can also learn much about decimals and percentages by using a calculator. Something as simple as noticing that one does not have to enter the zeros at the end of a decimal reinforces what decimals really mean.

Students can be taught to calculate percentages of increase and decrease by first adding to or subtracting from 100%, as appropriate. For example, to compute the cost of a $15 shirt after a 20% discount, the students can learn to press .8 ⊠ 15 to get the answer, instead of pressing .20 ⊠ 15, remembering or writing down the answer (3) and then pressing 15 ⊟ 3. This way of working with a percentage of decrease not only improves students' calculator skills but increases their understanding of percentages.

Calculators can also help to teach factoring. The surest way to factor a number is to divide by each prime up to the square root of the number. If you use the calculator to divide by 2, the smallest prime, until you get a dividend that is not a whole number, then divide by 3 until the dividend is not whole, and so on—up to the square root of the number—you can factor any number. The divisors that give whole-number dividends are the factors. In addition to teaching factoring, this practices the sequence of primes and shows that you can stop dividing when you reach the square root. Factoring in this way also teaches how to use the square-root key on the calculator.

Calculators at Home

Students who use calculators to do their homework may teach themselves some important mathematical concepts along the way. Students who do not use calculators may make too many unnecessary errors in computation. When the answer shown on the calculator display does not match the answer in the back of the book or given out in class, for example, the student may learn how to reconcile the two answers. In the process, the student gains a better understanding of the mathematical concepts involved—plus how to operate the calculator to maximum advantage.

Fractions, for example, do not occur on calculators. But calculators can still be used to solve problems involving fractions. One approach to solving fraction problems on a calculator is to use decimal equivalents. A decimal equivalent can be found by dividing the numerator of a fraction by the denominator. With this technique, a student soon learns the decimal equivalents for many common fractions.

Using a calculator can also teach students which fractions convert to decimals that terminate. For example, these fractions include halves (.5), fourths (.25), eighths (.125), tenths

(.1), sixteenths (.0625), twentieths (.05), and twenty-fifths (.04). The calculator can also show which decimals do not terminate. On most calculators, $\frac{1}{3}$ will be displayed as 0.3333333, while $\frac{2}{3}$ will be shown as 0.6666666. Calculations that involve those fractions will have small errors that must be eliminated before conversion from decimals back into the fraction form expected for the answer. (*See* Pt. IV, Sec. 3, "Fractional Numbers," for more discussion on how to do these conversions.)

You may realize that 0.6666666 is not the best approximation for $\frac{2}{3}$ to seven decimal places. The best approximation is 0.6666667. The first, unrounded approximation, however, is the one that will be given on most inexpensive calculators and even on some more expensive ones. All calculators that show 0.6666666 as the result of dividing 2 by 3 have at most eight decimal places in their displays. Such calculators do not have a check digit (not shown on the display) that tells them how to round, so the last calculated digit is the last one shown.

More complex calculators, especially those developed for scientific purposes, have more decimal places in their memories than are shown on the display. For example, a programmable calculator may work with eleven decimal places, even though only eight are shown. Thus, for a long series of calculations involving several decimals, the answer will probably be more accurate to the eight places shown. On such a calculator, the first digit not shown is used to round the final answer, so 2 divided by 3 is shown as 0.6666667.

The best way to cope with rounding problems on calculators is to adjust calculations so that the answer is the only number that the calculator rounds. This requires an understanding of the properties of fractions, which can be gained in class and in review.

You have seen that using a calculator for homework can be an important learning experience. But unthinking use of a calculator for simple drills is not desirable. Children, for example, can learn very little by doing a page of easy, whole-number addition or subtraction problems on a calculator.

In the later grades and in science courses, calculators become quite appropriate for homework—even essential. Again, the calculator does more for the student than merely find the answer. A student may be able to learn scientific notation from more complex calculators that use scientific notation in their displays. For example, a complex calculator may display the product of 12,345 times 67,890 like this:

$8.3810\ 08_{\times 10}$

or this:

$8.3810205\ _{08}$

Simpler calculators cannot deal with numbers this large. But on more complex calculators, the student would interpret such displays as scientific notation.

In each example, 08 means that the number shown at the left is to be multiplied by 10 raised to the eighth power. The number of decimal places in the number at the left indicates the precision with which the answer is reported. As students learn to interpret this notation—often called *floating-point notation*—on a calculator, they also learn scientific notation. Calculators that use floating-point systems also permit users to enter numbers in scientific notation, so students can practice both reading and writing it.

Students of second-year algebra or trigonometry used to spend much homework time looking up values for logarithms or trigonometric functions in tables in their textbooks. New textbooks omit the tables. Teachers of trigonometry (and some other mathematics courses) assume that students will use calculators to find the values that they need. Furthermore, calculators give values to more decimal places than did the tables in the textbooks, which makes their use even more beneficial.

The use of calculators instead of tables frees students from time-consuming operations that do not contribute to learning basic course content. Furthermore, people who later in life use trigonometry, logarithms, or statistics on a regular basis use calculators rather than tables.

Despite parents' and teachers' initial fears, the calculator has proved to be a helpful learning tool for students. Another helpful and increasingly important learning tool—the computer—is discussed in the next section.

Section 5

The Computer—A Modern Learning Tool

The inventions and ideas of many mathematicians and scientists led to the development of the computer. Today, computers can handle vast amounts of facts and figures and solve complicated problems at incredibly high speeds. The fastest computers are able to process millions of pieces of information in seconds.

Computers are used in many walks of life: business and industry; government and law enforcement; the military; engineering; the sciences; the fine arts; manufacturing; sales; and service and repair. They are also used in schools. In fact, computers were being used in schools even before the arrival of handheld calculators. And the educational use of computers rises at an amazing rate each year. A growing number of schools from elementary through college level use computers as a teaching aid, and the performance of many students has improved as a result.

While the day when every student or even every classroom will have a computer will not arrive soon, the possibility of that happening is not farfetched. Certainly, if present trends continue, it will not be long before every school has at least one computer of some kind. The possible uses of computers are so varied, and they are becoming so essential both to schools and to society, that their widespread acceptance is probably assured.

Computer Terms

Bit, which comes from the term *binary* digit, is the basic unit of information in a digital computing system. It may be either the digit 0 or 1.

Byte is a unit of eight bits in a computer memory.

Central Processing Unit, or CPU, is the section of a digital computer that manipulates data according to a set of stored instructions.

Data Base is a collection of information stored in a computer. The data are recorded on a magnetic disk unit or other direct-access storage device.

Hardware refers to the physical parts, such as the electronic, magnetic, and mechanical devices, that make up a computer system.

Interface is any input or output device. An interface serves as a communication link between a computer and its human operator or a machine controlled by the computer.

Logic Circuit is an electronic circuit that enables a digital computer to compare, select, and perform other logic operations.

Microprocessor is a miniature electronic device consisting of thousands of transistors and related circuitry on a silicon chip. The device is often called a "computer on a chip" because it has all the elements of a central processing unit.

Network is a system consisting of two or more computers connected by high-speed communication lines.

Program is a set of instructions to be carried out by a computer to solve a problem.

Simulation is the representation or imitation of a particular situation, operation, or system by a computer. The purpose is to predict and analyze what is likely to occur under various conditions.

Software refers to the programs used by a computer to perform a desired task.

Terminal is any device connected to a computer for remote input or output of data.

Early Uses in Schools

Computers have been in the schools for a long time. They were first used in the business offices of large school systems, primarily for financial and other records. Many schools did not actually own a computer but merely rented time on one for data processing (handling records). This practice is called *time sharing*. Computers were extremely large and expensive when schools first started using them, so they couldn't possibly be put in classrooms and only the largest school systems could afford access to them.

As computers became smaller and cheaper, more and more school systems were able to buy their own. Colleges and universities led the way. In fact, colleges and universities had the first scientific computers ever built. They were government-financed machines built toward the end of World War II to help in the war effort.

Once colleges owned computers, they began to look for new ways to use them. One of the first new uses was for scheduling classes. Scheduling turned out to be an ideal job for computers, and most colleges use computer scheduling to this day. When grade- and high-school systems began to acquire their own computers, they borrowed class-scheduling techniques from the colleges.

In the 1960s, as computers began to be used more and more by businesses as well as by schools and the federal government, mathematician Patrick Suppes began work to adapt the computer to a new task. He believed that computers could be programmed to teach children skills in such school subjects as English and mathematics. By the late 1960s and early 1970s, large corporations began to build on Suppes's experimental work. Such companies as RCA, Westinghouse, and Harcourt Brace Jovanovich set out to develop teaching materials that students could use on the terminals of large computers. They called this approach to learning *computer-assisted instruction* (CAI). CAI was extremely expensive. Not only was programming costly and time consuming, but the cost of terminals was especially high. Even though computer time was becoming less expensive and a large computer could handle hundreds of terminals, most schools could not afford to buy terminals in the first place.

So the educational programs developed at that time were eventually shut down or converted to other activities. Cost was the main problem. But another problem was that most CAI programs assumed that the best use of computers was for drill and practice. Schools might have been willing to spend more money on CAI programs if they had gone beyond drill and practice.

Another school use for computers was also promoted in the early 1970s. The record-keeping abilities of computers had proven to be a great advantage to financial offices. So, reasoned some, why not give the same record-keeping ability to teachers? The idea was that a teacher who had access to all the information that could be gathered about each student's work could tailor-make individual educational programs. This approach was termed *computer-managed instruction* (CMI).

Unfortunately, no one anticipated how difficult this process would be. A computer must be fed information before it can process it. Feeding the computer became a time-consuming task for teachers. Furthermore, a properly fed (and programmed) computer produced more information than any teacher could possibly use. CMI, while helpful in some instances, proved too unwieldy to become very popular.

By the mid-1970s, it was beginning to look as if the computer had been just another educational fad. Around that time, however, a little-noticed revolution was beginning. Chips, similar to the ones that control handheld calculators, had become quite cheap and readily available. As a result, a few pioneers recognized that, using these chips, they could build small computers for individual use. Companies began to market relatively primitive small computers for hobbyists. If any of these early "home" computers found their way into the schools, it was probably in their electrical shops.

Increases in the power and reductions in the cost of chips continued at a dizzying pace. By 1977, people began to predict that small, affordable computers would soon be available for business and home use. This prediction came true.

As more companies entered the field of producing small, inexpensive computers, schools became an obvious sales target. A few schools purchased the early models. There were not yet many educational programs for these computers, and teachers were wary of them. But it was clear from the beginning that children and computers got along very well.

Computer Literacy

Most people have only vague ideas about the nature of computers. So schools everywhere are promoting *computer literacy* campaigns to help people learn more about computers. The exact goals of computer-literacy programs vary from school to school. Some computer-literacy courses teach how to write programs for computers. Others focus on explaining the role of computers in society and the history of computer development. Some analyze the internal workings of computers, while others examine the information that computers produce. The only thing that all computer educators agree on is that computer literacy is crucial.

In most schools, computer literacy has become the responsibility of the mathematics department. Although math teachers do not necessarily know more about computers than other teachers, it is assumed that people who are comfortable with math will also be comfortable with computers. Furthermore, many well-known uses of computers involve mathematics. Finally, since schools are usually reluctant to start new departments, computer-literacy programs had to be added to an existing department. The most common choice was the math department.

Because there is so much debate about the true meaning of computer literacy, this section of *Math Power* will present a broad overview. You will learn a little bit about the different kinds of computers and how they work. You will also look at how computers are being used in schools today.

Inside Computers

Computers are frequently divided into two groups according to the jobs they perform. These groups are *general-purpose computers* and *special-purpose computers*. A general-purpose computer can handle many kinds of jobs and is not restricted to any particular user. For example, it can be used as effectively by hospitals and libraries as by banks and stores. On the other hand, a special-purpose computer is designed to do one specific job for a particular user. An example is a navigational computer on an airplane. It can be used only to guide a plane.

Computers differ in the way they work as well as in what they can do. On this basis, they can be classified into three general types: (1) digital computers, (2) analog computers, and (3) hybrid computers. Digital computers are by far the most common type.

Digital computers

Digital computers solve problems and do other tasks by counting, comparing, and rearranging digits in the arithmetic/logic unit. All the data, whether in the form of numbers, letters, or symbols, are represented by digits.

Digital computers use the digits of the *binary numeration system*. Unlike the familiar decimal number system, which uses 10 digits, the binary system uses only two digits: 0 and 1. These binary digits, called *bits,* can be easily represented by the thousands of tiny electronic circuits of a digital computer. The circuits operate much like an ordinary electric switch. When the switch is off, it corresponds to the binary digit 0. When on, it corresponds to the digit 1 (*see* diagram p. 186).

An electronic digital computer is able to perform all the basic arithmetic operations because binary digits, like decimal numbers, can be added, subtracted, multiplied, and divided. To solve a problem, it does the operations automatically one by one according to the program stored in its memory.

Most digital computers are general-purpose computers. They can be programmed to handle all sorts of complicated, multistep tasks. These computers are so widely used that the word *computer* often means a general-purpose digital computer.

Analog computers

Analog computers work directly with a physical quantity, such as weight, voltage, or speed, rather than with digits that represent the quantity. The computers solve problems by measuring the quantity in terms of another quantity. In a problem involving water pressure and water flow, for example, electrical voltage might serve as an *analogue* (likeness) for the water pressure, and electric current for the water flow. Many familiar devices, including speedometers, thermometers, and thermostats, operate on the same basic principle as analog computers. For example, a thermometer measures temperature in terms of the length of a thin line of liquid in a tube. An analog computer presents output data in a continuous form, often as a position on a scale. In some cases, the data are displayed as electrical signals on an instrument called an *oscilloscope*.

Analog computers are not so accurate as digital computers mainly because they work with continuous, varying quantities that cannot be measured exactly. However, they can solve certain types of problems faster than digital computers. Analog computers also may be more convenient to use. They do not require the preparation of detailed programs. An operator "tells" an analog computer how to solve a problem by simply connecting its electronic circuits or mechanical parts in a particular way.

Most analog computers are special-purpose computers. They solve engineering and scientific problems that can be described as systems of *differential equations*. These mathematical equations are expressions of natural laws that describe the rates of change of quantities. Electronic analog computers are especially well suited for designing and analyzing electrical networks. They also control *simulators* for airplanes, space vehicles, and oceangoing ships. These simulators reproduce the conditions under which such craft must operate. They are used either to check the performance of a craft or to train its crew in operating procedures.

Hybrid computers

Hybrid computers combine the features of analog and digital computers. They are as fast as analog computers and as accurate as digital computers.

A typical hybrid computer has many of the same kinds of parts as an analog computer. But like a digital computer, it processes data by manipulating digits. It has a device called an *analog-to-digital converter,* which changes input data in the form of analog quantities into binary digits. A hybrid computer also has a *digital-to-analog converter,* which changes digitally computed data back to an analog quantity. This conversion makes the processed data easier to interpret.

Hybrid computers are basically special-purpose computers. They are used chiefly in simulation projects and in *feedback systems* for automated equipment.

Parts of a Digital Computer

Digital computers vary widely in size. The size of a computer partly determines the jobs it can do. However, the performance of smaller computers is not necessarily limited. For example, a *microcomputer* is a small computer system that can range from desk-top size to pocket size. Microcomputers are widely used as "home" computers, but even the pocket-size models can translate thousands of words from one language into another. The *minicomputer* is a larger computer with higher performance. Minicomputers can handle all the data-processing needs of community libraries and many business firms. The largest computer, the *mainframe,* can fill a huge room. Mainframes can control a telephone switching network or serve as a data base for a major government agency.

Although digital computers differ greatly in size, they all have five basic parts. These parts consist of (1) the input equipment, (2) the main memory, (3) the control unit, (4) the arithmetic/logic unit, and (5) the output equipment.

In a mainframe, the main memory, control unit, and arithmetic/logic unit form a single unit called the *central processing unit* (CPU). Some mainframes have more than one CPU, which allows a number of operations to be performed at one time. At the other extreme, a microcomputer has a single CPU made up of one *large-scale integrated circuit* (LSI). This miniature electronic device, commonly called a *microprocessor,* contains thousands of transistors and other circuitry but is so small that it can fit in the palm of the hand.

Digital Computers and the Binary Number System

All data handled by digital computers, including words, are in the form of digits. But the computers use only the two digits of the binary number system—that is, 0 and 1. Different combinations of 0's and 1's represent letters and the various decimal numerals. The binary system is well suited for digital computers because their circuits have only two possible states and operate much like an ordinary light switch. When the switch is off, it corresponds to 0. When the switch is on, it stands for 1. The illustration shows how different combinations of the binary digits represent the decimal numerals 1 through 4.

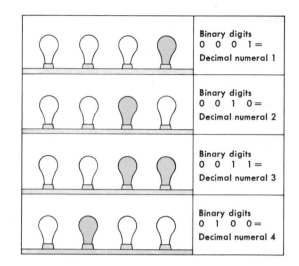

	Binary digits 0 0 0 1 = Decimal numeral 1
	Binary digits 0 0 1 0 = Decimal numeral 2
	Binary digits 0 0 1 1 = Decimal numeral 3
	Binary digits 0 1 0 0 = Decimal numeral 4

Input and output equipment functions as an *interface* between the CPU and the user—that is, it enables the machine and the human operator to communicate efficiently with each other. Such equipment, known as *peripheral equipment,* may be connected with a CPU or work independently of it. If the peripheral equipment is connected with a CPU, it is said to be *on-line*. If the equipment operates independently, it is *off-line*. Radio signals or telephone lines may link a CPU in one city with peripheral equipment in another city. Such equipment provides *remote terminals* for the CPU.

Input equipment

The input equipment transforms instructions and data into a code understandable to a computer. This code consists of a pattern of electrical signals that correspond to the 0's and 1's of the binary system.

There are various kinds of input devices. One common device is a *card reader,* which takes input information from punched cards. The pattern of punches in the cards represents letters, numbers, and other symbols. A related device is the *paper tape reader,* which senses data from holes in a roll of paper tape.

Most computers have a keyboard that enables the operator to enter alphabetical characters and numerals directly into the computer. Many keyboard units have a visual display, which consists of a *cathode-ray tube* (CRT). A CRT is a vacuum tube with a screen like that of a TV set. The CRT display makes it possible for the keyboard operator to check—and correct if

How a Digital Computer Works

An input device sends data and instructions to the main memory of a computer. The control unit then directs the data to the arithmetic/logic unit for processing. Finally, the control unit routes the processed data to an output device or an auxiliary storage unit, or back to the main memory.

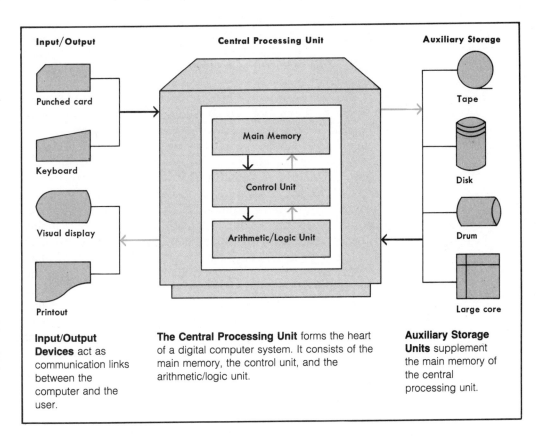

Input/Output   **Central Processing Unit**   **Auxiliary Storage**

Punched card

Keyboard

Main Memory

Control Unit

Arithmetic/Logic Unit

Visual display

Printout

Tape

Disk

Drum

Large core

Input/Output Devices act as communication links between the computer and the user.

The Central Processing Unit forms the heart of a digital computer system. It consists of the main memory, the control unit, and the arithmetic/logic unit.

Auxiliary Storage Units supplement the main memory of the central processing unit.

necessary—the data being entered into the computer. Some keyboard terminals of this type have a built-in microcomputer that controls their basic operations independently of the main computer. Input units with CRT displays called *interactive graphic devices* enable the user to communicate with the main computer by drawing a diagram on the screen with a light pen.

Some computers use *optical scanners* to change input data into electrical signals. The scanners optically sense bar codes and marks printed on grocery items, identification cards, and certain documents. Other digital computers are connected to *touch-tone telephones*. By pressing the buttons on the phone, the user can enter data into the computer.

Certain types of equipment handle input information and also function as output devices and *auxiliary storage units*.

Auxiliary storage units, or auxiliary memories, can store more information than a computer's main memory but do not operate as fast. The major types of auxiliary memories include (1) magnetic tape units, (2) magnetic disk units, (3) magnetic drum units, and (4) large-core storage units.

Magnetic tape units put information on tape similar to that used in tape recorders. The computer tape carries data in the form of tiny magnetic spots, or *cells*. More than 48,000 binary digits can be recorded and stored on 1 inch (2.54 centimeters) of magnetic tape.

Magnetic disk units record information by magnetizing cells on the surface of specially coated metal or plastic disks. The disks are stacked in a *disk pack* and held in a storage unit. Data and instructions recorded on disks can be retrieved more rapidly than information on tape. Locating data on tape may require unwinding the entire reel if the desired information is stored at the end of the tape. In contrast, the disk system provides direct access to a specific disk and the precise spot on that disk where the needed information is located. A unit consisting of small, flexible disks called *floppy disks* is widely used with minicomputers and microcomputers.

Magnetic drum units work much like disk units. However, they record information as magnetic spots on a rotating metal cylinder instead of on disks. The magnetic spots are arranged in a series of circular tracks along the surface of the drum. Information can be retrieved more quickly from drums than from either disks or tapes. But drums cannot hold as much data as disks or tapes.

Large-core storage units consist of thousands of tiny, doughnut-shaped iron cores. Each core encircles an intersection of wires on a rectangular grid. A core can be magnetized in either a clockwise or counterclockwise direction by an electric current passing through the wires. When magnetized one way, a core represents 1. When magnetized the opposite way, it stands for 0. Information is stored by magnetizing a group of cores in a certain combination of 1's and 0's. Large-core storage units are faster than tape, disk, or drum units. They are used in computer systems for space missions and other projects that require extremely fast retrieval of data.

Main memory

The main memory receives and stores data and instructions from an input device or an auxiliary storage unit. It also receives information from the control and arithmetic/logic units. The main memory stores only information that is currently needed by the CPU. After the CPU has finished with it, the information is transferred to auxiliary units for permanent storage or sent directly to an output device for immediate use.

The main memory consists of many memory cells. Each cell is a tiny device or electronic circuit capable of storing a binary digit. The cells are arranged into groups. Each group is assigned a number called an *address,* which makes it possible to locate specific bits of information quickly.

One type of memory used in many mainframes is the *magnetic core memory*. This memory closely resembles large-core auxiliary storage units. However, it has many more cores assembled on a larger wire grid, and the circuitry is more complex.

Mainframes designed for jobs that require extremely fast operating speeds use a *semiconductor memory*. This type of memory consists of integrated circuits, generally large-scale integrated circuits. A semiconductor memory is composed of one or more silicon chips. A chip only one-fourth the size of a postage stamp contains thousands of microscopic electronic circuits, each forming a memory cell for a binary digit. The compact size of a semiconductor memory makes it particularly suitable for minicomputers and microcomputers.

Control unit

The control unit directs and coordinates the operations of the entire computer according to instructions in the main memory. It has to select the instructions in proper order because their sequence determines each step in the operations. The control unit interprets the instructions and relays the appropriate commands to the arithmetic/logic unit. Each set of instructions is expressed through an *operation code* in binary form that specifies exactly what must be done to complete a job. The operation code also provides the addresses that tell where data for the processing operations are stored in the memory.

The control unit regulates the flow of data between the memory and the arithmetic/logic unit and routes processed information to the output device. In some cases, the actions generated by the control unit result in the storage of new data and instructions in the main memory and auxiliary units.

Arithmetic/logic unit

The arithmetic/logic unit, which is also called the *ALU,* manipulates data received from the main memory. It carries out all the arithmetic functions and logic processes required to solve a problem.

Data from the memory are held by the ALU temporarily in its own storage devices called *registers*. The registers consist of individual storage cells known as *flip-flops*. These miniature electronic circuits are connected to other circuits containing transistors and related switching devices. Three basic circuits, called the *AND-gate, OR-gate,* and *NOT-gate* or *inverter,* are combined in different ways to perform arithmetic and logic operations with electrical signals that represent binary digits. For example, one simple combination of these logic circuits performs addition. Another combination compares two numbers and then acts on the results of the comparison.

After an arithmetic or logic operation has been completed, the answer appears in the ALU's main register, which is known as the *accumulator*. The answer may be transferred from the accumulator to the memory for storage until it is needed for another operation, or it may be sent to the output device.

Output equipment

The output equipment, like the input equipment, serves as a communication link between the computer and the user. It translates the computer's electrical signals into a form comprehensible to the user. In some cases, the signals are altered so they can be used by machines that the computer operates.

Many computer systems have a CRT unit that displays output data as words, numbers, graphs, or pictures on a screen. Some of these units also can handle input material. Various computers use *automatic typewriters* or *line printers* to produce printed output data. Such output is called a *printout*. Automatic typewriters are used chiefly to print small amounts of data because they can type only one character at a time. Most line printers are high-speed devices that print a line of more than 100 letters and numbers at a time and from 60 to 2,000 lines a minute.

Other common output devices include *key punch machines*. These machines resemble typewriters and record data by punching patterns of holes in cards or paper tape. Output data presented in such a form or on magnetic tapes, disks, or drums can easily be put back into the computer when needed.

A few computer systems are equipped with *audio devices,* which transmit output information as spoken words through a

Main Memory and Auxiliary Storage

The main memory inside a computer stores data and instructions for immediate use. An auxiliary unit outside the computer provides additional storage. It can hold more information than the main memory but operates at a slower speed. The two types of main memories are *magnetic core* and *semiconductor* memories. Commonly used auxiliary devices include *magnetic tape* and *magnetic disk* units.

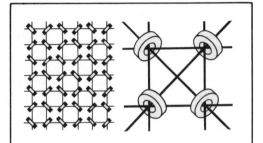

A Magnetic Core Memory has thousands of tiny rings. Each ring encircles an intersection of wires. A current passing through the wires magnetizes a ring, causing it to represent a binary digit.

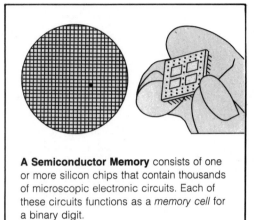

A Semiconductor Memory consists of one or more silicon chips that contain thousands of microscopic electronic circuits. Each of these circuits functions as a *memory cell* for a binary digit.

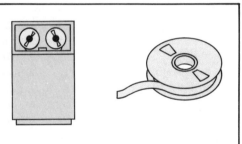

A Magnetic Tape Unit stores information on a reel of tape similar to that used in a tape recorder. The computer tape carries data and programs in the form of tiny magnetic spots.

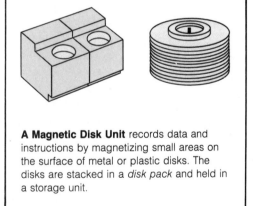

A Magnetic Disk Unit records data and instructions by magnetizing small areas on the surface of metal or plastic disks. The disks are stacked in a *disk pack* and held in a storage unit.

type of telephone. The audio responses consist of words and phrases selected from a collection of human voice recordings.

Programming a Digital Computer

Programming involves the preparation and writing of detailed instructions for a computer. These instructions tell a computer exactly what data to use and what sequence of operations to perform with the data.

In most cases, computer scientists and other computer specialists called *programmers* write the instructions. They refer to programs as *software* because the instructions have no physical parts. The term *hardware* is applied to the computer itself, including its electronic circuits and peripheral equipment.

Preparing a program

Preparing a program begins with a complete description of the job that the computer is to perform. This job description might be obtained from a business manager, an educator, an engineer, or a scientist. It explains what input data are required, what computing must be done, and what the output should be. Computer scientists or programmers use the job description to prepare diagrams and other pictorial aids that represent the steps needed to complete the task. They may also draw up a table listing all the variable conditions involved in the job. The computer specialists then produce a diagram that shows how all the major parts of the job fit together systematically. This diagram is called a *systems flow chart*.

In the case of a large or complicated project, the systems flow chart may be divided to break up the project into smaller jobs for which *subprograms* can be prepared. Different programmers work on the subprograms. A chief programmer writes the *main program,* which takes in all the subprograms.

The systems flow chart is often used to prepare another diagram, an *operations flow chart*. This kind of chart shows each step and instruction to create a clear picture of every detail of a job. It helps programmers write their instructions and reduces the chance of introducing errors. After a program has been written, it is tested on the computer for mistakes. Computer experts refer to mistakes as "bugs" and the testing procedure as "debugging."

Programmers use various methods to enter programs into a computer. In one method, they write the instructions on forms called *coding sheets*. Keypunch operators then put the instructions on punched cards, which are read by the computer's card reader. In a method called the *interactive mode,* programmers enter their instructions by means of a keyboard connected to a CRT display. All responses of the computer to the instructions appear on the screen immediately for the programmers to analyze. In most cases, programs resulting from this interaction between the computer and the programmers are recorded and stored on magnetic disks until needed.

An Operations Flow Chart is a kind of block diagram prepared by programmers to show the steps involved in a job. The example of a flow chart below gives the steps to be taken by a student arising in the morning and going to school. The symbols in the diagram are commonly used by programmers. For instance, a circle means stop or start. A diamond indicates a decision point.

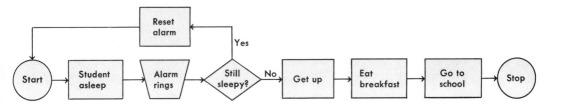

Using programming languages

A programmer writes the instructions for a computer in a *programming language*. Such a language consists of letters, words, and symbols as well as rules for combining those elements. Some programming languages closely resemble the language of mathematics. Others enable programmers to write instructions in simple, everyday expressions, such as "READ," "ADD," and "STOP." Programming languages of this kind are called *high-level languages*.

The language that a programmer uses depends largely on the job to be done. A commonly used programming language is BASIC (*B*eginner's *A*ll-purpose *S*ymbolic *I*nstruction *C*ode). BASIC is well suited for writing relatively simple programs for minicomputers and microcomputers. Many high schools that offer a course in programming teach BASIC because it is both easy to learn and easy to use. Suppose that a computer is to print the sum of 2 and 4. A program for this operation written in BASIC would read:

```
10   PRINT 2 + 4
20   END
```

Each statement, or instruction, of a BASIC program begins with a line number, such as the 10 and 20 above. This number serves as the statement's label, identifying its exact position in the sequence of instructions. The word or phrase that appears after the line number instructs the computer what to do. PRINT tells it to print the sum of 2 plus 4. END stops the program. If this program were written in another high-level language, it would look quite different.

Computers in School

Most children who use computers in school to learn math or other subjects do not know a computer language. Children must be carefully prepared to use computers. They begin by learning such basic information as where the on/off button is and whether anything should be done before turning the computer on.

For example, before the computer is turned on, some form of magnetic memory may need to be inserted. Some computers use cartridges that contain stored programs, but most computers use either tapes or disks. More and more people are turning to disks for storage because they are faster and easier to use. Children need to know how to handle disks so that memory is not accidentally erased by fingerprints or dust. Most disks are about the size of 45 rpm records, but they are enclosed almost completely in cardboard sheaths. Only a small opening allows the disk to be read. If most disks are inserted upside down, they will not work. (Some, called *flippy-floppies,* store programs on both sides.)

When a disk is inserted and the computer is turned on, most programs automatically begin. On the screen, a title will appear. After a few seconds, it may be replaced by the start of the program, or it may have another title to show the copyright and the name of the programmer. When the program begins to appear on the screen, it may use colors and artwork as well as words. Frequently, there are sound effects too. (Nearly all the small computers can generate at least a few beeps; many computers can play melodies.) Simply inserting the disk and turning the computer on enables the child to use it.

Computer programs are written to be *user friendly.* The computer screen provides simple and easy-to-follow directions. This usually does not present a problem for children who are old enough to read. They read the instructions and do something with the keyboard. If the response is correct, the computer will say so. If the response is incorrect or inappropriate, the computer screen will display further advice on what to do.

Many computer programs for both children and for adults are *menu driven.* That is, the screen displays a "menu" of different things that it can do. The user can make a choice by pressing the number or letter of one of the menu items. For example, the menu for an instructional program might show:

DO YOU WANT TO ADD OR SUBTRACT?
1   PRESS 1 FOR ADDITION
2   PRESS 2 FOR SUBTRACTION

If the child decides on subtraction and presses 2, the result may be another menu.

DO YOU WANT EASY, AVERAGE, OR HARD?
1 PRESS 1 FOR EASY
2 PRESS 2 FOR AVERAGE
3 PRESS 3 FOR HARD

There can be as many menus as needed to locate the exact place in the program that a child wants to select.

Frequently, a way of asking for help is included in programs or built right into a computer. Pressing a HELP button or typing an H will bring more detailed instructions.

Often programs are so user friendly that they address children by name. At the very beginning, before starting menus or actual work in a subject, the computer introduces itself and asks the individual children to type their names. Thereafter, throughout the program, the children are referred to directly by name. Many computers also use this feature to store the results of a practice session under each child's name. The child can then stop work and start again at the correct spot. Or the teacher can check the computer record to find out how well the child is doing.

Nearly all schools that use small computers use micros. In some schools, however, a mini is used with several terminals. In that case, the teacher probably starts the computer and inserts the program. The teacher may also start the computer for younger children.

Most often today, computers are kept in a separate computer room rather than in individual classrooms. But this situation seems to be changing as more and more schools get more and more computers. When there are computers in the classroom, several students can work on math or social studies with the computer while the teacher leads a reading group and other students work at their desks. Then, the groups are able to rotate activities.

Great flexibility is possible when schools can afford both computers and software. The varied uses to which computers have already been put in schools can only lead to speculation about how many other ways students will one day use computers to master their studies.

Part

IV

Complete Math Review Program

The math review program presented here is a complete refresher course. The twelve sections, organized by subject, start with basic math principles and progress to highly challenging mathematics. Each section prepares you for the next section to come; and many math exercises, plus answer keys, let you know when you are ready to go on.

Most students and others completing this program will reach a point when they are no longer reviewing but are learning new material. Students should use the new sections as a supplement to their ongoing school instruction. Adults can complete the lessons independently based on their understanding of the lessons already mastered.

Because this program has a built-in pattern of instruction, the sections are best worked in order. Do not skip early lessons even if they seem easy. You might miss an important principle that you will need for later lessons.

Throughout this part, you will be reminded to work thoughtfully, go slowly, and read carefully. You cannot rush through this review program and still benefit the most from it. Look at the answers only after you have studied the lessons well and worked out the exercises as directed. Also, a math notebook and some equipment are necessary: pencil, eraser, metric and customary rulers, compass, protractor, extra paper, scissors, for example. Don't try to work without the proper equipment; you might miss the most important point of an exercise. Lessons will show you what equipment you need.

In the early sections, use a calculator sparingly, especially if your computational skills are poor. Computational practice here will only make your math better for later sections, when calculator use is quite efficient, and in everyday home or classroom situations when a calculator is unavailable.

Are you ready? You will find the beginning of your math review program on the next page.■

(Preceding photo)
Math ability builds through a slow process of learning and review.

Understanding and Using Numbers

Starting at the Beginning

Mathematics has been used by humans from the beginning of their existence. As people learned to count and measure, it became necessary to invent a way of keeping records and computing.

In the beginning some people kept records by making piles of stones or sticks. Later, they put notches on the sticks. Thus the use of "tally sticks" was one of the earliest known devices for keeping written records.

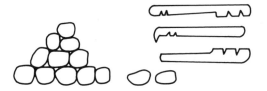

Written numbers (numerals) did not appear until the early civilizations began to develop. One such early system was a method of picture writing developed before 3000 B.C. by the Egyptians. Their system, called hieroglyphics, enabled them to write numerals for large and small amounts. Egyptians wrote | for our numeral 1, ∩ for 10, ⑨ (a scroll) for 100 and ⟩ (a lotus flower) for 1000. To form any numeral up to 9999, they simply grouped as many of each symbol as necessary. These symbols were written from right to left. For example, 1872 can be written in Egyptian numerals as follows:

Since new symbols had to be created for numbers greater than 9999, Egyptian numerals were cumbersome to write. The operations of addition, subtraction, multiplication, and division were also awkward to perform.

Another simple grouping system is Roman numerals. The Roman system came into existence much later than the Egyptian one. It introduces new symbols for 5, 50, and 500 as well as for 10, 100, and 1000. Roman numerals use the following symbols:

I for 1	C for 100
V for 5	D for 500
X for 10	M for 1000
L for 50	

The symbols are written from left to right. Thus 1872 in Roman numerals is written

MDCCCLXXII	M	=	1000
	D	=	500
	CCC	=	300
	LXX	=	70
	II	=	2
			1872

Notice that in each of these older systems large numbers are represented by using more symbols. For example, LXX means L + X + X = 50 + 10 + 10, which is written as 70. Subtraction is also used in writing Roman numerals. Nine is written as IX. The I before X means to take 1 away from 10. What do you think XL means? XL stands for 50 − 10 or 40. Thus 1929 is written MDCDXXIX.

Your Turn

Write an Egyptian numeral and a Roman numeral for each of the following:

1.	15	2.	39	3.	114
4.	51	5.	1442	6.	2046

(Answers appear at the end of the section.)

Throughout the history of mathematics there have been many different systems of notation. Our modern system of notation is the decimal system. The symbols are often called Hindu-Arabic numerals because many people believe the system began in India and developed further in the Arabian countries. Many different symbols were used, but the advent of printing helped to standardize the ten symbols: 0, 1, 2, 3, 4, 5, 6, 7, 8, and 9. These are used to represent any number regardless of size. Instead of a special symbol to represent each power of ten, the decimal system uses place value. This concept will be explored in detail. Different algorithms (written procedures) will be discussed along with relationships of addition, subtraction, multiplication, and division with whole numbers.

Numbers and Numerals

Mathematics is the study of numbers and their relationships. With the help of mathematics, people have built many structures such as bridges, buildings, and dams. Mathematics has helped astronauts make trips into space. It is used by businesspeople and consumers every day.

In mathematics one cannot work with things directly as one can in other areas such as science. An understanding of the relationships and the patterns of numbers depends upon an ability to work with and analyze many different ideas and concepts. For example, the concept of number can be used to describe various things. Three dogs and three doghouses are quite different things but the number three can be applied to either group. All three dogs may have different names. A dog's name is not the dog. Names are assigned to each of the dogs.

Just as names are assigned to people, animals, and other things, names are assigned to numbers. What is a number? It is a way of thinking, an idea, that enables people to compare different sets of objects. Numbers are not physical things that can be seen or touched. Names stand for numbers but are not the numbers themselves. Numerals and words are used to name numbers. For example, the number of corners on a triangle is three or 3.

In our modern decimal system of numeration, the ten digits 0, 1, 2, 3, 4, 5, 6, 7, 8, and 9 are used to build numerals. Numbers larger than nine are written in numeral form by placing the digits in a certain order according to place value.

The basis of our system of numeration is groups of ten or multiples of ten. Our system is also known as a place value or a positional system. In a place value system, every digit in a numeral has two different values associated with it—the value of the digit and the place value of the digit.

This chart shows some place values in the decimal system.

Millions	Hundred Thousands	Ten Thousands	Thousands	Hundreds	Tens	Ones

In the following chart, the digits are grouped in threes. The groups are named (reading from left to right) millions, thousands, and units. Notice also that within each group the names are the same.

MILLIONS			THOUSANDS			UNITS		
Hundreds	Tens	Ones	Hundreds	Tens	Ones	Hundreds	Tens	Ones
1	9	0	8	4	2	5	6	3

The place value of any position is ones, tens, or hundreds followed by the group name. In order to read a numeral correctly, it is necessary to consider both the value of the digits and the positions they occupy.

Reading from right to left the place value names are ones, tens, hundreds, thousands, ten thousands, hundred thousands, millions, ten millions, and hundred millions. Each digit gets its value from its place in the numeral. The value of each place is ten times the value of the place to its right.

To read the numeral 190842563 follow this rule.

RULE:
First, write the numeral.

1 9 0 8 4 2 5 6 3

Second, start at the right and use a comma to separate each group of three. (For four-digit numerals, the comma may be omitted.)

1 9 0, 8 4 2, 5 6 3

Third, use the chart above to name each group of three digits. Start at the left, read each group of three digits, and attach the name of that group.

190 million, 842 thousand, 563

Notice that the group name "units" is not read.

The word name for a number can be written by using the same process.

MILLIONS			THOUSANDS			UNITS		
Hundreds	Tens	Ones	Hundreds	Tens	Ones	Hundreds	Tens	Ones
1	9	0	8	4	2	5	6	3

The word name for this number would be written as:

> One hundred ninety million, eight hundred forty-two thousand, five hundred sixty-three.

Write the word for the digits named in each group of three followed by the group name. The "units" group name is not written.

Your Turn

Write the word for each of these.

1. 1030   2. 312,467   3. 954,123,004

Write the numeral for each of these.

4. four hundred seventy-three
5. twenty-four thousand, six hundred
6. two hundred million, five hundred ten thousand, one hundred sixty-four

(Answers appear at the end of the section.)

Another way that numerals are written is in expanded form. The numeral 496 tells us how many objects are in 4 piles of one hundred objects, 9 piles of ten objects, and 6 piles of one object each. Thus the number can be represented as follows:

$$496 = (4 \times 100) + (9 \times 10) + (6 \times 1)$$
$$= \quad 400 \quad + \quad 90 \quad + \quad 6$$

Notice that the multiplications are performed first, then the additions.

Using Exponents to Name Numbers

Numbers may be named in many ways. One useful device mathematicians use to name numbers is exponents. In this notation, a non-zero whole number exponent is used to indicate the number of times the base number is used as a factor (one of the numbers being multiplied).

$$2^3 \swarrow \text{exponent}$$
base $\nearrow$

In other words the exponent (3), in the above example, tells how many times the base (2) is used as a factor.

2^3 means $2 \times 2 \times 2$ or 8

Thus 10^2 means 10×10 or 100. Similarly, 10^3 means 10 is to be used as a factor three times.

$$10^3 = 10 \times 10 \times 10 = 1000$$

Notice that 10^1 means to use 10 as a factor once.

$$10^1 = 10$$

Although it may seem strange at first, mathematicians have defined 10^0. Why? It does not make much sense to "use 10 as a factor zero times." So they could have chosen to say that 10^0 was meaningless. But consider the following pattern:

$10^6 = 1,000,000$	Notice the
$10^5 = 100,000$	number of
$10^4 = 10,000$	zeros is
$10^3 = 1000$	the same as
$10^2 = 100$	the exponent.
$10^1 = 10$	
$10^0 = 1$	

Exponents can be used to name other numbers. For example, the number 6482 can be written in either of these ways.

$$(6 \times 1000) + (4 \times 100) + (8 \times 10) + (2 \times 1)$$
$$\text{or}$$
$$(6 \times 10^3) + (4 \times 10^2) + (8 \times 10^1) + (2 \times 10^0)$$

In each case, the number is written in expanded form.

Your Turn

Write the following in expanded form using exponents:

1. 357   2. 9125   3. 12,703

(Answers appear at the end of the section.)

Earlier the point was made that a number is an idea and that it exists only in abstraction. However, it should be noted that most people use "number" to mean either number or numeral. In the following pages, "number" will be used whenever the meaning can be clearly seen.

Rounding Numbers

A rounded number is an approximation of the exact value of a number. There are many occasions when there is a need to approximate the value of a number rather than state it exactly. For example, a reporter said that the attendance at the Rose Bowl Game was 98,000. Actually the official attendance record showed 97,659. In that situation the reporter rounded 97,659 "to the nearest thousand." This means that 97,659 is closer to 98,000 than to 97,000 or to any other whole number of thousands. Before rounding a number it is necessary to know to which place value the number is to be rounded. Then use this rule.

RULE:
When rounding a number to a given place,
1. **Underline the digit in the place to be rounded.**
2. **Circle the digit to the right of that place.**
3. **If the circled digit is less than 5 (0, 1, 2, 3, or 4), change all digits to the right of the given place to zeros.**
4. **If the circled digit is equal to or greater than 5 (5, 6, 7, 8, or 9), add 1 to the given place and replace all digits to the right with zeros.**

Example: Round 44,806 to the nearest thousand.

given place: thousand

$$4\ \underline{4}\ ,\ \textcircled{8}\ 0\ 6$$

Circle the digit to the right of given place.

Since the circled digit ⑧ is 5 or more, add 1 to the digit in the thousands place and change the digits to the right to zeros.

45,000

So 44,806 rounded to the nearest thousand is 45,000.

Example: Round 1749 to the nearest hundred.

given place: hundred

$$1\ \underline{7}\ \textcircled{4}9$$

Circle the digit to the right of given place.

Since 4 is less than 5 simply change the digits to the right of the hundreds place to zeros.

1700

So 1749 rounded to the nearest hundred is 1700.

Round each of the following to the indicated place.

1. 826 (tens)   2. 1045 (hundreds)
3. 155,834 (ten thousands)

(Answers appear at the end of the section.)

Note that when the digit to the right of the given place is 5, it is generally agreed that 1 should be added to the given place.

Adding Whole Numbers

Addition through counting

One way to think about addition is to think of counting. Addition is directly related to counting since the sum of two numbers can be obtained by counting. For example, to add 32 to 53 by counting, start with one group of 53 objects and another group of 32 objects. One-by-one, transfer the objects from the group of 32 to the group of 53. Count as you go along—starting with 53. Move one object, say 54. Move another object, say 55. Continue until all the objects are in one pile. There should be 85 objects, so 85 is the sum of 32 and 53. However, a faster way to find the sum is by computing.

Properties of addition

To determine which numerals should represent different groups of objects, use sets. (A set is defined to be a collection of objects.) The idea of sets is very useful in showing the meaning of addition. Study the following example.

To add the whole numbers 7 and 5, consider the sets of 7 books on one shelf and 5 books on another.

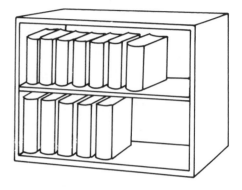

How many books are on the two shelves? The number of elements in the union of the two sets is the sum. Addition shows the joining of two parts to find an answer. The parts are called addends. The answer is called the sum. The " + " (plus) symbol indicates addition. The number of books on the bookshelf could be represented in either of these ways.

$$7 \leftarrow \text{addends} \quad \quad$$
$$\underline{+5} \quad \quad \quad \quad 7 + 5 = 12$$
$$12 \leftarrow \text{sum}$$

The addition can be shown by $7 + 5$ or $5 + 7$. The order of addition does not change the sum. This is the commutative property of addition of whole numbers. This property is useful when doing addition by first adding in one direction and then checking the addition by adding in the opposite direction.

$$73 + 91 = 164$$
$$\text{addends} \quad \quad \text{sum}$$
$$91 + 73 = 164$$

When adding more than two numbers the addends need to be paired because only two numbers can be added at one time. To add three numbers, for example, pair (associate) either of the end addends with the middle addend. In other words, the grouping of numbers in different ways when adding does not change the sum. This is called the associative property of addition.

$$(12 + 8) + 5 = 12 + (8 + 5)$$

The parentheses ( ) show which numbers are associated. The operation inside the parentheses is to be completed first.

Suppose one shelf had 4 books and the other shelf had no books. The addition could be shown by $4 + 0 = 4$. Notice that the sum is identical to the non-zero addend. Zero is called the identity element for addition because when zero is added to any given number the sum is the same (identical) number as the given number.

$$4 + 0 = 4 \qquad 0 + 7219 = 7219$$

The principles of place value, the commutative property, the associative property, and the identity element are helpful in addition and can make computation easier.

Addition facts

To add well requires a certain amount of memorization of facts. It is important to be sure that the addition facts are mastered before proceeding with a study of mathematics. Quick and accurate recall of addition facts makes the study of mathematics easier.

If you have trouble with addition facts, make and complete a table like the one shown below. It contains all the addition combinations. Recall that when zero is added to any addend, the sum is the same as the given addend. This is true only for zero. To complete the addi-

tion table, place the sum for a pair of addends in the square where the column of one addend and the row of the other addend intersect. Note that $5 + 4$ and $4 + 5$ have been completed for you. Do not write in the book. Copy the table on a separate sheet of paper or in your math notebook.

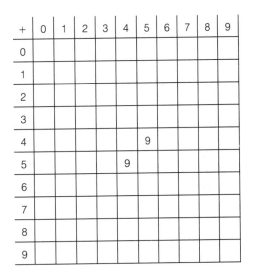

There are many shortcuts that can be discovered by observing patterns in the addition table. For example, by using the properties of addition, it is necessary to memorize only one-half of the table. Can you explain why this is so? If not, restudy the earlier section on properties of addition.

A complete addition facts table is included in Part VII, "Math Tables." Check your completed table with that table.

Addition of numbers greater than 10

To add two numbers, write the numerals so they align by place value. Then use addition facts to find the sum of the ones, the tens, the hundreds, and so on.

Align the   Add the   Add the   Add the
numerals.   ones.   tens.   hundreds.
              ↓   ↓   ↓

  4 3 6   4 3 6   4 3 6   4 3 6
+   6 2   +   6 2   +   6 2   +   6 2
        8   9 8   4 9 8

To add three or more numbers group the addends in pairs.

Add the ones.   Add the tens.
     ↓   ↓
   3 5   3 5
   2 1   2 1
 +1 2   +1 2
    8   6 8

$5 + 1 = 6$ $3 + 2 = 5$
   $6 + 2 = 8$ $5 + 1 = 6$

Your Turn

1.   45 2.   302 3.   15 4.   153
  +23   +194   20   514
                 +51   + 21

(Answers appear at the end of the section.)

Sometimes it is necessary to rename a number in order to add. Here are three ways of doing the same problem using renaming. Notice how the sum, 15 tens and 18 ones, is renamed as 168.

  49   4 tens + 9 ones
  54   5 tens + 4 ones
+65   + 6 tens + 5 ones
              15 tens + 18 ones

15 tens + (1 ten + 8 ones)
(15 tens + 1 ten) + 8 ones

16 tens + 8 ones

1 hundred + 6 tens + 8 ones or 168

This problem could also be stated and solved using expanded notation.

  49   40 + 9
  54   50 + 4
+65   + 60 + 5
         150 + 18 = 168

Any set of numbers could be added using either of these methods, but it would be better if an easier way could be found. The following is such a procedure. This procedure does not need to have the numbers written in expanded form. However, in the expanded form 18 is 1 ten plus 8 ones. In the short method the 8 is recorded in the ones column and the 1 above the tens column. This procedure is sometimes referred to as "carrying." When carrying a number just write it above the next column on the left. Here is the same problem reworked using the shorter method.

  1   Add the ones.
 49    $9 + 4 + 5 = 18$
 54   Write the 8 in the ones column.
+65   Write the 1 above the tens
  8   column.

  1   Add the tens.
 49    $1 + 4 + 5 + 6 = 16$
 54   Write the sum with the 6 in the
+65   tens column and the 1 in the
168   hundreds column.

This shorter method is the one most often used by students.

Your Turn

5.   82 6.   39 7.   412
  + 9   +28   +938

8.   32 9.   98
  59   21
 +18   +89

(Answers appear at the end of the section.)

Addition shortcuts

With practice, even large numbers can be added without the use of pencil and paper. Adding the tens first is a common method used in mental addition. Always group in a way that is easiest for you. In mental computation, some people work from left to right because that is the way they read, even though in written computation it is the usual custom to work from right to left. Study these examples to see how the sums can be found without paper and pencil.

A.
$$
\begin{array}{l}
\quad 34 \\
\underline{+68} \\
\quad 90 \ (30 + 60) \\
\underline{+12} \ (4 + 8) \\
\quad 102 \ (90 + 12)
\end{array}
$$

B.
$$
\begin{array}{l}
\quad 19 \\
\quad 16 \\
\underline{+24} \\
\quad 40 \ (10 + 10 + 20) \\
\quad 10 \ (6 + 4) \\
\underline{+ \ 9} \ (9) \\
\quad 59 \ (40 + 10) + 9
\end{array}
$$

Notice that when adding three numbers, finding groups of ten simplifies addition.

Your Turn

Mentally add the following.

10. $\begin{array}{r} 65 \\ +31 \end{array}$ 11. $\begin{array}{r} 34 \\ 26 \\ +18 \end{array}$ 12. $\begin{array}{r} 613 \\ +421 \end{array}$ 13. $\begin{array}{r} 97 \\ 12 \\ +48 \end{array}$

(Answers appear at the end of the section.)

Subtracting Whole Numbers

Subtraction related to addition

Subtraction is the inverse of addition. The process of subtraction can be based on any of the following three ways of thinking:

> **Example:** Find the second addend when the sum of two numbers is 12 and the first addend is 5.
>
> $5 + (\ ) = 12$
>
> 1. 5 from 12 leaves how many?
>
> or
>
> 2. How many must be added to 5 to get 12?
>
> or
>
> 3. 12 is how many more than 5?

In each case the answer is 7.

Some experts suggest that the "take away" method (thinking "5 from 12 leaves 7" or "12 minus 5 equals 7") is the most effective way of thinking about subtraction for many students. By thinking of subtraction as the process of taking one number from another, subtraction can be used to

1. Find the remainder when one number is taken from another.
2. Find the difference when two numbers are compared.
3. Find how many more are needed.
4. Find the second number when the sum of two numbers and one of the numbers is known.

Understanding the meaning and use of these processes is essential for successful use of subtraction in solving problems involving real-life applications.

In subtraction the smaller number, the one being taken away, is called the given addend or the subtrahend. It is always taken from the larger number, called the sum or the minuend. The answer to a subtraction problem is called the missing addend or the difference. A "−" (minus) is used to indicate subtraction. To indicate that 5 is subtracted from 12, the work can be shown either horizontally or vertically.

sum addend missing
addend

$$12 - 5 = 7$$

$$12 \leftarrow \text{sum} \qquad \text{(minuend)}$$
$$\underline{- \ 5} \leftarrow \text{addend} \qquad \text{(subtrahend)}$$
$$7 \leftarrow \text{missing} \qquad \text{(difference)}$$
$$\text{addend}$$

Unlike addition, subtraction is neither commutative nor associative. That is 12 − 5 does not equal 5 − 12. Likewise, (38 − 10) − 8 does not equal 38 − (10 − 8) because

$$\underline{(38 - 10)} - 8 \qquad 38 - \underline{(10 - 8)}$$

$$\underline{28 - 8} \qquad\qquad 38 - 2$$

20   not equal   36

Subtraction facts

In subtraction there are 100 basic facts. These facts are related to the 100 addition facts. Just as in addition, facts need to be memorized because they serve as a basis for subtracting larger numbers. The basic facts of subtraction are the inverses of the basic addition facts.

$$5 + 4 = 9 \qquad 9 - 4 = 5$$
$$4 + 5 = 9 \qquad 9 - 5 = 4$$

All subtraction work depends on a knowledge of these basic facts. Once you understand the meaning, any needed subtraction facts can be worked out from corresponding addition facts. However, should it be necessary to review the basic subtraction facts, *see* Part VII under "Math Tables."

Your Turn

1. $\begin{array}{r} 16 \\ - \ 9 \\ \hline \end{array}$ 2. $\begin{array}{r} 12 \\ - \ 5 \\ \hline \end{array}$ 3. $\begin{array}{r} 17 \\ - \ 8 \\ \hline \end{array}$

4. $\begin{array}{r} 14 \\ - \ 7 \\ \hline \end{array}$ 5. $\begin{array}{r} 16 \\ - \ 7 \\ \hline \end{array}$

(Answers appear at the end of the section.)

Subtracting larger numbers

To work a subtraction problem follow these steps.

1. Write the problem. Be sure the larger number is on top and the digits of the second number are aligned by place value underneath.
2. Start with the ones place and subtract.
3. Continue working to the left.

The example below shows the steps involved in subtraction.

Align digits.	Subtract ones.	Subtract tens.	Subtract hundreds.
	↓	↓	↓
$\begin{array}{r} 3\,4\,7 \\ - \ 4\,2 \\ \hline \end{array}$	$\begin{array}{r} 3\,4\,7 \\ - \ 4\,2 \\ \hline 5 \end{array}$	$\begin{array}{r} 3\,4\,7 \\ - \ 4\,2 \\ \hline 0\,5 \end{array}$	$\begin{array}{r} 3\,4\,7 \\ - \ 4\,2 \\ \hline 3\,0\,5 \end{array}$

Your Turn

6. $\begin{array}{r} 46 \\ -21 \\ \hline \end{array}$ 7. $\begin{array}{r} 320 \\ -110 \\ \hline \end{array}$ 8. $\begin{array}{r} 1469 \\ -1034 \\ \hline \end{array}$ 9. $\begin{array}{r} 7193 \\ - \ 182 \\ \hline \end{array}$

(Answers appear at the end of the section.)

Sometimes it is necessary to rename the larger number in order to subtract.

$$\begin{array}{r} 9\ 6\ 2 \\ -1\ 7\ 8 \\ \hline \end{array}$$

In the subtraction above, one cannot subtract 8 from 2 nor 7 from 6, so the larger number must be renamed. In subtraction always rename 1 ten as 10 ones and 1 hundred as 10 tens.

Use the drawings below to study how the renaming is done.

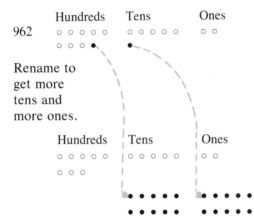

962

Rename to get more tens and more ones.

Now subtract.

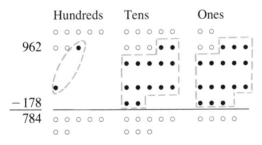

962

-178
784

Other ways to think of the subtraction are:

1. Think of it as completing a subtraction problem for each place.

Hundreds Place	Tens Place	Ones Place
8	15	12
-1	-7	-8
7	8	4

2. Use expanded form to complete the subtraction.

$$\begin{array}{rl} 962 = & (800 + 150 + 12) \\ -178 = & -(100 + \ \ 70 + \ \ 8) \\ \hline & 700 + \ \ 80 + \ \ 4 = 784 \end{array}$$

Renaming can be done using simpler steps. Some people find it easier to rewrite the example a different way. Study the following method. The numerals above the larger number are written to show the steps in renaming.

Rename and subtract the ones.	Rename and subtract the tens.	Subtract the hundreds.
	8 15	8 15
5 12	5 12	5 12
9 6 2	9 6 2	9 6 2
$-1\ \ 7\ \ 8$	$-1\ \ 7\ \ 8$	$-1\ \ 7\ \ 8$
4	8 4	7 8 4

Below are more examples that show the use of renaming.

$$\begin{array}{r} 9\ \ 10 \\ 0\ \ 10 \\ 1\ \ 0\ \ 0\ \ 4 \\ -\ \ \ \ 3\ \ 5\ \ 1 \\ \hline 6\ \ 5\ \ 3 \end{array}$$

$$\begin{array}{r} 2\ \ 14 \\ 3\ \ 11\ \ \ 4\ \ 12 \\ 4\ \ 1\ \ 3\ \ 5\ \ 2 \\ -2\ \ 9\ \ 1\ \ 8\ \ 6 \\ \hline 1\ \ 2\ \ 1\ \ 6\ \ 6 \end{array}$$

Your Turn

10.	123	11.	902	12.	3214
	-118		-729		-1406

13. $\begin{array}{r} 7682 \\ -6993 \\ \hline \end{array}$

(Answers appear at the end of the section.)

Multiplying Whole Numbers

Meaning of multiplication

In most school mathematics instruction, multiplication of whole numbers is presented as repeated addition. However, repeated addition is only one way of thinking about multiplication. In this section multiplication will also be presented as arrays. Repeated addition means that instead of adding

$$5 + 5 + 5 + 5 = 20,$$

the computation can be shown as

$$4 \times 5 = 20.$$

This shows that 5 has been multiplied by 4 and that 20 is the product of 4 and 5. Thus by definition multiplication is a shortened form for the addition of equal addends.

Multiplication can also be shown in terms of sets. For example, this diagram shows 4 sets of 5, or 20 members.

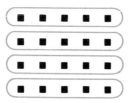

There are 4 sets of 5 objects each. A multiplication sentence is often used to describe the set.

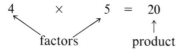

Sometimes the factor 4 is called the multiplier and the factor 5 the multiplicand.

Multiplication can be used to find the area of a rectangle. That means to find the number of square inches in its sur-face. In the case of this rectangle, it is separated into square inches.

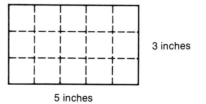

3 inches

5 inches

The surface contains 3 rows and each row contains 5 square inches. The area is 15 square inches because $3 \times 5 = 15$.

Multiplication properties

Multiplication as a shortened form of addition of equal numbers is usually learned by memorizing multiplication facts. Along with the multiplication facts it is necessary to learn certain properties, or laws, of multiplication.

The first three properties of multiplication are companions of the three properties of addition listed earlier. The law of order (commutative property) and the law of grouping (associative property) apply to multiplication as well as addition. These two properties are often useful in shortening the amount of computation needed to work some problems by making it easier to choose the easiest factor as the multiplier. The properties will be presented in an informal manner and discussed as one of the most common methods of checking addition.

Multiplication, like addition, has an identity element. Of particular importance is the fact that a number is not changed when it is multiplied by 1. This property will be applied quite often in developing some of the basic procedures with fractions.

How many sodas are shown in this crate?

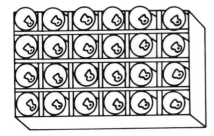

The sodas can be grouped as

4 sets of 6   or   6 sets of 4

Either way there are still 24 sodas.

4 × 6 = 6 × 4

This is an example of the commutative property of multiplication. Stated simply, it means that

RULE
Changing the order of two numbers does not change the product.

The law of grouping (associative property of multiplication) is used whenever more than two numbers are multiplied. In multiplication, like addition, only two numbers can be multiplied at a time. For example, the product of 4, 2, and 5 can be found several ways. Here are two ways.

(4 × 2) × 5 = ?   Think: 4 × 2 = 8
                            and   8 × 5 = 40
4 × (2 × 5) = ?   Think: 2 × 5 = 10
                            and 10 × 4 = 40

The associative property of multiplication can be stated this way.

RULE
The product of two or more numbers is the same regardless of the way in which the factors are grouped.

Both 0 and 1 have special roles as factors in multiplication. When a number is multiplied by zero, the product is zero.

6 × 0 = 0   0 × 175 = 0

If the product of two numbers is zero, then one of the numbers is zero or both are zero. Note that zero is a number, not just a placeholder.

When any number is multiplied by one (1), the number remains unchanged. A number which, when multiplied by another number, does not change the given number is called the identity element for multiplication. Therefore one (1) is the identity element.

5 × 1 = 5   1 × 75 = 75

Just as with addition and subtraction, multiplication is usually completed without thinking about the above properties. But an understanding of how they are used will be of help later in more advanced mathematics.

Multiplication facts

The multiplication properties make the multiplication facts easier to learn. However, in order to perform multiplication well, the facts should be memorized. For easy access, usually these facts are listed in a multiplication table. The multiplication table on the next page shows the products of all possible combinations of two single-digit numbers. There are 100 single-digit multiplication facts. The number of facts that must be memorized can be cut down considerably by carefully studying various patterns in the table.

Besides the facts for one and zero there are sixty-four multiplication facts that should be memorized. A study of the multiplication table will afford the opportunity for making interesting discoveries that can aid the memory process. For example, consider the column for 5. Notice that every product ends in 0 or 5. When moving down to the 8's column, at each step, the tens digit goes up one and the ones digit goes down two, except in moving from 40 to 48. Many other similar relationships can be discovered from this and other tables. Can you find the pattern for nines? (Answer given at end of this section.)

Use this table of basic multiplication facts to find the product of two factors. For example, to find the product of 7 and 8, find the number at which the row for 7 and the column for 8 come together. In this case that number is 56.

Multiplication Table

X	0	1	2	3	4	5	6	7	8	9
0	0	0	0	0	0	0	0	0	0	0
1	0	1	2	3	4	5	6	7	8	9
2	0	2	4	6	8	10	12	14	16	18
3	0	3	6	9	12	15	18	21	24	27
4	0	4	8	12	16	20	24	28	32	36
5	0	5	10	15	20	25	30	35	40	45
6	0	6	12	18	24	30	36	42	48	54
7	0	7	14	21	28	35	42	49	56	63
8	0	8	16	24	32	40	48	56	64	72
9	0	9	18	27	36	45	54	63	72	81

Notice the diagonal line within the table. Using the properties of multiplication, it is necessary only to memorize the facts above this line. This is because multiplication is commutative.

Your Turn

Use the multiplication table to find each product.

1. 3×6 2. 8×7 3. 9×4
4. 9×0 5. 6×6 6. 9×9

(Answers appear at the end of the section.)

More properties

Each of the properties discussed so far uses only one operation at a time. There also is a property that uses both addition and multiplication. This is called the distributive property of multiplication over addition. The distributive property is essential to explaining why the standard procedure (algorithm) that is used in multiplication works. For example, if a series of numbers is to be multiplied by the same multiplier, their sum may be multiplied or the numbers may be multiplied individually and their respective products added to secure the final sum.

$$2 \times (3 + 4) = (2 \times 3) + (2 \times 4)$$
$$2 \times 7 \quad = \quad 6 \quad + \quad 8$$
$$14 \quad = \quad 14$$

This example illustrates the distributive property of multiplication with respect to addition. The distributive property is commonly used when multiplying by a number that has two or more digits.

Here are four ways of finding the product of 4 and 35. Study these examples until you are sure that you understand how the distributive property is used in each case.

$$
\begin{aligned}
\text{a.} \quad 4 \times 35 &= (4 \times 30) + (4 \times 5) \\
&= \quad 120 \quad + \quad 20 \\
&= \quad 140
\end{aligned}
$$

b. $30 + 5$
$$\underline{\times \qquad 4}$$
$120 + 20$

c. $3\ 5$
$$\underline{\times \ 4}$$
$2\ 0$ 4×5
$1\ 2\ 0$ 4×30
$1\ 4\ 0$ 4×35

$\overset{2}{}$
d. $3\ 5$
$$\underline{\times \ 4}$$
$1\ 4\ 0$ $4 \times 5 = 20$ Write the 0, carry the 2. (4×3) $+\ 2 = 14$

Your Turn

7. 14 8. 21 9. 19 10. 39
$\underline{\times\ 2}$ $\underline{\times\ 8}$ $\underline{\times\ 6}$ $\underline{\times\ 5}$

(Answers appear at the end of the section.)

The basic properties of addition and multiplication are important because they show how the whole numbers behave when they are added and multiplied. There are other properties of addition and multiplication, but each can be explained using the properties discussed so far. Operations with whole numbers depend on these basic properties. In the following list, letters *a, b, c* stand for any whole numbers.

Addition properties

Commutative property:

$a + b = b + a$

Associative property:

$(a + b) + c = a + (b + c)$

Property of zero:

$a + 0 = a$

(Zero is the identity element for addition.)

Multiplication properties

Commutative property:

$a \times b = b \times a$

Associative property:

$(a \times b) \times c = a \times (b \times c)$

Property of one:

$a \times 1 = a$

(One is the identity element for multiplication.)

Distributive property:

$a \times (b + c) = (a \times b) + (a \times c)$

(Multiplication is distributed over addition.)

Multiplication shortcuts

Multiplication can be fun if you know some shortcuts. Study this pattern.

$$10 \times 5 = 50$$
$$100 \times 5 = 500$$
$$1000 \times 5 = 5000$$

It is easy to find a product when one of the factors is 10. To multiply by 10, write as many zeros to the right of the given number as there are zeros in the given multiplier.

RULE
If multiplying by 10, write one zero.
If multiplying by 100, write two zeros.
If multiplying by 1000, write three zeros.

Here is a way of multiplying when both factors are multiples of 10.

$$40 \times 50 = (4 \times 10) \times (5 \times 10)$$
$$= (4 \times 5) \times (10 \times 10)$$
$$= 20 \times 100$$
$$= 2000$$

Your Turn

11. 3 × 100   12. 8 × 1000   13. 9 × 10
14. 30 × 20   15. 20 × 90   16. 50 × 80

(Answers appear at the end of the section.)

You can do many multiplications by using what you already know about numbers. Study this example.

15 × 21 = ?

To find 15 × 21, notice that fifteen is three times as many as five, so

15 × 21 is three times 5 × 21
5 × 21 = ? (Find this product.)
so 15 × 21 = ?

You should have found that 5 × 21 was 105 and 3 × 105 was 315.

Your Turn

17. 25 × 12   18. 40 × 15
19. 15 × 18   20. 64 × 12

(Answers appear at the end of the section.)

Multiplying larger numbers

The multiplication facts and properties, along with the concept of place value, are useful in finding products of larger numbers. For example, one method of multiplying is to show each of the partial products and then add them.

```
        4 7 2
      × 3 8
        1 6 ←8 times 2
      5 6 0 ←8 times 70
    3 2 0 0 ←8 times 400
        6 0 ←30 times 2
    2 1 0 0 ←30 times 70
  1 2 0 0 0 ←30 times 400
  1 7 9 3 6
```

While this method helps to explain each of the multiplications, it is somewhat cumbersome. There are some shortcuts. The usual shortcut is to find the sum (mentally) of all the numbers multiplied by 8 and the sum of all the numbers multiplied by 30. Then find the sum of the partial products. Normally this process is written as

```
      4 7 2
    × 3 8
    3 7 7 6
  1 4 1 6
  1 7 9 3 6
```

Now the following generalization of the process of multiplication by numbers of two or more digits can be made.

RULE
To multiply a number of more than one digit, multiply by the digit in the ones' place, then by the digit in the tens' place, and so on. Place the right-hand digit of each product immediately under the digit of the number being used as a multiplier. Then add the partial products to obtain the complete product.

Below are more examples that use the shortcut for multiplication of larger numbers.

```
      5 6 7          1 2 3
    × 3 1          × 4 6
      5 6 7          7 3 8
  1 7 0 1          4 9 2
  1 7 5 7 7        5 6 5 8
```

```
        9 3 2
      × 2 3 0
    2 7 9 6 0
  1 8 6 4
  2 1 4 3 6 0
```

Your Turn

21. 295   22. 321   23. 1245
    × 34   × 9   × 129

24. 9864
    × 854

(Answers appear at the end of the section.)

Estimating products

Often it is not necessary to find an exact product. In many cases a good estimate will suffice. Furthermore, comparing an exact product with an estimated product is a good way to determine whether the exact product is reasonable. Try answering these questions with an estimate.

   a. A girl delivers 42 papers on each of two daily trips along her route. How many papers will she deliver in 30 days?
   b. A computer company sold 8215 computers during a three-month period. At this rate how many can it expect to sell in one year?

To estimate an answer, round the numbers and complete the multiplication. In problem a., round the numbers to 40 and 30: 40 × 2 × 30 = 2400. The girl will deliver about 2400 papers in 30 days. In problem b., round the number to 8000. Since there are 4 three-month periods in one year, the answer will be about 8000 × 4, or about 32,000 computers per year.

Your Turn

Estimate the answer to each problem.

25. Ms. Jamison drove about 1950 miles each month. How far did she drive in 10 months?

26. The Arjay Company sold 10,231 cards in one week. At that rate, how many cards will be sold in 6 weeks?
27. Jack packed 398 objects in each of 210 boxes. How many objects were packed in all?

(Answers appear at the end of the section.)

Dividing Whole Numbers

Division related to multiplication

Division is the most difficult of the four fundamental operations. Part of this difficulty occurs because people learn the process of division mechanically without understanding the basic meanings involved. If division is learned in simple progressive stages much of this difficulty can be overcome.

Just as subtraction is defined as the inverse of addition, division is defined as the inverse of multiplication. The example 8 ÷ 2 = 4 means:

   8 is the product of two numbers
   4 is one of the two numbers
   2 is the other number

This can be written as

$$8 \div 2 = 4$$

dividend divisor quotient

The symbol " ÷ " is the division symbol. To divide 8 by 4 is to determine the number (quotient) that when multiplied by 4 (divisor) gives the number 2 (dividend); 8 ÷ 4 = 2 because 2 × 4 = 8. In general, the quotient of two numbers is that number which multiplied by the divisor gives the dividend.

Division as continued subtraction

Division can also be interpreted as continued subtraction. The example $8 \div 4 = 2$ can be interpreted as follows:

$$
\begin{array}{r}
8 \\
-4 \\
\hline
4 \\
-4 \\
\hline
0
\end{array}
$$

Notice that 4 can be subtracted from 8 in succession twice to give a zero remainder. The example $8 \div 4 = 2$ can also be written this way:

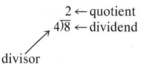

Division as measurement

Division can be interpreted as measurement. Thus, $24 \div 6$ means: "How many 6's are in 24?" Consider this example. Suppose 24 oranges are to be divided into groups of equal size, each one containing 6 oranges. The question is, "How many groups are there?" Since $4 \times 6 = 24$, the answer is 4 groups. However, the answer can be found in a concrete (physical) way by putting 6 oranges in one bag, then another group of 6 oranges in another bag, and continuing until all of the 24 oranges have been separated into groups of 6. Count the number of bags or groups to find that there are 4 groups. This process of separation is known as measurement division because the size of the group is known. The question again is, "How many groups are there?"

Division as partition

Division can be interpreted as partition. Thus, $24 \div 6$ means 24 is divided into 6 equal parts. Once again consider the 24 oranges in the example above. This time the oranges must be separated into 6 equal groups. The question now becomes, "How many oranges are in each group?" Create 6 groups by placing an orange in each of 6 bags until all 24 oranges have been placed. When finished, count the oranges in each group. The answer, of course, is 4. This method of separation is called partition division because of the partition of the total into groups of the same size.

Two different questions are asked by measurement-division and partition-division. When the size of the groups is known, the answer tells the number of groups. When the number of groups is known, the answer indicates the size of each group. The answer in each case is determined by the question. The division is the same for both questions.

In summary, division can be interpreted four ways, as

1. the inverse of multiplication
2. continued subtraction
3. measurement
4. partition

Knowing the basic multiplication facts makes division easier. One can also study the table of division facts. *See* Part VII, "Math Tables."

Your Turn

1. $15 \div 5$ 2. $36 \div 6$ 3. $63 \div 7$

4. $8\overline{)64}$ 5. $6\overline{)48}$ 6. $7\overline{)56}$

(Answers appear at the end of the section.)

Remainders in division

Notice that if only whole numbers are known, division is not always possible. For example, 4 ÷ 5 cannot be a whole number since there is no whole number that when multiplied by 5 gives the result 4. The need for division of this type leads to fractions. Fractions will be discussed in a later section.

With whole number division, sometimes the division is not exact. For example, 12 ÷ 5 does not give an exact whole number quotient. When the division is not exact there is a remainder. Thus, 16 ÷ 5 = 3, with a remainder of 1. There is one caution that should be observed.

Division by zero is not possible. Zero can be divided by 5 because 5 groups of 0 equals 0; however, 5 cannot be divided by 0 because no matter how many zeros there are, their sum can never be 5. Thus 0 ÷ 5 = 0 because 0 × 5 = 0. But 5 ÷ 0 has no answer because no number times 0 equals 5.

In division, it is necessary to know not only the multiplication facts, but also their inverses, the division facts. Certain division problems will have remainders, such as

17 ÷ 5 = 3, R 2 because
17 = 5 × 3 + 2

Your Turn

7. 21 ÷ 5   8. 62 ÷ 9   9. 15 ÷ 2
10. 82 ÷ 9   11. 45 ÷ 7   12. 32 ÷ 6

(Answers appear at the end of the section.)

Digit value and location

One of the most important decisions that must be made in division is the location and value of each digit in the quotient. In the problem 749 ÷ 4 the quotient will be in hundreds because there are more than 100 fours in 749. There are fewer than 1000 fours.

$$1 \times 4 = 4$$
$$10 \times 4 = 40$$
$$100 \times 4 = 400 \leftarrow \text{Too small}$$
$$1000 \times 4 = 4000 \leftarrow \text{Too large}$$

Answer between 100 and 1000.

Thus, the first digit in the quotient is in the hundreds place. The following discussion shows how the division algorithm works. Note that this algorithm is also the basis for long division.

749 ÷ 4

a.
```
      1
  4) 7 4 9
     4 0 0
     3 4 9
```
Estimate the hundreds. 4)7 is about 1, so 4)749 is about 100. Write 1 in the hundreds place. 100 × 4 = 400. Subtract.

b.
```
      1 8
  4) 7 4 9
     4 0 0
     3 4 9
     3 2 0
       2 9
```
Estimate the tens. 4)34 is about 8, so 4)349 is about 80. Write 8 in the tens place. 80 × 4 = 320. Subtract.

c.
```
      1 8 7 R 1
  4) 7 4 9
     4
     3 4
     3 2
       2 9
       2 8
         1
```
Estimate the ones. 4)29 is about 7. Write 7 in the ones place. 7 × 4 = 28. Subtract. Show the remainder.

You can see that 187 R 1 is correct by multiplying the quotient by the divisor and then adding the remainder.

$$4 \times 187 + 1 = 749$$

Here is a summary of the steps of division with whole numbers. Repeat the steps as often as necessary to complete the division.

1. Estimate
2. Multiply
3. Subtract
4. Compare
5. Bring down
6. Check

Here are two more examples.

```
  512          463 R 1
3)1536       7)3242
  15           28
   3           44
   3           42
   6           22
   6           21
   0            1
```

Your Turn

13. 2)230   14. 4)8124   15. 6)8215

(Answers appear at the end of the section.)

Dividing larger numbers

In long division, the idea is to start by taking as many of the divisor values from the dividend value as you wish to take. You think of a separate division problem for each place of the quotient. Basically the steps used for a one-digit divisor can be used for larger numbers. Often the most difficult part is estimating the quotient for each part.

PROCESS   Think in this manner to estimate the first digit.

```
      8 4      70 × 60 = 4200←Too small
62)5 2 4 0     80 × 60 = 4800←Too small
   4 9 6       90 × 60 = 5400←Too big
     2 8 0     The product is between 80
     2 4 8     and 90.
       3 2
```

CHECK: $(84 \times 62) + 32 = 5240$

How many groups of 62 each can be made from a group of 5240? The answer is 84 groups of 62 each, with a remainder of 32. As more skills are developed through practice, fewer and fewer steps will be needed to estimate quotients.

Your Turn

Find each quotient. Don't forget to estimate the quotient and to check your answers.

16. 98)2 0 5 8   17. 25)1 4 5 0

18. 15)4 2 0 5   19. 93)7 8 4

20. 34)1 7 3 8   21. 156)3 1 3 5 9

(Answers appear at the end of the section.)

Operations with 0 and 1

Find the answers to these problems.

1. $0 \div 5 = ?$ 2. $2 \times 0 = ?$
3. $0 + 0 = ?$ 4. $0 - 0 = ?$
5. $6 - 6 = ?$ 6. $0 \times 3 = ?$

In each case the answer should be zero. Recall that zero has some special properties. Below is a summary of some of the important ideas concerning zero and one. The letter *a* stands for any whole number.

RULE
When zero is added to or subtracted from any whole number, the result is the same whole number.

$a + 0 = a$ and $a - 0 = a$

where a is any whole number.

RULE
When zero is multiplied by any whole number, the result is zero.

$a \times 0 = 0$ or $0 \times a = 0$

where a is any whole number.

RULE
When zero is divided by a whole number the result is zero.

$0 \div a = 0$

where a is any whole number.

RULE
Division by zero is meaningless.

$a \div 0$ has no answer.

RULE
When zero is divided by zero no single answer is possible.

$0 \div 0$ has no one answer.

Thus division by zero is undefined.

RULE
When a number is divided by one the result is the number.

$a \div 1 = a$

where a is any whole number.

Recall that the number one is called the identity element for multiplication because

$a \times 1 = a$ for any number a

Since multiplication and division are inverse operations, the following observations can be made.

RULE
If a number is multiplied by a number greater than 1, the product will be greater than the multiplicand. Since division is the inverse of multiplication, if a given number is divided by a number greater than 1, the quotient will be smaller than the dividend.

Complete this statement.

When the divisor is _____ than 1, the quotient is always _____ than the dividend.

Give an example to show that this statement is true.

Order of Operations

Look at the two solutions for this problem. Only one is correct.

a. $\underline{3 + 7} \times 2$ b. $3 + \underline{7 \times 2}$

       $\underline{10 \times 2}$ $\underline{3 + 14}$

      20   17
  INCORRECT   CORRECT

In a., the addition is completed first, then the multiplication. In b., the multiplication is completed first, then the addition. The method used in b. is the correct method. To find the answer to problems when more than one operation is involved, rules called the order of operations are used. These rules are necessary so that correctly computed answers will be the same and situations such as the one shown can be avoided.

The following general rule has been universally adopted for computing answers to problems containing mixed operations without parentheses.

RULE:

If a problem contains a series of operations involving additions, subtractions, multiplications, and divisions, perform first the multiplications and divisions in the order in which they occur. Then do the indicated additions and subtractions in order from left to right.

Example:
$$81 \div 9 - 3 \times 2 + 4$$
$$9 \quad - \quad 6 \quad + \quad 4$$
$$3 \quad + \quad 4$$
$$7$$

Another example:
$$21 - 7 \times 2 + 5$$
$$21 - 14 + 5$$
$$7 + 5$$
$$12$$

Sometimes problems may be grouped with parentheses. To compute answers to problems with parentheses, follow this rule:

RULE:

Do the work within parentheses first. Complete all multiplications and divisions in order from left to right. Then, add or subtract in order from left to right.

The important thing to keep in mind is that operations enclosed within parentheses must be performed first, to give a single number. Then operations not enclosed within sets of parentheses are performed.

Example:
$$(6 \times 8) + (12 - 4) - 7$$
$$48 \quad + \quad 8 \quad - \quad 7$$
$$56 \quad - \quad 7$$
$$49$$

Another example:
$$(6 + 8) \times (12 - 4) \div 7$$
$$14 \quad \times \quad 8 \quad \div \quad 7$$
$$112 \quad \div \quad 7$$
$$16$$

Your Turn

Perform the indicated operations.

1. $45 \div 5 + 20 + 4 - 3$
2. $3 + 72 \div 8 \times 3 - 6 \times 2$
3. $(9 \div 3) \times 3 + (6 \times 8) \div 2 \times 4 - 3$
4. $8 - 4 \times (5 - 2) \div 3 - 2$

(Answers appear at the end of the section.)

Solving Word Problems

What methods should you use to solve problems like these?

1. Typing at the rate of 72 words per minute, how long would it take to type 2304 words?
2. Light travels at a speed of 186,252 miles per second. How far would it travel in one minute?
3. If your income is $18,250 per year and you pay $2436 in taxes, what is your after-tax pay?
4. A football team gained 196 yards rushing and 215 yards passing. How many yards were gained altogether?

In order to solve problems such as these correctly, you need to know, among other things, which computations to perform. Do you add, multiply, subtract, or divide to find the answer? Sometimes this is not easy to decide. Furthermore, you must also keep in mind that just doing the computations correctly does not guarantee that the computed answer is the solution to the problem. One way to tackle this situation is to use a set of organized steps that can be followed with most routine problems. There are as many such procedures, or plans, as there are problem solvers.

It is important to note that all steps need not be considered necessary in every problem that you encounter. The procedures used are not the important thing. What is important is the development of an organized set of questions to ask when confronted with a problem-solving situation. Here is one set of procedures that can be used.

Read

Read the problem carefully. Be sure that you identify what is given and what has to be found.

Understand

Analyze the information. Be sure that you understand the meaning of each word. Sometimes familiar words may be used in such a way that they take on new meanings. In example 4. above, the use of the word *altogether* suggests that the amounts of yardage should be added. Looking for any special words or situations in a problem can aid in understanding the problem. Once you discover these key words you may find it useful, at times, to restate the problem in your own words.

Plan

Decide which operation to use. Plan the solution. Plan the entire solution at once. Write down your plan, if you need to. Sometimes your plan might include one or more of the following:

a.   making a table
b.   drawing a diagram
c.   using a calculator
d.   working backward

In example 1., one question that could be asked is "How do I find out how many 72's there are in 2304?" This is a clue that the answer can be found by division.

Estimate

Estimate the solution. Use rounding whenever possible. Establish boundaries—what is the least and the most the answer could be. In example 2., by rounding 186,282 to 200,000 an estimate of the product can be made before you compute.

$$200,000 \times 60 = 12,000,000$$

The estimate shows that the actual answer should be close to 12,000,000.

Solve

Perform all necessary operations. Ask yourself if the answer is really the solution to the problem.

Check

Check your solution. Make sure the arithmetic is correct by using the inverse operation. Compare it with the original estimate. Decide if the answer is reasonable. Estimation is a good way to check certain problems. It is especially important when computing with a calculator because you can easily press a wrong key or not press a key firmly enough. Also you might forget to clear the calculator before starting a new problem.

Now use these steps to solve the four problems at the beginning of this discussion. Explanations are given below.

1. Information Given: 72 words per minute
   Find: 2304 words to type
   Typing time
   Plan: Divide.
   Estimate: 23 ÷ 7 is a little more than 3, so 2300 ÷ 70 is a little more than 30.
   Solve: 32 minutes
   Check: 72 × 32 = 2304 and 32 is close to the estimate of 30.

2. Information Given: Speed: 186,252 miles per second
   60 seconds in 1 minute
   Find: Distance traveled in one *minute*
   Plan: Multiply.
   Estimate: 200,000 × 60 = 12,000,000
   Solve: 11,175,120 miles
   Check: 11,175,120 ÷ 60 = 186,252
   11 million is close to 12 million.

3. Information Given: Income $18,250
   Taxes $2436
   Find: After-tax pay
   Plan: Subtract.
   Estimate: 20,000 − 2000 = 18,000
   Solve: $15,814
   Check: 15,814 + 2436 = 18,250
   Estimate seems off by 2000. Would have been closer if

estimate had been 18,000 − 2000.

4. Information Given: 196 yards rushing
   215 yards passing
   Find: Total yards gained
   Plan: Add.
   Estimate: 200 + 200 = 400
   Solve: 411 yards
   Check: 411 − 196 = 215
   Estimate is close.

Your ability to solve word problems will improve as you encounter and solve many different types of problems.

Your Turn

The following problems include a variety of different problem-solving situations. Review the problem-solving steps and the examples. Refer to them as needed to help solve the problems.

1. A basketball team scored 2632 points in 28 games. Find the average number of points scored per game.
2. A publishing company must package 20,000 books in cartons of 52 books each. How many cartons will be filled? How many books will be left over?
3. If an automobile averages 27 miles per gallon of gasoline, and if its tank holds 14 gallons, how far can it travel on a full tank?
4. If the odometer of an automobile reads 21,053 at the beginning of a trip and 22,976 at the end of the trip, how long was the trip?
5. A parking lot attendant wants to find the number of cars a parking lot will hold. There are 14 rows for cars. Each row holds 21 cars. What answer should the attendant get?

(Answers appear at the end of the section.)

Many problems involving applications of mathematics are found in various areas, such as business, consumerism, science, and technology. In almost all of these applications, it is necessary to set up and use a problem-solving procedure and then complete the necessary computation. Sometimes the solutions to such problems require more than one operation. Following are some illustrations of these types of problems. Give the operations you would use to solve each problem.

Your Turn

6. The average speed of a satellite is 300 miles per minute and it has been circling the earth for 6 hours. How far has it traveled?
7. If 25 pounds of dog food sell for $7.00, and a 10-pound package of the same dog food sells for $2.00, which is the better buy?
8. One employee has 3 weeks' vacation. Another employee has 5 weeks' vacation. How many more vacation days does the second employee have than the first?
9. In a parking lot there are 8 used cars for every 2 new cars. If there are 50 cars in all, how many cars are new and how many cars are used?
10. For 140 days of work, new division managers received $12,600 each. How much should they receive for 180 days of work?

The operations needed to solve the problems above are:

6. Multiply by 60 to find speed in miles per hour. Then multiply by 6 to solve the problem.
7. Divide to find the cost per pound of each package. Then compare costs.

8. Work the problem in either of these ways:

   $(5 - 3) \times 5$ or $(5 \times 5) - (3 \times 5)$

9. Add 8 and 2, divide 50 by that sum, then multiply the quotient by 2 to find how many new cars and by 8 to find how many used cars.
10. Divide 12,600 by 140 to find pay per day. Then multiply by 180.

Now find the solutions to problems 6–10 above. Then solve these problems:

11. A salesperson drove 529 miles. The company pays 25 cents for each mile driven. How much should the company pay the salesperson?
12. A room is 12 feet long by 10 feet wide. Mr. and Mrs. Williams want to buy carpeting for the room. The carpeting costs $12 per square foot. How much will the carpeting cost for the entire room?
13. A photographer developed 6 rolls of film. Two rolls had 36 pictures on each roll. Four rolls had 20 pictures on each roll. How many pictures were developed?
14. The library has 3219 fiction books and 2098 nonfiction books. The library wants to get more books for a total of 8000 books. How many more books should the library get?
15. The temperatures for one week in July were 70, 82, 91, 94, 87, 84, and 80. What was the average temperature during that week?

(Answers appear at the end of the section.)

Answers

Starting at the Beginning (pp. 199–200)

1. $||||\cap$; XV   2. $|||||||||\cap\cap\cap$; XXXIX   3. $||||\cap\,^9$; CXIV   4. $|\cap\cap\cap\cap\cap$; LI

5. $||\cap\cap\cap\cap\,^9\,^9\,^9\,^9\,^{\frac{3}{2}}$; MCDXLII   6. $|||||||\cap\cap\cap\,^{\frac{3}{2}}\,^{\frac{3}{2}}$; MMXLVI

Numbers and Numerals (pp. 200–202)

1. one thousand, thirty   2. three hundred twelve thousand, four hundred sixty-seven

3. nine hundred fifty-four million, one hundred twenty-three thousand, four   4. 473

5. 24,600   6. 200,510,164

Using Exponents to Name Numbers (pp. 202–203)

1. $(3 \times 10^2) + (5 \times 10^1) + (7 \times 10^0)$ 2. $(9 \times 10^3) + (1 \times 10^2) + (2 \times 10^1) + (5 \times 10^0)$

3. $(1 \times 10^4) + (2 \times 10^3) + (7 \times 10^2) + (0 \times 10^1) + (3 \times 10^0)$

Rounding Numbers (pp. 203–204)

1. 830   2. 1000   3. 160,000

Adding Whole Numbers (pp. 204–207)

1. 68   2. 496   3. 86   4. 688   5. 91   6. 67   7. 1350   8. 109   9. 208

10. 96   11. 78   12. 1034   13. 157

Subtracting Whole Numbers (pp. 207–209)

1. 7   2. 7   3. 9   4. 7   5. 9   6. 25   7. 210   8. 435   9. 7011

10. 5   11. 173   12. 1808   13. 689

Multiplying Whole Numbers (pp. 210–215)

Multiplication table answer: Going down the 9's column, the ones digit increases one and the tens digits decreases one.

1. 18   2. 56   3. 36   4. 0   5. 36   6. 81   7. 28   8. 168   9. 114
10. 195   11. 300   12. 8000   13. 90   14. 600   15. 1800   16. 4000
17. 300   18. 600   19. 270   20. 768   21. 10,030   22. 2889   23. 160,605
24. 8,423,856   25. 20,000 miles   26. 60,000 cards   27. 80,000 objects

Dividing Whole Numbers (pp. 215–218)

1. 3   2. 6   3. 9   4. 8   5. 8   6. 8   7. 4 R1   8. 6 R8   9. 7 R1
10. 9 R1   11. 6 R3   12. 5 R2   13. 115   14. 2031   15. 1369 R1   16. 21
17. 58   18. 280 R5   19. 8 R40   20. 51 R4   21. 201 R3

Order of Operations (pp. 219–220)

1. 30   2. 18   3. 102   4. 2

Solving Word Problems (pp. 220–223)

1. 94 points   2. 384 cartons with 32 books left   3. 378 miles   4. 1923 miles   5. 294 cars
6. 108,000 miles   7. 10-pound package   8. 10 days   9. 10 new cars; 40 used cars
10. $16,200   11. $132.25   12. $1440   13. 152 pictures   14. 2683 books
15. 84 degrees

Section 2

Number Theory

The Greek mathematician Pythagoras found many unusual things about whole numbers. He was intrigued, for example, by the discovery that the pitch of a musical note from a string depends upon the length of the string. He found that the relationship between the pitch and the length of the string could be described by whole numbers or by various combinations of them.

Some of the properties that were discovered involved odd numbers and even numbers. Another property that was discovered was whether a number is prime or composite. This kind of study of the whole numbers and the various relations among them is now called number theory. Some of these concepts were discussed in the previous section. Now such concepts will be discussed in a number theory context. Other number theory concepts will also be presented.

Common Stumbling Blocks

Inadequate computational skills are probably the greatest hindrance to under-standing number theory. A clear understanding of the four basic operations is essential before any progress can be made in studying number theory. A good memory and the ability to recognize patterns are also beneficial. Although some new vocabulary such as factorization, sequences, and sets will be encountered, it is not necessary to be familiar with these concepts before studying this section.

Important Techniques and Concepts

Mathematical words, like other words, are defined in terms of other words whose meanings are already agreed upon. One such mathematical term is the term *set*. A set is a collection of objects. Sets of objects are encountered every day. Perhaps one set that you are familiar with is a standard deck of cards.

Each card is a member of the deck. If you count the cards, the counting will come to an end at 52. This is because there is a definite number of cards in a deck. A set with a definite (finite) number of members is called a finite set. The

members of a finite set can be counted. If a set is not finite, then it is infinite. Even though counting every grain of sand in the world would be difficult, it could be done. There is an end, a final number that would say how many grains of sand there are. This set is finite.

An infinite set is a set with an infinite number of members. The set of whole numbers has an infinite number of members and is therefore an infinite set. There is no largest whole number.

There are two ways to show that things are members of a set and that things are not members:

1. Describe the set in words.

   Example: "The set of odd numbers less than 10"

2. List the members of the set.

   Example: {1, 3, 5, 7, 9}

The numbers used for counting, sometimes called the natural numbers, are used every day by each of us. They are named by this set.

{1, 2, 3, 4, . . .}

(The dots inside the braces indicate that the set of numbers extends indefinitely in that direction.)

This set of numbers is called the whole numbers.

{0, 1, 2, 3, 4, . . . }

If the only reason for having whole numbers was to count sets of objects, these numbers would not be of much interest. However, the whole numbers themselves are not the subject of this study. Instead, some subsets of whole numbers will be studied.

Subsets of Whole Numbers

Set A is a subset of a set B if each member of A is also a member of B. To indicate this write

A ⊂ B (read "A is a subset of B").

For example, the set N of the natural numbers is a subset of the set W of whole numbers:

N ⊂ W

To picture this, a diagram can be drawn. (The letter U stands for the universal set, the set that contains all numbers.)

N = {1, 2, 3, . . .}
W = {0, 1, 2, . . .}

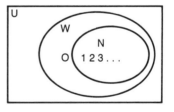

When you think of the whole numbers that have some special property, you think of a subset of W.

There are different subsets of whole numbers. Many of these subsets have special properties. The study of subsets of whole numbers with special properties is called number theory.

The whole numbers are probably used more often in everyday life than any other numbers. So it is natural for you to compute with them without a second thought. However, in the next examples the focus will be specifically on two subsets that can be formed as a result of multiplication and addition.

Example A: Use the set of whole numbers $\{0, 1, 2, 3, \ldots\}$ and multiply each number in the set by 2. List the set of numbers you get. What name is usually given to this set?

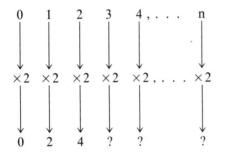

A number that is 2 times a whole number is called an even number.

$$E = \{0, 2, 4, 6, 8, \ldots\}$$

Example B: Start with the set of even numbers $\{0, 2, 4, 6, 8, \ldots\}$ and add 1 to each number in the set. Write the results. What is this set usually called?

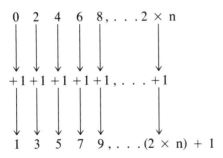

A number that is one more than an even number is called an odd number.

$$O = \{1, 3, 5, 7, 9, \ldots\}$$

Your Turn

Study this table and then answer the questions that follow.

×	0	1	2	3	4	5	6	7	8	9
0	0	0	0	0	0	0	0	0	0	0
1	0	1	2	3	4	5	6	7	8	9
2	0	2	4	6	8	10	12	14	16	18
3	0	3	6	9	12	15	18	21	24	27
4	0	4	8	12	16	20	24	28	32	36
5	0	5	10	15	20	25	30	35	40	45
6	0	6	12	18	24	30	36	42	48	54
7	0	7	14	21	28	35	42	49	56	63
8	0	8	16	24	32	40	48	56	64	72
9	0	9	18	27	36	45	54	63	72	81

1. Select any two odd numbers. Multiply them. Is the product odd or even?
2. Select any two even numbers. Multiply them. Is the product odd or even?
3. Select an odd number and an even number. Multiply them. Is the product odd or even?

Make an addition table or use the table given in Part VII, "Math Tables." Study the various combinations of odd and even numbers and then answer these questions.

4. Select any two odd numbers. Add them. Is the sum even or odd?
5. Select any two even numbers. Add them. Is the sum even or odd?
6. Select an even number and an odd number. Add them. Is the sum even or odd?

(Answers appear at the end of the section.)

Using a number line you can also think of odd and even numbers this way.

From the number line, you see that even numbers are whole numbers that have 2 as a factor. Odd numbers are whole numbers that do not have 2 as a factor.

The words *factor* and *divisor* are frequently used in number theory. Review the meaning of these two words by studying the following statement.

The numbers 1, 2, 3, 6, 9, and 18 are the divisors (or factors) of 18.

This statement can be made because when 18 is divided by any of these numbers (1, 2, 3, 6, 9, or 18) the remainder is zero.

> **RULE:**
> **A factor is a number that divides the product so that the quotient is a whole number with zero as a remainder.**

$$
\begin{array}{r} 8 \\ 2\overline{)16} \\ 16 \\ \hline 0 \end{array}
\qquad
\begin{array}{r} 5 \\ 3\overline{)15} \\ 15 \\ \hline 0 \end{array}
\qquad
\begin{array}{r} 4 \\ 4\overline{)18} \\ 16 \\ \hline 2 \end{array}
$$

2 is a
factor
of 16.

3 is a
factor
of 15.

4 is not
a factor
of 18.

If a number is a factor of a second number, then the second number is divisible by that factor.

16 is divisible by 2.
15 is divisible by 3.
18 is not divisible by 4.

In general,

> **RULE**
> **If a, b, and c are whole numbers and if $a \times b = c$, then**

1. a **is a factor of** c.
2. b **is a factor of** c.

$2 \times 7 = 14$ 2 is a factor of 14.
7 is a factor of 14.

Your Turn

7. What are the divisors of 12?
8. Is 30 divisible by 5?
9. Is 48 divisible by 5?
10. Is 9 a factor of 56?
11. Is 32 a factor of 4?

(Answers appear at the end of the section.)

Usually factors of numbers are stated in pairs. The pairs of factors of 18 are

1 × 18
2 × 9
3 × 6

Notice the following pairs are not listed:

6 × 3
9 × 2
18 × 1

This is because the factors are the same as those in the first list.

You can always divide the product by one of a pair of factors to get the other factor.

Example: List the pairs of factors of 56. One factor is 7.

7 × ? = 56
56 ÷ 7 = 8

So 7 × 8 is one pair of factors of 56. Using the same idea, the following pairs of factors are found:

7 × 8
4 × 14
2 × 28
1 × 56

Next you will see that zero also has factors. Since

$$0 \times 0 = 0$$
$$0 \times 1 = 0$$
$$0 \times 2 = 0$$
$$0 \times 3 = 0$$

. . . and so on, every whole number is a factor of zero. Study this chart.

$1 = 1 \times 1$	The only factor of 1 is 1.
$2 = 1 \times 2$	The only factors of 2 are 1 and 2.
$3 = 1 \times 3$	The only factors of 3 are 1 and 3.
$4 = 1 \times 4 = 2 \times 2$	The only factors of 4 are 1, 4, and 2.
$5 = 1 \times 5$	The only factors of 5 are 1 and 5.

Notice that every number except 1 has at least two factors.

Your Turn

List all the factors for the following:

12. 6   13. 10   14. 19   15. 42

(Answers appear at the end of the section.)

Prime numbers

Whole numbers that have no factors other than 1 and the number itself are prime numbers. The number 1 is usually not considered to be a prime number. All other whole numbers are composite numbers. All composite numbers may be ex-

pressed as a product of primes. Composite numbers have more than two distinct factors.

The numbers 1 and 0 are neither prime nor composite. Zero has an endless number of factors and the number one has only one factor, itself.

Sieve of Eratosthenes

One famous method for finding prime numbers is called the Sieve of Eratosthenes. This method of screening out the primes is named in honor of the Greek mathematician who discovered it more than 2000 years ago.

Use this method to find all prime numbers between 1 and 50. Begin by listing these numbers in a table on a separate paper.

```
 1   2   3   4   5   6   7   8   9  10
11  12  13  14  15  16  17  18  19  20
21  22  23  24  25  26  27  28  29  30
31  32  33  34  35  36  37  38  39  40
41  42  43  44  45  46  47  48  49  50
```

Follow the steps below. Notice that examples are provided to show how each step is completed for the numbers through 30. You are to complete the examples through 50 on your paper.

Step 1: Mark out 1. It is not considered a prime because it has only one factor.

Step 2: Circle 2. It is a prime. Cross out all numbers greater than 2 that have a factor of 2. A / was used in the example. This should leave only odd numbers that are not crossed out.

```
 ☒  ②   3   4̸   5   6̸   7   8̸   9  1̸0
11  1̸2  13  1̸4  15  1̸6  17  1̸8  19  2̸0
21  2̸2  23  2̸4  25  2̸6  27  2̸8  29  3̸0
```

Step 3: Find the next number that is not crossed out—3. Circle 3. It is a prime. Cross out all numbers greater than 3 that have a factor of 3. A \ was used. Notice that some numbers are now crossed out twice.

X̶ ② ③ 4̶ 5 6̶ 7 8̶ 9̶ 1̶0̶
11 1̶2̶ 13 1̶4̶ 1̶5̶ 1̶6̶ 17 1̶8̶ 19 2̶0̶
2̶1̶ 2̶2̶ 23 2̶4̶ 25 2̶6̶ 2̶7̶ 2̶8̶ 29 3̶0̶

Step 4: Circle the next number that is not crossed out. Five is a prime. Cross out all numbers that have a factor of 5. A — was used.

X̶ ② ③ 4̶ ⑤ 6̶ 7 8̶ 9̶ 1̶0̶
11 1̶2̶ 13 1̶4̶ 1̶5̶ 1̶6̶ 17 1̶8̶ 19 2̶0̶
2̶1̶ 2̶2̶ 23 2̶4̶ 2̶5̶ 2̶6̶ 2̶7̶ 2̶8̶ 29 3̶0̶

Step 5: Circle the next number that is not crossed out. Seven is a prime. Cross out all numbers that have a factor of 7. A | was used.

X̶ ② ③ 4̶ ⑤ 6̶ ⑦ 8̶ 9̶ 1̶0̶
11 1̶2̶ 13 1̶4̶ 1̶5̶ 1̶6̶ 17 1̶8̶ 19 2̶0̶
2̶1̶ 2̶2̶ 23 2̶4̶ 2̶5̶ 2̶6̶ 2̶7̶ 2̶8̶ 29 3̶0̶

Step 6: Circle the next number that is not crossed out. Eleven is a prime. Look for the numbers that have a factor of 11. Notice that all these numbers (22, 33, and 44) have already been crossed out. This means you have found all the primes less than 50.

The sieving process, for finding primes, can be used with whole numbers as high as you care to go.

Your Turn

1. Use the Sieve of Eratosthenes to find all prime numbers less than 100.
2. Is every odd number, other than 1, a prime number?
3. Is every even number, other than 2, a composite number?

Notice that 30 was crossed out 3 times. This shows that 2, 3, and 5 are prime factors of 30.

4. What are 2 prime factors of 28?
5. What are 3 prime factors of 42?

(Answers appear at the end of the section.)

Goldbach's conjecture

Christian Goldbach, an eighteenth-century mathematician, claimed that every even number greater than 2 can be expressed as the sum of two prime numbers. This conjecture has not been proved, although most mathematicians believe it is true.

$$\underset{\underset{32}{\downarrow}}{\text{Even}} = \underset{\underset{13}{\downarrow}}{\text{Prime}} + \underset{\underset{19}{\downarrow}}{\text{Prime}}$$

Your Turn

Verify Goldbach's conjecture by finding two primes whose sum is

6. 24   7. 40   8. 28   9. 46

(Answers appear at the end of the section.)

With the exception of 2, the prime numbers are odd, so two consecutive primes have a difference of two. Pairs of primes that have a difference of two are called prime twins. The following numbers are prime twins:

5, 7   11, 13   29, 31

Mathematicians believe there are an infinite number of such pairs.

Your Turn

10. List three more prime twins.

(Answers appear at the end of the section.)

Finding prime numbers

When working with fractions and higher mathematics problems, it is often necessary to know whether a number is a prime. Many formulas have been devised to find some prime numbers. In mathematics it is said that prime numbers are "generated" by these formulas. One such expression, $4p - 1$, produces many primes for whole number values of p. When, in a mathematical expression, a number and a letter (like $4p$) are written next to each other with no space, that means to multiply. So $4p$ means $4 \times p$ and $4p - 1$ means $(4 \times p) - 1$.

Example: $4p - 1$
If $p = 1$, $(4 \times 1) - 1 = 3$ (prime)
If $p = 2$, $(4 \times 2) - 1 = 7$ (prime)
If $p = 10$, $(4 \times 10) - 1 = 39$ (composite)

But when $p = 10$, the number found is not prime. The rule produces some numbers that are not prime.

Your Turn

Find the value of $4p - 1$ for each of the following. Tell whether the result for each is prime or composite.

11. 3   12. 4   13. 7   14. 14

(Answers appear at the end of the section.)

No one has ever found a formula that always produces prime numbers, but many people have tried. Another formula that sometimes works is

$$n^2 + n + 41$$

For example, if $n = 3$ then

$$n^2 + n + 41$$
$$3^2 + 3 + 41$$
$$9 + 3 + 41$$
$$12 + 41$$
$$53, \text{ which is prime.}$$

This formula produces prime numbers for every value of n from 1 through 39. However, it fails for $n = 40$.

Arrays

Some whole number subsets may be pictured graphically by using arrays. There are two types of arrays. A linear array is an arrangement with only one row or column.

A rectangular array is a set with more than one row and column.

It is possible to think of a prime number as a number that cannot be represented by a rectangular array. A composite number can be represented by both a linear and a rectangular array.

Prime factorization

Every composite number may be expressed as a product of prime numbers. This may be done by writing all the prime factors of the number. Although a number may be factorable in more than one way, each method leads to the same set of prime factors. This process of factoring a number is called prime factorization. To factor a number, divide the number by the primes 2, 3, 5, 7, 11, . . . (in that order) until you find a divisor.

$$18 = 2 \times 9 = 2 \times 3 \times 3$$

The number 18 can be written as 2×9. But 9 is not prime. However, 9 can be factored further as 3×3. Thus, $18 = 2 \times 3 \times 3$. When a factor appears more than once, you can also use exponents to show the factorization.

$$18 = 2 \times 3^2$$

When factoring larger numbers, you may wish to use either of the following methods.

Example: Give the prime factorization of 840.

$$2)\overline{8\ 4\ 0}$$
$$2)\overline{4\ 2\ 0}$$

840

$$2)\overline{2\ 1\ 0} \qquad 10 \quad \times \qquad 84$$

$$3)\overline{1\ 0\ 5} \quad 5 \times 2 \times \quad 4 \quad \times \quad 21$$

$$5)\ \underline{3\ 5} \quad 5 \times 2 \times 2 \times 2 \times 3 \times 7$$
$$7$$

Thus, $840 = 2 \times 2 \times 2 \times 3 \times 5 \times 7$
$$= 2^3 \times 3 \times 5 \times 7$$

Your Turn

Give the prime factorization for these numbers.

15. 1050   16. 686   17. 1215
18. 1120   19. 252   20. 504

(Answers appear at the end of the section)

Divisibility rules

A useful name for the product of factors is *multiple*. Both 8 and 96 are multiples of 2. All multiples of a number have that number as a factor. There are certain patterns that will help you find multiples of a number. Even numbers, for example, are all multiples of 2. If the last digit is even, the number is even.

RULE:
Test for 2: **A number is divisible by 2 if its last digit is 0, 2, 4, 6, or 8.**

214 is divisible by 2 because it ends with 4.

230 is divisible by 2 because it ends with 0.

397 is not divisible by 2 because it ends with 7. Seven is odd.

756 is divisible by 2 because it ends with 6.

Your Turn

Test for 3: See if you can find a pattern for getting the multiples of 3.

Number	Sum of the Digits
10	$1 + 0 = 1$
11	$1 + 1 = 2$
12	$1 + 2 = 3$
13	$1 + 3 = ?$
14	$1 + 4 = ?$
15	$1 + 5 = ?$
16	$1 + 6 = ?$
17	$1 + 7 = ?$
18	$1 + 8 = ?$
19	$1 + 9 = ?$
20	$2 + 0 = ?$

The pattern shows that a number is divisible by 3 only if the sum of digits is divisible by ___?___.

(Answers appear at the end of the section.)

RULE:
Test for 4: **In order to tell whether a number is divisible by 4, you need to inspect the last two digits (tens and ones) of the number. If the number formed by the last two digits of a number is divisible by 4, then the number is divisible by 4.**

932 is divisible by 4 because 32 (the number formed by the last two digits) is divisible by 4.

121 is not divisible by 4 because 21 is not divisible by 4.

RULE:
Test for 5: **Any number is divisible by 5 if it ends in 5 or 0.**

23,790 ends with 0, thus it is divisible by 5.

4325 ends with 5, thus it is divisible by 5.

RULE:
Test for 6: **To test for 6, you need to test for both 2 and 3, since 6 = 2 × 3. A number is divisible by 6 if the ones digit is divisible by 2 and if the sum of the digits is divisible by 3.**

768 is divisible by 6 because the last digit is divisible by 2 and 7 + 6 + 8 is divisible by 3.

RULE:
Test for 7: **There is no easy test for 7.**

RULE:
Test for 8: **A number is divisible by 8 if the number formed by the last 3 digits of a number is divisible by 8.**

2488 is divisible by 8 because 488 is divisible by 8.

12,460 is not divisible by 8 because 460 is not divisible by 8.

RULE:
Test for 9: **Any number is divisible by 9 if the sum of its digits is divisible by 9.**

4077 is divisible by 9 because the sum of its digits, 18, is divisible by 9.

21,468 is not divisible by 9 because the sum of its digits, 21, is not divisible by 9.

RULE:
Test for 10: **Any number is divisible by 10 if it ends in zero.**

350 is divisible by 10 because the ones digit is zero.

Your Turn

Copy the chart below on a separate sheet of paper. Use all the tests for divisibility discussed above to complete the chart. Write "Y" in the rectangle if the number is divisible by the number at the top of that column. Otherwise, write "N."

	2	3	4	5	6	8	9	10
Example: 3220	Y	N	Y	Y	N	N	N	Y
1. 648								
2. 4036								
3. 6201								
4. 32,019								
5. 144,000								
6. 27,006,345								

(Answers appear at the end of the section.)

Progressions

One way to develop number awareness is to explore different number patterns. From very early times people have observed patterns in nature. The seasons of the year, the seventeen-year locust, and the half-life of radioactive elements are a few of the many recurring patterns in everyday life that are taken for granted. Now some of these patterns will be discussed, expressed as number sequences, and then classified by different types of arithmetic and geometric progressions.

Number sequences

You can often find a pattern in certain groups of numbers. Suppose you know that January 3 is a Sunday. Then because of the pattern on which our calendar is based, the next Sunday will be January 10. The following Sunday will be seven days later on January 17. The next Sunday will be January 24, and the last Sunday in January will be seven days after January 24, on January 31. These dates form a pattern that can be listed as

3, 10, 17, 24, 31

This list of numbers is called a number sequence. A number sequence is a set of numbers in which each number follows the last according to a uniform rule. The numbers in a sequence are called terms of the sequence.

Arithmetic sequences

In the sequence of days above, notice that a pattern was used, adding seven each time, to get the next term. A number sequence that is obtained by adding the same number is called an arithmetic sequence. Here are two sequences that you will recognize: the sequences of odd numbers and of even numbers.

$O = \{1, 3, 5, 7, 9, \ldots\}$
$E = \{2, 4, 6, 8, 10, \ldots\}$

The rule for each sequence happens to be the same.

RULE:
Add two to each number to get to the next one. That is, if n represents the first term, the next term is $n + 2$.

The number added to each term of an arithmetic sequence is actually the difference between any two adjacent terms in the sequence. For example, the difference between each term here is 5.

1, 6, 11, 16, 21, 26

To find the difference of the terms in a sequence, select any two adjacent terms and subtract the first from the second. In the above sequence you might choose 16 and 21 as the adjacent terms and then subtract to find the common difference. Of course, any two adjacent numbers in the set can be selected. If the first term and the common difference for an arithmetic sequence are known, then it is possible to write as many terms of the sequence as are needed.

Your Turn

Complete these arithmetic sequences.

1. 4, 5, 6, 7, ?, ?, ?, 11
2. 32, 35, ?, 41, ?, ?, 50
3. 11, 23, 35, ?, ?, ?, ?
4. ?, 35, 51, ?, ?
5. 15, ?, 45, 60, ?, ?

Draw the next two figures to complete these sequences.

6.

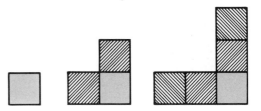

7.

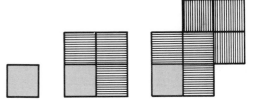

8. Complete this table of arithmetic sequences.

Time (Seconds)	Distance (Feet)
0	21
1	62
2	103
3	?
4	?
5	226
6	267
7	?
8	349
9	?
10	431

(Answers appear at the end of the section.)

One easy way to find any term. What is the 20th term of the sequence in the last exercise? Did you get the answer, 800? Instead of counting and adding up to the 20th term, there is an easier way to find the answer. The same sequence of distances can be found by thinking about the sequence in this manner:

First term	21
Second term	$21 + 1 \times 41$
Third term	$21 + 2 \times 41$
Fourth term	$21 + 3 \times 41$
Fifth term	$21 + 4 \times 41$
•	•
•	•
•	•
Twentieth term	$21 + 19 \times 41$

Notice that to find the twentieth term nineteen 41's were added to 21. This technique can be used to find any term in an arithmetic sequence.

Your Turn

Figure out the terms in each of the following sequences.

9. The 12th term of 3, 12, 21, . . .
10. The 35th term of 12, 17, 22, 27, . . .
11. The 313th term of 3, 9, 15, 21, . . .

(Answers appear at the end of the section.)

Gauss's method to find any term. Karl Friedrich Gauss, an eighteenth-century German mathematician, was an outstanding young student. The following story is often told about his years as a schoolboy.

One of Karl's teachers was very lazy. This teacher would give the class an addition example like this:

$$4586 + 4594 + 4602 + 4610 \ldots$$

and so on, with as many as a hundred numbers. The teacher would then sit back and relax while the students tried to work the examples. Sometimes their work could take several hours to complete. Gauss noticed that the teacher always made up problems so that adjacent numbers were the same amount apart. (In the example shown, each number has a common difference of 8.)

In those days the custom was to have the students bring their slates to the teacher's desk as they finished their work, and then return to their seats. One day, the teacher had no sooner finished telling the class the numbers before Karl had written the answer down on his slate and put it on the teacher's desk. The teacher couldn't believe that Karl had done the work; but when the teacher checked the slate, he found that Karl's answer was correct. The young lad had figured out a short way of doing the addition. While the other students in the class were adding two numbers at a time, Gauss would proceed as follows:

Problem: Find the sum of the first hundred counting numbers.

Gauss noticed that the numbers could be paired. Each pair had a sum of 101.

$$1+2+3+4 + \ldots + 97+98+99+100$$

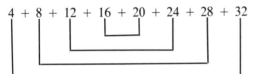

$$4 + 97 = 101$$
$$3 + 98 = 101$$
$$2 + 99 = 101$$
$$1 + 100 = 101$$

Since there are 50 sums of 101, the total is 50 × 101, or 5050.

Example: Find the sum of this sequence. 4, 8, 12, 16, 20, 24, 28, 32

$$4 + 8 + 12 + 16 + 20 + 24 + 28 + 32$$

4 pairs with a sum of 36
4 × 36 = 144
The sum is 144.

Example: Find the sum of the first twenty-five even numbers.

Think: 2 + 4 + . . . + 48 + 50

12 pairs with a sum of 52 *and* the middle even number, 26. (12 × 52) + 26 = 650

Notice that when there is an odd number of terms in the sequence, the middle term must be added.

Your Turn

Find the sum of the numbers in each of these sequences.

12. 4, 7, 10, 13, 16
13. 25, 29, 33, 37, 41, 45
14. 12, 24, 36, 48, 60, 72, 84
15. 1 + 2 + 3 + . . . + 49 + 50
16. 1 + 3 + 5 + . . . + 73 + 75

(Answers appear at the end of the section.)

Geometric sequences

When each term of a sequence is obtained by always multiplying the previous term by the same number, the sequence is called a geometric sequence.

$$3, \quad 9, \quad 27, \quad 81, \quad 243$$

$$\times 3 \quad \times 3 \quad \times 3 \qquad ?$$

What is the common multiplier?

The sequence 3, 9, 27, 81, 243 is a geometric sequence because each term is three times the number before it. The sequence 4, 16, 64, 256, . . . is also geometric. To find the next number in this sequence, multiply the last listed number by the common multiplier, 4. So the next term in the sequence is 4 × 256 or 1024.

There are a variety of applications of geometric sequences. For example, the chain letter gimmick that people sometimes send to their friends is based on a geometric sequence.

A chain letter works this way. You receive a letter with a list of 6 names. You send a postcard to the person named at the top, cross that name out and add your own name at the bottom. You then send out six copies of the letter to your friends and ask them to do the same. When your six friends send out six letters each, there will be 36 letters sent out in all. If none of the 36 persons getting these letters breaks the chain, 216 more letters will be sent, and then 1296, and so on. This sequence can be listed as follows:

1, 6, 36, 216, 1296, . . .

If the chain is unbroken, your name will be on the 6 letters you send first, then on the 36 letters sent by your 6 friends, and so on. How many postcards will you receive if the chain is unbroken?

(Answer appears at the end of the section.)

Your Turn

Complete each of the following geometric sequences.

17. 8, 48, 288, 1728, ?, ?
18. 1, 11, 121, ?, ?, ?
19. 13, 39, ?, ?, ?, 3159
20. 28, 784, ?, 614656, ?

(Answers appear at the end of the section.)

Figurate numbers

Here are some sets of dots that form different figures. Count the dots in each and see if you can sketch the next figure.

1.

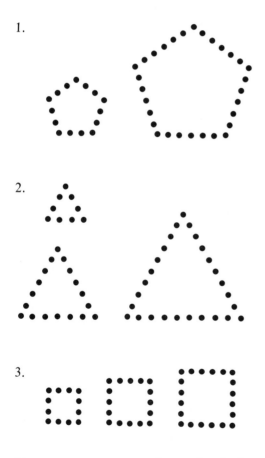

2.

3.

(Answers appear at the end of the section.)

Numbers that can be represented by arrays of dots such as the ones above are called figurate numbers. Some special types of figurate numbers are rectangular numbers, square numbers, and triangular numbers.

Rectangular numbers. Think of the patterns made by the dots on a set of dice, a pile of logs, or the keys on a calculator. All these regular patterns can be used to picture numbers along with their factors. For example, the number 6 can be pictured as follows:

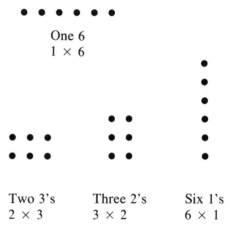

One 6
1×6

Two 3's   Three 2's   Six 1's
2×3 3×2 6×1

Your Turn

Draw all possible rectangles of dots for the following:

4. 12   5. 18   6. 25
7. 20   8. 9   9. 16

(Answers appear at the end of the section.)

Square numbers. Did you notice that some of the patterns you drew in the previous exercise were squares? (A square is a special kind of rectangle.) For example, 25 can be shown as

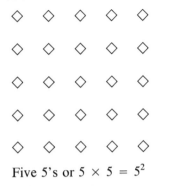

Five 5's or $5 \times 5 = 5^2$

This array is in the form of a square. It has the same number of columns as rows. So 25 is called a square number. The number 25 has two equal factors, 5 and 5, which are called square roots.

Your Turn

Study this list of square numbers. Add the next 3 square numbers.

$$1^2 = 1 \times 1 = 1$$
$$2^2 = 2 \times 2 = 4$$
$$3^2 = 3 \times 3 = 9$$
$$4^2 = 4 \times 4 = 16$$

10. $5^2 =$
11. $6^2 =$
12. $7^2 =$

(Answers appear at the end of the section.)

Compare the pattern formed with this figure.

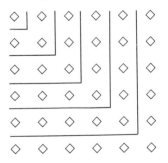

Your Turn

Now complete the following up to 10^2:

$$2^2 = 1^1 + 3$$
$$3^2 = 2^2 + 5$$
$$4^2 = 3^2 + 7$$
$$5^2 = 4^2 + 9$$

13. $6^2 =$
14. $7^2 =$
15. $8^2 =$
16. $9^2 =$
17. $10^2 =$

(Answers appear at the end of the section.)

Below is another pattern. Study it.

$$1^2 = \ \ 1 = 1$$
$$2^2 = \ \ 4 = 1 + 3$$
$$3^2 = \ \ 9 = 1 + 3 + 5$$
$$4^2 = 16 = 1 + 3 + 5 + 7$$
$$5^2 = 25 = 1 + 3 + 5 + 7 + 9$$

Your Turn

Complete the above pattern for sums through 10^2.

18. 6^2 19. 7^2 20. 8^2 21. 9^2 22. 10^2
23. What are the numbers on the right called?

(Answers appear at the end of the section.)

Odd numbers are related to square numbers in a special way. Review the last list of sums above to see if you can discover the relationship. Here is a hint:

First odd number: $1 = 1^2$
First 2 odd numbers: $1 + 3 = 2^2$
First 3 odd numbers: $1 + 3 + 5 = ?$

Triangular numbers. Imagine a stack of pencils arranged with their erasers showing as follows.

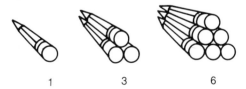

1   3   6

These numbers, as shown in the groups of pencils, are called triangular numbers. Study the figure below. What is the relationship between the triangular numbers and the square numbers?

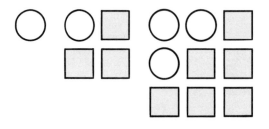

Complete these sets of triangular numbers and square numbers. What is the relationship between the two sets?

Square numbers 1, 4, 9, . . . 64
Triangular numbers 1, 3, 6, . . . 36

Read the next section on the Fibonacci sequence to find the relationship.

Fibonacci sequence. The Fibonacci sequence is a sequence of numbers in which every number after the second number is equal to the sum of the two preceding numbers.

1, 1, 2, 3, 5, 8, 13, 21, 34, . . .

This sequence was originally presented by Leonardo of Pisa around the year 1200 when he introduced algebra in Italy. He was also known as Leonardo Fibonacci and is considered the greatest mathematician of the thirteenth century. Numbers

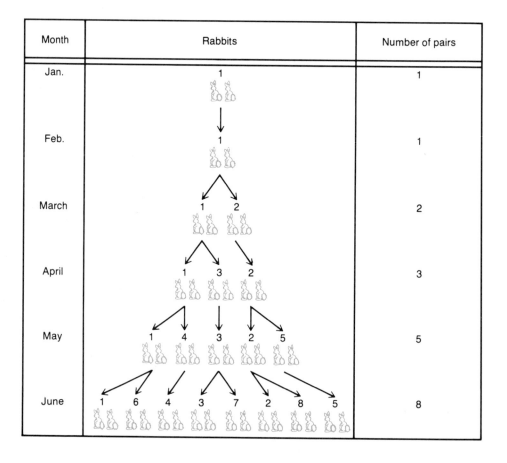

from the Fibonacci sequence occur in a variety of places in nature.

One of the number patterns that Fibonacci discovered was related to rabbits. Assume that a pair of rabbits produces a new pair of rabbits in their second month and then one pair in every month thereafter. This pattern continues for all new rabbits. None of the rabbits dies. The number of pairs of rabbits that will be present is shown in the diagram, on page 240. The rabbit population is represented by the Fibonacci numbers. Fibonacci was wrong about the way rabbits breed, but his pattern has been of great interest to mathematicians.

You may have noticed that the number-pairs of rabbits fit the pattern of the Fibonacci sequence. This sequence is neither arithmetic nor geometric.

The first two terms of the sequence are 1, and each succeeding term is found by adding the two preceding terms.

1,   1,   2,   3,   5,   8, . . .

1   1

$$1 + 1 = 2$$

$$1 + 2 = 3$$

$$2 + 3 = 5$$

$$3 + 5 = 8$$

$$5 + 8 = ?$$

Your Turn

24. List the next eight terms in the Fibonacci sequence.

(Answers appear at the end of the section.)

Fibonacci patterns have been found in the nodes of a pine cone, in the petals of flowers, in the leaves of plants, and in the scales of pineapples.

You can quickly determine the sum of any ten consecutive Fibonacci numbers by using the following procedure.

The sum is always 11 times the seventh number in the sequence. Consider this portion of the Fibonacci sequence.

144
233
377
610
987
1597
2584 → (11 × 2584) = 28,424
4181
6765
10946

Thus, the sum of these ten numbers of the sequence is 28,424. (You might want to check this by adding all the numbers.)

Your Turn

25. Find the sum of the first 8 terms of the Fibonacci sequence. The sum is one less than the tenth term of the sequence.

26. According to the rabbit problem, how many pairs of rabbits can be produced in a year?

27. Starting with 2, construct a sequence using the same rule used in the Fibonacci sequence.

28. In the sequence in exercise 27., what is the third number in the sequence? the eighth?

29. How does the eighth number in your new sequence compare with the eighth in the Fibonacci sequence?

(Answers appear at the end of the section.)

Answers

Subsets of Whole Numbers (pp. 227–230)

1. odd   2. even   3. even   4. even   5. even   6. odd   7. 1, 2, 3, 4, 6, 12
8. yes   9. no   10. no   11. no   12. 1, 2, 3, 6   13. 1, 2, 5, 10   14. 1, 19
15. 1, 2, 3, 6, 7, 14, 21, 42

Prime Numbers (pp. 230–233)

1. 2, 3, 5, 7, 11, 13, 17, 19, 23, 29, 31, 37, 41, 43, 47, 53, 59, 61, 67, 71, 73, 79, 83, 89, 97
2. no   3. yes   4. 2, 7   5. 2, 3, 7
For 6–10 answers may vary. Sample answers are given.
6. 5 and 19   7. 3 and 37   8. 11 and 17   9. 7 and 39
10. 17 and 19, 41 and 43, 59 and 61   11. 11, prime   12. 15, composite   13. 27, composite
14. 55, composite   15. $2 \times 3 \times 5^2 \times 7$ 16. 2×7^3 17. $3^5 \times 5$ 18. $2^5 \times 5 \times 7$
19. $2^2 \times 3^2 \times 7$ 20. $2^3 \times 3^2 \times 7$

Divisibility Rules (pp. 233–234)

Patterns for test of divisibility by 3: 4, 5, 6, 7, 8, 9, 10, 2; 3

	2	3	4	5	6	8	9	10
1. 648	Y	Y	Y	N	Y	Y	Y	N
2. 4036	Y	N	Y	N	N	N	N	N
3. 6201	N	Y	N	N	N	N	Y	N
4. 32,019	N	Y	N	N	N	N	N	N
5. 144,000	Y	Y	Y	Y	Y	Y	Y	Y
6. 27,006,345	N	Y	N	Y	N	N	Y	N

Arithmetic and Geometric Sequences (pp. 235–238)

1. 4, 5, 6, 7, 8, 9, 10, 11   2. 32, 35, 38, 41, 44, 47, 50   3. 11, 23, 35, 47, 59, 71, 83
4. 19, 35, 51, 67, 83   5. 15, 30, 45, 60, 75, 90

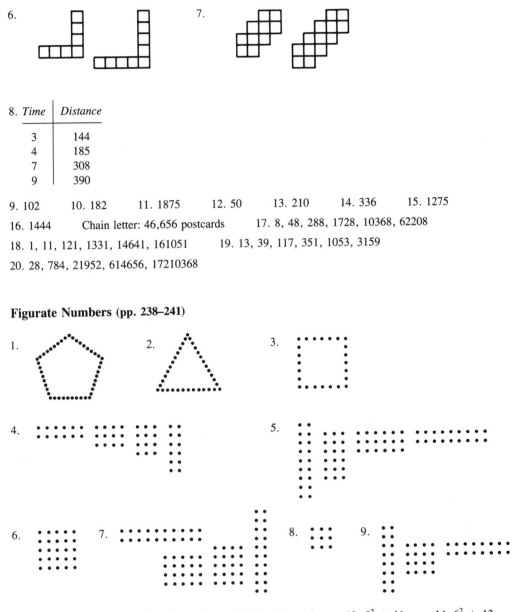

6.

7.

8.

Time	Distance
3	144
4	185
7	308
9	390

9. 102   10. 182   11. 1875   12. 50   13. 210   14. 336   15. 1275

16. 1444   Chain letter: 46,656 postcards   17. 8, 48, 288, 1728, 10368, 62208

18. 1, 11, 121, 1331, 14641, 161051   19. 13, 39, 117, 351, 1053, 3159

20. 28, 784, 21952, 614656, 17210368

Figurate Numbers (pp. 238–241)

1.

2.

3.

4.

5.

6.   7.   8.   9.

10. $5 \times 5 = 25$ 11. $6 \times 6 = 36$ 12. $7 \times 7 = 49$ 13. $5^2 + 11$ 14. $6^2 + 13$

15. $7^2 + 15$ 16. $8^2 + 17$ 17. $9^2 + 19$ 18. $36 = 1 + 3 + 5 + 7 + 9 + 11$

19. $49 = 1 + 3 + 5 + 7 + 9 + 11 + 13$ 20. $64 = 1 + 3 + 5 + 7 + 9 + 11 + 13 + 15$

21. $81 = 1 + 3 + 5 + 7 + 9 + 11 + 13 + 15 + 17$

22. $100 = 1 + 3 + 5 + 7 + 9 + 11 + 13 + 15 + 17 + 19$ 23. odd numbers or arithmetic sequences

24. 13, 21, 34, 55, 89, 144, 233, 377   25. 54   26. 144

27. 2, 2, 4, 6, 10, 16, 26, 42, 68, 110   28. 4, 42   29. It is twice as large.

Section 3

Fractional Numbers

In Section 1 of Part IV, it was shown that numbers came about out of a need for counting. As civilizations advanced people became concerned about sharing goods and dividing things into various parts, such as land and proportional shares of a harvest.

Many questions about the physical world that were unanswerable with just the set of whole numbers are answerable with the set of fractions. Questions involving the sharing of a supply of goods, for example, usually lead to ideas involving fractional numbers.

Success in working with fractions requires the mastery of many concepts. A large number are presented here. You should study all the examples carefully. Do not try to complete more than a few pages of this section at each sitting.

Meanings of Fractions

A fraction symbol may be thought of in any one of several ways. The difficulty that people have with fractions has often resulted from the fact they were not aware that there are several meanings to the symbol. Therefore, it is very important to have an understanding of each of these points of view. A fraction symbol may be examined from four different points of view:

1. A fraction may be thought of as representing one or more of the equal parts of a unit.

For example, if the length of an inch is divided into four equal parts, the length of one part is $\frac{1}{4}$ inch and the length of three parts is $\frac{3}{4}$ inch. The $\frac{3}{4}$ represents 3 of the 4 parts into which the whole is separated. In other words $\frac{3}{4}$ tells you to separate the base unit into 4 equal parts and think of 3 of the parts.

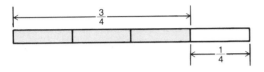

2.   A fraction may be considered as representing one of several equal parts of several units.

For example, in this diagram $\frac{3}{4}$ shows three of the four equal parts of four units.

There are 4 fractional units each of which is $\frac{1}{4}$ of a base unit.

The symbol $\frac{5}{6}$ shows that there are 5 fraction units, each of which is $\frac{1}{6}$. Thinking of fractions this way does not require the performance of any operations. The operation is already understood. The numerator tells how many units there are, and the denominator the kind of unit.

five $\frac{1}{6}$'s or $\frac{5}{6}$ ← parts shaded
               ← parts in one unit

3.   A fraction can be thought of as indicating division.

$\frac{12}{6}$ ← parts shaded
    ← parts in one unit

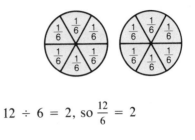

$12 \div 6 = 2$, so $\frac{12}{6} = 2$

Example: How many $\frac{1}{4}$ inches are in 3 inches?

$\dfrac{3}{\frac{1}{4}}$ means $3 \div \frac{1}{4} = ?$

Study the drawing below to find the answer.

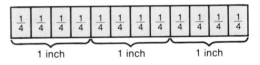

$\dfrac{3}{\frac{1}{4}}$ represents the number of shaded parts. There are 12 parts, so $\dfrac{3}{\frac{1}{4}} = 12$.

This example suggests that there is no limit on the kind of numbers that can be used as denominators and numerators of fractions except that the denominator cannot be zero.

4. A fraction may be interpreted as a ratio; that is, the comparison of two quantities.

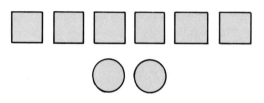

If two numbers are compared, there are two ways of making the comparison. To compare 6 with 2 you might ask, "6 is how much more than 2?" To find the answer, subtract and say 6 is 4 more than 2.

$$6 - 2 = 4$$

A different question could be asked, such as "6 is how many times as great as 2?" In that case divide 6 by 2 and say that 6 is 3 times as great as 2.

$$\frac{6}{2} = 3$$

Thus two numbers can be compared by subtraction or by division. The division comparison is called a ratio.

These four interpretations of the fraction symbol serve useful purposes in helping to understand some of the operations with fractions.

Important words

In a study of fractions it is also necessary to become familiar with and use the appropriate vocabulary. The list of technical words needed includes the following: numerator, denominator, simplest form, proper fraction, improper fraction, mixed numeral, and invert. It should be noted that one does not learn the meaning of technical terms in mathematics by memorizing definitions but through concrete experiences in which the terms are used.

Several of the terms that are convenient to use when talking about fractions are descriptive. In a fraction, the numeral above the line of a fraction represents a number that is the numerator. The numeral below the line represents a number that is the denominator of the fraction.

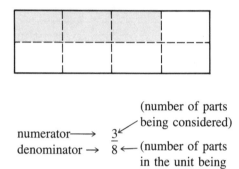

(number of parts being considered)

numerator ⟶ 3
denominator ⟶ 8 ⟵ (number of parts in the unit being considered)

Before 2000 B.C. the Babylonians used fractions. One of the first kinds of fractions to be used was the unit fraction. A unit fraction has a numerator of 1.

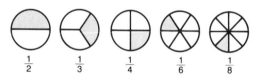

$$\frac{1}{2} \qquad \frac{1}{3} \qquad \frac{1}{4} \qquad \frac{1}{6} \qquad \frac{1}{8}$$

Each drawing shows a unit fraction. Each of these unit fractions is of a different size. When the numerator of each fraction is the same and the denominator of each succeeding fraction is larger, the value of each fraction becomes smaller. The larger the denominator, the smaller the value a unit fraction has.

When the numerator of a fraction is smaller than the denominator, the fraction is called a proper fraction. When the numerator is equal to or greater than the denominator, the fraction is called an improper fraction.

Naming fractions

Fractional numbers, like whole numbers, can be matched with points on a number line. On the number line below, fractional numbers have been matched with some points on the line. Obviously, points representing fractions will fall between those representing whole numbers. On this number line the distance between the whole number points has been divided into equal parts. Each numeral represents the distance from 0 to a given point in terms of the distance from 0 to 1.

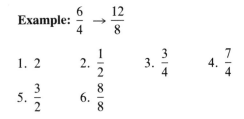

Notice that the distance from 0 to point j is 2 units plus $\frac{2}{4}$ of a unit. This distance can be written in any of these ways.

$$2\frac{2}{4} \qquad \frac{10}{4} \qquad 2\frac{1}{2}$$

The examples above all name the same number, but in different ways. A number represented by a whole number and a fraction is called a mixed numeral.

The marks on a ruler separate inches into fractional parts. The drawing below represents two inches on a ruler. This drawing is not actual size, it is bigger.

Your Turn

Use the drawing of a ruler to give another name for each of the following:

Example: $\frac{6}{4} \rightarrow \frac{12}{8}$

1. 2   2. $\frac{1}{2}$ 3. $\frac{3}{4}$ 4. $\frac{7}{4}$

5. $\frac{3}{2}$ 6. $\frac{8}{8}$

(Answers appear at the end of the section.)

Mixed numerals and fractions

Often when fractions are added or multiplied, the results may be a an improper fraction. Sometimes it is desirable, although not always necessary, to change an improper fraction to mixed numeral form. A quick way to do so is to divide the numerator by the denominator. To rename any improper fraction as a mixed numeral, use the following procedure.

Example: Rename $\frac{5}{3}$ as a mixed numeral. First divide the numerator by the denominator.

$1 \leftarrow$ This is the whole number part.
$3\overline{)5}$

$\underline{3}$ The remainder is the
$2 \leftarrow$ numerator of the fraction part.

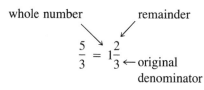

whole number   remainder

$$\frac{5}{3} = 1\frac{2}{3} \leftarrow \text{original}$$
denominator

$1\frac{2}{3}$ is a mixed numeral. Sometimes you will need to rename a mixed numeral as an improper fraction.

Example: Rename $5\frac{2}{3}$ as an improper fraction.

1. Multiply the whole number by the denominator.

$\times \; c5\frac{2}{3}$ $(5 \times 3) = 15$

2. Add that answer to the numerator.

$+ \; c5\frac{2}{3}$ $(5 \times 3) + 2 = 17$
$\times$

3. Place that answer over the original denominator.

$+ \; c5\frac{2}{3} \longrightarrow \frac{17}{3} = \frac{17}{3}$
$\times$

Your Turn

Rename each mixed numeral below as a fraction.

7. $1\frac{1}{2}$ 8. $2\frac{3}{4}$ 9. $1\frac{5}{6}$

10. $3\frac{2}{5}$ 11. $6\frac{2}{7}$ 12. $5\frac{3}{8}$

Express each fraction below as a mixed numeral.

13. $\frac{6}{5}$ 14. $\frac{10}{3}$ 15. $\frac{9}{4}$

16. $\frac{21}{8}$ 17. $\frac{35}{16}$ 18. $\frac{57}{7}$

(Answers appear at the end of the section.)

Equivalent fractions

The drawing of the enlargement of part of a ruler on page 247 shows that there are many names for the same distance. When fractions name the same number, they are called equivalent fractions. You could draw pictures to find equivalent fractions, but doing so might be inconvenient. An easier way is to build "families" of equivalent fractions. These families can be built by using multiplication.

$$\overset{\times 2}{\frac{2}{3}} = \frac{4}{6} \qquad \overset{\times 3}{\frac{2}{3}} = \frac{6}{9}$$
$\times 2$ $\qquad$ $\times 3$

$$\overset{\times 4}{\frac{2}{3}} = \frac{8}{12}$$
$\times 4$

$\frac{2}{3}, \frac{4}{6}, \frac{6}{9}$, and $\frac{8}{12}$ are equivalent fractions.

Families can also be built by division.

$$\overset{\div 2}{\frac{18}{24}} \quad \frac{9}{12} \qquad \overset{\div 3}{\frac{18}{24}} \quad \frac{6}{8}$$
$\div 2$ $\qquad$ $\div 3$

$$\overset{\div 6}{\frac{18}{24}} \quad \frac{3}{4}$$
$\div 6$

$\frac{18}{24}, \frac{9}{12}, \frac{6}{8}$, and $\frac{3}{4}$ are equivalent fractions.

Your Turn

Use multiplication to build three equivalent fractions for each of the following:

19. $\frac{1}{5}$ 20. $\frac{4}{7}$ 21. $\frac{5}{6}$

Use division to build three equivalent fractions for each of the following:

22. $\dfrac{24}{36}$ 23. $\dfrac{60}{40}$ 24. $\dfrac{12}{60}$

(Answers appear at the end of the section.)

Simplest Form of Fractions

In the families of equivalent fractions shown on page 248 of the previous section, $\dfrac{2}{3}$ and $\dfrac{3}{4}$ are expressed in lowest terms or in simplest form. To express a fraction in lowest terms or in simplest form, divide the numerator and the denominator by the same number. A fraction is said to be in lowest terms when no number except 1 will divide both of its terms. For example, $\dfrac{4}{8}$ may be reduced to lowest terms, but $\dfrac{5}{8}$ is already in lowest terms since 1 is the only number that will evenly divide both 5 and 8. The fraction $\dfrac{4}{8}$ may be reduced to $\dfrac{1}{2}$ by dividing both terms of the fraction by 4. Notice that when the fraction is reduced, fewer parts are found but the parts are larger.

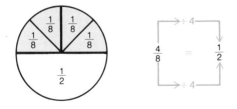

Thus, to reduce a fraction to lowest terms, divide the numerator and the de-

nominator by the largest number that will exactly divide both of them. This number is called the greatest common factor of the terms.

Greatest common factor

In the number theory section, factors and multiples of whole numbers were discussed. You will now see how these concepts relate to fractions.

Suppose there are 16 women and 12 men at a party. The hostess wishes to form the greatest number of teams possible for playing a game so that each team has the same number of women and each team has the same number of men. What is the greatest number of teams that she can form in this way? The hostess made a chart.

Number of Teams	Number of Men	Number of Women
1	12	16
2	6	8
3	4	—
4	3	4
6	2	—
8	—	2
12	1	—
16	—	1
	↑ Factors of 12.	↑ Factors of 16.

She could have written the factors this way.

W = {1, 2, 4, 8, 16}
M = {1, 2, 3, 4, 6, 12}

The factors common to both M and W are 1, 2, and 4. The greatest (largest) common factor of W and M is 4. Thus, the largest number of teams with equal numbers of men and equal numbers of women on each team would be 4.

The greatest common factor is often referred to as the GCF. There is another way to find the GCF of 12 and 16. Factor 16 and 12 into products of prime numbers. Choose the prime factors common to both numbers.

$$16 = 2 \times 2 \times 2 \times 2$$
$$12 = 2 \times 2 \times 3$$

Now find the product of the common factors.

$$GCF = 2 \times 2 = 4$$

So, the GCF of 12 and 16 is 4.

Here is another example. Find the greatest common factor of 24 and 36.

$$36 = 2 \times 2 \times 3 \times 3$$
$$24 = 2 \times 2 \times 2 \times 3$$

GCF of 24 and 36 = $2 \times 2 \times 3$, or 12.

The famous Greek mathematician Euclid invented still another way of finding the GCF of two numbers. Divide the larger number by the smaller and then divide the remainder into the previous divisor until the remainder is 0. The last divisor is the GCF of the two numbers. This example shows how to find the GCF of 75 and 125 using Euclid's method.

$$
\begin{array}{r}
1 \\
75\overline{)125} \\
75 \\
\hline
50
\end{array}
\qquad
\begin{array}{r}
1 \\
50\overline{)75} \\
50 \\
\hline
25
\end{array}
\qquad
\begin{array}{r}
2 \\
25\overline{)50} \\
50 \\
\hline
0
\end{array}
$$

Since 25 is the last divisor, it is the GCF of 75 and 125.

Your Turn

Find the greatest common factor (GCF).

1. 25 and 40
2. 44 and 60
3. 63 and 72
4. 35 and 45
5. 36 and 90
6. 48 and 84

(Answers appear at the end of the section.)

Simplifying fractions

As mentioned earlier, a fraction can be reduced to lowest terms (simplified) by dividing the numerator and denominator by the largest number that will divide both exactly. For example, to simplify

$$\frac{30}{42}$$

first find the GCF of 30 and 42.

$$30 = 2 \times 3 \times 5$$
$$42 = 2 \times 3 \times 7$$

The GCF of 30 and 42 is 2×3, or 6. To write the fraction in simplest form, divide as shown using the GCF.

$$\frac{30}{42} = \frac{5}{7} \quad \overset{\div 6}{\underset{\div 6}{}}$$

simplest form

Example: Simplify $\frac{42}{35}$

Find the GCF of 42 and 35.

$$42 = 2 \times 3 \times 7$$
$$35 = 5 \times 7$$

Divide, using the GCF.

$$\frac{42}{35} = \frac{6}{5} \quad \overset{\div 7}{\underset{\div 7}{}}$$

$\frac{6}{5}$ is NOT in simplest form yet. It is an improper fraction. Change $\frac{6}{5}$ to a mixed numeral.

$$\frac{6}{5} \rightarrow 5\overline{)6} \rightarrow 1\frac{1}{5}$$
$$\frac{5}{1} \qquad \text{simplest form}$$

RULE:
A proper fraction is in simplest form when the only number that will divide the numerator and denominator is 1.

An improper fraction must be changed to a mixed numeral. When the fraction part of a mixed numeral is in simplest form, then the mixed numeral is in simplest form.

Your Turn

Simplify each of the following:

7. $\dfrac{25}{40}$ 8. $\dfrac{72}{63}$ 9. $\dfrac{36}{90}$ 10. $\dfrac{24}{10}$ 11. $\dfrac{35}{45}$

(Answers appear at the end of the section.)

Multiplying Fractions

Multiplying whole numbers and fractions

This drawing shows a part of the blade of a saw. The teeth of the blade are made on an automatic perforating machine, according to specified dimensions.

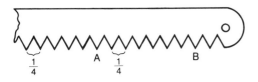

To find the distance from A to B, you could add $\dfrac{1}{4}$ seven times. For example,

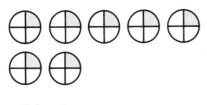

= 7 fourths

Length of AB $= \dfrac{1}{4} + \dfrac{1}{4} + \dfrac{1}{4} + \dfrac{1}{4} + \dfrac{1}{4} + \dfrac{1}{4} + \dfrac{1}{4}$

$= \dfrac{7}{4}$

$= 1\dfrac{3}{4}$

The length from A to B is $1\dfrac{3}{4}$ units.

However, it is usually easier and faster to multiply. For example,

Length of AB $= 7 \times \dfrac{1}{4}$

$= \dfrac{7 \times 1}{4}$ or $\dfrac{7}{4}$

$= 1\dfrac{3}{4}$

Did you notice that you needed to recall your multiplication facts in order to do this problem? Study the following rule.

RULE:
To multiply a whole number by a fraction, multiply the numerator of the fraction by the whole number and place the product over the denominator.

The following rule of multiplication of fractions shows a standard procedure for multiplying fractions.

RULE:
If a, b, c, and d are whole numbers, and b and d are not 0, multiplication of fractions is defined as
$$\dfrac{a}{b} \times \dfrac{c}{d} = \dfrac{a \times c}{b \times d}$$

Since the number 7 can be written as $\dfrac{7}{1}$, the problem above can be written as

$$\dfrac{7}{1} \times \dfrac{1}{4} = \dfrac{7}{4} \text{ or } 1\dfrac{3}{4}$$

Now study this example to see why this works.

The shaded area in this diagram represents $\frac{1}{2}$.

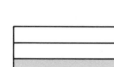

$$\frac{5}{6} \times \frac{3}{7} = \frac{5}{\underset{2}{6}} \times \frac{\overset{1}{3}}{7} \blacktriangleright \frac{5 \times 1}{2 \times 7} = \frac{5}{14}$$

The shaded area represents $\frac{1}{3}$ of this diagram.

The area shaded twice represents $\frac{1}{3}$ of $\frac{1}{2}$ of the drawing.

Study the figure carefully. Into how many parts has the figure been divided? How do the parts compare in size and how many parts are there? What kind of parts are they? How many parts are in the area that is shaded twice?

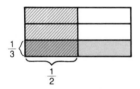

The figure has been separated into 6 equal parts. One of the 6 parts is shaded twice. Notice that $\frac{1}{3}$ of $\frac{1}{2}$ is $\frac{1}{6}$ of the drawing. Usually this is written as a multiplication problem.

$$\frac{1}{2} \times \frac{1}{3} = \frac{1}{6}$$

By now it should be clear that the product of the numerators will tell how many units there are and the product of the denominators will indicate what kind of units.

You may be familiar with the shortcut of dividing the numerators and denominators of the fractions by common factors before multiplying.

The technique of drawing slash marks through the numerator and denominator to show division by common factors is often called cancelling. While this is a good technique, it can lead to errors if one isn't careful about which terms should and should not be divided out. Another technique is to display the prime factors of both the numerator and the denominator and then use values of one to simplify the product. Study this example. Notice that each colored pair of numerals has a value of 1. These are the common factors.

$$\frac{14}{40} \times \frac{10}{15} = \frac{7 \cdot 2 \cdot 2 \cdot 5}{2 \cdot 2 \cdot 2 \cdot 5 \cdot 5 \cdot 3}$$

$$= \frac{7}{30}$$

The use of prime factors to simplify multiplication with fractions not only eliminates some of the misunderstandings associated with the cancelling technique, but emphasizes the uses of basic concepts and sound mathematical thinking.

Your Turn

Find each product in simplest form.

1. $\frac{2}{3} \times \frac{1}{5}$ 2. $\frac{7}{8} \times \frac{2}{3}$ 3. $\frac{1}{2} \times \frac{1}{2}$

4. $\frac{4}{9} \times \frac{3}{4}$ 5. $6 \times \frac{2}{3}$ 6. $\frac{9}{10} \times 10$

7. $5 \times \frac{7}{8}$ 8. $\frac{3}{5} \times \frac{7}{8}$ 9. $\frac{15}{19} \times \frac{3}{5}$

(Answers appear at the end of the section.)

Mixed numerals in multiplication

If mixed numerals are used in multiplication, it is usually better to change them to improper fractions before multiplying. Although other procedures are possible, this method is the preferred one.

$$3\frac{1}{4} \times 2\frac{2}{3} = \frac{13}{4} \times \frac{8}{3}$$ Change the mixed numerals to improper fractions.

$$= \frac{26}{3}$$ Multiply.

$$= 8\frac{2}{3}$$ Simplify.

Below are examples that show how a mixed numeral is multiplied by a fraction and by a whole number.

$$2\frac{4}{5} \times \frac{3}{7} = \frac{14}{5} \times \frac{3}{7} \qquad 5\frac{7}{9} \times 3 = \frac{52}{9} \times \frac{3}{1}$$

$$= \frac{6}{5} \qquad\qquad\qquad = \frac{52}{3}$$

$$= 1\frac{1}{5} \qquad\qquad\qquad = 17\frac{1}{3}$$

Your Turn

Find each product in simplest form.

10. $1\frac{1}{2} \times 2\frac{1}{2}$ 11. $5\frac{7}{8} \times \frac{4}{5}$ 12. $8 \times 2\frac{3}{4}$

13. $\frac{7}{10} \times 4\frac{2}{7}$ 14. $3\frac{1}{3} \times 3\frac{1}{3}$ 15. $9\frac{1}{4} \times 3\frac{1}{5}$

(Answers appear at the end of the section.)

Dividing Fractions

In the first section of Part IV, you saw that division is the inverse of multiplication. Recall that in division the product is given, but one of the factors is missing. What are the missing factors in the following examples?

$$\underline{\ ?\ } \times 5 = 15$$
$$3 \times \underline{\ ?\ } = 15$$

If two such factors are multiplied and their product is 1, for example,

$$\frac{2}{3} \times \frac{3}{2} = 1$$

then each factor is called the multiplicative inverse, or reciprocal, of the other. Thus,

the reciprocal of $\frac{2}{3}$ is $\frac{3}{2}$

the reciprocal of $\frac{1}{8}$ is $\frac{8}{1}$

the reciprocal of $\frac{4}{5}$ is $\frac{5}{4}$

the reciprocal of 12 is $\frac{1}{12}$

If you are given a fraction, you can find its reciprocal by interchanging (inverting) the numerator and denominator.

Using reciprocals in division

In dividing whole numbers such as 15 divided by 5, you are asking "how many 5's are there in 15?" Likewise in this problem,

$$2 \div \frac{1}{4}$$

you are asking, how many $\frac{1}{4}$'s are there in 2? In a problem such as $\frac{7}{8} \div \frac{3}{4}$, you want to know how many $\frac{3}{4}$'s are in $\frac{7}{8}$. The following rule can be used when dividing with fractions or whole numbers.

RULE:
To divide any number by a fraction or a whole number, multiply the dividend by the reciprocal of the divisor (or invert the divisor and multiply).

Study these examples.

$$\frac{3}{4} \div \frac{2}{5} = \frac{3}{4} \times \frac{5}{2}$$ Multiply by the reciprocal of the divisor.

$$= \frac{15}{8}$$ Multiply.

$$= 1\frac{7}{8}$$ Simplify. ← This is the answer.

$$\frac{2}{3} \div 6 = \frac{2}{3} \div \frac{6}{1}$$ Write 6 as the fraction.

$$= \frac{2}{3} \times \frac{1}{6}$$ Multiply by the reciprocal of the divisor.

$$= \frac{1}{9}$$ ← This is the answer.

Your Turn

Find each quotient in simplest form.

1. $2 \div \frac{1}{4}$ 2. $\frac{7}{8} \div \frac{3}{4}$ 3. $\frac{5}{9} \div 2$

4. $\frac{1}{8} \div \frac{4}{5}$ 5. $\frac{4}{5} \div \frac{1}{8}$ 6. $10 \div \frac{5}{8}$

(Answers appear at the end of the section.)

Mixed numerals in division

When the dividend or divisor (or both) is named by a mixed numeral, rename each as a fraction, then perform the division.

$$2\frac{2}{5} \div 1\frac{1}{3} = \frac{12}{5} \div \frac{4}{3}$$ Rename the mixed numerals as improper fractions.

$$= \frac{12}{5} \times \frac{3}{4}$$ Multiply by the reciprocal of the divisor.

$$= \frac{9}{5}$$ Multiply.

$$= 1\frac{4}{5}$$ Simplify.

$$\frac{5}{6} \div 8\frac{3}{4} = \frac{5}{6} \div \frac{35}{4}$$ Rename.

$$= \frac{5}{6} \times \frac{4}{35}$$ Rewrite as multiplication.

$$= \frac{2}{21}$$ Multiply.

Your Turn

Find each quotient in simplest form.

7. $3\frac{3}{8} \div 1\frac{5}{6}$ 8. $2\frac{1}{2} \div 1\frac{1}{4}$ 9. $1\frac{1}{4} \div 2\frac{1}{2}$

10. $9 \div 2\frac{1}{5}$ 11. $4\frac{5}{8} \div 3$ 12. $\frac{7}{10} \div 1\frac{7}{10}$

(Answers appear at the end of the section.)

Least Common Multiple

The problem of finding least common multiples is important to the arithmetic of fractions. The least common multiple (LCM) of several numbers is the smallest number other than zero that is a multiple of all of them. Each of the given numbers is, therefore, a factor of the LCM. So to find the LCM of two or more numbers, simply locate the smallest number (other than zero) that is a multiple of all the numbers.

Think of this situation. Armando has blocks that are 6 inches tall. Sue has blocks that are 4 inches tall. Pamela has blocks that are 9 inches tall. They have each made a stack of their blocks, one on top of another. How tall will the stacks of blocks be the first time that all three stacks are of the same height? This can be shown with a picture.

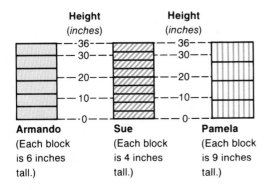

Armando	Sue	Pamela
(Each block is 6 inches tall.)	(Each block is 4 inches tall.)	(Each block is 9 inches tall.)

The least common multiple of 6, 4, and 9 is 36. This is the first time that all three stacks are of equal height.

Use the picture to find what number is the least common multiple of 6 and 4. You should see that the first time the stacks are the same height at 12 inches. Twelve is the LCM of 6 and 4. What is the LCM of 6 and 9? What is the LCM of 4 and 9?

(Answers appear at the end of the section.)

Using prime factorization to find LCM

It might be too time consuming to draw a picture every time you need to find the least common multiple of two or more numbers. A more efficient method is shown below. This method uses the concepts of multiples, factors, and of prime factorizations. These concepts were discussed in the number theory section start-

ing on page 226. You may wish to review those concepts before continuing this section.

To find the least common multiple of two or more numbers, prime factorization can be used. For example, to find the LCM of 120 and 288, find their factorizations.

$$120 = 2 \times 2 \times 2 \times 3 \times 5$$
$$288 = 2 \times 2 \times 2 \times 2 \times 2 \times 3 \times 3$$

The number 2 occurs three times as a factor in the first number and five times in the second number. Therefore the number $2 \times 2 \times 2 \times 2 \times 2$ must be a factor of the LCM, since it is a factor of 288.

Similarly, the number 3×3 is a factor of the LCM since it is also a factor of 288. The number 5, named in the factorization for 120, is also a factor of the LCM. Therefore, the LCM of 120 and 288 is $2 \times 2 \times 2 \times 2 \times 2 \times 3 \times 3 \times 5$, or 1440.

Here are two more examples to study.

Find the LCM of 12 and 10.

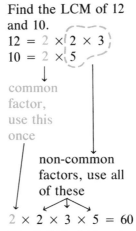

$$2 \times 2 \times 3 \times 5 = 60$$

The LCM of 12 and 10 is 60.

Find the LCM of 4, 6, and 9.

$4 = 2 \times 2$
$6 = 2 \times 3$
$9 = \quad 3 \times 3$

common factors, use one of each

non-common factors, use all of these

$2 \times 3 \times 2 \times 3 = 36$

The LCM of 4, 6, and 9 is 36.

Your Turn

Give the least common multiple for each of the following sets of numbers:

1. 8 and 12
2. 3 and 9
3. 12 and 15
4. 20 and 8
5. 4 and 12
6. 4, 6, and 8

(Answers appear at the end of the section.)

Comparing fractions

Suppose you had $\frac{3}{4}$ pound of seed A and $\frac{5}{6}$ pound of seed B. Of which type of seed did you have the most? To find out, you could compare the fractions $\frac{3}{4}$ and $\frac{5}{6}$. One way to do so is to find a common denominator and build equivalent fractions. If you can find the least common multiple of 3 and 4, you can easily compare these fractions. Study the steps below.

$\frac{3}{4} \;⑦\; \frac{5}{6}$ The least common multiple of 4 and 6 is 12.

$\frac{3}{4} = \frac{?}{12} \quad \frac{5}{6} = \frac{?}{12}$ Build equivalent fractions with a denominator of 12

$4 \times ? = 12 \quad 6 \times ? = 12$

Now multiply the numerator of each fraction by the same number by which the denominator was multiplied to get 12.

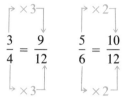

$$\frac{3}{4} = \frac{9}{12} \qquad \frac{5}{6} = \frac{10}{12}$$

Now compare the fractions $\frac{9}{12}$ and $\frac{10}{12}$. If two fractions have the same denominator, the fraction with the larger numerator is the larger fraction. So,

$$\frac{10}{12} > \frac{9}{12} \qquad \frac{5}{6} > \frac{3}{4}$$

is greater than   is greater than

Below are two more examples.

Which is greater,

$\frac{3}{5}$ or $\frac{5}{8}$?

The LCM of 5 and 8 is 40.

$$\frac{3}{5} = \frac{24}{40} \qquad \frac{5}{8} = \frac{25}{40}$$

$$\frac{25}{40} > \frac{24}{40} \quad \frac{5}{8} > \frac{3}{5}$$

$\frac{5}{8}$ is greater than $\frac{3}{5}$

Which is greatest,

$\frac{1}{2}, \frac{4}{7},$ or $\frac{7}{12}$?

The LCM of 2, 7, and 12 is 84.

$\frac{1}{2} = \frac{42}{84} \qquad \frac{4}{7} = \frac{48}{84}$

$\frac{7}{12} = \frac{49}{84}$

$\frac{49}{84} > \frac{48}{84} > \frac{42}{84}$

$\frac{7}{12} > \frac{4}{7} > \frac{1}{2}$

$\frac{7}{12}$ is the greatest.

Your Turn

Use the LCM to find the greater fraction in each pair.

7. $\frac{1}{2}$ and $\frac{17}{33}$ 8. $\frac{4}{7}$ and $\frac{10}{19}$ 9. $\frac{1}{8}$ and $\frac{3}{40}$

Use the LCM to find the greatest fraction in each group.

10. $\frac{2}{3}, \frac{3}{4},$ and $\frac{7}{10}$ 11. $\frac{3}{5}, \frac{5}{8},$ and $\frac{11}{15}$

(Answers appear at the end of the section.)

Adding and Subtracting Fractions

One cannot add or subtract common fractions unless they are expressed in terms of the same fraction scale. This is consistent with what is done in addition and subtraction with whole numbers. For example, you add ones to ones, tens to tens, and so on. You add like numbers. However, in addition and subtraction of common fractions, the denominator tells the kind of unit that is to be added or subtracted instead of the place-value of the digit. The denominators, which name the kind of units to be added, must be the same in the sum as well as in each addend. Fractions of this type, that is, fractions that have the same denominator, are called like fractions. Thus, $\frac{2}{6}$ and $\frac{1}{6}$ are like fractions; $\frac{3}{8}$ and $\frac{2}{4}$ are not.

Adding and subtracting like fractions

The following examples show how to add with fractions when they have the same denominator.

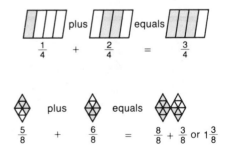

From each of the above diagrams it should be clear that you can find the sum by counting the number of parts that are shaded.

Just as 4 pounds + 3 pounds = 7 pounds,

so

4 eighths + 3 eighths = 7 eighths

$$\frac{4}{8} + \frac{3}{8} = \frac{7}{8}$$

RULE:
To add like fractions, add the numerators and place the sum over the common denominator. Express the sum in simplest form.

The work of adding $\frac{4}{8}$ and $\frac{3}{8}$ may also be arranged vertically and added this way.

$$\frac{4}{8}$$
$$\frac{3}{8}$$
$$+\frac{8}{8}$$

4 + 3 = 7

$$\frac{7}{8}$$

However, in actual practice, addition of fractions usually occurs in some type of horizontal arrangement. So many of the examples will be presented that way. Choose the method that is best for you.

The following examples show how to subtract with fractions having the same denominator.

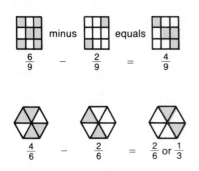

RULE:
To subtract with fractions having a common denominator, subtract the numerators only. The denominator of the difference is the common denominator. Express the answer in simplest form.

Your Turn

Add or subtract. Express each answer in simplest form.

1. $\frac{3}{5} - \frac{1}{5}$ 2. $\frac{2}{9} + \frac{5}{9}$

3. $\frac{7}{8} + \frac{5}{8}$ 4. $\frac{11}{12} - \frac{7}{12}$

5. $\frac{3}{4} + \frac{3}{4}$ 6. $\frac{8}{9} - \frac{5}{9}$

7. $\frac{5}{6} - \frac{1}{6}$ 8. $\frac{3}{8} + \frac{7}{8}$

9. $\frac{6}{7} - \frac{2}{7}$ 10. $\frac{11}{18} - \frac{4}{18}$

(Answers appear at the end of the section.)

Adding and subtracting unlike fractions

When denominators are unlike, the situation is similar to addition and subtraction of quarts and gallons or feet and inches. Since only like quantities can be added, the sum of 3 feet and 10 inches is

<u>3 feet</u>   10 inches
                ↓
36 inches + 10 inches = 46 inches

You cannot add or subtract unlike fractions directly, either. In order to do so, you must rewrite the fractions, using equivalent fractions, so that all resulting fractions have the same denominator.

Example: Add $\frac{3}{8}$ and $\frac{7}{12}$.

$$\frac{3}{8} \rightarrow 3 \times 3 \rightarrow \frac{9}{24}$$

$$+\frac{7}{12} \rightarrow 2 \times 7 \rightarrow \frac{14}{24}$$

$$\frac{23}{24}$$

In this case, notice that the new denominator, 24, is the smallest number that both the different denominators divide into with zero as a remainder. You may recall that this number is called the LCM of the fractions. The LCM is also the least common denominator (LCD) of the fractions. You can find the LCD of two fractions by using prime factorization or by listing multiples of the denominators.

Example: Find the LCD for this problem

$$\frac{5}{9} + \frac{3}{8}$$

1. First list all the multiples of both 8 and 9.
   Multiples of 8 = {8, 16, 24, 32, 40, 48, 56, 64, 72}
   Multiples of 9 = {9, 18, 27, 36, 45, 54, 63, 72, 81}
2. The first number that appears in both lists is the least common multiple.
   Least Common Multiple = 72
3. Since the least common multiple is also the LCD, then the LCD for 8 and 9 is 72.

It is the LCD that is used to add $\frac{5}{9}$ and $\frac{3}{8}$.

$$\frac{5}{9} + \frac{3}{8}$$
$$\downarrow \qquad \downarrow$$
$$\frac{40}{72} + \frac{27}{72} = \frac{67}{72}$$

Use the same procedure when subtracting unlike fractions.

$$\frac{11}{16} = \frac{33}{48}$$
$$-\frac{7}{24} = \frac{14}{48}$$
$$\overline{\qquad \frac{19}{48}}$$

At this time you may wish to review the section on comparing fractions for further discussion on the LCM and LCD.

Your Turn

Add or subtract. Express all answers in simplest form.

11. $\frac{2}{3} + \frac{1}{2}$ 12. $\frac{3}{4} + \frac{5}{6}$

13. $\frac{1}{7} + \frac{3}{8}$ 14. $\frac{5}{9} - \frac{1}{3}$

15. $\frac{9}{10} - \frac{3}{5}$ 16. $\frac{1}{3} - \frac{1}{7}$

17. $\frac{5}{6} - \frac{1}{4}$ 18. $\frac{1}{2} + \frac{1}{3} + \frac{1}{4}$

(Answers appear at the end of the section.)

Mixed numerals in addition

When mixed numerals are used in addition, add the whole number parts and the fraction parts separately. The work is easier if you find the LCD before you rename each fractional number. In some cases it may be necessary to simplify the answer as shown in these examples.

$$7\frac{13}{24}$$
$$+2\frac{7}{24}$$
$$\overline{9\frac{20}{24}} = 9\frac{5}{6}$$

$$8\frac{7}{8}$$
$$+9\frac{5}{8}$$
$$\overline{17\frac{12}{8}} = 18\frac{1}{2}$$

Remember that a mixed numeral is in simplest form when the fractional part is in simplest form. If you need to review simplifying mixed numerals, turn to page 250 of this section. You can also add three or more mixed numerals in the same manner.

$7\frac{11}{12} = 7\frac{33}{36}$

$2\frac{5}{6} = 2\frac{30}{36}$

$+3\frac{8}{9} = 3\frac{32}{36}$

$12\frac{95}{36} = 14\frac{23}{36}$

The LCM of 12, 6, and 9 is 36.

Use 36 as the common denominator.

Add the fractions.
Add the whole numbers.

Your Turn

Add. Express each answer in simplest form.

19. $2\frac{1}{4}$
   $+1\frac{1}{4}$

20. $5\frac{2}{3}$
   $+ \frac{1}{6}$

21. $13\frac{5}{8}$
   $+ 9\frac{2}{3}$

22. $39\frac{1}{2}$
    $5\frac{3}{4}$
   $+28\frac{2}{3}$

(Answers appear at the end of the section.)

Mixed numerals in subtraction

In order to subtract when mixed numerals are involved, you must also find the LCD of both fractions. First subtract the fractions, then subtract the whole numbers. Study these examples.

$4\frac{3}{4} = 4\frac{15}{20}$
$-2\frac{2}{5} = 2\frac{8}{20}$
$2\frac{7}{20}$

$10\frac{5}{8} = 10\frac{15}{24}$
$-5\frac{1}{12} = 5\frac{2}{24}$
$5\frac{13}{24}$

To check subtraction, you can use addition.

$2\frac{7}{20} + 2\frac{8}{20} = 4\frac{15}{20}$

$= 4\frac{3}{4}$

It checks.

$5\frac{13}{24} + 5\frac{2}{24} = 10\frac{15}{24}$

$= 10\frac{5}{8}$

It checks.

When you try to subtract a mixed numeral from a whole number, the whole number must be renamed as shown.

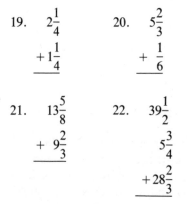

$6 = 5\frac{4}{4}$
$-2\frac{1}{4} = 2\frac{1}{4}$
$3\frac{3}{4}$

$6 = 5 + 1$
$1 = \frac{4}{4}$
$6 = 5 + \frac{4}{4}$

$3\frac{3}{4} + 2\frac{1}{4} = 5\frac{4}{4}$ or 6

It checks.

Study the example below.

$5\frac{2}{5} = 5\frac{8}{20}$
$-2\frac{3}{4} = 2\frac{15}{20}$

↓

cannot subtract; rename →

$5\frac{8}{20} = 4\frac{28}{20}$
$-2\frac{15}{20} = 2\frac{15}{20}$
$2\frac{13}{20}$

Notice that $5\frac{2}{5}$ was first renamed with a denominator of 20. A larger fraction was needed in order to complete the subtraction. This is how to think about the renaming of $5\frac{8}{20}$.

$$5\frac{8}{20} = 4 + 1 + \frac{8}{20}$$

$$= 4 + \frac{20}{20} + \frac{8}{20} \text{ or } 4\frac{28}{20}$$

Your Turn

Subtract. Express each answer in simplest form.

23. $\quad 5\frac{2}{3}$
 $\quad -1\frac{1}{3}$

24. $\quad 8\frac{7}{8}$
 $\quad -6\frac{1}{6}$

25. $\quad 15\frac{5}{6}$
 $\quad -9\frac{2}{3}$

26. $\quad 34$
 $\quad -15\frac{7}{10}$

27. $\quad 3\frac{1}{2}$
 $\quad -\frac{2}{5}$

28. $\quad 6\frac{1}{10}$
 $\quad -5\frac{4}{5}$

29. $\quad 46\frac{3}{10}$
 $\quad -45\frac{3}{4}$

30. $\quad 100\frac{2}{3}$
 $\quad -53\frac{5}{7}$

(Answers appear at the end of the section.)

Decimal Fractions

Defining decimal fractions

A decimal numeral is another way to write a fraction that has a denominator of 10, 100, or 1000, and so on. For example, you can write $\frac{5}{10}$ as 0.5 and read it as "five tenths." You can write $\frac{5}{100}$ as 0.05 and read it as "five hundredths." You can write $\frac{5}{1000}$ as 0.005 and read it as "five thousandths."

Decimal notation is an extension of the place-value notation for whole numbers with ten as the base. In decimal notation, a dot, called the decimal point, is placed to the left of as many digits of the numerator as there are zeros in the denominator of the number expressed as a fraction. In the above examples,

$\frac{5}{10}$ becomes 0.5

The decimal point is inserted to the left of *one digit* because there is *one zero* in the denominator of the fraction.

$\frac{5}{100}$ becomes 0.05

The decimal point is inserted to the left of *two digits* because there are *two zeros* in the denominator of the fraction.

$\frac{5}{1000}$ becomes 0.005

The decimal point is inserted to the left of *three digits* because there are *three zeros* in the denominator of the fraction.

Just as in whole number place-value notation, the place each digit occupies has a value ten times the value of the place to its right, and the position each number holds has a different name. This chart shows some of these place-value names.

Tens	Ones		Tenths	Hundredths	Thousandths	Ten Thousandths	Hundred Thousandths	Millionths	Ten Millionths
3	6	.	4	9	8	5			

Reading from left to right, notice that the first digit after the decimal tells how many one-tenths ($\frac{1}{10}$), the second tells how many $\frac{1}{100}$'s, the third tells how many $\frac{1}{1000}$'s.

$$36.4985 = 3 \times 10 + 6 \times 1 +$$

$$4 \times \frac{1}{10} + 9 \times \frac{1}{100} +$$

$$8 \times \frac{1}{1000} + 5 \times \frac{1}{10,000}$$

This decimal is read as thirty-six and four thousand, nine hundred eighty-five ten-thousandths.

Comparing decimals

Which is larger, 0.833 or 0.85? You can use equivalent fractions to show that 0.85 is larger than 0.833. First, write each decimal as a fraction. Then build equivalent fractions with a common denominator. Find the least common multiple of the denominators, then use it as the new common denominator.

$$\frac{833}{1000} \longrightarrow \frac{833}{1000}$$

$$\times 10$$

$$\frac{85}{100} \qquad \frac{850}{1000}$$

$$\times 10$$

$$\frac{850}{1000} > \frac{833}{1000}$$

Notice that the value of the decimal is not changed by adding a zero to the right of the decimal place. Recall also that the symbol ">" means "is greater than" and the symbol "<" means "is less than." Therefore, 0.85 is greater than 0.833 and this can be written as

$$0.85 > 0.833$$

Below is a scale that shows the location of several decimals. Notice that the place value and the digits determine which decimal is greater, not the number of digits in the decimal.

0   0.25   0.375 0.5   0.75   0.875 1

Your Turn

Write each fraction as a decimal.

1. $\frac{1}{10}$ 2. $\frac{583}{1000}$ 3. $\frac{1}{100}$

4. $\frac{35}{100}$ 5. $\frac{4123}{10000}$

Use < or > to compare these decimals.

6. 0.8 _____ 0.3   7. 0.1234 _____ 0.0987
8. 0.5 _____ 0.51   9. 0.7 _____ 0.67891

(Answers appear at the end of the section.)

Adding and Subtracting Decimals

Addition and subtraction of decimals are simpler than addition and subtraction of common fractions. This is because it is not necessary to find common denominators when working with decimals.

When adding and subtracting decimals, set up the problem so that you are adding tenths to tenths, hundredths to hundredths, and so on. You can accomplish this by arranging the numerals with decimal points lined up vertically. Then bring down the decimal point and add or subtract as if the numbers were whole numbers.

ADD: 0.425 + 1.0073 + 0.28 + 25

Placing zeros after the digit to the right of the decimal point does not change the value of the decimal. The numbers 25, 25.0, 25.0000 are all the same.

$$
\begin{array}{r}
0.425\,0 \\
1.0073 \\
0.280\,0 \\
\underline{25.0000} \\
26.7123
\end{array}
$$

SUBTRACT: 0.943 − 0.85

$$
\begin{array}{r}
0.943 \\
\underline{-\,0.850} \\
0.093
\end{array}
$$

The following rule summarizes the procedure for adding and subtracting decimals.

RULE:
To add or subtract with decimals, write them in a column, making sure the decimal points are in a line. Then proceed as with whole numbers.

Here are more examples to study.

2.4 + 0.043 + 32.54

$$
\begin{array}{r}
2.400 \\
0.043 \\
\underline{+32.540} \\
34.983
\end{array}
$$

43 − 5.93

$$
\begin{array}{r}
^{9\ 10} \\
2\ \ 10 \\
4\,\cancel{3}.\,\cancel{0}\,\cancel{0} \\
\underline{-\ \ 5.93} \\
37.07
\end{array}
$$

Your Turn

1. 0.154 + 0.32   2. 32.4 + 6.91 + 2.431
3. 99.1 + .932   4. 1.32 + 4.2 + 5.9
5. 15.32 − 2.2   6. 231.4923 − 0.6381
7. 0.845 − 0.42   8. 1.8435 − 1.7935

(Answers appear at the end of the section.)

Multiplying Decimals

Numbers named by decimals are multiplied as if they were whole numbers—except for the placement of the decimal point in the result. To see how this works, study the effect of shifting from decimal form to fractional form:

Example: Multiply 0.438 by 4.75.

$$
\begin{aligned}
0.438 \times 4.75 &= \frac{438}{1000} \times \frac{475}{100} \\
&= \frac{208050}{100000} \\
&= 2\frac{805}{10000} \text{ or } 2.0805
\end{aligned}
$$

If the multiplication is arranged in vertical form, notice the pattern.

$$
\begin{array}{r}
0.4\,3\,8 \leftarrow 3 \text{ decimal places} \\
\times\ \ 4.7\,5 \leftarrow 2 \text{ decimal places} \\
\hline
2\,1\,9\,0 \\
3\,0\,6\,6 \\
\underline{1\,7\,5\,2\ \ \ } \\
2.0\,8\,0\,5\,0 \leftarrow 5 \text{ decimal places}
\end{array}
$$

This suggests the following rule for multiplying decimals.

RULE:
Multiply the numbers without regard for the decimal points. Then point off in the product from the right as many decimal places as there are in the sum of the decimal places of two factors.

Here are more examples to study.

$$
\begin{array}{r}
0.0\,4 \\
\times\ 0.0\,0\,9 \\
\hline
0.0\,0\,0\,3\,6
\end{array}
\qquad
\begin{array}{r}
1\,2.9 \\
\times 0.3\,9 \\
\hline
1\,1\,6\,1 \\
\underline{3\,8\,7\ \ } \\
5.0\,3\,1
\end{array}
$$

Your Turn

1. 4.305 × 0.51   2. 0.592 × 0.035
3. 20.4 × 0.618   4. 653.4 × 2.89

5. 0.025 × 1.872   6. 40.6 × 0.008

(Answers appear at the end of the section.)

Dividing Decimals

Many people experience difficulty in dividing decimals. If you can decide where to locate the decimal point in the quotient, the division of decimals is completed in the same manner as division of whole numbers. Basically there are three types of division problems that may involve decimals.

Example 1: When the dividend contains a decimal and the divisor is a whole number. Divide 135.9 by 45.

Place the decimal
point in the
quotient directly
above the decimal
point in the
dividend.

$$\begin{array}{r} 3.0\,2 \\ 45\overline{)1\,3\,5.9\,0} \\ \underline{1\,3\,5} \\ 9\,0 \\ \underline{9\,0} \\ 0 \end{array}$$

There are many rules that may be given for the division of decimals, but the process just shown for dividing a decimal by a whole number is the simplest. However, it is easy to reduce any problem involving division with decimals to one in which the divisor is a whole number.

Example 2: Divide 6.3 by 0.3.

The decimal points in
both the dividend and
the divisor are moved
to the right one
place to multiply by
10 and thereby make
the divisor a whole
number.

$$0.3\overline{)6.3}$$

$$3\overline{)6\,3.}$$

$$\begin{array}{r} 2\,1. \\ 3\overline{)6\,3.} \end{array}$$

Divide 2535 by 3.25.

The decimal point
must be moved two
places to the right.
Notice that two
zeros were added.
The decimal point is
placed directly above
the new position of
the decimal point in
the dividend.

$$3.25\overline{)2535.00}$$

$$325\overline{)253500.}$$

$$\begin{array}{r} 780. \\ 325\overline{)253500.} \end{array}$$

You divide decimals by eliminating the decimal point from the divisor. This procedure works because the concept of equivalency is true with decimals, just as it is with common fractions. That is, you can remove a decimal point in the divisor by multiplying both the dividend and divisor by the appropriate multiple of 10. Remember that fractions can mean division and that

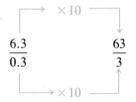

So, 6.3 divided by 0.3 is equal to 63 divided by 3.

There is one other case in which division leads to decimals. This is when division of whole numbers does not "come out even." To complete such division, simply place a decimal point after the dividend and add as many zeros as necessary. Study the examples below.

Example 3:

12 ÷ 25

$$\begin{array}{r} 0.4\,8 \\ 25\overline{)1\,2.0\,0} \\ \underline{1\,0\,0} \\ 2\,0\,0 \\ \underline{2\,0\,0} \\ 0 \end{array}$$

$142 \div 16$

```
        8.8 7 5
16)1 4 2.0 0 0
    1 2 8
    1 4 0
    1 2 8
      1 2 0
      1 1 2
          8 0
          8 0
            0
```

Your Turn

Divide.

1. $72 \div 0.9$
2. $9.6 \div 1.2$
3. $2.40 \div 16$
4. $2.94 \div 0.003$
5. $128.64 \div 4.8$
6. $0.4332 \div 0.76$
7. $18 \div 5$
8. $48.418 \div 5.63$

(Answers appear at the end of the section.)

Rounding Decimals

Suppose you know that 16 pens cost $12.50 and you want to know how much one pen costs. You can divide to find the answer.

```
       0.7 8 1 2 5
16)1 2.5 0 0 0 0
   1 1 2
     1 3 0
     1 2 8
         2 0
         1 6
           4 0
           3 2
             8 0
             8 0
               0
```

One pen costs $0.78125. But amounts of money are given in dollars and cents.

You must round 0.78125 to the nearest hundredth to find the answer.

Study how this is done.

3.92655

Round 0.78125 to the nearest hundredth.

given place: hundredth

0.7 8 ① 2 5

Circle the digit to the right of the given place.

Since the circled digit is less than 5, simply drop the digits to the right of the given place.

0.78125 to the nearest hundredth is 0.78.

If the circled digit is 5 or more, add one to the digit in the given place and drop the digits to the right.

Round 3.2849 to the nearest thousandth.

3.2 8 4 ⑨
Greater than 5
3.2 8 5 to the nearest thousandth.

Round 0.15 to the nearest tenth.

0.1 ⑤
↑Equal to 5

0.2 to the nearest tenth.

Decimals and Fractions

Changing fractions to decimals

When you use a calculator or when you work problems involving money, you may find it easier to work with decimals than with fractions. For this reason you need to know how to change a fraction to a decimal.

This is quite easy; simply divide the numerator by the denominator.

Change $\frac{7}{8}$ to a decimal.

Change $\frac{7}{25}$ to a decimal.

$$
\begin{array}{r}
0.8\,7\,5 \\
8)\overline{7.0\,0\,0} \\
6\,4 \\ \hline
6\,0 \\
5\,6 \\ \hline
4\,0 \\
4\,0 \\ \hline
0
\end{array}
\qquad
\begin{array}{r}
0.2\,8 \\
25)\overline{7.0\,0} \\
5\,0 \\ \hline
2\,0\,0 \\
2\,0\,0 \\ \hline
0
\end{array}
$$

$\frac{7}{8} = 0.875$ $\frac{7}{25} = 0.28$

Repeating decimals

Sometimes, when a fraction is changed to a decimal, the division does not "come out even," even if you add many zeros after the decimal point.

Example: Find the decimal equivalent for $\frac{2}{3}$.

$\frac{2}{3}$ means 2 divided by 3. $3)\overline{2}$

Notice that you can continue the division indefinitely and get 6's in the quotient.

$$
\begin{array}{r}
.66\overline{6} \\
3)\overline{2.000}
\end{array}
$$

Since the repetition begins with 6, a bar is placed over the 6 to show that the quotient repeats. Thus $0.\overline{6}$ is a repeating decimal. The bar over the 6 shows that this is a repeating decimal and that 6 is the part that repeats.

Decimals may begin to repeat with any digit, for example,

$\frac{7}{30} = 0.2\overline{3}$ $\frac{23}{24} = 0.958\overline{3}$

Also more than one digit may repeat.

$\frac{5}{11} = 0.\overline{45}$ $\frac{3}{7} = 0.\overline{428571}$

In summary, if a remainder of 0 occurs in the divisor, the quotient is a terminating decimal. If after a series of divisions, a remainder other than 0 repeats, then the quotient is a repeating decimal. Often before a repeating decimal can be used in computing, it must be rounded. The number of digits retained in rounding depends on the degree of precision required in the computation. If you need to review how to round decimals, refer to page 265 of this section.

Example: Change $\frac{4}{7}$ to a decimal. Round answer to nearest hundredth.

$\frac{4}{7} = 0.\overline{571428}$

Rounded to the nearest hundredth.

$\frac{4}{7} \approx 0.57$

$\approx$ stands for "is about equal to" or "approximately."

Your Turn

Change each fraction to a decimal. Indicate repeating fractions with a bar. Then round answers to nearest hundredth.

Example: $\frac{9}{11} = 0.\overline{81} \approx 0.82$

1. $\frac{5}{6}$ 2. $\frac{9}{16}$ 3. $\frac{2}{3}$

Divide. Round each answer to the nearest tenth.

4. $17.25 \div 25$ 5. $3.6 \div 0.84$
6. $0.889 \div .09$ 7. $12.5 \div 0.016$
8. $770.7 \div 33$ 9. $09.20 \div 70$

(Answers appear at the end of the section.)

Changing decimals to fractions

The ability to express decimals as fractions and fractions as decimals is essential for successful work with fractions. The following procedure may be used when changing a decimal to a fraction.

RULE:
To change a decimal to an equivalent fraction, omit the decimal point and write the digits as the numerator of the fraction. For the denominator, write 1 followed by as many zeros as there are decimal places in the decimal. Then simplify the fraction. Study these examples.

$$0.25 = \frac{25}{100} \text{ or } \frac{1}{4}$$

$$0.1875 = \frac{1875}{10,000} \text{ or } \frac{3}{16}$$

$$0.125 = \frac{125}{1000} \text{ or } \frac{1}{8}$$

$$3.75 = \frac{375}{100} \text{ or } \frac{15}{4} = 3\frac{3}{4}$$

This procedure works well for most fractions. However, when the fraction is a complex fraction, you need to employ a slightly different procedure. (A complex fraction is one where the numerator and the denominator, or both, is a fraction or a mixed numeral, like $0.2\frac{3}{4}$).

RULE:
When the fraction is a complex fraction, multiply the numerator and the denominator by the denominator of the fraction in the numerator. Reduce the resulting fraction to lowest terms.

For example,

$$0.12\frac{2}{3} = \frac{12\frac{2}{3}}{100}$$

$$= \frac{12\frac{2}{3} \times 3}{100 \times 3}$$

$$= \frac{\frac{38}{3} \times 3}{100 \times 3} = \frac{38}{300} \text{ or } \frac{19}{150}$$

Your Turn

Express each of the following as common fractions in simplest form.

10. 0.85   11. 0.68   12. $0.12\frac{1}{2}$

13. $0.06\frac{1}{4}$ 14. 0.875   15. $0.5\frac{1}{3}$

(Answers follow.)

Answers

Meanings of Fractions (pp. 244–249)

1. $\frac{16}{8}, \frac{8}{4}$, or $\frac{4}{2}$ 2. $\frac{4}{8}$ or $\frac{2}{4}$ 3. $\frac{6}{8}$ 4. $\frac{14}{8}$ 5. $\frac{12}{8}$ or $\frac{6}{4}$ 6. $\frac{4}{4}, \frac{2}{2}$, or 1   7. $\frac{3}{2}$

8. $\frac{11}{4}$ 9. $\frac{11}{6}$ 10. $\frac{17}{5}$ 11. $\frac{44}{7}$ 12. $\frac{43}{8}$ 13. $1\frac{1}{5}$ 14. $3\frac{1}{3}$ 15. $2\frac{1}{4}$ 16. $2\frac{5}{8}$

17. $2\frac{3}{16}$ 18. $8\frac{1}{7}$

19–24. Answers may vary. Examples are given.

19. $\frac{2}{10}, \frac{3}{15}, \frac{4}{20}$ 20. $\frac{8}{14}, \frac{16}{28}, \frac{24}{42}$ 21. $\frac{10}{12}, \frac{15}{18}, \frac{30}{36}$ 22. $\frac{12}{18}, \frac{6}{9}, \frac{2}{3}$ 23. $\frac{30}{20}, \frac{15}{10}, \frac{3}{2}$

24. $\frac{6}{30}, \frac{2}{10}, \frac{1}{5}$

Simplest Form of Fractions (pp. 249–251)

1. 5   2. 4   3. 9   4. 5   5. 18   6. 12   7. $\frac{5}{8}$ 8. $1\frac{1}{7}$ 9. $\frac{2}{5}$ 10. $2\frac{2}{5}$

11. $\frac{7}{9}$

Multiplying Fractions (pp. 251–253)

1. $\frac{2}{15}$ 2. $\frac{7}{12}$ 3. $\frac{1}{4}$ 4. $\frac{1}{3}$ 5. 4   6. 9   7. $4\frac{3}{8}$ 8. $\frac{21}{40}$ 9. $\frac{9}{19}$ 10. $3\frac{3}{4}$

11. $4\frac{7}{10}$ 12. 22   13. 3   14. $11\frac{1}{9}$ 15. $29\frac{3}{5}$

Dividing Fractions (pp. 253–254)

1. 8   2. $1\frac{1}{6}$ 3. $\frac{5}{18}$ 4. $\frac{5}{32}$ 5. $6\frac{2}{5}$ 6. 16   7. $1\frac{37}{44}$ 8. 2   9. $\frac{1}{2}$

10. $4\frac{1}{11}$ 11. $1\frac{13}{24}$ 12. $\frac{7}{17}$

Least Common Multiple (pp. 254–257)

Answers from page 255: 18, 36

1. 24   2. 9   3. 60   4. 40   5. 12   6. 24   7. $\frac{17}{33}$ 8. $\frac{4}{7}$ 9. $\frac{1}{8}$

10. $\frac{3}{4}$ 11. $\frac{11}{15}$

Adding and Subtracting Fractions (pp. 257–261)

1. $\frac{2}{5}$ 2. $\frac{7}{9}$ 3. $1\frac{1}{2}$ 4. $\frac{1}{3}$ 5. $1\frac{1}{2}$ 6. $\frac{1}{3}$ 7. $\frac{2}{3}$ 8. $1\frac{1}{4}$ 9. $\frac{4}{7}$ 10. $\frac{7}{18}$

11. $1\frac{1}{6}$ 12. $1\frac{7}{12}$ 13. $\frac{29}{56}$ 14. $\frac{2}{9}$ 15. $\frac{3}{10}$ 16. $\frac{4}{21}$ 17. $\frac{7}{12}$ 18. $1\frac{1}{12}$

19. $3\frac{1}{2}$ 20. $5\frac{5}{6}$ 21. $23\frac{7}{24}$ 22. $73\frac{11}{12}$ 23. $4\frac{1}{3}$ 24. $2\frac{17}{24}$ 25. $6\frac{1}{6}$ 26. $18\frac{3}{10}$

27. $3\frac{1}{10}$ 28. $\frac{3}{10}$ 29. $\frac{11}{20}$ 30. $46\frac{20}{21}$

Decimal Fractions (pp. 261–262)

1. 0.1   2. 0.583   3. 0.01   4. 0.35   5. 0.4123   6. >   7. >   8. <
9. >

Adding and Subtracting Decimals (pp. 262–263)

1. 0.474   2. 41.741   3. 100.032   4. 11.42   5. 13.12   6. 230.8542
7. 0.425   8. 0.05

Multiplying Decimals (pp. 263–264)

1. 2.19555   2. 0.02072   3. 12.6072   4. 1888.326   5. 0.0468   6. 0.3248

Dividing Decimals (pp. 264–265)

1. 80   2. 8   3. 0.15   4. 980   5. 26.8   6. 0.57   7. 3.6   8. 8.6

Decimals and Fractions (pp. 265–267)

1. $0.8\overline{3} \approx 0.83$ 2. $0.5625 \approx 0.56$ 3. $0.\overline{6} \approx 0.67$ 4. 0.7   5. 4.3   6. 9.9
7. 781.3   8. 23.4   9. 0.1   10. $\frac{17}{20}$ 11. $\frac{17}{25}$ 12. $\frac{1}{8}$ 13. $\frac{1}{16}$ 14. $\frac{7}{8}$

15. $\frac{8}{15}$

Section 4

Ratio, Proportion, and Percent

Except for the introduction of some new terminology and language, the study of ratio, proportion, and percent offers no new difficulty other than that found in the work with fractional numbers. If you understand how to compute with common fractions and decimals, then computations involving ratio, proportion, and percent will be easy.

Several examples, worked out in detail, for each topic are presented for study throughout this section. Plan to follow the processes through these step-by-step examples and then do the sample exercises.

In the previous section it was shown that decimals and ratios are special kinds of fractions. In this section you will see that percentage is also a special kind of fraction. In order to learn about percent, however, you will first need to understand the concept of ratio and proportion. This is necessary since you will be using the proportion method as one way to solve percent problems. Ratio and proportion are therefore presented before the discussion on percent.

Ratios

Two numbers may be compared by subtraction or by division. If you compare 12 with 3 by subtraction, you see that 12 is nine more than 3.

$$12 - 3 = 9$$

Comparison by division shows that 12 is four times as large as 3.

$$12 \div 3 = 4$$

When two quantities are compared by an indicated division, a fraction is formed. This fraction is called the ratio. For example, suppose you want to name the ratio of the number of inches in a foot to the number of inches in part of a foot.

12 inches ← 1 foot
3 inches ← part of a foot

Notice that when 12 is compared to 3, 12 is divided by 3: $\frac{12}{3}$. This ratio can be named as $\frac{12}{3}$, $\frac{4}{1}$, 4 to 1, or 4:1.

In the example, if the procedure is reversed, that is, if you compare 3 to 12, then 3 is divided by 12 as $\frac{3}{12}$, which equals $\frac{1}{4}$, 1 to 4, or 1:4. Notice that since a ratio is a fraction it can be reduced to lowest terms by the same method that was used with fractions. (*See* Pt. IV, Sec. 3, page 249.)

Converting to like units

When ratios are used for comparison in this way, the units must be the same. The ratio of the two lengths in the above example were compared using the same units, inches. It would be incorrect to say that the ratio of 3 inches to 1 foot is 3 to 1. Either the 1-foot length must be changed to inches or the 3-inch length must be changed to feet. Study the following examples.

Evangeline is 5 feet, 6 inches, and her father is 5 feet, 10 inches. What is the ratio of Evangeline's height to her father's height? (The ratio can be found using either feet or inches as a unit.)

Using inches:

5 feet 6 inches = 66 inches
5 feet 10 inches = 70 inches

So the ratio is $\dfrac{66}{70} = \dfrac{33}{35}$

Using feet: 5 feet 6 inches = $5\frac{1}{2}$ feet

5 feet 10 inches = $5\frac{5}{6}$ feet

So the ratio is
shown by

$$5\frac{1}{2} \div 5\frac{5}{6} = \frac{11}{2} \div \frac{35}{6}$$

$$= \frac{11}{2} \times \frac{6}{35}$$

$$= \frac{33}{35}$$

Your Turn

Reduce these ratios to simplest terms.

1. $\dfrac{4}{12}$ 2. $\dfrac{15}{30}$ 3. $\dfrac{24}{16}$ 4. $\dfrac{21}{7}$

Write a fraction in lowest terms to name each of the following ratios.

5. 24 to 72   6. 64 to 96
7. 5 hours to 45 minutes
8. 36 seconds to 1 minute

9. Pat bought $10\frac{1}{4}$ yards of blue material

and $5\frac{1}{2}$ yards of red material.

a. Find the ratio of red material to blue material.
b. Find the ratio of blue material to red material.

(*Answers appear at the end of the section.*)

Rates

A rate is a special kind of ratio. The only difference between the ratios you just studied and rates is in the kind of sets compared. For example, a rate may be used to compare the number of eggs to the number of cartons as follows:

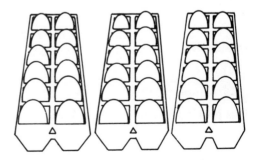

Number of Eggs $\longrightarrow$ 36
Number of Cartons $\longrightarrow$ 3
ratio: 36 to 3 or
ratio in simplest form: 12 to 1 or $\dfrac{12}{1}$

Example: Express this rate as a ratio in simplest form:

400 miles in 6 hours

miles $\rightarrow$ $\dfrac{400}{6}$ = $\dfrac{200}{3}$
hours $\rightarrow$

ratio in simplest form: 200 to 3 or $\dfrac{200}{3}$

From these examples, you can see that a rate is used to compare two sets with different kinds of quantities. Notice that rates are written the same way as other ratios. You work with them the same way.

Your Turn

Express in rates in simplest form.

10. 90 miles to 2 hours
11. 6 cans for $8
12. 10 seconds to 100 feet
13. 25 cents to 2 pencils

(Answers appear at the end of the section.)

Proportions

A proportion is a statement that two ratios are equal. It can be a sentence in words or it can be a statement with numbers and letters.

Using the equivalent ratios $\dfrac{14}{16}$ and $\dfrac{21}{24}$, you can write the proportion

$$\frac{14}{16} = \frac{21}{24}$$

This proportion can also be expressed as

14:16 = 21:24

In both forms the proportion is read as

"14 is to 16 as 21 is to 24."

There are four terms in a proportion.

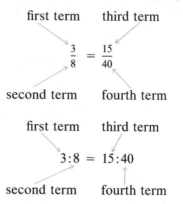

The first and fourth terms of a proportion, in this case 3 and 40, are called the extremes. The second and third terms, or the middle terms, in this case 8 and 15, are called the means.

RULE:
In any proportion, the product of the means equals the product of the extremes.

In the proportion $\dfrac{2}{3} = \dfrac{14}{21}$,

$$\underbrace{3 \times 14}_{\text{product of means}} = \underbrace{2 \times 21}_{\text{product of extremes}}$$

This is sometimes called the cross-multiplication rule. This rule makes it possible to see if two ratios are equal. If the product of the means equals the product of the extremes, then the ratios form a proportion. If the product of the means does not equal the product of the extremes, then the ratios do not form a proportion.

The ratios $\dfrac{5}{6}, \dfrac{4}{5}$ cannot form a proportion because

$$6 \times 4 \neq 5 \times 5$$
$$24 \neq 25$$

$\dfrac{3}{5}$ and $\dfrac{18}{30}$ can form a proportion because

$$5 \times 18 = 3 \times 30$$
$$90 = 90$$

This rule can also be used to solve a problem by finding the missing term in a proportion.

Solving proportions

The ratio of Kim's height to her friend Martha's height is 7 to 8. If Martha is 66 inches tall, how tall is Kim?

Ratio of heights ▶ $\dfrac{\text{Kim's Height}}{\text{Martha's Height}} = \dfrac{7}{8}$

The other actual height ratio is $\dfrac{?}{66}$.

You can now use these two ratios to write a proportion

$$\frac{7}{8} = \frac{?}{66}$$

Solve it using the cross-multiplication rule.

The product of the extremes is
$7 \times 66 = 462$.
The product of the means is $8 \times ?$.

As you can see, the missing term can be found by dividing by the product, 462, by the known factor, 8.

$$462 \div 8 = 57.75 \text{ inches}$$

Thus, Kim is 57.75 inches tall.

Usually the missing term in a proportion is represented by a letter. Thus the problem above could have been

$$\frac{7}{8} = \frac{n}{66}$$
$$8 \times n = 7 \times 66$$
$$8 \times n = 462$$

The "$=$" sign tells you that $8 \times n$ and 462 are the same number. Therefore, if $8 \times n$ and 462 are both divided by 8, the resulting numbers on both sides of the equals sign will also be the same. That is,

$$\frac{8 \times n}{8} = \frac{462}{8}$$
$$n = 57.75$$

You can check these results by replacing n in the original proportion with 57.75.

$$\frac{7}{8} = \frac{57.75}{66}$$
$$8 \times 57.75 = 7 \times 66$$
$$462 = 462 \qquad \text{It checks.}$$

RULE:
To solve a proportion, first show the product of the means equal to the product of the extremes. Then divide each product by the number that multiplies the unknown letter.

Your Turn

Use the cross-multiplication rule to solve the following proportions.

1. $\dfrac{2}{3} = \dfrac{4}{n}$ $\_\_ \times n = \_\_$ $\times \_\_$ $n = ?$

2. $\dfrac{n}{5} = \dfrac{24}{30}$ $n \times \_\_ = \_\_$ $\times \_\_$ $n = ?$

3. $\dfrac{4}{9} = \dfrac{n}{27}$ 4. $\dfrac{24}{18} = \dfrac{4}{n}$

5. $4:n = 20:30$ 6. $8:14 = 12:n$

(Answers appear at the end of the section.)

Solving problems using proportions

Proportions are especially useful in solving many types of word problems. The first step is to determine a ratio showing the numbers that are being compared. Study the following examples.

Example:

If 250 gallons of fuel oil cost $300, what will 800 gallons cost?

First set up the ratios:

$$\frac{\text{Initial fuel oil}}{\text{Needed fuel oil}} = \frac{\text{Initial cost}}{\text{Final cost}}$$

$$\frac{250}{800} = \frac{300}{n}$$

$$250 \times n = 800 \times 300$$
$$250 \times n = 240{,}000$$
$$n = \frac{240{,}000}{250}$$
$$n = 960$$

Therefore 800 gallons of fuel oil will cost $960.

Example:

A photograph 3 inches wide by 5 inches high is to be enlarged so that it is 12 inches wide. How high will the photograph be?

First write a proportion in which each ratio compares height to width.

$$\frac{3}{5} = \frac{12}{n}$$
$$3 \times n = 5 \times 12$$
$$3 \times n = 60$$
$$n = \underline{\quad?\quad}$$

So the enlarged photograph will be ____?____ inches wide.

(Answer appears at the end of the section.)

Here is a summary of the steps for solving word problems with proportions.

1. Let a letter stand for the unknown.
2. Write a proportion. Be sure the same units occupy corresponding positions in the two ratios of the proportion.
3. Use the cross-multiplication rule to show that the product of the means equals the product of the extremes.
4. Divide the product by the number that multiplies the unknown.

5. Check by substituting the results in the original proportion.

Your Turn

Use proportions to solve each of the following problems.

7. If 3 bottles of gasoline antifreeze cost $1.10, how much do 12 bottles cost?
8. Sandra earns $864 in two months. At this rate, how much will she earn in 6 months?
9. A recipe for 50 persons uses 3 cups of sugar. How many cups of sugar are needed for 35 persons?
10. If 12 boxes are required to hold 40 pounds of meat, how many boxes will be required to hold 30 pounds of meat?
11. An economy car can go 330 miles on $16\frac{1}{2}$ gallons. How many gallons will be needed to go 500 miles?

(Answers appear at the end of the section.)

Percent

You are no doubt already aware from everyday experiences of many uses of percent. "Percent" is used often in what seems to be so many different ways that it is easy to forget that the word has a special meaning.

The word percent comes from the Latin word *per centum,* meaning "per hundred."

Example: One year 100 rookies went to pro-football training camps. At the end of the sessions 34 rookies signed pro-football contracts.

34 of the 100 may be expressed as a ratio $\frac{34}{100}$, which means 34 per hundred. The symbol for percent is

%. Thus $\frac{34}{100}$ is the same as 34%, and either $\frac{34}{100}$ or 34% can be pictured as follows:

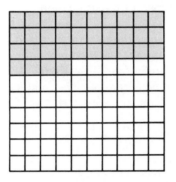

The large square is divided into 100 small squares. Each small square is $\frac{1}{100}$, or 1% of the large square. Thirty-four of the small squares are shaded. The shaded part is 34% of the large square.

Since percent means hundredths, you can express a given percent as a decimal fraction or as a common fraction. Because a percent is the same as a common fraction with a denominator of 100, solutions to these problems are possible.

Example a: Express $\frac{3}{5}$ as a percent.

Multiply the denominator by 20 to get 100. Multiply the numerator by the same number.

$$\frac{3 \times 20}{5 \times 20} = \frac{60}{100} \text{ or } 60\%. \text{ Thus } \frac{3}{5} = 60\%.$$

RULE:
Any fraction can be expressed as a percent by changing it to an equivalent fraction with a denominator of 100.

Example b: Express 0.8 as a percent.
Since 0.8 means $\frac{8}{10}$, convert $\frac{8}{10}$ to an equivalent fraction with a denominator of 100.

$$\frac{8 \times 10}{10 \times 10} = \frac{80}{100} \text{ or } 80\%$$

Thus 0.8 = 80%

RULE:
A decimal can be changed to a percent by expressing it as a fraction first.

As you probably noticed, the percent symbol represents two decimal places. So a decimal that has two places can be changed to a percent by simply removing the decimal point and using the percent sign: 0.55 = 55% and 5.13 = 513%.

Example c: Express 16 as a percent. Recall that any whole number may be expressed as a fraction with a denominator of 1. So write 16 as $\frac{16}{1}$ and then change it to an equivalent fraction with a denominator of 100.

$$\frac{16 \times 100}{1 \times 100} = \frac{1600}{100} \text{ or } 1600\%$$

Therefore $16 = \frac{16}{1} = 1600\%$.

Expressing a fraction as a percent by converting it to an equivalent fraction with a denominator of 100 is not always the easiest way to do it. Sometimes it is easier first to change the fraction into a decimal. For example, to change $\frac{8}{9}$ to a percent, it is easier to change the fraction to a decimal rounded to the nearest hundredth, and then convert the resulting decimal to percent.

$$\begin{array}{r} 0.8\,8\,8 \\ 9\overline{)8.0\,0\,0} \\ \underline{7\,2} \\ 8\,0 \\ \underline{7\,2} \\ 8\,0 \\ \underline{7\,2} \\ 8 \end{array}$$

Thus, $\frac{8}{9} \approx 0.89$ or 89%.

Renaming percents

Today the meaning of percent is much broader than the original concept of "per hundred." Of course, 10% still means 10 out of 100. But the concept can now be extended to show other meanings. For example, 200% means twice the original number, and 2000% means twenty times the original number.

You may have noticed a headline similar to the following in your newspaper.

OIL PRICES RISE
150% IN TEN YEARS

In this headline, the 150% shows that oil prices rose $1\frac{1}{2}$, or 1.5, times the price ten years ago. In this case 150% has been renamed first as a fraction ($1\frac{1}{2}$) and as a decimal (1.5).

In order to rename a percent as a *decimal,* you need only to recall that the second decimal place after the decimal point is called hundredths. Therefore 0.75, read 75 hundredths, is the same as $\frac{75}{100}$, or 75 per hundred. This means that hundredths is the same as per hundred, or percent; so $75\% = \frac{75}{100} = 0.75$.

$$25\% = \frac{25}{100} \text{ or } 0.25$$

$$37.5\% = \frac{37.5}{100} \text{ or } 0.375$$

$$16\frac{1}{4}\% = \frac{16\frac{1}{4}}{100} \blacktriangleright 0.16\frac{1}{4} = 0.1625$$

Another way to change a percent to a decimal is to move the decimal point two places to the left and remove the percent sign.

$$12.6\% = 0.126$$
$$4.25\% = 0.0425$$
$$3\frac{1}{2}\% = 0.03\frac{1}{2} \text{ or } 0.035$$

A percent may be renamed as a *fraction* by two different methods.

1. Remove the percent sign and write the number as the numerator of a common fraction with the denominator 100. Then reduce the fraction to lowest terms.

$$24\% = \frac{24}{100} \text{ or } \frac{6}{25}$$

2. Change the percent to a decimal and then change the decimal to a common fraction in lowest terms.

$$150\% = 1.5 \blacktriangleright 1\frac{5}{10} = 1\frac{1}{2}$$
$$60\% = 0.60 \blacktriangleright \frac{60}{100} = \frac{3}{5}$$

Your Turn

Rename the following percents as decimals and then as fractions in lowest terms.

Example: $12.5\% \rightarrow .125, \frac{1}{8}$

1. 62.5%   2. 8%
3. 45%   4. 125%
5. 0.6%   6. 30%

(Answers appear at the end of the section.)

Solving percent problems

Most everyday problems involving percents deal with the comparison of two numbers. One number is compared to a second number, which is called the base. For example, if you buy a house for $50,000 and sell it five years later for

$80,000, your profit is $80,000 − $50,000, or $30,000. If you want to know what percent profit you made, then you will need to compare your profit ($30,000) to the original cost ($50,000). The original cost is the base. In fraction form this is expressed as follows:

$$\frac{30,000}{50,000} \text{ or } \frac{3}{5}$$

Now change $\frac{3}{5}$ to a percent.

$$3 \div 5 = 0.6$$

Move the decimal point two places to the right and use a percent sign:

$$\frac{3}{5} = 0.6 \text{ or } 60\%$$

So, you will make a profit of 60%.

Another way to solve percent problems is the proportion method. This method starts with the fact that a percent is a ratio: it is the comparison of a number with 100.

To solve a percent problem using the proportion method, it is necessary to create a proportion from the conditions stated in the problem. Usually a letter is used to represent the number you want to find. This number may be represented by one of the following three terms in the proportion:

→ the amount *A*
→ the base *B*
→ the percent *R*

To solve any percent problem, the numbers for two of these three terms must be given. To work out a problem, you must be able to identify which two of the three terms the given numbers represent.

"*R*" is the easiest term to identify because it is written with the word *percent*, or with the symbol (%). "*B*" is the num-

ber that represents 100 percent (base) and usually follows the words *percent of*. This leaves "*A*", which is the remaining number after *R* and *B* have been identified.

Here are three ways in which percent problems may be stated. All three terms have been identified in each example.

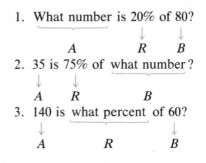

1. What number is 20% of 80?
   $\quad\quad\quad A \quad\quad R \quad\quad B$
2. 35 is 75% of what number?
   $\quad A \quad R \quad\quad\quad\quad B$
3. 140 is what percent of 60?
   $\quad A \quad\quad\quad\quad R \quad\quad\quad B$

Your Turn

In the following problems, identify each problem as being type 1, 2, or 3. Do not solve the problems yet.

7. What number is 35% of 160?
8. What percent of 48 is 12?
9. 20% of what number is 220?
10. What number is 5% of 750?
11. 147 is what percent of 350?

(Answers appear at the end of the section.)

From these examples and previous practice problems, you may have observed that there are three basic types of percent problems. The three types are:

1. to find *A*, when *R* and *B* are given.

   Type (1) problems are usually stated in the form:

   What number is 20% of 80?
   or   Find 20% of 80.
   or   20% of 80 is what number?

2. to find *B*, when *R* and *A* are given.

   Type (2) problems are usually stated in the form:

   25 is 70% of what number?

or 70% of what number is equal to 25?

or 25 is 70% of a number. Find the number.

3. to find R, when A and B are given.

Type (3) problems are usually stated in the form:

12 is what percent of 16?

or Find what percent 12 is of 16.

or What percent of 16 is 12?

The following percent-proportion can be used to solve all three types of percent problems.

$$\frac{R}{100} = \frac{A}{B}$$

See if you can identify the A, R, and B parts in the problems on page 277 and then set up the proportions. Once again do not solve the problems yet. You will later.

(Answers appear at the end of the section.)

Another way to solve percent problems is to use the formula method. As indicated earlier in the section on whole numbers, the word *of* usually indicates multiplication. The word *is* describes the relationship "is equal to" or "=". Since this relationship is also true when working with percent, write the following formula:

$R\%$ of B is A or $R\% \times B = A$

When any two of R, B, and A are known, it is easy to find the other value.

The following examples will be worked using both the percent-proportion and the percent-formula methods. Study each example, pick the method you prefer, and use it for solving percent problems.

Study each example carefully. Notice that you must never divide or multiply with percent numbers. Percent numbers are not arithmetic numbers. All percents must be renamed as fractions or decimals before you can use them in division or multiplication.

Example a: What number is 30% of 150?

Method 1

$$\frac{R}{100} = \frac{A}{B}$$

$R = 30$, $B = 150$, and A is unknown.

$$\frac{30}{100} = \frac{A}{150}$$
$$100 \times A = 30 \times 150$$
$$100 \times A = 4500$$
$$A = \frac{4500}{100}$$
$$A = 45$$

So, 45 is 30% of 150.

Method 2
Translate the values directly into the percent formula:

$$R\% \times B = A$$
$$30\% \times 150 = A$$
$$0.30 \times 150 = A$$
$$45 = A$$

So, 30% of 150 is 45.

Example b: 900 is 30% of what number?

Method 1
$R = 30$, $A = 900$, and B is unknown.

$$\frac{30}{100} = \frac{900}{B}$$
$$100 \times 900 = 30 \times B$$
$$90000 = 30 \times B$$
$$\frac{90000}{30} = B$$
$$3000 = B$$

So, 900 is 30% of 3000.

Method 2
Translate the values directly into the percent formula:

$R\% \times B = A$
$30\% \times B = 900$
$0.30 \times B = 900$
$B = \dfrac{900}{0.30}$
$B = 3000$

So, 900 is 30% of 3000.

Example c: 32 is what percent of 40?

Method 1
$A = 32$, $B = 40$, and R is unknown.

$\dfrac{R}{100} = \dfrac{32}{40}$
$R \times 40 = 100 \times 32$
$R \times 40 = 3200$
$R = \dfrac{3200}{40}$
$R = 80$

So, 32 is 80% of 40.

Method 2
Translate the values directly into the percent formula:

$R\% \times B = A$
$\dfrac{R}{100} \times 40 = 32$
$\dfrac{R}{100} = \dfrac{32}{40}$ or 0.8
$R = 80$

So, 32 is 80% of 40.

Your Turn

12.–16. Now, return to the examples just discussed where you identified A, B, and R and solve them using either method.

(Answers appear at the end of the section.)

The basic principles you have learned apply to yet other problems involving percent. First, identify the given values for R, B, or A and then identify what is to be found. Next, it is usually helpful to determine the two parallel situations that can be translated into a proportion. Finally, set up appropriate procedures for solving the problem using either the percent-proportion or the percent-formula methods. Study the following problems.

Example a: During three football games, a quarterback completed 44 out of 72 passes. What percent of passes were completed?

Step 1: Rearrange the problem so it is easy to see the relationships. 44 is what percent of 72?

Step 2: Determine the given values and identify the unknown.

$A = 44$
$B = 72$
$R = ?$

Step 3: Determine what the two parallel conditions are.

1. The number of passes completed is $R\%$.
2. The number of passes thrown is 100%.

Step 4: Set up a proportion.
$\dfrac{R}{100} = \dfrac{44}{72}$

Step 5: Solve the proportion.
$R \times 72 = 100 \times 44$
$R = \dfrac{4400}{72}$
$R = 61.\overline{1}$

So, the quarterback completed 61.1% of the passes.

Example b: A baseball team played 130 games and won 70% of them. How many games did the team win?

Step 1: Rearrange the problem so it is easy to see the relationships.
What number is 70% of 130?

Step 2: Determine the given values and identify the unknown.

$B = 130$
$A = ?$
$R = 70$

Step 3: Determine what the two parallel conditions are.

1. The number of games played is 130.
2. The number of games won is A.

Step 4: Set up the proportion.

$$\frac{70}{100} = \frac{A}{130}$$

Step 5: Solve the proportion.

$100 \times A = 70 \times 130$
$$A = \frac{9100}{100}$$
$$A = 91$$

So, the team won 91 games.

Example c: On an examination a student worked 18 problems correctly. She received a score of 75%. How many problems are on the test?

Step 1: Rearrange the problem so the relationships are easy to see.
75% of what number is 18?

Step 2: Determine the given values and identify the unknown.

$B = ?$
$A = 18$
$R = 75$

Step 3: Determine what the parallel conditions are.

1. A student worked 18 problems correctly.
2. The number of problems on the test is B.

Step 4: Now write the proportion.

$$\frac{18}{B} = \frac{75}{100}$$

Step 5: Solve the proportion.

$B \times 75 = 18 \times 100$
$$B = \frac{1800}{75}$$
$$B = 24$$

So, there were 24 problems on the test.

Your Turn

Solve each problem using proportion.

17. Jason made 15 out of 20 baskets in a game. What percent of baskets were made?
18. In one game Judy got a hit 50% of the times she batted. If she batted 6 times, how many hits did she get?
19. Pete got 72 out of 75 questions correct on a test. What percent did he get correct?
20. Anita sank 60% of the free throws she attempted. If she made 15 free throws, how many did she attempt?

(Answers appear at the end of the section.)

Commission

Many salespeople are paid on a commission basis. They receive a certain percent of sales based on the amount of goods they sell. The amount they receive is called commission. The percent they receive is called the rate of commission.

Example: Suppose you sell used cars and receive a commission of 28%. About how much will you earn on each sale if the average selling price of a car is $7500?

28% means $\frac{28}{100}$. The ratio of your commission is $\frac{A}{7500}$.

Now write the proportion:

$$\frac{28}{100} = \frac{A}{7500}$$

Complete the problem on your own.

(Answer appears at the end of the section.)

Your Turn

Solve these problems.

21. If a salesperson's commission is 8%, how many dollars' worth of goods must be sold in order to earn $1200?
22. A salesperson received $360 for selling goods priced at $4500. What percent commission was received?
23. What rate of commission would a salesperson receive for selling a house for $85,000 and receiving a commission of $4250?
24. A salesperson receives a weekly salary of $150 with a 10% commission on all sales. What must the total weekly sales be if the weekly income is $800?

(Answers appear at the end of the section.)

Discounts

In order to stimulate sales, merchants sometimes sell goods and services at a reduced price. The percent of reduction is the rate of discount. The amount of reduction is the discount. The price after the discount is the sale price.

Example: The list price of a sofa is $750. On a special sale it is offered at 20% off. What is the sale price?
Rearrange: What number is 20% of $750?

So, $B = 750$, $A = ?$, $R = 20$
and,

$$\frac{20}{100} = \frac{A}{750}$$

$$A = 150$$

Thus, the discount is $150. Now, to get the sale price you must subtract the discount from the list price.

$$\begin{aligned} \text{sale price} &= \text{list price} - \text{discount} \\ &= 750 - 150 \\ &= 600 \end{aligned}$$

The sale price is $600.

Your Turn

Here are a few problems to check your understanding of discount.

Complete this table:

Item	Original Price	Discount Rate	Sale Price
25. 8″ fry pan	$13	33%	_____
26. 10″ fry pan	$15	_____	$9.00
27. 12″ fry pan	$18	50%	_____
28. 1 qt saucepan	_____	25%	$7.50
29. 2 qt saucepan	$20	_____	$10.80
30. 3 qt saucepan	$22	20%	_____

31. A stereo on sale for $425 is advertised as 15% off the regular price. What was the regular price?
32. A newspaper advertisement lists a lawn mower at $179.95. The same mower is billed to the retail dealer at $35.99 less than the advertised price. What is the rate of discount?
33. A catalog lists a certain pair of shoes at $45. The same pair of shoes is billed to merchants at $30. What is the rate of discount? (Caution: The discount is *not* $30.)

34. An automobile dealer is offering 25% off of the sticker price of a certain new-car model. If the sticker price is $14,296, what is the sale price?

(Answers appear at the end of the section.)

The following newspaper advertisements do not show how much you will save on the listed items.

Remember that it is always necessary to know the original price, otherwise you cannot make comparisons. Other advertisements contain such phrases as "30% more miles per gallon," or "33% fewer cavities when you use." More than what? Fewer than what? There should always be some reference to a given base for the percent to have any meaning.

Other ways of finding percent

Sometimes when solving percent problems it is helpful to be able to find 1%, 10%, and 1000% of a number. This is especially helpful when you need to do the computations mentally. To compute with such values always move the decimal point in the number the same as you would to multiply by 0.01, 0.1, or 10. This is true because the decimals or whole numbers equal to these percents are as follows:

$$1\% = 0.01 \quad 10\% = 0.1 \quad 1000\% = 10$$

Thus,

$$1\% \text{ of } 136 \text{ means } 0.01 \times 136 \text{ or } 1.36$$
$$10\% \text{ of } 136 \text{ means } 0.1 \times 136 \text{ or } 13.6$$
$$1000\% \text{ of } 136 \text{ means } 10 \times 136 \text{ or } 1360$$

In many cases where rates are expressed as fractions of a percent, such as $\frac{1}{8}\%$, $\frac{1}{2}\%$, and $\frac{3}{4}\%$, the above relationships can help you solve the problem more quickly. For example,

$\frac{1}{8}\%$ means $\frac{1}{8}$ of 1%;

$\frac{1}{2}\%$ of $645 means $\frac{1}{2}$ of 1% of $645.

Likewise, to find $6\frac{1}{4}\%$ of $8275, you might proceed as follows:

$$6\% \text{ of } 8275 \rightarrow 0.06 \times 8275 = 496.50$$
$$\frac{1}{4}\% \text{ of } 8275 =$$

$$\frac{\frac{1}{4}}{100} \times 8275 \rightarrow \frac{2068.75}{100} = 20.69$$

Now add: $496.50 + 20.69 = 517.19$

Thus $6\frac{1}{4}\%$ of $8275 is $517.19.

You can also use a similar approach if you wish to solve a problem like, "72 is 8% of what number?" A problem of this type can be solved by asking what is 1% of the number, and then by multiplying by 100.

$$8\% \text{ of the number is } 72$$
$$\frac{8}{8} = 1 \text{ or } 1\%; \frac{72}{8} = 9$$

So, 1% of the number is 9. 100% of the number is 900. 72 is 8% of 900.

Now check this using the procedure that was developed previously.

$$0.08 \times B = 72$$
$$B = \frac{72}{0.08}$$
$$B = 900 \qquad \text{It checks.}$$

Another technique that can be used with some problems is to first express the relationships in the problem as a fraction and then express the fraction as a percent. For example, suppose you want to find what percent 80 is of 640, then you could write:

$$\frac{80}{640} = \frac{1}{8} \rightarrow 0.125 = 12.5\%$$

If you memorize the decimals and fractional equivalents of the most frequently used percents, you will find that this will be helpful in doing most computations. Here is a list for your convenience.

$80\% = \frac{4}{5} = 0.80 \qquad 87\frac{1}{2}\% = \frac{7}{8} = 0.875$

$75\% = \frac{3}{4} = 0.75 \qquad 83\frac{1}{3}\% = \frac{5}{6} = 0.833$

$60\% = \frac{3}{5} = 0.60 \qquad 66\frac{2}{3}\% = \frac{2}{3} = 0.666$

$50\% = \frac{1}{2} = 0.50 \qquad 62\frac{1}{2}\% = \frac{5}{8} = 0.625$

$40\% = \frac{2}{5} = 0.40 \qquad 37\frac{1}{2}\% = \frac{3}{8} = 0.375$

$25\% = \frac{1}{4} = 0.25 \qquad 33\frac{1}{3}\% = \frac{1}{3} = 0.333$

$20\% = \frac{1}{5} = 0.20 \qquad 12\frac{1}{2}\% = \frac{1}{8} = 0.125$

Your Turn

Use any method you like to complete these problems.

35. $\frac{3}{4}\%$ of 800 = ?

36. 0.5% of 1200 = ?

37. $3\frac{3}{5}\%$ of 1800 = ?

38. 38 is 5% of what number?

39. 160 is 40% of what number?

40. 85 is what percent of 1500?

41. What percent of 32 is 16?

42. What number is $8\frac{1}{2}\%$ of $60,000?

(Answers appear at the end of the section.)

Percent of increase or decrease

When you buy an item "on sale" or at discount, you buy it for a certain percent less than the regular price. In other words the regular price of the item has been decreased by a certain percent. On the other hand, when the cost of goods goes up, the prices have risen by a certain percent. Sometimes it is desirable to know the percent of increase or decrease. This can be quite helpful when you do comparison shopping.

To find the percent of increase or decrease, find the amount of increase or decrease and then determine what percent this is of the original amount.

Here are some problems to show how this procedure works.

Example a: In 1975 the average family income in the United States was $13,719. In 1981, the average family income was $22,388. What was the percent of increase?

The amount of increase is $8669.

The ratio of increase in income to the original income is 8669 to 13,719. This ratio, written as a fraction, is $\frac{8669}{13,719}$.

In decimal form $\frac{8669}{13,719}$ = 0.632 (rounded to the nearest thousandth)

Thus $\frac{8669}{13,719}$ = 0.632 = 63.2%

Therefore an increase from $13,719 to $22,388 represents a 63.2% increase in average family income from 1975 to 1981.

Example b: In 1965, 9.3 million cars were produced by American companies. In 1981, 6.3 million cars were produced by the same companies. Find the percent of decrease.

The amount of decrease is 3 million.

The ratio of decrease in car production to the original number produced is 3 to 9.3. This ratio, written as a fraction is $\frac{3}{9.3}$.

In decimal form $\frac{3}{9.3}$ = 0.323 (rounded to the nearest thousandth)

Thus 0.323 = 32.3%

Therefore, a decrease from 9.3 million to 6.3 million represents a 32.3% decrease in car production from 1965 to 1981.

Your Turn

Copy and complete this table.

	Original Number	New Number	Increase or Decrease	Percent of Increase or Decrease
43.	24	40	_____	_____
44.	150	50	_____	_____
45.	225	475	_____	_____
46.	500	190	_____	_____

Find the amount of the percent of decrease in price for these items. Round answers to the nearest percent.

47.

$377   Originally $509 Color television at big $132 savings. Electronic tuning. Auto-color. #465

48.

$499   Originally $699 25″ color console television. In-home service contract available. #4706

For the last two problems in this section, you will determine percent of savings. The problem involves phone rates by two competing phone companies.

Calls	Min.	Company A	Company B	% of Savings
49. N.Y. to L.A.	10	$3.09	$2.06	_____%
50. Tulsa to Spokane	3	$ .91	$ .77	_____%

(Answers appear at the end of the section.)

Answers

Ratios (pp. 270–272)

1. $\dfrac{1}{3}$ 2. $\dfrac{1}{2}$ 3. $\dfrac{3}{2}$ 4. $\dfrac{3}{1}$ 5. $\dfrac{1}{3}$ 6. $\dfrac{2}{3}$ 7. $\dfrac{20}{3}$ 8. $\dfrac{3}{5}$ 9. a. $\dfrac{22}{41}$

b. $\dfrac{41}{22}$ 10. $\dfrac{45}{1}$ 11. $\dfrac{3}{4}$ 12. $\dfrac{1}{10}$ 13. $\dfrac{25}{2}$

Proportions (pp. 272–274)

1. $2 \times n = 3 \times 4; n = 6$ 2. $n \times 30 = 5 \times 24; n = 4$ 3. $n = 12$ 4. $n = 3$
5. $n = 6$ 6. $n = 21$

Answer from page 274: 20

7. \$4.40   8. \$2592   9. $2\dfrac{1}{10}$ cups   10. 9 boxes   11. 25 gallons

Percent (pp. 274–284)

1. $0.625; \dfrac{5}{8}$ 2. $0.08; \dfrac{2}{25}$ 3. $0.45; \dfrac{9}{20}$ 4. $1.25; 1\dfrac{1}{4}$ 5. $0.006; \dfrac{3}{500}$ 6. $0.30; \dfrac{3}{10}$
7. 1   8. 3   9. 2   10. 1   11. 3

Answers for page 278:   7. $B = 160; R = 35; A$ is unknown   8. $A = 12; B = 48; R$ is unknown
9. $A = 220; R = 20; B$ is unknown   10. $B = 750; R = 5; A$ is unknown
11. $A = 147; B = 350; R$ is unknown
12. $A = 56$ 13. $R = 25\%$ 14. $B = 1100$ 15. $A = 37.5$ 16. $R = 42\%$
17. 75%   18. 3 hits   19. 96%   20. 25 attempted

Answer for page 281: \$2100

21. \$15,000   22. 8%   23. 5%   24. \$6500   25. \$8.71   26. 40%   27. \$9.00

28. \$10.00   29. 46%   30. \$17.60   31. \$500   32. 20%   33. $33\dfrac{1}{3}\%$

34. \$10,722   35. 6   36. 6   37. 64.8   38. 760   39. 400   40. $5\dfrac{2}{3}\%$

41. 50%   42. \$5100   43. 16; 66.7%   44. 100; 66.7%   45. 250; 111.1%
46. 310; 62%   47. 26%   48. 29%   49. 33%   50. 15%

Section 5

Informal Geometry

If you have ever drawn a circle, measured an area, or connected two points with a straight line, you have used geometry. Geometry is the part of mathematics that studies the properties, such as shape and size, and the relationships of plane and space figures.

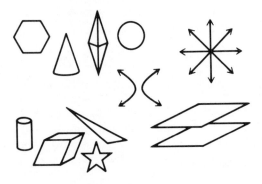

Geometry is used by architects, engineers, astronomers, industrial designers, athletes, artists, and everyone, everyday. The name comes from two Greek words, *ge* (earth) and *metrei* (measure), and suggests why the subject has been studied for as long as records have been kept.

Geometry can be studied in two ways. In informal geometry, various figures are described and their boundaries (perimeters and surfaces) and the regions they enclose (areas and volumes) are measured. In formal geometry, mathematicians have abstracted ideas from life and made a set of rules (logic) with which they draw conclusions.

An understanding of geometry is useful to everyone. Geometric patterns are a vital part of everyone's daily life. These patterns enable you to describe and understand your world, from the microscopic world of cells to the universe viewed with a telescope. Geometric patterns and concepts are used in designing homes, offices, and factories; in setting out plants and trees; in designing and us-

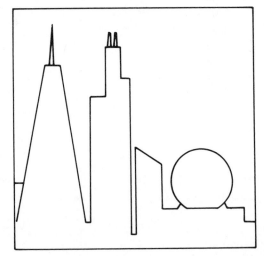

ing cars, planes, trains, and ships; in making clothes; and in enlarging photographs. A shell or the arrangement of petals on a flower can be described by means of geometric patterns.

The manufacture of items for daily life uses two basic geometric concepts: similar figures (those with the same shape but not necessarily the same size), and congruent figures (those with both the same shape and the same size).

Figures such as those just shown are built from simple parts that you will learn about in this section.You will need the following materials as you work:

> straightedge (such as a ruler)
> metric ruler
> protractor (used to measure angles)
> compass (used in constructions)
> unlined paper and several pencils

Note that a straightedge is used for drawing straight lines and is not used for measuring. The edge of a book can be used as a straightedge. A ruler can be used both as a straightedge and as a measuring tool.

Throughout the section you will find *experiments* and *constructions*. To gain the greatest benefit from this section, you should work through the experiments and constructions as you encounter them.

You will also find many new terms, definitions, observations, and rules here. If you have not started a mathematics notebook, as suggested at the beginning of Part IV, you may now wish to start one. Further, do not try to work through too many pages at one sitting.

Figures in a Plane

Points

A point is represented with a dot, but mathematically, takes up *no* space.

Experiment

On a piece of paper, draw any two lines that cross. The crossing-place, or intersection, is a point. You can make the following observation:

> **RULE:**
> **Two intersecting lines determine one and only one point.**

Lines and line segments

For a mathematician, a line extends endlessly (or infinitely) in both directions. You can show this "ongoingness" by putting arrows on the diagram.

A   B

In the real world, there are only pieces of lines, or line segments. (In everyday language, line segments are referred to as lines.)

Experiment

On a piece of paper, mark two separate points. Use a straightedge to connect the points. You have drawn a line segment. It consists of the two endpoints and all the points in between. Now draw different paths connecting the two original points.

Any drawing different from the first one will not have the property called straightness. A line segment must be straight. The line segment is the shortest distance between the two points. (Compare the drawings that you have made to see which is the shortest.) You can make the following observations:

> **RULE:**
> **Two points determine one and only one line (or line segment).**

RULE:
The shortest distance between two points is a line segment.

Note the pattern formed:

Lines	*Points*
One	At least two
Two intersecting	One

A point is named by a capital letter, such as point (T). A line is named by two capital letters with a line above them $(\overleftrightarrow{AB})$. A line segment also uses two capital letters, but it has no arrowheads on the segment above the letters $(\overline{RV})$.

Examples:
$\overleftrightarrow{DE}$ and $\overleftrightarrow{FE}$ intersect at point E.

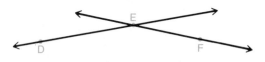

$\overline{RV}$ and $\overline{TZ}$ intersect at point W.

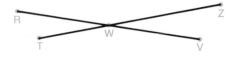

In referring to line segments or <u>lines</u>, write either "line segment RV" or "RV." Never write "line segment $\overline{RV}$."

Since only two points are needed to determine a line, it is very easy to set up boundaries for property. Put two stakes in the ground, fasten a string to join them, and tighten to take out the slack.

Straight lines are seen everywhere: in buildings, streets, sidewalks, walls, ceil-ings, floors, football fields, baseball diamonds, and rows of plants on a farm. Look about and see how many straight lines (or line segments) you can spot.

Experiment

Draw a line segment and letter the endpoints A and B. Mark any point between A and B and name it C. Next, mark a point between A and C and name it D. Then mark a point between A and D and name it E.

The diagram is quickly filling up with points. Soon it will be too hard to see the new point you are drawing, but you can continue to put a point between A and the last point selected forever—at least in your thoughts. You can see that between any two points, however close, you can place another *mathematical* point. (Remember that points take up no space.) Observe the following:

RULE:
There are infinitely many points on a line or line segment.

RULE:
Between any two points on a line or line segment, there are infinitely many points.

Think about the last observation. Isn't it a bit surprising? Infinity is a concept that holds many surprises. Try this next experiment.

Experiment

Draw the figure below.

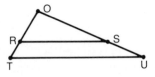

Pick any point on $\overline{TU}$ and connect it to point O. The connecting segment crosses $\overline{RS}$ at a point. Thus, there is a point on $\overline{RS}$ for every point on $\overline{TU}$, and vice versa. You can then say that there are "just as many" points on the shorter segments, $\overline{RS}$, as there are on the longer segment, $\overline{TU}$.

Rays

Sometimes you want part of a line that includes one endpoint and extends infinitely in one direction. Mathematicians call this figure a ray.

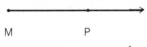

M   P

To name a ray, name the endpoint and a point not on the endpoint $(\overrightarrow{MP})$. Notice that the first letter used in naming a ray names the endpoint of the ray.

B   A   C   D   E   F

This is ray AB. ($\overrightarrow{AB}$).

This is ray CD, ray CE, or ray CF.

Think of a ray of sunshine that starts at the sun and continues forever.

s
u
n   ray

Your Turn

Name each of the following with a symbol instead of words.

1. line segment CD
2. line ZX
3. ray MN
4. Two points determine how many lines?

5. Two intersecting lines determine how many points?

(Answers appear at the end of the section.)

Planes

Look at a piece of paper lying on a table. Think of the paper extending in all directions.

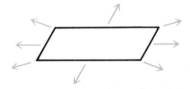

Mathematicians call this figure a plane. In the real world, you work with parts of planes, such as a piece of paper or a wall of a room.

How many points are needed to determine a plane? If you have one point, you can pass many planes through it. (Think of the corner of the room where the planes of two walls and the floor come together in a point.) If you have two points, you have a straight line. Many planes can pass through a straight line. (Think of the pages of a newspaper, each page a plane coming from the fold line.)

many planes

many planes

What about three points? Think of balancing a piece of stiff paper on three legs of an upturned stool, even if the legs are not all the same length. The paper will remain flat and touch all three legs.

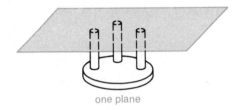

one plane

Observe the following:

RULE:
Three points, not all on a straight line, determine one and only one plane.

Angles

Angles are seen in many figures. To a mathematician, an angle is a figure formed by two rays with the same endpoint. The endpoint is called the vertex of the angle.

This angle is named as ∠F (angle F) or ∠AFB (with the vertex named in the middle).

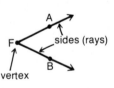

sides (rays)

vertex

In everyday terms, think of an angle as a corner. The hands of the clock below form an angle.

A special instrument, called a protractor, is used to measure an angle. The instrument is half a circle, marked with 180 divisions that are called degrees.

To measure an angle, place the center of the base of the protractor on the vertex of the angle and line up the base with one of the sides of the angle. Then read the number where the other side of the angle intersects the marked circle of the protractor.

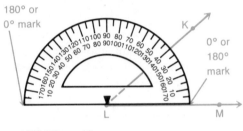

180° or 0° mark

0° or 180° mark

m∠KLM = 40

The "m" means "the measure of." The measure of ∠KLM is 40°. Draw angles such as angles B, C, D shown below and label them angles E, F, and G. Then find the measure of angles B, C, and D with a protractor.

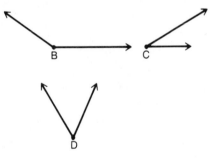

(Answers appear at the end of the section.)

Angles are often grouped by their size into the following classifications:

zero angle   0°

acute angle   0° < m∠A < 90°
                     Angle A has a
                     measure between 0°
                     and 90°.

right angle	90°
obtuse angle	90° < m∠A < 180° Angle A has a measure between 90° and 180°.
straight angle	180°
reflex angle	180° < m∠A < 360° Angle A has a measure between 180° and 360°.

Adjacent angles

Names are also given to certain pairs of angles. Adjacent angles have a common vertex and a common side, but no common interior points.

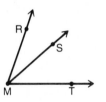

∠RMS and ∠SMT are adjacent angles.	∠1 and ∠2 are adjacent angles. (An angle can also be named by an interior number placed by the vertex.)

Complementary and supplementary angles

Complementary angles are two angles whose measures add to 90°. Supplementary angles are two angles whose measures add to 180°. Complementary angle pairs and supplementary angle pairs do not have to be located physically near each other.

∠A and ∠B are
complementary
angles.

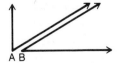

∠C and ∠D are
supplementary
angles.

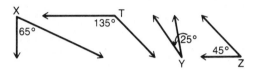

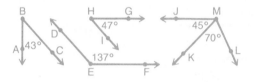

∠X is the complement of ∠Y. ∠Y is the complement of ∠X. ∠T is the supplement of ∠Z. ∠Z is the supplement of ∠T.

Your Turn

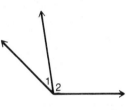

Use the angles above to name

1. a pair of adjacent angles
2. a pair of complementary angles
3. a pair of supplementary angles

Give the measure of the complements for angles with these measures.

4. 30°   5. 45°   6. 18°   7. 61°

Give the measure of the supplements for angles with these measures.

8. 30°   9. 45°   10. 136°   11. 90°

(Answers appear at the end of the section.)

Congruent angles

All angles of a particular measure (for example, 42°) are similar to one another—they have the same shape. Since the sides of any angle can be extended indefinitely, the lengths of the sides do not matter. Thus, all angles of a particular measure are congruent; they have both the same size and the same shape.

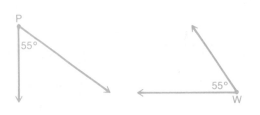

∠P ≅ ∠W   Angle P *is congruent to* angle W. The symbol ≅ shows congruence.

Vertical angles are pairs of angles formed by intersecting lines.

∠1 and ∠2 are a pair of vertical angles. ∠3 and ∠4 are a pair of vertical angles.

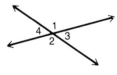

∠QEJ and ∠WEK are a pair of vertical angles. ∠QEW and ∠JEK are a pair of vertical angles.

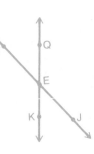

Experiment

Draw two intersecting lines and label them as shown above. Find the measure of ∠QEJ, ∠QEW, ∠WEK, and ∠JEK. You should have found that

∠QEJ ≅ ∠WEK and ∠JEK ≅ ∠QEW

This leads to the following observation:

RULE:
Intersecting lines form two pairs of vertical angles. Vertical angles are congruent.

Your Turn

12. Name the two pairs of vertical angles formed by the lines at the right.

13. Is ∠ABC ≅ ∠DBC?

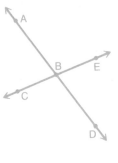

14. If m∠ABC = 72°, what is the measure of ∠EBD? of ∠ABE?

(*Answers appear at the end of the section.*)

You can construct an angle congruent to a given angle without the use of a protractor. For constructions, use a compass and a straightedge. Work through each step as it is discussed.

Construction

You are given ∠X. To construct ∠Y ≅ ∠X, draw a working line, *m*, and pick a point Y for the vertex of the new angle.

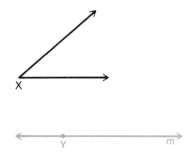

Open the compass to a convenient width, place the point of the compass on the vertex of ∠X, and make an arc that intersects both sides. Now place the point of the compass on the vertex picked for ∠Y, and make an arc like the first one. Be careful not to change the size of the compass opening.

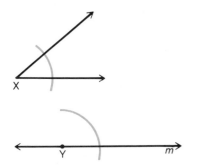

Next, place the point of the compass on the intersection of the arc and one side of ∠X. Adjust the compass opening so that the pencil point meets the intersection of the arc and the other side of ∠X. Without changing the compass opening, mark the same opening from one side of ∠Y along the arc.

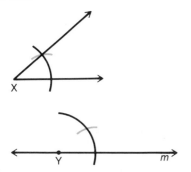

Draw the second side of ∠Y by connecting the vertex with the intersection of the arc and the opening mark. You now have constructed an angle that matches the size of ∠X as closely as your writing tool will permit.

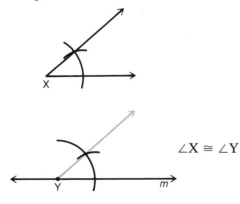

∠X ≅ ∠Y

Two more constructions with angles are very useful. It is often handy to be able to separate an angle into two congruent angles, that is, to bisect the angle. In particular, bisecting a straight angle gives two 90° angles, that is, two right angles. When two lines meet to form right angles, the lines are perpendicular. Thus, when you bisect a straight angle, you erect a perpendicular to a line at the point where the vertex lies.

To bisect any angle, use the following construction.

Construction

You are given ∠P. Open the compass to a convenient width, place the point of the compass on the vertex, and draw an arc that intersects each side of the angle. Name the intersections points R and S.

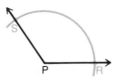

Place the point of the compass first at R and then at S, and from each of these points draw arcs that intersect in the interior of the angle, point T. Connect point T to the point P.

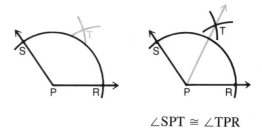

∠SPT ≅ ∠TPR

In the next construction, you bisect a straight angle to obtain perpendicular lines.

Construction

You are given straight angle PQR. Bisect ∠PQR as just described.

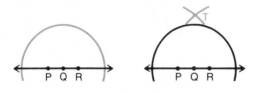

Extend the bisector through point Q. You now have four right angles and two perpendicular lines.

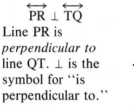

$\overleftrightarrow{PR} \perp \overleftrightarrow{TQ}$

Line PR is *perpendicular to* line QT. ⊥ is the symbol for "is perpendicular to."

Carpenters have to make sure that the vertical supports of a building are perpendicular to the horizontal frame. They also have to check the frames for the doors and windows to be sure that the verticals and horizontals make right angles, that is, that they are perpendicular. For this work, they have a metal angle called a T square with which they check their work.

Lines in a plane

In a plane, two lines either intersect or are parallel. Parallel lines are pairs of lines that do not meet however far they are extended. Parallel lines are everywhere the same distance apart, that is, they are equidistant. The distance between parallel lines is measured along a line perpendicular to each of the parallel lines, as shown in the figure. The length

of the segment intercepted (cut off) by the parallel lines is said to be the distance between them.

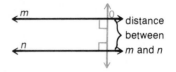

$m \parallel n$
Line *m* is parallel to line *n*.

⌐ is the symbol for a right angle.

∥ is the symbol for "is parallel to."

When a pair of lines is crossed by a third line, called a transversal, a number of angles are formed.

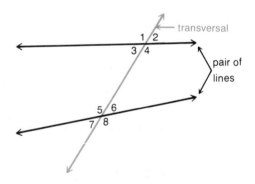

Alternate interior angles are a pair of angles, one on each side of the transversal, between the pair of lines. Angles 3 and 6 are one pair of alternate interior angles. Angles 4 and 5 are another pair of alternate interior angles.

Corresponding angles are pairs of angles, each on the same side of the transversal of a pair of lines, one interior and one exterior to the lines. Angle pairs 1 and 5, 2 and 6, 3 and 7, and 4 and 8 are pairs of corresponding angles.

When the pair of lines crossed by the transversal are parallel, the pairs of alternate interior angles are congruent and the pairs of corresponding angles are congruent.

For the figure below, give the reason for the following congruencies:

$\angle 4 \cong \angle 5$	$\angle 3 \cong \angle 7$
$\angle 3 \cong \angle 6$	$\angle 2 \cong \angle 6$
$\angle 1 \cong \angle 5$	$\angle 4 \cong \angle 8$

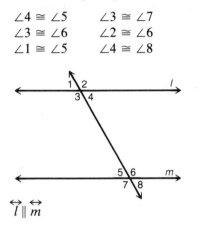

$\overset{\leftrightarrow}{l} \parallel \overset{\leftrightarrow}{m}$

Also, do you recall why $\angle 1 \cong \angle 4$, $\angle 2 \cong \angle 3$, $\angle 5 \cong \angle 8$, $\angle 6 \cong \angle 7$? (Hint: what do you call such pairs of angles?)

(Answers appear at the end of the section.)

Your Turn

In the figure below, you have a pair of parallel lines, a transversal, and the measure of one angle. Use what you know about supplementary and vertical angles, and about alternate interior and corresponding angles of parallel lines crossed by a transversal, to find the measures of all the angles, 2 through 8. The measure of $\angle 1 = 150°$.

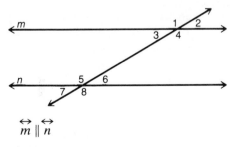

$\overset{\leftrightarrow}{m} \parallel \overset{\leftrightarrow}{n}$

(Answers appear at the end of the section.)

Polygons

Many figures can be constructed by joining line segments at their endpoints. If the line segments do not cross and the figure is closed, the many-sided figures formed are called polygonal figures, or polygons.

If all the angles of a polygonal figure measure less than 180°, the figure is said to be convex. If any angle is greater than 180°, the figure is said to be concave.

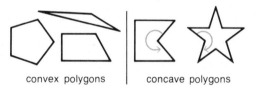

Green arrows show that at least one angle is greater than 180°.

Triangles

The polygon with the smallest number of sides is the triangle. As triangles take on many shapes, they have been grouped for convenience into sets. They may be grouped by the relation of the sides or by the size of the angles.

By sides, the triangles are grouped as:

scalene	no two sides congruent

isosceles	at least two sides congruent
equilateral	all sides congruent

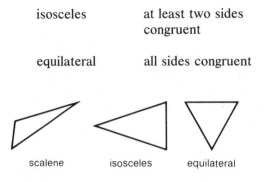

scalene   isosceles   equilateral

You can see that every equilateral triangle is also an isosceles triangle.

By angles, triangles are grouped as:

acute	all angles <90°
right	one angle = 90°
obtuse	one angle >90°

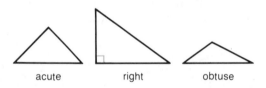

acute   right   obtuse

Triangles are extremely useful figures. They are rigid figures. When a force is applied to them, they remain stable until the material forming the sides gives

way. For this reason, the triangle is used as a support and as a construction element. Triangles make good shelf supports. Triangles are also often used as a design element in the support structure of bridges and towers.

You can check the stable property of the triangle in the following experiment.

Experiment

Take a carpenter's folding rule and make a triangular shape, one segment for each side of the triangle.

Press on the figure. You will see that the triangle does not change its shape. Now make a square figure with the carpenter's rule and press on it.

The angles change their size; the shape of the figure changes. (For another application of this property, *see* p. 17.)

Construction

It is easy to construct an equilateral triangle. Choose a length for one side of the triangle, $\overline{RS}$. Copy this length m with your compass on a working line, as shown in the figure. Now, from each end of $\overline{AB}$ make arcs of the same length as $\overline{AB}$. The point of the intersection of these arcs is the vertex of the equilateral triangle.

R   S

$\xleftarrow{\hspace{2cm}}$ m A B $\xrightarrow{\hspace{2cm}}$

$\overline{AB} \cong \overline{RS}$

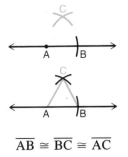

$$\overline{AB} \cong \overline{BC} \cong \overline{AC}$$

An interesting fact about the three angles of a triangle can be seen from the next experiment.

Experiment

Cut a triangle from a piece of paper. Select one side to be the base of the triangle. Call the base AB. Slide vertex A along the base until the vertical segment formed intersects the vertex above the base.

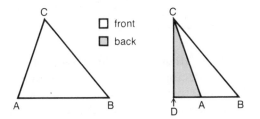

Crease sharply, then open. Call the point where the crease meets the base, point D. Now fold so that points A and B meet at point D. Next bring point C down to point D. You can see that the three angles of the triangle, A, B, and C, form a straight angle, which has a measure of 180°.

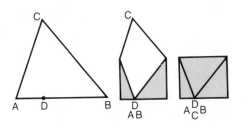

Observe the following:

> **RULE:**
> **The sum of the measures of the angles of a triangle is 180°.**

The equilateral triangle has three congruent angles. It can also be called an equiangular triangle. Since the sum of the measures of the angles is 180°, each of the angles measures 60°. You then have an easy construction for a 60° angle.

Construction

Begin the construction of an equilateral triangle, as described on page 296. When two sides are drawn, they form a 60° angle.

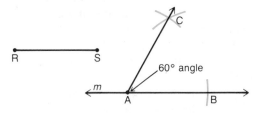

Right triangles. One of the classes of triangles mentioned earlier is the right triangle. The two sides of the right triangle that form the right angle are called the legs; the side opposite the right angle is called the hypotenuse.

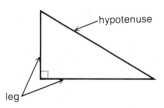

Since the right angle has a measure of 90°, and the sum of the measures of the angles of a triangle is 180°, the sum of the measures of the two remaining angles must be 90°. From this observation you can conclude that:

RULE:

Two of the angles of a right triangle must be acute angles (<90°) and the two acute angles of a right triangle are complementary.

Experiment

With your straightedge and protractor, draw a right triangle with an acute angle measuring 30°. What must the measure of the other acute angle be?

(Answer appears at the end of the section.)

Write the measures of the three angles of the triangle in a column, reading from smallest to largest. Now, measure the length of the side opposite each angle to the nearest millimeter. Record the values next to the angle measures. Do the lengths of the sides fall in the same order?

Draw other triangles (acute and obtuse). Measure and record the angles and the lengths of the sides opposite the angles, in the same order. Is the shortest angle always opposite the smallest side? Is the longest side always opposite the largest angle in the triangle? From this experiment you should observe that:

RULE:

The longest side of a triangle lies opposite the largest angle; and the shortest side, opposite the smallest angle. In a right triangle, the longest side, the hypotenuse, lies opposite the right angle.

Cevians. There are certain interesting line segments that can be drawn in a triangle. These line segments, which connect the vertex to a particular point on the opposite side, are called cevians.

One of the cevians is the angle bisector. The second cevian is the median. It is the line segment that connects any vertex to the midpoint of the opposite side.

The arc marks, ⟩⟩, indicate equality of angle measure.

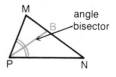

$$\angle MPB \cong \angle BPN$$

The tic marks, |, indicate equality of segment measure.

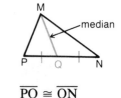

$$\overline{PQ} \cong \overline{QN}$$

The third cevian is the altitude. It is the line segment from a vertex perpendicular to the opposite side, or to the extension of the opposite side.

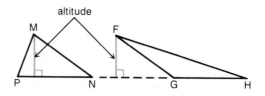

Each triangle has three each of the angle bisectors, medians, and altitudes. The angle bisectors and medians always lie in the interior of the triangle. For one group of triangles, two of the altitudes lie in the exterior, and for another group, two sides of the triangle are altitudes. Sketch a triangle for each group.

(Answers appear at the end of the section.)

In order to draw the medians of a triangle, you have to be able to find the midpoint of a line segment. Mathematicians use a compass and a straightedge other than a ruler.

Construction

Select a line segment, $\overline{AB}$. Open the compass to more than half the length of the line segment. From each of the points A and B, make arcs above and below $\overline{AB}$ so that they intersect, as shown in the figure below. Connect the points of intersection, P and Q. $\overleftrightarrow{PQ}$ is the perpendicular bisector of $\overline{AB}$, and the point at which it intersects $\overline{AB}$ is then the midpoint, M.

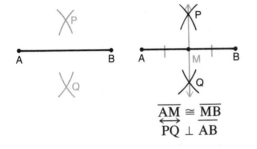

$$\overline{AM} \cong \overline{MB}$$
$$\overleftrightarrow{PQ} \perp \overline{AB}$$

To construct an altitude of a triangle, you must first be able to construct a line that goes through a given point and is perpendicular to a given line. This is often referred to as dropping a perpendicular to a line from a point not on that line.

Construction

To drop a perpendicular to a line from a point not on that line, use the following construction.

You are given line segment AB and point P not on line AB. Open the compass so that when you make an arc from P, it will intersect $\overleftrightarrow{AB}$ in two places, points C and D. You have now created line segment CD and can proceed to construct its perpendicular bisector, as you did in the preceding construction.

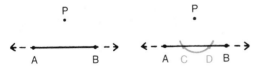

From each of the points C and D make arcs that intersect below $\overline{AB}$. Connect the point of intersection of these arcs

with point P. Call the intersection of this line with $\overline{AB}$ point Q.

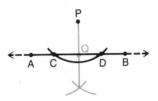

$\overline{PQ}$ is the perpendicular to $\overline{AB}$ from point P. It is also the shortest path to $\overline{AB}$ from point P. Try drawing other paths and compare them with $\overline{PQ}$.

With this construction, you can draw the altitude from any vertex of a triangle to the opposite side (or to the extension of the opposite side, if necessary).

Your Turn

1. Construct an equilateral triangle. From one vertex, construct an altitude, an angle bisector, and a median. What do you observe? Make the same three constructions from one vertex of a scalene triangle. Compare the results.

2. Cut out a triangle. Working with one vertex at a time, fold the triangle so that the two sides are brought together. Crease sharply, then open. You have folded the angle bisector. Fold the other two angle bisectors. What do you find when you have folded all three angle bisectors? Try this experiment again with a different kind of triangle.

3. Examine the three medians of a triangle. You can get these also by folding. To find the midpoint of a side, bring two vertices of the triangle together and pinch the side between them to mark the midpoint. Then crease the triangle along the line segment that connects a vertex and the midpoint of the opposite side. What

do you note about the three medians?
4. Cut out an acute triangle. To crease an altitude, slide a vertex along an adjacent side until the crease that is forming comes from the vertex opposite that side. Crease each altitude sharply, then open. What do you note about the three altitudes?

(Answers appear at the end of the section.)

Similar triangles. For all figures, there are two very special relationships. Figures may have the same shape, as shown below. These are called similar figures.

$\triangle LMN \sim \triangle OPQ$
Triangle LMN *is similar to* triangle OPQ. $\sim$ is the symbol for "is similar to."

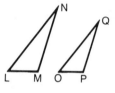

For similar polygons, the corresponding angles are congruent and the pairs of corresponding sides have the same ratio.

One way to show that two triangles are similar is to determine that two pairs of corresponding angles are congruent. The third angles of the triangles will be congruent, since the sum of the angles of every triangle is 180°.

A second way to show that two triangles are similar is to determine that the three pairs of corresponding sides have the same ratio.

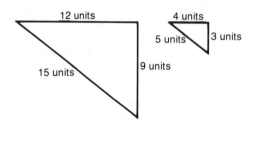

Set up the ratios so they show:

$$\frac{\text{longest side}}{\text{longest side}} \qquad \frac{\text{shortest side}}{\text{shortest side}} \qquad \frac{\text{third side}}{\text{third side}}$$

Using the triangles shown, the ratios are

$$\frac{15}{5} \qquad \frac{9}{3} \qquad \frac{12}{4}$$

Remember that ratios can be simplified, just as fractions are simplified.

$\dfrac{15}{5} = \dfrac{15 \div 5}{5 \div 5} = \dfrac{3}{1}$ The ratios are all 3:1, so the

$\dfrac{9}{3} = \dfrac{9 \div 3}{3 \div 3} = \dfrac{3}{1}$ sides are said to be proportional and the triangles

$\dfrac{12}{4} = \dfrac{12 \div 4}{4 \div 4} = \dfrac{3}{1}$ are similar.

A third method of demonstrating that two triangles are similar is to show that two pairs of corresponding sides are proportional, and the angles formed by those sides (called the included angle) in the two triangles are congruent.

Experiment

Draw any triangle (such as ABC in the figure). Construct a second triangle DEF in the following way.

With your compass, mark off a segment EF equal in length to twice the length of $\overline{BC}$ (mark off $\overline{BC}$ twice on a working line). You have set the ratio of similitude to be 1:2.

Construct $\angle E \cong \angle B$ and $\angle F \cong \angle C$. (Use the construction for congruent angles.)

Use your compass to check whether you can mark off $\overline{AB}$ twice on $\overline{DE}$, and $\overline{AC}$ twice on $\overline{DF}$.

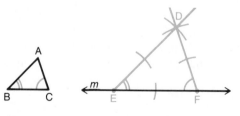

Construct an altitude AP from A to $\overline{BC}$, and a corresponding altitude DQ from D to $\overline{EF}$. Is the ratio $\dfrac{\overline{AP}}{\overline{DQ}} = \dfrac{1}{2}$?

Construct a pair of corresponding medians in the two triangles and also a pair of corresponding angle bisectors, and check the ratio of these pairs of line segments. Summarize your findings.

(Answers appear at the end of the section.)

Similar figures are frequently used. An architect often makes a model of a building being planned so that the buyer can see how it will look when completed. Museums feature scale models of important constructions: buildings, bridges, ships, planes, and trains. Photographers create similar figures when they enlarge or reduce photographs. Modern copying machines can provide reduced figures of drawings. A mechanical instrument called a pantograph, which consists of linkages, enables you to make mechanical drawings that are similar to the original being copied. In all of the applications of similar figures, the shape of the figure remains the same but the size is changed.

Experiment

Draw a triangle, such as △MNO in the next figure. Pick a point P on side MN, and through this point, draw a line parallel to base NO. You can make this construction by making ∠MPQ ≅ ∠N. Copy ∠N at vertex P, using the congruent angle construction shown on page 292. Since the pair of corresponding angles are congruent, and ∠M is congruent to itself, the triangles MNO and MPQ are similar triangles. What can you say about the pairs of corresponding sides of these triangles?

You can see that you are able to make $\overline{MP}$ any fraction of $\overline{MN}$ that you

choose. In particular, if point P is the midpoint, you bisect $\overline{MN}$, and since $\overline{MQ}$ will have a measure half that of $\overline{MO}$, you are bisecting $\overline{MO}$ as well.

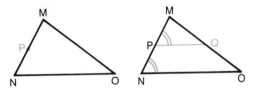

It is to be noted that all right triangles with a particular value of an acute angle are similar, as shown in the figure below. This property is used in the branch of mathematics called trigonometry.

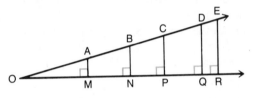

△OAM ~ △OBN ~ △OCP ~ △ODQ ~ △OER . . .

Experiment

Similar triangles can be used to make indirect measurements. Suppose you wish to measure the height of a building. Obtain a small mirror and place it on the ground. Position yourself so that by looking in the mirror you can just see the top of the building.

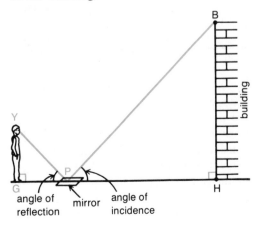

Triangles YGP and BHP are similar triangles. Each has a right angle, and all right angles are congruent since each has a measure of 90°. Also, from the laws of physics, $\angle YPG \cong \angle BPH$, since the angle of incidence of a ray of light has the same measure as the angle of reflection. Thus, the two triangles are similar. The corresponding sides are then proportional. Thus

$$\frac{\overline{BH}}{\overline{YG}} = \frac{\overline{HP}}{\overline{GP}}$$

You can readily measure three of these quantities: $\overline{YG}$, the height to your eye level; $\overline{GP}$, the distance from you to the mirror; $\overline{HP}$, the distance from the building to the mirror. Solve the proportion to find the fourth quantity, $\overline{BH}$. (For another application of this principle, *see* vol. 2, p. 525.)

Congruent triangles. Pairs of triangles and other figures may have both the same shape and the same size. (These are similar figures with a ratio of similitude of 1:1.) Such pairs of figures are called congruent figures, as shown in the diagram.

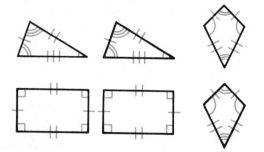

Manufacturing relies heavily on the production of congruent figures. All of the parts for a particular model of a car must be exactly alike, for example. All jeans from a particular manufacturer in a given size are alike. When you copy patterns carefully, whether for a dress, a suit, or a bookcase, you make the new item exactly like the original one.

You want to have congruency in these instances.

It is easy to construct a triangle that is congruent to a given triangle. A triangle has six parts: three angles and three sides. If you match the six sets of corresponding parts, you will have congruent triangles.

However, it can be shown that it is not necessary to use all six parts. If you select certain sets of three, the triangle will be completely determined.

In the next construction, you will see how only one triangle can be formed with three particular sides. Note before you begin that not every set of three segments will form a triangle. Picture trying to make a triangle with sides of 1 cm, 1 cm and 10 cm. The two short sides would never intersect if attached to the ends of the 10 cm side. If you lengthened the short sides to 5 cm each, they would just fall on the 10 cm side. You still could not obtain a triangle. The path along any two sides must be longer than the shortest path between the two endpoints of the third side, which is the line segment that connects them.

RULE:
For every triangle, the sum of the lengths of any two sides must be greater than the length of the third side.

Construction

You are given three line segments, as shown below.

Mark off $\overline{AB}$ on a working line. Adjust the compass opening to the length of $\overline{AC}$, and with the point of the compass on A, make an arc above $\overline{AB}$. Now, readjust the compass to the length of $\overline{BC}$ and make an arc, having the point of the compass on B. The two arcs will intersect at a point, point C. Connect points A and B to point C.

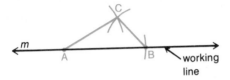

There are four sets of three parts of a triangle that will guarantee congruency. These are as follows:

Parts needed:	Referred to as:
side-angle-side	SAS
angle-side-angle	ASA
angle-angle-side	AAS
side-side-side	SSS

The letters in the right-hand column are the abbreviations that are usually used.

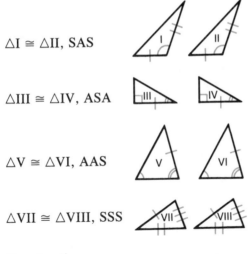

$\triangle I \cong \triangle II$, SAS

$\triangle III \cong \triangle IV$, ASA

$\triangle V \cong \triangle VI$, AAS

$\triangle VII \cong \triangle VIII$, SSS

Construction

Construct a triangle with two given sides and a given value for the included angle (SAS).

Given parts:

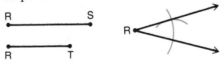

Start with a working line. Mark off line segment RS. Construct an angle congruent to the given angle at point R.

Mark off a line segment equal to the other given segment and label it RT. Draw line segment ST to complete the construction of the triangle.

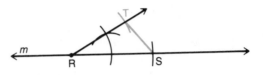

If you are given two sides and a not-included angle, you cannot guarantee congruence. The figure below shows two triangles that correspond to the given two sides and the not-included angle. Clearly, they are not congruent.

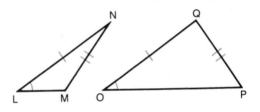

$\overline{LN} \cong \overline{OQ}$; $\overline{MN} \cong \overline{PQ}$; $\angle L \cong \angle O$

Your Turn

For each set of congruent parts of a pair of triangles, tell whether the triangles are congruent. If they are congruent, state the reason, such as SSS or ASA.

1. three sides
2. three angles
3. two sides and the included angle
4. two angles and the included side

5.   two angles and any side
6.   two sides and any angle

(Answers appear at the end of the section.)

Quadrilaterals

Another important class of polygons is that of the quadrilaterals, or four-sided figures. This is an immense family of figures, with which you should become thoroughly familiar.

Trapezoids. Trapezoids are figures that have exactly two sides parallel. If the two non-parallel sides are congruent, the trapezoid is an isosceles trapezoid.

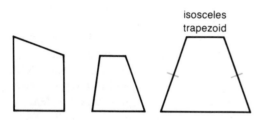

isosceles
trapezoid

The median, or midline, of a trapezoid is the line segment connecting the midpoints of the two non-parallel sides of the trapezoid.

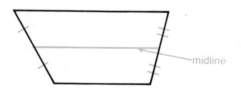

midline

Experiment

Draw four trapezoids and bisect their non-parallel sides. Connect the midpoints of the non-parallel sides to form the midlines. Measure the upper bases, lower bases, and midlines to the nearest millimeter. Copy table and record the values. Compute the sum of the bases and the average of the bases (half the sum).

	Upper base	Lower base	Sum of bases	½ Sum of bases	Midline
1					
2					
3					
4					

What observation can you make about the length of the midline of a trapezoid?

(Answer appears at the end of the section.)

Observe this series of figures.

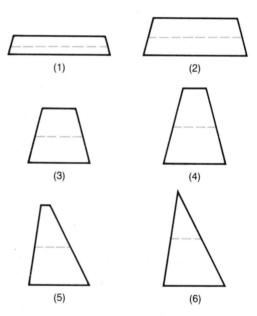

(1)   (2)

(3)   (4)

(5)   (6)

You can think of a triangle as a trapezoid whose upper base is a point (with length 0). From the first part of this experiment, how long should a midline of a triangle be? Check your conclusion by measuring the lower base and the midline. (Note: There are three midlines in each triangle.)

Parallelograms. Quadrilaterals with opposite pairs of sides parallel are called parallelograms.

If the parallelogram has one right angle, then all four angles are right angles. Such a figure is called a rectangle.

rectangle   rectangle; square

If a parallelogram has a pair of adjacent sides congruent, then all four sides are congruent. Such a figure is called a rhombus.

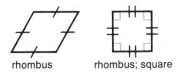

rhombus   rhombus; square

If the rhombus has a right angle, the figure is called a square. You can also think of a square as a rectangle with a pair of adjacent sides congruent.

Two other interesting quadrilaterals are the kite and the chevron. These figures each have two pairs of adjacent, congruent sides. The pairs of sides are not congruent. The kite is a convex figure, while the chevron is a concave figure.

kite   chevron

The quadrilateral family, then, is the set of all plane polygons that have exactly four sides. You have looked at some of the subsets of the quadrilaterals: parallelograms, trapezoids, kites and chevrons, for example. These sets also have subsets. A subset of the trapezoids is the set of isosceles trapezoids. Subsets of the parallelograms are rectangles and rhombuses. The squares form a subset of both the rectangles and the rhombuses. You can show the quadrilateral family as below.

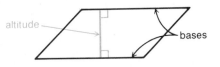

It is customary to call the horizontal sides of a parallelogram the bases, upper and lower. The altitude is a line segment connecting the bases (or their extension) and perpendicular to them.

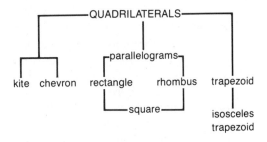

The line segment that connects a vertex of a polygon to a non-adjacent vertex is called a diagonal. Quadrilaterals each have two diagonals.

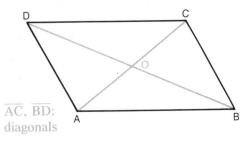

$\overline{AC}$, $\overline{BD}$: diagonals

Your Turn

There are several interesting observations that can be made after folding and cutting quadrilaterals. See how many observations you can make.

1. Draw a parallelogram as above and cut out the figure. Fold along one diagonal and cut the figure into two triangles. What can you say about these triangles?
2. Cut a parallelogram as above, then cut a rhombus, a square, and a rectangle. Fold the two diagonals for each figure. What observation can you make about the angles made by the diagonals of the rhombus and the square that is not true for the diagonals of the rectangle and the parallelogram?
3. Measure and record the lengths of the diagonals for each of the figures and record the results with the name of the figure. What observation can you make about the lengths of the diagonals of the square and the rectangle that is not true for the diagonals of the parallelogram and the rhombus?
4. Make a copy of the parallelogram shown in the figure and cut it into four parts along the diagonal lines. By matching parts, determine which line segments are congruent. Copy the original figure and mark it to show the congruent parts. What observation can you make?
5. A diagonal of a quadrilateral divides the figure into two triangles. You know the sum of the measures of the angles of a triangle. What do you conclude about the sum of the measures of the angles of a quadrilateral?

(Answers appear at the end of the section.)

Rectangular shapes are seen everywhere. Look at the ceiling, walls, floor, windows, door of your room, the cover of your book, the pages of a newspaper, a magazine, the faces of a box, the doors of a cabinet, an index card, a check, a sheet of notebook paper, an envelope, a stamp. How many other objects around you have rectangular shapes?

Square shapes are also widely used, as for floor tiles. Can you find square shapes among familiar objects?

A very special rectangle is the golden rectangle. It is considered to have the most pleasing proportion (ratio of length to width) of any rectangle. The ratio is approximately 1.618:1, and it is represented by the Greek letter φ (phi).

Artists and architects have long been aware of the golden ratio and used it in their works. The Parthenon of ancient Greece has the proportions of the golden ratio, and it was also used in works of such artists as Leonardo da Vinci and Piet Mondrian.

Perhaps people find the golden ratio so pleasing because it occurs frequently in nature. Even the human body embodies the golden ratio. Leonardo da Vinci analyzed the proportions of the human head, demonstrating the appearance of the golden ratio in many of the measurements. He prepared the illustrations for a book on the golden ratio published at the beginning of the sixteenth century.

If you divide any term of the Fibonacci sequence (discussed on page 240) by the term preceding it, you get an approximation of the golden ratio. The higher the terms, the better is the approximation. (Calculate a few values from the Fibonacci sequence: 1,1,2,3,5,8,13,21,34, 55,89,144,233,377,610 . . .) As the Fibonacci sequence occurs in nature in pine cones, chrysanthemums, and certain shells, among other things, you see that the golden ratio is part of your world. You can easily construct a golden rectangle.

Construction

Draw a square, ABCD. Bisect the base AB. Call the midpoint of the base point M. Open the compass to the length MC and make an arc from point M that intersects the extension of base AB at point E. Construct a perpendicular at point E. Extend $\overline{DC}$ until it intersects the perpendicular at point F. Rectangle AEFD is a golden rectangle. Also rectangle BEFC is a golden rectangle. Measure the sides of each rectangle and check the ratios.

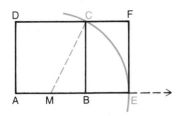

The next experiment reveals an interesting property of all quadrilaterals.

Experiment

Draw four different quadrilaterals.

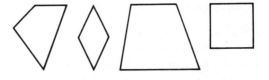

Mark the midpoints of each side of each figure. Connect the midpoints of each figure consecutively. What do the new figures appear to be?

(Answer appears at the end of the section.)

Polygons with more than four sides

You can construct polygons with any numbers of sides. A five-sided figure is called a pentagon. The most famous example of this figure is the military headquarters building near Washington, D.C., which gets its name, the Pentagon, from its shape.

The six-sided figure, the hexagon, is frequently encountered. It is the shape used by bees in the construction of their honeycombs. Interestingly, this shape gives the maximum strength with the least amount of material.

Figures with additional numbers of sides are:

No. of Sides	Name
7	Septagon
8	Octagon
9	Nonagon
10	Decagon

Regular polygons

A polygon that has all sides congruent and all angles congruent is called a regular polygon. The equilateral triangle and the square are two examples of regular polygons. You can construct a regular hexagon from a circle.

Construction

With a compass, make a circle. Keeping the same compass opening, put the point of the compass anywhere on the circle and mark off arcs, moving the point of the compass from one arc mark to the next around the circle until you return to the starting point, as shown in the figure. Connect the adjacent arc marks, as shown. You now have a regular hexagon.

You can obtain the sum of the measures of the angles of any polygon by using diagonals. You have already found that the sum of the measures of the angles of a triangle is 180°. Subdivide the polygon into triangles by drawing all possible diagonals from any *one* vertex of the polygon. Then the product of the number of triangles formed in this manner and 180° gives the total number of degrees for all of the angles of a polygon of a given number of sides.

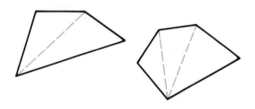

Your Turn

1. Make a general rule so that you can calculate the sum of the measures of angles for a polygon with any number of sides, *n*.

Copy and complete the following table first:

No. of sides	No. of diagonals	No. of triangles	Sum of measures of angles
3	0	1	180°
4	1	2	360°
5	2	3	540°
6			
7			
8			
10			
20			
100			

2. Determine the sum of the measures of the angles of a polygon with 150 sides.

3. If the polygon is regular, all of the angles have the same measure. From your table, find the sum of the measure of each angle for a hexagon. To find the measure of one angle of a regular hexagon, divide this figure by 6. What is the measure of each angle of a regular hexagon?

(Answers appear at the end of the section.)

Experiment

From the data in the table, you can find the measure of each angle of a regular polygon with any number of sides. Find the measures of angles of regular polygons with 3, 4, 6, 10, and 20 sides. Make a table and record the sum of the measures of the angles for these polygons. Divide each sum by the number of angles in that polygon to find the measure of one of the angles.

Can you write a rule (formula) that will compute the measure of one angle of a regular polygon of any number of sides (*n*)? If so, write the formula and use it to compute the measure of one angle of a regular polygon of 150 sides.

From the results of your experiment, you can say that the measure of the angle of a regular polygon increases as the number of sides increases; that it gets closer and closer to ___?___°, but that it can never get so large as ___?___°.

You can express this finding by stating that you have a sequence of values for the measures of the angles of regular polygons that increases as the number of sides of the polygons increases, and that the sequence has a limiting value (called a limit) of ___?___°.

(Answers appear at the end of the section.)

The exterior angle of a polygon is the supplement of the interior angle, as shown in the figure.

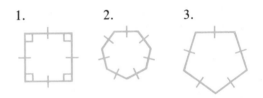

exterior angle

Find the measures of the exterior angles of the regular polygons for which you just calculated the measures of the interior angles. For example, a regular polygon with three sides—an equilateral triangle—has a sum of 180°, and each angle has a measure of 60°. The exterior angle of each angle has a measure of 120°, since supplementary angles have a sum of 180° (180° − 60° = 120°). The sum of the three exterior angles of an equilateral triangle is then 360° (3 × 120° = 360°).

Find the sum of the exterior angles for polygons of 4, 6, 10 and 20 sides. What seems true about the sum of the measures of the exterior angles of a polygon? Draw a non-regular polygon of any number of sides that you choose, extend the sides to form exterior angles, and measure the angles with your protractor. Find the sum of the measures. Do you get the same results that you did from your calculations?

(Answers appear at the end of the section.)

Your Turn

Name each regular polygon.

1.   2.   3.

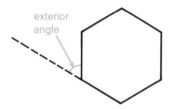

4.   Give the measure of one interior angle of each figure above.
5.   Give the sum of the measures of the exterior angles for each figure above.

(Answers appear at the end of the section.)

Circles

Another plane figure is the circle. The circle is a pleasing shape that is used for all kinds of figures in art, architecture, and industrial design. The circle also occurs frequently in nature.

A circle is a set of points in a plane that are all equally distant from a fixed point called the center. A line segment that connects two points on the circle is called a chord. Any chord that contains the center of the circle is called a diameter. Any segment that connects the center of the circle to a point on the circle is called a radius (plural: radii).

$\overline{AB}$ is a diameter.
$\overline{OC}$ is a radius.

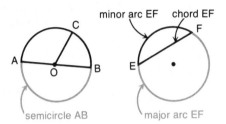

A portion of the circle that connects the two endpoints of a chord is called an arc. If the chord is not a diameter, then the two arcs will be different in size. The smaller arc is called the minor arc, and the larger arc is called the major arc. A diameter of a circle divides the circle into two arcs that are congruent. Each of these arcs is called a semicircle.

It was discovered early that the ratio of the distance around the circle (called the circumference) to the length of the diameter is the same for all circles. It was also found that this number cannot be written as a whole number or a whole number plus a fraction. No matter how finely the diameter is divided, the circumference is never a whole number of these subunits. The Greek mathematicians expressed this idea by saying that the two numbers, one for the measure of the circumference and the other for the measure of the diameter, are "incommensurable."

Experiment

You can find the measure of a circumference by "straightening out" the curve in the following way. Use your compass and draw a large circle on stiff paper. Mark the center, and draw a diameter. Measure and record the length of the diameter in millimeters.

Now cut out the circle and mark a spot on the circumference. Match this mark to the 0 point on your ruler.

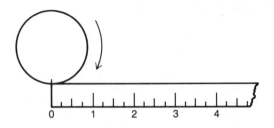

Roll the circle along the ruler until you reach the marked spot. You have traveled a distance along a straight line equal to the distance around the circle. Note and record the reading on the ruler. Now divide the length of the circumference by the length of the diameter. You obtain a figure a little larger than 3.

The ratio of the length of the circumference to the length of the diameter is an irrational number—it has a non-terminating number, π, or about 3.14.

The diameter is twice the length of the radius. The circumference is about 3.14 times the length of the diameter. If a circle has a radius of 4 inches, the diameter is 2 × 4 or 8 inches. The circumference is about 3.14 × 8 or 25.12 inches.

Your Turn

1. A circle has a radius of 12 inches. What is the diameter of that circle? What is the circumference?
2. A circle has a diameter of 6 feet. What is the radius of that circle? What is the circumference?
3. You have a circular garden that has a radius of 5 feet. You want to put a fence around the circumference of the garden. How many feet of fence will you need?

(Answers appear at the end of the section.)

Symmetry

Some of the figures you have worked with have a special property called symmetry. For plane figures, there are two kinds of symmetry: line symmetry and point symmetry.

If a figure has line symmetry, you can fold it along the line of symmetry (also called the axis of symmetry) and match two congruent figures. For example, if the figure 8 is folded on its axis of symmetry, the two halves will match exactly.

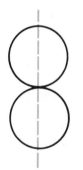

The axis of symmetry acts as a mirror. The figure has reflectional symmetry.

In a more formal way each point of the figure has a corresponding point, and the axis of symmetry is the perpendicular bisector of every segment that connects two corresponding points of the figure.

Figures may have more than one axis of symmetry. A square, for example, has

four axes of symmetry. Determine how many axes of symmetry each of the following figures has. (You can cut out the figures and check symmetry by folding.)

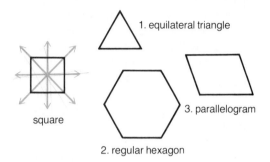

square

1. equilateral triangle

3. parallelogram

2. regular hexagon

Your Turn

Find which of the capital letters shown below have at least one axis of symmetry.

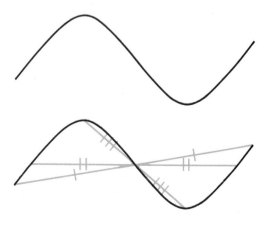

(Answers appear at the end of the section.)

A plane figure may also have point symmetry. Each point of a point-symmet-

ric figure has a corresponding point, and the symmetry point (also called the center of symmetry) is the midpoint of the line segment connecting each point with its corresponding point. The figure shown on the last page has point symmetry.

Figures that are point-symmetric are part of a group that have rotational symmetry. If a figure can be rotated less than 360° around a point so that it will coincide with itself, it has rotational symmetry. For example, the square has rotational symmetry. If it is rotated 90°, 180°, or 270° about the point at which its diagonals intersect, it coincides with itself.

Symmetry is used in design work. Symmetric designs appear in wallpapers and wrapping papers. Symmetry is admired for the orderliness that it adds to a design. Buildings are quite often constructed to be symmetrical.

Symmetry exists widely in nature. Some of the most beautiful designs in nature that exhibit symmetry are those of snowflake crystals.

Symmetry appears in various areas of mathematics other than geometry. In Section 1 of this part, you looked at the addition and the multiplication tables.

Did you notice that the tables can be folded across the diagonal, so that the entries on the two sides match? The diagonal is the axis of symmetry for the tables. This symmetry makes the task of memorizing the tables much easier.

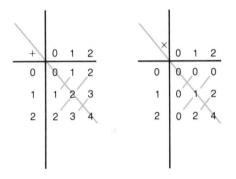

Relations in mathematics may be symmetric or asymmetric. One of the symmetric relations in mathematics is equality. The equal sign acts like a mirror. If $a = b$, then $b = a$. This property is used for the process known as factoring in algebra. Another relationship that is symmetric is that of congruency. If $\triangle ABC \cong \triangle XYZ$, then $\triangle XYZ \cong \triangle ABC$. A relation that is asymmetric is the $<$ relation. If $a < b$, then $b \not< a$. (The slash means "not.")

Your Turn

Tell whether each of the following is symmetric.

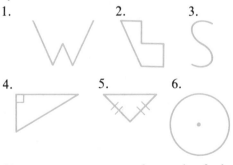

1.   2.   3.

4.   5.   6.

(Answers appear at the end of the section.)

Figures in Space

Think of a box. Now consider that each side of this box could expand, as shown in the figure. As the box grows larger, it fills a region called space.

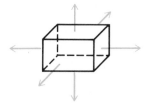

So far, you have considered a variety of figures in the plane. Now you will consider some of the three-dimensional figures that are encountered in space. A study of figures in the plane helps you to understand and describe the three-dimensional figures.

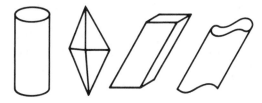

Lines in space

Lines in space may have three different relations. As in a plane, lines may intersect or they may be parallel. In addition, however, lines that do not intersect may not remain the same distance apart, as do parallel lines. These lines can pass one another without touching. Such lines are called skew lines. You can see these lines when you look about a room. Picture the one line that is formed by the intersection of two walls, and a second line that is formed by the floor and a wall opposite one of the first two walls.

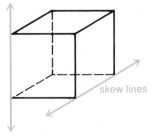

Planes in space

Pairs of planes in space either intersect or they are parallel—everywhere equidistant. The distance between two planes is measured along the shortest path between them. This is a line segment perpendicular to each of the planes, just as the distance between two lines is measured by the length of a segment that is perpendicular to each of the lines.

A line that is perpendicular to a plane is perpendicular to every line in the plane that passes through the point at which the line pierces the plane.

The intersection of two planes is a line (like the intersection of two walls of a room, mentioned above). A third plane that intersects a pair of intersecting planes may meet them in a line or at a point. Two walls and the floor of a room come together at one point in the corner of the room. The pages of a newspaper can represent a number of planes meeting in a line, the fold line.

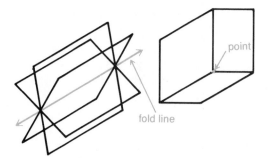

fold line

point

A line may be parallel to a plane (everywhere the same distance from the plane), it may intersect the plane, or it may lie in the plane. If a line intersects a plane, it does so at exactly one point. If two points of a line lie in a plane, all the points of the line lie in the plane.

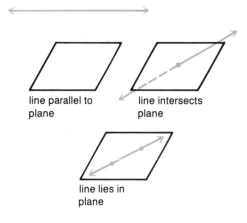

line parallel to plane

line intersects plane

line lies in plane

A line divides a plane into three distinct sets of points: two half planes and the line itself.

Angles in space

You have considered angles in the plane. They are formed by the union of two rays with a common endpoint.

One type of angle encountered in space is the dihedral angle. It is formed by the union of two half planes that inter-

sect, and their common line of intersection, called the edge.

$\overline{CD}$ is the edge.

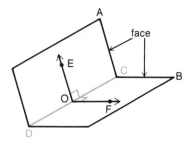

face

dihedral angle A-CD-B; plane angle EOF

A dihedral angle is measured by its plane angle. The plane angle is formed by two rays, each perpendicular to the edge and meeting at a common endpoint. The measure of the dihedral angle is the measure of the plane angle.

There are also polyhedral angles. Polyhedral angles are formed by three or more planes that meet at a point, called the vertex of the polyhedral angle. The corner of a room where two walls and the ceiling meet is a polyhedral angle. The portions of the planes that form the polyhedral angle are called the faces of the polyhedral angle.

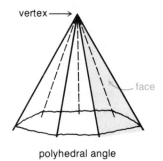

vertex

face

polyhedral angle

The angles formed by the edges of the faces are called the face angles of the polyhedral angle. The angles formed by two faces meeting at an edge are called the dihedral angles of a polyhedral angle.

Polyhedral angles present an interesting situation. Two polyhedral angles can have congruent face angles and congruent dihedral angles and yet not be congruent polyhedral angles. If the face and dihedral angles of one are congruent to those of the second polyhedral angle *in the same order,* then the two polyhedral angles will be congruent. If the order of the face and dihedral angles of the second polyhedral angle is reversed, then you have a pair of symmetric angles, as shown in the figure.

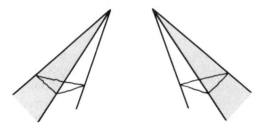

You may wish to cut out pairs of congruent triangles to form two symmetric angles and check that indeed they are not congruent angles.

Your Turn

1. When two planes intersect, how many lines are formed?
2. If two lines in space do not intersect and are not parallel, what are they called?
3. If the endpoints of a line segment lie in a plane, do all the points of that line segment lie in that plane?
4. Three planes that intersect, can intersect in a _____ or a _____ .
5. Name the dihedral angle shown at the right.

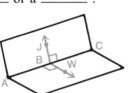

6. Name the plane angle in the last figure.

(Answers appear at the end of the section.)

Polyhedrons

Three-dimensional figures formed by the union of polygons are called polyhedrons. The figures must be simple, that is, the polygons (or faces) intersect only at the edges. The figures must also be closed. In a closed figure, any line segment connecting an interior point with an exterior point intersects the surface of the figure.

Prisms

One special group of polyhedrons consists of figures that have a pair of opposite faces that are parallel. These figures are called prisms. There are a variety of prisms that are classified by the shape of the polygons that form the parallel faces. Thus there are triangular, quadrangular, pentagonal, hexagonal, and octagonal prisms, corresponding to prisms with three, four, five, six, and eight sides for the polygons that form their bases.

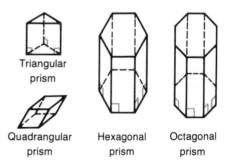

Triangular prism

Quadrangular prism

Hexagonal prism

Octagonal prism

The side faces of a prism are called the lateral faces. If the lateral faces are perpendicular to the bases of the prism, it is called a right prism. All other prisms are called oblique prisms. In the last illustration, the quadrangular prism is oblique; the triangular, hexagonal and octagonal prisms are right prisms.

Regular polyhedrons

A special group of polyhedrons are those that have all faces congruent and all polyhedral angles congruent. These are called the regular polyhedrons, just as polygons with all sides congruent and all angles congruent are called regular polygons. These figures are called the Platonic solids, after the ancient Greek philosopher Plato, who held mathematics in the highest esteem.

So high was Plato's regard for the importance of the knowledge of mathematics to an educated individual, that he placed a sign over the entrance to his academy. Roughly translated, the sign read, "Geometry required here." Plato felt that a knowledge of geometry (the major branch of mathematics at that time, and the branch that includes a study of logic) was necessary for anyone who entered his academy and who wished to learn about the nature of the universe.

How many regular polyhedrons can be formed? You can deduce the answer by considering the material with which you can work, and one additional fact. First observe that a circle about any point in a plane contains 360 degrees. If you wish to create a "corner " in space, a vertex of a regular polyhedron, you must have a sum of face angles about that point totaling less than 360°. Second, note that there must be at least three faces to form a polyhedral angle. Next, consider the measures of the interior angles of regular polygons that are available for use as the faces.

From the previous study of the regular polygons, you can form a table, as follows.

Number of sides	Measure of angle	Sum of 3 angles
3	60°	180°
4	90°	270°
5	108°	324°
6	120°	360°

From this table you can create the regular polyhedrons discussed next and only them—no others. There could be three regular triangles at a vertex. The angle sum would be 180°. There could be four regular triangles at a vertex. The angle sum would be 240°. This is still less than 360°, so there will be a space figure. There could be five regular triangles at a vertex. The angle sum would be 300° (5 × 60°), so a polyhedron could be formed. There cannot be 6 regular triangles about a point, as the angle sum is 360° and the triangles would form a plane figure.

You may wish to cut out a set of congruent equilateral triangles and form the polyhedral angles with three, four, and five faces. Check what happens when you try to use six faces.

Next, consider the square. There can be 3 squares at a point. The squares will form the corner of a familiar figure, the cube. Four squares will give an angle sum of 360°—too much.

Can you use a pentagon? Three pentagons will give an angle sum of 324°. Three pentagons will form a regular polyhedron.

What about a hexagon? For three hexagonal faces, the angle sum is 360°. The hexagon cannot be a face of a regular polyhedron.

For any regular polygon with more than six sides, the angle sum for three faces is greater than 360°. Thus, no polygon with more than five sides can be used as a face of a regular polyhedron, as the face angles produce too large an angle sum to form a vertex of a polyhedral angle.

Now you can construct five regular polyhedrons: three with triangular faces, one with square faces, and one with pentagonal faces. The regular polyhedron with the smallest number of faces is the tetrahedron; the four faces are triangles. Next in order of the number of faces is the hexahedron (the cube) with six faces. The faces are squares. The next figure is the octahedron with eight faces. The faces are triangles. The fourth figure is this sequence is the dodecahedron. It has twelve faces; the faces are pentagons. Finally, there is the icosahedron, with twenty sides; the faces are triangles.

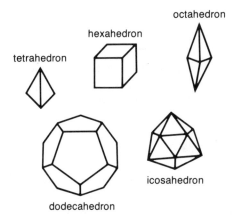

octahedron

hexahedron

tetrahedron

dodecahedron

icosahedron

In the illustrations that follow, the "nets" for each of these beautiful polyhedrons are shown. If you cut out an enlarged copy of these nets and fold on the dotted lines, you can make a model of each of the Platonic solids. These can be taped together.

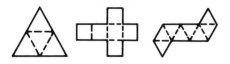

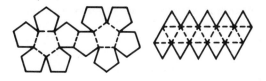

There are a number of other solids of great beauty. Solids can be made with two or more regular polygons forming the faces. Here are four of the thirteen Archimedean solids (named for the ancient Greek mathematician, Archimedes).

truncated cube   rhombicuboctahedron

cuboctahedron   rhombicosidodecahedron

Even the names of the figures are fascinating: truncated icosadodecahedron and rhombicosidodecahedron, for example. You may wish to look up more information on these figures and perhaps try to make a few models for yourself.

Gemstones are cut with many polygonal faces so that they reflect light and appear very brilliant. Some of the shapes used are shown in the diagram.

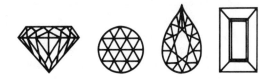

Some more lovely figures can be made by applying tetrahedrons to the faces of some of the solids that have been discussed. The new figure formed becomes starlike; the process is called stellation.

Pyramids

A *pyramid* is a three-dimensional polyhedron that has a polygon for the base and triangular sides (faces) that meet in a point. The point at which the faces meet is called the vertex. A line from the vertex and perpendicular to the base is called the altitude.

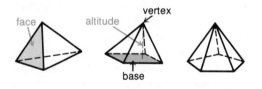

Pyramids are classified by the shape of their bases: triangular, square, rectangular, and hexagonal, for example.

Pyramidal shapes were much admired by the ancient Egyptians. They used this form to create burial monuments for their revered rulers, the pharaohs. Pyramids were also constructed in southern Mexico and Central America by the Mayans. The ruins of the pyramids can still be viewed today.

Cylinders

Another interesting group of figures has curved surfaces rather than polygonal surfaces. A circular cylinder has circular bases. In a circular cylinder, all the points on the surface are a fixed distance from a line through the center called the central axis. If the central axis is perpendicular to both bases of a cylinder, then it is a right cylinder. Otherwise, it is an oblique cylinder.

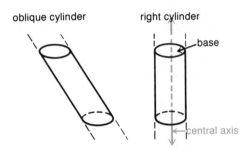

The cylindrical shape is familiar. It is the shape of many drinking glasses, pipes, cans, and other containers.

Spheres

One of the most familiar space figures is also the simplest—the sphere. It is the space version of a circle—a set of points all at a fixed distance from a given point.

When people travel into space, an awareness of the shape of the earth is necessary in order to return home. A knowledge of geometry is essential. The earth approximates a sphere. The shape of the earth became much more evident as it was viewed from space. It is not a perfect sphere—it is a little flattened at the poles and it bulges a bit in the middle from spinning about. But, nevertheless, it is our best-loved sphere.

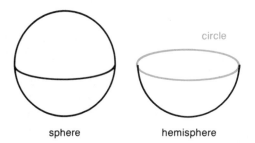

circle

sphere   hemisphere

A sphere can be cut into two equal pieces, called hemispheres. The cut forms a circle. Any position on earth can be measured by using circles of the sphere. These are discussed in the measurement section (*see* p. 322).

In the twentieth century, a fascinating group of figures has been developed by Buckminster Fuller. These figures serve as building structures. They differ markedly in construction from any structures that have previously been built. The structures are based on spheres with outer supporting shells that use the rigid triangles in their design. They are called geodesic domes. Two famous geodesic domes are the U.S. Pavilion in Montreal, Canada, and the Epcot Center at Disney World in Orlando, Florida.

Cones

A *cone* is a three-dimensional figure that has a closed curve for a base and a surface that comes to a point (the vertex). Ice-cream cones are familiar examples of cones. If a cone is cut apart and laid flat, it looks like this:

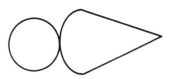

The axis of a cone is a line segment that connects the vertex with a point at the center of the base. When the base is a circle, the axis is perpendicular to the base and the cone is a right circular cone.

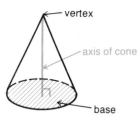

vertex

axis of cone

base

The exercise below will test your knowledge of some polyhedrons. Many of these space figures will be studied in future sections of this book.

Your Turn

Identify each drawing with its name.

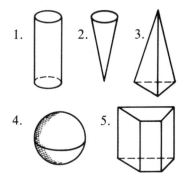

a. pyramid
b. cone
c. sphere
d. cylinder
e. prism

(Answers appear at the end of the section.)

Answers

Figures in a Plane (pp. 287–312)

Answers for page 289.
1. $\overrightarrow{CD}$ 2. $\overleftrightarrow{ZX}$ 3. $\overrightarrow{MN}$ 4. One   5. One

Answers for page 290.
Your answers may vary. The angles shown in the book have these measures:
$m\angle B = 150°$, $m\angle C = 30°$, $m\angle D = 60°$

Answers for page 291.
1. m $\angle JMK$ and $\angle KML$ 2. $\angle ABC$ and $\angle GHI$ 3. $\angle DEF$ and $\angle ABC$ 4. 60°
5. 45°   6. 72°   7. 29°   8. 150°   9. 135°   10. 44°   11. 90°

Answers for page 292.
12. $\angle ABC$ and $\angle DBE$; $\angle CBD$ and $\angle ABE$ 13. No   14. 72°; 108°

Answers for page 295.
$\angle 4 \cong \angle 5$, $\angle 3 \cong \angle 6$—Alternate interior angles are congruent.
$\angle 3 \cong \angle 7$, $\angle 2 \cong \angle 6$, $\angle 1 \cong \angle 5$, $\angle 4 \cong \angle 8$—Corresponding angles are congruent.
$\angle 1 \cong \angle 4$, $\angle 2 \cong \angle 3$, $\angle 5 \cong \angle 8$, $\angle 6 \cong \angle 7$—Vertical angles are congruent.
$m\angle 2 = 30°$, $m\angle 3 = 30°$, $m\angle 4 = 150°$, $m\angle 5 = 150°$, $m\angle 6 = 30°$, $m\angle 7 = 30°$, $m\angle 8 = 150°$

Answers for page 298: 60°.

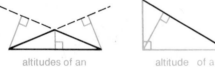

altitudes of an
obtuse triangle

altitude of a
right triangle

Answers for page 299–300.
1. In an equilateral triangle, the altitude, median, and angle bisector are all the same line segment. This is not so for a scalene triangle.   2. The three angle bisectors intersect at one point.   3. The three medians intersect at one point.   4. The three altitudes intersect at one point.

Answers for page 301.
The ratio for the altitudes, medians, and angle bisectors is also $1:2$.

Answers for pages 303–304.
1. Yes, SSS   2. No   3. Yes, SAS   4. Yes, ASA   5. Yes, ASA or AAS
6. Only if the angle is an included angle.

The length of the midline of a trapezoid is equal to one-half the sum of the bases.

Answers for page 306.
1. The triangles are congruent.   2. The diagonals of a rhombus and of a square are perpendicular.
3. The diagonals of a square and of a rectangle are congruent to each other.   4. $\overline{DO} \cong \overline{OB}$; $\overline{AO} \cong \overline{OC}$; The diagonals of a parallelogram bisect each other.   5. The sum of the measures of the angles of a quadrilateral is 360°.

Answer for page 307.
The figures that are formed are parallelograms.

Answers for page 308.
1. $(n - 2) \times 180$, where n is the number of sides of the polygon.

No. of sides	No. of diagonals	No. of triangles	Sum of measures
6	3	4	720°
7	4	5	900°
8	5	6	1080°
10	7	8	1440°
20	17	18	3240°
100	97	98	17,640°

2. 26,640°   3. 120°

Answers for page 309.
The general rule to find the measure of one angle of a regular polygon is

$$\frac{(n - 2) \times 180}{n}$$

One angle of a polygon with 150 sides has a measure of 177.6°.
180; 180; 180
The sum of the measures of the exterior angles is 360°. This holds for non-regular polygons also.

1. square   2. septagon   3. pentagon   4. 90°; $128\frac{4°}{7}$; 108°   5. 360°

Answers for page 310.
1. 24 inches; 75.36 inches   2. 3 feet; 18.84 feet   3. 31.4 feet

Answers for page 311.
1. 3;   2. 6;   3. None
I, K, and M have at least one axis of symmetry.

Answers for page 312.
1. Yes (line)   2. No   3. Yes (point)   4. No   5. Yes (line)   6. Yes (point and line)

Figures in Space (pp. 313–319)

Answers for page 315.
1. One   2. skew lines   3. Yes   4. line; point   5. dihedral angle J-AC-W

6. plane angle JBW

Answers for page 319.
1. d   2. b   3. a   4. c   5. e

Section 6

Measurement

Every day questions are asked such as, "How far?", "How long a time?", "How heavy?" A numerical answer, which is a comparison between the unknown quantity and a known (standard) quantity, is expected. You may find that the distance to your school is 3 miles, the time allowed for lunch is 40 minutes, and your weight is 120 pounds.

Measurement assigns a number to a particular characteristic of a person, an object, or a concept. Measurement is used in business, science, and manufacturing, as well as for many tasks of daily living. A branch of study is said to be "scientific" only when measurements are made and the concepts are expressed quantitatively, that is, with numbers.

Before beginning this section, review your work with fractions, decimals, and percents. Also review the lessons on the properties of geometric figures, as mea-

surement of perimeter, area, and volume are to be developed.

It is important in studying measurement to learn the system of measures to be used. Tables of units for both the customary (English) and metric units are presented here. The relations should be memorized for the customary system. The relationships are quite easy to learn for the metric system; the same prefixes are used for length, mass, and capacity.

Methods of Measurement

Direct measurement

Two classes of objects can be measured. The objects may be discrete, that is, separate. The measurement is then accomplished by counting. The count, if properly made, is always exact. The number of autos parked in a particular lot, for example, is found by counting each car.

The second class of objects to be measured consists of objects with characteristics that are continuous. Consider the room you are in. It has the characteristic of length. Suppose that the length is 12 feet. Along the 12-foot side, lengths can be measured that correspond to any number between 0 and 12. With appropriate measuring instruments, you can locate points corresponding to lengths of 6 feet, $6\frac{1}{2}$ feet, or $6\frac{1}{4}$ feet. Conversely, if you select a particular point, you can determine the length to that point with varying degrees of precision: to the nearest foot, the nearest half-foot, and to the nearest quarter-foot.

You cannot, however, make an exact measurement of a characteristic that is continuous. Theoretically, at least, you can always conceive of a measuring instrument that has finer subdivisions than the one being used. The new scale would provide you with a measurement of greater precision (accuracy).

Indirect measurement

There are also situations in which you wish to measure a quantity of discrete items but counting is not practical. For example, suppose that you wish to find how many grains of sand are in a large conical pile of sand. Each grain of sand is distinct, and there is a finite number of grains. While the task of counting them is theoretically possible, it is formidable.

The problem can be solved in another way. You can select a small measure, fill it, and count the grains of sand in it. As the next step, you would determine the volume of the pile of sand and then deter-

mine how many times your small container would be needed to fill a volume equal to that of the sand pile. Finally, the product of the number of containers needed and the number of grains of sand in this sample container would provide a good estimate of the total number of grains of sand in the pile.

This technique, called sampling, is also used to count, by microscope, the number of red cells, white cells, and platelets in a specimen of blood. Sampling techniques have numerous other applications, for example, finding purity of air, water, or soil.

These examples have illustrated that (1) a direct measurement is made by counting or with the use of an instrument marked with one or more standard units and applied directly to the object to be measured and (2) an indirect measurement is based on one or more direct measurements related to the desired one, combined with a computation to obtain the desired result. Indirect measurements are often computed with the use of a formula. For example, the length of the circumference (distance around) a circle can be computed from the length of the diameter of the circle ($C = \pi d$) or from the length of the radius ($C = 2\pi r$).

Your Turn

Which of the following measurements can be made directly?

1. The diameter of a dime
2. The height of Mt. Everest
3. A pint of milk

Which of the following measurements can be made exactly, and which must be inexact? Explain why.

4. The number of pages in a telephone book.
5. The distance to the star Sirius.

6. The temperature on the roof of the Empire State Building in New York City at 12 noon today.

(Answers appear at the end of the section.)

History of Measurement

In simple agricultural societies, there was a need for basic units of measure, but no serious problems arose regarding their standardization. When commerce spread over a large region and relatively complex machines were developed, standardization of units was needed. There was too much confusion if all people involved in the region weren't using the same measures, called *standard measures*.

Early measurement units

The earliest units used for making measurements were the handiest ones possible—parts of the human body. You always carry these measuring units with you. Even today measurements are made by using a hand or a foot as the basic measure.

Some of the early units used are the following:

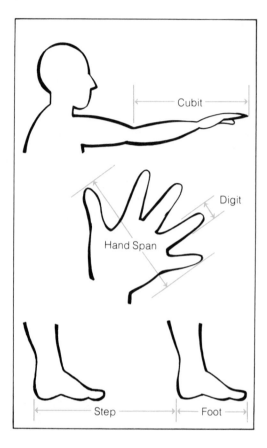

digit	width of finger
hand or palm	width of palm
hand span	distance from tip of thumb to tip of little finger when the hand is fully stretched out
cubit	length of arm from elbow to tip of middle finger with hand stretched out
foot	length of foot
step	distance from heel of forward foot to heel of back foot as one makes a single step
pace	two steps

Quite clearly, these units were not "standard." Individuals vary widely in their body dimensions. Even when one group of people agreed upon a value for a measure, other communities used a different value. The cubit used in Rome differed, for example, from the cubit used in Egypt.

Despite the variation in the basic unit, accurate measurements could be made with simple instruments. For example, it has been found that in Egypt, with the use of a knotted string to lay off the length of a side of the Great Pyramid, the error was as small as 0.042 feet in a 755-foot side. This relative error in the measurement of 0.006 parts per one hundred (0.006%) reflects high accuracy.

Customary units

The early units gave rise to the units that now form the customary system of units. The foot is reflected in the modern foot. The inch was established by the Romans to be $\frac{1}{12}$ of a foot. The decision to use twelve subdivisions was made on the practical basis that 12 has more divisors than any other integer close in value. Twelve can be evenly divided in halves, thirds, fourths, and sixths. This makes the computation of fractional parts a little easier, as $\frac{2}{12}, \frac{3}{12}, \frac{4}{12}, \frac{6}{12}, \frac{8}{12}$, and $\frac{9}{12}$ can be simplified. The Romans also liked to create subdivisions with new names (such as the inch and the ounce) so that quantities could be combined frequently without the use of fractions. For example, it is easier to add 4 feet 2 inches to 5 feet 8 inches and obtain 9 feet 10 inches rather than to add $4\frac{1}{6}$ and $5\frac{2}{3}$.

The Romans established a distance measure of 1000 paces. As their pace was approximately five feet, a thousand paces was 5000 feet, about equal to the mile.

In the twelfth century, the yard was established by Henry I of England to be the distance from the tip of his nose to the thumb of his outstretched arm. In the fourteenth century, Edward II decreed one inch to be the length of three barleycorns, dry and round, laid lengthwise. He then established the foot to be 12 of these inch measures. The measurement of a hand was established as 4 inches. (The hand is still in use to measure the height of horses.) By the sixteenth century, the yard was established as three feet.

A number of suggestions were made through the centuries from ancient times to modern times for standardizing the basic units. Suggestions were also made for using ten subdivisions for the basic units, since the basis of our system of numeration is ten. The computations required for working with sub-units of powers of ten are much easier than the computations in the English system. Multiplying or dividing by a power of ten merely requires the decimal point to be shifted to the right or left. In the English system, one must multiply or divide by 12 (inches per foot), 3 (feet per yard), 5,280 (feet per mile), 16 (ounces per pound), and other subdivisions related to units of length, weight, or capacity.

The divided nature of society in the Middle Ages made it impossible to achieve a general agreement. Standard units were used throughout the empire of the most famous medieval ruler, Charlemagne (742–814). After his time, local communities in his empire went back to their individual systems of measures.

The standardization in measurement finally came in modern times. The necessity for a uniform system and one that made computation easier reflected the needs of society following the Industrial Revolution. One cannot successfully construct a machine such as the steam engine with rough, uncertain measurements. The piston must be made to fit the cylinder. The technological developments in engineering and science required an improved system of measurement and standardization of the basic units.

Metric units

France took the lead in developing a new system. In 1790, the French Academy of Sciences appointed a committee to study the problems and devise a new system. For length, the basic unit of one meter was proposed (in French, *mètre*). This unit was to be $\frac{1}{10,000,000}$ of the distance from the North Pole to the Equator along a meridian. The meter (39.37 in.) is a little larger than the English yard (36 in.).

Other units were obtained as subunits or multiples of the meter in powers of ten. Basic units were also chosen for mass and capacity. The prefixes for the sub-units and multiples are the same for length, mass and capacity, making the learning of names easier.

The change in France did not come about rapidly. People were permitted to choose the system to be used until 1840. In that year, the metric system, as it is called, was made the only legal system in France.

The metric system is now used worldwide. It is the official system in every major country except the United States. In the United States it became legal to use the metric system in 1866, but the customary system remained the official one. Today the United States has two systems in operation. The customary system is used in everyday situations. But scientists use the metric system for their work. It is very important that they use this system, as scientific reports are published and studied worldwide.

Businesses also make wide use of the metric system. Many businesses manufacture items that are sold in other countries, and the parts have to be measured and constructed in the metric system for successful use in those countries.

One of the most outstanding examples of international cooperation is that of the agreements on standards of measurement. An international treaty made in 1875 provided for an International Bureau of Weights and Measures. This bureau adopted the metric system. The bureau maintains the standards.

In the United States, the differences in weights and measures inherited from colonial times became a matter of national concern. In 1830 the problem was investigated, and two years later a decision was made on standardizing weights and measures for the United States. Our National Bureau of Standards maintains all the standards for measurements in the country. In 1893, it was decided to define the yard in terms of the meter and the pound in terms of the kilogram. In 1959, the official equivalency was set at 1 yard = 0.9144 meters (making 1 inch = 2.54 centimeters). Thus, the foundation of our own system of measurement is metric.

Much thought has been given to adopting the metric system as the official system for measurement in the United States. There are two reasons for not making the changeover. First, it is difficult and expensive to convert from one system to another. All of the measuring tools, rulers, scales, and other instruments would have to be replaced. It is also difficult to think in a new system at the beginning, although world travelers confirm that once one begins using the new system, the change is not difficult. One makes so many measurements every day, there is plenty of opportunity for practice.

Second, the inch and the foot are really convenient units of measurement for daily use. There are no comparable basic units in the metric system. An inch is approximately $2\frac{1}{2}$ centimeters in the metric system, and a foot is approximately $30\frac{1}{2}$ centimeters. It would appear that the United States will be using two systems of measurement for some time, so it is very important to be able to work within both systems.

Precision of Measurement

All measurements made of a quantity that is continuous are *inexact*. The precision of a measurement depends on the smallest subdivision of the measuring instrument used. If the measurement is made in inches, for example, higher precisions can be obtained by using a ruler subdivided into sixteenths or thirty-seconds or sixty-fourths. Theoretically, no matter how fine the subdivision, it is always possible to obtain a higher precision with still finer subdivisions. Thus, no measurement can be perfectly precise.

The precision of a measurement is determined by the size of the unit used for the measure. Suppose you measure a pencil as 6 inches to the nearest inch. It is understood that the length of the pencil is $5\frac{1}{2}$ or more inches up to, but not including, $6\frac{1}{2}$ inches, since any measure in that interval would round to 6 inches. The greatest possible error of the measurement is one-half an inch, half of the smallest interval used for the measurement.

Suppose now that you measured the pencil to the nearest half-inch. Then the length is in the interval of $5\frac{3}{4}$ inches up to, but not including, $6\frac{1}{4}$ inches. The greatest possible error is $\frac{1}{4}$ inch. Another way to express these measurements is $6 \pm \frac{1}{2}$ in. and $6 \pm \frac{1}{4}$ in. The smaller the subdivision used in the measurement, the less the possible error and the higher the precision of the measurement.

The accuracy of a measurement can be expressed by comparing the *greatest possible error* (GPE) of the measurement with the measurement itself. The ratio of the possible error to the measurement is called the *relative error*. The relative error expresses the accuracy of the measurement. For example, when the six-inch pencil is measured to the nearest inch, the relative error is

$$\frac{\text{GPE} \longrightarrow 0.5}{\text{measure} \longrightarrow 6} = 0.083 \text{ or } 8.3\%$$

When the six-inch pencil is measured to the nearest half-inch, the relative error is

$$\frac{0.25}{6} = 0.0417 \text{ or } 4.2\%$$

The precision of a measurement is not improved by arithmetic computations. For example, the circumference of a circle can be computed with

$$C = 2\pi r$$

where r represents the length of the radius of the circle, and C is the circumference. Remember that when terms such as 2, π, and r are written next to one another, multiplication is indicated.

$$C = 2 \times \pi \times r$$

Suppose that r is given as 1 foot, to the nearest foot. You also know that 3.14159 is a decimal approximation for π. Then

$$\begin{aligned} C &= 2 \times 3.14159 \times 1 \\ &= 6.28318 \end{aligned}$$

If the answer is stated as 6.28318 feet, the impression is given that the circumference is precise to a hundred-thousandth of a foot. However, it was inappropriate to use five decimal places for the approximation of π. Since the radius is known to the nearest foot, the circumference is precise only to the nearest foot. The answer should be 6 feet. (If the length of the radius was precise to the nearest tenth of a foot, it would have been written 1.0 foot.) It is important not to be misled by keeping all the decimal places that may be introduced by computation.

For example, a length was determined as the sum of three measurements: 15.38 meters, 21.49 meters, and 18.567 meters. Addition would be used to find the total length. The first two measurements are precise to the nearest hundredth of a meter, while the third measurement is precise to the nearest thousandth of a meter. The sum should be rounded to the nearest hundredth, the lowest precision of the individual measurements.

$$
\begin{array}{r}
15.38 \\
21.49 \\
+\,18.567 \\
\hline
55.437
\end{array}
$$

The total length is 55.44 meters, not 55.437 meters.

Your Turn

Give the GPE for the measurements.

1. 10 inches
2. 16.2 centimeters
3. $5\frac{1}{4}$ inches
4. 18.462 meters

Determine the relative error for each measurement below.

5. 10 inches, to the nearest inch
6. 10 inches, to the nearest $\frac{1}{8}$ inch
7. 16.2 centimeters
8. 18.46 meters

Solve each problem. Be sure to state your answer with the proper precision. Then find the relative error of the answer.

9. One side of a triangle is 16.237 meters. Another side is 15.30 meters. Find the difference between the lengths of the sides.
10. Suppose a length is the sum of four lengths: $1\frac{1}{4}$ feet, 2 feet, $1\frac{1}{4}$ feet, and $2\frac{1}{2}$ feet. Find that total length.

(Answers appear at the end of the section.)

Linear Measure

Customary units

The units of linear measure in the customary system are given below.

Customary (English) units for measures of length

---

12 inches (in.) =	1 foot (ft)
1 ft =	1 yard (yd)
$16\frac{1}{2}$ ft =	1 rod
1760 yd =	1 mile (mi)
5280 ft =	1 mi

Note that the only abbreviation for a unit of length that is followed by a period is "in." for inch. This is to avoid confusion between the word "in" and the abbreviation "in."

The following represents a ruler with line segments. Notice that one endpoint of each line segment aligns with the beginning of the ruler. The location of the other endpoint of the line segment determines the length of the segment.

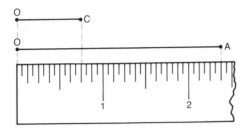

$\overline{OA}$ = 2 inches, to the nearest inch

$\overline{OA}$ = $2\frac{3}{8}$ inches, to the nearest $\frac{1}{8}$ inch.

$\overline{OC}$ = $\frac{3}{4}$ inch, to the nearest $\frac{1}{4}$ inch

$\overline{OC}$ = $\frac{3}{4}$ inch, to the nearest $\frac{1}{16}$ inch

Your Turn

Give the length of each line segment to the nearest inch and then to the nearest $\frac{1}{4}$ inch.

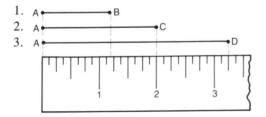

1. A B
2. A C
3. A D

(Answers appear at the end of the section.)

Converting customary units

Sometimes it is necessary to convert, or change, units within the customary system. Conversion can be made easier if

you keep in mind that it requires a smaller quantity of a larger basic unit than of a smaller basic unit. To change from a smaller unit to a larger unit, division is used. Thus, a length of 24 inches is the distance covered by 2 feet (a smaller quantity of a larger basic unit). To change inches to feet, divide by 12 (24 ÷ 12 = 2). Conversely, a measure with a large unit can be changed to a smaller unit by multiplication. To change 9 yards to inches, multiply by 36. Thus 9 yards = 324 inches (a larger quantity of a smaller basic unit). Below are more examples.

Change 10,560 feet to miles.
10,560 feet = ? miles
5280 feet = 1 mile
Think: Going from small to large, so divide
$$\frac{10,560}{5280} = 2$$
So, 10,560 feet = 2 miles

Change 75 yards to feet.
75 yards = ? feet
1 yard = 3 feet
Think: Going from large to small, so multiply
75 × 3 = 225
So, 75 yards = 225 feet

Your Turn

4. Change 30 rods to feet.
5. Change 15,372 inches to feet.
6. Change 15,372 inches to yards.
7. Change 8 miles to yards.

(Answers appear at the end of the section.)

Computations with customary units

In solving problems, it is often necessary to add, subtract, multiply, or divide measures. Note that a measure is a number while a measurement is a number and a unit. Computations involve numbers, but the units cannot be ignored. Often computations require renaming, or converting, units. Study the four examples below. Notice that it is sometimes necessary to simplify an answer. One should not leave an answer such as 18 inches unless specifically asked for the number of inches. The answer in simplified form is 1 foot, 6 inches.

1. Find the sum of 2 yards, 2 feet and 1 yard, 2 feet.

To add, add like units (yards to yards, feet to feet).

$$
\begin{array}{r}
2 \text{ yd } 2 \text{ ft} \\
+1 \text{ yd } 2 \text{ ft} \\
\hline
3 \text{ yd } 4 \text{ ft}
\end{array}
$$
←—This is not in simplest form. Change 4 ft to 1 yd 1 ft. Then simplify to find the answer.

$$\overbrace{3 \text{ yd} + 1 \text{ yd } 1 \text{ ft}}$$

4 yd 1 ft

2. Subtract 7 feet, 6 inches from 10 feet, 1 inch.

Subtract like units. Since you cannot subtract 6 from 1, rename.

$$
\begin{array}{r}
10 \text{ ft } 1 \text{ in.} \\
- \ 7 \text{ ft } 6 \text{ in.}
\end{array}
$$

10 ft 1 in. = 9 ft + 1 ft + 1 in.
　　　　　 = 9 ft + 12 in. + 1 in.
　　　　　 = 9 ft + 13 in.

$$
\begin{array}{r}
9 \text{ ft } 13 \text{ in.} \\
-7 \text{ ft } \ 6 \text{ in.} \\
\hline
2 \text{ ft } \ 7 \text{ in.}
\end{array}
$$
Now subtract.

3. Multiply 3 miles, 1000 feet by 12.

$$
\begin{array}{r}
3 \text{ mi } 1000 \text{ ft} \\
\times \qquad 12 \\
\hline
36 \text{ mi } 12{,}000 \text{ ft}
\end{array}
$$
Multiply each measure (number) by 12. Change 12,000 ft to miles and feet by division.

$$\frac{12{,}000}{5280} = 2 \text{ R } 1440$$

38 mi 1440 ft

Simplify the answer.

4. Divide 8 yards, 6 inches by 3.

8 yd 6 in.

$$\overbrace{(8 \times 36) + 6}$$

294 in.

Because of the difficulty of changing units while dividing, it is advisable to change to the smaller units before dividing. Complete the division. Then simplify the answer.

$$
\begin{array}{r}
98 \\
3\overline{)294}
\end{array}
$$

Find yards.

$$
\begin{array}{r}
2 \ \leftarrow \text{yards} \\
36\overline{)98} \\
72 \\
\hline
26
\end{array}
$$

Find feet.

$$
\begin{array}{r}
2 \ \leftarrow \text{feet} \\
12\overline{)26} \\
24 \\
\hline
2 \ \leftarrow \text{inches}
\end{array}
$$

98 in. = 2 yd 2 ft 2 in.

Computations with customary units are cumbersome, but with practice you can become skilled.

Your Turn

Complete each computation. Be sure to express each answer in simplest form.

8.
$$
\begin{array}{r}
5 \text{ mi } \ 900 \text{ yd} \\
+1 \text{ mi } 1200 \text{ yd}
\end{array}
$$

9.
$$
\begin{array}{r}
6 \text{ ft } 8 \text{ in.} \\
-2 \text{ ft } 4 \text{ in.}
\end{array}
$$

10.
$$
\begin{array}{r}
1 \text{ yd } 2 \text{ ft} \\
\times \qquad 8
\end{array}
$$

11.
$$
\begin{array}{r}
2 \text{ yd } 1 \text{ ft } 3 \text{ in.} \\
-1 \text{ yd } \qquad 9 \text{ in.}
\end{array}
$$

12. 9 ft 7 in. ÷ 5

13. 11 yd ÷ 4

(Answers appear at the end of the section.)

Metric units

The metric system of measures uses the following set of prefixes for length, mass, and capacity. The subdivisions use Latin terms, and the multiples use Greek terms. The most frequently used prefixes are shown.

Prefix	Decimal
milli-	0.001
centi-	0.01
deci-	0.1
deka-	10.
hecto-	100.
kilo-	1000.

Recent developments in technology that permit measuring immense and minute quantities have necessitated the use of prefixes such as those given below.

Prefix	Decimal
pico-	0.000000000001
nano-	0.000000001
micro-	0.000001
giga-	1,000,000,000.
tera-	1,000,000,000,000.

The next table shows how the prefixes are used with metric units of length.

Metric units for measures of length
1 millimeter (mm) = 0.001 meter (m)
1 centimeter (cm) = 0.01 m
1 decimeter (dm) = 0.1 m
meter (basic unit)
1 dekameter (dam) = 10 m
1 hectometer (hm) = 100 m
1 kilometer (km) = 1000 m

Note that each unit in the list is ten times greater than the unit above it. So 1 km = 10 hm, 1 dm = 10 cm, 1 dm = 100 mm.

Following is a representation of a metric ruler. The numerals 1, 2, 3, 4, 5 are centimeters. Each centimeter is separated into ten equal parts. Each of these ten equal parts is 1 millimeter.

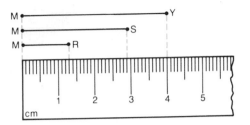

$\overline{MR}$ = 1.3 cm or 13 mm
$\overline{MS}$ = 2.9 cm or 29 mm
$\overline{MY}$ = 4 cm or 40 mm

Your Turn

Give the length of each line segment in centimeters and in millimeters.

14. Z•——•V
15. Z•————————•W
16. Z•———————————————•X

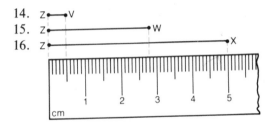

(Answers appear at the end of the section.)

Converting metric units

Converting from one unit to another in the metric system is much easier than converting in the customary system. The same basic principle applies:

Going from	To	You
small unit	large unit	divide
large unit	small unit	multiply

For example, suppose you want to change 150 centimeters to meters.

150 cm = ? m   Think: Going from
                    small to large, so
                    divide.
100 cm = 1 m   Relation of
                    cm to m. So divide
                    150 by 100.
$$\frac{150}{100} = 1.5$$ Notice that the dec-
                    imal point has
                    moved, but the digits
150 cm = 1.5 m   have not changed.

Study how 0.523 kilometer is changed to
hectometers.

    0.523 km = ? hm
    Going from large to small, so multi-
    ply. Since 10 hm = 1 km, multiply by
    10. To do so, just move the decimal
    point one place to the right.
    0.523 km = 5.23 hm

Your Turn

17. Change 5390 meters to kilometers.
18. Change 0.3 millimeter to centimeters.
19. Change 50 centimeters to decimeters.
20. Change 20 dekameters to decimeters.
21. Change 0.001 kilometer to centimeters.

*(Answers appear at the end of the
section.)*

Computing with metric units

Solving problems involving computation
with metric measures is much simpler
than with customary units. But be careful
to add and subtract only like units and
express answers in simplest form.

    Example 1. Find the sum of 42 centi-
    meters, 1.2 meters, and 5.23 meters.

    0.42 m   Change 42 cm to meters.
    1.2 m   Then add. Be sure
    +5.23 m that the sum is stated in
    6.85 m   the units required to
             solve the problem.

Example 2. Subtract 0.5 decimeter
from 659 millimeters. You could find
the answer in decimeters or in
millimeters.

In decimeters	In millimeters
6.59 dm	659 mm
−0.5 dm	− 50 mm
6.09 dm	609 mm

Example 3. Multiply 3.24 kilometers by 8.

    3.24 km
    ×   8
    25.92 km

Example 4. Divide 15.40 hectometers by 5.

    3.08 hm
    5)15.40 hm

Notice that the metric system is based on
the decimal system, therefore computation is completed as for decimals.

Your Turn

22. Add 55 centimeters and 209 millime-
    ters. Show the answer in millimeters.
23. Multiply 432 hectometers by 0.1.
24. Subtract 0.032 meters from 41.1 cen-
    timeters. Show the answer in meters.
25. Divide 0.042 kilometers by 3.
26. Find the sum of 4.2 meters, 4.2 deci-
    meters, and 4.2 centimeters. Express
    your answer first in meters, then in
    decimeters, then in centimeters.
27. Find the difference between 52.43 deka-
    meters and 52.43 hectometers. Ex-
    press your answer first in dekame-
    ters, then in hectometers.

*(Answers appear at the end of the
section.)*

Perimeter Measure

With linear measures, the perimeter, or
distance around a geometric figure, can

be determined. Because some of the figures are measured so frequently, the equations used for the computations are written with special letters. An equation written in this manner is called a formula. The use of a formula speeds up the work, as it is not necessary each time to make up the equation to be used for the problem.

You will be working with geometric figures as you solve the formulas below. Before beginning, you may wish to review the material on geometric figures in the last section.

Parallelograms

The opposite sides of a parallelogram are congruent in pairs. The length is denoted by ℓ and the width by w. The perimeter is given by

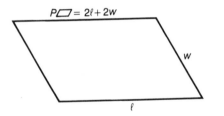

Note: $2\ell + 2w$ means $(2 \times \ell) + (2 \times w)$

Regular polygons

All sides of a regular polygon are congruent. The length of a side is denoted by s. The perimeter is the product of the length of one side and the number of sides, n.

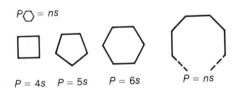

Scalene triangles

The lengths of the sides are denoted by a, b, and c. The perimeter is given by

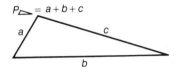

Example: Find the perimeter of a regular pentagon with a side of 8 cm.

$$P = ns$$
$$n = 5$$
$$s = 8 \text{ cm}$$
$$P = 5 \times 8 \text{ or } 40 \text{ cm}$$

Suppose that two rectangles are similar. Their corresponding sides are then proportional (*see* discussion of similar figures, p. 300). Study the discussion below to find the ratio of their perimeters.

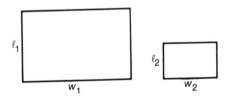

There are two rectangles with sides whose lengths are in the ratio 2:1. Since a rectangle is a parallelogram, the perimeters may be written as

$$p_1 = 2 \times (\ell_1 \times w_1) \text{ and}$$
$$p_2 = 2 \times (\ell_2 + w_2).$$

As the sides of the larger rectangle are twice those of the smaller one, they may be written as

$$\ell_1 = 2\ell_2 \text{ and } w_1 = 2w_2$$

assuming that the first rectangle is the larger one. The perimeter of the first rectangle can then be written, by substitution, as

$$p_1 = 2 (2\ell_2 + 2w_2)$$
$$= 4 (\ell_2 + w_2)$$

The ratio of the perimeters of the two rectangles is then

$$\frac{p_1}{p_2} = \frac{4 (\ell_2 + w_2)}{2 (\ell_2 + w_2)} \text{ or } \frac{2}{1}$$

The same ratio holds for the perimeters as for the sides.

Your Turn

1. Find the perimeter of a rectangle with width $4\frac{3}{8}$ in. and length $12\frac{1}{4}$ in.
2. Find the perimeter of a regular hexagon with a side of length 1.4 cm.
3. A pyramid with a square base has a perimeter of 900 m. Find the length of a side of the base of the pyramid.
4. Two squares have sides in the ratio 6:1. The perimeter of the larger square is 24 ft. What is the perimeter of the smaller square?
5. Write a formula for the perimeter of an isosceles triangle that takes into account its special characteristic.

(Answers appear at the end of the section.)

Circles

The perimeter of a circle is called the circumference. It was discovered in ancient times that the ratio of the circumference of a circle to its diameter is a constant value, a little over three. This value is denoted by the Greek letter π ("pi").

$$\frac{C}{d} = \pi$$

The formula for the circumference, C, of a circle is usually written as

$$C = \pi d$$

Since the diameter of a circle is twice the radius, r, the circumference may also be given by the formula

$$C = 2\pi r$$

For most of the computations made for daily work, the decimal approximation 3.14, or the fractional approximation $\frac{22}{7}$, is an adequate approximation for π.

Example: 1. Find the circumference of a circle with a radius of 42 in. Use $\frac{22}{7}$ for π.

$$C = 2\pi r$$
$$= 2 \times \frac{22}{7} \times 42$$
$$= 264 \text{ in.}$$

Doing the computational work correctly is important. It is equally important, as you have seen, not to be misled by computing results with a much higher precision than is justified by the data. The caution is particularly necessary when using calculators or computers, as it is easy to obtain results that suggest high precision. In actuality, the apparent high precision is introduced by the calculation. The art of measurement is far from a mere exercise in arithmetic. It requires an even higher degree of that particularly human skill, judgment.

In example 1., it is necessary to examine the accuracy of the figure computed as the circumference. If 42 is considered to be an exact figure, then it is proper to keep the result as 264 in. However, if the radius length was obtained as a result of measurement, the figure is inexact. Writing it as 42 indicates that the measurement was made to the nearest inch. The GPE is $\frac{1}{2}$ inch, and the radius is

$42 \pm \frac{1}{2}$ in. The length of the radius has a

relative error of $\frac{\frac{1}{2}}{42}$ (= 0.012), or about

1%. The circumference of 264 in. also has

a GPE of $\frac{1}{2}$ inch, so the relative error is

$\frac{\frac{1}{2}}{264} = 0.00189$, or about 0.2%. A relative

error of 0.2% for the answer shows more accuracy than a relative error of 1% for the measurement of the radius. The accuracy was improved by calculations. If the answer is rounded to the nearest ten,

260, the greatest possible error is $\frac{1}{2} \times 10$,

or 5. Then the relative error is $\frac{5}{260}$ or

1.9%, which is greater than the relative error of 1%. Therefore, use 260 for the answer.

Finding the relative error of the measurements and the answer for every problem encountered would take a lot of time. A procedure has been developed that is generally applicable and simplifies the process. The product is expressed with the same number of significant digits as the lowest number of significant dig-

Numeral	Significant digits	Explanation
147	3	All are significant.
1470	3	Zero is a place-holder.
1407	4	Zero shows no tens.
0.233	3	The zero before the decimal is a place-holder.
0.071	2	The zero directly after the decimal point is a place-holder.
0.710	3	The last zero shows no thousandths.
500	1, 2, or 3	See below.

its in the factors. Significant digits, in simple terms, are any digits not used as place-holders.

If a measurement is given as "500 km," it is assumed the result of the measurement was rounded to the nearest hundred and 500 has one significant digit. The greatest possible error of this measurement is $\frac{1}{2}$ of 100 or 50 km. If a measurement is given as "500 km, to the nearest km," there are 3 significant digits because the zeros show that there are no tens and no ones—the GPE of this measurement is 0.5 km.

Hence, the general rule for rounding a product obtained in computing area measurements is to keep as many significant digits in the product as there are in the measure with the smallest number of significant digits. In example 1., 42 has 2 significant digits, therefore the answer should also have 2 significant digits. Round 264 to 260 to obtain the answer.

Example 2. Find the diameter of a circle whose circumference is 3.50 meters. Use the value 3.14 for π.

$$C = \pi d$$
$$3.50 = 3.14 \times d$$
$$d = \frac{3.50}{3.14} \text{ or } 1.11 \text{ m}$$

The answer is given with 3 significant digits since 3.50 has 3 significant digits.

Example 3. Find the difference in the circumference of two circles. The smaller circle has a diameter of 8 in., and the larger circle a diameter of 9 in.

$$C = \pi d$$
$$C_1 = 9\pi$$
$$C_2 = 8\pi$$
$$C_1 - C_2 = 9\pi - 8\pi$$
$$= \pi \text{ or } 3.14$$

Since both 8 in. and 9 in. have one significant digit, the answer should have one significant digit. Rounding 3.14 in. to the nearest inch, the larger circle is approximately 3 in. larger than the smaller circle in circumference.

Example 4. How far does a bicycle travel in one complete revolution of a wheel, if the diameter of the wheel is 26.0 in.? The bicycle will travel a distance equal to the circumference of the wheel.

$$C = \pi d$$
$$C = 26.0 \times 3.14$$
$$= 81.64 \text{ or } 81.6 \text{ in.}$$

Your Turn

6. Find the circumference of a circle with a radius of 5.05 m.
7. Find the diameter of a circle with a circumference of 154 ft. Use $\frac{22}{7}$ for π.
8. The circumference of a circle is 1.5 yd. What is the circumference of a circle with a radius six times the length of that of the first circle?

(Answers appear at the end of the section.)

Area Measure

An important measure to determine is that of area. In almost every instance, area measurements are made indirectly, with the aid of computation. For an area measurement, a number is assigned to a region of a surface that indicates the number of standard units that will cover that region.

Parallelograms could be used as the standard unit to cover the surface, but they would not be practical for rectangular regions, such as floors, ceilings, and walls. The simplest regular polygons available are those with the smallest number of sides: the equilateral triangle with three sides, and the square with four sides. The square is the best choice for the standard unit of area measure. Fewer squares than triangles are needed to cover a surface, and they are easily arranged.

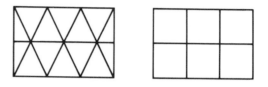

As most of the surfaces to be measured require a significant number of unit squares, it is not possible to place the squares physically on the surface to accomplish the measurement of area. Therefore, areas are computed from other measurements that can be made more easily.

Rectangles

Consider the measurement of a rectangular region. The squares are placed in rows. By counting the number of squares in a row and the number of rows needed, the area can be calculated.

Suppose that you have six squares in a row and a total of four rows covering a region, then a total of 6 + 6 + 6 + 6 = 24 squares are needed. The rapid way to make this calculation is, of course, to perform the repeated addition by multiplication. Thus, the product of the number of squares per row and the number of rows gives the total number of square units needed.

For example, if 16 squares per row and 10 rows are needed to fill the area of a rectangle, 160 squares are needed. The number of squares per row can be determined by making a linear measurement, as can the number of rows. A linear measurement is an easy and a convenient measurement to make. The process can be expressed with a formula for the area of a rectangle:

$$\text{Area}_\square = \text{length} \times \text{width, or}$$
$$A_\square = \ell w$$

The number of squares needed can be computed when a fractional part of a square is required. For example, suppose that $2\frac{1}{2}$ squares fit in one row, and 4 rows are needed. Then

$$A = 4 \times 2\frac{1}{2}$$
$$= 10$$

The area is 10 square units.

When finding area, the answers are expressed in square units. Below are examples of units of area.

In words	In symbols
square centimeters	cm^2
square inches	$in.^2$
square miles	mi^2
square meters	m^2

It is important once again to decide how to determine the precision of the computed measurement. When an actual measurement is made, two inexact numbers are multiplied together to provide the measure of the area of a rectangle. How will the appropriate precision then be determined?

Suppose that you have a rectangle with length 5.1 cm and width 2.5 cm. The GPE for each of these measurements is $\frac{1}{2}(0.1)$ or 0.05 cm. This means that

for ℓ: $5.05 \le \ell < 5.15$ and
for w: $2.45 \le w < 2.55$

The product, ℓw, obtained is 12.75. Because of the inexactness of the measurements,

$$12.3725 \le \ell w < 13.1325$$

That is, the product is equal to or greater than the product of the two smallest values and less than the product of the two largest values, with the given precision of the length and the width. The actual product is 5.1×2.5 or 12.75. How should this product be expressed? Since both factors, 5.1 and 2.5, have two significant digits, two significant digits will be used in the product. Hence, the product is rounded to 13. The area is 13 cm^2.

Your Turn

Find the area of each rectangle. Each length was found by measurement. Therefore, you must be sure answers are stated with the correct number of significant digits.

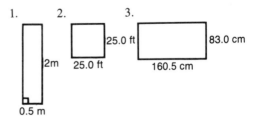

(*Answers appear at the end of the section.*)

From the area of the rectangle, the area of other figures can be obtained.

Parallelograms

Draw a parallelogram, such as ABCD, and draw altitude $\overline{DE}$, as shown.

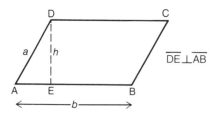

$$\overline{DE} \perp \overline{AB}$$

Cut off △ADE and move to the position on the right, with $\overline{AD}$ fitted along congruent side BC.

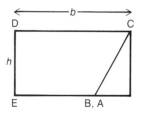

The new figure formed is a rectangle. The area of the figure has not changed through this rearrangement, so the area of the parallelogram is equal to the area of the rectangle.

The length of the rectangle is denoted b, and the width of the rectangle is the altitude (height) h of the parallelogram. Thus, the area of the rectangle is the product bh, and it is the area of the parallelogram as well. It is important to note that the area of the parallelogram is not obtained as the product of the sides directly.

Example: Find the area of this figure.

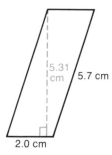

2.0 cm

Note: Not all measures that are given are used. Be careful to use the measure of the base and the height to find the area.

$$A = bh$$
$$= 2.0 \times 5.31$$
$$= 10.62$$
$$A = 11 \text{ cm}^2 \text{ Rounded to 2 significant digits because 2.0 has 2 significant digits.}$$

Your Turn

4. Find the area of a parallelogram with a height of 13.0 m and a base of 20.4 m.
5. A parallelogram has a base of 12 in. and a height of 10 in. The other side has a measure of 16 in. All measurements are to the nearest inch. Find the area.

(Answers appear at the end of the section.)

Triangles

A triangle can be considered to be half a parallelogram. If $\overline{AD}$ is drawn parallel to $\overline{BC}$ and $\overline{DC}$ is drawn parallel to $\overline{AB}$, parallelogram ABCD is created, based on triangle ABC.

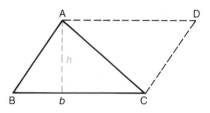

Since $\overline{AB} \cong \overline{DC}$, $\overline{BC} \cong \overline{AD}$, and $\overline{AC} \cong \overline{AC}$, the two triangles are congruent, and the area of each is half the area of the parallelogram. The area of a triangle is then given by

$$A_\triangle = \frac{1}{2}bh$$

where b is the base (any side) and h is the altitude to that side. When working with metric measures, it is easier to state the formula as

$$A = 0.5bh$$

Examples: Find the areas of the following triangles.

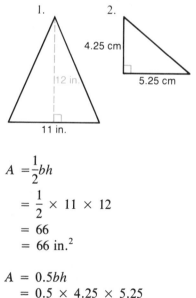

1.

2.

4.25 cm

|12 in

5.25 cm

11 in.

$$A = \frac{1}{2}bh$$
$$= \frac{1}{2} \times 11 \times 12$$
$$= 66$$
$$= 66 \text{ in.}^2$$

$$A = 0.5bh$$
$$= 0.5 \times 4.25 \times 5.25$$
$$= 11.15625$$
$$= 11.2 \text{ cm}^2$$

Your Turn

Find the area of each triangle.

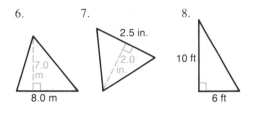

6.

7.

8.

2.5 in.

7.0 m

8.0 m

2.0 in.

10 ft

6 ft

(Answers appear at the end of the section.)

Trapezoids

A trapezoid can be divided into two triangles by a diagonal, and its area obtained from the areas of the triangles.

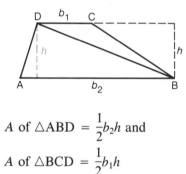

$$A \text{ of } \triangle ABD = \frac{1}{2}b_2h \text{ and}$$

$$A \text{ of } \triangle BCD = \frac{1}{2}b_1h$$

The total area is then the sum:

$$A \text{ of trapezoid } ABCD = \frac{1}{2}b_1h + \frac{1}{2}b_2h$$

$$A_\square = \frac{1}{2}h \, (b_1 + b_2)$$

Another way to associate the factors in the formula leads to a slightly different formula.

$$A_\square = h\left(\frac{b_1 + b_2}{2}\right)$$

The average of the two bases of the trapezoid is the median, m. The median is the line segment joining the midpoints of the two non-parallel sides of the trapezoid.

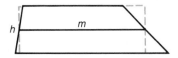

Note that the rectangle with length m and height h is equivalent in area to the trapezoid. The area of the trapezoid can then be written as:

$A = hm$

Example: The two bases of a trapezoid are 15.5 and 30.5 inches, respectively. The height is 4.0 in. Find the area.

$A = hm$

$m = \frac{1}{2}(b_1 + b_2)$

$\quad = \frac{1}{2}(15.5 + 30.5)$

$\quad = 23$

$A = 4(23)$ or 92 in.^{2} (Two significant digits may be kept.)

Your Turn

Find the area of each trapezoid.

9.   10.   11.

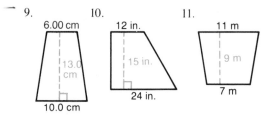

(Answers appear at the end of the section.)

Polygons

The area of a regular polygon can be obtained by calculating the area of one of the triangles formed by drawing line seg-

ments to two adjacent vertices, and then multiplying by the number of triangles that can be formed (equal to the number of sides).

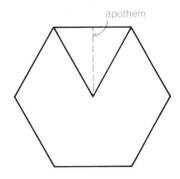

The altitude of the triangle is called the apothem of the regular polygon. Let a represent the length of the apothem. Then the area of one triangle is

$A_\triangle = \frac{1}{2}bh$

$A_\triangle = \frac{1}{2}sa$ Where s is the length of a side of the polygon and a is the apothem of the polygon.

The total area of the polygon is

$A_\bigcirc = \frac{1}{2}nsa$

Since ns is the perimeter, p, of the polygon, the formula may be written as

$A_\bigcirc = \frac{1}{2}ap$

In general, the area of polygonal figures that are non-standard shapes can be obtained by partitioning them into standard shapes—rectangles, triangles, squares—and finding the area of each of the parts.

Example: The figure below can be partitioned into rectangles and a triangle, and the area of each of the parts can then be determined.

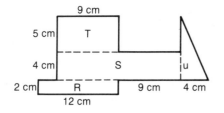

Assume that all measurements are exact—in other words ignore precision and significant digits.

Area of R = 2 × 12 or 24 cm²
Area of S = 4 × (9 + 9)
            = 4 × 18 or 72 cm²
Area of T = 5 × 9 or 45 cm²
Area of U = 0.5 × 4 × (4 + 5)
            = 0.5 × 4 × 9 or 18 cm²
Area of
the polygon = 24 + 72 + 45 + 18
            = 159 cm²

Your Turn

Find the area of each polygon. Assume all measurements are exact.

12. A regular pentagon with sides of 5 in. and apothem of 4.3 in.
13. A regular octagon with sides of 0.8 cm and apothem of 1.8 cm.

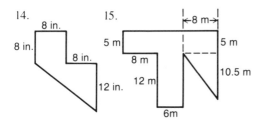

14.
15.

(Answers appear at the end of the section.)

Circles

The area of a circle can be approached from the knowledge of the area of polyg-

onal figures. Suppose that a circle is subdivided. It could be cut into four parts, and the sectors rearranged, as shown.

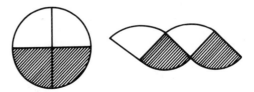

It could be more finely divided, into twelve congruent sectors, and these parts also rearranged.

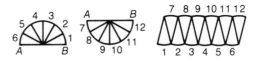

As the subdivisions are made smaller, the rearranged figure begins to assume the shape of a parallelogram. The base of the parallelogram is half the circumference, or πr, and the altitude approaches the length of the radius, r. The area then approaches the area of the parallelogram:

A = bh
$A_\odot$ = $(\pi r) \times (r)$ or
$A_\odot$ = πr^2

By more advanced methods, it can be shown that if the measurement of r is exact, the formula is exact. Since $r = \dfrac{d}{2}$, the formula can also be written:

$$A = \pi \frac{d^2}{4}$$

Example: The diameter of a penny is 2.0 cm. Find the area. Use 3.14 for π.

$$A_\odot = \pi \frac{d^2}{4}$$

$$A_\odot = (3.14)\frac{2^2}{4} \text{ or } 3.14 \text{ cm}^2$$

Since the diameter was measured to the nearest tenth, the measurement has two significant figures. Thus the area is rounded to 3.1 cm^2.

Your Turn

Find the area of each circle. The measure of the radius or diameter shows the accuracy of the measurement. Use 3.14 for π.

16.   17.   18.

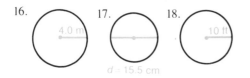

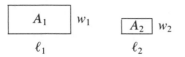

(Answers appear at the end of the section.)

Observations on area

It is interesting to observe the effect on the area of enlarging a figure to form a new, similar figure. It was seen that the perimeters of similar figures have the same ratio as the sides of the figures. Suppose that you have two similar rectangles, such that the ratio of similitude of the first to the second is 2:1.

The areas

| A_1 | w_1 |
| ℓ_1 | |

| A_2 | w_2 |
| ℓ_2 | |

can be expressed as

$$A_2 = \ell_2 w_2 \text{ and } A_1 = \ell_1 w_1$$

Since $\ell_1 = 2\ell_2$ and $w_1 = 2w_2$

$$A_1 = (2\ell_2)\,(2w_2)$$

The ratio of the two areas is then

$$\frac{A_1}{A_2} = \frac{(2\ell_2)\,(2w_2)}{\ell_2 w_2} \text{ or } \frac{4}{1}$$

Thus the areas are in the ratio of the square of the ratio of similitude.

Example: A rectangle has an area of 12 in.^{2} What is the area of a similar rectangle whose sides are in the ratio 3:1 with the original figure?

$$\frac{A_2}{A_1} = \left(\frac{3}{1}\right)^2 \text{ or } 9$$

$$A_2 = 9\,(12) \text{ or } 108 \text{ in.}^2$$

The circle is one figure with a curved boundary for which a formula has been devised to determine the area. In general, however, the problem of determining the area for regions with curved boundaries is a difficult one. One approach is to partition the region with familiar polygonal figures whose areas are readily calculated. The concept goes back to Archimedes. For example, the region below could be approximated by rectangles. These rectangles can be inscribed or circumscribed about the curve, or some of each type can be used. The region could also be filled with trapezoids.

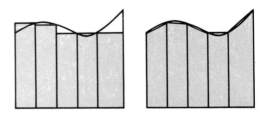

The finer the subdivision made, the better the approximation.

Part of the material of the branch of mathematics called the calculus studies the problem of finding areas of regions bounded by curves. The work done by Archimedes in ancient times came very close to the techniques developed for the calculus.

Experiment

The technique of estimating an area with the area of polygonal figures can be seen from the following experiment. As the equations for curves are generally more difficult to work with than the equation of a line, a straight line boundary will be used for the region.

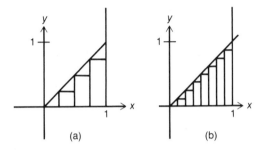

(a)   (b)

The lines whose equations are $y = x$, $y = 0$ and $x = 1$ form a triangle. Inscribe three rectangles as shown in (a), and then seven rectangles, as shown in (b). Find the area of each rectangle, then add to obtain the approximation of the area of the triangle. The area of the triangle is

$$A = \frac{1}{2}bh$$

$$A = \frac{1}{2}(1)(1)$$

$$A = 0.5 \text{ square units}$$

(The height of the rectangles is easily determined, since y, the height, is equal to x.)

Volume Measure

The measurement of volume assigns a number to a three-dimensional region indicating the number of standard elements that partition the space. The standard element used is the cube.

When finding volume, the units of volume are cubic units. Below are examples of units of volume.

In words	In symbols
cubic centimeters	cm^3
cubic feet	ft^3
cubic inches	$in.^3$
cubic meters	m^3

Prisms and cylinders

A rectangular prism can be filled with layers of cubes. To obtain the number of cubes in one layer, the number of cubes in one row is multiplied by the number of rows needed. Thus, the number of cubes needed to fill one layer is equal numerically to the area of the base. The number of layers needed is equal numerically to the height of the prism.

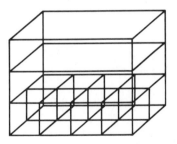

The volume of the rectangular prism can then be determined by multiplying the area of the base by the height.

$$V_{\square} = Bh, \text{ where } B \text{ is the area of the base.}$$

Example: A box available from the post office is 12.0 in. by 16.0 in. by 4.0 in. Find the volume of the box.

$$V_{\square} = Bh$$
$$V_{\square} = (12)(16)(4)$$
$$V_{\square} = 768 \text{ in.}^3$$

Since the measurement of 4.0 in. has two significant digits, the volume is 770 cubic inches.

The volume of a prism with any polygonal base can be determined from the formula $V = Bh$. The base may be triangular, pentagonal, hexagonal, for example.

The volume of a cylinder similarly is determined as the product of the area of the base and the height. As the base of the cylinder is a circle, the formula is

$$V_{cyl} = \pi r^2 h$$

Examples: Find the volume for the prism and the cylinder. Assume all measurements are exact.

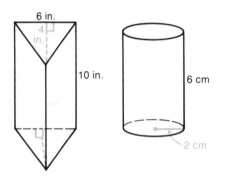

$$V = Bh$$
$$= 0.5 \times 4 \times 6 \times 10$$
$$= 120$$
$$= 120 \text{ in.}^3$$

$$V = \pi r^2 h$$
$$= 3.14 \times 2^2 \times 6$$
$$= 75.36$$
$$= 75.36 \text{ cm}^3$$

Your Turn

Find the volume of each prism and cylinder. Assume all measurements are exact.

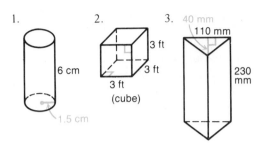

1.   2.   3.

(Answers appear at the end of the section.)

Pyramids, cones, and spheres

The volume of a pyramid has been found to be $\frac{1}{3}$ the volume of a prism with the same base and the same height. Similarly, the volume of a cone is equal to $\frac{1}{3}$ the volume of a cylinder with the same base and the same height.

$$V_{Pyr} = \frac{1}{3}Bh$$

$$V_{Co} = \frac{1}{3}\pi r^2 h$$

The volume of a sphere is given by

$$V_{Sph} = \frac{4}{3}\pi r^3$$

Examples: Find the volume of each solid. Assume the measurement for the sphere is exact.

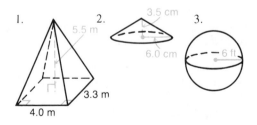

1.   2.   3.

1. $V = \frac{1}{3}Bh$

$\quad = \frac{1}{3} \times (4 \times 3.3) \times 5.5$

$\quad = \frac{1}{3} \times 13.2 \times 5.5$

$\quad = 24.2$

$\quad = 24 \text{ m}^3$

$B = $ Area of
the base,
or 4×3.3

The answer is rounded to two significant digits because the measures are given in two significant digits.

2. $V = \frac{1}{3}\pi r^2 h$

$\quad = \frac{1}{3} \times 3.14 \times 6 \times 6 \times 3.5$

$\quad = 131.88$

$\quad = 130 \text{ cm}^3$

Rounded to two significant digits because 3.5 has two significant digits.

3. $V = \frac{4}{3}\pi r^3$

$\quad = \frac{4}{3} \times \frac{22}{7} \times 6 \times 6 \times 6$

$\quad = 905\frac{1}{7}$

$\quad = 905\frac{1}{7} \text{ ft}^3$

Not rounded because measurement was assumed to be exact.

Your Turn

Find the volume of each solid. In exercises 5. and 6., assume the measurements are exact.

4.   5.   9 m   6.   15 in.

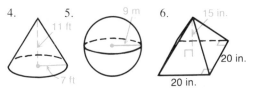

20 in.

7 ft   20 in.

(Answers appear at the end of the section.)

Capacity Measure

In addition to volume measurements, capacity is measured with a variety of units in the customary system of measures. For dry measure, there are pints, quarts, pecks, and bushels. For liquid measure, there are teaspoons, tablespoons, cups, pints, quarts, gallons, and other measures not so well known.

<u>Dry measure</u>
2 pints (pt) = 1 quart
8 quarts (qt) = 1 peck
4 pecks (pk) = 1 bushel

<u>Liquid measure</u>
16 fluid ounces
(fl oz) = 1 pint
2 pints = 1 quart
4 quarts = 1 gallon (gal.)

The metric system has a uniform system of measure of capacity. The basic unit is the liter, which is very close to our quart measure. One liter is equivalent to 1.057 quarts. The liter is equal to 1000 cm^3 (cubic centimeters). The same set of prefixes is used with the liter that were used with the meter. The following table shows the most common metric units of capacity.

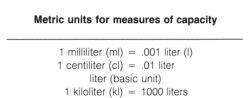

Metric units for measures of capacity

1 milliliter (ml) = .001 liter (l)
1 centiliter (cl) = .01 liter
liter (basic unit)
1 kiloliter (kl) = 1000 liters

To convert from one metric unit of capacity to another, use the same methods as for converting from one metric unit of length to another.

Examples: 1. Judy had 164 pints of milk. How many gallons did she have?

$$164 \text{ pt } = ? \text{ gal.}$$
$$= 164 \div 8$$
$$= 20\frac{1}{2}$$
$$= 20\frac{1}{2} \text{ gal.}$$

Going from small to large, so divide.
1 gal. = 8 pt

2. Dan has 2 bushels of corn. How many quarts does he have?

$$2 \text{ bu } = ? \text{ qt}$$
$$= 2 \times 32$$
$$= 64$$
$$= 64 \text{ qt}$$

Going from large to small, so multiply.
1 bu = 32 qt

3. Ralph has 2 liters of milk. John bought 1000 milliliters of milk. How many liters of milk do they have?

$$1000 \text{ ml } = ? \text{ L}$$
$$= 1 \text{ L}$$

Change one unit in order to add the measures.

$$2 \text{ L } + 1 \text{ L } = ?$$
$$= 3 \text{ L}$$

They have three liters of milk.

Your Turn

1. Delia's aquarium holds 14 gallons of water. The only container she has with which to fill the aquarium is a one-pint jar. How many times must she fill the jar and empty it into the aquarium to fill the aquarium?
2. Glenn fed his horses 1664 quarts of oats. How many bushels was that?
3. Sing-ho used an eyedropper marked in milliliters to fill a small vial with medicine. The eyedropper held 25 milliliters. It required 64 times of filling the eyedropper to fill a vial with the medicine. How many liters did the vial hold?

(Answers appear at the end of the section.)

Other Measures

Weight in the customary system is measured in ounces, pounds, and tons.

$$16 \text{ ounces } = 1 \text{ pound}$$
$$2000 \text{ pounds } = 1 \text{ ton (sometimes called the short ton)}$$

Weight is a force. It is the product of the mass of an object (which is invariable) and the acceleration due to gravity, g. The value of g varies depending on your height above sea level. Most persons have become very conscious of the variability of weight after seeing pictures of the astronauts in a weightless condition in their space capsules.

The metric system measures mass; the customary system measures weight. If the variability of weight due to the variation of the acceleration due to gravity is not taken into account, standard relations can be used between the two systems.

The basic unit of mass in the metric system is the gram. It is the weight of 1 cm^3 of water at 4° Celsius (when it is at maximum density). A gram is a tiny unit. A nickel weighs about 5 grams. Since the gram is so small a unit, 1000 grams, or 1 kilogram (kg), is the unit of weight in general use for daily work. A kilogram is about 2.2 pounds. The metric ton, or long ton, is 2240 pounds.

There are two scales of temperature in common use, the Fahrenheit scale and the Celsius scale. On the Fahrenheit scale (°F) water freezes at 32° and boils at 212°. On the Celsius scale (°C), water freezes at 0° and boils at 100°. The Celsius system is used with the metric system and in scientific work. The relation between the two systems is given by the formula:

$$C = \frac{5}{9}(F - 32)$$

Your Turn

1. A beef roast weighs 3 pounds. One serving of the roast is 6 ounces. How many servings can be made from the 3-pound roast?
2. A roll of coins contains 40 nickels. Each nickel weighs about 5 grams. How many grams does that roll of coins weigh? Express that as part of a kilogram.
3. If the temperature outside is 50°F, what is it in degrees Celsius?

(Answers appear at the end of the section.)

The world of measurement has a bewildering array of units. Only the most widely used units have been discussed in this section. There are many special units used by particular trades or industries. There are units to measure electrical pressure (volts) and the quantity of electricity flowing (amperes). There are units for the measure of light intensity, sound intensity, and magnetism. Force and energy are measured. The fuel equivalent of food is measured in calories.

Velocity and acceleration are measures of speed. An auto's performance is measured by the number of miles it will travel on one gallon of gasoline. There are picas and points for printers, microfarads, henries, and ohms for electronics specialists.

Astronomers measure with light-years. There are measures for time, measures for angles, and every country has a system of measures for its money.

Choose any field and explore its measures. As you do, you will find an intriguing blend of old and new, history and science. There is much to be enjoyed in the amazing world of measurement.

Answers

Methods of Measurement (pp. 322–324)

1. directly   2. indirectly   3. directly   4. exact; The pages can be counted.   5. inexact; The distance can only be estimated.   6. inexact; A smaller, more accurate, unit of measurement should be used.

Precision of Measurement (pp. 327–328)

1. $\frac{1}{2}$ inch   2. 0.05 centimeter   3. $\frac{1}{8}$ inch   4. 0.0005 meter   5. 5%   6. 0.625%

7. about 0.3%   8. about 0.03%   9. 0.94 meters; about 0.5%   10. 7 feet; about 7%

Linear Measure (pp. 328–332)

1. 1 inch; $1\frac{1}{4}$ inches   2. 2 inches; 2 inches   3. 3 inches; $3\frac{1}{4}$ inches   4. 495 ft

5. 1281 ft   6. 427 yd   7. 14,080 yd   8. 7 mi 340 yd   9. 4 ft 4 in.   10. 13 yd 1 ft

11. 1 yd 6 in.   12. 1 ft 11 in.   13. 2 yd 2 ft 3 in.   14. 0.5 cm; 5 mm   15. 2.8 cm; 28 mm

16. 5 cm; 50 mm   17. 5.39 km   18. 0.03 cm   19. 5 dm   20. 2000 dm   21. 100 cm

22. 759 mm   23. 43.2 hm   24. 0.379 m   25. 0.014 km   26. 4.662 m; 46.62 dm;

466.2 cm   27. 471.87 dam; 47.187 hm

Perimeter Measure (pp. 332–336)

1. $33\frac{1}{4}$ in.   2. 8.4 cm   3. 225 m   4. 4 ft   5. $p = 2a + b$ Where a is the measure of

the congruent sides and b is the measure of the third side.   6. 31.7 m   7. 49 ft   8. 9 yd

Area Measure (pp. 336–343)

1. 1 m^2 2. 625 ft^2 3. 13,330 cm^2 4. 265 m^2 5. 120 in.^{2} 6. 28 m^2

7. 2.5 in.^{2} 8. 30 ft^2 9. 104 cm^2 10. 270 in.^{2} 11. 80 m^2 12. 53.75 in.^{2}

13. 5.76 cm^2 14. 160 in.^{2} 15. 224 m^2 16. 50 m^2 17. 189 cm^2 18. 300 ft^2

Volume Measure (pp. 343–345)

1. 42.39 cm^3 2. 27 ft^3 3. 506,000 mm^3 4. 600 ft^3 5. 3052.08 m^3 6. 2000 in.^{3}

Capacity Measure (pp. 345–346)

1. 112 times   2. 52 bu   3. 1.6 liters

Other Measures (pp. 346–347)

1. 8 servings   2. 200 g; 0.2 kg   3. 10°C

The Basics of Algebra

Algebra is a branch of mathematics that deals with relations and properties of numbers by means of symbols. Symbols have already been used in some of the previous sections of this book to show certain relationships. Since algebra uses the same basic operations as arithmetic, it is often defined as generalized arithmetic. However, it goes further than arithmetic in studying the nature of the numbers themselves.

Algebra has two important kinds of applications. One application is the use of formulas to solve physical problems. The other application is the use of algebra within other branches of mathematics. In fact, in all of mathematics, algebra is considered to be the language of mathematics.

Although you still need to use words to some degree, you will find that algebra is more precise than words. Whereas in arithmetic you are confined to writing statements about particular numbers, the language of algebra permits you to write statements about all numbers in a given set. In everyday life when you speak or write English, you use words and sentences to express your ideas. However, as you may recall from Section 1 of this part, the expression of mathematical ideas depends upon the use of symbols as well as sentences.

In algebra, symbols are used to form phrases and sentences. Every algebraic sentence has at least one letter symbol called a variable. A variable is a letter that stands for a number that is to be found or for the value of an unknown number. The letters a, b, and c in the following mathematical sentences are examples of variables:

$$a = 6 \qquad b - 1 = 3 \qquad c = 2a$$

A variable is associated with a set. Any element of the set may be used to replace the variable. In this section the set that will be used to replace the variable is the set of real numbers. Two number systems have already been discussed, the natural numbers and the whole numbers. In this section you will see how these two sets, with other sets of numbers, make up the real number system.

Algebraic computations require both organization and patience. As one misstep can produce an incorrect result, it is essential to:

1. Make haste slowly—do not rush through the work;
2. Write out the work carefully, indicating as briefly as possible what steps are being performed, so that you can understand the work in case it is necessary to reread it;
3. Check the work both as you go along and at the end of the problem;
4. Compare the result with an estimate, if it is possible to make one, to ascertain that the result is reasonable.

You should recheck all computations carefully whenever you work with algebra problems that involve basic computation. Sometimes errors occur with the use of decimals and fractions. It is easy to misplace a decimal point or forget to simplify a result. Other errors occur with the use of signed numbers. It is especially important to use good notation and to check each step carefully when working with signed numbers.

Number Systems

Integers

Visual representations, such as sketches or pictures, are frequently used in mathematics to clarify abstract concepts. One of these is the number line. In earlier sections it was shown how whole numbers

could be represented by equally spaced points along the number line. The number line can be extended to the left with a set of equally spaced points continued as before.

Numbers used to name the points to the left of 0 on the number line are called negative numbers. Numbers used to name points to the right of 0 on the number line are called positive numbers. The number associated with point A, the coordinate of A, can be written as $+3$, or simply 3. The coordinate of point B is -2 or negative 2. This leads to the following definition:

> **DEFINITION:**
> **The set of integers (J) consists of the positive numbers, the negative numbers, and the number zero.**

(Recall from your earlier work that 0 is not a natural number and that the numbers called whole numbers include the natural numbers and 0.)

As you can see there is a negative integer that corresponds to every positive integer on the number line. Thus associated with the positive integer, $+5$, there is a negative integer, -5. Because $+5$ on the number line is in the direction opposite from -5 and the two points are the

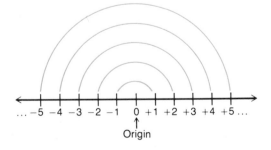

same distance from the origin, 0, the numbers -5 and $+5$ are called opposites.

Similarly -2 and $+2$ are opposites of each other and -18 and $+18$ are opposites of each other. However, 0 is its own opposite. In algebra, the idea of opposites is very important.

The following definition summarizes this discussion.

DEFINITION:
The opposite of a signed number is located the same number of units from zero on the other side of zero on the number line.
If a is a positive number then,

$-(a) = -a$

The opposite of a positive number is a negative number.

$-(-a) = a$

The opposite of a negative number is a positive number.

Your Turn

Write the opposite of each of the following numbers.

1. -1 2. $+8$ 3. -7 4. -9

5. $+3.5$ 6. $-2\frac{1}{2}$ 7. -1.3 8. $+\frac{7}{8}$

(Answers appear at the end of the section.)

Rational numbers

Now consider the portion of the number line from $+1$ through $+2$.

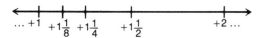

Halfway between the points with coordinates $+1$ and $+2$, there is a point with

coordinate $+1\frac{1}{2}$. Halfway between the points with coordinates $+1$ and $+1\frac{1}{2}$, there is a point with coordinate $+1\frac{1}{4}$. Halfway between the points with coordinates $+1$ and $+1\frac{1}{4}$ is a point with coordinate $+1\frac{1}{8}$. This process could be continued indefinitely.

This is one way of showing that there are many more numbers on the number line than just the integers. Since the interval between each integer can be divided into halves, thirds, fourths, the number line also may be related to fractions so that there is a point on the number line corresponding to each fraction. This leads to the following definition:

DEFINITION:
The set of numbers that consists of the fractional numbers and their opposites is the set of rational numbers.

Integers such as -3, -1, $+1$, and $+3$ can also be shown as $-\frac{3}{1}$, $-\frac{1}{1}$, $+\frac{1}{1}$, and $+\frac{3}{1}$. Thus it should be noted that the set of integers is a subset of the set of rational numbers.

In general, a rational number is a number of the form $\frac{a}{b}$, where a and b are any integers, except b may not be zero. The number of points corresponding to the rational numbers are unlimited, or infinite, because there is always another fraction between any two fractions. Since this is true, mathematicians say that the rational numbers are a dense set. Although they are dense, there will still be points on the number line whose coordinates are not rational numbers.

Irrational numbers

Numbers that are not rational are called irrational numbers. For example, $\sqrt{2}$ is such a number. To locate a point on the number line that corresponds to the irrational number $\sqrt{2}$, on the number line construct a square with the side measuring the unit length.

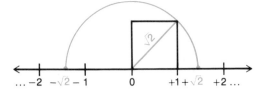

The length of the diagonal of the square measures $\sqrt{2}$. By drawing an arc, using the diagonal as radius, on the number line you can locate the points corresponding to $\sqrt{2}$ and $-\sqrt{2}$. Another irrational number is π (pi). For a circle that has a diameter of 1 unit, the circumference, or distance around, is π units. (For example, if the diameter is 1 centimeter, the circumference is π centimeters.)

The symbol π represents an irrational number. Neither π, $\sqrt{2}$, nor any rational number can be represented exactly as a fraction $\frac{a}{b}$.

Real numbers

The examples above show that there is a point corresponding to every distance from zero. Some of these numbers are rational numbers and others are irrational. Thus the real number line is the full set of points that correspond to the set of real numbers. This leads to the following definition:

DEFINITION:
The union of the set of rational numbers and the set of irrational numbers is called the set of real numbers.

From this definition, it should be clear that every point on the number line can be associated with exactly one real number and for each real number there is one and only one point on the number line. In other words, there is a one-to-one correspondence between the set of real numbers and the set of points on the number line. This is called the completeness property of the set of real numbers.

The diagram below shows the relationships among all the numbers studied so far.

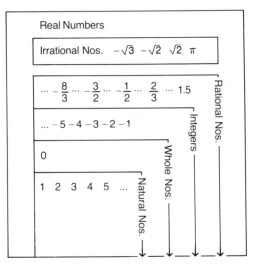

Properties of Real Numbers

In Section 1 of this part, it was pointed out that an expression like $a \times b$ is called the product of a and b. It was also determined that the numbers a and b are called factors.

In algebra, this multiplication can be written several ways. For example, $a \times b$ can be written as $a \cdot b$, $a(b)$, $(a)(b)$, $(a)b$, or simply ab. Since the multiplication symbol is easily confused with the letter x, generally the symbol $\times$ is not used in algebra to indicate multiplication. Likewise, in algebra, division is indicated by using fractional notation. For example, the expression $a \div b$ is written as a/b or $\frac{a}{b}$ (read "a divided by b").

Just as chemicals have properties (characteristics, such as a liquid being flammable), the numbers used in algebra have certain properties that describe them and that show the difference between them and other kinds of numbers. Some of the properties of real numbers are assumed to be true. Statements concerning these assumptions are called axioms or postulates. Earlier in the discussion on whole numbers, properties of that system were presented. At that time the properties were all stated in numerical form. However, in algebra it is necessary to state universal sets of generalizations. Thus, properties are almost always written as statements that use letters (variables). The following are postulates of some properties of the real numbers with respect to addition and multiplication.

Addition
1. Closure under addition:
   For every two real numbers a and b, $a + b$ is a real number.
2. Associativity of addition:
   If a is any real number, b is any real number, and c is any real number, then $(a + b) + c = a + (b + c)$.
3. Identity element of addition:
   If a is any real number, $a + 0 = a$.
4. Additive inverse:
   If a is any real number, then a and $-a$ are additive inverses and $a + (-a) = 0$.
5. Commutativity of addition:
   If a is any real number and b is any real number, then $a + b = b + a$.

Multiplication
6. Closure under multiplication:
   For every two real numbers a and b, $(a)(b)$ is a real number.
7. Associativity of multiplication:
   If a is any real number, b is any real number, and c is a real number, then $(ab)c = a(bc)$.
8. Identity element of multiplication:
   If a is any real number, then $a \cdot 1 = 1 \cdot a = a$.
9. Multiplicative inverse:
   If a is any real number and $a \neq 0$, there is a number $\frac{1}{a}$ such that $a\left(\frac{1}{a}\right) = \frac{1}{a}(a) = 1$. The numbers a and $\frac{1}{a}$ are called multiplicative inverses or reciprocals.
10. Commutativity of multiplication:
    If a is any real number and b is any real number, then $a(b) = b(a)$.
11. Distributivity of multiplication over addition:
    If a, b, and c represent real numbers, then $a(b + c) = ab + ac$.

The eleven properties listed above are called the field properties, and any set of elements that possesses all of these properties is called a field.

In addition to the axioms and postulates, certain definitions must be agreed upon. Most definitions can be written as generalizations. You will be more successful in your future work if you learn these definitions.

DEFINITION OF SUBTRACTION:
For real numbers a, b, and c, if $a + b = c$, then $c - b = a$, and if $c - b = a$, then $a + b = c$.

DEFINITION OF DIVISION:
For real numbers a, b, and c, where $b \neq 0$, if $a \cdot b = c$, then $c \div b = a$, and if $c \div b = a$, then $a \cdot b = c$.

Operations with Signed Numbers

Numbers represented on the number line make it easy to recognize two important properties: a direction from zero and a distance from zero. (Recall that the direction from zero is indicated by a plus or minus sign, and that a positive number may be written without a sign.) The other property, the distance from zero, is called the absolute value of the number.

DEFINITION:
The absolute value of a number is its distance from zero on the number line. If x stands for any real number, then the absolute value of x is written $|x|$.

For example:

$|+3| = 3$ Because $+3$ is 3 units from zero.

$|-3| = 3$ Because -3 is 3 units from zero.

Adding signed numbers

Since real numbers have both a distance from zero and a direction from zero, addition and subtraction of two real numbers can be thought of in those terms. There are two distinct rules for adding numbers: one for adding two numbers with the same sign and another for adding a negative number and a positive number.

RULE 1:
If two real numbers have the same sign, that is, both $+$ or $-$, add their absolute values and use their common sign as the sign for the sum.

RULE 2:
If two real numbers have opposite signs, subtract the smaller absolute value from the larger and use the sign of the number farthest from zero as the sign of the difference.

When you have an addition problem, first decide which of these two rules you are dealing with and then apply it.

Example a. Add $-3 + (-4)$ (Rule 1)

$$|-3| \longrightarrow 3 \qquad\qquad -3$$
$$|-4| \longrightarrow \underline{4} \qquad\qquad \underline{+ \ -4}$$
$$7 \qquad\qquad \longrightarrow -7$$

Like signs, so find sum of absolute values.

Common sign is negative, so use negative sign for sum.

Example b. Add $+5 + (+8)$ (Rule 1)

$$|+5| \longrightarrow 5 \qquad\qquad +5$$
$$|+8| \longrightarrow \underline{8} \qquad\qquad \underline{+ \ +8}$$
$$13 \qquad\qquad \longrightarrow +13$$

Like signs, so find sum of absolute values.

Common sign is positive, so use positive sign for the sum.

Example c. Add $-9 + (+6)$ (Rule 2)

$$|-9| \longrightarrow 9 \qquad\qquad -9$$
$$|+6| \longrightarrow \underline{6} \qquad\qquad \underline{+ \ +6}$$
$$3 \longrightarrow \qquad -3$$

Opposite signs, so find difference of absolute values.

Negative number is farther from 0 than positive number, so sum is negative.

Example d. Add $-4 + (+7)$ (Rule 2)

$$|-4| \longrightarrow 4 \qquad\qquad -4$$
$$|+7| \longrightarrow \underline{7} \qquad\qquad \underline{+ \ +7}$$
$$3 \qquad\qquad \longrightarrow +3$$

Opposite signs, so find difference of absolute values.

Positive number is farther from 0 than negative number, so sum is positive.

As you may have noticed, the examples above all contain more than one plus sign. This is true because $+$ and $-$ signs can be used in two ways, either as signs of direction or as signs of operation.

When the signs indicate addition and subtraction, they are called operation signs and are read plus and minus. When the signs indicate direction, they are called direction signs and are read positive and negative. Thus, in the last example, the + sign before the parentheses is an operation sign, while the other two signs are direction signs.

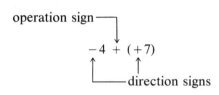

Hence, −4 + (+7) is read: negative 4 plus positive 7. Note: Positive numbers can be written without a + sign. So this example could be written as −4 + (7) or as −4 + 7.

Your Turn

1. +8 + (−5)
2. −5 + (−3)
3. −7 + (−3)
4. +6 + (+2)
5. −12 + (+7)
6. −14 + (+10)
7. −31 + (−21)
8. −18 + (+16)
9. +15 + (−17)
10. +23 + (−28)

(Answers appear at the end of the section.)

Subtracting signed numbers

Now that you have learned to add signed numbers, you can subtract them by using addition. Remember that subtraction is defined in terms of addition. Use the rule for addition to solve any subtraction problem.

RULE:
For all real numbers *a* and *b*,
$$a - b = a + (-b)$$

Thus to subtract *b* from *a* means to add the negative of *b* to *a*. In everyday terms

this rule simply means that in order to subtract one real number from another, you simply add the opposite of the number being subtracted. In the following examples notice that each subtraction is first changed to addition, then the rule for addition is used. This procedure is recommended until you have learned the rules well and practiced a great deal.

Study these examples. Notice that when writing positive numbers, it is not necessary to write the + sign.

Example a. $8 - 5 = 8 + (-5)$
$$= 3$$
Different signs, so find difference and use sign of larger.

Example b. $5 - 8 = 5 + (-8)$
$$= -3$$
Different signs, so find difference and use sign of larger.

Example c. $-9 - 6 = -9 + (-6)$
$$= -15$$
Same sign, so find the sum. Use common sign.

Example d. $13 - (-7) = 13 + 7$
$$= 20$$
Same sign, so find the sum. Use common sign.

Example e. $-4 - (-3) = -4 + 3$
$$= -1$$
Different signs, so find difference and use sign of larger.

Example f. $-4 - (-4) = -4 + 4$
$$= 0$$
Different signs, so find the difference. Zero has no sign.

Example g. $4 - 4 = 4 + (-4)$
$$= 0$$
Different signs, so find the difference. Zero has no sign.

Your Turn

11. $-10 - 2$
12. $10 - 2$
13. $10 - (-2)$
14. $-8 - (-9)$
15. $9 - 15$
16. $-6 - (-6)$
17. $23 - (-4)$
18. $-3 - 3$
19. $-5 - 22$

(*Answers appear at the end of the section.*)

As you become more skillful in adding and subtracting signed numbers, you will notice shortcuts. You may discover that you do not always need to change subtraction problems to addition of the opposite in order to get the answer. If so, you should feel free to use any shortcuts you wish as long as you are able to get the right answers consistently. Of course, you should check with your teacher before using such shortcuts in schoolwork.

Multiplying signed numbers

Products and quotients of signed numbers can be found in the same way as products and quotients of whole numbers. Thus in computing multiplication and division problems involving signed numbers, the main thing to remember is to assign the correct sign for each product or quotient. First consider the rule for multiplication.

RULE:
If the factors have like signs, the sign of the product is positive; if the factors have different signs, the sign of the product is negative.

For example,

$(3)(5) = 15$
$(-3)(-5) = 15$
$(3)(-5) = -15$
$(-3)(5) = -15$

Following is a proof of the above rule.

Prove: If a and b are real numbers, and $a > 0$, $b > 0$, then $(-a)(-b) = ab$
First: Define the equality of two real numbers.
Definition: If a and b are real numbers, then $a = b$ if and only if $a - b = 0$.
Second: Define subtraction.
Definition: If a and b are real numbers, then $a - b = a + (-b)$.

Using these two definitions, the proof can be done in three parts.

1. Prove $-(-a) = a$
   Proof: Show that $-(-a) - a = 0$
   $-(-a) - a = -(-a) + -a$

   > Definition of subtraction

   $= 0$
   > Addition of opposites

   So, $-(-a) = a$
   > Definition of equality

This result can now be used to prove $(-a)(b) = -(ab)$.

2. Prove $(-a)(b) = -(ab)$
   Proof: Proceed as above. To prove two real numbers are equal, show that their difference equals zero.
   $(-a)(b) - [-(ab)]$
   $= (-a)(b) + [-(-ab)]$
   Definition of subtraction

   $= (-a)(b) + ab$
   From Proof 1

   $= (-a)(b) + (a)(b)$
   Factor

   $= (-a + a)(b)$
   Distributive property

   $= 0 \, (b)$
   Addition of opposites

   $= 0$ So, $(-a)(b) = -(ab)$

Now consider the case where both factors are negative.

3. Prove $(-a)(-b) = ab$

Proof:

$(-a)(-b) - (ab)$
$= (-a)(-b) + [-(ab)]$
Definition of subtraction

$= (-a)(-b) + (-a)(b)$
From Proof 2

$= -a(-b + b)$
Distributive property

$= (-a) \cdot 0$
Addition of opposites

$= 0$
So, $(-a)(-b) = ab$

The generalized nature of this proof can be reduced by substituting different values for the variables. Try this on your own using $a = -2$ and $b = 3$.

Dividing signed numbers

You already know from your work with whole numbers that division is the inverse of multiplication. That is, if the product of two numbers is divided by either of the factors, the quotient is the other factor. For example if $(12)(2) = 24$, then $24 \div 12 = 2$. Study the following examples. See if you can detect a pattern.

$(3)(6) = 18 \qquad 18 \div 6 = 3$
$(-3)(-6) = 18 \qquad 18 \div (-6) = -3$
$(-3)(6) = -18 \qquad -18 \div 6 = -3$
$(3)(-6) = -18 \qquad -18 \div (-6) = 3$

The examples lead to rules similar to those for multiplication.

RULES:
The quotient of two numbers with like signs is positive. The quotient of two numbers with unlike signs is negative.

For example,

$(-35) \div (7) = -5$
$(35) \div (-7) = -5$
$(-35) \div (-7) = 5$
$(35) \div (7) = 5$
$(-24) \div (-6) = 4$
$(-24) \div (6) = -4$

Your Turn

20. $(3)(-7)$ 21. $(-8)(2)$
22. $(-4)(6)$ 23. $(-5)(-8)$
24. $-5 \div (-5)$ 25. $20 \div (-4)$
26. $-16 \div (4)$ 27. $-14 \div (-7)$

(Answers appear at the end of the section.)

Order of Operations

Parentheses are often used in algebra to show which operation to do first.

$2 (5 + 4)$

In this example, the parentheses indicate that $5 + 4$ is to be computed first, and then the answer is to be multiplied by 2.

Occasionally a problem involving more than one operation may be written without parentheses.

$3 + 7 \times 2$

There are two ways that you can do this problem. Only one way is correct.

$3 + 7 \times 2 \qquad\qquad 3 + 7 \times 2$
$10 \times 2 = 20 \qquad\quad 3 + 14 = 17$
Wrong   **Correct**

The first solution is marked wrong and the second is marked correct because of a rule that is always followed in algebra.

RULE:
1. **If there are parentheses, first perform the operations inside them.**
2. **Then do any multiplications or divisions.**
3. **Finally, do all additions and subtractions.**

Your Turn

1. 4(8 + 3)
2. −7(2 + 5)
3. 2 + 5 × 6
4. −3 + 2 × 4
5. −4 + 2(−3)
6. − 5 + (−5)(−5)
7. 6(3 − 8) + 1
8. 10(−4 − 9) + 2

(Answers appear at the end of the section.)

Variables and Phrases

In algebra variables are used as abbreviations for names. You can add and subtract only those values that have the same variables. For example, 3 gallons + 5 quarts can be abbreviated as $3g + 5q$. But you cannot add them because each variable represents a different quantity. In order to add, you need to change the problem so that there is one common variable.

Algebraic expressions whose parts are not separated by + or − signs are called terms. Thus $3g$ and $5q$ are terms. Other examples of algebraic terms are: $3a$, b, xy, $2x^2y$ and $-12c$. Each of these expressions contains one term and is called a monomial. An expression containing two terms, such as $x + y$, $2a - 1$, or $a^2 - b$, is called a binomial. Expressions with three terms are called trinomials. Thus, $a + b - c$, $2x^2 + 6y - 16$, and $y^2 - 8x + 16$ are trinomials.

An algebraic expression that is either a monomial or a sum of monomial terms is called a polynomial. Thus, each of the above monomials, binomials, and trinomials is also a polynomial.

Your Turn

List the monomial terms in each of the following polynomials.

1. $x + 3$
2. $a^2 + 6a + 5$
3. $2x^2 + 16x + 12$
4. $a + b + c + d$
5. $3x^2y + 27y^2$

Tell which of the above polynomials are binomials and which are trinomials.

(Answers appear at the end of the section.)

You can perform operations with polynomials in the same way that you do with signed numbers. However, you must follow these rules.

1. Variables cannot be added unless they are the same. You must change them all to the same variable before adding.
2. To add variables, add the numbers (coefficients) in front of the letters.
3. A variable with no number in front of it is the same as the variable with the number 1 in front of it.

Example a.
$$5x + 8x + 9x = (5 + 8 + 9)x$$
$$= 22x$$

Example b.
$$3.5y + 46.2y + (-21.9y) = 27.8y$$

In the next example notice that all the terms with the variable a are added, and then all the terms with b are added. However, you cannot add a and b terms because they represent different things.

Example c.

$6a - 2b - 6b + 4a + 2a$

First group like terms together:

$6a + 4a + 2a - 2b - 6b$

Then combine like terms by adding the coefficients: $12a - 8b$

This cannot be combined any further, so $12a - 8b$ is the answer.

As you can see all the rules that you learned in your earlier study of signed numbers also apply when working with polynomials.

Your Turn

Simplify.

6. $4a + 7 + 6a$
7. $3a + 5b + (-5a) + (-7a)$
8. $-10x + 7y - 5x + 3y + 9x$
9. $x + y + z - 2x - 3y - 4z$
   (Note: x means $1x$)
10. $-\frac{2}{3}a + 3\frac{1}{2}a - 1\frac{1}{3}b$

(Answers appear at the end of the section.)

The polynomials in the exercises above are often referred to as number phrases. A number phrase is simply a phrase that names a number. A number phrase containing a variable, such as $x + 5$, is called an open phrase because the number it expresses is open to various possible values. For example, if x is replaced by 2, the resulting expression is $2 + 5$, or 7. But if x is replaced by -5, the resulting expression is $-5 + 5$, or 0.

In algebra it is often necessary to translate word phrases into number phrases and vice versa. The table shows some examples of such translations.

By placing one of the listed symbols between any two numbers or open phrases, you can construct a number sentence.

Word phrase	Open phrase
A number	n
A number plus 5 A number increased by 5 A number added to 5 5 more than a number A number augmented by 5	$n + 5$
A number minus 3 A number less 3 3 less than a number Take 3 from a number. Subtract 3 from a number.	$n - 3$
The product of 2 and a number A number multiplied by 2 2 times a number	$2n$
The quotient of a number and 4 A number divided by 4 $\frac{1}{4}$ of a number	$\frac{n}{4}$ or $\frac{1}{4}n$

$=$	is equal to
$\neq$	is not equal to
$<$	is less than
$>$	is greater than
$\leq$	is less than or equal to
$\geq$	is greater than or equal to

These symbols act as verbs. Using these symbols you can write open sentences that can be judged true or false. The subject of an open sentence is the name of the number, and the truth or falsity of the sentence depends upon the number selected as the subject.

Your Turn

Write an open sentence for each of the following.

11. Three times a number is equal to 15.
12. A number that is divided by 2 is less than 10.
13. Fifteen plus a number is greater than or equal to 5.

14. Four less than a number is not equal to 7.
15. Six is less than or equal to a number plus 3.

(Answers appear at the end of the section.)

Evaluating Algebraic Expressions

When the variable in an algebraic expression has been replaced by numbers (substitution), the expression can be evaluated. The order in which the operations should be done is the same as discussed earlier when computing with signed numbers.

Substitution of numbers is used most often with formulas. A formula is just a way of expressing a rule by using algebraic symbols and operations. A formula commonly used is the one for finding the perimeter of a rectangle.

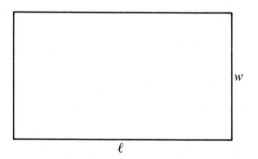

ℓ

The formula is $P = 2\ell + 2w$. Therefore, a rectangle whose length is 28 cm and width is 12 cm has a perimeter of

$$
\begin{aligned}
P &= 2\ell + 2w \\
&= 2(28) + 2(12) \\
&= 56 + 24 \\
&= 80 \text{ cm}
\end{aligned}
$$

The key idea in evaluation is that you must work carefully step by step. By re-membering the following hints you can reduce the possibility of making errors in computation.

1. If the expression is a multiplication, substitute the number values and then multiply.

Evaluate: $5xy$, where $x = -2$, $y = 4$
$$
\begin{aligned}
& 5xy \\
&= 5(-2)(4) \\
&= -40
\end{aligned}
$$

2. If the expression is a sum or difference of terms, find a numerical value for each term first, then add or subtract the terms.

Evaluate: $3a^2 - b$,
where $a = -2$, $b = -3$
$$
\begin{aligned}
& 3a^2 - b \\
&= 3(-2)(-2) - (-3) \\
&= 3(4) - (-3) \\
&= 12 + 3 \\
&= 15
\end{aligned}
$$

Notice that if the expression has a square or other power of a given variable, you must find the value of that factor first and then multiply.

Your Turn

Evaluate each phrase.

1. $3ab$, where $a = 2$ and $b = 7$
2. $x - y$, where x is 7 and y is -3
3. $2c + 4d$, where c is 5 and d is -1
4. $3m^2 + m - 2$, where m is -4

(Answers appear at the end of the section.)

Solving Equations

An algebraic equation is commonly called an open sentence that uses the symbol equal. In other words, an equation is a quick way of saying that the symbols before and after the equals sign represent the same number.

In the equation $3x = 18$, the expression on the left of the equals sign is called the left member, and the expression on the right of the equals sign is called the right member. The variable x, whose value is to be found, is called the unknown. The root of an equation is a value of the unknown that, when substituted in the equation, makes one member equal to another. The process of finding the root is called solving the equation.

To solve equations, you need to understand and use two basic rules.

RULE 1:
If equal quantities are added to or subtracted from both sides of an equation, then the solution does not change.

$$\begin{aligned} \text{If} \quad & a = b, \\ \text{then} \quad & a + c = b + c. \\ \text{Also if} \quad & a = b, \\ \text{then} \quad & a - c = b - c. \end{aligned}$$

This rule enables you to solve equations that contain addition and subtraction operations.

Example a. Solve: $x + 5 = 12$
$$\begin{aligned} x + 5 &= 12 \\ x + 5 - 5 &= 12 - 5 \end{aligned}$$
Subtract 5 from each side.
$$x = 7$$
So, the solution is 7.

Example b. Solve: $x - 3 = 11$
$$\begin{aligned} x - 3 &= 11 \\ x - 3 + 3 &= 11 + 3 \end{aligned}$$
Add 3 to each side.
$$x = 14$$
So, the solution is 14.

Sometimes when solving an equation, it is necessary to use a rule more than once. Study this example:

Example c.
Solve: $-4x + 5 + 2x = 20 - 3x$
To solve an example of this type, first combine like terms and then add $3x$ to both sides. This will make x disappear from the right side of the equation.

$$\begin{aligned} -4x + 2x + 5 &= 20 - 3x \\ -2x + 5 &= 20 - 3x \end{aligned}$$
Combine like terms.

$$-2x + 3x + 5 = 20 - 3x + 3x$$
Add $3x$ to each side.

$$\begin{aligned} x + 5 &= 20 \\ x + 5 - 5 &= 20 - 5 \end{aligned}$$
Subtract 5 from each side.

$$x = 15$$

You can check your work by substituting the solution into the original equation.

Check:
$$\begin{aligned} -4x + 5 + 2x &= 20 - 3x \\ -4(15) + 5 + 2(15) &\stackrel{?}{=} 20 - 3(15) \\ -60 + 5 + 30 &\stackrel{?}{=} 20 - 45 \\ -25 &= -25 \end{aligned}$$
It checks.

RULE 2:
If both sides of an equation are multiplied or divided by the same non-zero number, then the solution does not change.

$$\begin{aligned} \text{If} \quad & a = b \\ \text{then} \quad & ac = bc \\ \text{If} \quad & a = b \\ \text{then} \quad & \frac{a}{c} = \frac{b}{c} \text{ if } c \neq 0. \end{aligned}$$

This rule enables you to solve equations that involve multiplication and division operations.

Example d. Solve: $5x = 65$

$5x = 65$

$\dfrac{5x}{5} = \dfrac{65}{5}$ Divide each side by 5.

$x = 13$

Example e. Solve: $\dfrac{x}{4} = 16$

$\dfrac{x}{4} = 16$

$\dfrac{x}{4} \cdot (4) = 16(4)$ Multiply each
              side by 4.

$x = 64$

The next two examples illustrate the use of both rules in solving equations.

Example f. Solve: $3x - 5 = 7$

$3x - 5 = 7$

$3x - 5 + 5 = 7 + 5$

            Add 5 to each side.

$3x = 12$

$\dfrac{3x}{3} = \dfrac{12}{3}$

            Divide each side by 3.

$x = 4$

So, the solution is 4.

Check:

$3x - 5 = 7$

$3(4) - 5 \overset{?}{=} 7$

$12 - 5 \overset{?}{=} 7$

$7 = 7$ It checks.

Example g. Solve: $2x + \dfrac{3}{4} = \dfrac{5}{8}$

$2x + \dfrac{3}{4} = \dfrac{5}{8}$

$2x + \dfrac{3}{4} - \dfrac{3}{4} = \dfrac{5}{8} - \dfrac{3}{4}$ Subtract $\dfrac{3}{4}$
                      from each side.

$2x = -\dfrac{1}{8}$

$\dfrac{2x}{2} = -\dfrac{1}{8} \div 2$

            Divide each side by 2.

$x = -\dfrac{1}{16}$

As you can see, when more than one operation is used in a problem, the first rule is used to undo any additions or subtractions and the second rule is used to undo any multiplications or divisions. Notice also that if a variable is being multiplied by a number like -5, you must divide by the -5 so that you end up with just the variable on one side of the equation. Remember that in the final answer the variable should never be left with a negative sign, such as $-x$. It does not matter on which side of the equals sign the variable is located. Most people prefer to have the variable on the left because they read from left to right. But, it really does not matter because $x = 5$ means $5 = x$.

Other equations that require several steps for their solution are equations that contain parentheses. Equations with parentheses all require simplification before the above rules can be used.

Example h. Solve: $3(2x + 4) = 4x - 2$

$3(2x + 4) = 4x - 2$

$6x + 12 = 4x - 2$

$6x - 4x + 12 = 4x - 4x - 2$

Use the distributive property to simplify left side of the equation.

$2x + 12 = -2$

$2x + 12 - 12 = -2 - 12$

$2x = -14$

$x = -7$

Your Turn

Solve each of the following equations. Be sure to check your work.

1. $-3x = 27$
2. $x - 8 = -21$
3. $2y + 1 = 15$
4. $4(a + 2) = 2a + 8$
5. $2x = 4 - 3(x - 2)$

6. $-\dfrac{w}{8} = 4$

7. $5x + 6 = 3x - 6$

8. $4(2b + 3) = -3(b - 1) + 20$
9. $-5(r - 3) - 2(2r + 1) = -8$
10. $3x - 1 = 7 - 4(6 - 2x)$

(Answers appear at the end of the section.)

Applications

In this section you will work with word problems. When working word problems it is very important to read the problem carefully. You may have to read a problem several times before you understand it. This is not unusual. A review of the problem-solving steps that were first introduced in the whole number section can be helpful. Here is a modified version of those steps.

Read
Read the problem carefully. Decide what is given and what is to be found.
Understand
Analyze the information. Look for any special words or situations that can aid in understanding the problem.
Plan
Select a variable to represent what is to be found. Write an equation to show the relationship.
Solve
Solve the equation. Ask yourself if the answer you get is really the solution to the problem.
Check
Check your result to make sure that the answer satisfies the requirements of the problem.

Study the following examples and then try solving the problems in the exercises that follow.

One of the most common types of problems in algebra involves finding a specific number.

Example a. The difference between two numbers is 105. The smaller number is 65. What is the larger number?

You are asked to find a number. Let n stand for the number and then translate the problem.

The difference between a number and 65 is 105.
$$n - 65 = 105$$

Now solve the equation.
$$n - 65 = 105$$
$$n = 170$$

Since $170 - 65 = 105$, then 170 is the correct number because it satisfies the equation.

Example b. The sum of two numbers is 82. One number is twelve less than the other. Find the two numbers.

In this problem you are asked to find two numbers. Let n stand for one number and $n - 12$ stand for the other. Then translate the problem.

(First Number) +
(Second Number) is 82.
$$n + n - 12 = 82$$

Solve the equation.

$$n + n - 12 = 82$$
$$2n - 12 = 82$$
$$2n = 94$$
$$n = 47$$

So, 47 is one number and $47 - 12$ is the other. The two numbers are 47 and 35.

Many problems involve the use of formulas. One often-used formula is the distance formula:

Distance = Rate × Time
$$d = r \times t$$

However, to solve certain types of distance problems, you need to use this formula along with other concepts that you have learned in your work with algebra. Consider this example.

Example c. Two buses leave the same city and travel in opposite directions. One of the buses averages 12 mi/h (miles per hour) less than the other. After 3 hours the buses are 324 miles apart. What is the average speed of each bus?

Let n = the number of miles per hour for the rate of the first bus. Set up a table to show the relationships.

Rate × Time = Distance

	(mi/h)	(h)	(mi)
First bus	n	3	$3n$
Second bus	$n - 12$	3	$3(n - 12)$

Now write an equation.

$$3(n - 12) + 3n = 324$$
$$3n - 36 + 3n = 324$$
$$6n - 36 = 324$$
$$6n = 360$$
$$n = 60$$

So, the first bus has an average speed of 60 mi/h.
The second bus has an average speed of $(n - 12)$, or 48 mi/h.

Check:

Distance of first bus = 3(60) or 180
Distance of second bus = 3(60 − 12)
or 144
Total distance = 324

Another common problem type in algebra is the mixture problem.

Example d. How many pounds of cashew nuts, worth $0.90 per pound, must be mixed with 20 lb of peanuts, worth $0.80 per pound, to make a mixture worth $0.85 per pound?

Let n stand for the number of pounds of cashews to be mixed with the $0.80 per pound peanuts. To see the relationships more clearly, it is suggested that you set up a table.

	Cashews	**Peanuts**	**Mixture**
No. lb	n	20	$20 + n$
$ per lb	$0.90	$0.80	$0.85
Value in $	$(0.90)(n)$	$(0.80)(20)$	$(0.85)(20 + n)$

The weight of the cashews plus the weight of the peanuts equals the total weight of the mixture. Therefore the weight of the mixture is $20 + n$.

Likewise, the value of the cashews plus the value of the peanuts equals the total value of the mixture. Thus the value of the mixture is $0.85(20 + n)$.

Now write the equation and solve it.

$$(0.80)(20) + 0.90n = 0.85(20 + n)$$
$$16 + 0.90n = 17 + 0.85n$$
$$1600 + 90n = 1700 + 85n$$
$$5n = 100$$
$$n = 20$$

So, 20 pounds of cashew nuts are needed.

Check:

The value of 20 lb
of cashews @ $0.90 = $18.00
The value of 20 lb
of peanuts @ $0.80 = $16.00
Total value of 40 lb = $34.00
The value of 40 lb @ $0.85 = $34.00

Age problems are also common in algebra.

Example e. Barbara is five years older than Diane. Two years ago Barbara's age was six times Diane's age. Find the age of each girl now.

If n = Diane's age now, then this means that Barbara is $n + 5$ years old. If Diane is n years old now, then two years ago she was $n - 2$ years old. If Barbara is $n + 5$ years old now, then two years ago she was $n + 5 - 2 = n + 3$ years old.

Displaying these relationships in a table will help you understand the problem better. Arrange the people in rows and the different times in columns.

	Age now	Age two years ago
Diane	n	$n - 2$
Barbara	$n + 5$	$n + 3$

From reading the problem again, it is also clear that two years ago Diane's age was six times Barbara's age. So writing an equation for this gives:

Barbara's age = Six times
Diane's age
$$n + 3 = 6(n - 2)$$
$$n + 3 = 6n - 12$$
$$12 + 3 = 6n - n$$
$$15 = 5n$$
$$3 = n$$

Thus, Diane is 3 years old and Barbara is 8 years old. Check the answers.

Your Turn

1. The difference between two numbers is 91. The larger number is 213. Find the smaller number.

2. Four more than twice a number is 76. What is the number?

3. Two airplanes leave at the same time from the same airport and travel in opposite directions. One plane averages 120 mi/h less than the other. After $2\frac{1}{2}$ hours the planes are 2250 miles apart. What is the average speed of each plane?

4. How many pounds of hybrid seed, retailing for $3.25 per pound, should be mixed with 50 lb of regular seed, retailing for $1.75 per pound, to make a mixture worth $2.25 per pound?

5. A man is twice as old as his daughter. Together the sum of their ages is 63. What are their ages?

6. George is twice as old as his sister. Four years ago he was four times as old as his sister. Find their ages now.

(*Answers appear at the end of the section.*)

Operations with Polynomials

Multiplication

In Section 1 of this part you used the fact that multiplication with whole numbers can be thought of as repeated addition. A similar relationship exists between exponents and repeated multiplication. For example, a is a double factor in $a \cdot a$ and 3 occurs as a factor two times in the product $3 \cdot 3$. These products are also called powers and could be written as $a \cdot a = a^2$ and $3 \cdot 3 = 3^2$, respectively. In general, any power can be represented by a symbol of the form a^n, where a stands for any repeated factor. Further, any factor that shows no exponent is considered to have an exponent of one (1). So, $a = a^1$ and $4b = 4^1b^1$. A factor with an exponent of zero is defined as being equal to one (1). So, $a^0 = 1$ and $4^0 = 1$. In algebra the following rules are used when operating with monomials.

RULE 1:
The power of a product is the product of the powers.

$(ab)^s = a^s b^s$

Example a. $(4a)^2 = (4a)(4a)$
$$= (4 \cdot 4)(a \cdot a)$$
$$= 4^2 a^2$$
$$= 16a^2$$
The numeral may also be left in exponential form.

Example b. $(-3b)^2 = (-3b)(-3b)$
$$= (-3 \cdot -3)(b \cdot b)$$
$$= (-3)^2 b^2$$
$$= 9b^2$$
Note that $(-3a)^2$ and $-3a^2$ have different meanings, so the parentheses are very important: $(-3a)^2$ means $(-3a)(-3a)$ and $-3a^2$ means $(-3)(a)(a)$.

RULE 2:
To multiply two expressions with the same base, add the exponents and keep the common base.

$(a^r)(a^s) = a^{r+s}$

Example a. $(x^2)(x^3) = x^{2+3}$
Add exponents.
$$= x^5$$

Example b. $(a^2b^5)(ab^4)$
$$= a^2 \cdot a^1 \cdot b^5 \cdot b^4$$
Rearrange.
$$= (a^{2+1})(b^{5+4})$$
Add exponents.
$$= a^3 b^9$$

RULE 3:
A power raised to another power is the base raised to the product of the powers.

$(a^r)^s = a^{r \cdot s}$

Example a. $(x^2)^3 = x^{2 \cdot 3}$
Multiply the powers.
$$= x^6$$

Example b. $(4x^2y)^4 = (4^{1 \cdot 4})(x^{2 \cdot 4})(y^{1 \cdot 4})$
$$= 4^4 x^8 y^4$$
$$= 256 x^8 y^4$$

Division

Since division is the inverse operation of multiplication, the properties of exponents for division are similar to the properties for multiplication with exponents. In general, the following rule applies.

RULE 4:
In division with the same base, subtract the exponent in the denominator from the exponent in the numerator and raise the base to the exponent that results.

$$\frac{a^r}{a^s} = a^{r-s}$$

Example a. $\dfrac{y^6}{y^2} = y^{6-2}$ or y^4

Example b. $\dfrac{y^4}{y^7} = y^{4-7}$
$$= y^{-3}$$
Notice the negative exponent.

In the last example the result contained a negative exponent. If the exercise is simplified in the following manner, you can see the meaning of a negative exponent.

$$\frac{y^4}{y^7} = \frac{yyyy}{yyyyyyy}$$

Since $\frac{y}{y} = 1$, you can simplify this expression.

$$= \frac{1}{yyy}$$

$$= \frac{1}{y^3}$$

Since $y^4 \div y^7$ is equal to y^{-3} and also $\frac{1}{y^3}$, y^{-3} must be equal to $\frac{1}{y^3}$. A negative exponent means that the base raised to that positive power is used for the denominator of a unit fraction.

$$a^{-b} = \frac{1}{a^b}$$

Square roots

Since $a \cdot a = a^2$, then $\sqrt{a^2} = a$. The symbol $\sqrt{}$ is called a radical sign and indicates a number that when multiplied by itself yields the number under the radical sign. In the first example, $\sqrt{a^2} = a$, because $a \cdot a = a^2$. However $(-a)(-a)$ also equals a^2. Therefore $\sqrt{a} = +a$ or $-a$, which is often written as $\pm a$. If $a^2 = 4$, then $\sqrt{4} = \pm 2$ because $2 \cdot 2 = 4$ and $(-2)(-2) = 4$. However, if $a^2 = 2$, there is no rational number that represents $\sqrt{2}$. The square root of two is an irrational number. When working with variables, divide the exponent by 2 to find the square root of a monomial.

$\sqrt{4a^2b^4}$ Think:

$$\sqrt{4} = 2; \sqrt{a^2} = a;$$

$\sqrt{4a^2b^4} = \pm 2ab^2$ $\sqrt{b^4} = b^2$

$\sqrt{2x^6}$ Think:

$\sqrt{2}$ is irrational;

$\sqrt{2x^6} = \pm x^3\sqrt{2}$ $\sqrt{x^6} = x^3$

Notice that if the square root of the whole number is irrational, for now it is left in the radical form.

Using the above rules, you are now ready to perform some basic operations with monomials. Consider multiplication, for example. In multiplication of monomials, first rewrite the products using the commutative and associative properties. Simplify by multiplying coefficients and adding exponents of like bases.

$$(-4x^3)(5x^4) = (-4 \cdot 5)(x^3 \cdot x^4) = -20x^7$$

In division remember to divide coefficients and subtract exponents.

Example:

$$\frac{21a^2b^3}{7a^5b} = \frac{21}{7} \cdot \frac{a^2}{a^5} \cdot \frac{b^3}{b}$$

$$= 3(a^{-3})(b^2)$$

$$= \frac{3b^2}{a^3}$$

(Notice that the negative exponent is not left in the answer.)

It is not desirable to make generalizations based on only one example. Later, in the intermediate algebra section, you will learn more about procedures for operations with polynomials.

Your Turn

Simplify and combine terms. Do not leave numerals in exponential form. Do not leave any negative exponents.

1. $a \cdot a \cdot a \cdot a$
2. $\sqrt{16a^4b^2}$
3. $(-5x)^3 \cdot x$
4. $-5x^3 \cdot x$
5. $(3x^5)(2x^3)$
6. $(a^6)^3$
7. $(-2a^2b)^4$
8. $(5a^3b)(-3ab^2)$
9. $\frac{14x^3y^2}{7x^2}$
10. $\frac{30x^6y^2}{6x^4y^7}$

(*Answers appear at the end of the section.*)

Answers

Number Systems (pp. 350–352)

1. $+1$ 2. -8 3. $+7$ 4. $+9$ 5. -3.5 6. $+2\frac{1}{2}$ 7. $+1.3$ 8. $-\frac{7}{8}$

Operations with Signed Numbers (pps. 354–357)

1. $+3$ 2. -8 3. -10 4. $+8$ 5. -5 6. -4 7. -52 8. -2
9. -2 10. -5 11. -12 12. 8 13. 12 14. 1 15. -6 16. 0
17. 27 18. -6 19. -27 20. -21 21. -16 22. -24 23. 40
24. 1 25. -5 26. -4 27. 2

Order of Operations (pp. 357–358)

1. 44 2. -49 3. 32 4. 5 5. -10 6. 20 7. -29 8. -128

Variables and Phrases (pp. 358–360)

1. x; 3; binomial   2. a^2; $6a$; 5; trinomial   3. $2x^2$; $16x$; 12; trinomial   4. a; b; c; d
5. $3x^2y$; $27y^2$; binomial   6. $7 + 10a$ 7. $-9a + 5b$ 8. $-6x + 10y$
9. $-x - 2y - 3z$ 10. $2\frac{5}{6}a - 1\frac{1}{3}b$ 11. $3n = 15$ 12. $\frac{n}{2} < 10$ 13. $15 + n \geq 5$
14. $n - 4 \neq 7$ 15. $6 \geq n + 3$

Evaluating Algebraic Expressions (p. 360)

1. 42 2. 10 3. 6 4. 42

Solving Equations (pp. 360–363)

1. $x = -9$ 2. $x = -13$ 3. $y = 7$ 4. $a = 0$ 5. $x = 2$ 6. $w = -32$
7. $x = -6$ 8. $b = 1$ 9. $r = 2\frac{1}{3}$ 10. $x = 3\frac{1}{5}$

Applications (pp. 363–365)

1. $n = 122$ 2. $n = 36$ 3. $s_1 = 510$ mi/h; $s_2 = 390$ mi/h   4. $h = 25$ pounds

5. $m = 42$ years; $g = 21$ years   6. $g = 12$ years; $s = 6$ years

Operations with Polynomials (pp. 365–367)

1. a^4 2. $4a^2b$ 3. $-125x^4$ 4. $-5x^4$ 5. $6x^8$ 6. a^{18} 7. $16a^8b^4$

8. $-15a^4b^3$ 9. $2xy^2$ 10. $\dfrac{5x^2}{y^5}$

Section 8

Intermediate Algebra

You were introduced to algebra in the last section. This section will broaden your knowledge. First, a review and expansion of the significance of this branch of mathematics would be useful.

Although some problems that are classified as algebra problems were solved by the ancient Egyptians and Babylonians, very little was accomplished with algebra in early times. Most of what is now known has been developed fairly recently. Negative numbers were not treated as being valid numbers in Western mathematics until the sixteenth century, although they were recognized by Chinese mathematicians at least as early as 200 B.C.

Algebra began to develop with the flourishing of Islamic culture among the Arabs. The name "algebra" comes from the title of a work by the mathematician Muhammad ibn Musa al-Khowarizmi who lived in the early part of the ninth century. He wrote a work on algebra with the title *Hisab al-jabr wal-muqabala,* and the term *al-jabr* was taken and westernized to become *algebra*. It referred to all of the equation-solving aspects of algebra. Another term used frequently today comes from the name of his book. The title was written *liber Algorismi* (book of al-Khowarizmi), from which the word *algorism*, or more commonly, *algorithm*, came.

A deep interest in problems relating to solution of equations was developed in the Italian city-states in the sixteenth century, and important advances were made. By the seventeenth century, it was seen that algebra and geometry could be blended together, and coordinate geometry was developed (independently) by René Descartes and Pierre de Fermat of France. New developments were made in both algebra and geometry as mathematicians adopted a fresh point of view.

Mathematics benefited greatly from the invention of printing. Information could be spread more quickly and more widely than before. Also, the printing of material encouraged the agreement to use a standard notation that would be understood by all who worked in the field, regardless of country or language.

If you picked up a mathematics text for students who lived in another country, you would find that you could understand many of the problems because the common algebraic language is used. The use of this "universal language" is in no small part responsible for the tremendous growth of mathematics in the last few centuries.

With the basic techniques that are used in algebra, you can solve a variety of problems. Once you translate the special quantities and relationships into mathematical terms and sentences, the techniques used are standard.

Expressions with Parentheses

When simplifying expressions with parentheses, use the following steps.

1. Do all the work indicated inside.
2. Remove the parentheses by performing the addition or subtraction indicated.
3. Simplify the resulting expression.
4. Check your work.

Example:

$5 + (6x - 2 - x)$	Given.
$5 + (5x - 2)$	Combine like terms in parentheses.
$5 + 5x - 2$	Remove parentheses (terms added).
$5x + 3$	Combine like terms.
Check:	One method of
Let $x = 3$	checking an expres-
$5 + (18 - 2 - 3)$	sion is by substitu-
$5 + 13$	ting a value for x
18	in the original and
Let $x = 3$	final expressions;
$15 + 3$	value of expression should not change.
18	Both expressions have value 18 when $x = 3$.

Important: In removing parentheses, you must observe whether an addition or a subtraction is indicated (plus sign or minus sign before the parentheses). In the example given, there was an addition (plus sign), so the parentheses could simply be dropped.

If there is a subtraction indicated (minus sign before the parentheses), add another step to the above three steps.

1a. Label each term with the proper number sign, change all number signs of terms within the parentheses, and change the subtraction preceding the parentheses to addition.

You subtract by adding the inverse.

Example:
Given: $2 - (x - 7)$

$2 \mp (+x - +7)$	Change to show
$2 \oplus (\ominus x - \ominus 7)$	addition of inverse.
$2 - x + 7$	Now drop
$-x + 9$	parentheses.

If the parentheses indicate a multiplication, distribute the term preceding the parentheses over the terms within the parentheses, using the distributive property.

Example:
$2(x - 7)$

$2 \cdot (x - 7)$

$2x - 14$

If a binomial is in parentheses preceding a second binomial, perform a double distribution.

Example:
$(x + 3)(x - 7)$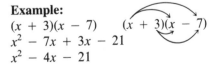
$x^2 - 7x + 3x - 21$
$x^2 - 4x - 21$

This technique is sometimes referred to as the F-O-I-L method (first-outer-inner-last). It is a good way to remember the double distribution technique.

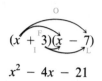

$$x^2 - 4x - 21$$

When you have done a number of these double distributions, you will probably be able to combine the two x terms mentally and just write the result. (Remember, though, not to use any shortcut technique until you feel ready for it.)

Solving linear equations

Use the above technique for removing parentheses to help solve a linear equation.

Example:

$4(2x - 1) = 12 - 3(x - 2)$
  Given.

$8x - 4 = 12 - 3x + 6$
  Perform indicated distribution.

$8x - 4 = 18 - 3x$
  Combine like terms.

$$\underline{ \; 3x \quad = \quad 3x }$$
$11x - 4 = 18$
  Add $3x$ to both members.

$$\underline{ \; 4 = 4 }$$
$11x = 22$
  Add 4 to both members.

$x = 2$
  Multiply each member by $\frac{1}{11}$.

Check:

$4(2x - 1) = 12 - 3(x - 2)$
  Substitute 2 for x

$4(2 \cdot 2 - 1) \overset{?}{=} 12 - 3(2 - 2)$
$4 \cdot 3 \overset{?}{=} 12 - 3 \cdot 0$
$12 = 12$ It checks.

Applications

Problems can be solved with these techniques. Given that the three angles of a triangle have measures of $(x - 3)°$, $(x + 7)°$, and $2x°$, find the measure of each angle.

1. *Read and understand.* You are given algebraic terms for the value of each angle measure.
2. *Plan.* You know from your work in geometry that the sum of the measures of the angles of a triangle is 180°. Add the given measures and set the sum equal to 180°.
3. *Solve.*

   $(x - 3) + (x + 7) + 2x = 180$
   $x - 3 + x + 7 + 2x = 180$
   $4x + 4 = 180$
   $4x = 176$
   $x = 44°$
   $x - 3 = 41°; x + 7 = 51°; 2x = 88°$

4. *Check.*

   $41° + 51° + 88° \overset{?}{=} 180°$
   $180° = 180°$ It checks.

Polynomials in One Variable

Expressions with more than one term are called polynomials. Polynomials may contain one or more variables. $x - 4$, $3x - 16$, and $x^3 - 3x^2 + 18x + 25$ are three polynomial expressions in one variable. The degree of a polynomial is the highest power of a term.

$x^5 - 4x^3 + 7$ has degree 5.
$x^3 + 2$ has degree 3.

$x - 2y$ and $2x^2 + xy + 3y$ are polynomials in two variables. The degree of the first expression is 1, and of the second expression, 2. The polynomial $3x^4y^3 - 5x^2y + 12x + 6$ has degree 7, as the term with the highest degree is the first term: $4 + 3 = 7$. Note that when a term has more than one variable, the powers of the variables are added.

Polynomials with two and three terms appear so frequently, they have special names. A polynomial of two terms is called a binomial, and of three terms, a trinomial. The terms of a polynomial are generally arranged in descending or ascending order. When a polynomial has terms with more than one variable, the terms are arranged in ascending or descending order of one of the variables. $x^3 - 4x^2 - 8$ is a polynomial written in descending order.

$2 - 5xy^3 - 2x^3y^2 + 9x^4y^2$ is a polynomial written in ascending order with respect to the variable x.

To add polynomials, combine like terms. Like terms are terms that contain the same variables of the same power.

$8x^3$	$-2x^3$	like terms
$8x^3$	$8x^2$	unlike terms
$-2x^2y$	$4x^2y$	like terms
$-2x^2y$	$4x^2y^2$	unlike terms

Example:
Add $5x^3 - 3x^2 + 15$ and $x^3 - 4x - 2$. Write the result in descending order.

$$\begin{array}{r} 5x^3 - 3x^2 \quad\quad + 15 \\ + \ x^3 \quad\quad - 4x - 2 \\ \hline 6x^3 - 3x^2 - 4x + 13 \end{array}$$

To subtract polynomials, change the signs of the subtrahend and proceed as in addition. In other words, add the additive inverse of the subtrahend.

Example: From $5x^3 - 3x^2 + 15$, subtract $x^3 - 4x - 2$. (*Hint:* Be careful to identify the subtrahend. Here, $(x^3 - 4x - 2)$ is the subtrahend.)

$$\begin{array}{r} 5x^3 - 3x^2 \quad\quad + 15 \\ -x^3 \quad\quad + 4x + 2 \\ \hline 4x^3 - 3x^2 + 4x + 17 \end{array}$$

Remember that to subtract you add the opposite. ←Change the sign of each term and add.

Note that the terms are arranged so that they will appear in descending order in the result.

Your Turn

1. Add $3x^3 + x^2 - 1$ and $x^3 - 5x^2 - 4x + 3$.
2. Subtract $5x^2 - x - 9$ from $8x^3 + 2$.
3. Add $6x^4 + 3x - 6$ and $5x^3 - 2x + 6$.
4. Subtract $7x^2 - 2x + 3$ from $9x^3 + 2x^2 - 3x$.

(*Answers appear at the end of the section.*)

To multiply a polynomial by a monomial, distribute the monomial over the polynomial.

Example:
Multiply $(3x^2 - 2x + 5)$ by 4.

$4(3x^2 - 2x + 5)$
$4(3x^2) + 4(-2x) + 4(5)$
$12x^2 - 8x + 20$

The second step may be performed mentally and need not be recorded.

Your Turn

5. Multiply $(x^3 - 4x^2 - 5x + 9)$ by 5.
6. Multiply $(4x^3 - 6x + 3)$ by $-5x$.

(*Answers appear at the end of the section.*)

To multiply a polynomial by a binomial, distribute each term of the binomial over the polynomial.

Example:
Multiply $(3x^2 - 4x + 2)$ by $(x - 2)$.

$$(x - 2)(3x^2 - 4x + 2)$$
$$= x(3x^2) + x(-4x) + x(2) +$$
$$(-2)(3x^2) + (-2)(-4x) + (-2)(2)$$
$$= 3x^3 - 4x^2 + 2x - 6x^2 + 8x - 4$$

Now combine like terms and arrange the terms in descending order.

$$= 3x^3 - 10x^2 + 10x - 4$$

Your Turn

7. Multiply $(2x^3 - 9x + 12)$ by $(x - 3)$.
8. Multiply $(4x^2 - 2x + 3)$ by $(4 - x)$.
9. Multiply $(5x^3 + 2x^2 + 3x)$ by $(x^2 + 4)$.

(Answers appear at the end of the section.)

In general, to multiply two polynomials, distribute the terms of one polynomial over the terms of the other polynomial, then combine terms and arrange in descending order.

Example:
Multiply $(x^2 - x + 2)$ by $(2x^2 + x - 4)$

$$(x^2 - x + 2)(2x^2 + x - 4)$$
$$= x^2(2x^2 + x - 4) + (-x)(2x^2 + x - 4)$$
$$+ 2(2x^2 + x - 4)$$
$$= 2x^4 + x^3 - 4x^2 - 2x^3 - x^2 + 4x +$$
$$4x^2 + 2x - 8$$
$$= 2x^4 - x^3 - x^2 + 6x - 8$$

Your Turn

Multiply. Combine like terms and arrange terms in descending order in product.

10. $(3x^2 - x + 2)(2x^3 - 3)$
11. $(5x^2 - 4x)(2x^2 + 3x + 4)$
12. $(7x + 6)(7x + 6)$

(Answers appear at the end of the section.)

Special Products

There are some special products that appear frequently. It is useful to identify them.

Square of a binomial

Suppose you had a square like the one shown below. Remember that to find the area of a square you multiply the length of one side by itself.

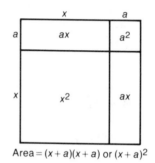

Area $= (x + a)(x + a)$ or $(x + a)^2$

Note that the monomial written inside each smaller rectangle shows the area of that rectangle. If you add the area measures of the rectangles, you will find the area of the large square.

$$\text{Area} = x^2 + ax + ax + a^2$$
$$= x^2 + 2ax + a^2$$
Therefore, $(x + a)^2 = x^2 + 2ax + a^2$

This can also be shown algebraically.
Suppose that $a = 3$; then you can multiply to find $(x + 3)$.

$$(x + 3)^2 = (x + 3)(x + 3)$$
$$= x^2 + 6x + 9$$

Note the pattern:

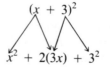

$$x^2 + 2(3x) + 3^2$$

You can state the pattern in words: The square of a binomial equals the sum of the square of the first term, twice the product of the two terms, and the square of the second term.

Watch the signs. For the binomial $(x - 3)^2$, think: $[x + (-3)]^2$.
$$(x - 3)^2 = x^2 + 2(-3x) + (-3)^2$$
$$= x^2 - 6x + 9$$

Your Turn

1. $(x - 5)^2$ 2. $(x + 6)^2$
3. $(2x - 3)^2$ 4. $(5x + 1)^2$

(Answers appear at the end of the section.)

Sum and difference of terms

Another special product that is of interest is the product of the sum and difference of two terms.

Example:
$$(x + 2)(x - 2)$$
$$= (x^2 - 2x + 2x - 4)$$
$$= x^2 - 4$$

Study the pattern: The product of the sum and difference of two terms is the square of the first term minus the square of the second term. Note that when all the terms in the product are written out, the second and third terms in the expression add to zero.

Your Turn

5. $(x - 8)(x + 8)$
6. $(x - 1)(x + 1)$
7. $(2x + 3)(2x - 3)$
8. $(9x - 2)(9x + 2)$

(Answers appear at the end of the section.)

Factoring

Very often, a polynomial has to be expressed as an equivalent expression that is the product of polynomials. Each of the new polynomials is a factor of the new expression; hence, this process is called "factoring."

The reason for rewriting the polynomial expression in factored form is that in some algebraic operations it is easier to work with factors than with addends.

For example, consider the expression:

$$\frac{2x^3 - x^2 - 22x - 24}{2x^2 - 5x - 12}$$

If this expression is written in factored form, it is

$$\frac{(x + 2)(2x + 3)(x - 4)}{(2x + 3)(x - 4)}$$

Since factors may be grouped in any manner (associative property), and since $\frac{(2x + 3)}{(2x + 3)}$ and $\frac{(x - 4)}{(x - 4)}$ can be replaced with the equivalent 1, the equivalent polynomial expression becomes $(x + 2)(1)(1)$, or simply $x + 2$.

In order to accomplish factoring, the distributive property of multiplication over addition, and the symmetry property of equality are used. Since $6(x + 2) = 6x + 12$ by the distributive property, then by the symmetry property of equality $6x + 12 = 6(x + 2)$. When the binomial $6x + 12$ is written as $6(x + 2)$, the expression has been factored.

In order to accomplish factoring successfully, keep in mind the patterns of the products obtained in the multiplication of polynomials. Factoring merely reverses these patterns by the symmetry principle. Factoring techniques are grouped according to the patterns established in multiplication.

Common monomial factor

When a monomial is distributed over a polynomial, the monomial becomes a factor in each of the terms of the polynomial. Hence, when you look for a common monomial factor of a polynomial expression, examine each term of the expression to see whether there is a common factor in each of the terms.

Example:
Given the expression, $2x^3 + 8x^2 - 16x$, find the greatest common monomial factor. Put each term in common factored form. (This step can be done mentally.)

$$2x^3 = 2 \cdot x \cdot x \cdot x = 2x(x^2)$$
$$8x^2 = 2 \cdot 2 \cdot 2 \cdot x \cdot x = 2x\,(4x)$$
$$16x = 2 \cdot 2 \cdot 2 \cdot 2 \cdot x = 2x\,(8)$$

Note that the greatest common factor of these three terms is $2x$, since 2 and x are common factors. Write $2x$ as one factor of the product, and the sum of the quotients of the terms resulting from division by $2x$ as the other factor.

$$2x^3 + 8x^2 - 16x = (2x)(x^2 + 4x - 8)$$

Your Turn

Find the common factor, if any, and factor each of the following:

1. $3x^2 + 12x + 9$ 2. $9x^3 + 2x^2 + 7x$
3. $72x + 9$ 4. $18x^3 + 7x + 3$

(*Answers appear at the end of the section.*)

Difference of two perfect squares

You saw that, as one special product, the product of the sum and difference of two terms was the difference of the squares of the two terms. By symmetry then, the difference of the factors that are squares can be factored into the product of the sum and difference of the two terms.

Example:
Factor $81y^2 - 100$.
$$81y^2 = (9y)^2 \qquad 100 = 10^2$$
$$(81y^2 - 100) = (9y + 10)(9y - 10)$$

It is handy to have on hand a table of squares of whole numbers. A few of these values are listed below.

No.	Square	No.	Square
1	1	11	121
2	4	12	144
3	9	13	169
4	16	14	196
5	25	15	225
6	36	16	256
7	49	17	289
8	64	18	324
9	81	19	361
10	100	20	400

Example:
Factor $18b^8c - 2c^3$.
Are $18b^8c$ and $2c^3$ perfect squares? No. Look for a common factor. Then factor.

$$18b^8c - 2c^3 = 2c(9b^8 - c^2)$$
$$= 2c(3b^4 - c)(3b^4 + c)$$

Note that c^2 means $1c^2$ and c^2 is a perfect square. Also study how the exponents of the variables are determined. $(x^4)(x^4) = x^8$, so when x^8 is factored as a perfect square, the factors contain x^4.

Your Turn

Factor each of the following:

5. $4a^2 - 25$ 6. $64x^2y^4 - 49$
7. $12x^2 - 48$ 8. $18x^8y - 242y$

(Answers appear at the end of the section.)

Factoring trinomials

Perfect square trinomials

The square of a binomial is a trinomial. Such a trinomial is called a "perfect square trinomial." For example, $(x + 2)^2 = x^2 + 4x + 4$ and $(x - 2)^2 = x^2 - 4x + 4$. When the distribution is reversed by symmetry, look for the pattern: the first and third terms of the trinomial (arranged in descending order) are perfect squares, and the middle term is twice the product of the square roots of the first and third terms.

Example:
Find whether $x^2 - 6x + 9$ is a perfect square trinomial.

$$x^2 - 6x \qquad + 9$$
$$\downarrow \qquad\qquad \downarrow$$
$$(x)^2\,(2)(-3)x\;(\pm 3)^2$$

Choose the negative sign, since the middle term is negative. The trinomial is a perfect square trinomial and can be factored as the square of a binomial.

$$x^2 - 6x + 9 = (x - 3)^2$$

Example:
Factor $3b^3c^2 + 30b^2c + 75b$.
Start by factoring any common factors. Then complete the factoring.

$$3b^3c^2 + 30b^2c + 75b$$
$$= 3b(b^2c^2 + 10bc + 25)$$
Think: $1 \cdot 1 = 1,\ 5 \cdot 5 = 25,$
$$\qquad\qquad 2(1 \cdot 5) = 10.$$
$$= 3b(bc + 5)(bc + 5)$$
$$= 3b(bc + 5)^2$$

Your Turn

Factor each of the following. Be sure to look for common factors and perfect squares.

9. $a^2 - 14a + 49$
10. $4c^2 + 4c + 1$
11. $5d^2 - 30d + 45$
12. $4x^2y^2 - 12xy + 9$
13. $9x^2 - 3x + 9$
14. $49s^2t + 84st + 36t$

(Answers appear at the end of the section.)

Note that the product of the sum and difference of two terms is the difference of their squares, and the product of a binomial with itself is a trinomial. None of the products obtained with two binomials produced the *sum* of two perfect squares, hence (aside from a possible common monomial factor) the sum of two perfect squares cannot be factored over the real numbers. The polynomial $(x^2 + 1)$ is then said to be in prime factored form.

General trinomials

The product of two binomials is obtained by a double distribution:

$$
\begin{aligned}
(x + 2)(x + 3) &= x(x + 3) + 2(x + 3) \\
&= x^2 + 3x + 2x + 2 \cdot 3 \\
&= x^2 + (3 + 2)x + 2 \cdot 3 \\
&= x^2 + \quad 5x \quad + \quad 6
\end{aligned}
$$

Notice the pattern:

$$x^2 = x \cdot x$$
$$5x = (2 + 3)x$$
$$6 = 2 \cdot 3$$

The coefficient of the middle term is the sum of 2 and 3, and the third term is the product of 2 and 3. Then to factor a trinomial with terms arranged in descending order and a first term of $(1)x^2$, find two numbers whose algebraic sum gives the coefficient of the middle term and whose product gives the end term.

Example: Factor $x^2 + 7x + 6$.

Start with the third term, $+6$. Two number pairs have a product of 6: 3,2 and 6,1. The product is positive, so either both members of the pair are positive or both are negative. Now consider the coefficient of the middle term. Since the sign is positive, both terms must be positive. The sum of 3 and 2 is 5, the sum of 6 and 1 is 7. You need the number pair, 6,1. Now write the binomial factors of this trinomial.

$$x^2 + 7x + 6 = (x + 6)(x + 1)$$

Always check a factorization by performing the indicated multiplication and comparing the product with the original expression.

$(x + 6)(x + 1) = x^2 + 6x + 1x + 6$
or $x^2 + 7x + 6$ It checks.

Suppose the trinomial were $x^2 + 5x - 6$. The same number pairs are considered, 3,2 and 6,1, but one member of the pair is a negative number since the product is negative (-6). For the coefficient of the middle term, the possibilities to consider are 6 and -1, -6 and 1, 3 and -2, and -3 and 2. Of the results, 5, -5, 1, and -1, the desired one is 5, which comes from the number pair, $6, -1$. The factorization of the trinomial $x^2 + 5x - 6$ is $(x + 6)(x - 1)$.

Your Turn

Factor each of the following.

15. $x^2 - 6x + 8$ 16. $x^2 + 6x + 9$
17. $x^2 + 8x - 20$ 18. $x^2 - 10x - 24$

(Answers appear at the end of the section.)

As you will sometimes have to check several number pairs, it is useful to proceed in an organized manner. The following technique allows you to explore all the possibilities for the factorization of a trinomial. With this method, you are assured that all the possibilities for the factorization have been tried.

First, examine the trinomial for a common monomial factor. For complete factorization, you have to list a common monomial factor as one of the factors. When more than one type of factoring is necessary, removing the common monomial factor in the first step allows you to work with smaller coefficients in the following steps.

Second, it is often possible to obtain a factorization by inspection. You may look at $x^2 + 4x + 3$ and "see" that the number pair to be used is 3,1. Therefore, $(x + 3)(x + 1)$ is the desired factorization. Check your guess by performing the indicated multiplication. Use the following method when you cannot obtain a factorization of a trinomial by inspection.

Example: Factor $x^2 + 7x + 12$.

$$(1,12)$$
$$(2,6)$$
$$(3,4)$$

First look for a common monomial factor. In this polynomial there is none. Next, list, as above, the number pairs with a product of 12. For convenience in checking, write them in this fashion: (the 1's in the first column represent the coefficients of x^2 for each of the factors).

$$\begin{vmatrix} 1 \\ 1 \end{vmatrix} \diagdown \begin{matrix} 1 \\ 12 \end{matrix} \qquad \begin{vmatrix} 1 \\ 1 \end{vmatrix} \diagdown \begin{matrix} 2 \\ 6 \end{matrix} \qquad \begin{vmatrix} 1 \\ 1 \end{vmatrix} \diagdown \begin{matrix} 3 \\ 4 \end{matrix}$$

Check the middle coefficient by calculating the sums of the "cross-products" $(1)(12) + (1)(1)$; $(1)(6) + (2)(1)$;

(1)(4) + (3)(1). These are indicated by the $\diagdown\!\!\!\!\diagup$ in the diagram. The last set, (1)(4) + (3)(1) = 7, is used to obtain the middle coefficient. Then write the factorization:

$$x^2 + 7x + 12 = (x + 4)(x + 3)$$

Example:
Factor $x^2 - x - 12$.

Proceed just as you did when factoring $x^2 + 7x + 12$, except that one of the numbers in the pair is negative, since the product (-12) is negative. Write out two rows of possible arrangements. With practice, you can write just one row and do the sign work mentally.

$$\begin{vmatrix} 1 & -1 \\ 1 & 12 \end{vmatrix} \quad \begin{vmatrix} 1 & -2 \\ 1 & 6 \end{vmatrix} \quad \begin{vmatrix} 1 & -3 \\ 1 & 4 \end{vmatrix}$$

$$\begin{vmatrix} 1 & 1 \\ 1 & -12 \end{vmatrix} \quad \begin{vmatrix} 1 & 2 \\ 1 & -6 \end{vmatrix} \quad \begin{vmatrix} 1 & 3 \\ 1 & -4 \end{vmatrix}$$

When the cross-products are examined, you find the number pair $(3, -4)$ is the pair that produces the correct product, -1. Stop the process as soon as you find a pair that produces the correct result—you do not always have to try all the possibilities. The desired factorization is:

$$x^2 - x - 12 = (x - 4)(x + 3)$$

As you practice factoring trinomials, you will find that you are able to get quite a few factorizations "by sight." Suppose that you were asked to factor the expression $x^2 + 10x + 12$. Proceed in exactly the same manner as for $x^2 + 7x + 12$. For this expression, however, none of the possible combinations produces a sum of 10 for the middle coefficient. Hence, the polynomial $x^2 + 10x + 12$ is in prime factored form. Thus, by systematically

writing all possible combinations, you can tell when it is possible to factor a trinomial over the integers. You know that all possible arrangements have been examined.

Note particularly that $x^2 + 2(5x + 6)$ is not considered to be a factorization of the trinomial, as there are two addends, x^2 and $2(5x + 6)$, rather than two (or more) factors.

Your Turn

Factor each of the following. Be sure to check for a common monomial first.

19. $9x^2 - 36x + 36$
20. $x^3 + x^2 - 30x$
21. $3x^2 - 24x + 36$
22. $x^2y^2 + 10xy + 24$

(Answers appear at the end of the section.)

This organized method of obtaining factors of trinomials is also useful for more difficult factorization, that of trinomials that have a coefficient different from 1 for the first term. It is a little more difficult only because, in general, there will be more combinations to consider.

Example: Factor $15x^2 + 28 + 12$.

1,15	1,12	12,1
3,5	2,6	6,2
	3,4	4,3

$$\begin{vmatrix} 1 & 1 \\ 15 & 12 \end{vmatrix} \qquad \begin{vmatrix} 1 & 12 \\ 15 & 1 \end{vmatrix} \qquad \begin{vmatrix} 1 & 2 \\ 15 & 6 \end{vmatrix}$$

$$\begin{vmatrix} 1 & 6 \\ 15 & 2 \end{vmatrix} \qquad \begin{vmatrix} 1 & 3 \\ 15 & 4 \end{vmatrix} \qquad \begin{vmatrix} 1 & 4 \\ 15 & 3 \end{vmatrix}$$

$$\begin{vmatrix} 3 & 1 \\ 5 & 12 \end{vmatrix} \qquad \begin{vmatrix} 3 & 12 \\ 5 & 1 \end{vmatrix} \qquad \begin{vmatrix} 3 & 2 \\ 5 & 6 \end{vmatrix}$$

$$\begin{vmatrix} 3 & 6 \\ 5 & 2 \end{vmatrix} \qquad \begin{vmatrix} 3 & 3 \\ 5 & 4 \end{vmatrix} \qquad \begin{vmatrix} 3 & 4 \\ 5 & 3 \end{vmatrix}$$

You have twelve arrangements—quite a few. Notice the first pairs for 12 are shown as (1,12) and (12,1). If the coefficient of x is not 1, then the order of the second pair is important. Notice that the sum for (1,15) and (1,12) is 27, while the sum for (1,15) and (12,1) is 181. You should find that the pairs (3,5) and (2,6) will produce the desired coefficient, 28.

$$15x^2 + 28x + 12 = (3x + 2)(5x + 6)$$

If the last term is negative, there will be twice as many cases. However, there is still a definite number of cases to be checked, and either you find a factorization over the integers or else you have determined definitely that the expression is not factorable over the integers.

Your Turn

Factor each of the following.

23. $4a^2 - 14a + 6$
24. $12a^2 + 8a - 15$
25. $10b^2 - 9b - 9$
26. $3b^2 - 24b + 36$
27. $20c^2 - 405$
28. $24c^3 - 18c^2 - 102c$

(*Answers appear at the end of the section.*)

Quadrinomials

Sometimes quadrinomials are factored by grouping. Note the product:

$$(x - a)(x - b) = x(x - b) +$$
$$(-a)(x - b)$$
$$= x^2 - bx - ax + ab$$

To reverse the process, group together two terms with x and two terms with a.

Example: Factor $x^2 - 2rx + 3sx - 6rs$. Group the terms in pairs of two and factor a common monomial factor from each pair:

$$(x^2 - 2rx) + (3sx - 6rs)$$
$$x(x - 2r) + 3s(x - 2r)$$

Note that the two groups of terms have a common binomial factor. Write this factor as one factor, and the sum of the quotients as the other factor:

$$x^2 - 2rx + 3sx - 6rs =$$
$$(x - 2r)(x + 3s)$$

Example: Factor $3x^2 + 6x - 6ax - 12a$

$= 3(x^2 + 2x - 2ax - 4a)$ Factor the common monomial.

$= 3[(x)(x + 2) + (-2a)(x + 2)]$ Group and factor.

$= 3[x + (-2a)](x + 2)$ Use the common factor and the sum of the other two quotients.

$= 3(x - 2a)(x + 2)$ Simplify.

Your Turn

Factor each of the following:

29. $2x^2 + 10x + ax + 5a$
30. $6b - 3y + 2by - y^2$
31. $36c^2 - 48c - 24cd + 32d$
32. $15n + 10\,np - 6p - 4p^2$

(*Answers appear at the end of the section.*)

There is another set of products that produces an interesting pattern and provides an easily remembered factorization.

$(x + 1)(x^2 - x + 1)$
$= x(x^2 - x + 1) + 1(x^2 - x + 1)$
$= x^3 - x^2 + x + x^2 - x + 1$
$= x^3 + 1$

$(x - 1)(x^2 + x + 1)$
$= x(x^2 + x + 1) + (-1)(x^2 + x + 1)$
$= x^3 + x^2 + x - x^2 - x - 1$
$= x^3 - 1$

By symmetry you can see that both the sum and the difference of two perfect cubes can be factored. The trinomial factors, $x^2 - x + 1$ and $x^2 + x + 1$, are in prime factored form and thus cannot be factored further. It is useful to have on hand a few values of cubes of the positive integers.

No.	Cube	No.	Cube
1	1	7	343
2	8	8	512
3	27	9	729
4	64	10	1000
5	125	11	1331
6	216	12	1728

Example:
Factor $729r^3 - 125$.
$= (9r - 5)(81r^2 + 45r + 25)$

The first factor is the difference of the cube roots of the factors. The second factor contains three terms. The first and last are the squares of the terms of first factor and the middle term is the opposite of the product of the terms of the first factor.

$9r - 5$
$(9r)(9r) + -(9r)(-5) + (-5)(-5)$
$81r^2 + -(-45r) + 25$
$81r^2 + 45r + 25$

You can try to factor the last factor, but you will find that it is in prime factored form, so you are finished.

Your Turn

Factor each perfect cube.

33. $27b^3 - 1$ 34. $d^3 + 125$
35. $a^3 - c^3$ 36. $1000x^3 + 512$

(Answers appear at the end of the section.)

Quadratic Equations

A quadratic equation is an equation in which two is the highest degree of a term. If all non-zero terms are put together on one side of the equal sign, you will have an expression with one, two, or three terms equal to zero.

$$x^2 = 0$$
$$x^2 - 4 = 0$$
$$x^2 - 6x + 5 = 0$$

These are quadratic equations. If factorization is allowed for all the real numbers, every quadratic expression can be factored into two binomials.

Zero factor-zero product theorem

You will now consider a theorem that can easily be deduced from your arithmetic experience. It is called the zero factor-zero product theorem. Note that:

$$a \cdot 0 = 0$$
$$0 \cdot a = 0$$
$$0 \cdot 0 = 0$$

In other words, the product of two factors is zero if and only if one or both of the factors is zero.

Thus, if a trinomial is written as a product of two factors equal to zero, then one or both of the factors is equal to zero. By setting each of the linear factors equal to zero, you can find the values that make the quadratic expression equal to zero. These values are called the solution to the equation, or the "roots" of the equation. Since there are two factors for every quadratic, there will be two roots for every second degree equation. It may happen, as with the perfect square trinomial, that the two linear factors are identical. In that case, the two roots are identical.

The method is used in the following way. Suppose you are given that $x^2 + 4x = -3$. First, get all non-zero terms on one side of the equal sign.

$$\begin{array}{rl} x^2 + 4x & = -3 \\ +3 & +3 \\ \hline x^2 + 4x + 3 = & 0 \end{array}$$

Next, factor the trinomial:

$$(x + 3)(x + 1) = 0$$

Since the product is zero, one or the other or both of the linear factors is equal to zero. Set each of the factors equal to zero.

$$\begin{array}{ll} x + 3 = 0 & x + 1 = 0 \\ x = -3 & x = -1 \end{array}$$

The two solutions of the equation are $\{-3, -1\}$. Check by substituting them into the original equation.

Check: $x^2 + 4x = -3$
$(-3)^2 + 4(-3) \overset{?}{=} -3$
$9 - 12 \overset{?}{=} -3$
$-3 = -3$

$(-1)^2 + 4(-1) \overset{?}{=} -3$
$1 - 4 \overset{?}{=} -3$
$-3 = -3$

Example:
Solve this equation.
$24a^2 + 16a = 30$

$$\begin{array}{rll} 24a^2 + 16a & = 30 & \text{Add } -30 \text{ to} \\ -30 & -30 & \text{both sides.} \\ \hline 24a^2 + 16a - 30 & = 0 \end{array}$$

$2(12a^2 + 8a - 15) = 0$ Find the common factor, if there is one.

$2(6a - 5)(2a + 3) = 0$ Complete factoring.

Now set each factor equal to zero.

$2 = 0$ False. This is called an extraneous factor. It is not a root of the equation.

$\begin{array}{ll} 6a - 5 = 0 & \text{One factor.} \\ +5 \ +5 & \text{Add 5 to each side.} \\ \hline 6a = 5 \end{array}$

$\dfrac{6a}{6} = \dfrac{5}{6}$ Divide each by 6.

$a = \dfrac{5}{6}$ ← A root of the equation, if it checks.

Check: $24a^2 + 16a = 30$

$24\left(\dfrac{5}{6}\right)\left(\dfrac{5}{6}\right) + 16\left(\dfrac{5}{6}\right) \overset{?}{=} 30$

$\dfrac{50}{3} + \dfrac{40}{3} \overset{?}{=} 30$

$\dfrac{90}{3} = 30$

It checks.

$\begin{array}{ll} 2a + 3 = 0 & \text{Other factor.} \\ 2a = -3 & \text{Add } -3 \text{ to both} \\ & \text{sides.} \end{array}$

$a = -\dfrac{3}{2}$ Divide both sides by 2.
A root, if it checks.

Check: $24a^2 + 16a = 30$

$24\left(-\dfrac{3}{2}\right)\left(-\dfrac{3}{2}\right) + 16\left(-\dfrac{3}{2}\right) \overset{?}{=} 30$

$54 + -24 = 30$ It checks.

The two solutions are $\left\{\dfrac{5}{6}, -\dfrac{3}{2}\right\}$.

Your Turn

Solve each quadratic equation by factoring and then setting each factor equal to zero.

1. $x^2 + 3x = -2$
2. $a^2 + 3a = 18$
3. $2d^2 - 19d = -24$
4. $10b^2 - 9b = 9$

(*Answers appear at the end of the section.*)

Completing the square

You have already seen that some equations cannot be factored over the integers. Other methods of solving quadratic equations have been devised. One such method is called completing the square.

Previously you learned that if the product of two factors is equal to zero, each factor can be set equal to zero to find the roots of the equation. Completing the square requires that you write an equivalent equation so that the polynomial is a perfect square. Then you can solve the equation by finding the square root of both sides of the equation and setting the results equal to each other. Suppose you had the equation

$$x^2 + 4x + 3 = 0$$

Since 3 is not a perfect square, this equation is not a perfect square. The question is how to change the equation to make the polynomial on the left side of the equals sign a perfect square. This can be accomplished in a systematic way.

$x^2 + 4x + 3 = 0$ Given equation.
$x^2 + 4x = -3$ Add -3 to each side. The object is to get the constant by itself on the other side.

Now you must determine what constant will make $x^2 - 4x + ?$ a perfect square. To find this term when the coefficient of x^2 is 1, take $\frac{1}{2}$ of the coefficient of x and square it.

$\frac{1}{2}$ of 4 = 2 and $2^2 = 4$

$$
\begin{array}{rl}
x^2 + 4x & = -3 \\
+ 4 & +4 \\
\hline
x^2 + 4x + 4 & = 1
\end{array}
$$
Add that constant to both sides of the equation.

$(x + 2)^2 = 1$ Factor the polynomial.
$x + 2 = \pm 1$ Find the square root of each side of the equation.
So $x + 2 = 1$ Set the square root of the equation equal to each value of the square root of the constant.
$x + 2 = -1$

Now solve the given quadratic equation by solving each of the linear equations.

$$
\begin{array}{rr}
x + 2 = & 1 \\
- 2 & -2 \\
\hline
x = & -1
\end{array}
\qquad
\begin{array}{rr}
x + 2 = & -1 \\
- 2 & -2 \\
\hline
x = & -3
\end{array}
$$

Check: $x^2 + 4x + 3 = 0$
$(-1)^2 + 4(-1) + 3 \overset{?}{=} 0$
$1 + (-4) + 3 = 0$ It checks.

$(-3)^2 + 4(-3) + 3 \overset{?}{=} 0$
$9 + (-12) + 3 = 0$ It checks.

You have found that $\{-1, -3\}$ are roots of the quadratic equation.

Notice that when the square root of each side was taken, only the constant was given the $\pm$ symbol. Actually both sides could have the $\pm$ symbol. However, it is only necessary to consider either the positive value or the negative value of the equation. Study the examples below to find out why.

The other two possible arrangements that are not shown above would be

$$
\begin{array}{rl}
-(x + 2) = & 1 \\
-x - 2 = & 1 \\
-x = & 3 \\
\dfrac{-x}{-1} = & \dfrac{3}{-1} \\
x = & -3
\end{array}
\qquad
\begin{array}{rl}
-(x + 2) = & -1 \\
-x - 2 = & -1 \\
-x = & 1 \\
\dfrac{-x}{-1} = & \dfrac{1}{-1} \\
x = & -1
\end{array}
$$

Note that the same two roots are obtained when the negative value of the square root of the equation is used.

Therefore, it is only necessary to consider the positive value of the square root of the equation.

Example: Solve $x^2 - 6x - 7 = 0$.

$$x^2 - 6x - 7 = 0$$

$\quad x^2 - 6x \quad = 7$ Add 7 to each side.

$x^2 - 6x + 9 = 16$ Add the square of $\frac{1}{2}$ of the coefficient of x to each side.

$\quad (x - 3)^2 = 16$ Factor.

$\quad\quad x - 3 = \pm 4$ Find the square root of each side.

$$
\begin{array}{ll}
x - 3 = 4 & x - 3 = -4 \\
\underline{+3 \quad +3} & \underline{+3 \quad +3} \\
x = 7 & x = -1
\end{array}
$$
Solve each equation.

Check: $x^2 - 6x - 7 = 0$

$7^2 - 6 \cdot 7 - 7 = 0 \quad (-1)^2 - 6(-1) - 7 = 0$
$49 - 42 - 7 = 0 \qquad\quad 1 + 6 - 7 = 0$

Both solutions check.

$\{7, -1\}$ are roots of the equation.

Your Turn

Find the roots of each equation by completing the square.

5. $x^2 - x - 6 = 0$
6. $x^2 + 8x - 9 = 0$

(*Answers appear at the end of the section.*)

Quadratic formula

Completing the square works well for finding the roots of some equations, but is not efficient for all quadratic equations. If the general application of completing the square is examined where a and b are the coefficients of x^2 and x respectively and c is the constant, a formula is obtained that will work to solve any quadratic equation. Start with the equation $ax^2 + bx + c = 0$.

$ax^2 + bx + c = 0$ Given equation.

$\dfrac{a}{a}x^2 + \dfrac{b}{a}x + \dfrac{c}{a} = \dfrac{0}{a}$ Divide by a so x^2 has coefficient of 1.

$x^2 + \dfrac{b}{a}x = -\dfrac{c}{a}$ Subtract the constant from both sides.

$x^2 + \dfrac{b}{a}x + \left(\dfrac{b}{2a}\right)^2 =$
$\left(\dfrac{b}{2a}\right)^2 - \dfrac{c}{a}$ Find the square of $\frac{1}{2}$ of the coefficient of x and add that to both sides to make a perfect square.

$x^2 + \dfrac{b}{a}x + \left(\dfrac{b}{2a}\right)^2 =$
$\dfrac{b^2}{4a^2} - \dfrac{c}{a}$

$\left(x + \dfrac{b}{2a}\right)^2 = \dfrac{b^2 - 4ac}{4a^2}$ Factor.

$x + \dfrac{b}{2a} = \dfrac{\pm\sqrt{b^2 - 4ac}}{2a}$ Find the square root of each side.

$x = -\dfrac{b}{2a} \pm \dfrac{\sqrt{b^2 - 4ac}}{2a}$ Solve for x.

$x = \dfrac{-b \pm \sqrt{b^2 - 4ac}}{2a}$ Simplify.

Example: Use the quadratic formula to solve this equation: $3x^2 + 6x - 4 = 0$.

$$
\begin{array}{ll}
3x^2 + 7x - 6 = 0 & a = 3 \\
 & b = 7 \\
 & c = -6
\end{array}
$$

$$x = \dfrac{-b \pm \sqrt{b^2 - 4ac}}{2a}$$

$$= \frac{-7 \pm \sqrt{7^2 - 4(3)(-6)}}{2(3)}$$ Substitute for a, b, and c.

$$= \frac{-7 \pm \sqrt{49 + 72}}{6}$$ Simplify.

$$= \frac{-7 \pm \sqrt{121}}{6}$$

$$= \frac{-7 \pm 11}{6}$$

$$x = \frac{-7 + 11}{6}$$ Solve each equation. (One using positive value and one using negative value.)

$$= \frac{4}{6} \text{ or } \frac{2}{3}$$

$$x = \frac{-7 - 11}{6}$$

$$= \frac{-18}{6} \text{ or } -3$$

Check:

$$3\left(\frac{2}{3}\right)\left(\frac{2}{3}\right) + 7\left(\frac{2}{3}\right) - 6 \overset{?}{=} 0$$

$$\frac{4}{3} + \frac{14}{3} - 6 \overset{?}{=} 0$$

$$\frac{18}{3} - 6 \overset{?}{=} 0$$

$$6 - 6 = 0$$

It checks.

$$3(-3)(-3) + 7(-3) - 6 \overset{?}{=} 0$$
$$27 - 21 - 6 \overset{?}{=} 0$$
$$27 - 27 = 0$$

It checks.

The roots are $\frac{2}{3}$ and -3.

Your Turn

Use the quadratic formula to solve each equation.

7. $6x^2 + x - 2 = 0$
8. $2x^2 - 13x + 6 = 0$
9. $x^2 - 3x - 18 = 0$
10. $4x^2 - 20x + 25 = 0$

(Answers appear at the end of the section.)

By using the letters a, b, and c to represent the coefficients of x^2, x and the constant term, you have an equation for x that will produce the two roots of any quadratic equation. The invention of this equation, or formula, is a significant achievement. You no longer have to go through the steps of completing the square to solve a quadratic; you do not have to depend on finding the factors. You merely arrange the three members of the trinomial in standard form (all in one member of the equation in descending order), identify the a, b and c (being very careful to note the signs properly), and compute the x values from the formula.

Discriminant of a quadratic equation

In the quadratic formula, you see the expression $\sqrt{b^2 - 4ac}$. The expression $b^2 - 4ac$ is called the discriminant. You can determine the nature of the roots of the quadratic from the discriminant without actually carrying out the calculation. Thus, this expression "discriminates" among the roots.

One basic axiom states the Law of Trichotomy, which says that a quantity must be one of three things: less than zero (negative), equal to zero, or greater than zero (positive). Hence there are three possibilities for the discriminant.

If the discriminant is greater than zero, the roots are real numbers. If the discriminant is a perfect square, the roots will be rational numbers. If the discriminant is not a perfect square, the roots will be irrational numbers. In either case, the roots will be unequal. If the discriminant is equal to zero, the roots will be real and equal. The roots will be given by

$$\frac{-b + 0}{2a} \text{ and } \frac{-b - 0}{2a} \text{ or } -\frac{b}{2a}$$

If $b^2 - 4ac$ is a negative number, the roots are complex. The table below summarizes the types of roots found in a quadratic equation in the form

$$ax^2 + bx + c = 0$$

Value of the discriminant ($b^2 - 4ac$)	Type of roots of the quadratic equation
equal to 0	real and equal
greater than 0 and a perfect square	rational and distinct (not equal)
greater than 0 but not a perfect square	irrational and distinct
less than 0	complex (involving i) and distinct

Your Turn

For each quadratic equation, decide whether the roots will be real and equal, complex, rational, or irrational. Do not solve the equations.

11. $2x^2 - 5x + 6 = 0$
12. $x^2 + 4x + 1 = 0$
13. $x^2 - 10x - 3 = 0$
14. $x^2 - 6x + 9 = 0$
15. $6x^2 - 13x + 2 = 0$

(Answers appear at the end of the section.)

Complex roots

The quadratic formula is not without its problems, however. For example, solve the quadratic equation $x^2 + 1 = 0$ with the use of the quadratic formula. If the equation is rewritten in the form

$$x^2 = -1$$

you know at once that you are in trouble. None of the real numbers when multiplied by itself produces a negative num-

ber. If the two roots are positive, the product will be positive. If the two roots are negative, the product will be positive. No square of a real number produces a negative number.

On the other hand, you have a formula produced by perfectly sound logic and mathematical reasoning. There is no restriction on the values for a, b, and c, other than that a cannot be zero (in which case there would not be a quadratic equation, anyway). So try the formula.

$x^2 + 1 = 0$	Given.
$a = 1; b = 0; c = 1$	
$x = \pm\dfrac{\sqrt{-4}}{2}$	By quadratic formula.

The formula requires that you obtain the square root of a negative number. But there is no real number for $\sqrt{-4}$. What choice can a mathematician make? One can, of course, reject solutions requiring the square roots of negative numbers as being meaningless, much as negative numbers were for centuries rejected.

The other possible resolution of the dilemma is to invent a new number, one which, when squared, produces a negative real number. Just such numbers were invented in the sixteenth century by the Italian mathematician, Rafael Bombelli. It is difficult for a new number to gain a foothold in the conservative world of mathematics. This new number did not have an easy time.

Numbers that were invented a very long time ago, so long ago that no trace of their invention remains, are so much a part of the world that they are regarded as having the same status as objects in the physical world. (They are, of course, abstract ideas, no matter how accepted they are.)

The new numbers representing square roots of negative quantities were termed by their inventor "imaginary numbers." The letter i was used to represent $\sqrt{-1}$. The square roots of other negative numbers were represented as:

$$\sqrt{-4} = 2i;$$

$$-\sqrt{-4} = -2i;$$

$$\sqrt{-100} = 10i$$

In the nineteenth century, the Irish mathematician William Rowan Hamilton was able to make a satisfactory interpretation of imaginary numbers and of complex numbers, which are a combination of real and imaginary numbers (for example, $1 + i$). The new numbers are no more or less invented or unnatural than the old numbers, but it is not easy to change ways of thinking. Imaginary numbers are now a very important part of the world of mathematics. If you wish to learn more about them, *see* Part VI, Section 2, "The Square Root of 2."

Irrational roots

When the discriminant is greater than zero, but not a perfect square, an irrational number is obtained. Such a number has for its numeral a nonterminating, non-repeating decimal. Therefore, an approximation of the number can be written. For some purposes, the irrational number is left as an indicated square root, to be evaluated at some later time. For example, you may write $6 \pm \sqrt{2}$ as a solution until you need to combine the integer 6 with a decimal approximation of $\sqrt{2}$.

If you need a decimal approximation of an irrational number, you can obtain the square root value in several ways. One way is to use a handheld calculator. Some calculators have a key for $\sqrt{x}$ that will produce an approximation of the square root of x.

A second method is to use a table of square roots. Below is a table of square roots of the positive integers from 1 to 100.

N	$\sqrt{N}$	N	$\sqrt{N}$	N	$\sqrt{N}$	N	$\sqrt{N}$
1	1.000	26	5.099	51	7.141	76	8.718
2	1.414	27	5.196	52	7.211	77	8.775
3	1.732	28	5.292	53	7.280	78	8.832
4	2.000	29	5.385	54	7.348	79	8.888
5	2.236	30	5.477	55	7.416	80	8.944
6	2.449	31	5.568	56	7.483	81	9.000
7	2.646	32	5.657	57	7.550	82	9.055
8	2.828	33	5.745	58	7.616	83	9.110
9	3.000	34	5.831	59	7.681	84	9.165
10	3.162	35	5.916	60	7.746	85	9.220
11	3.317	36	6.000	61	7.810	86	9.274
12	3.464	37	6.083	62	7.874	87	9.327
13	3.606	38	6.164	63	7.937	88	9.381
14	3.742	39	6.245	64	8.000	89	9.434
15	3.873	40	6.325	65	8.062	90	9.487
16	4.000	41	6.403	66	8.124	91	9.539
17	4.123	42	6.481	67	8.185	92	9.592
18	4.243	43	6.557	68	8.246	93	9.644
19	4.359	44	6.633	69	8.307	94	9.695
20	4.472	45	6.708	70	8.367	95	9.747
21	4.583	46	6.782	71	8.426	96	9.798
22	4.690	47	6.856	72	8.485	97	9.849
23	4.796	48	6.928	73	8.544	98	9.899
24	4.899	49	7.000	74	8.602	99	9.950
25	5.000	50	7.071	75	8.660	100	10.000

To find the approximation for $\sqrt{67}$, look down the columns labeled N to locate 67. Read the entry in the column $\sqrt{N}$ just to the right. You will find the value 8.185.

Your Turn

Use the table above to find the square root of the following numbers:

16. 15   17. 56   18. 99   19. 88

(Answers appear at the end of the section.)

Square roots can also be computed by hand computation, or by hand computation assisted by a calculator. An informal technique, called the bracket method, is a third way to find a square root. In this method you find the square root by systematic guessing and improving the guess.

Example: Determine the square root of 54 correct to two decimal places.
1. From your knowledge of perfect squares, you can bracket the number between two perfect squares.

$$49 < 54 < 64$$

The number 54 is larger than the perfect square 49 but less than the next perfect square, 64. Therefore,

$$7 < R < 8$$

2. You are looking for a number, R, so that $R \times R = 54$, or $54 \div R = R$.

If the divisor $Q \rightarrow$ the quotient
is too small, $\rightarrow D\overline{)54}$ will be
larger than
the divisor.

If the divisor is too large, the quotient will be smaller than the divisor. Guess a value for R, a number between 7 and 8. Since 54 is closer to 49 than it is to 64, guess 7.3. A handheld calculator can be used to aid the computation. First do the division.

$$7.3\overline{)54.0}^{\,7.4}$$

The divisor is too small; the quotient is larger than the divisor. You have obtained, however, better bounds on the root. It is now known that

$$7.3 < R < 7.4$$

3. For the second guess, the first guess 7.3 is averaged with the first quotient. The average is $\frac{7.3 + 7.4}{2}$, or 7.35. The same procedure used with

the first guess will be followed with the second guess, 7.35.

$$7.35\overline{)54.00}^{\,7.35}$$

The quotient agrees with the divisor to two decimal places. Thus, $\sqrt{54}$, correct to two decimal places, is 7.35.

It is not essential, with this method, that you make very good guesses. Your knowledge of the values of the squares of the positive integers enables you to place the root between two perfect squares. You can then use any number in this interval as your next estimate of the root. For example, in finding $\sqrt{54}$, you first determined that the root was a number between 7 and 8. Say then, for your first guess, that you choose the number 7.9. Then $54 \div 7.9 = 6.8$. Average 6.8 and 7.9 and obtain $\frac{6.8 + 7.9}{2}$, or 7.35. This is the same value that was obtained when 7.3 and 7.4 were averaged.

Your Turn

Use any method to find the square root for the following:

20. 34   21. 88   22. 142   23. 250

(*Answers appear at the end of the section.*)

Solving more quadratic equations

Now you can solve all quadratic equations that have rational roots.

Example: Solve $6x^2 + 7x - 10 = 0$

$$6x^2 + 7x - 10 = 0 \qquad a = 6$$
$$b = 7$$
$$c = -10$$

$$x = \frac{-7 \pm \sqrt{(7)(7) - 4(6)(-10)}}{2(6)}$$

$$= \frac{-7 \pm \sqrt{49 + 240}}{12}$$

$$= \frac{-7 \pm \sqrt{289}}{12} \qquad \sqrt{289} = 17$$

$$= \frac{-7 \pm 17}{12}$$

$$x = \frac{-7 + 17}{12} \qquad x = \frac{-7 - 17}{12}$$

$$x \approx 0.83 \qquad x = -2$$

Check:

$$6(0.83)(0.83) + 7(0.83) - 10 \stackrel{?}{=} 0$$
$$4.13 + 5.81 - 10 \stackrel{?}{=} 0$$
$$.06 \approx 0$$

The answer is close, considering that rounding was used in the computation.
Check:

$$6(-2)(-2) + 7(-2) - 10 \stackrel{?}{=} 0$$
$$24 - 14 - 10 \stackrel{?}{=} 0$$
$$0 = 0$$
$$\text{It checks.}$$

Example:

Solve $4x^2 - 2x - 1 = 0$ $\qquad a = 4$
$\qquad b = -2$
$\qquad c = -1$

$$x = \frac{2 \pm \sqrt{4 + 16}}{8}$$

$$= \frac{2 \pm \sqrt{20}}{8} \qquad \sqrt{20} \approx 4.47$$

$$x = \frac{2 + 4.47}{8} \qquad x = \frac{2 - 4.47}{8}$$

$$x \approx 0.81 \qquad x \approx -0.31$$

The check is left to you.

Your Turn

Solve each quadratic equation.

24. $2x^2 - 3x + 1 = 0$
25. $6a^2 - 2a - 7 = 0$
26. $4b^2 + 7b + 3 = 0$
27. $9a^2 - 30a + 25 = 0$

(Answers appear at the end of the section.)

Pythagorean Theorem

Recall that one of the most famous theorems in mathematics is the Pythagorean Theorem. It states that if a and b represent the lengths of the two legs of a right triangle, respectively, and c represents the length of the hypotenuse, then

$$a^2 + b^2 = c^2$$

The relationship for certain right triangles was known to the Egyptians by at least 1000 B.C. They used the fact that a triangle made with lengths of 3 and 4 for the legs and 5 for the hypotenuse would be a right triangle. With the use of ropes that were knotted at even intervals, they could set up a right angle and thus two lines that were perpendicular. This technique was useful for setting out property lines of rectangular plots.

There is evidence that the Babylonians knew that the Pythagorean Theorem held for certain triangles even before the Egyptians, and before the Babylonians, the Chinese had noted it. It is not clear that anyone, however, knew that the property held for all right triangles until the time of the Greeks. This proof was one of the proofs developed by the Pythagoreans in ancient times. As they did not record which individual was responsible for a particular work, the leader Pythagoras is given credit.

The proof of the theorem first given was undoubtedly a geometric proof. A geometric proof is presented by Euclid. All the geometric proofs are based on the equality of areas. One would state that the area of the square with the hypotenuse as a side is equal to the sum of the areas of squares each with one of the legs of the right triangle as a side.

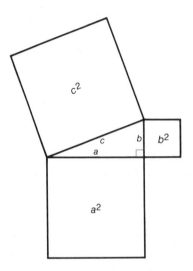

The easiest proof is the algebraic one. It is based on similar triangles. If the altitude is drawn to the hypotenuse of a right triangle, there are three similar triangles: the original and the two new triangles formed by the altitude.

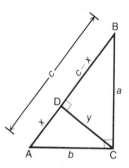

The three triangles are similar, as the corresponding angles of each are congruent.

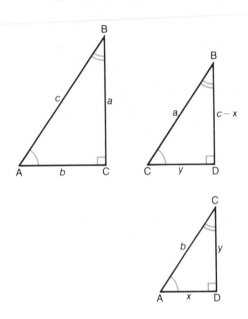

Since corresponding sides of similar triangles are proportional, the following proportions hold:

From triangles ACB and CDB:

(1) $\dfrac{c}{a} = \dfrac{a}{c - x}$

From triangles ACB and ADC:

(2) $\dfrac{c}{b} = \dfrac{b}{x}$

From your earlier work with ratios and proportions, you know that the product of the means is equal to the product of the extremes. It follows then that:

(3) $a^2 = c^2 - cx$ from (1) and
(4) $b^2 = cx$ from (2)

If (3) and (4) are added:

(5) $a^2 + b^2 = c^2$

The 3,4,5 right triangle is but one right triangle in which the sides have measures that are integral numbers. An infinite listing can be made of such number triples, called Pythagorean triples. The number sets fall into two groups.

The "primitives" have no common factor. Thus, 3,4,5 is a primitive triple. The second group consists of multiples of the primitive triples. Some multiples of the primitive 3,4,5 are 6,8,10; 9,12,15; and 12,16,20.

Pythagorean triples can be calculated with a method developed by Euclid. To find a number triple, use the formula $p^2 - q^2$ for a $(p > q)$; $2pq$ for b, and $p^2 + q^2$ for c.

Example:
Find a Pythagorean triple that uses 16 and 1.
Let $p^2 = 16$ and $q^2 = 1$. Then $p = 4$ and $q = 1$.

$a = 16 - 1$ or 15
$b = 2\,(4)(1)$ or 8
$c = 16 + 1$ or 17

The triple is 8,15,17.

Check: $8^2 + 15^2 \stackrel{?}{=} 17^2$
$64 + 225 \stackrel{?}{=} 289$
$289 = 289$

Your Turn

Find Pythagorean triples using the following values for p^2 and q^2, as shown above.

1. 25 and 16   2. 9 and 4
3. 36 and 1

(Answers appear at the end of the section.)

If the lengths of two sides of a right triangle are known, the length of the third side can be calculated using the Pythagorean Theorem. If the unknown side is the hypotenuse, the lengths of the legs are squared and added, and the length of the third side is obtained as the square root of the sum.

Example: Find the length of the hypotenuse of a right triangle with legs of

length 3 and 5, correct to two decimal places.

$$a^2 + b^2 = c^2$$

Let $a = 3$ and $b = 5$. Find c.

$$3^2 + 5^2 = c^2$$
$$9 + 25 = c^2$$
$$34 = c^2$$
$$c = \sqrt{34}, \text{ or about } 5.83$$

Notice that only the positive value of the square root is used. It is impractical to consider the negative value when talking about length.

If the lengths of the hypotenuse and one leg are given, solve the formula for a^2: $a^2 = c^2 - b^2$. The following example shows how to compute the length of the unknown leg.

Example: Find the length of a leg of a right triangle with a hypotenuse of 41 and one leg of 40.

$$a^2 = c^2 - b^2$$

Let $c = 41$ and $b = 40$.

$$a^2 = 41^2 - 40^2$$
$$a^2 = 1681 - 1600$$
$$a^2 = 81$$
$$a = \sqrt{81} \text{ or } 9$$

Your Turn

Find the length of one leg of a right triangle, given that the lengths of the hypotenuse and the second leg are:

4. $c = 10, b = 8$
5. $c = 2, b = 1$
6. $c = 4, b = 3$

(Express non-integral values correct to two decimal places.)

(Answers appear at the end of the section.)

Once you are able to find the length of one of the sides of a right triangle, given the lengths of the other two sides, you can solve a number of problems, such as the following one.

Example: Find the length of the diagonal of a rectangle, given that the length of the rectangle is 24 and the width of the rectangle is 7.

The diagonal of the rectangle forms a right triangle. The two sides of the rectangle form the legs of the right triangle.

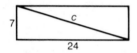

The Pythagorean Theorem can be used.

$$c^2 = a^2 + b^2$$
$$c^2 = 7^2 + 24^2$$
$$c^2 = 49 + 576$$
$$c^2 = 625$$
$$c = 25$$

The formula $a^2 + b^2 = c^2$ has led mathematicians to wonder whether the relationship $a^n + b^n = c^n$ holds when a, b, and c are positive integers and n is an integer greater than 2. The question was answered in a tantalizing fashion by the mathematician Pierre de Fermat, who said that the relationship would not hold for any n greater than 2. From the seventeenth century to the present, mathematicians have been trying to prove that hypothesis, known as "Fermat's Last Theorem." Was Fermat mistaken when he thought that he had a proof? Mathematicians think he had found one. In the course of their efforts to find a proof, they have demonstrated that there are no such values of a, b, and c for all values of n up to a very large number. However, they have not been able to develop a proof that shows the statement to be true for all values of n, so they cannot be absolutely sure of the truth of the statement. The quest for the proof continues.

There are a number of intriguing problems such as this one in mathematics. They are easy to state, but difficult to solve. They appeal to everyone who likes to solve a puzzle. If you would like to try some, turn to Part VI of *Math Power.*

Answers

Polynomials in One Variable (pp. 372–374)

1. $4x^3 - 4x^2 - 4x + 2$ 2. $8x^3 - 5x^2 + x + 11$ 3. $6x^4 + 5x^3 + x$

4. $9x^3 - 5x^2 - x - 3$ 5. $5x^3 - 20x^2 - 25x + 45$ 6. $-20x^4 + 30x^2 - 15x$

7. $2x^4 - 6x^3 - 9x^2 + 39x - 36$ 8. $-4x^3 + 18x^2 - 11x + 12$

9. $5x^5 + 2x^4 + 23x^3 + 8x^2 + 12x$ 10. $6x^5 - 2x^4 + 4x^3 - 9x^2 + 3x - 6$

11. $10x^4 + 7x^3 + 8x^2 - 16x$ 12. $49x^2 + 84x + 36$

Special Products (pp. 374–375)

1. $x^2 - 10x + 25$ 2. $x^2 + 12x + 36$ 3. $4x^2 - 12x + 9$ 4. $25x^2 + 10x + 1$
5. $x^2 - 64$ 6. $x^2 - 1$ 7. $4x^2 - 9$ 8. $81x^2 - 4$

Factoring (pp. 375–381)

1. $3(x^2 + 4x + 3)$ 2. $x(9x^2 + 2x + 7)$ 3. $9(8x + 1)$ 4. cannot be factored
5. $(2a - 5)(2a + 5)$ 6. $(8xy^2 - 7)(8xy^2 + 7)$ 7. $12(x - 2)(x + 2)$
8. $2y(3x^4 - 11)(3x^4 + 11)$ 9. $(a - 7)^2$ 10. $(2c + 1)^2$ 11. $5(d - 3)^2$
12. $(2xy - 3)^2$ 13. $3(3x^2 - x + 3)$ 14. $t(7s + 6)^2$ 15. $(x - 4)(x - 2)$
16. $(x + 3)^2$ 17. $(x + 10)(x - 2)$ 18. $(x - 12)(x + 2)$ 19. $9(x - 2)^2$
20. $x(x + 6)(x - 5)$ 21. $3(x - 6)(x - 2)$ 22. $(xy + 6)(xy + 4)$
23. $2(2a - 1)(a - 3)$ 24. $(2a + 3)(6a - 5)$ 25. $(5b + 3)(2b - 3)$
26. $3(b - 6)(b - 2)$ 27. $5(2c - 9)(2c + 9)$ 28. $6c(4c^2 - 3c - 17)$
29. $(2x + a)(x + 5)$ 30. $(3 + y)(2b - y)$ 31. $4(3c - 2d)(3c - 4)$
32. $(5n - 2p)(3 + 2p)$ 33. $(3b - 1)(9b^2 + 3b + 1)$ 34. $(d + 5)(d^2 - 5d + 25)$
35. $(a - c)(a^2 + ac + c^2)$ 36. $8(5x + 4)(25x^2 - 20x + 16)$

Quadratic Equations (pp. 381–389)

1. $x = -1; x = -2$ 2. $a = -6; a = 3$ 3. $d = 1\frac{1}{2}; d = 8$ 4. $b = -\frac{3}{5}; b = 1\frac{1}{2}$

5. $x = 3; x = -2$ 6. $x = -9; x = 1$ 7. $x = -\frac{2}{3}; x = \frac{1}{2}$ 8. $x = \frac{1}{2}; x = 6$

9. $x = 6; x = -3$ 10. $x = 2\frac{1}{2}; x = 2\frac{1}{2}$ 11. complex   12. irrational   13. irrational

14. real and equal   15. rational   16. 3.873   17. 7.483   18. 9.950   19. 9.381

20. 5.83   21. 9.38   22. 11.92   23. 15.81   24. $x = \frac{1}{2}; x = 1$

25. $a \approx -.93; a \approx 1.26$ 26. $b = -\frac{3}{4}; b = -1$ 27. $a = 1\frac{2}{3}; a = 1\frac{2}{3}$

Pythagorean Theorem (pp. 389–392)

1. 9, 40, 41   2. 5, 12, 13   3. 35, 12, 37   4. 6   5. 1.73   6. 2.65

Section 9

Graphs and Statistics

The twentieth century could be called the Age of Information. More data are now available than ever before in human history. There is a tremendous amount of information gathering for individual countries by scientific groups and all levels of government, and for the world as a whole through such agencies as the United Nations and the World Health Organization.

Populations are counted. Not only are their numbers recorded but also the age, sex, occupation, family status, income, and education of the individual members. Medical scientists report on disease problems and keep records on birth and death rates in various countries. Agricultural and manufacturing output is analyzed worldwide: how many bushels of wheat, corn, and soybeans are harvested; how many barrels of oil are produced; how many tons of coal are mined.

Scientists in many different fields conduct large numbers of experiments and record their data in numerous scientific journals. Astronomers take data on the sun, the moon, the stars, and the galaxies. Rockets sent into space record data on other planets and on the nature and distribution of matter in space. Often they obtain data that could not be obtained from within the earth's atmospheric envelope. Other satellites circle the planet and beam back data about the earth itself. Weather phenomena are monitored and recorded: levels of rainfall and snowfall, temperatures, and storms such as hurricanes and typhoons. Each day newspapers and journals print data on the economy of the nation. These include stock prices, employment, rate of inflation, and the money supply.

Data can also be stored more easily than ever before. High-speed computers record charge sales in a store, deposits and withdrawals from a bank account, and purchases of airline tickets. The abundance of data presents serious problems. How can this flow of information be managed? How can the data be arranged and presented so they are easily and quickly understood?

The collection of techniques used to organize, to analyze, and to present data forms a branch of mathematics called statistics. The techniques used can be broadly placed in two groups. By means of the first group of techniques, data are organized and then presented in various types of tables or graphs. With the second group of techniques, data are analyzed. Two of the most important patterns investigated by analysis are the pattern of central tendency and the pattern of variance. Many sets of data cluster around an average, or *mean*. This is the pattern of central tendency. The data may be tightly clustered or they may be spread out widely. The way in which they spread out is the pattern of variance.

In the following discussion, the basic techniques for organizing, displaying, and analyzing data are presented. Some of the techniques that are used are quite straightforward, like, for example, finding an average. Other techniques are not. Judgment is needed when deciding on the type of presentation to be used or on the scales for a particular graph. Some experimentation may be required in order to reach a decision.

Graphs

In general, graphs present a wide variety of data in an easy-to-read format for quick and ready comprehension. However, graphs can also mislead. Great care must be taken to avoid presenting the material so that it gives an impression different from the one desired. Three useful kinds of graphs are line graphs, bar graphs, and circle graphs.

Line graphs

Line graphs are often found in newspapers and magazines. An example of a graph that might appear in a magazine is shown next. It shows the average price of a used home in thousands of dollars for two towns. The data points are shown for each month of one year.

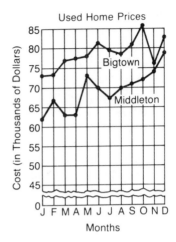

The graph was probably drawn from information in a table like the one below.

	Middleton	Bigtown
Jan.	62,500	73,000
Feb.	67,000	73,300
Mar.	63,000	77,000
Apr.	63,000	77,500
May	73,000	78,000
June	70,000	81,500
July	67,500	79,500
Aug.	70,000	78,500
Sept.	71,000	81,000
Oct.	72,000	86,000
Nov.	74,000	76,000
Dec.	79,000	83,000

Line graphs are usually used to show changes in amounts or results over a period of time. For example, the line graph above makes it easier to see how home prices are changing in the two towns. (They are going up.) From the table it would be hard to compare prices in the two towns, while the graph makes such comparisons easy.

To make the line graph, the horizontal axis is used to represent the months of the year. The vertical axis represents the cost of homes in thousands of dollars.

Notice that the step, or interval, between the amounts is 5, which represents $5000. So to show home sales of $70,000 in August, the person making the graph found the A for August at the bottom of the graph; followed the vertical line above A upward to the point where that line intersected the line for 70 ($70,000); and then placed a dot at that intersection. After all dots were located for a given set of data (one town), the dots were connected with line segments to complete the line graph.

Your Turn

1. The following data were reported on retail sales in two counties for the period of one year. Make a line graph to display the data. Mark the vertical axis from 1.025 billion to 1.625 billion in steps of 0.075 billion. Put the months on the horizontal axis. Mark the data points and connect them with line segments.

Month	Retail sales (billions of dollars)
Jan.	1.100
Feb.	1.025
Mar.	1.075
Apr.	1.085
May	1.190
June	1.175
July	1.145
Aug.	1.125
Sep.	1.145
Oct.	1.155
Nov.	1.225
Dec.	1.540

2. Did retail sales increase or decrease for the year shown on your graph?
3. In which month were retail sales the highest?
4. In which month were retail sales the lowest?

(Answers appear at the end of the section.)

Bar graphs

Bar graphs are generally used to compare amounts or results. Suppose you took a survey and wanted to show the results in graphic form to make comparisons easier. The results of your survey might be displayed in a table like the one below.

Student vacation preferences

Season	Number of students
Spring	40
Summer	45
Winter	30
Autumn	10

To graph this information, use the horizontal axis to show the seasons. Use the vertical axis to show the number of students, using a step of 10. (Any convenient step can be used. Ten is used here because of space considerations. Deciding what step to use and the size of the bars depends on personal judgment and preference.) The graph would look like this:

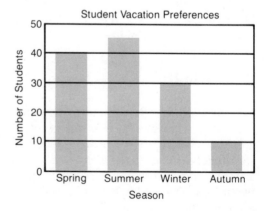

Notice that at a glance you can compare the results and tell the most popular and the least popular season for vacations (summer and autumn, respectively).

Your Turn

5. Use the information below to make a bar graph. Be sure to label the axes.

Enrollment of schools in Bigtown

School	Enrollment
Washington	400
Keller	300
Carver	200
Jackson	250
King	500

6. Which school had the greatest student enrollment?
7. Which school had the smallest student enrollment?

(Answers appear at the end of the section.)

Another type of bar graph enables you to compare two (or more) groups of data with respect to a common characteristic. This is called a dual bar graph.

Recently published data show the median income of full-time year-round workers, 25 years of age and over, based on educational achievement. The data were presented separately for men and for women.

For each of the four educational levels shown—8 years elementary school, 4 years high school, 1 year or more college, 5 years or more college—two bars are shown side-by-side, one for males and one for females.

Multiple bar graphs bring out comparisons very quickly. Note how much easier it is to see the comparison from the graph than from the table of data.

Education	Median income	
	Male	Female
Elem. 8 yr	$14,674	$ 8,857
High School, 4 yr	19,469	11,537
College, 1 yr or more	23,454	14,831
College, 5 yr or more	27,690	18,100

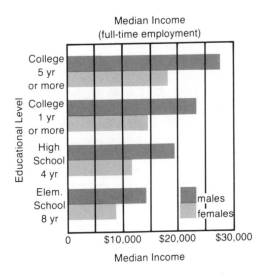

Median Income
(full-time employment)

Your Turn

8. Use the information in the table below to make a dual bar graph. Be sure to label the axes.

Men and women in various jobs with Build-It Company

Type of job	Number of males	Number of females
Custodial	10	8
Clerical	12	15
Secretarial	4	14
Sales	24	16
Middle management	8	18
Top management	8	6

9. Which type of job has the largest difference between the male and female employees?
10. Which type of job has the largest total number of people employed?
11. Are there more male or more female employees in the Build-It Company?

(Answers appear at the end of the section.)

Circle graphs

A graph designed to show relative proportions is the circle graph. The angle of a sector of the circle is made proportional to the percent of an item of the data list to be displayed.

The following breakdown of normal weekday activities was made by a computer operator.

Activity	No. of hr
Working	8
Commuting	1
Shopping and errands	1
Cooking, eating, and personal care	3
Recreation	2
Working around the house	2
Sleeping	7
Total	24

A table is made for the circle graph by calculating the ratio of the time for each activity group to 24 hours, and then calculating that fraction of 360° for the angle of the sector to be used in the circle graph. The table of the computer operator's daily activities appears as follows when all the data are computed and then inserted.

Activity	Hr	Ratio	Angle
Working	8	$\frac{8}{24}$	120°
Commuting	1	$\frac{1}{24}$	15°
Shopping and errands	1	$\frac{1}{24}$	15°
Cooking, eating, and personal care	3	$\frac{3}{24}$	45°
Recreation	2	$\frac{2}{24}$	30°
Working around house	2	$\frac{2}{24}$	30°
Sleeping	7	$\frac{7}{24}$	105°
		Total	360°

The graph then appears as follows.

Circle graphs are often used to display budgets. For example, information supplied by the Office of Management and Budget for one fiscal year shows the U.S. government obtains its funds from the following sources:

For each incoming dollar, the source is:	
Individual income tax	$0.39
Social security receipts	0.28
Corporate income tax	0.08
Excise taxes	0.05
Borrowing	0.15
Other	0.05
Total	$1.00

A chart can be formed, as for the previous graph, to obtain the angles to represent each income source.

Source	% of $	Angle
Inc. tax	.39	.39 × 360 = 140°
Soc. sec.	.28	.28 × 360 = 101°
Corp. inc. tax	.08	.08 × 360 = 29°
Excise taxes	.05	.05 × 360 = 18°
Borrowing	.15	.15 × 360 = 54°
Other	.05	.05 × 360 = 18°

The angle measures are used for the circle graph as shown below.

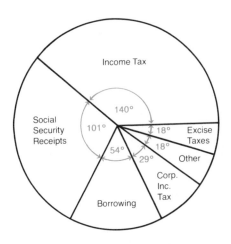

Your Turn

12. Make a table of the major activities of your day and present the data in a circle graph. You may wish to make two graphs, one for weekdays and one for weekends, and compare them.

13. The Office of Management and Budget gave figures on the breakdown of each dollar the U.S. government spent, as follows:

Direct benefit payments to individuals	$0.43
National defense	0.29
Grants to states and localities	0.11
Net interest	0.12
Other	0.05
Total	$1.00

Present these data in a circle graph.

(Answers appear at the end of the section.)

Using Statistics

Statistics is the science of collecting and using facts. In everyday conversation, the term *statistics* is often used to refer to data or numbers derived from a set of data. The numbers derived are, of course, only a part of the subject of statistics. These numbers are not always easily interpreted.

Suppose, for example, that a study was made by a school district on the number of schoolage children per family in that school district. The school district surveyed exactly 600 families and found there were 1500 school-age children in these families. Thus, the average number of schoolage children per family was $\frac{1500}{600}$, or 2.50. How will this figure, or "statistic," be treated?

Obviously, only a whole number can properly describe the number of children.

Should the number 2.50 be rounded to a whole number either because only whole numbers were used to derive it, or because only whole numbers have "real" meaning for this problem? The answer for statistical analysis is that since there are 3 and 4 significant digits in each of the numerals 600 and 1500 in this particular problem, it is proper to have 3 significant digits in the quotient. Also, for statistical purposes, it would be misleading to round the figure of 2.50. This number does have statistical meaning.

For example, suppose that the school district wished to estimate the enrollment for the following year. It is expecting 100 families to move into newly completed apartments in the summer in a housing development similar to others that have been built recently. If the same family patterns hold for the new families as for the families surveyed, the school district might use *statistical inference* (that is, predicting on the basis of the statistical analysis of a sample). It would guess that 100 families × 2.5 school-age children per family would bring 250 new students into the schools in the new term.

Note the "if" in the prediction. It is not difficult to obtain statistical figures, but it is considerably harder to interpret and apply them, especially in decision-making problems that involve predictions. Great care and judgment must be exercised in interpreting and making use of statistical results.

Organizing Data

The techniques of organizing and interpreting data can best be shown with an example: On a midterm examination in mathematics, a teacher recorded the following grades.

88	65	84	91	66
79	90	62	76	90
100	71	71	48	80
76	73	92	73	25
65	38	78	73	94
82	68	65	84	76
43	81	70	96	75
80	100	84	80	73
70	78	85	87	95
79	69	94	88	78

How well did the class do on this examination? How can individual students decide how well they did in comparison to the other students? It is very difficult to answer these questions just by looking at the set of grades, or "raw data," as they are called.

In order to obtain such information, the teacher analyzed the data in the following way:

1. All grades were listed in order from the highest to the lowest, and each grade was recorded with a tally mark. The chart appeared as follows:

100//	90//	80///	70//	60	50	40	30
99	89	79 //	69 /	59	49	39	29
98	88//	78 ///	68 /	58	48 /	38 /	28
97	87/	77	67	57	47	37	27
96/	86	76///	66/	56	46	36	26
95/	85/	75 /	65 ///	55	45	35	25 /
94//	84 ///	74	64	54	44	34	24
93	83	73/////63		53	43 /	33	23
92/	82/	72	62 /	52	42	32	22
91/	81/	71//	61	51	41	31	21

2. Next, the following quick analysis was made. The range, or difference between the highest and the lowest recorded values (grades, in this study), were noted.

highest grade	lowest grade	range
100	− 25	= 75

The range of grades was rather large. How many times each grade occurred (the frequency of the grades) was examined, and the grade with the highest frequency was noted. This grade was 73. The value with the highest frequency is called the mode. (There may be more than one mode in a set of data.)

The mode does not give too much information in this analysis, since several grades had frequencies of 3: 84, 80, 78, 76 and 65. However, as all these grades with higher frequencies were passing grades (65 or above was passing for the test), it began to appear that the examination results were fairly good for the class as a whole. Also, the 7 grades with a frequency of 2 were also passing grades.

3. The next step was to determine the *median* grade. The median is one measure of central tendency. It is the value (in this case, the grade) that is in the middle of the data set when the data are put in order from highest to lowest. As there are 50 grades in this set, the center lies between the 25th and the 26th entry. When the center falls between two values, it is customary to average the two values in order to determine the median. The 25th and the 26th values are both 78 in this study, so the median grade is 78.

The teacher now has one figure that shows how the class did as a whole. The central grade (by this measure) is well above the passing mark (65 for this test), so the teacher feels that the class performance was quite good. The individual students can also judge how well they did with respect to the class as a whole. They can see whether they were above or below the center value and by how much their grade differed.

4. The next step was to find the average grade, or the *mean*. The average is obtained in the standard way: all the values are added and the sum is divided by the number of addends. In this study, the total of all the grades is obtained and then divided by 50, the number of tests. The sum of the grades is written as Σg, where the Greek capital S (sigma) represents "sum." In order to show that 50 items are to be added, the symbol $\sum_{i=1}^{i=50} g_i$ is used. It means that the sum, $g_1 + g_2 + g_3 + \ldots + g_{49} + g_{50}$, is to be obtained. In this study, $\sum_{i=1}^{i=50} g_i = 3{,}828$. The mean is then $\frac{\Sigma g}{n} = \frac{3{,}828}{50}$ or 76.56, where n is the number of grades. As each of the entries has at least two significant digits, the mean is rounded to 77.

In this study, the mean, 77, is very close to the value of the median, 78, and the mode, 73. This does not always happen. You can average 100, 100, and 0 and obtain a mean of 67, a median of 100, and a mode of 100. The fact that the mean and the median are close in value is an indication that the data are clustering around a central value. The teacher also notes that only four grades fell below a value of 63, so the wide range first noted (a spread of 75 in the grades) does not indicate that many poor grades are being balanced by a number of very high grades to produce a satisfactory average. It is also noted that these four students, 8% of the class, are doing far less well than the other members of the class and are evidently in need of remedial help.

The teacher is quite pleased that the class average, 77, is well above the passing grade for the exam, 65. The teacher feels that the examination was properly constructed, which is particularly important because the test is a standardized examination made up by a committee working with state requirements for the course. It was not tailored to suit this particular class. The results indicate that the students have mastered the techniques and concepts a group of mathematician-educators considered important.

On the basis of class performance in doing homework and participating in the classroom discussions and demonstrations, the teacher believed, before giving the examination, that the average or mean should have fallen somewhere between 75 and 80. The teacher is now confident that the test is a good reflection of the students' performances. If the results had been poorer than expected, these possibilities might have been considered:

1. whether a good "feel" for the students' ability to progress had been developed;
2. whether the classroom program being followed was appropriate for the mastery of the state-mandated goals;
3. whether the exam was appropriately designed to test the points it was supposed to cover.

On the basis of the analysis, the teacher decided to continue in the general way in which the first half of the term had been conducted. But consideration would be given to the problem of the four students with the very low grades and also of the students who had just passed.

Here is another example with a small set of data. Make sure you understand it before going on to the exercise.

Allowances per week of 10 students

$5.00	$10.00	$8.00	$20.00	$3.00
$6.00	$11.00	$9.00	$12.00	$2.00

When listed in order, from least to greatest, the amounts are

$ 2.00	There is one of each amount;
3.00	there is no mode.
5.00	
6.00	The range is 20 − 2, or 18.
8.00	
9.00	The median is the average of
10.00	the middle (fifth and sixth)
11.00	values.
12.00	Median = $\dfrac{8.00 + 9.00}{2}$ or $8.50
20.00	

The mean is the sum of the amounts ($86.00) divided by the number of allowances (10).

$$\text{Mean} = \frac{\sum\limits_{i=1}^{i=10} g_i}{10} = \$8.60$$

Your Turn

In the classified advertisements recently, a number of positions were listed for well-qualified secretaries with several years of experience. The salaries listed were as follows:

$16,000	$16,900
$22,000	$18,000
$15,000	$15,600
$14,300	$12,500
$15,600	$14,500
$18,000	$14,300
$17,000	$17,500
$15,600	$16,500
$14,000	$14,300
$14,300	$16,800

1. Find the range.
2. Find the mode.
3. Find the median.
4. Find the mean.

(Answers appear at the end of the section.)

There are other ways to arrive at a mean for a set of data besides the one that has been demonstrated. When there are very large sets of data, they are often put into groups and an average value obtained for each grouping. Then a weighted average is determined by multiplying the average value for the group by the frequency of the items in that group. The method is easily seen by reconsidering the data set of grades, previously analyzed. You will also then be able to compare the results obtained with the two slightly different techniques.

The table below organizes the data into 5-point grade spans. If the number of items in the data set had been larger, they could have been grouped into 10-point rather than 5-point grade spans.

Group	Frequency	Group average	Product
96–100	3	98	294
91–95	5	93	465
86–90	5	88	440
81–85	6	83	498
76–80	11	78	858
71–75	7	73	511
66–70	5	68	340
61–65	4	63	252
56–60	0	58	0
51–55	0	53	0
46–50	1	48	48
41–45	1	43	43
36–40	1	38	38
31–35	0	33	0
26–30	0	28	0
21–25	1	23	23
		Total	3810

The sum of the products of the average value for a group and the frequency for that group is 3810. Divide this by the number of grades (50). The mean, or average, obtained with the grouping is 76.2, or 76 when rounded to two significant digits. This value is very close to the mean of 77 previously obtained by adding each of the values separately and then dividing by 50.

Your Turn

5. Group the data below using a 10-point span (50–59, 60–69, and so on) and make a chart.

Tickets sold

50	122	95	100	72	138	101
70	76	54	102	65	57	73
104	82	110	125	99	126	79
137	143	120	131	56	125	93

6. Find the mean.

(Answers appear at the end of the section.)

Displaying Data

The data have been collected, organized, and analyzed. The next step is to represent the data with a graph that will communicate the important values quickly.

Using the data at left, a histogram can be made. A *histogram* is a bar graph used in statistics to display a frequency distribution in which vertical rectangles or columns are constructed, with the width of each rectangle being a class interval and the height a distance corresponding to the frequency in that class interval. The horizontal axis in this example is labeled with scores, as shown in the following figure, and the vertical axis shows the frequency. Each group in the last table is represented by a bar: 96–100, 91–95, 86–90, 81–85, and so on. The height of each bar corresponds to the frequency. The mean value is also shown on the graph as the vertical line. You could also show the median and the mode. However, care must be taken not to clutter the graph. The graph shows the distribution of grades in an easily read format.

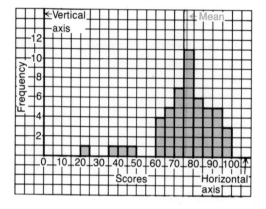

Another method of displaying the data is with a line graph called a frequency polygon. The data for the frequency polygon come from the same table.

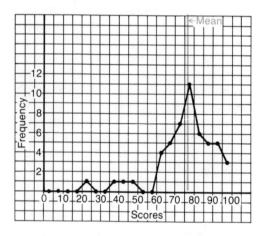

Another interesting way to display the data requires that four other columns of data be calculated. These new sets of data are the

a. Cumulative frequency—the sum of the frequencies as one proceeds

from the lowest grouping to the highest;

b. The relative frequency—the ratio of the frequency for a group to the total frequency (50 for this study);

c. The cumulative relative frequency—the ratio of the cumulative frequency to the total frequency.

In the last column to the right, the cumulative relative frequency is listed in percent.

Group	Freq.	Cum. freq.	Rel. freq.	Cum. rel. freq.	Cum. rel. freq. (%)
0–5	0	0	0	0	0
6–10	0	0	0	0	0
11–15	0	0	0	0	0
16–20	0	0	0	0	0
21–25	1	1	0.02	0.02	2
26–30	0	1	0	0.02	2
31–35	0	1	0	0.02	2
36–40	1	2	0.02	0.04	4
41–45	1	3	0.02	0.06	6
46–50	1	4	0.02	0.08	8
51–55	0	4	0	0.08	8
56–60	0	4	0	0.08	8
61–65	4	8	0.08	0.16	16
66–70	5	13	0.10	0.26	26
71–75	7	20	0.14	0.40	40
76–80	11	31	0.22	0.62	62
81–85	6	37	0.12	0.74	74
86–90	5	42	0.10	0.84	84
91–95	5	47	0.10	0.94	94
96–100	3	50	0.06	1.00	100

The S-shaped cumulative relative frequency curve, expressed in percent, is shown in the graph that follows. For the cumulative relative frequency curve (plotted here in percent for ease in reading), the frequency is plotted for the group value at the right side of each group interval (that is, 5, 10, 15, 20, and so on.)

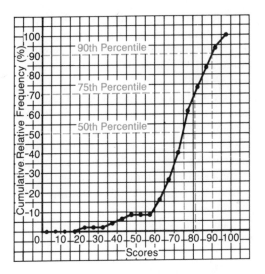

Interesting information can be obtained from this curve. Three horizontal dotted lines have been drawn to the curve, and the vertical lines drawn from the intersection of these horizontal lines with the curve show the corresponding reading on the horizontal axis. The horizontal lines are called the "percentiles." At the 90th percentile, students know that their scores are in the top 10% of the group; 90% of the students have lower scores. For the 75th percentile, the students' scores are in the top 25%; 75% of the scores are lower. The 50th percentile corresponds to the mean; half the scores are above that line and half are below.

Your Turn

A class of high-school students recently conducted a survey on the television-viewing habits of students in their class. One hundred students responded to a questionnaire. The students were asked to keep track for four weeks of the time they spent viewing television and then to compute and report an average daily time. When the responses were received, the data were listed and grouped. Following are the results of the survey.

H = hours spent viewing television each day, on the average; $a < H \le b$

Group a–b	Frequency
0 –0.5	5
0.5–1.0	9
1.0–1.5	16
1.5–2.0	21
2.0–2.5	24
2.5–3.0	15
3.0–3.5	6
3.5–4.0	3
4.0–4.5	1
Total	100

1. Calculate the cumulative frequency.
2. Calculate the cumulative relative frequency in percent:

$$\text{Cum. rel. freq. (\%)} = \left(\frac{\text{Cum. freq.}}{N} \right) \times 100;$$

N = 100 in this study.
3. Graph the cumulative relative frequency. Put the hours, 0, 0.5, 1.0, 1.5, . . . 4.5, on the horizontal axis. Connect the data points with a smooth curve.
4. Robin watches 2 hours of television per day, on the average. What is Robin's percentile?
5. If Nita is in the 30th percentile, she watches up to approximately how many hours per day, on the average?

(Answers appear at the end of the section.)

Variance

You have seen the various ways by which the central tendency of data is measured: the mean, the median, and the mode. So far, only one measure of the scatter of data has been mentioned, the range. This is the difference between the highest and the lowest values in the data set. The measure of the scatter—that is, how much the data spread out from the mean—is very important for the interpretation of the data. A grade of 80 when the mean is 75 has one interpretation if most of the grades are close to the mean (say between 70 and 80); but it has a different interpretation if many of the grades are in the mid-nineties. Several methods have been developed to measure the scatter.

In the study of data on page 400, a set of grades was examined. The mean for this set was 77, but the grades ranged from 25 to 100. One way to measure the scatter is to determine the difference between a grade and the mean. If the algebraic signs of the differences are kept, however, the positive and negative values will cancel out when the deviations are added up, as the mean was calculated to be right in the middle. You may recall that half of the area of the histogram lay on each side of the mean. Since only the distance of a data point from the mean is of interest, the absolute value of the difference, or variation, is taken. In the usual notation, the data point is denoted by X. X_i stands for a particular data point. $\overline{X}$ stands for the average X-value, or mean. Thus, the formula for the deviations can be written as

$$|X_i - \overline{X}|$$

To obtain an average deviation, all the deviations are added and the sum is divided by n, the number of data used. The formula can then be written with the symbol for sum, Σ, as follows:

$$\frac{1}{n}\sum_{i=1}^{i=n} |X_i - \overline{X}|$$

The absolute value sign is awkward to use in computational work, so mathematicians devised another way to eliminate the negative values. If you take the positive square root of the square of a number, you obtain the positive value of the number. For example, $\sqrt{(5)^2} = 5$ and $\sqrt{(-5)^2} = 5$. The technique for eliminating the negative signs is used to obtain a measure of scatter called the variance. It is obtained by taking the average of the sum of the squares of the deviations from the mean.

The steps in the procedure are as follows.

1. The mean of the data set is determined.

2. The deviations of the data from the mean value are determined. Each data point from the original set may be used; or, when the data set is large, the average values for each class in a grouped set may be used.

    It is very important to remember that when grouped data are used, the deviation for a group has to be multiplied by the number of values in that group.

3. The squares of the deviations are summed.

4. The sum of the squares of the deviations is divided by n, the total number of entries. It is important, if you work with grouped data, to remember that n is the original number of values of the variable. The value that has been obtained, the average of the squares of the deviations from the mean, is the variance.

A very important value is obtained from the variance. The square root of the variance is called the standard deviation.

It is the most widely used number for expressing the variation of the data from the mean. It is denoted by the lower case Greek letter *s*, σ (sigma).

$$\sigma = \sqrt{\frac{1}{n} \sum_{i=1}^{i=n} |X_i - \overline{X}|^2}$$

The formula for the standard deviation summarizes all the steps used to obtain the variance; then the square root of the variance is obtained. The formula looks rather complicated. However, as you can see from the steps listed above, all that is required is arithmetic. (It helps to have a handheld calculator to do the arithmetic, of course.)

The standard deviation of the data is determined below for the set of grades that was examined earlier in this section. As there were 50 values in the original set, the reduced set of 12 groups is used.

X_i	f	$|X_i - \overline{X}|$	$|X_i - \overline{X}|^2$	$f|X - \overline{X}|^2$
98	3	21	441	1323
93	5	16	256	1280
88	5	11	121	605
83	6	6	36	216
78	11	1	1	11
73	7	−4	16	112
68	5	−9	81	405
63	4	−14	196	784
48	1	−29	841	841
43	1	−34	1156	1156
38	1	−39	1521	1521
23	1	−54	2916	2916
$\overline{X}$ = 77			Total	11,170

The first column lists the average value for each of the twelve groups, under the heading X_i. The next column lists the number of entries in each group, f. The third column lists the deviations

from the mean, 77. The heading is $|X_i - \overline{X}|$. The fourth column lists the squares of the deviations, $|X_i - \overline{X}|^2$. The last column multiplies each deviation squared by the frequency for that group so that the square of the deviation is applied to every data entry in the appropriate group. The total at the bottom of the last column, then, is the sum of the squares of the deviations for all fifty grades. The quotient obtained when that figure is divided by 50 is the variance, and the square root of the variance is the standard deviation.

The average deviation squared is obtained by dividing the sum by 50, the number of original values.

$$\frac{11,170}{50} = 223$$

The standard deviation, σ, is the square root of the variance.

$$\sigma = \sqrt{223} \text{ or } 15$$

In more advanced work, statisticians study the shape of the frequency polygon. When there are a large number of data, this polygon takes on a bell-shaped curve for many sets of data. In such circumstances, about 68% of the data lie within a band the width of two standard deviations, one on each side of the mean. In this study, this means that about 68% of the grades fall in the range from 77 − 15 to 77 + 15, or from 62 to 92. Again, for data that are considered to be "normally distributed," 95% of the data fall within a 4σ band (2 standard deviations on each side of the mean). Thus, a small value for the standard deviation shows that the data cluster tightly about the mean, while a large standard deviation indicates that the data are widely scattered.

Using the frequency polygon (line graph), the standard deviations can be shown as on the following page.

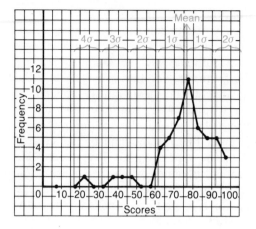

Notice that most scores fall within one standard deviation, either positive or negative. The very low scores do not fall within 2 standard deviations. These students need special help.

Your Turn

On a test students received the following scores.

98	95	55	87	94	99	93	66
23	88	46	65	58	87	78	86
87	80	75	60	55	67	95	96
88	94	55	64	56	69	87	98
99	77	85	80	79	87	98	87

1. Use ranges of 10 (91–100, average 96; 81–90, average 86, and so on) to find the mean.
2. Make a frequency polygon (line graph) showing the results.
3. Find the standard deviation and show that on the frequency polygon.
4. Were most of the scores within 2 standard deviations?

(Answers appear at the end of the section.)

Answers

Graphs (pp. 395–399)

1.

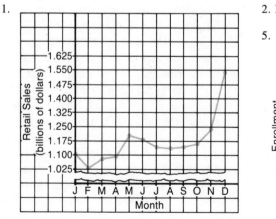

2. Increase   3. December   4. February

5.

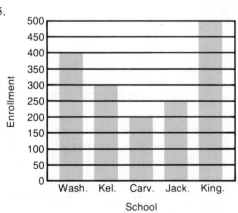

6. King   7. Carver

8.

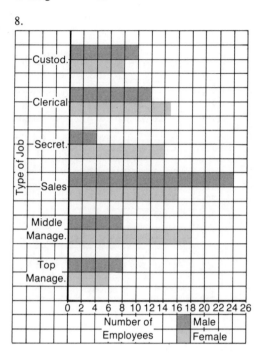

9. Secretarial and middle management

10. Sales   11. Female

12. Answers will vary.

13.

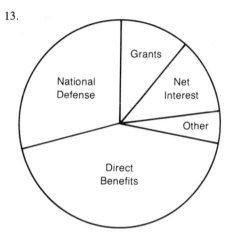

Organizing Data (pp. 400–403)

1. 9500

2. 14,300

3. 15,600

4. 15,935

5. _____

Group	Frequency	Group average	Product
140–149	1	145	145
130–139	3	135	405
120–129	5	125	625
110–119	1	115	115
100–109	4	105	420
90–99	3	95	285
80–89	1	85	85
70–79	5	75	375
60–69	1	65	65
50–59	4	55	220
		Total	2740

6. 98

Displaying Data (pp. 403–405)

1.–2.   3.

Group a–b	Frequency	Cumulative frequency	Cumulative relative frequency (%)
0–0.5	5	5	5
0.5–1.0	9	14	14
1.0–1.5	16	30	30
1.5–2.0	21	51	51
2.0–2.5	24	75	75
2.5–3.0	15	90	90
3.0–3.5	6	96	96
3.5–4.0	3	99	99
4.0–4.5	1	100	100

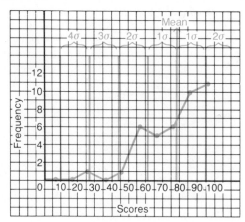

4. 51%   5. 1.5 hours

Variance (pp. 405–408)

1. Mean = 78

2.

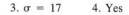

3. $\sigma = 17$ 4. Yes

Section 10

Formal Geometry

Of all of the sections in Part IV, this is the one which should be read the most slowly and carefully. It is best to study one section until it is thoroughly mastered before proceeding to the next. The chief problem that may be encountered is that of trying to work through the material with incomplete understanding of some of the concepts. Formal geometry is a step-by-step process, and each portion is essential for the one that comes next and rests on it. Your understanding of formal geometry may require some review of other sections in Part IV.

In this section, you should not be concerned with measurements or with finding a numerical solution to a problem. You will be examining the foundation of mathematics: its principles and its rules of reasoning. The reward for the effort that has to be made is that an understanding of the nature of formal geometry will provide you with an insight into the essential nature of all of mathematics.

History of Geometry

A gift from the Greek mathematicians who lived and worked over two thousand years ago has determined the nature of mathematics from that time to the present. The gift is formal geometry.

Much practical geometry had been developed in the ancient world. Both the Babylonians and the Egyptians used applied geometry to carry out surveying, construction, and astronomical work. They developed practical methods for making direct and indirect measurements. However, there is no indication of the use of a formal system of logic to demonstrate the truth of certain statements. This aspect of geometry, which is considered to be the essential part of geometric thought, was an invention of Greek mathematician-philosophers.

The Greek mathematicians were seeking order and structure in the world.

411

They sought to discover the ultimate nature of the universe and the manner in which it operates. They carried out their work by abstracting general principles from experience, primarily with geometric aspects of objects. They probably chose to work with mathematical objects rather than biological ones because mathematical objects are much easier to analyze. The characteristics of mathematical objects are uniform and easy to describe.

Another aspect of the geometry developed was a formal system of logic with strict rules. The structure and the rules of reasoning can be applied to other objects as well. Thus, for all these centuries, the study of formal geometry has been thought to develop one's reasoning abilities.

The chief reason for studying formal geometry is to learn to construct a formal argument based upon a strictly observed set of rules. The material studied is not of great importance, as the geometry used to solve problems today is the analytic geometry that will be considered in the section on coordinate geometry.

The geometric objects used in the system are idealized objects—points, lines, planes, and space figures that can exist only in one's thoughts. The objects encountered in the world of experience are rough "copies" of the ideal objects. For example, an ideal point takes up no space at all, while a real point has to have some dimension, however small.

Thales of Miletus

The work began, so far as the records show, with the mathematician Thales of Miletus. Thales, often called the Father of Geometry and known as one of the Seven Wise Men of ancient Greece, lived in the sixth century B.C. When he was still young, he made a fortune selling oil during a time of scarcity and was able to retire early. A talented individual filled with curiosity, he had traveled considerably in the region. He had learned the practical geometry that existed, and he came to see that generalizations or abstractions could be made that drew the knowledge together in a logical, consistent manner. Most importantly, he was not satisfied with the approximate answers that one obtains by means of inductive reasoning (reasoning from particular cases to a general rule). He saw a way to reason deductively, by accepting a few inductive propositions and then arguing from the general case to a particular instance. Thales demonstrated five geometric propositions:

1.   A circle is bisected by its diameter.

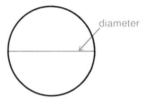

2.   The base angles of an isosceles triangle are congruent.

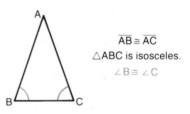

$\overline{AB} \cong \overline{AC}$
△ABC is isosceles.
$\angle B \cong \angle C$

3.   The pair of opposite (vertical) angles formed by two intersecting lines are congruent.

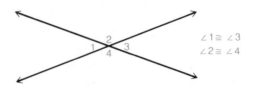

$\angle 1 \cong \angle 3$
$\angle 2 \cong \angle 4$

4. Two triangles with an angle-angle-side or angle-side-angle correspondence are congruent (AAS and ASA theorems).

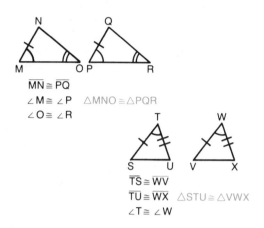

$\overline{MN} \cong \overline{PQ}$
$\angle M \cong \angle P$ $\triangle MNO \cong \triangle PQR$
$\angle O \cong \angle R$

$\overline{TS} \cong \overline{WV}$
$\overline{TU} \cong \overline{WX}$ $\triangle STU \cong \triangle VWX$
$\angle T \cong \angle W$

5. An angle inscribed in a semicircle is a right angle.

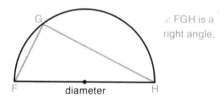

$\angle FGH$ is a right angle.

Pythagoras

Thales taught his subject as well as inventing it. His most brilliant student was Pythagoras, whose history will be reviewed here.

Pythagoras headed a brotherhood that studied number theory, music, astronomy, and geometry. At that period, mathematics was intertwined with religious and philosophical thought. These ideas were not separated then as they are now.

The Pythagoreans developed the work begun by Thales. In geometry, they developed definitions of terms, put the theorems in an orderly sequence, and indicated that they were building a mathematical structure. They started with a firm foundation and derived each new theorem from the material that had come before.

While many of the achievements of the Pythagoreans are credited to their leader, Pythagoras, there is no way of knowing the author of a particular concept or theorem. One of the important theorems proved by the Pythagoreans states that the sum of the measures of the angles of a triangle is equal to the measure of two right angles. They also worked out the solution of the quadratic equation by geometric means to obtain the real roots of a quadratic.

The most famous theorem associated with the Pythagoreans bears their name—the Pythagorean Theorem. It states that the square of the length of the hypotenuse of a right triangle is equal to the sum of the squares of the lengths of the two legs of the triangle.

A number of people in different locations knew the property for special sets of natural numbers (for example, the 3, 4, 5 right triangle). The Chinese had studied such sets around 1000 B.C., and the Egyptians had studied them 1000 years before that time. The property for the 3, 4, 5 right triangle was apparently used by surveyors to set up right angles. A knotted rope with segments of equal length was wrapped around stakes; the angle formed by the sides of lengths 3 and 4 formed a right angle.

There is no indication, however, that at these early times anyone knew that the property held not only for the 3, 4, 5, and other special right triangles but indeed for all right triangles. It is not known which proof Pythagoras gave for this theorem, but there can be little doubt that it was a geometric proof.

The Pythagorean Theorem is the most popular theorem in all of mathematics. It holds a fascination that is as strong today as it was some 2500 years ago. In his second edition of the book entitled *The Pythagorean Proposition* (1968), Elisha Loomis presents 367 different proofs of the theorem, and more have been devised since the book was published. One proof was developed by the twentieth president of the United States, James Garfield.

Professor Loomis makes some very interesting observations about the various proofs for the Pythagorean Theorem. First, he places all the proofs in just four groups: (a) algebraic, (b) geometric, (c) vector (called the quaternion group), and (d) dynamic (proofs that use mass and velocity). He concluded from his study of the proofs that the number of algebraic and geometric proofs is limitless. He also found that all the geometric proofs are based on the comparison of areas. He further discovered that all of the geometric proofs are based on just ten types of geometric figures, and no trigonometric proof is possible, since trigonometry is based on the Pythagorean Theorem. That would be arguing in a circle.

An algebraic proof of the Pythagorean Theorem and computations based on the theorem are presented in the section on intermediate algebra.

Euclid

All the work that had been done to 300 B.C. was drawn together by the Greek mathematician who is probably the best known of all—Euclid. Very little is known of the details of Euclid's life. He lived around 300 B.C. and founded a school at Alexandria. There is no doubt about his achievements, however. He produced a work called *The Elements,* consisting of thirteen parts, or books. The first six books cover plane geometry; other portions cover arithmetic, number theory, the theory of proportions, the irrational numbers, and solid geometry.

The Elements is the second most successful book that has ever been written. It is surpassed only by the Bible. It has been translated into almost all of the languages of the earth. More importantly, it is an effective book at the present time, although it is 2300 years old.

Some changes have been introduced, of course, but it is the basis for almost every elementary textbook on plane geometry that is written and used.

Euclid gathered together all of the mathematical knowledge of his time, but he did not simply collect and edit the material. He developed further the ideas of formal geometry to provide a carefully structured, rigorous system that has remained effective from his time to the present. The nature and workings of this system will be examined next.

Induction and Deduction

Formal geometry uses reasoning by deduction, as opposed to reasoning by induction. You can see how the two types of reasoning differ in this example.

Suppose that you have measured the angles of several triangles and make the discovery that the sum of the measures of the angles seems to be almost the same for every triangle you examined. When you found the result for three triangles, you thought you might have made a mathematical discovery. You then eagerly checked three more triangles. To the best of your ability to measure, you decided the value is approximately 180°.

You say approximately because, with your protractor, the sum might be 179°, 180°, or 181°.

There is a second problem to consider. You might measure the angles of another six triangles, or those of one hundred triangles, but you cannot be absolutely certain that you will never find a triangle for which the sum of the measures of the angles is a different value.

You can make a statement induced from (drawn from) this set of experiences. You can state that the sum of the measures of the angles of a triangle is 180° ± 1° (that is, the sum is within 1° of 180°). The results have been expressed as a range of values. You have drawn a conclusion inductively from experience.

You can even deal with the second problem—the likelihood of finding a very different kind of triangle. If you take a sufficiently large sample of triangles, you can add a statement, based on probability theory (*see* Pt. VI, Sec. 5), about the degree of probability that the inductive statement is true.

On the other hand, with deductive reasoning, you can argue from a set of agreed-upon statements to a guaranteed conclusion that the sum of the measures of the angles of a triangle (*every* triangle) is 180°. The results are ironclad. You state the result with complete confidence for the system within which you are working. The proof of this theorem will be presented under "Proofs" later in this section.

It is very important to note that the result will be guaranteed for a *particular* system. Before investigating the nature of proofs, you will examine more carefully how a system is built that provides such certainty. At the close of this discussion of formal geometry, the question of other systems will be considered.

Building a System

A system's basic materials are (1) defined terms and (2) statements that have been proved, or proved theorems. There are also a small number of undefined terms as well as some unproved statements, called postulates or axioms.

Undefined terms

Why should it be necessary to have undefined terms and unproved statements in a rigorous system? Because of the nature of definition and of proof, these undefined terms and unproved statements have to be used to get the system started.

Terms are defined by means of simpler terms. For example, a polygon is the union of line segments, intersecting only at their end points, and with no two adjacent segments collinear. Then *line segment* must be defined as a set consisting of two points and all the points between them. Then *points* have to be defined. If this is continued it will go on endlessly.

$$\text{Term} \longleftarrow \frac{\text{simpler}}{\text{term}} \longleftarrow \frac{\text{simpler}}{\text{term}} \longleftarrow \cdots$$

A definite starting point for definitions is needed. A starting point is obtained by accepting certain terms as being undefined. These terms are described but are not defined in the manner of other terms in the system. It is felt that these terms are so well understood from common human experience that accepting them would cause no difficulty. The terms *point, line,* and *plane* are accepted as undefined terms.

Postulates

The same problem exists with proofs that exists with definitions. Arguments are based on statements that have been proved, but in order to get the system started, some statements are needed with which to work. Thus, a set of statements, called postulates, is accepted without proof.

How is this special set of statements obtained? The postulates that are used in ordinary plane (or Euclidean) geometry were arrived at from experience—they are inductive. They correspond to what is found in the physical world; this fact makes Euclid's geometry very useful.

It is possible to set up a geometry system with a different set of postulates, as you will see later. The only caution is that the postulates must not contradict one another.

Euclid chose five postulates for his system. There are several other postulates that are embedded in his work. In addition, Euclid used several axioms (which he called common notions) in his proofs. The term *postulate* was used for assumed statements that apply to the particular area of study (in this case, geometry), while the term *axiom* refers to assumed statements that are applicable to the entire field of study.

The five basic postulates used by Euclid can be stated in modern terms as follows.

1. Two points determine a straight line.
2. A straight line can be extended indefinitely in either direction.
3. A point (for the center) and a length (for the radius) determine a circle.
4. All right angles are congruent.
5. Through a point not on a line exactly one line can be drawn parallel to the given line.

The Fifth Postulate is famous. For centuries it made mathematicians uneasy. Many were sure that this statement need not be postulated but, rather, could be proved from the other postulates. Attempts to prove the Fifth Postulate were unsuccessful, although a few mathematicians believed that they had succeeded. The attempts, however, were highly fruitful in that they brought about much development in mathematics. In modern times it has been established that the famous Fifth should indeed have the status of postulate; it cannot be proved from the other postulates.

Euclid did not state the Fifth Postulate in the form in which it is stated above. He said that parallel lines are lines in the same plane that do not meet, however far they are extended. One can see that this postulate appears to be different from the other postulates.

Axioms

Of the various axioms that are listed in the work of Euclid by those who followed him (his original document no longer exists), five are usually thought of as being in his presentation. These are:

1. Things equal to the same thing are equal to each other. (This is now stated as the transitivity property of equality.)
2. If equals are added to equals, the sums are equal. (This is now stated as the addition property of equality.)
3. If equals are subtracted from equals, the differences are equal. (This property is covered by the addition property of equality, since work with signed numbers is now possible. Subtraction is simply the addition of a negative number.)

4. The whole is equal to the sum of its parts and is greater than any of its parts. (This property is now stated by defining "betweenness" for points on a line segment, and the angle addition postulate.)
5. Things that can be made to coincide are equal to each other. (Congruency is defined as a relationship between figures that has two parts: similarity of the figures and equality of their areas.)

Among the axioms listed by Euclid, several are now used for algebra.

Postulates used today

The lists of postulates presented in modern textbooks are considerably longer than Euclid's list. From twenty to thirty postulates may be listed in an elementary textbook on geometry. It is a fundamental concept in mathematics that the number of postulates should be kept to a minimum. From Aristotle to the present, mathematicians have stressed that no more should be assumed or presented for a proof than is absolutely necessary. However, in order to simplify beginning work, it may be useful or easier to list and use as postulates some statements that could be proved as theorems.

Following is a list of postulates that are generally given in textbooks. It is important in using a particular text that you note the postulates chosen by the author and the order in which they are given. One cannot use a postulate or a theorem until it is presented. Each author has a choice as to how to arrange the material, and it is necessary to follow the author's presentation in working with a textbook.

You may wish to review the section on informal geometry at this point. In it are experiments that present some of the postulates in the list and show that the postulates are consistent with experience.

1. Two points determine exactly one line.
2. Three points determine exactly one plane.
3. A line contains at least two points; a plane contains at least three non-collinear points; space contains at least four non-coplanar points.
4. If two points of a line lie in a plane, then all points of that line lie in the plane.
5. Two planes are either parallel or they intersect. If two planes intersect, their intersection is a line.
6. The points of a line can be placed in a one-to-one correspondence with the set of real numbers. The correspondence can be made so that any point can be assigned the number 0 and any other point can be assigned a positive number.
7. The set of measures of angles can be placed in a one-to-one correspondence with the numbers from 0 to 180.
8. If D is a point in the interior of angle ACB, then $m\angle ACD + m\angle DCB = m\angle ACB$.
9. Two triangles are congruent if the corresponding parts consisting of two sides and the included angle (SAS) are congruent.
10. Two triangles are congruent if the corresponding parts consisting of three sides (SSS) are congruent.
11. Two triangles are congruent if the corresponding parts consisting of two angles and one side (ASA) are congruent.
12. Through a point not on a given line, exactly one line can be drawn parallel to the given line.
13. Every polygonal region can be assigned a positive number (for

area). The side of an arbitrary square region can be assigned the number 1, and the area of the region is then obtained as the square of the side (s^2), or 1.

14. The area of the union of two or more polygonal regions with no interior points in common is equal to the sum of the areas of the individual regions.

Your Turn

Tell whether each of the following is an undefined term, an axiom, or a postulate.

1. Two points determine a straight line.
2. If $a = b$, then $a + c = b + c$.
3. A point is a location on a plane or in space.

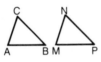

4. If $\angle A \cong \angle M$, $\overline{AC} \cong \overline{MN}$, and $\overline{AB} \cong \overline{MP}$, then $\triangle ABC \cong \triangle MPN$.
5. If $a = b$ and $c = b$, then $a = c$.

(Answers appear at the end of the section.)

Logic in Geometry

Before you undertake some proofs in geometry, you have to look more closely at the nature of the statements that are made and the rules by which new statements can be formed. The statements with which you work are called conditional statements. All of them can be put in an "If——, then——" form, even though they are not always written this way. For example, the statement "Base angles of an isosceles triangle are congruent" can be put in the if-then form as

"If a triangle is isosceles, then its base angles are congruent." The two parts of the statement are called the hypothesis (the "if" part) and the conclusion (the "then" part). A sentence such as "Close the door" is a command that cannot be put into the if-then form; it cannot be used in the deductive system of reasoning.

In addition, it must be possible to assign a value of truth or falsity to the statements that are used. A statement such as "They are intelligent people" is not acceptable, since it is not known to whom the pronoun *they* refers.

Your Turn

Put the following sentences into the if-then form, if possible.

1. The fact that the car runs implies that the fuel tank contains fuel.
2. A square is a parallelogram.
3. The fact that the car won't start implies that the car is out of gas.

(Answers appear at the end of the section.)

New statements can be formed from simple statements in a number of ways. A new statement can be formed by negating a statement. The statement "Triangle ABC is an isosceles triangle" can be negated as "Triangle ABC is not an isosceles triangle." Simple statements can be joined to form compound statements with the connecting words *and, but,* or *or.*

Considerable difficulty can be encountered in developing the skill of proving arguments in formal geometry because it is often taken for granted that everyone knows the rules of reasoning or that everyone can understand them without an explanation.

Logic can be written with letters to represent sentences and special symbols to represent relationships, just as letters are used to represent numbers and special symbols to represent relationships in algebra and geometry. This development of logic and its symbolism has been extremely important in the development of computers.

Here are some of the rules used to form logical arguments. Let sentences be represented with the letters p, q and r.

TRANSITIVITY:
If p, then q.   If q, then r.
Therefore, if p, then r.

Example: If $\triangle ABC$ is equilateral, then $\triangle ABC$ is isosceles.
If $\triangle ABC$ is isosceles, two of the angles are congruent.
Therefore, if $\triangle ABC$ is equilateral, then two of the angles are congruent.

SYLLOGISM:
If p, then q.
If p is true, then q is true.

Example: If two triangles are congruent, then the corresponding parts are congruent.
Therefore, since $\triangle ABC \cong \triangle RST$, the corresponding parts are congruent.

INDIRECT REASONING:
If p or q is true, then either p is true, q is true, or both are true.

Example: $\sqrt{2}$ is either a rational or an irrational number.

Since a number cannot be both rational and irrational (by definition), either p or q must be true ($\sqrt{2}$ is rational or irrational). If one of the possibilities can be shown to be false, then the other possibility has to be true. Assume that $\sqrt{2}$ is a rational number. Based on that assumption you can ar-

rive at a contradiction, indicating that the assumption was false. Therefore, $\sqrt{2}$ is an irrational number.

You can also form new statements from previous statements by making changes in the if and then parts. You can form three statements from a given statement that are somewhat alike but express different ideas. Because they appear to be similar, you have to be very careful about the wording and use of such statements. The names of these forms are converse, inverse, and contrapositive. Below are examples of each type.

Statement: If p, then q.
Converse: If q, then p.

Example:
Statement: If I live in San Francisco, then I live in California.
Converse: If I live in California, then I live in San Francisco.
Note that the converse is false, even though the statement is true. Therefore the converse of a statement is not necessarily true.

A common error in geometric proofs is to make an argument from the converse of what is to be proven. When a converse is formed, it must be treated as a new statement to be examined for truth or falsity.

Statement: If p, then q.
Inverse: If not p, then not q.

Example:
Statement: If I live in San Francisco, then I live in California.
Inverse: If I do not live in San Francisco, then I do not live in California.
Note that the inverse is not true, even though the statement is true. Therefore the inverse of a statement is not necessarily true.

In geometric proofs the inverse must also be examined as a new statement with regard to its truth or falsity.

> Statement: If *p,* then *q.*
> Contrapositive: If not *q,* then not *p.*

Example:

> Statement: If I live in San Francisco, then I live in California.
> Contrapositive: If I do not live in California, then I do not live in San Francisco.
> Note that both the contrapositive and the statement are true.

In geometric proofs you can use the contrapositive because when you prove the contrapositive true, you also prove the statement true, and vice versa.

Another error to watch for in completing proofs is forming a circular argument. In this error one uses the conclusion as a statement in the supporting argument. Suppose that you wish to prove that two lines are perpendicular, and in the proof you use the statement that the two lines are perpendicular. You are arguing in a circle. In a long proof it is not difficult to make such an error.

Your Turn

Write the converse, the inverse, and the contrapositive for the following statements. Then tell whether each statement you wrote is true or false.

4. If the car is out of gas, then it will not start.
5. If a number ends in 0 or 5, then the number is exactly divisible by 5.
6. If the river floods, then Hays Street is closed.

(Answers appear at the end of the section.)

Definitions

You have examined axioms, postulates, the form of theorems (if-then statements), and undefined terms. You also have to examine defined terms. A definition places a term in a set and then presents the characteristics that distinguish it from other members of the set. A definition requires two statements, both a statement and its converse. For example, a triangle is isosceles if at least two sides are congruent. The converse statement is "If at least two sides of a triangle are congruent, then the triangle is an isosceles triangle." As it is awkward to write both statements for each definition, a special form has been developed. The converse of if *p,* then *q* is if *q,* then *p.* It can also be written as only if *p,* then *q.* Thus, to write a statement and its converse you can write the two sentences together as if and only if *p,* then *q.* You are then making both statements. A short way of writing if and only if is with the symbol "iff." Thus, when you write definitions, use this symbol for brevity: A triangle is an isosceles triangle iff at least two sides are congruent.

Proofs

To make the task of reading and understanding proofs easier, a column form has been developed for the presentation of the proof. In this method, each statement made is listed in a column on the left, and the reason supporting the statement appears in a column on the right. A reason may be a definition, an axiom, a postulate, a previously proved theorem, or allowable constructions.

The column form of presentation makes understanding the proof easier. It also forces the writer to be careful in the presentation. In more advanced work, proofs are often presented in paragraph form, with supporting statements left out when the writer believes the reasoning is "clear" to an advanced mathematician.

In addition to the statements and reasons, the original statement is translated into a specific case, and a figure is drawn and labeled to represent the general item in the proof. For example, if you are to prove that "Base angles of an isosceles triangle are congruent," you would pick a special triangle, label the vertices, and state all the given information in terms of this special triangle. It has to represent all isosceles triangles. In developing a figure, you must be very careful not to add any characteristics that do not belong to the general figure. For example, if you have a theorem about triangles in general, you should not choose an isosceles triangle to represent the general triangle, as the isosceles triangle has special characteristics. It is also customary to state the given information (hypothesis) in terms of the particular figure chosen, and to state the conclusion to be obtained (the "to prove"). It is also a good idea to make a plan for the proof, although it is not necessary to show the plan as part of the proof.

Devising the plan for the proof is the most interesting part of proof work and, of course, the most challenging. One interesting technique is to argue back from the conclusion to the given. This method of developing a proof is called the analytic method. The method of proceeding from the given to the conclusion is called the synthetic method.

In writing the proofs, the small cycles of argument if *p*, then *q* and *p*, therefore *q*, are written in an abbreviated form, and thus at the beginning it is not always clear how the argument is proceeding. Consider a short argument, two perpendicular lines form an angle whose measure is 90°. (See Proof A below.)

Begin with the definition of perpendicular lines: Two lines are perpendicular iff they form a right angle. You then select two lines, AB and CD, as representatives. Call their point of intersection O. (It is not necessary to state that two lines intersect in one point; omit some obvious statements.) Then argue that since all perpendicular lines form a right angle, and $\overleftrightarrow{AB}$ and $\overleftrightarrow{CD}$ are a pair of perpendic-

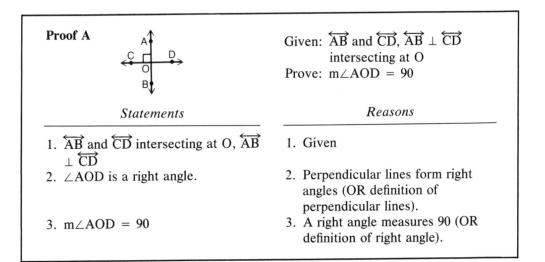

Proof A

Given: $\overleftrightarrow{AB}$ and $\overleftrightarrow{CD}$, $\overleftrightarrow{AB} \perp \overleftrightarrow{CD}$
intersecting at O
Prove: m∠AOD = 90

Statements	*Reasons*
1. $\overleftrightarrow{AB}$ and $\overleftrightarrow{CD}$ intersecting at O, $\overleftrightarrow{AB}$ $\perp \overleftrightarrow{CD}$	1. Given
2. ∠AOD is a right angle.	2. Perpendicular lines form right angles (OR definition of perpendicular lines).
3. m∠AOD = 90	3. A right angle measures 90 (OR definition of right angle).

ular lines, *these* perpendicular lines form a right angle. Next use the definition of a right angle: an angle is a right angle iff it has a measure of 90°. Argue that, since all right angles have a measure of 90°, and this angle, ∠AOD, is a right angle, then *this* angle has a measure of 90°. Note how the argument is shortened in the column proof presentation.

Two more formal proofs are presented next. The first proves that vertical angles are congruent. The second proves that the sum of the measures of the angles of a triangle is 180° for every triangle in the Euclidean geometry system.

For the proof that vertical angles are congruent, make the following plan.

Show that the two vertical angles are each the supplement of the same angle, and that therefore they are congruent. Sometimes the theorem that supplements of the same or of congruent angles are congruent is proved before the vertical angle proof, and then can be used in the proof.

There are many variations for this proof. Some authors define a linear pair (two angles formed by two opposite rays and any ray between) and use a postulate that if two angles form a linear pair, then they are supplementary. Other authors first prove a theorem that supplements of the same (or congruent) angles are congruent, and can then use that theorem to

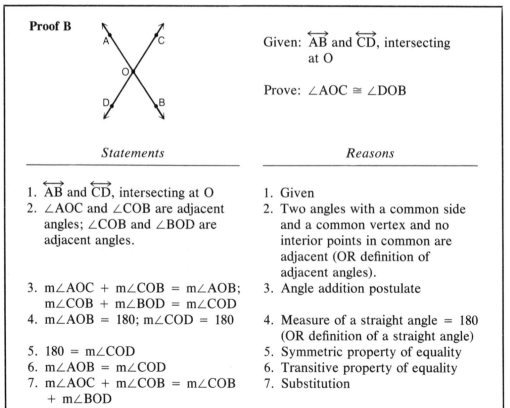

Proof B

Given: $\overleftrightarrow{AB}$ and $\overleftrightarrow{CD}$, intersecting at O

Prove: ∠AOC ≅ ∠DOB

Statements	*Reasons*
1. $\overleftrightarrow{AB}$ and $\overleftrightarrow{CD}$, intersecting at O	1. Given
2. ∠AOC and ∠COB are adjacent angles; ∠COB and ∠BOD are adjacent angles.	2. Two angles with a common side and a common vertex and no interior points in common are adjacent (OR definition of adjacent angles).
3. m∠AOC + m∠COB = m∠AOB; m∠COB + m∠BOD = m∠COD	3. Angle addition postulate
4. m∠AOB = 180; m∠COD = 180	4. Measure of a straight angle = 180 (OR definition of a straight angle)
5. 180 = m∠COD	5. Symmetric property of equality
6. m∠AOB = m∠COD	6. Transitive property of equality
7. m∠AOC + m∠COB = m∠COB + m∠BOD	7. Substitution
8. m∠AOC = m∠BOD	8. Addition property of equality (addition of additive inverse)

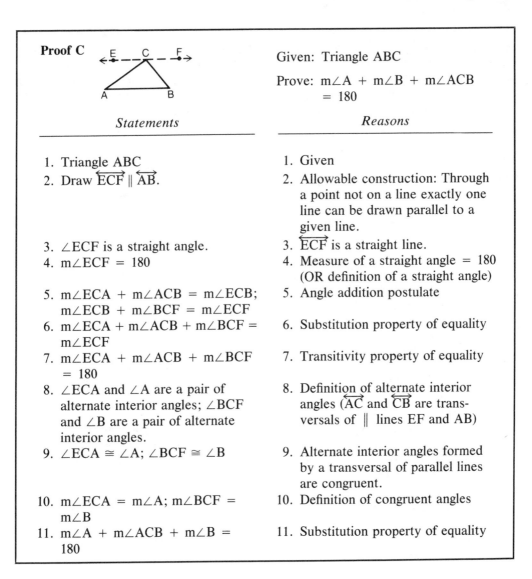

Proof C

Given: Triangle ABC

Prove: m∠A + m∠B + m∠ACB
     = 180

Statements	*Reasons*
1. Triangle ABC	1. Given
2. Draw $\overleftrightarrow{ECF} \parallel \overrightarrow{AB}$.	2. Allowable construction: Through a point not on a line exactly one line can be drawn parallel to a given line.
3. ∠ECF is a straight angle.	3. $\overleftrightarrow{ECF}$ is a straight line.
4. m∠ECF = 180	4. Measure of a straight angle = 180 (OR definition of a straight angle)
5. m∠ECA + m∠ACB = m∠ECB; m∠ECB + m∠BCF = m∠ECF	5. Angle addition postulate
6. m∠ECA + m∠ACB + m∠BCF = m∠ECF	6. Substitution property of equality
7. m∠ECA + m∠ACB + m∠BCF = 180	7. Transitivity property of equality
8. ∠ECA and ∠A are a pair of alternate interior angles; ∠BCF and ∠B are a pair of alternate interior angles.	8. Definition of alternate interior angles ($\overrightarrow{AC}$ and $\overleftrightarrow{CB}$ are transversals of ∥ lines EF and AB)
9. ∠ECA ≅ ∠A; ∠BCF ≅ ∠B	9. Alternate interior angles formed by a transversal of parallel lines are congruent.
10. m∠ECA = m∠A; m∠BCF = m∠B	10. Definition of congruent angles
11. m∠A + m∠ACB + m∠B = 180	11. Substitution property of equality

shorten the theorem on vertical angles. Yet other authors do not bother to state that 180 = m∠COD by the symmetry property of equality before using the transitivity property, as they feel the statement is "obvious."

Thus, there is no single proof that is standard for all textbooks. You must study a geometry textbook in the order in which the theorems are presented to understand it.

The theorem stating that the sum of the measures of the angles of a triangle is 180° uses the parallel postulate. The plan is to state that the measure of a straight angle is 180°, and then substitute two angles of the triangle for two of the angles that make up the straight angle. [Note that a scalene triangle (a general triangle) is chosen for the figure in Proof C.]

An elementary geometry textbook will prove from 100 to 200 theorems.

These are statements about polygonal plane figures and circles, the various line segments that can be drawn in them, and the relationships that hold. Many books also present some material on prisms, pyramids, spheres, and cones. The student will prove many more theorems, using the theorems that have already been proved along with the undefined and defined terms, postulates from geometry, and axioms from algebra. In this way one learns the structure and logic of math.

Your Turn
Complete each proof.

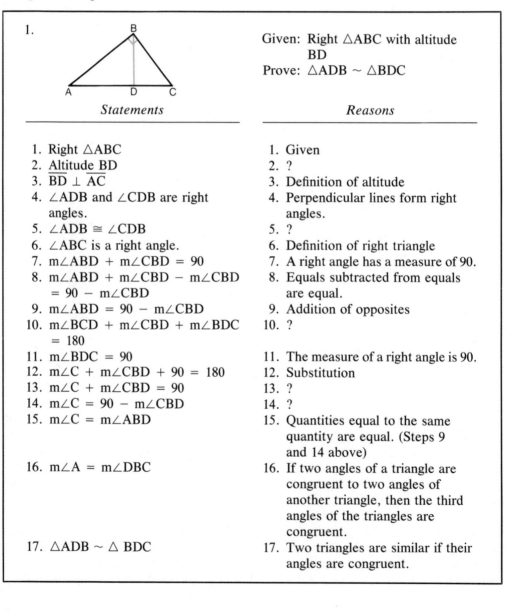

1.

Given: Right $\triangle$ABC with altitude BD

Prove: $\triangle$ADB ~ $\triangle$BDC

Statements	*Reasons*
1. Right $\triangle$ABC	1. Given
2. Altitude BD	2. ?
3. $\overline{BD} \perp \overline{AC}$	3. Definition of altitude
4. $\angle$ADB and $\angle$CDB are right angles.	4. Perpendicular lines form right angles.
5. $\angle$ADB $\cong$ $\angle$CDB	5. ?
6. $\angle$ABC is a right angle.	6. Definition of right triangle
7. m$\angle$ABD + m$\angle$CBD = 90	7. A right angle has a measure of 90.
8. m$\angle$ABD + m$\angle$CBD − m$\angle$CBD = 90 − m$\angle$CBD	8. Equals subtracted from equals are equal.
9. m$\angle$ABD = 90 − m$\angle$CBD	9. Addition of opposites
10. m$\angle$BCD + m$\angle$CBD + m$\angle$BDC = 180	10. ?
11. m$\angle$BDC = 90	11. The measure of a right angle is 90.
12. m$\angle$C + m$\angle$CBD + 90 = 180	12. Substitution
13. m$\angle$C + m$\angle$CBD = 90	13. ?
14. m$\angle$C = 90 − m$\angle$CBD	14. ?
15. m$\angle$C = m$\angle$ABD	15. Quantities equal to the same quantity are equal. (Steps 9 and 14 above)
16. m$\angle$A = m$\angle$DBC	16. If two angles of a triangle are congruent to two angles of another triangle, then the third angles of the triangles are congruent.
17. $\triangle$ADB ~ $\triangle$BDC	17. Two triangles are similar if their angles are congruent.

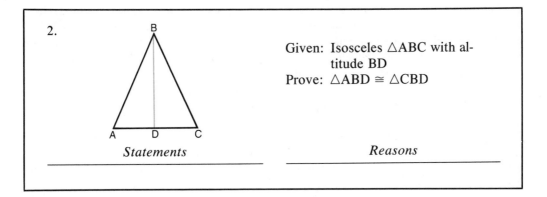

2.

Given: Isosceles △ABC with altitude BD

Prove: △ABD ≅ △CBD

Statements	*Reasons*

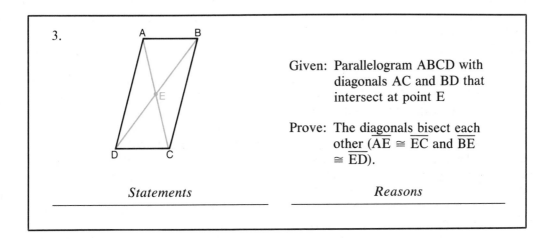

3.

Given: Parallelogram ABCD with diagonals AC and BD that intersect at point E

Prove: The diagonals bisect each other ($\overline{AE} \cong \overline{EC}$ and $\overline{BE} \cong \overline{ED}$).

Statements	*Reasons*

(Answers appear at the end of the section.)

Other Geometries

It was mentioned earlier that for two thousand years, mathematicians were uncertain as to whether the Fifth Postulate of Euclid (that parallel lines in a plane will never meet) was to be considered an assumption or whether it could be proved from the other postulates. Euclid himself was concerned about this postulate and tried to prove it. It does not appear "self-evident," as do the other postulates that

Euclid used. Girolamo Saccheri, an Italian priest of the eighteenth century, tried to clear the matter up in the book *Euclid Freed of Every Flaw*. Instead Saccheri actually showed that a new geometry was possible, although he did not realize it. The "clearing up" came in the nineteenth century with the independent discoveries of two mathematicians, Janos Bolyai, a Hungarian, and Nikolai Lobachevsky, a Russian.

If the statement on parallels is a postulate independent of the others, then it should be possible to replace it and construct a consistent geometry. On the other hand, if it is a theorem that can be derived from the other postulates, then replacing it with a contradictory statement would lead to a contradiction in the results that follow. Both Bolyai and Lobachevsky were able to replace the parallel postulate and obtain a new, logically consistent geometry. They replaced the Fifth Postulate of Euclid with one that states that through a point not on a given line no lines can be drawn parallel to the given line. The new geometry is logical and consistent. Of course, theorems based on this postulate will change, so that the nature of the space that is described also changes.

As Lobachevsky published his work first, the geometry that was developed became known as Lobachevskian geometry. Bolyai's work was referred to one of the greatest mathematicians of all time, Karl Friedrich Gauss. In a letter of response, Gauss stated that he had developed this idea himself. However, he never published his findings. One wonders whether Gauss felt it was not sufficiently important to do so or whether he thought that his reputation would suffer.

The new geometry did not get much attention at first. Lobachevsky's ideas were met with hostile criticism. In his lifetime he never received the honor that he deserved for his great contribution to mathematics.

Nevertheless, the question of the Fifth Postulate had been, after two thousand years, resolved. Another mathematician, Bernhard Riemann, a German mathematician, invented another type of geometry that he termed "non-Euclidean" geometry. Riemann replaced Euclid's Fifth Postulate with the assumption that through a point not on a line, no lines could be drawn parallel to a given line. Riemann had to make some other changes as well to develop his system; but again, he produced a logical geometry.

It is not difficult to make a model that will illustrate Riemann's system. However, it is necessary to rethink ideas about the nature of the concepts that are undefined. One model proposed for this geometry is the surface of a sphere. Since there are no flat portions on a sphere, you have to consider what you mean by a line on a sphere.

On a plane surface it can be shown that a straight line segment is the shortest distance between two points. You can think of a line in a dynamic way as connecting two points that are constantly moving apart. On a sphere, the shortest path between two points is an arc of a great circle. (A great circle is the intersection of the surface of the sphere with any plane that includes the center point of the sphere.) All circles are closed figures, so a "line" on the sphere differs from a line on the plane. It does not extend indefinitely. Further, all "lines" on the sphere intersect, as can be seen in the diagram below. Thus, the postulate that through a point not on a line, no lines can be drawn parallel to a given line is perfectly appropriate for the geometry of a spherical surface.

A theorem that is very important concerns the sum of the measures of the angles of a triangle. For a triangle in a plane this sum is 180°. The theorem is based on the parallel postulate. Thus, this should change when the parallel postulate is changed. For Lobachevskian geometry the sum of the measures of the angles of a triangle is less than 180°; for Rieman-

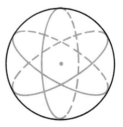

nian geometry the sum is greater than 180°. Any other theorem that depends on the parallel postulate chosen is also subject to change.

The works of Saccheri, Bolyai, Lobachevsky and Riemann have provided a new view of geometry. Euclidean geometry remains the geometry of everyday life. It is still the most practical for most of the problems that occur in ordinary experiences. Nevertheless, there are situations that call for the application of other geometries. In constructing a model of the universe for his theories, the mathematician-physicist Albert Einstein used a Riemannian geometry.

Keep in mind that you live on a sphere, not on a flat plane. If you travel far enough in one direction, you will return to your starting point. Flagpoles at opposite ends of the United States are not parallel, due to the earth's spherical shape, as you can see in the illustration below. Astronauts and those responsible for their safe return from space are certainly mindful that the astronauts will land on a sphere.

What is the "true" geometry? One can speak of relative truth—truth relative to a particular system with its postulates and undefined terms—or to validity. Logical systems can be constructed and tested on models by predicting and then checking experimental results. However, one cannot be 100% certain that any of the systems describe all of the "real world." The idea of absolute truth in mathematics does not apply.

Since early in the development of formal geometry, mathematicians have striven to develop a system that is both consistent and complete. A consistent system would not allow for two contradictory theorems to be proved true. A complete system would provide that every statement that can be made about the elements of the system and their relationships can be proved either true or false. Even if work is never completed, a mathematician would like to know that the postulates and the undefined terms have been chosen so as to make the system "perfect."

The hope for a consistent and complete system was forever destroyed in the twentieth century by the contemporary mathematician Kurt Gödel, who now works in the United States. In 1931 he published a paper showing that a system only as complex as arithmetic could not be both complete and consistent. If there is a set of postulates that do not generate contradictory theorems, there will be one or more theorems that are undecidable within the system.

Sometimes it seems to a beginning student that mathematics has all been written. One has only to read the books about it and then produce the proofs (which one assumes can all be done with enough time and motivation). Mathematics is, however, much more exciting than that. It is not a closed and completed book. Which of the systems that are made are undecidable? What other systems can be postulated? Do the new systems have real-world models? New discoveries are made every day, and these discoveries are as exciting as any human adventure can be. Formal geometry is a challenge to one's highest level of thought.

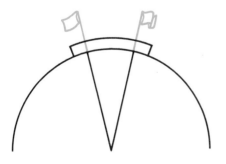

Answers

Building a System (pp. 415–418)

1. postulate   2. axiom   3. undefined term   4. postulate   5. axiom

Logic in Geometry (pp. 418–420)

1. If a car runs, then the fuel tank must contain fuel.
2. If a figure is a square, then the figure is a parallelogram.
3. If a car will not start, then the car is out of gas.

4. Converse: If the car will not start, then it is out of gas. False

   Inverse: If the car is not out of gas, then it will start. False

   Contrapositive: If the car will start, then it is not out of gas. True

5. Converse: If a number is exactly divisible by 5, then it ends in 0 or 5. True

   Inverse: If a number does not end in 0 or 5, then it is not divisible by 5. True

   Contrapositive: If a number is not exactly divisible by 5, then it does not end in 0 or 5. True

6. Converse: If Hays Street is closed, then the river is flooded. False

   Inverse: If the river is not flooded, then Hays Street is not closed. False

   Contrapositive: If Hays Street is not closed, then the river is not flooded. True

Proofs (pp. 420–425)

1. _____
                              Reasons
   _____

   2. Given

   5. All right angles are congruent.

   10. The sum of the measures of the angles of a triangle is 180°.

   13. Equals subtracted from equals are equal.

   14. Equals subtracted from equals are equal.

   Your proof may be different from the ones given for 2. and 3.

2.

Statements	*Reasons*
1. Isosceles △ABC	1. Given
2. $\overline{AB} \cong \overline{BC}$	2. Definition of isosceles triangle
3. $\overline{BD} \cong \overline{BD}$	3. Any line segment is congruent to itself.
4. Altitude BD	4. Given
5. $\overline{BD} \perp \overline{AC}$	5. Definition of altitude
6. ∠BDC and ∠BDA are right angles.	6. Perpendicular lines form right angles.
7. ∠BDC ≅ ∠BDA	7. All right angles are congruent.
8. ∠A = ∠C	8. Angles opposite congruent sides are congruent.
9. ∠ABD ≅ ∠CBD	9. If two angles of a triangle are congruent to two angles of another triangle, then the third angles of the triangles are congruent.
10. △ABD ≅ △CBD	10. SAS (Postulate 9, page 417)

3.

Statements	*Reasons*
1. Parallelogram ABCD	1. Given
2. Diagonals AC and BD intersect at E.	2. Given
3. $\overline{AB} \parallel \overline{DC}$	3. Definition of a parallelogram
4. ∠BAC ≅ ∠DCA	4. Alternate interior angles are congruent.
5. ∠ABD ≅ ∠BDC	5. Alternate interior angles are congruent.
6. $\overline{AB} \cong \overline{CD}$	6. Opposite sides of a parallelogram are congruent.
7. △ABC ≅ △CDE	7. ASA
8. $\overline{AE} \cong \overline{CE}$ and $\overline{DE} \cong \overline{BE}$	8. Corresponding parts of congruent triangles are congruent.

Coordinate Geometry

A tremendous advance was made in mathematics by joining the techniques of algebra with the concepts of geometry. This branch of mathematics is called analytic geometry, or coordinate geometry.

The basic idea behind coordinate geometry is that you can give an address to every point in a plane. This is not a startling idea because there is an address for most houses in cities and towns. How are houses numbered? This is done with a grid system composed of two sets of parallel lines, each set perpendicular to the other.

If you are going to plan a city, you can start with two principal streets at right angles to each other. Call them Main and Center streets. Streets parallel to one of the principal streets can be named First, Second, Third and so on. Streets running parallel to the second principal street might be given alphabetical names, beginning with A, B, C and so on. Points at which the grid lines intersect can then be identified as the intersection of First and A, Third and B, Fifth and D, Second and D, Fifth and C.

Cartesian Coordinates

A modern coordinate system is called a Cartesian coordinate system. The word *Cartesian* comes from the name of Descartes, a French mathematician who devised the basic ideas of coordinate geometry in the seventeenth century. The Latin form of Descartes' name, which he used to sign his papers, is Cartesius. The coordinate system of Cartesius is called the Cartesian coordinate system.

As with the grid system, begin with two perpendicular lines. These lines are called the coordinate axes. The point where they intersect is the starting point of the system. This point, called the origin, is the point of intersection of the two lines. Next select a length to represent one unit of the measuring system. Start from 0 and mark this unit on the line, to the right of 0 on the horizontal line, and above 0 on the vertical line. (Use a compass to mark this line segment congruent to the length that you selected.)

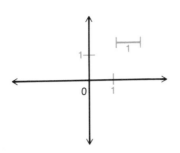

By marking this segment again and again, you have points corresponding to the set of whole numbers. Mark both the horizontal and the vertical axes in this manner. The numbers increase as you go to the right on the horizontal axis, and as you go up on the vertical axis. (The numbers could equally well increase as you move left or move down, just as east can be represented as the left side of a map equally as well as the right side. However, conventions have been established for both graphs and maps, and everyone follows them.)

Complete the coordinate system by marking unit lengths to the left and below 0. These points are labeled with negative numbers, starting at 0 and proceeding left or down. The *axes* now represent all real numbers.

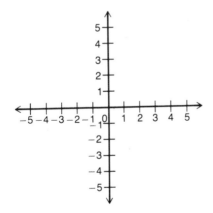

You can locate points on the axes corresponding to rational numbers with

the use of geometric constructions. The construction for bisecting a line segment will give the midpoint of that segment, so points corresponding to 0.5, 1.5, and 2.5 can be obtained. You can bisect again and again to locate fourths, eighths, sixteenths. Segments can be divided into any number of segments of equal length—thirds, fifths, sevenths—so you can locate the points corresponding to the rational numbers: $\frac{1}{3}, \frac{2}{3}, \frac{3}{5}, \frac{4}{7}$. Points corresponding to certain irrational numbers, such as $\sqrt{2}$, can be located by constructing an isosceles right triangle. The Pythagorean Theorem shows that the length of the hypotenuse is $\sqrt{2}$.

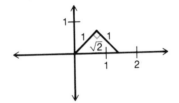

There are other irrational numbers that cannot be constructed in this fashion, but you know there are points that correspond to these numbers. For example, there is a point representing the irrational number π that lies between 3.1415 and 3.1416. The important question is whether there is a point for every number and a number for every point. Indeed, there is a one-to-one correspondence between the set of real numbers and the points on a line.

Ordered pairs

With this coordinate system, every point in the plane is named by a pair of numbers. The first number tells how far to move from the vertical axis to the right or to the left to arrive at the vertical line that passes through the desired point. The second number tells how far above or below the horizontal axis to move to arrive at a horizontal line that passes through the desired point. The two numbers given in the order (horizontal move, vertical move) are called the coordinates of the point. The coordinates of the origin are (0,0).

The diagram shows how to plot (locate) the points (3,4) and (−2,−3).

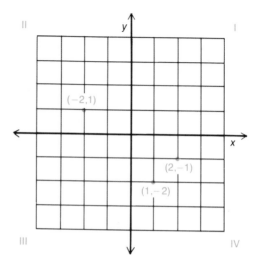

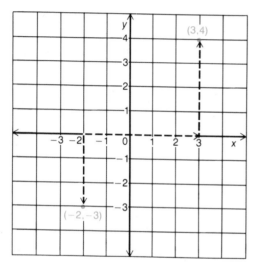

The horizontal axis is usually called the *x*-axis, and the vertical axis is called the *y*-axis. The symbol *(x,y)* is used to refer to the coordinates of a point and is called an ordered pair. The first coordinate is called the abscissa, and the second coordinate is called the ordinate. It is important to note that the order of the numbers of the coordinate pair is just as important as the magnitude (size) of the numbers themselves. The pair (−2,1) is not the same as the pair (1,−2) nor (2,−1). As shown in the diagram, they are distinct points.

Your Turn

On a piece of graph paper mark the two coordinate axes, and label each from −10 to 10. Plot the points with the following coordinates, and name each point with the letter shown.

A (1,9)	B (3,6)	C (−3,6)
D (−3,−6)	E (3,−6)	F (8,8)
G (−8,−8)	H (−6,3)	

(Answers appear at the end of the section.)

Quadrants

The two axes divide the plane into four regions called quadrants. The quadrants are numbered from I to IV, in a counterclockwise direction, as shown in the drawing above the preceding exercises.

By looking at the coordinates of a point, you can tell whether the point lies on one of the axes or in the interior of a quadrant. Further, if the point lies within a quadrant, the signs of the coordinates tell in which quadrant it is located. Can you tell in which quadrant $(-3, -4)$ is located without plotting the point? Did you say Quadrant III? All points with negative abscissas lie to the left of the vertical axis in Quadrants II and III. All points with negative ordinates lie below the horizontal axis in Quadrants III and IV. Therefore, a point with a negative abscissa and a negative ordinate lies in Quadrant III. The findings are summarized in the following table:

Abscissa	Ordinate	Quadrant
+	+	I
−	+	II
−	−	III
+	−	IV

Study how the following points are plotted.

A (3,0)   B (−6,0)
C (0,2)   D (0, −1)

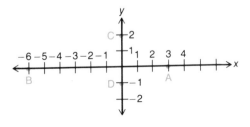

You can make the following observation. Points that lie on the x-axis have an ordinate of 0. A y-value of 0 indicates that the point is neither above nor below the horizontal axis. Points that lie on the y-axis have an abscissa of 0. An x-value of 0 indicates that the point is neither to the left nor to the right of the vertical axis. Thus you can tell by the coordinates of a point whether it lies on one of the axes.

Your Turn

From the coordinates of each point, tell whether it lies on the x-axis, the y-axis; or, if it is in one of the quadrants, tell in which quadrant it is located.

A (5,0)   B (−3,8)   C (−6,0)
D (6,2)   E (0,1)   F (0, −7)
G (−4,−4)   H (−1,4)   I (9, −1)

(Answers appear at the end of the section.)

Cartesian products

Geometric information about the points can be deduced without the use of a drawing. The ability to obtain information about sets of points by analyzing their algebraic representation is the heart of analytic, or coordinate, geometry.

The sets of points that have been analyzed and represented by algebraic equations are many. They range from straight lines to the curves that were examined in informal geometry and many more. They also include many sets of points that represent data used by physicists, chemists, engineers, designers, economists, and others working with numerical data. Modern technology could not exist without analytic geometry.

To obtain the number pairs corresponding to the points in a plane without making a graph, proceed in the following way. Think of writing two identical sets, each composed of all the real numbers. Then think of forming all the possible pairs of numbers by taking one number from the first set and one number from the second set for each pair of numbers. The new set of number pairs is called the Cartesian product of the two sets. Since the set of real numbers is an infinite set, there is an infinite set of number pairs to attach to the points of an infinitely extending plane. You can see how the process works with the use of a small, finite set. Form the Cartesian product of the set $\{-2, -1, 0, 1, 2\}$ with itself. You obtain:

$$\{(-2,-2), (-2,-1), (-2,0), (-2,1),$$
$$(-2,2), (-1,-2), (-1,-1), (-1,0),$$
$$(-1,1), (-1,2), (0,-2), (0,-1),$$
$$(0,0), (0,1), (0,2), (1,-2), (1,-1),$$
$$(1,0), (1,1), (1,2), (2,-2), (2,-1),$$
$$(2,0), (2,1), (2,2)\}$$

The points are shown in the graph.

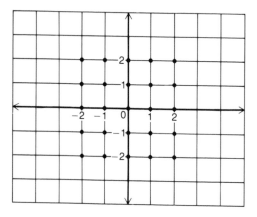

The points are located at the intersection of the horizontal and vertical lines that pass through the integers on the axes. These points are referred to as the lattice points on the graph.

Distance

Distances on a grid

With the coordinate system, you can find how far it is from the origin to a point or how far it is from one point to another. To find the distance between two points on the *x*-axis, find the difference between the *x*-coordinates of the two points, as this number will give the length of the line segment that connects the points. (Note that distance is always positive; it does not matter in which direction you measure the distance). The distance between the point (2,0) and the point (11,0) is $11 - 2$, or 9, units. Similarly you can find the distance between two points on any horizontal line. The distance between the points on a line 3 units above the *x*-axis, (2,3) and (11,3), is $11 - 2$ or 9 units.

You can also find the distance between two points on the *y*-axis by the difference of the ordinates of the points. The distance between the point (0,2) and (0,11) is $11 - 2$, or 9, units. The distance between two points on a line 3 units to the left of the *y*-axis, $(-3,2)$ and $(-3,11)$ is $11 - 2$, or 9, units.

Suppose you want to find the distance between points $(-8,-4)$ and $(-2,-4)$. You still find the difference between the abscissas.

$$-8 - (-2) = -8 + 2 \text{ or } -6$$

However, distances are always positive, so find the absolute value of the difference, which is 6. This method also works for finding the length of a line segment that crosses the *x*-axis or *y*-axis. Find the distance between $(-2,-8)$ and $(-2,4)$.

$$-8 - 4 = -8 + (-4) \text{ or } -12$$

The distance is $|-12|$, or 12.

Your Turn

Find the distance between each pair of points.

1. (4,2) and (10,2)
2. (−3,8) and (−7,8)
3. (0,−9) and (0,3)
4. (−1,−5) and (−1,7)

(Answers appear at the end of the section.)

Distance formula

The Pythagorean Theorem is used to find the distance between any two points in the plane. Suppose you need to find the distance between the points (4,1) and (10,9). Connect the two points with line segment AB. Compute the length.

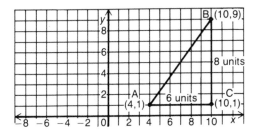

Note that you can find the length of $\overline{AC}$ and $\overline{CB}$, as these are horizontal and vertical segments, respectively. These segments are at right angles, since they lie on lines that are mutually perpendicular. Thus, △ABC is a right triangle, $\overline{AB}$ is the hypotenuse, and its length can be found with the use of the Pythagorean Theorem. In the problem, the length of $\overline{AC}$ is 10 − 4, or 6. The length of $\overline{CB}$ is 9 − 1, or 8. By the Pythagorean Theorem,

$$(\overline{AB})^2 = (\overline{AC})^2 + (\overline{CB})^2$$
$$(\overline{AB})^2 = 6^2 + 8^2$$
$$= 36 + 64$$
$$= 100$$
$$\overline{AB} = 10$$

The general formula for the distance between two points in the plane can be written on the basis of this problem. It is customary to call the distance between two points lying on a horizontal line Δx. The Δ (Greek capital D) is used in mathematics to indicate "difference" or "change in." Δ is read "delta." Take note of this symbol. Δx is a number (obtained as a difference of two numbers). It is not a product of some quantity delta with a number x. When you write the ratio $\dfrac{\Delta y}{\Delta x}$, you cannot factor the delta symbol from the numerator and denominator. Here Δx indicates the change in the x-coordinates of the points. The distance between two points lying on a vertical line is represented by Δy. With this notation you can represent the distance, d, between two points in the plane by:

$$d = \sqrt{(\Delta x)^2 + (\Delta y)^2}$$

This equation is known as the distance formula.

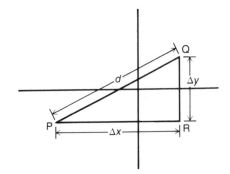

Your Turn

Find the distance between the following pairs of points.

5. (2,18) and (7,6)
6. (−3,2) and (12,10)
7. (7,−4) and (−2,−16)

(Answers appear at the end of the section.)

Linear Equations

Algebraic equations that represent lines are called linear equations. The use of an algebraic equation to represent a set of points is advantageous in several ways.

1. It can easily be determined whether a particular point belongs to a given set of points. A point belongs to a set if and only if its coordinates satisfy the equation for the set. You may not be able to make a precise determination from a drawing.
2. Given one coordinate for a point, you can calculate the other coordinate of a point on a line with the use of the equation for that set. In this manner you can produce the coordinates for many points in the set.

As an example of how the second technique is used, suppose that an equation relates the height of a moving object with the time, t. Then, given values of time, you could calculate the corresponding heights that will be reached by the object. Further suppose that you are working with a satellite, over which you have control. With a high-speed computer, you can calculate the height of the satellite well in advance of its arrival at that particular position. You are then in a position to act on the information and alter the path of the satellite in accordance with a particular need.

Graphing lines in a plane

In informal geometry you saw that two points determine a line. You can draw that geometric figure and also write an equation for the line, given the coordinates of the two points. Graph $\overleftrightarrow{AB}$, which

contains the points $(-2, -1)$ and $(2,7)$. Locate the points on a graph, and connect them with a line.

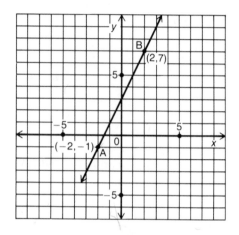

Slope of a line

You can write the equation of a line using a method that makes use of a special characteristic of the line. This characteristic is called the slope of the line. The slope gives a measure of the steepness (slant) of the line. You know that when you walk or ride a bicycle up a steep hill, you have to make much more effort than when you travel on a level road. You can get a measure of the steepness by the effort you must make.

Here is how to make a mathematical measure of the steepness of a line. From any point on the line draw a horizontal segment and, from another point, draw a vertical segment, extending the segments until they intersect. The lengths of the segments give the horizontal and vertical distances between the two points on the line. The horizontal distance is sometimes called the run, and the vertical distance, when it is positive, is called the rise.

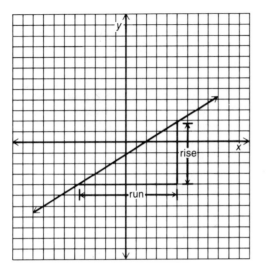

The slope of the line is defined as the ratio of the rise to the run.

$$\text{slope} = \frac{\text{rise}}{\text{run}}$$

The letter m is used to represent the slope.

You have also called the horizontal and vertical distances between two points on a line Δx and Δy. Δx is obtained as the change in the x-coordinates of the two points and Δy as the change in the y-coordinates of the two points.

$$\Delta x = x_2 - x_1 \text{ and}$$
$$\Delta y = y_2 - y_1$$

You can then write two equations for the slope, m:

$$m = \frac{\Delta y}{\Delta x} \text{ or}$$

$$m = \frac{y_2 - y_1}{x_2 - x_1}$$

Note that you can also use the formula

$$m = \frac{y_1 - y_2}{x_1 - x_2}$$

since

$$\frac{y_1 - y_2}{x_1 - x_2} = \frac{-(y_1 - y_2)}{-(x_1 - x_2)}$$

$$= \frac{-y_1 + y_2}{-x_1 + x_2} = \frac{y_2 - y_1}{x_2 - x_1}$$

In each case, the subscripts of x and y are taken in the same order. You must be very careful to observe this rule when you calculate the slope of a line.

You can calculate the slope for the line graphed on page 436. Use the two points that were used to establish the line, A $(-2, -1)$ and B $(2, 7)$.

$$m = \frac{7 - (-1)}{2 - (-2)}$$

$$= \frac{8}{4} \text{ or } 2$$

Some lines fall as you go from left to right.

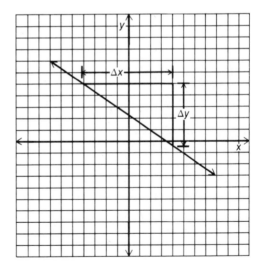

You can again draw the segments Δy and Δx for the vertical and horizontal distances between the two points. Since Δy is negative, it is confusing to call it a rise. However, Δy can still be used to indicate the change in the y-coordinates or "change in y," and Δx for the change in the x-coordinates, or "change in x." The slope $m = \dfrac{\Delta y}{\Delta x}$ is negative for a line that falls as you go from left to right.

You also may have a horizontal line.

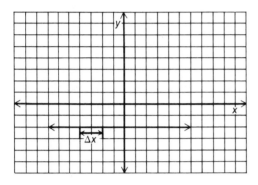

For any Δx that you choose, $\Delta y = 0$ for a horizontal line. Therefore the slope of a horizontal line is zero. For vertical lines Δx, for any two points that you choose, is zero.

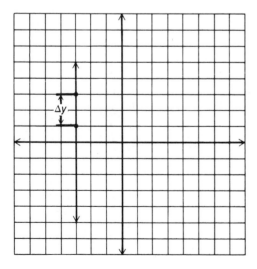

Thus you cannot form the ratio $\dfrac{\Delta y}{\Delta x}$ for a vertical line, since you cannot divide by

zero. The slope for a vertical line is undefined. Vertical lines are sometimes said to have "no slope." It is important to keep in mind that "no slope" is short for "no slope *number*." Vertical lines certainly are steep. Again, keep in mind the difference in meaning between zero slope for horizontal lines (the lines have a slope number—it is zero) and no slope for vertical lines (the slope for vertical lines is not defined).

Note that any convenient pair of points can be used to obtain Δx and Δy for the slope ratio. As shown in the diagram, you have a set of similar triangles formed by different values of Δx and Δy for a line. The ratios of the two sides of the triangles formed remain constant, so you are able to use any of the figures that prove convenient.

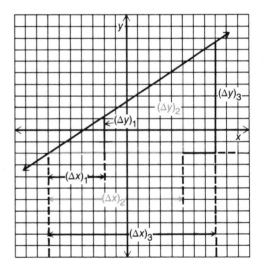

You can then determine the slope of a line from the coordinates of two distinct points on the line.

Example: Given a line through the points $(2,3)$ and $(4, -9)$ find the slope of the line.

$$m = \frac{\Delta y}{\Delta x}$$

$$\Delta y = y_2 - y_1$$

$$\Delta y = -9 - 3 \text{ or } -12$$

$$\Delta x = x_2 - x_1$$

$$\Delta x = 4 - 2 \text{ or } 2$$

$$m = \frac{-12}{2} \text{ or } -6$$

Your Turn

Given lines through the following pairs of points, determine the slope of these lines. If the slope is undefined, write "undefined."

1. A (0,0) and B (5,10)
2. C (−4,2) and D (3,−9)
3. E (−3,5) and F (10,5)
4. G (3,−8) and H (11,−6)
5. I (5,−8) and J (5,10)

(Answers appear at the end of the section.)

You can now write equations for all lines: those with positive or negative slope, and those with zero slope and no slope as well. It is simple to write equations for horizontal and vertical lines. You saw that on a horizontal line, the x values of the coordinate pairs vary, while the y values, which give the height, remain constant for all the points. Express this by writing an equation of the form:

$$y = \text{constant}$$

For example, the equation for the x-axis is $y = 0$. No matter what x-coordinate a point has on this line, the y value is zero. A line that is one unit below the x-axis and parallel to it has the equation

$$y = -1$$

A vertical line has an equation of the form:

$$x = \text{constant}$$

Every point on a vertical line has the same x coordinate; the y coordinates vary for different positions on the line.

You can thus write equations for horizontal lines (lines with zero slope) and vertical lines (lines with "no slope").

Special forms of equations

For lines with positive or negative slope, use information on the coordinates of two points or on the coordinates of one point and the slope.

Example: Write an equation for a line passing through the points A (2,5) and B (4,15). Let P (x,y) represent a general point of the line. Use the fact that the slope is everywhere the same for a straight line to develop the equation. Calculate the slope twice, using two pairs of points, A and P and A and B. Then set the two values equal to each other.

$$m \text{ (line through A and P)} = \frac{y - 5}{x - 2}$$

$$m \text{ (line through A and B)} = \frac{15 - 5}{4 - 2}$$

$$\frac{y - 5}{x - 2} = \frac{15 - 5}{4 - 2}$$

You now have an equation for the line, but you should simplify it and put it in a more convenient form.

$$\frac{y - 5}{x - 2} = \frac{10}{2}$$

$$= 5$$

$$y - 5 = 5(x - 2)$$

You can write a general equation for the line in what is called the two-point form if you use letter coordinates for points A and B. Use A (x_1, y_1) and B

(x_2, y_2). Then the equation would be written:

$$\frac{y - y_1}{x - x_1} = \frac{y_2 - y_1}{x_2 - x_1}$$

and simplified as

$$y - y_1 = \frac{y_2 - y_1}{x_2 - x_1}(x - x_1)$$

This is the general two-point form of an equation for a line. You can substitute values for the coordinates of two points of a line, simplify, and obtain an equation for the line through those points.

Your Turn

Use the two-point form of the equation of a line to obtain the equations for lines that contain the following pairs of points:

6. $(2, -2)$ and $(1, -5)$
7. $(-1, -1)$ and $(-3, -3)$
8. $(7, 6)$ and $(-4, -9)$

(Answers appear at the end of the section.)

You probably noticed that the expression

$$\frac{(y_2 - y_1)}{(x_2 - x_1)}$$

is the slope of the line, which is denoted by m. You can rewrite the two-point form of the equation substituting m for $\frac{y_2 - y_1}{x_2 - x_1}$ and obtain the point-slope form of an equation for a line.

$$y - y_1 = m(x - x_1)$$

This is a useful form of the equation if you know the slope and the coordinates of a point.

Example: Write, in point-slope form, an equation for a line with a slope of 3 and containing the point $(-2, 7)$. Sub-

stitute the given values into equation and obtain:

$$y - 7 = 3(x - -2) \text{ or}$$
$$y - 7 = 3(x + 2)$$

The point-slope of the equation is sometimes written in another way:

$$y = y_1 + m(x - x_1)$$

The term Δx has been used to represent a change in x. If you use Δx for $(x - x_1)$ you can write:

$$y = y_1 + m(\Delta x)$$

In words, the new y value is equal to the sum of the old y value and the product of the change in x values and the slope. This form of the equation is useful in many applications.

Another form of the equation that is useful is the slope-intercept form. If a line is not parallel to the y-axis (that is, not vertical), it must intersect the y-axis at some point. Let the coordinates of this point of intersection be $(0, b)$. The letter b is called the y-intercept of the line; that is, the y-value of the point of intersection of the line and the y-axis. Substitute the values $(0, b)$ for (x_1, y_1) in the point-slope form of the equation. You then obtain

$$y = b + m(x - 0) \text{ or}$$
$$y = mx + b$$

Example: Write an equation in slope-intercept form for a line with a slope of -2 and a y-intercept of 9. Use the equation and obtain:

$$y = -2x + 9$$

Example: Determine the slope and the y-intercept of a line whose equation is $2x + 5 = 4y$. Put the equation in slope-intercept form by dividing both members by 4.

$$y = \frac{2}{4}x + \frac{5}{4} \text{ or}$$

$$y = \frac{1}{2}x + \frac{5}{4}$$

The slope of the line is $\frac{1}{2}$ and the y-intercept is $\frac{5}{4}$.

Thus far you have learned many different formulas and equations. To summarize, for points A (x_1, y_1) and B (x_2, y_2)

Distance between two points, A and B

$$d = \sqrt{(\Delta x)^2 + (\Delta y)^2}$$

or

$$d = \sqrt{(x_1 - x_2)^2 + (y_1 - y_2)^2}$$

Slope, m, of a line containing points A and B

$$m = \frac{y_1 - y_2}{x_1 - x_2}$$

Equation for a horizontal line through point A

$$y = y_1$$
(Note: y_1 is a constant.)

Equation for a vertical line through point A

$$x = x_1$$
(Note: x_1 is a constant.)

Two-point form of the equation for a line through points A and B

$$y - y_1 = \frac{y_2 - y_1}{x_2 - x_1}(x - x_1)$$

Point-slope form of the equation for a line through point A with a slope of m

$$y = y_1 + m(x - x_1)$$

Slope-intercept form of the equation for a line with a slope of m and a y-intercept of b

$$y = mx + b$$

Your Turn

Write the point-slope form of the equation for each line, given the slope and the coordinates of one point.

9. $m = 3$, A $(4, -3)$
10. $m = -1$, A $(-2, 1)$

Write the slope-intercept form of the equation for each line, given the slope and the y-intercept.

11. $m = 5$, $b = -2$
12. $m = -4$, $b = 8$

Find the slope for a line through each given pair of points. Then write the equation of that line in point-slope form and in slope-intercept form.

13. A $(0, 0)$, B $(-3, -6)$
14. A $(1, 1)$, B $(0, 0)$

(Answers appear at the end of the section.)

There are still other useful forms of a line. If a line is neither vertical nor horizontal, it will intersect both coordinate axes. Denote the intersection of the line and the x-axis with the coordinates $(a, 0)$. Use the two-point form of the equation for a line to obtain an equation. The two points are the points of intersection with the x-axis and the y-axis, with coordinates $(a, 0)$ and $(0, b)$. The equation is then

$$y - 0 = \frac{b - 0}{0 - a}(x - a)$$

Simplify and obtain:

$$y = -\frac{b}{a}(x - a)$$
$$ay = -bx + ab$$
$$bx + ay = ab$$

This form of the equation is usually written with the right-hand member equal to 1. Given that a and b are both different from zero, you can divide all terms by ab and obtain:

$$\frac{x}{a} + \frac{y}{b} = 1$$

This is called the intercept form of the line because you can read directly the values of the abscissa of the point of intersection with the x-axis (a) and the ordinate of the point of intersection of the line with the y-axis (b) from the equation.

Example: Write the equation of the line $y = 2x - 3$ in intercept form and find the values of a and b. Put the equation in intercept form, as follows:

$$2x - y = 3$$
$$\frac{2x}{3} + \frac{(-y)}{3} = 1$$

The equation is still not in the proper form, as the numerators in the left member must be x and y, not $2x$ and $-y$. Rewrite the first term, using the fact that multiplying x by $\frac{2}{3}$ is equivalent to dividing x by the reciprocal of $\frac{2}{3}$; that is, by $\frac{3}{2}$. Also associate the -1 in the numerator of the second term with the denominator, using the fact that a negative sign in a fraction can be used in the numerator, the denominator, or in front of the fraction.

$$\frac{x}{\left(\frac{3}{2}\right)} + \frac{y}{-1} = 1$$

Now read the values for a and b:

$$a = \frac{3}{2} \text{ and } b = -1$$

General linear equation

Finally, write a general linear equation. It will have an x term or a y term or both,

and a constant, c. The equation

$$Ax + By + C = 0, (A^2 + B^2) \neq 0$$

is a general linear equation. The statement that $A^2 + B^2$ is not equal to zero guarantees that both the x-term and the y-term are not lost.

Linear equations can be graphed in several ways. Given an equation for a line, you can calculate the coordinates of points, as was done previously. Select a value for the x-coordinate and calculate a value for the corresponding y-coordinate. While only two points are needed to determine the line, it is customary to calculate a third point to use as a check. Also, it is easier to draw the line properly if the two points are not too close.

Example: To graph the line that has the equation $2x + 3y = -6$, select three values for x, substitute those values in the equation, and solve for y.

If $x = 0$, then $2(0) + 3y = -6$
$$0 + 3y = -6$$
$$y = -2 \ (0, -2)$$

If $x = 3$, then $2(3) + 3y = -6$
$$6 + 3y = -6$$
$$y = -4 \ (3, -4)$$

If $x = -3$, then $2(-3) + 3y = -6$
$$-6 + 3y = -6$$
$$y = 0 \ (-3, 0)$$

You can plot the three ordered pairs. Connect the points to graph the line.

Your Turn

Calculate three points for each of the lines whose equations are given. Then graph and label each line with its equation.

$$2x + 5y = 0$$
$$-3x + 2y = 4$$
$$3x + 2y = 4$$

(Answers appear at the end of the section.)

You can also use the slope and the y-intercept to plot a line.

Example: Graph the line whose equation is $y = 2x - 5$. The y-intercept is -5. Note that the standard form of the equation is $y = mx + b$. Read the given equation as $y = 2x + (-5)$ to match the coefficients with the m and b of the standard form. The slope of the line is 2, which may be written as $\frac{2}{1}$. Locate the y-intercept, and indicate the slope with $\Delta x = 1$ and $\Delta y = 2$. The line can then be drawn, as shown.

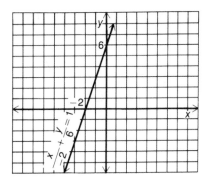

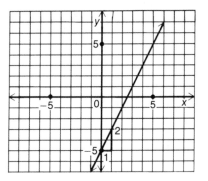

| Establish one point at the y-intercept, $(0, -5)$. | From $(0, -5)$ move 1 unit to the right and 2 units up to locate a second point on the line. |

Then draw the line through those two points. You can also draw a line from the intercept form of the equation.

Example: Graph the equation $\frac{x}{-2} + \frac{y}{6} = 1$. Read the values $a = -2$ and $b = 6$ from the intercept form of the equation. Then plot the x-intercept, a, on the x-axis and the y-intercept, b, on the y-axis. Connect the two points, as shown, to draw the line.

Your Turn

Graph and label the lines for these equations.

$$\frac{x}{4} + \frac{y}{2} = 1 \qquad \frac{x}{-3} + y = 1$$

$$y = 4x - 3 \qquad y = -2x + 6$$

(Answers appear at the end of the section.)

Solving equations simultaneously

Another technique is used in a variety of problems. In a plane, two lines are either parallel or they intersect. If the lines intersect, you can obtain the point of intersection by solving the equations for the lines simultaneously (at the same time). One technique to obtain the solution is to solve for x (or y) in one of the equations and substitute this expression in the other equation.

Example: Determine the point of intersection of the two lines whose equations are $x + 2y = 5$ and $2x - y = 8$. Solve the first equation for x.

$$x = 5 - 2y$$

Substitute this expression for x in the second equation.

$$2(5 - 2y) - y = 8$$

Clear the parentheses, combine like terms, and solve for y.

$$10 - 4y - y = 8$$
$$10 - 5y = 8$$
$$2 = 5y$$
$$y = \frac{2}{5}$$

Solve for x by substituting this value of y in one of the two original equations.

$$x + 2\left(\frac{2}{5}\right) = 5$$
$$x = 5 - \frac{4}{5}$$
$$x = \frac{25 - 4}{5} \text{ or } \frac{21}{5}$$

The coordinates of the point of intersection of the two lines are $\left(\frac{21}{5}, \frac{2}{5}\right)$. Check your work by using the technique of substituting the coordinates into each of the two original equations to see whether the point lies on each line.

   The graph of the two lines shown below indicates the difficulty in trying to determine the coordinates of the point of intersection from the graph. It is difficult to determine the coordinates exactly.

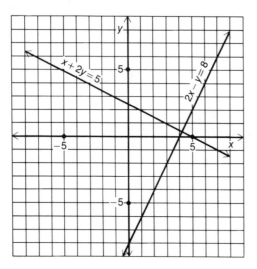

Your Turn

Find the point of intersection for each pair of lines by solving the equations simultaneously.

15. $x - 2y = 7$ and $3x - y = 6$
16. $3x + 4y = 12$ and $x + y = -1$
17. $-4x + y = 6$ and $2x + 6y = 10$

(Answers appear at the end of the section.)

Parallel and perpendicular lines

You may also have difficulty in determining from the inspection of a graph whether two lines are parallel. The lines in the graph below appear to be parallel, but are they parallel? You can make that determination from an inspection of the equations for the lines.

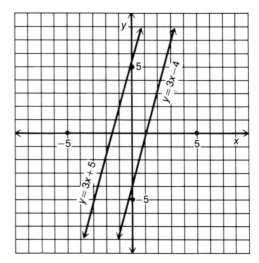

Two lines with the same slope and different y-intercepts will be parallel.

   Example: The lines shown in the diagram have the equations:

$$3x - y = -5 \text{ and}$$
$$3x - y = 4$$

The equations are shown in the standard slope-intercept form.

$$y = 3x + 5$$
$$y = 3x - 4$$

The first line has a slope of 3 and a y-intercept of 5. The second line has a slope of 3 and a y-intercept of -4. The two lines have the same slope and different y-intercepts; they are parallel.

Perpendicular lines have slopes that are negative reciprocals. The lines shown below in the graph have the equations:

$$y = 2x + 1 \text{ and}$$
$$y = -\frac{1}{2}x - 6$$

The slope of the second line, $-\frac{1}{2}$, is the negative reciprocal of 2, the slope of the first line. The lines are perpendicular.

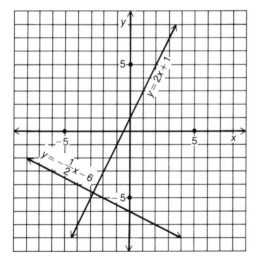

Your Turn

Tell whether each pair of lines are parallel, perpendicular, or neither.

18. $2x - y = 6$ and $3x + y = 5$
19. $x + 3y = 1$ and $2x + 6y = 10$
20. $6x - y = 2$ and $3x - \frac{1}{2}y = -2$

21. $5x + 2y = 8$ and $-2x + 5y = 20$

(Answers appear at the end of the section.)

Using linear equations

The equations for lines are called linear equations. The highest degree of a term is one. When you can write these equations and interpret the slope and the y-intercept, you can solve a number of problems easily with the use of graphing techniques. The use of algebra to solve these equations makes the process easy and provides a precision that cannot be achieved by graphing.

Here are a few of the large number of ways that you can solve problems with linear equations.

You can check whether a point belongs to a line. If a point belongs to a line, its coordinates satisfy the equation of the line.

> **Example:** Are points P (2,7) and Q (3,10) on the line whose equation is $y = 4x - 1$?
>
> Substitute (2,7) for (x,y) in the equation.
>
> $$7 \stackrel{?}{=} 4(2) - 1$$
> $$7 = 7$$

The point P (2,7) belongs to the line. Substitute (3,10) for (x,y).

$$10 \stackrel{?}{=} 4(3) - 1$$
$$10 \neq 11$$

The point (3,10) does not belong to the line.

You can use an equation to find any value of y (called the dependent variable) for a given value of x (called the independent variable).

> **Example:** When acceleration, a, is constant, the velocity of a moving body is

given by the equation: $v = v_0 + at$. Use v as the dependent variable (instead of y); t for the independent variable (instead of x); and v_0 for the intercept of the line with the vertical axis (the value of the velocity when the time $t = 0$). If a body is moving under constant acceleration and has an initial velocity of 3 km/sec, find the velocity after 4.5 seconds. Use 9.8 (km/sec)/sec for the acceleration.

$$v = v_0 + at$$
$$v = 3 + 9.8(4.5)$$
$$v = 3 + 44.1$$
$$ = 47.1 \text{ km/sec}$$

A number of formulas are linear equations. Formulas are simply equations that are used very frequently and that usually have special letters for the variables. One such formula relates temperature in degrees Celsius (C) to temperature in degrees Fahrenheit (F).

$$C = \frac{5}{9}(F - 32)$$

You can write this equation in slope-intercept form by clearing the parentheses.

$$C = \frac{5}{9}F - \frac{160}{9}$$

Example: Find the temperature of boiling water in degrees Celsius, given the temperature is 212°F.

$$C = \frac{5}{9}F - \frac{160}{9}$$
$$= \frac{5}{9}(212) - \frac{160}{9}$$
$$= 117\frac{7}{9} - 17\frac{7}{9}$$
$$= 100 \text{ or } 100°C$$

A set of lines that deserves attention are the lines whose equations have the form: $y = kx$. This family of lines has a y-intercept of 0—they all pass through the origin.

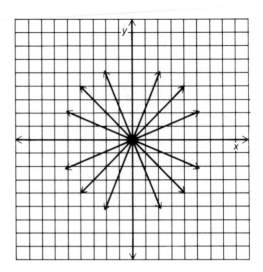

These lines are interesting because they express the relationship that two variables are directly proportional. There are many phenomena that can be described by direct proportionality.

For example, a law of physics, Hooke's Law, states that the elongation of a spring being stretched is directly proportional to the force applied (within elastic limits, of course). You can then determine the amount by which a spring is lengthened when you know the force being used. The relationship is expressed by the equation:

$$s = kf$$

where s is the elongation and f is the applied force. The constant, k, is called the constant of proportionality. Many other relationships follow this simple rule of direct variation. You calculate total cost as the product of price per item (constant) and the number of items (variable), simple interest as the product of interest rate (constant) and amount invested (variable), circumference of a circle as the product of π (constant) and the diameter (variable), and inches as the product of 12 (constant) and the number of feet (variable). These are but a few examples of direct relationships that can be expressed by an equation of the form $y = kx$.

Your Turn

Check whether the following points belong to the line whose equation is $y = 2x + 2$.

22. $(1, -4)$ 23. $(-2, -2)$ 24. $(6,1)$

Use equations to solve each problem.

25. Find the velocity after 6 seconds for a body moving under constant acceleration with an initial velocity of 5.5 km/sec. Use 9.8 (km/sec)/sec for the acceleration.
26. Normal human body temperature is 98.6°F. What is that temperature in degrees Celsius?
27. Find the total cost of 6 items that cost $15 each.
28. Find the cost of 15 items if the total cost is $240.

Challenge: Rewrite the formula relating degrees Celsius and degrees Fahrenheit so that F is the independent variable and C is the dependent variable.

(Answers appear at the end of the section.)

Quadratic Equations

Some of the most interesting mathematical figures are called conic sections. They were described by Appolonius in the third century B.C. However, not until algebraic equations were written with good notation for variables and studied was it understood that all of the equations of second degree describe the conic sections (or the degenerate conic sections). In this section a few of these equations and their conic sections will be discussed.

You can fashion a conic surface. Take a stick and locate some convenient point near the center. Hold this point fixed, and make one end of the stick trace a circle. The stick will trace out two circular cones in space. (Assume that this surface can continue indefinitely.)

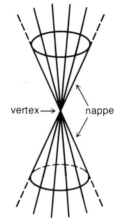

Each conical surface is called a nappe. You can section—that is, cut—the conic surface with a plane in various ways to obtain an interesting set of figures. These figures are called the conic sections: the circle, the ellipse, the parabola, and the hyperbola.

You can also intersect the conic surface with a plane so as to obtain a pair of intersecting lines, one line, or a point. These three figures are sometimes called the "degenerate" conic sections. As you examine the chief conic sections, you will see how this latter group got its name.

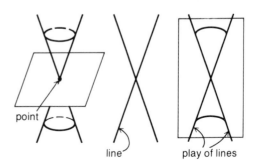

point   line   play of lines

The conic sections are particularly interesting because every body that moves in space under the action of gravity—the earth, the planets, their moons, satellites, comets, and stars—all follow a path that is one of the conic sections. Thus the interest in the conic sections is as old as people's first astronomical understandings and as new as the twentieth-century interest in the exploration of space.

The general equation of second degree has three second degree terms, two linear terms and one constant term. It is written as

$$Ax^2 + Bxy + Cy^2 + Dx + Ey + F = 0$$

Of course, one or more of the terms may have a coefficient of zero, but it cannot be true that A, B and C are all zero, as then there would not be an equation of second degree.

Circles

You can obtain a circle if you cut the conical surface with a plane at right angles to the axis of symmetry. As you move the cutting plane closer to the vertex of the conical surface, the circles grow smaller. Finally, the plane will pass through the single point, the vertex. You could say that the set of circles has *degenerated* to a point. That is why the point is called one of the "degenerate" conics.

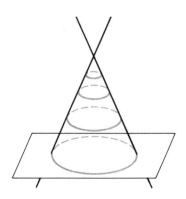

The circle is a unique figure in that it has infinitely many lines of symmetry. Any line drawn through the center of the circle is a line of symmetry.

If the center of the circle is the origin of the coordinate system, the equation of the circle is given by:

$$x^2 + y^2 = k^2$$

The constant k^2 is the radius squared, so that you can write $x^2 + y^2 = r^2$. When you read the equation of a circle you can determine the radius at once. For example, the circle whose equation is $x^2 + y^2 = 25$ is a circle with the center at the origin and a radius of 5 units.

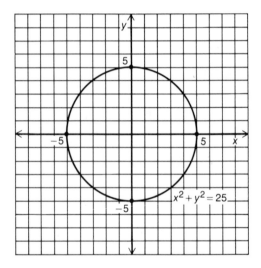

When a set of points is moved to another position in the plane, the equation changes appropriately. You can see the effect of a translation of a set of points in the plane in the diagram.

Suppose you had an original graph with axes x and y, and points, P, with coordinates (x,y). The whole system is then translated h units to the right and k units up, and the coordinate axes in the new position are labeled X and Y. The coordinates of the points, P, with respect to

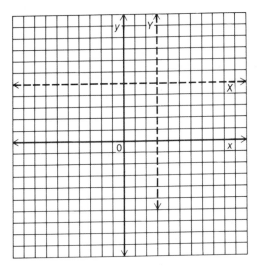

the new coordinate axes are (X, Y). The new coordinates are related to the old co-ordinates, as can be seen from the diagram, by the linear equations:

$$x = X + h$$
$$y = Y + k$$

You can then solve these equations for X and Y and obtain:

$$X = x - h$$
$$Y = y - k$$

If you substitute these coordinates into the equations, you can determine by in-spection how the set of points has been translated.

For example, suppose you have a cir-cle located in the plane with the center at the origin of the translated axes. The new axes have their origin at the point whose coordinates are (3,5) in the original sys-tem. With respect to the new coordinate system, the equation of the circle is

$$X^2 + Y^2 = 25$$

With respect to the old coordinate sys-tem, the equation of the circle can be ob-tained by replacing X with $x - h$ or $x - 3$, and Y with $y - k$, or $y - 5$, in this

case. You then have the equation of the circle with respect to the original coordi-nate system:

$$(x - 3)^2 + (y - 5)^2 = 25$$

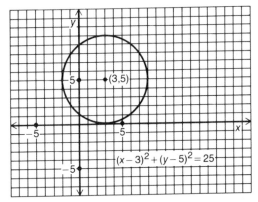

When you are familiar with the effect of translation on the equation, you can read the translation from the equation, once it is put into standard form. The new equa-tion tells that the circle has a center at (3,5) and a radius of 5. You can put the equation in the proper form by the now-familiar process of completing the square.

Example: The equation of a circle is $x^2 - 6x + y^2 + 8y = 0$. Determine the location of the center of the circle, and the length of the radius. Rewrite the equation by completing the square to form two trinomials, one with x as the variable and the other with y as the variable.

$$(x^2 - 6x + \underline{9}) +$$
$$(y^2 + 8y + \underline{16}) = 9 + 16$$
$$(x - 3)^2 + (y + 4)^2 = 25$$
$$(x - 3)^2 + (y - -4)^2 = 5^2$$

The equation is now in a standard form, ready for analysis. The center of the circle is at the point whose coordi-nates are $(3, -4)$, and the radius of the circle is 5 units.

Your Turn

Give the coordinates of the center and the length of the radius for each circle.

1. $x^2 + y^2 = 100$
2. $x^2 - 10x + y^2 - 24y = 0$
3. $x^2 + 2x + y^2 - 12y + 28 = 0$

(Answers appear at the end of the section.)

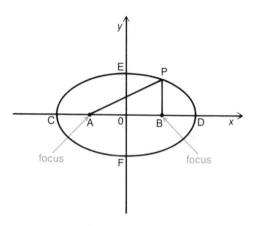

Ellipses

If you cut the conical surface with a plane that is not perpendicular to the axis of symmetry, you obtain an ellipse. If you move the cutting plane closer and closer to the vertex of the conical surface, you obtain a sequence of ellipses that grow smaller and smaller. The limiting figure for the sequence is a point, as it was for the circle.

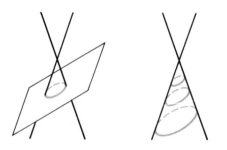

The ellipse can be described as a set of points in a plane for which the sum of the distances from two fixed points is constant. Each of the fixed points is called a focus of the ellipse (plural: foci).

In the figure, the sum of the lengths of $\overline{AP}$ and $\overline{PB}$ is always the same. The lines x and y are axes of symmetry for the ellipse. The segments CD and EF that lie on these axes are called the major axis and minor axis, respectively. The major

axis is the segment connecting the points C and D, the vertices of the ellipse. The center of the ellipse is the midpoint of the major axis, 0.

The equation of an ellipse is given in standard form by

$$\frac{x^2}{a^2} + \frac{y^2}{b^2} = 1$$

The quantities a and b are shown in the diagram. The major axis has length $2a$ and the minor axis has length $2b$; so a and b are the lengths of the semi-major and semi-minor axes, respectively.

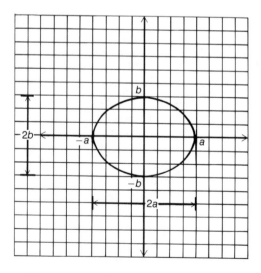

Example: An ellipse with its center at the origin has an equation $9x^2 + 16y^2 = 144$. Put the equation in standard form, and determine the length of the major axis and the minor axis. The right-hand side of the equation is to be 1, so divide every term by 144.

$$\frac{x^2}{16} + \frac{y^2}{9} = 1$$

From the equation, you can see that a is 4 and b is 3. The major axis is $2a$, or 8, units in length, and the minor axis is $2b$, or 6, units in length.

If the ellipse is translated h units to the right and k units up, the new equation reads:

$$\frac{(x - h)^2}{a^2} + \frac{(y - k)^2}{b^2} = 1$$

Example: You are given the equation for an ellipse in the form

$$x^2 - 6x + 9y^2 + 36y = -9$$

Complete the square for two trinomials, one for x and one for y.

$$(x^2 - 6x + 9) + (9y^2 + 36y + 36) = -9 + 9 + 36$$

$$(x - 3)^2 + (3y + 6)^2 = 36$$

$$(x - 3)^2 + 3^2(y - -2)^2 = 36$$

$$\frac{(x - 3)^2}{36} + \frac{9(y - -2)^2}{36} = 1$$

$$\frac{(x - 3)}{6^2} + \frac{(y - -2)}{2^2} = 1$$

The center is at $(3, -2)$. The major axis is 12 units in length. The minor axis is 4 units in length.

Your Turn

Put each equation for an ellipse in standard form. Tell where the center is and the lengths of the major axis and minor axis.

4. $x^2 + 9y^2 = 9$
5. $16x^2 - 32x + 25y^2 - 100y = 284$
6. $4x^2 + 24x + 9y^2 = 0$

(Answers appear at the end of the section.)

Parabolas

A parabola is a figure that is obtained by a plane passing through the conic surface parallel to one of the elements that form the surface (that is, one of the positions that the stick took when the surface was traced out).

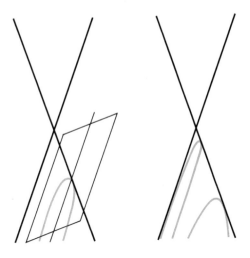

As you move the cutting plane closer to the edge of the conical surface, you get narrower parabolas. The limiting figure for this sequence of parabolas is a straight line, when the cutting plane just touches one element of the conical surface.

A parabola can also be described as a set of points in a plane for which the distance from a fixed point called the focus is the same as the distance from a fixed line called the directrix.

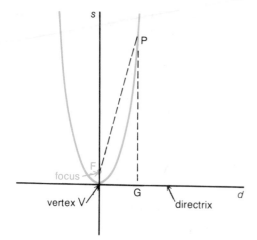

In the figure, point F is the focus, line d is the directrix. The length of $\overline{PF}$ is the same as the length of $\overline{PG}$. Line s is the axis of symmetry for the figure. Point V is called the vertex of the figure. Notice that the figure is rounded at V; there are no sharp corners on a parabola.

The parabola has a useful reflecting property. If a light ray comes from a source placed at the focus and is reflected from the parabola, it will travel in a line parallel to the axis of symmetry.

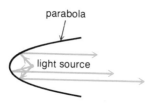

Also, a light ray coming in parallel to the axis and striking the parabola will be reflected through the focal point. This reflecting property has practical applications. The reflectors of the headlights of an auto are made in a three-dimensional parabolic shape (a paraboloid) with the headlight lamp at the focal point. In this manner a parallel set of rays emerges from the headlight.

A parabola with a vertical axis of symmetry has for its equation:

$$y = ax^2 + bx + c$$

With a horizontal axis of symmetry, the equation of the parabola is

$$x = ay^2 + by + c$$

To graph the parabola whose equation is $y = x^2$, first make a table.

x	y (=x²)	ordered pair
−3	9	(−3,9)
−2	4	(−2,4)
−1	1	(−1,1)
0	0	(0,0)
1	1	(1,1)
2	4	(2,4)
3	9	(3,9)

Plot the ordered pairs and draw the parabola, remembering it is a smooth curve.

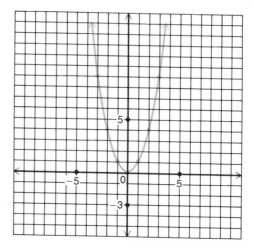

Suppose that you wish to move the parabola, translating it 3 units to the right and 5 units down. You can alter the equation to reflect the translation by replacing

x with $(x - 3)$ and y with $(y - -5)$, or $(y + 5)$. You then obtain:

$$(y + 5) = (x - 3)^2$$

If you expand and combine like terms, you obtain:

$$y + 5 = x^2 - 6x + 9$$
$$y = x^2 - 6x + 4$$

Now suppose that you had been given the problem of determining the translation, given the equation $y = x^2 - 6x + 4$. You would reverse the steps you just carried out; that is:

$$y = x^2 - 6x + 4$$

Complete the square for the trinomial in x.

$$y = (x^2 - 6x + 9) - 9 + 4$$

Notice that 9 was added and subtracted from the right-hand member of the equation so as not to change its value. Watch that step very carefully.

$$y = (x - 3)^2 - 5$$
$$y + 5 = (x - 3)^2$$
$$y - -5 = (x - 3)^2$$

The set of points has been translated 3 units to the right and 5 units down.

Your Turn

Graph each parabola. Start by making a table, then locate the ordered pairs.

1. $y = x^2 - 2x + 1$
2. $y = -(x)^2 - 2x - 1$

(Answers appear at the end of the section.)

Hyperbolas

A hyperbola is formed when a plane cuts a conic surface parallel to the axis of symmetry. The cutting plane will pass through both nappes of the conic surface

and thus form two branches. Each branch looks something like a parabola, but there is an important difference. All the points of each branch of a hyperbola lie between two intersecting lines called asymptotes. The points of a parabola cannot be contained between such a pair of lines.

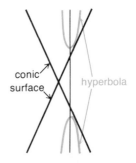

If you move the cutting plane closer to the axis of symmetry you obtain a sequence of hyperbolas. When the cutting plane passes through the vertex and the axis of symmetry, the section is a pair of intersecting lines, which form the limiting figure for this sequence of hyperbolas.

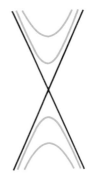

A hyperbola can be described as a set of points for which the difference of the distances of any point on the curve from two fixed points (called foci) is constant. In the figure, $\overline{PC} - \overline{PD}$ is constant for any point P on the hyperbola.

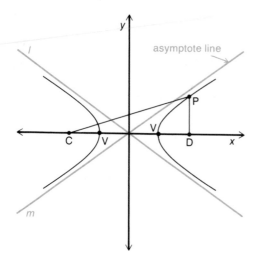

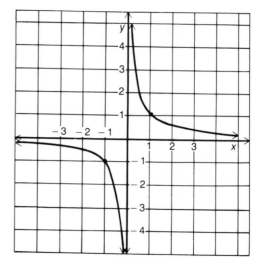

Lines *l* and *m* are the asymptote lines. The points forming the branches of the hyperbola approach these limit lines but never touch them. The lines *x* and *y* are the axes of symmetry for the figure.

One of the simplest equations with which you can work is that of the rectangular hyperbola, $xy = k$. It is especially interesting because it describes inverse variations. You can write it as $y = k\frac{1}{x}$. This relationship says that as *x* increases, *y* decreases. Calculate a few points for the curve and then graph it. For the graph, choose $k = 1$.

The graph then has the appearance as shown. As the values approach 0, the right branch of the hyperbola increases enormously—when the divisor is a very small number, less than 1 and positive, the quotient is a very large number. For example, $1 \div \frac{1}{1,000,000}$ is 1,000,000. To the left of the y-axis, the values are negative and increase as you go further to the left, approaching 0, but remain negative.

An example of inverse variation is one in which a gas is confined in a container such as a tire or a balloon. A law of physics says that if the temperature remains constant, the product of the pressure (*P*) and volume (*V*) remain constant.

You can write this as $PV = k$ or $P = k\frac{1}{V}$. The smaller the volume, the higher the pressure. If a balloon is squeezed to make the volume smaller, the pressure on the balloon increases; and if the volume is made very small, the balloon will burst.

Your Turn

Graph each hyperbola. Start by making a table, then locate the ordered pairs.

x	$\frac{1}{x}$	*x*	$\frac{1}{x}$
−5	$-\frac{1}{5}$	5	$\frac{1}{5}$
−4	$-\frac{1}{4}$	4	$\frac{1}{4}$
−3	$-\frac{1}{3}$	3	$\frac{1}{3}$
−2	$-\frac{1}{2}$	2	$\frac{1}{2}$
−1	−1	1	1
0	undefined		

1. $y = 3\left(\dfrac{1}{x}\right)$ 2. $y = 2\left(\dfrac{1}{x}\right) + 2$

(Answers appear at the end of the section.)

Finally it is worth remarking that you have been studying the Cartesian coordinate system exclusively, and the algebraic development that is consistent with it. There are, however, other coordinate systems available. You could construct a grid system where the two sets of lines are mutually oblique rather than perpen-

dicular. You might like to draw such a system and graph the sets of points on them to see the effect it produces. Another system, quite widely used for certain figures and certain problems, is a polar coordinate system. Figures known as roses, lemniscates, cardioids, and spirals are more easily graphed on a polar coordinate system, and the equations written with polar coordinates are easier to work with for these figures. You may wish to investigate these other coordinate systems for yourself.

Answers

Cartesian Coordinates (pp. 430–434)

Answers for page 432.

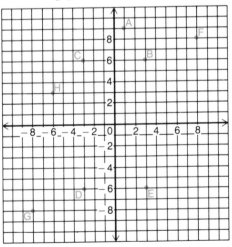

Answers for page 433.

A on x-axis   B in Quadrant II
C on x-axis   D in Quadrant I
E on y-axis   F on y-axis
G in Quadrant III   H in Quadrant II
I in Quadrant IV

Distance (pp. 434–435)

1. 6   2. 4   3. 12   4. 12   5. 13   6. 17   7. 15

Linear Equations (pp. 436–447)

1. 2   2. $-\frac{11}{7}$ 3. 0   4. $\frac{1}{4}$ 5. undefined   6. $y + 2 = 3(x - 2)$

7. $y + 1 = 1(x + 1)$ or $y = x$ 8. $y - 6 = \frac{15}{11}(x - 7)$ 9. $y = -3 + 3(x - 4)$

10. $y = 1 - 1(x + 2)$ 11. $y = 5x - 2$ 12. $y = -4x + 8$

13. $m = 2; y = -6 + 2(x + 3)$ or $y = 0 + 2(x + 0); y = 2x$

14. $m = 1; y = 1 + 1(x - 1)$ or $y = 0 + 1(x - 0); y = 1x$ or $y = x$

Answers for page 442.

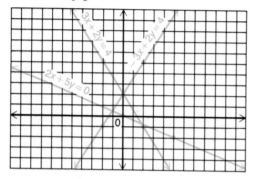

Answers for page 443

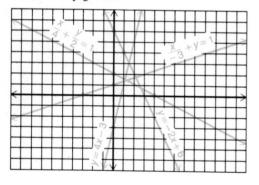

15. $x = 1; y = -3$ 16. $x = -16; y = 15$ 17. $x = -1; y = 2$ 18. neither

19. parallel   20. parallel   21. perpendicular

Answers for page 447.

22. No   23. Yes   24. No   25. 64.3 km/sec   26. 37°C   27. $90

28. $16   Challenge: $F = \frac{9}{5}C + 32$

Quadratic Equations (pp. 447–455)

1. $(0,0)$; $r = 10$ 2. $(5,12)$; $r = 13$ 3. $(-1,6)$; $r = 3$ 4. $(0,0)$; axes: 6 units, 2 units

5. $(1,2)$; axes: 10 units, 8 units   6. $(-3,0)$; axes: 6 units, 4 units

Answers for page 453.

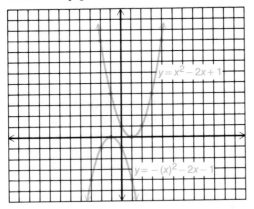

Answers for page 455.

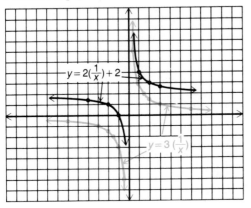

Section 12

Trigonometry

The right triangle is the basis of trigonometry, a branch of mathematics that combines arithmetic, algebra, and geometry. Trigonometry has an interesting, ancient history. The word *trigonometry* comes from two Greek words interpreted as "the measurement of triangles." Early trigonometry developed from "shadow reckoning." A stick and its shadow can be used to determine heights indirectly by means of similar figures. The rays of the sun (consider these parallel) create similar triangles with figures and their shadows.

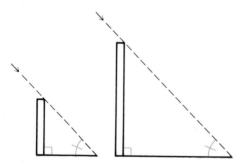

From geometry it was seen that two triangles are similar if two angles of one are congruent respectively to two angles of another. Since all right angles are congruent, two right triangles are similar if an acute angle of one is congruent to an acute angle of the second. As the triangles are similar, the corresponding sides are proportional. It is not a long step to note that the ratios for a particular right triangle depend on the measure of one of the acute angles. One triangle with a particular angle becomes a reference triangle. Its ratios apply to all right triangles with an acute angle of the same measure.

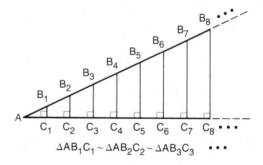

$$\triangle AB_1C_1 \sim \triangle AB_2C_2 \sim \triangle AB_3C_3 \quad \bullet \bullet \bullet$$

The ratios are said to be "functions of the angle." The study and application of the ratios for the acute angles of a right triangle make up what is called "right-angle trigonometry."

The trigonometric tables in ancient times did not record the ratios used today but rather recorded a set of values related to them. The triangle was placed in a circle. One side of the triangle became a chord of the circle. The lengths of the chords were related to the radius of the circle, and a table of chords was produced. During the Middle Ages the Hindus and the Arabs replaced the chords in their tables with half-chords.

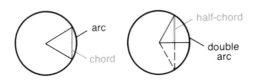

The half-chord of the double arc is equivalent to the ratio $\frac{a}{c}$ used in modern mathematics.

Most of the early applications of trigonometry were in astronomy. However, in the thirteenth century Fibonacci applied trigonometry to surveying. Trigonometry began to emerge as a separate study in the 15th century.

With the development of printing, algebra grew rapidly, since printing made possible standardization of symbols. Negative numbers came into common use, which reduced the number of computational steps needed for many trigonometric problems. The development of algebraic notation contributed significantly to the growth of trigonometry. After the development of algebra, the nature of the trigonometric ratios was studied as a subject in its own right. Trigonometry was significantly expanded.

In ancient times, angles were considered to be parts of polygons such as triangles. As the sum of the measures of all three angles of a triangle is 180°, there could be no angle so large as or larger than 180°. Strictly formal geometry works only with angles from 0° up to but not including 180°. But trigonometry involves angles of any measure. In the modern world there are machines whose parts can rotate. Mathematics must be able to describe circular motion, including angles with measures that exceed 180°. Further, since rotation can be both clockwise and counterclockwise, directions of rotation have been established as positive and negative. The basis for trigonometry is still the right triangle, but the scope of trigonometry has been enlarged enormously.

Right-Triangle Trigonometry

Consider two right triangles, ABC and DEF, with right angles C and F and $\angle A \cong \angle D$.

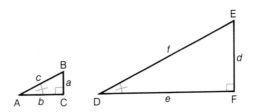

The triangles are similar (angle-angle theorem of geometry), and therefore the corresponding sides are proportional (definition of similarity). Thus, the proportion can be written:

$$\frac{a}{d} = \frac{b}{e}$$

From the section on ratio and proportion, recall that the product of the means is equal to the product of the extremes: *bd*

= *ae*. If both members of this equation are divided by *ad*, a new proportion is obtained:

$$\frac{bd}{ad} = \frac{ae}{ad} \text{ or } \frac{b}{a} = \frac{e}{d}$$

Thus, the ratio of two sides of *one* triangle is equal to the ratio of the two corresponding sides of the second triangle. Six ratios can be formed for two sides of one triangle: $\frac{a}{b}, \frac{b}{a}, \frac{a}{c}, \frac{c}{a}, \frac{b}{c}, \frac{c}{b}$. As will be shown, the values of these ratios for sides of a right triangle have been given special names, calculated, and recorded in reference tables that are available for use.

Now the problem of finding lengths indirectly (without actually measuring the length) can be solved in two somewhat different ways. The first method, shadow reckoning, is based on the properties of similar triangles. The second method also makes use of the properties of similar triangles but employs a reference triangle whose ratios are recorded in a table for convenient use. As the second (reference) triangle is not drawn in a diagram representing the problem, it is often forgotten that this table-value method is based on the properties of similar triangles and that the values in the table represent the ratios for the lengths of the sides of a right triangle.

Example: (*Method I*) A stick one meter long casts a shadow three meters long. Find the height of a building that casts a shadow 45 meters long.

To help make a plan for solving the problem, a drawing should be made. The height of the building will be denoted by *h*.

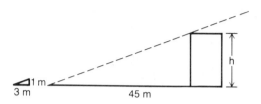

Since the triangles are similar, the ratio of the sides of one triangle is equal to the ratio of the sides of the second triangle.

$\dfrac{1}{3} = \dfrac{h}{45}$	Set up the proportion.
$1 \times 45 = 3h$	Solve the proportion by using cross-products.
$\dfrac{45}{3} = \dfrac{3h}{3}$	Divide both sides by 3.
$15 = h$	The height of the building is 15 meters.

Your Turn

1. Find the height of a tree casting a 20-foot shadow when a 1-foot stick casts a 2-foot shadow.

   Make a drawing and choose a letter to denote the height of the tree. Write a proportion and solve it.

2. Here is a slightly different problem. Find the length of a shadow of a 15-foot flagpole when a 1-foot stick casts a 1.5-foot shadow.

(*Answers appear at the end of the section.*)

In the second method, a table of values for the ratio of two sides of a right triangle for different angles is used. The ratio $\frac{a}{b}$ is given for several values of $\angle A$.

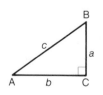

angle A	$\dfrac{a}{b}$
10°	$\dfrac{18}{100}$
20°	$\dfrac{36}{100}$
30°	$\dfrac{58}{100}$
40°	$\dfrac{84}{100}$
50°	$\dfrac{119}{100}$
60°	$\dfrac{173}{100}$
70°	$\dfrac{275}{100}$
80°	$\dfrac{567}{100}$

Triangle ABC is used as a reference triangle for any triangle with an acute angle whose measure is listed in the table.

Before solving a problem with the aid of the table, it is useful to learn two new terms. Two terms that are often used in problems on the indirect measurement of height are the *angle of elevation* and the *angle of depression*. These are a pair of angles formed by the line of sight and horizontal lines, as shown.

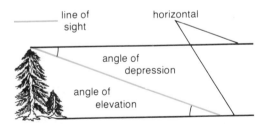

The angles are congruent, as they are alternate interior angles formed by a transversal (the line of sight) on a pair of parallel lines (two horizontal lines).

Example: *(Method II)* At a distance of 100 feet from a building, the top of the building has a 20° angle of elevation with ground level. Find the height of the building.

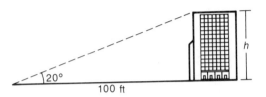

The ratio $\dfrac{a}{b}$ for a triangle with an acute angle of 20° is, from the table, $\dfrac{36}{100}$. The ratio for the triangle formed by the building, the ground and the line of sight is $\dfrac{h}{100}$, where h is the height of the building. The two triangles are similar, so the ratios form a proportion.

$$\frac{h}{100} = \frac{36}{100}$$

$$h = 36$$

The height of the building is 36 feet.

The measurement of the angle of elevation is more conveniently made from eye level than from ground level. The problem can then be arranged as follows.

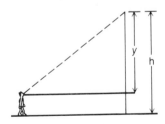

The height of the building above eye level (y) is measured. For the height of the building, the height of the eye level of the observer is then added to the value of y.

Example: Find the height of the flagpole on the next page.

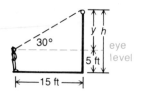

Note that

$$h = y + 5$$

$$\frac{a}{b} = \frac{y}{15} \qquad \text{Write the ratio.}$$

$$\frac{y}{15} = \frac{58}{100} \qquad \begin{array}{l}\text{Set up the propor-}\\\text{tion, using the ta-}\\\text{ble on page 461.}\end{array}$$

$$100y = 15(58) \qquad \text{Solve.}$$

$$\begin{aligned}y &= 8.7 \qquad &\text{The flagpole is}\\h &= y + 5 \qquad &\text{about 14 feet tall,}\\&= 8.7 + 5 \qquad &\text{rounded to the}\\&&\text{nearest foot.}\end{aligned}$$

Your Turn

From the table on page 461, find the values of the $\frac{a}{b}$ for angles with measures of:

3. 60°   4. 70°   5. 20°
6. A basketball player notes that the angle of elevation from eye level to the beam at the intersection of the end wall and the ceiling of the gym is 40°. The player is 18 feet from the end wall. Eye level is 6 feet for this player. How high is the beam to the nearest foot?

(Answers appear at the end of the section.)

Experiment

You can make indirect measurements by finding the angle of elevation of tops of buildings, trees, and poles. You can find the angle of elevation with an instrument that is easily constructed: a clinometer.

You will need a piece of cardboard (4″ × 6″ or larger), a large soda straw, scotch tape, a piece of string, a weight to attach to the string, a protractor, a straightedge, and a pencil. With the protractor, mark the 90° arc and the angle measures, as shown. Extend the angle lines at 10° intervals across the cardboard. Attach the soda straw at the top, and the string at the upper right corner. Attach the weight to the string.

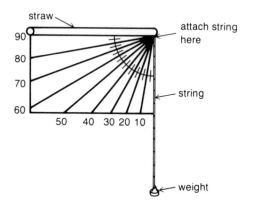

To measure an angle of elevation, sight the top of the object to be measured through the straw and read the angle marked by the string.

Basic trigonometric ratios

Six ratios can be formed from the measures of the sides of a right triangle: three basic ratios and their reciprocals. The capital letters A, B, and C are used in three ways: they denote the vertices of the right triangle, the angles that have these vertices, and the measures of these angles. The lower case letters *a*, *b*, and *c* denote the sides of the right triangle and the measures of the sides. The meaning of the symbols is clear from the way in which they are used in the problem. C represents the right angle of the triangle; and the side opposite ∠C, the hypotenuse, is denoted by c.

The six ratios are defined with respect to ∠A. Side a lies opposite ∠A and is called the side opposite (with respect to A). Side b is one of the sides that form ∠A and is called the side adjacent (with respect to A). Note that with respect to ∠B, side b is the side opposite, and side a is the side adjacent. It is very important in naming the sides to state which of the two acute angles of the right triangle you are using as the reference. The ratios are named and defined as follows:

$$\text{sine A} = \frac{\text{length of side opposite}}{\text{length of hypotenuse}}$$

$$\text{cosine A} = \frac{\text{length of side adjacent}}{\text{length of hypotenuse}}$$

$$\text{tangent A} = \frac{\text{length of side opposite}}{\text{length of side adjacent}}$$

$$\text{cotangent A} = \frac{\text{length of side adjacent}}{\text{length of side opposite}}$$

$$\text{secant A} = \frac{\text{length of hypotenuse}}{\text{length of side adjacent}}$$

$$\text{cosecant A} = \frac{\text{length of hypotenuse}}{\text{length of side opposite}}$$

These ratios are abbreviated as follows:

$$\sin A = \frac{a}{c} \qquad \cot A = \frac{b}{a}$$

$$\cos A = \frac{b}{c} \qquad \sec A = \frac{c}{b}$$

$$\tan A = \frac{a}{b} \qquad \csc A = \frac{c}{a}$$

Your Turn

7. Given right triangle XYZ, with Y the right angle, label the sides x, y and z. (Each side uses the letter of the vertex opposite it.)

8. Write the six trigonometric ratios for angle X and then for angle Z. (Determine which are the side opposite and the side adjacent with respect to X and then Z before writing the ratios.)

(Answers appear at the end of the section.)

Trigonometric relations

Angles A and B are complementary, since their sum must be 90°. (The sum of the angles of a triangle is 180°, and the measure of a right angle is 90°.) The cosine of angle A is $\frac{b}{c}$. With respect to angle B, the side b is the side opposite, so that $\frac{b}{c}$ is the sine of angle B. Thus the cosine of an angle is the sine of the complement of that angle. The term cosine comes from *complement's sine*. In the same way, it is seen that

$$\sin A = \cosine B$$
$$\tangent A = \cotangent B$$
$$\secant A = \cosecant B$$

From the definitions of the ratios, certain relations among them are easy to see. For example, there are six reciprocal relations.

$$\sin A = \frac{1}{\csc A} \text{ and } \csc A = \frac{1}{\sin A}$$

$$\cos A = \frac{1}{\sec A} \text{ and } \sec A = \frac{1}{\cos A}$$

$$\tan A = \frac{1}{\cot A} \text{ and } \cot A = \frac{1}{\tan A}$$

Another way to express these relationships is as follows:

Check:

$$(\sin A)(\csc A) = 1 \qquad \frac{a}{c} \cdot \frac{c}{a} = 1$$

$$(\cos A)(\sec A) = 1 \qquad \frac{b}{c} \cdot \frac{c}{b} = 1$$

$$(\tan A)(\cot A) = 1 \qquad \frac{a}{b} \cdot \frac{b}{a} = 1$$

Another relationship can also be seen:

$$\tan A = \frac{\sin A}{\cos A}$$

Example: Show, by substitution, that

$$\tan A = \frac{\sin A}{\cos A}$$

$\tan A = \frac{a}{b}$, $\sin A = \frac{a}{c}$, and $\cos A = \frac{b}{c}$

Substituting: $\dfrac{a}{b} \overset{?}{=} \dfrac{\dfrac{a}{c}}{\dfrac{b}{c}}$

$$\overset{?}{=} \frac{a}{c} \div \frac{b}{c}$$

$$\overset{?}{=} \frac{a}{c} \cdot \frac{c}{b}$$

$$\frac{a}{b} = \frac{a}{b}$$

Your Turn

Show by substitution that the following relationships hold:

9. $\cot A = \dfrac{\cos A}{\sin A}$

10. $\sec A = \dfrac{1}{\cos A}$

11. $\cot A = \dfrac{1}{\tan A}$

(Answers appear at the end of the section.)

Developing trigonometric ratios

If the three sides of a right triangle have known lengths, it is easy to write the trigonometric ratios for each of the acute angles of that triangle.

Example: Write the six trigonometric ratios for right triangle ABC, with respect to $\angle A$, given $a = 3$, $b = 4$ and $c = 5$.

$$\sin A = \frac{3}{5} \qquad \csc A = \frac{5}{3}$$

$$\cos A = \frac{4}{5} \qquad \sec A = \frac{5}{4}$$

$$\tan A = \frac{3}{4} \qquad \cot A = \frac{4}{3}$$

Your Turn

Write the six trigonometric ratios for angle A:

12. Given right $\triangle ABC$, $a = 12$, $b = 5$, and $c = 13$.

13. Given right $\triangle ABC$, $a = 24$, $b = 7$, and $c = 25$.

(Answers appear at the end of the section.)

It is also possible to write the trigonometric ratios if just one ratio is given.

Example: Write the six trigonometric ratios with respect to angle B for right triangle ABC given $\sin B = \frac{3}{7}$ and C as the right angle. In order to write the ratios, it is necessary to find a value for the length of the side adjacent to ∠B. The side opposite ∠B has length $3m$, where m is any number >0, and the hypotenuse has the length $7m$. Since ratios are to be formed, the value of m is not needed $\left(\dfrac{3m}{7m} = \dfrac{3}{7}\right)$.

The side opposite and the hypotenuse will be assigned lengths of 3 and 7, respectively. The length of the third side can be obtained with the use of the Pythagorean Theorem.

$$a^2 + b^2 = c^2$$
$$a^2 + 3^2 = 7^2$$
$$a^2 + 9 = 49$$
$$a^2 = 49 - 9 \text{ or } 40$$
$$a = \sqrt{40} \text{ or } 2\sqrt{10}$$

The ratios are then:

$$\sin B = \frac{3}{7} \qquad \csc B = \frac{7}{3}$$

$$\cos B = \frac{2\sqrt{10}}{7} \qquad \sec B = \frac{7}{2\sqrt{10}}$$

$$\tan B = \frac{3}{2\sqrt{10}} \qquad \cot B = \frac{2\sqrt{10}}{3}$$

Your Turn

Given right triangle ABC and $\cot A = \dfrac{12}{5}$, find the following ratios:

14. sin A   15. cos A   16. tan A
17. csc A   18. sec A

(Answers appear at the end of the section.)

Trigonometric tables

A table of trigonometric ratios for angles from 1° through 89° in steps of 1° is presented on page 466. A large number of problems can be solved easily with the use of the table. Care must always be taken in reading a value from a table. It is handy to keep an index card in your book so you can line up properly in the horizontal direction when reading the table. Read the value of angle from one of the columns headed "angle" and then select the value under the desired heading. Watch the headings carefully.

Example: Find sin 57° and tan 19° from the table. From the table, sin 57° = .8387 and tan 19° = .3443.

Your Turn

Use the table to find the following:

19. sin 35°   20. cos 58°
21. tan 75°   22. sin 32°

(Answers appear at the end of the section.)

Pythagorean relationships

Several very important relationships extend the use of the trigonometric ratios. The Pythagorean Theorem can be expressed in trigonometric terms. For all right triangles, it has been proved that

$$a^2 + b^2 = c^2$$

where a and b are the lengths of the legs of the triangle and c is the length of the hypotenuse. Each term may be divided by c^2:

$$\frac{a^2}{c^2} + \frac{b^2}{c^2} = \frac{c^2}{c^2}$$

Trigonometric ratios

Angle	Sin	Cos	Tan	Angle	Sin	Cos	Tan
1°	.0175	.9998	.0175	46°	.7193	.6947	1.0355
2°	.0349	.9994	.0349	47°	.7314	.6820	1.0724
3°	.0523	.9986	.0524	48°	.7431	.6691	1.1106
4°	.0698	.9976	.0699	49°	.7547	.6561	1.1504
5°	.0872	.9962	.0875	50°	.7660	.6428	1.1918
6°	.1045	.9945	.1051	51°	.7771	.6293	1.2349
7°	.1219	.9925	.1228	52°	.7880	.6157	1.2799
8°	.1392	.9903	.1405	53°	.7986	.6018	1.3270
9°	.1564	.9877	.1584	54°	.8090	.5878	1.3764
10°	.1736	.9848	.1763	55°	.8192	.5736	1.4281
11°	.1908	.9816	.1944	56°	.8290	.5592	1.4826
12°	.2079	.9781	.2126	57°	.8387	.5446	1.5399
13°	.2250	.9744	.2309	58°	.8480	.5299	1.6003
14°	.2419	.9703	.2493	59°	.8572	.5150	1.6643
15°	.2588	.9659	.2679	60°	.8660	.5000	1.7321
16°	.2756	.9613	.2867	61°	.8746	.4848	1.8040
17°	.2924	.9563	.3057	62°	.8829	.4695	1.8807
18°	.3090	.9511	.3249	63°	.8910	.4540	1.9626
19°	.3256	.9455	.3443	64°	.8988	.4384	2.0503
20°	.3420	.9397	.3640	65°	.9063	.4226	2.1445
21°	.3584	.9336	.3839	66°	.9135	.4067	2.2460
22°	.3746	.9272	.4040	67°	.9205	.3907	2.3559
23°	.3907	.9205	.4245	68°	.9272	.3746	2.4751
24°	.4067	.9135	.4452	69°	.9336	.3584	2.6051
25°	.4226	.9063	.4663	70°	.9397	.3420	2.7475
26°	.4384	.8988	.4877	71°	.9455	.3256	2.9042
27°	.4540	.8910	.5095	72°	.9511	.3090	3.0777
28°	.4695	.8829	.5317	73°	.9563	.2924	3.2709
29°	.4848	.8746	.5543	74°	.9613	.2756	3.4874
30°	.5000	.8660	.5774	75°	.9659	.2588	3.7321
31°	.5150	.8572	.6009	76°	.9703	.2419	4.0108
32°	.5299	.8480	.6249	77°	.9744	.2250	4.3315
33°	.5446	.8387	.6494	78°	.9781	.2079	4.7046
34°	.5592	.8290	.6745	79°	.9816	.1908	5.1446
35°	.5736	.8192	.7002	80°	.9848	.1736	5.6713
36°	.5878	.8090	.7265	81°	.9877	.1564	6.3138
37°	.6018	.7986	.7536	82°	.9903	.1392	7.1154
38°	.6157	.7880	.7813	83°	.9925	.1219	8.1443
39°	.6293	.7771	.8098	84°	.9945	.1045	9.5144
40°	.6428	.7660	.8391	85°	.9962	.0872	11.4301
41°	.6561	.7547	.8693	86°	.9976	.0698	14.3007
42°	.6691	.7431	.9004	87°	.9986	.0523	19.0811
43°	.6820	.7314	.9325	88°	.9994	.0349	28.6363
44°	.6947	.7193	.9657	89°	.9998	.0175	57.2900
45°	.7071	.7071	1.0000				

Example: Give the value for each of the trigonometric functions for $\angle B$. Then find the lengths of sides a and b to the nearest whole unit.

$c = 120$

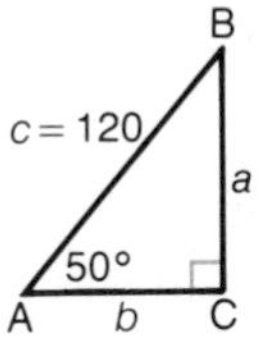

$a = ?$
$b = ?$
$c = 120$
$m\angle A = 50$
$m\angle B = ?$
$m\angle C = 90$

$$m\angle B = 180 - (50 + 90)$$
$$= 40$$
$\sin B = 0.6428$ from table
$\cos B = 0.7660$ from table
$\tan B = 0.8391$ from table
$\sec B = ?$

$$\tan^2 B + 1 = \sec^2 B$$
$$(0.8391)^2 + 1 = \sec^2 B$$
$$\sqrt{1.7040888} = \sec B$$

$\sec B = 1.3054$ $1.3054 = \sec B$

$\csc B = ?$ $\csc B = \dfrac{1}{\sin B}$

$$= \dfrac{1}{0.6428}$$

$\csc B = 1.5557$ $= 1.5557$
$\cot B = ?$ $\cot^2 B + 1 = \csc^2 B$
$$\cot^2 B = \csc^2 B - 1$$
$$= (1.5557)^2 - 1$$
$$\cot B = \sqrt{1.4202}$$

$\cot B = 1.1917$ $= 1.1917$

$\sin B = \dfrac{b}{c}$ $\cos B = \dfrac{a}{c}$

$0.6428 = \dfrac{b}{120}$ $0.7660 = \dfrac{a}{120}$

$$b = 120(0.6428)$$
$$= 77.136$$
$b = 77$ to the nearest whole unit

$$a = 120\,(0.7660)$$
$$= 91.92$$
$a = 92$ to the nearest whole unit

You can check the results by using the tangent function.

$$\tan B = \dfrac{b}{a}$$

$0.8391 \overset{?}{=} \dfrac{77}{92}$

$0.8391 \approx 0.8370$ Close enough, since results were rounded

This may be written as

$$\left(\frac{a}{c}\right)^2 + \left(\frac{b}{c}\right)^2 = 1$$

By substituting sin A for $\frac{a}{c}$ and cos A for $\frac{b}{c}$,

$$(\sin A)^2 + (\cos A)^2 = 1$$

This is usually written more briefly as

$$\sin^2 A + \cos^2 A = 1$$

This is the trigonometric form of the Pythagorean Theorem. Watch the notation carefully. The number that is sin A or cos A is the quantity that is to be squared.

If, instead of dividing by c^2, the terms are divided by b^2 or a^2, two other Pythagorean relationships are obtained:

$$\tan^2 A + 1 = \sec^2 A \text{ and}$$
$$1 + \cot^2 A = \csc^2 A$$

With the techniques used, right triangles have been "solved." That is, if certain sets of measures of three of the six parts (three angles and three sides) of a triangle are known, the measures of the remaining angle(s) and the remaining side(s) can be calculated.

Your Turn

Use the trigonometric table on page 466 and the Pythagorean relationships to find the lengths of the sides for each triangle to the nearest whole unit. Also find the value of sec B, csc B, and cot B for each triangle.

23.

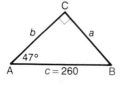

24.

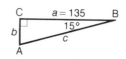

(Answers appear at the end of the section.)

Oblique Triangles in Trigonometry

In the section on informal geometry, it was shown that for all triangles, the sets SSS, SAS, ASA, and AAS uniquely determine the triangle. Then it follows that it should be possible to calculate the remaining parts for non-right (or oblique) triangles as well as right triangles.

Law of Sines

The right triangle can be used to find relationships to solve oblique triangles. Consider a general acute triangle, ABC, with altitude CD drawn to the base AB. The altitude is perpendicular to the base and so forms two right triangles. Let h be the measure of the altitude, and x and y the measures of the two segments of the base, so that $x + y = c$.

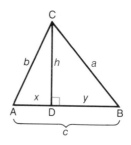

Then

$$\frac{h}{b} = \sin A \qquad \frac{h}{a} = \sin B$$

If both members of the first equation are multiplied by b, and both members of the second equation by a, you have

$$b \sin A = h$$
$$h = a \sin B$$

By the transitive property of equality,

$$b \sin A = a \sin B$$

Both members of the new equation can be divided by the product ab, to give the relationship:

$$\frac{\sin A}{a} = \frac{\sin B}{b}$$

By drawing the altitude from B to side b, it can be shown that

$$\frac{\sin A}{a} = \frac{\sin C}{c}$$

(You may wish to derive this yourself, to be sure that you understand the process.) Again, by the property of transitivity, the relationship can be derived:

$$\frac{\sin A}{a} = \frac{\sin B}{b} = \frac{\sin C}{c}$$

This relationship is called the *Law of Sines*.

It would be highly desirable if this relationship held for all triangles, including those with an angle whose measure was greater than 90°. In order to accomplish this generalization, a new definition would have to be made for the trigonometric ratios. Just such a definition has been made, and it forms the basis of general trigonometry, to be considered shortly.

With the Law of Sines, you can determine all parts of a triangle if the measures of two of the angles and one of the sides are known.

Example: A ship at sea is in radio contact with two shore stations, 150 miles apart. Station A radios that the direction of communication from the ship makes an angle of 35° with a line from Station A to Station B. Station B radios that the ship's communication makes an angle of 65° with a line between the two stations. The ship wants to know how far it is from Station B (to the nearest mile).

The calculation can be made with the Law of Sines. First make a diagram of the problem.

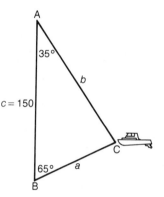

$$c = 150 \text{ miles}$$
$$m\angle A = 35 \qquad m\angle B = 65$$
$$m\angle C = 180 - (35 + 65) \text{ or } 80$$

$$\frac{\sin A}{a} = \frac{\sin C}{c}$$

$$\sin A = 0.5736 \qquad \text{(from table)}$$
$$\sin C = 0.9848$$
$$\frac{0.5736}{a} = \frac{0.9848}{150}$$

$$a = \frac{150\,(0.5736)}{0.9848}$$

$$a = 87.37$$

To the nearest mile, $a = 87$ miles.

Your Turn

Use the Law of Sines to find a and b in each figure, to the nearest foot.

1.

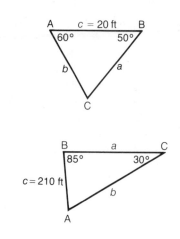

2.

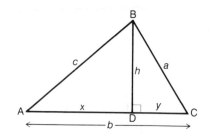

3. Ann and Bob are standing 300 feet apart. Across a river from them is Chad. Bob notes that the angle formed by lines between him and the other two is 55°. Ann notes that the angle formed by lines between her and the others is also 55°. How far from Ann is Chad?

(Answers appear at the end of the section.)

Law of Cosines

The Law of Sines is helpful for the AAS and ASA cases, but it does not give the needed information when three sides of a triangle (SSS) or two sides and the included angle (SAS) are known. Another relationship is needed for these calculations.

Once again, consider an acute triangle ABC. Altitude BD is drawn to base AC. Let h denote the length of the altitude, and x and y the two segments of the base, b, so that $b = x + y$.

The altitude is perpendicular to the base and thus creates two right triangles, ABD and CBD. (The derivation of the Law of Cosines is rather long. For this reason, equations have been given numbers to help you follow the logic and sub-

stitutions used.) Using the Pythagorean Theorem and △ABD, you get:

(1) $c^2 = x^2 + h^2$

From △ABC:

(2) $x = b - y$

From △CBD:

(3) $\dfrac{h}{a} = \sin C$

(4) $\dfrac{y}{a} = \cos C$

Square equation (2).

(5) $x^2 = (b - y)^2$
            $= b^2 - 2by + y^2$

Substitute x^2 from equation (5) in equation (1).

(6) $c^2 = b^2 - 2by + y^2 + h^2$

To eliminate the special segments introduced, h and y, solve equation (4) for y and then find y^2. Also solve equation (3) for h and then find h^2.

(4) $\dfrac{y}{a} = \cos C$ (3) $\dfrac{h}{a} = \sin C$

(7) $y = a \cos C$ (9) $h = a \sin C$

(8) $y^2 = a^2 \cos^2 C$ (10) $h^2 = a^2 \sin^2 C$

Substitute for h^2, y, and y^2 in equation (6).

(6) $c^2 = b^2 - 2by + y^2 + h^2$
(11) $= b^2 - 2b(a \cos C) +$
              $a^2 \cos^2 C + a^2 \sin^2 C$

Rewrite the expression, factoring a^2 from the last two terms.

(12) $c^2 = b^2 - 2b(a \cos C) + a^2(\cos^2 C + \sin^2 C)$

Recall the Pythagorean Theorem in trigonometric form.

(13) $\sin^2 C + \cos^2 C = 1$

Substitute equation (13) in equation (12).

(14) $c^2 = b^2 - 2b(a \cos C) + a^2 (1)$

Rearrange the terms to arrive at:

(15) $c^2 = a^2 + b^2 - 2ab \cos C$

As any of the sides can be called a, b, or c, it is clear that this relation can also be written:

$$a^2 = b^2 + c^2 - 2bc \cos A$$
$$\text{and}$$
$$b^2 = a^2 + c^2 - 2ac \cos B$$

This relation is known as the Law of Cosines.

This law states that the Pythagorean relation holds for all triangles with the addition of a correction term. The Law of Cosines is also called the Generalized Pythagorean Theorem. Once again, if the trigonometric ratios are defined for angles of 90° and greater, then the Law of Cosines would hold for obtuse triangles as well as acute triangles.

The Law of Cosines enables you to solve triangles when the lengths of all three sides are known, or when the lengths of two sides and the measure of the angle formed by those two sides are known.

Example: Two planes leave an airport on paths that make an angle of 50°. One plane travels at 375 miles per hour, the other at 450 miles per hour. How far apart are the two planes after two hours? Let c represent the length of the unknown side of the triangle. Side a measures 375 × 2, or 750, and side b = 450 × 2, or 900. Since m∠C = 50°, cos C = 0.6428 from the table.

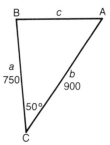

The Law of Cosines can be used for this problem.

$$c^2 = a^2 + b^2 - 2ab \cos C$$

Substitute the values for a, b, and cos C.

$$c^2 = (750)^2 + (900)^2 \\ - 2 (750)(900)(0.6428)$$
$$c^2 = 562,500 + 810,000 - 867,780$$
$$c^2 = 504,720$$
$$c = \sqrt{504,720}, \text{ or } 710 \text{ miles to the nearest mile.}$$

Your Turn

Use the Law of Cosines to find the third side of each triangle, to the nearest meter.

4.

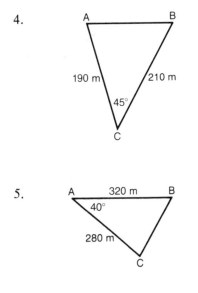

5.

6. Suppose you know that two sides of a triangle are 14 meters and 18 meters long. You also know that the angle formed by those two lines was 42°. Find the length of the third side.

(Answers appear at the end of the section.)

Solving triangles is a very important technique in applied mathematics. Surveyors, for example, solve triangles to make indirect measurements in a number of situations. Not only may they have to measure heights that cannot be measured directly, but they may have to make ground measurements across water that make direct measurement impossible.

General Trigonometry

The desire to apply trigonometry to angles of measure 90° and greater as well as to acute angles led to a more general definition of the trigonometric ratios. The modern system conceives an angle as having an initial side and a terminal side. The angle is placed in a rectangular coordinate system, with the vertex of the angle at the origin, the initial side lying along the positive ray of the *x*-axis, and the terminal ray rotated to any desired position. The measure of the angle is the amount of rotation necessary to bring the terminal ray to its position. Rotation in the counterclockwise direction is termed *positive* and rotation in the clockwise direction is *negative*. The measure of the rotation can thus be any real number, positive or negative.

For any position of the terminal ray, the intersection of the ray with the circle has (x,y) coordinates. The distance from the origin to this point is denoted by r, a positive number. By the Pythagorean Theorem, $x^2 + y^2 = r^2$, so $r = \sqrt{x^2 + y^2}$.

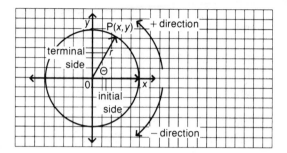

General trigonometric ratios

The six trigonometric ratios are now defined as shown below. (The angle of rotation will be denoted by θ, the Greek letter *theta*.)

$$\sin \theta = \frac{y}{r} \qquad \cot \theta = \frac{x}{y}$$

$$\cos \theta = \frac{x}{r} \qquad \sec \theta = \frac{r}{x}$$

$$\tan \theta = \frac{y}{x} \qquad \csc \theta = \frac{r}{y}$$

For angles between 0° and 90°, a reference triangle can be drawn. It can be seen that the trigonometric ratios obtained are the same as for right-triangle trigonometry.

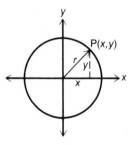

However, in right-triangle trigonometry, there can be no trigonometric ratios for angles of 0° or 90°, since these values cannot be measures of the acute angle of a right triangle. In the new system, it is not necessary to have the reference triangle to define the ratios; they depend only on the x and y coordinates of the endpoint of the rotating radius.

For simplicity, consider that the angle is placed in a unit circle; that is, a circle with radius of 1 unit in whatever measuring system you wish to work. Then x = cos θ and y = sin θ. As the coordinates for θ = 0° are (1,0), cos 0° = 1 and sin 0° = 0.

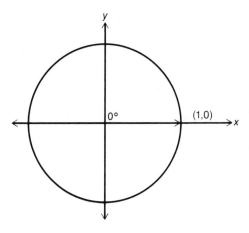

At θ = 90°, the coordinates of the endpoint of the terminal side are (0,1); hence, cos 90° = 0 and sin 90° = 1.

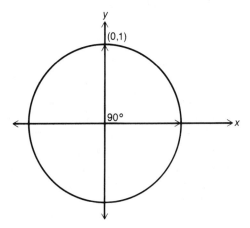

As $\angle\theta$ increases from 0° to 90°, sin θ increases from 0 to 1 and cos θ decreases from 1 to 0.

In the second quadrant, the x numbers are negative and the y numbers are positive. Hence, cos θ is negative for angles between 90° and 180°, and sin θ is positive. Once again, a reference triangle can be drawn. The length of the sides correspond to the numerical values of x and y and provide the correct numerical ratio. However, it must be noted that the angle does not lie in the reference triangle; this occurs only when the angle is between 0° and 90°. Also, for the correct ratio the signs of x and y must be used. (Remember that r represents a distance and is always positive.)

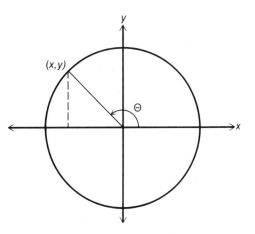

When θ = 180°, the coordinates of the endpoint of the rotating segment are $(-1,0)$. Then cos θ = -1 and sin θ = 0.

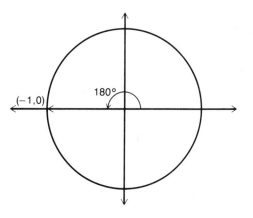

The correct signs for the tangent ratio can be determined for each quadrant by considering the signs of x and y in that quadrant.

Example: What is the sign of the tangent ratio for angles whose terminal sides fall in the second quadrant? Tan $\theta = \frac{x}{y}$. In the second quadrant, the x number is negative and the y number is positive, so the ratio $\frac{x}{y}$ is negative.

Your Turn

1. What are the coordinates of the endpoint of the rotating segment in a unit circle when $\theta = 270°$? What is sin 270°? What is cos 270°?

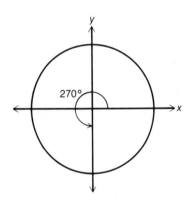

2. Find sin 360°, cos 360° and tan 360°.

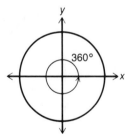

(Answers appear at the end of the section.)

Some relations among trigonometric ratios for angles of different measures can be seen directly from diagrams. In the diagram below, x_1 and x_2 have the same numerical value but opposite signs. Similarly, y_1 and y_2 have the same numerical value and opposite signs.

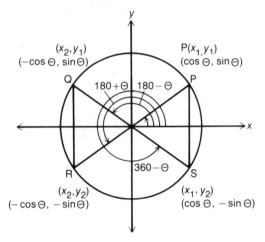

From symmetry, the following relations can be observed. (θ is an acute angle.)

$$\sin (180° - \theta) = \sin \theta$$
$$\sin (180° + \theta) = -\sin \theta$$
$$\sin (360° - \theta) = -\sin \theta$$

and

$$\cos (180° - \theta) = -\cos \theta$$
$$\cos (180° + \theta) = -\cos \theta$$
$$\cos (360° - \theta) = \cos \theta$$

Thus, all of the values that the trigonometric ratios can take on as the terminal side of the angle rotates from 90° to 360° occur in the first quadrant as θ goes from 0° to 90°. (The values, of course, are just repeated as θ becomes larger than 360°; the terminal arm of the angle moves through the same set of positions. If the rotation is negative, the values of the ratios are repeated in reverse order; that is, in clockwise order.)

The only thing that changes for angles larger than 90° is the sign of the ratio. Thus, all values of the ratios refer back to the right triangle, with the exception of the values of the ratios for 0° and 90° that are now added to the system. Thus, the table of values for angles from 0° to 90° is the only table needed. However, it is necessary to determine whether the ratio should be positive or negative.

To find a trigonometric ratio for an angle greater than 90°, the following procedure is followed.

1. Determine an acute reference angle for the given angle. The measure of the reference angle is the number of degrees (less than 90°) between the terminal arm of the given angle and the positive or negative ray of the x-axis. The positive ray is used for angles whose terminal side lies in Quadrant I or IV, and the negative ray is used when the terminal side lies in Quadrant II or III.

2. Find the trigonometric ratio for the reference angle.

3. Attach the proper sign ($+$ or $-$) to the ratio, according to the signs of x and y in the quadrant in which the terminal arm falls.

4. If the angle is a quadrantal angle (that is, the terminal arm coincides with a ray of the x-axis or y-axis), use the known coordinates of the endpoint of the terminal side in a unit circle to determine the ratios (as was done in the example).

Example: Find sin 240°, cos 240° and tan 240°.

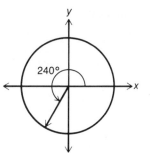

The terminal side of the angle falls in Quadrant III. The reference angle θ is 240° $-$ 180° or 60°.

$$\sin 60° = 0.8660$$
$$\cos 60° = 0.5000$$
$$\tan 60° = 1.7321$$

In Quadrant III, x is negative and y is negative (r is always positive). Thus $\frac{y}{r} = \sin \theta$ is negative; $\frac{x}{r} = \cos \theta$ is negative, and $\frac{x}{y} = \tan \theta$ is positive. Then

$$\sin 240° = -0.8660$$
$$\cos 240° = -0.5000$$

and

$$\tan 240° = 1.7321$$

Your Turn

Find sin A, cos A, and tan A of each of the following values of A.

3. 190°   4. 300°   5. 110°

(Answers appear at the end of the section.)

Condensing the table

The table of trigonometric ratios can be made even smaller than the one used earlier. As was shown previously, the function of an angle is the cofunction of its complement. Thus, only the values from

Trigonometric functions of angles

Degrees	Sin	Cos	Tan	Cot	Sec	Csc	
0	.0000	1.0000	.0000	. . . . . .	1.0000	. . . . . .	90
1	.0175	.9998	.0175	57.2900	1.0002	57.299	89
2	.0349	.9994	.0349	28.6363	1.0006	28.654	88
3	.0523	.9986	.0524	19.0811	1.0014	19.107	87
4	.0698	.9976	.0699	14.3007	1.0024	14.336	86
5	.0872	.9962	.0875	11.4301	1.0038	11.474	85
6	.1045	.9945	.1051	9.5144	1.0055	9.5668	84
7	.1219	.9925	.1228	8.1443	1.0075	8.2055	83
8	.1392	.9903	.1405	7.1154	1.0098	7.1853	82
9	.1564	.9877	.1584	6.3138	1.0125	6.3925	81
10	.1736	.9848	.1763	5.6713	1.0154	5.7588	80
11	.1908	.9816	.1944	5.1446	1.0187	5.2408	79
12	.2079	.9781	.2126	4.7046	1.0223	4.8097	78
13	.2250	.9744	.2309	4.3315	1.0263	4.4454	77
14	.2419	.9703	.2493	4.0108	1.0306	4.1336	76
15	.2588	.9659	.2679	3.7321	1.0353	3.8637	75
16	.2756	.9613	.2867	3.4874	1.0403	3.6280	74
17	.2924	.9563	.3057	3.2709	1.0457	3.4203	73
18	.3090	.9511	.3249	3.0777	1.0515	3.2361	72
19	.3256	.9455	.3443	2.9042	1.0576	3.0716	71
20	.3420	.9397	.3640	2.7475	1.0642	2.9238	70
21	.3584	.9336	.3839	2.6051	1.0711	2.7904	69
22	.3746	.9272	.4040	2.4751	1.0785	2.6695	68
23	.3907	.9205	.4245	2.3559	1.0864	2.5593	67
24	.4067	.9135	.4452	2.2460	1.0946	2.4586	66
25	.4226	.9063	.4663	2.1445	1.1034	2.3662	65
26	.4384	.8988	.4877	2.0503	1.1126	2.2812	64
27	.4540	.8910	.5095	1.9626	1.1223	2.2027	63
28	.4695	.8829	.5317	1.8807	1.1326	2.1301	62
29	.4848	.8746	.5543	1.8040	1.1434	2.0627	61
30	.5000	.8660	.5774	1.7321	1.1547	2.0000	60
31	.5150	.8572	.6009	1.6643	1.1666	1.9416	59
32	.5299	.8480	.6249	1.6003	1.1792	1.8871	58
33	.5446	.8387	.6494	1.5399	1.1924	1.8361	57
34	.5592	.8290	.6745	1.4826	1.2062	1.7883	56
35	.5736	.8192	.7002	1.4281	1.2208	1.7434	55
36	.5878	.8090	.7265	1.3764	1.2361	1.7013	54
37	.6018	.7986	.7536	1.3270	1.2521	1.6616	53
38	.6157	.7880	.7813	1.2799	1.2690	1.6243	52
39	.6293	.7771	.8098	1.2349	1.2868	1.5890	51
40	.6428	.7660	.8391	1.1918	1.3054	1.5557	50
41	.6561	.7547	.8693	1.1504	1.3250	1.5243	49
42	.6691	.7431	.9004	1.1106	1.3456	1.4945	48
43	.6820	.7314	.9325	1.0724	1.3673	1.4663	47
44	.6947	.7193	.9657	1.0355	1.3902	1.4396	46
45	.7071	.7071	1.0000	1.0000	1.4142	1.4142	45
	Cos	Sin	Cot	Tan	Csc	Sec	Degrees

0° through 45° need be listed. For sin 60°, read cos 30°. In order to make the table reading a bit easier and still take advantage of this property of the trigonometric ratios, the angles are listed in two columns and the headings in two different horizontal rows, as in the table shown on page 476.

For angles from 0° to 45°, the angle is read in the left-hand column and the top headings are used. For angles from 45° to 90°, the angles are read in the right-hand column and the headings at the bottom of the table are used.

Example: Find sin 70°, cos 70° and tan 70°. Read up the right-hand column until you reach 70°. Then use the column headings at the bottom of the table.

sin 70° = 0.9397
cos 70° = 0.3420
tan 70° = 2.7475

Example: Find sin 250°, cos 250°, and tan 250°. The reference angle is x, where 180 + x = 250. Since x = 70, use 70° as the measurement of the reference angle.

Function	Reference angle	Sign of function for angle	Value of function for angle
sine	70°	−	−0.9397
cosine	70°	−	−0.3420
tangent	70°	+	2.7475

From the examples, you should see that all of the functions are positive in Quadrant I. In each of the other quadrants, one pair of reciprocal functions is positive and the other four functions are negative. The results can be arranged as in the figure below.

Positive ratios (all others negative)

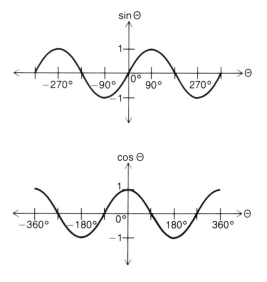

"C-A-S-T" is an easy way to remember how to label the quadrants to help you attach the proper signs to the ratios.

Your Turn

Find the value of each function for the given measure.

6. sin 290°   7. cos 290° 8. tan 290°
9. sin 52°   10. cos 100° 11. tan 310°

(Answers appear at the end of the section.)

Graphing Trigonometric Functions

The trigonometric functions have been graphed. Graphs of sin θ, cos θ and tan θ are shown below.

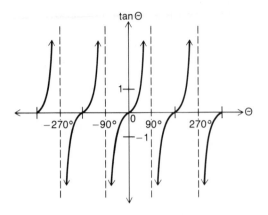

Your Turn

Use the graphs shown for sin θ, cos θ, and tan θ to tell at what angle measures the functions have the following values:

Example: sin θ = −1
Answers: −90°, 270°

1. sin θ = 0   2. sin θ = 1
3. cos θ = 0   4. cos θ = −1
5. cos θ = 1   6. tan θ = 0

(Answers appear at the end of the section.)

Note that the sine and cosine functions have the same shape but start (at 0°) at different points on the curve. The values for sin θ and cos θ range from −1 to +1, inclusive. The height of the graph (wave) above the centerline is called the *amplitude*. The number of degrees needed to obtain a complete set of points is called the *period*. The period of this sine wave is 360°.

The tangent function has no value for angles of 90°, −90°, 270° and −270°. When the terminal side of the angle is in these positions, the coordinates of the endpoint on a unit circle are (1,0) and (−1,0). However, a ratio cannot be formed with zero as a denominator. As the denominator of the ratio, *x*, gets close to 0 (that is, for example, when the rotation approaches 90°), the ratio $\frac{y}{x}$ gets very large. Think of *x* as being $\frac{1}{1,000,000}$. The rotating side is almost vertical, so *y* is almost 1. The ratio is then approximately $1 \div \frac{1}{1,000,000}$ or 1 × 1,000,000—close to a million.

The nature of the trigonometric functions is a very important part of modern trigonometry. The functions are important in their own right, as they occur in situations unrelated to the solution of triangles. For example, the sine function is important in electricity and electronics. The electrical alternating current voltages that supply power for lights and machines is generated in the shape of a sine wave. Thus it is critical to know the nature of this function in order to understand how equipment operates with this energy source.

The radio waves that carry communications are also sine waves. They can be formed very rapidly—that is, a large number of waves can be generated in a given time. The wave so formed is said to have a high frequency. It can be measured in thousands of cycles per second.

These applications of trigonometry are further examples of the variety of uses to which trigonometry has been put in modern times. Modern trigonometry may be rooted in the concepts of ancient times, but it has taken on dimensions the ancients never imagined.

Answers

Right-Angle Trigonometry (pp. 459–468)

1. 10 feet   2. 22.5 feet   3. $\dfrac{173}{100}$ 4. $\dfrac{275}{100}$ 5. $\dfrac{36}{100}$ 6. 21 feet

7.

8.
$$\sin X = \frac{x}{y} \qquad \cot X = \frac{z}{x} \qquad \sin Z = \frac{z}{y} \qquad \cot Z = \frac{x}{z}$$
$$\cos X = \frac{z}{y} \qquad \sec X = \frac{y}{z} \qquad \cos Z = \frac{x}{y} \qquad \sec Z = \frac{y}{x}$$
$$\tan X = \frac{x}{z} \qquad \csc X = \frac{y}{x} \qquad \tan Z = \frac{z}{x} \qquad \csc Z = \frac{y}{z}$$

9. $\cot A = \dfrac{b}{a}$, $\cos A$
$= \dfrac{b}{c}$, $\sin A = \dfrac{a}{c}$
$$\cot A \stackrel{?}{=} \frac{\cos A}{\sin A}$$
$$\frac{b}{a} \stackrel{?}{=} \frac{\dfrac{b}{c}}{\dfrac{a}{c}}$$
$$\stackrel{?}{=} \frac{b}{c} \div \frac{a}{c}$$
$$\stackrel{?}{=} \frac{b}{c} \cdot \frac{c}{a}$$
$$\frac{b}{a} = \frac{b}{a}$$

10. $\sec A = \dfrac{c}{b}$,
$\cos A = \dfrac{b}{c}$
$$\sec A \stackrel{?}{=} \frac{1}{\cos A}$$
$$\stackrel{?}{=} \frac{1}{\dfrac{b}{c}}$$
$$\stackrel{?}{=} \frac{1}{1} \div \frac{b}{c}$$
$$\stackrel{?}{=} \frac{1}{1} \cdot \frac{c}{b}$$
$$\frac{c}{b} = \frac{c}{b}$$

11. $\cot A = \dfrac{b}{a}$, $\tan A = \dfrac{a}{b}$
$$\cot A \stackrel{?}{=} \frac{1}{\tan A} \qquad \frac{b}{a} \stackrel{?}{=} \frac{1}{\dfrac{a}{b}}$$
$$\stackrel{?}{=} \frac{1}{1} \div \frac{a}{b}$$
$$\stackrel{?}{=} \frac{1}{1} \cdot \frac{b}{a}$$
$$\frac{b}{a} = \frac{b}{a}$$

12. $\sin A = \dfrac{12}{13}$ $\cot A = \dfrac{5}{12}$
$\cos A = \dfrac{5}{13}$ $\sec A = \dfrac{13}{5}$
$\tan A = \dfrac{12}{5}$ $\csc A = \dfrac{13}{12}$

13. $\sin A = \dfrac{24}{25}$ $\cot A = \dfrac{7}{24}$
$\cos A = \dfrac{7}{25}$ $\sec A = \dfrac{25}{7}$
$\tan A = \dfrac{24}{7}$ $\csc A = \dfrac{25}{24}$

14. $\dfrac{5}{13}$ 15. $\dfrac{12}{13}$ 16. $\dfrac{5}{12}$ 17. $\dfrac{13}{5}$ 18. $\dfrac{13}{12}$ 19. 0.5736

20. 0.5299   21. 3.7321   22. 0.5299

23. $a = 190$; $b = 177$; $\sec B = 1.3672$; $\csc B = 1.4663$; $\cot B = 1.0724$

24. $b = 36$; $c = 140$; $\sec B = 1.0353$; $\csc B = 3.8639$; $\cot B = 3.7322$

Oblique Triangles in Trigonometry (pp. 468–472)

1. $a = 18$ ft; $b = 16$ ft   2. $a = 381$ ft; $b = 418$ ft   3. 262 feet   4. 154 m

5. 209 m   6. 12 m

General Trigonometry (pp. 472–477)

1. $(0, -1)$; -1; 0   2. 0; 1; 0   3. sin A $= -0.1736$; cos A $= -0.9848$; tan A $= 0.1763$

4. sin A $= -0.8660$; cos A $= 0.5000$; tan A $= -1.7321$

5. sin A $= 0.9397$; cos A $= -0.3420$; tan A $= -2.7475$ 6. -0.9397 7. 0.3420

8. -2.7475 9. 0.7880   10. -0.1736 11. -1.1918

Graphing Trigonometric Functions (pp. 477–478)

1. $-360°$; $-180°$; $0°$; $180°$; $360°$ 2. $-270°$; $90°$ 3. $-270°$; $-90°$; $90°$; $270°$

4. $-180°$; $180°$ 5. $-360°$; $0°$; $360°$ 6. $-360°$; $-180°$; $0°$; $180°$; $360°$